Table of Websites Mentioned

Canada Deposit Insurance Corporation (CDIC)
http://www.cdic.ca/

CANSIM (Statistics Canada's socio-economic database)
http://cansim2.statcan.ca/

C.D. Howe Institute
http://www.cdhowe.org/

Bank of Canada
http://www.bank-banque-canada.ca/

Bank of Canada Review
http://www.bankofcanada.ca/en/review/index.html

The Daily (Statistics Canada)
http://www.statcan.ca/english/

Department of Finance, Canada
http://www.fin.gc.ca

Fiscal Reference Tables (Department of Finance, Canada)
http://www.fin.gc.ca/purl/frt-e.html

GPO Access (U.S. Government Printing Office)
http://www.access.gpo.gov/eop

Historical Statistics of Canada (Statistics Canada)
http://www.statcan.ca/english/freepub/11-516-XIE/sectiona/toc.htm

International Monetary Fund
http://www.imf.org/

Monthly Labor Review Online
http://stats.bls.gov/opub/mlr/mlrhome.htm

National Income and Expenditure Accounts (Statistics Canada)
http://www.statcan.ca/english/sdds/1901.htm

Productivity Growth in Canada (Statistics Canada)
http://www.statcan.ca/english/IPS/Data/15-204-XIE.htm

National Bureau of Economic Research (NBER)
http://www.nber.org

Organisation for Economic Co-operation and Development (OECD)
http://www.oecd.org

Statistics Canada
http://www.statcan.ca/

U.S. Census Bureau
http://www.census.gov/

The World Bank
http://www.worldbank.org/

SECOND
CANADIAN
EDITION

MACROECONOMICS

J. BRADFORD DeLONG
University of California, Berkeley

MARTHA L. OLNEY
University of California, Berkeley

ARMAN MANSOORIAN
York University

LEO MICHELIS
Ryerson University

McGraw-Hill
Ryerson

Toronto   Montréal   Boston   Burr Ridge, IL   Dubuque, IA   Madison, WI   New York
San Francisco   St. Louis   Bangkok   Bogotá   Caracas   Kuala Lumpur   Lisbon   London
Madrid   Mexico City   Milan   New Delhi   Santiago   Seoul   Singapore   Sydney   Taipei

I dedicate this book to my wife, Arpiné,
for her love and support.
A.M.

To the Memory of my Mother.
L.M.

Macroeconomics
Second Canadian Edition

Statistics Canada information is used with the permission of the Minister of Industry, as Minister responsible for Statistics Canada. Information on the availability of the wide range of data from Statistics Canada can be obtained from Statistics Canada's Regional Offices, its World Wide Web site at http://www.statcan.ca, and its toll-free access number 1-800-263-1136.

ISBN-13: 978-0-07-095162-4
ISBN-10: 0-07-095162-4

1 2 3 4 5 6 7 8 9 10 FR 0 9 8 7

Printed and bound in Canada

Editorial Director: Joanna Cotton
Publisher: Lynn Fisher
Sponsoring Editor: Bruce McIntosh
Marketing Manager: Joy Armitage Taylor
Senior Developmental Editor: Maria Chu
Editorial Associate: Stephanie Hess
Senior Production Coordinator: Andrée Davis
Senior Supervising Editor: Anne Nellis
Copy Editor: Trish O'Reilly
Cover Design: Greg Devitt
Interior Design: Greg Devitt
Cover Image Credit: Matthew J. Atanian/Getty Images
Composition: S R Nova PVT Ltd., Bangalore, India
Printer: Friesens

Library and Archives Canada Cataloguing in Publication

DeLong, J. Bradford
    Macroeconomics / J. Bradford DeLong, Martha L. Olney, Arman Mansoorian, Leo Michelis. -- 2nd Canadian ed.

Includes bibliographical references and index.
ISBN-13: 978-0-07-095162-4
ISBN-10: 0-07-095162-4

    1. Macroeconomics–Textbooks. I. Mansoorian, Arman II. Michelis, Leo III. Title.

HB172.5.D438 2007   339   C2006-903686-1

ABOUT THE AUTHORS

J. Bradford DeLong is professor of economics at the University of California at Berkeley, where he has been teaching since 1995. Before starting to teach at Berkeley, he was deputy assistant secretary for economic policy in the United States Department of the Treasury (1993 to 1995), where an enormous range of issues crossed his desk — from what the Federal Reserve will do next week to whether the Uruguay Round of the GATT should be ratified to the macroeconomic implications of the (unsuccessful) health care reform. Before working at the Treasury he was an associate professor at Harvard University, where he was both an undergraduate student (B.A. 1982) and a graduate student (Ph.D. 1987). He has also taught at Boston University and MIT.

Professor DeLong is also a research associate of the National Bureau of Economic Research and a visiting scholar at the Federal Reserve Bank of San Francisco. And he is a former coeditor of the *Journal of Economic Perspectives*.

Professor DeLong's research interests range from the origins of the Great Depression to the effect of irrational speculation on stock market values to whether there is a "new economy," and, among other things, to the causes of long-run economic divergence across nations. He is a prolific writer and has contributed more than 100 articles to publications ranging from *The American Economic Review* to *Fortune* and *Foreign Affairs* to *The New York Times*. His own website contains an impressive amount of material — including reviews of books and scholarly articles and analyses of current events — and is widely considered to be one of the best academic economics websites available. Brad DeLong lives in Lafayette, California, with his wife and two children.

Martha L. Olney received her B.S. in 1978 from the University of Redlands and Ph.D. in 1985 from the University of California, Berkeley. She is an adjunct professor of economics at U.C. Berkeley, where she has taught since 1992. Previously, she was a tenured member of the economics faculty at University of Massachusetts, Amherst. Professor Olney has also taught at Stanford University. Her research is in the areas of consumer spending and consumer indebtedness, focusing especially on the interwar years.

Professor Olney is the author of *Buy Now, Pay Later: Advertising, Credit, and Consumer Durables* (University of North Carolina Press, 1991). Honoured several times for her excellence in teaching, Professor Olney is the recipient of Distinguished Teaching Awards from the University of California, Berkeley, and University of Massachusetts, Amherst. The Economic History Association awarded her the Jonathan Hughes Prize for Excellence in Teaching Economic History in 1997. Martha Olney lives in El Cerrito, California, with her partner and their son.

Arman Mansoorian is a professor of economics at York University. He completed his undergraduate education at the London School of Economics before moving to Canada, where he completed his Ph.D. at Queen's University in 1989. His fields of specialization are macroeconomics and fiscal federalism. He has had several publications, including articles in *Economic Journal*, *International Economic Review*, the *Journal of International Economics*, the *Journal of Public Economics*, the *Journal of Money Credit and Banking*, *Economic Letters*, the *Journal of Economic Dynamics and Control*, *Regional Science and Urban Economics*, and the *Canadian Journal of Economics*. Professor Mansoorian has served as Director of the Economics Graduate Program and Chair of the Department of Economics at York. Before joining York University, he was an assistant professor at the University of Western Ontario and Dalhousie University.

Leo Michelis is a professor of economics at Ryerson University and the current Director of the Graduate Program in International Economics and Finance. Before joining Ryerson in 1996, he taught at York University and the University of Western Ontario. Professor Michelis received his B.A. and M.A. degrees from York University, and his Ph.D. degree from Queen's University in 1993. His areas of special interest in teaching and research are macroeconomics, international finance, and econometrics. He has published articles in the *Journal of Econometrics*, the *Journal of Applied Econometrics*, *Econometric Theory*, the *Journal of Economic Dynamics and Control*, the *Canadian Journal of Economics*, *Economics Letters*, *Applied Economics*, the *Journal of International Money and Finance*, the *Journal of Quantitative Economics*, and the *Journal of Economic Integration*. In addition to *Macroeconomics*, he is the co-editor of two books on economic integration and is a contributing author for several books.

BRIEF CONTENTS

CONTENTS

PART IV STICKY-PRICE MACROECONOMICS 235

PREFACE

It is more than three-quarters of a century since John Maynard Keynes wrote his *Tract on Monetary Reform*, which first linked inflation, production, employment, exchange rates, and policy together in a pattern that we today can recognize as "macroeconomics." It is two-thirds of a century since John Hicks and Alvin Hansen drew their IS and LM curves. It is more than one-third of a century since Milton Friedman and Ned Phelps demolished the static Phillips curve, and since Robert Lucas, Thomas Sargent, and Robert Barro taught us what rational expectations could mean. All this time, intermediate macroeconomics has become more complicated, as new material is added while old material remains.

It seemed to us that if we could successfully streamline the presentation of material, both traditional and modern, the result would be a more understandable and comprehensible book. We hope that we have succeeded — that this book does move more smoothly through the water than its competitors and will prove to be a better textbook for third-millennium macroeconomics courses. This conclusion is based on five changes made in the standard presentation of modern macroeconomics. These changes are not radical; rather they are shifts in emphasis and changes of focus. They do not require recasting of courses, but they are very important in bringing the organization of the book into line with what students learning macroeconomics today need to know.

MAJOR CHANGES TO THE SECOND CANADIAN EDITION

The Second Canadian Edition has a number of very important features, some of which are:

◆ The book contains a clear discussion of the important macroeconomic issues that have confronted the Canadian economy in recent years.

◆ **Chapter 1** now includes a detailed discussion of Canadian economic history and the productivity slowdown in the Canadian economy that were previously discussed in Chapter 4 of the first edition.

◆ **Chapter 2** is devoted exclusively to the discussion of the historical performance and measurement of the six important macroeconomic variables: real GDP, the unemployment rate, the inflation rate, the interest rate, the stock market, and the exchange rate.

◆ **Chapter 3** includes a new box devoted to the Harrod-Domar model and its relation to other growth models.

◆ **Chapter 4** includes a new section devoted to a detailed discussion of income inequality: how income inequality is measured and why it is important in studying macroeconomic performance.

◆ **Chapter 5** contains a more streamlined discussion of the components of domestic spending, and the mathematical content has been simplified.

◆ **Chapter 6** includes a clearer presentation of the equilibrium flexible-price model. The more technical treatment of this model has been moved to a new appendix at the end of the chapter.

◆ **Chapter 7** includes an expanded treatment of financial innovations and how they affect the economy. It also introduces the liquidity preference in a linear form. In addition, it now includes a more detailed treatment of the inflation tax.

◆ **Chapter 8** is now devoted exclusively to the income-expenditure framework and the multiplier, with fixed interest rates.

◆ **Chapter 9** is now devoted exclusively to the IS-LM model and the macroeconomic equilibrium with fixed prices. The treatment of the LM curve has been expanded. The government expenditure multiplier and the money supply multiplier have been derived in this framework and their importance discussed in detail.

◆ **Chapter 10** is now devoted exclusively to the aggregate supply–aggregate demand model. It uses this model to explain the prolonged Canadian recession of the early 1990s (the Great Canadian Slump).

◆ **Chapter 11** has a discussion of the Hodrick-Prescott (HP) filter and how it is used to estimate the natural rate of unemployment and potential output.

◆ **Chapter 12** includes a new section on monetary policy, the liquidity trap, and deflation.

◆ **Chapter 13** updates the discussion of the various measures of the government budget and the national debt. It also includes a new section on the Ricardian equivalence, which was discussed in Chapter 17 of the first Canadian edition.

◆ **Chapter 14** includes a more refined discussion of the different theories of business cycles.

◆ **Chapter 16** has a new section on currency unions and currency boards.

MAJOR INNOVATIONS

The first two changes in the book have to do with **economic growth**.

◆ **Provide a more student-friendly way of learning growth theory.**

◆ **Provide sufficient coverage of growth facts so that students learn the how and why of both growth over time and growth across countries.**

The presentation of long-run growth — both the facts and the theory — in modern macroeconomics textbooks needs to be beefed up, and we have done this. Economic growth is worth much more than one or even two short chapters — here the growth chapters are among the longest in this book. Students have no business leaving macroeconomics courses without understanding the nature and causes of the wealth of nations. They need to see and understand broad cross-country and cross-time patterns: the industrial revolution, the spread of industrialization, the history of the Canadian economy, and its performance relative to the U.S. economy, income inequality, the East Asian miracle, and the American century.

We provide a more easily grasped presentation of the fairly complex "Solow model" by carefully building, step-by-step, the basic theoretical concepts that often confuse undergraduates (e.g., the idea of a steady-state equilibrium growth path). The textbook has a detailed discussion of the important endogenous growth models due to Romer, Rebelo, and Barro, and their comparison with the Solow model in a manner that is unrivalled by any other intermediate macroeconomics textbook.

The third change, long overdue, has to do with the **open economy**.

◆ **Treat the economy as open from the beginning of the book.**

It is time to simply forget about the "closed-economy case" and ask students to analyze an open economy from the very beginning of the book. Virtually every economic policy issue and news event has an important international dimension. Presenting the closed-economy case first gives students a lot of wrong impressions — about the size of the Keynesian multiplier, about the freedom countries have to conduct independent monetary and fiscal policies, and about the relationship between saving and investment — that then have to be unlearned in the "open economy macro" chapters. Moreover, moving the international material into the main narrative thread enhances streamlining. All of the "in the closed-economy chapters we said this, but really. . . " passages in the textbook are no longer needed. Throughout the book, save in Chapters 15 and 16, the default assumption is that the exchange rate is freely floating. This assumption was not true in the past and may not be true in the distant future, but it is true now and for the foreseeable future and is thus a reasonable working assumption.

In one of the later chapters, Chapter 15, we provide a more detailed discussion of the balance of payments, the workings of the economy under fixed and flexible exchange rate systems, international parity conditions, and the exchange rate overshooting model of Dornbusch in a manner that is unrivalled by any other intermediate macroeconomics textbook.

The fourth change, also long overdue, has to do with **monetary policy**.

◆ **Deal with interest rates, not money stocks.**

In today's world, where central banks set interest rates but not money stocks, the LM curve's underlying assumption that the money stock is fixed is artificial. A major reason for giving the LM curve a central place is historical; it allows one to present the Keynesian-monetarist debate of the 1970s as a debate about the relative slopes of IS and LM curves. Steep LM curve or shallow IS curve and monetarists are right — the money stock is the principal determinant of output, unemployment, and inflation. Shallow LM or steep IS curve and the Keynesians are right. (Never mind that Milton Friedman always thought that this was an unwise and unfair way of presenting the debate.)

However, this debate has been dead for a generation, and conducting much of the discussion of the determination of real GDP in a framework in which the money stock is fixed gives students the wrong intuitions. The LM curve cannot be eliminated; there are monetary regimes under which the central bank does not fix the interest rate. But it can be downplayed. It is much better to downplay the LM curve and focus on the key factors of the position of the IS curve and the real interest rate that is determined by the term structure and central bank policy. This brings the presentation in the textbook much closer to what students will find when they open up the newspaper. This makes our tasks as teachers much easier because there is no longer an artificial gap between the models taught and the actions seen in the world.

Furthermore, the space saved by downplaying the LM curve can be used for a serious discussion of the term structure of interest rates. The Bank of Canada, along with most central banks in industrialized countries, controls short-term, nominal, safe interest rates; and the principal determinants of aggregate demand are long-term, real, risky interest rates. The slippage between these two is a limitation on the government's ability to stabilize the economy. Treating this topic seriously allows us to begin to teach the importance of expectations and the limits of policy relatively early in the book, rather than leaving these topics for the policy chapters at the book's end.

The fifth change has to do with the **inflation rate**, as opposed to the price level.

◆ **Focus on the inflation rate — not the price level**

In policy discussions and the media, the variable that is very widely discussed is the inflation rate — and not the general price level. Yet, in most intermediate textbooks the focus of the analysis of the aggregate supply–aggregate demand (AS-AD) model is on the determination of the price level. In this book we show how the AS-AD model can be modified in order to discuss the determination of the inflation rate instead of the price level. Interest rate setting as described by the Taylor rule is used to derive the AD curve with the inflation rate measured on the vertical axis and real GDP on the horizontal axis, while a simple extension of the conventional aggregate supply equation is used to derive an AS curve with the inflation rate on the vertical axis and real GDP on the horizontal axis. This model is then used to determine the equilibrium inflation and real GDP in an economy, as well as to discuss the prolonged recession in the Canadian economy in the 1990s, which is widely believed to be the result of low inflation rate targets set by the Bank of Canada.

The sixth change has to do with the **Phillips curve** and **aggregate supply**.

◆ **Focus on the Phillips curve**

A very close integration of the AS-AD framework with the Phillips curve helps students follow policy discussions relating to the determinants of the unemployment rate.

Other shifts of emphasis and presentation include Chapter 11, "The Phillips Curve and Expectations," which explains that rational, adaptive, and static expectations are not incompatible, but rather different strategies for dealing with the problems of inflation — each of which can be useful in the right economic environment.

PEDAGOGY

Much of the pedagogical work in this book is aimed at smoothing over what often turn out to be rough spots for the students. One important way that people learn is by watching other people solve problems and then repeating the process themselves. Thus, students will note that this book contains a greater-than-usual number of worked examples. This will be especially helpful for those who hesitate before making conceptual leaps.

Boxes provided throughout the book try to reinforce the main narrative without disrupting it. They are an attempt to solve the perennial problem of how to provide additional depth and background to those who need (or want) it without boring or distracting those who wish to move on. *Macroeconomics* contains **five** kinds of boxes:

Tools boxes remind students of some of the algebraic and conceptual tools economists use.

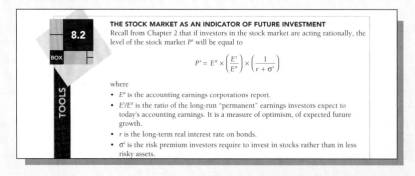

8.2

BOX

TOOLS

THE STOCK MARKET AS AN INDICATOR OF FUTURE INVESTMENT
Recall from Chapter 2 that if investors in the stock market are acting rationally, the level of the stock market P^s will be equal to

$$P^s = E^a \times \left(\frac{E^s}{E^a}\right) \times \left(\frac{1}{r + \sigma^s}\right)$$

where
- E^a is the accounting earnings corporations report.
- E^s/E^a is the ratio of the long-run "permanent" earnings investors expect to today's accounting earnings. It is a measure of optimism, of expected future growth.
- r is the long-term real interest rate on bonds.
- σ^s is the risk premium investors require to invest in stocks rather than in less risky assets.

Details boxes provide for those who want to dig deeper into a particular subject.

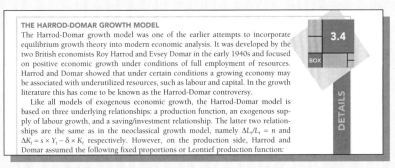

THE HARROD-DOMAR GROWTH MODEL

The Harrod-Domar growth model was one of the earlier attempts to incorporate equilibrium growth theory into modern economic analysis. It was developed by the two British economists Roy Harrod and Evsey Domar in the early 1940s and focused on positive economic growth under conditions of full employment of resources. Harrod and Domar showed that under certain conditions a growing economy may be associated with underutilized resources, such as labour and capital. In the growth literature this has come to be known as the Harrod-Domar controversy.

Like all models of exogenous economic growth, the Harrod-Domar model is based on three underlying relationships: a production function, an exogenous supply of labour growth, and a saving/investment relationship. The latter two relationships are the same as in the neoclassical growth model, namely $\Delta L_t/L_t = n$ and $\Delta K_t = s \times Y_t - \delta \times K_t$ respectively. However, on the production side, Harrod and Domar assumed the following fixed proportions or Leontief production function:

BOX 3.4 · DETAILS

Policy boxes provide for those who want to know how the current thread of the book affects the making of economic policy.

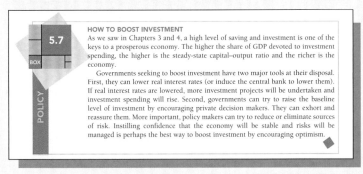

BOX 5.7 · POLICY

HOW TO BOOST INVESTMENT

As we saw in Chapters 3 and 4, a high level of saving and investment is one of the keys to a prosperous economy. The higher the share of GDP devoted to investment spending, the higher is the steady-state capital–output ratio and the richer is the economy.

Governments seeking to boost investment have two major tools at their disposal. First, they can lower real interest rates (or induce the central bank to lower them). If real interest rates are lowered, more investment projects will be undertaken and investment spending will rise. Second, governments can try to raise the baseline level of investment by encouraging private decision makers. They can exhort and reassure them. More important, policy makers can try to reduce or eliminate sources of risk. Instilling confidence that the economy will be stable and risks will be managed is perhaps the best way to boost investment by encouraging optimism.

Examples boxes show how the concepts, ideas, and models of the current main thrust of the book can be applied.

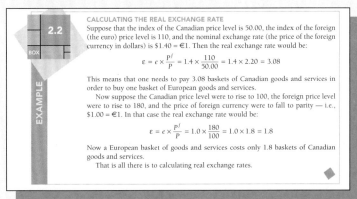

BOX 2.2 · EXAMPLE

CALCULATING THE REAL EXCHANGE RATE

Suppose that the index of the Canadian price level is 50.00, the index of the foreign (the euro) price level is 110, and the nominal exchange rate (the price of the foreign currency in dollars) is $1.40 = €1. Then the real exchange rate would be:

$$\varepsilon = e \times \frac{P^f}{P} = 1.4 \times \frac{110}{50.00} = 1.4 \times 2.20 = 3.08$$

This means that one needs to pay 3.08 baskets of Canadian goods and services in order to buy one basket of European goods and services.

Now suppose the Canadian price level were to rise to 100, the foreign price level were to rise to 180, and the price of foreign currency were to fall to parity — i.e., $1.00 = €1. In that case the real exchange rate would be:

$$\varepsilon = e \times \frac{P^f}{P} = 1.0 \times \frac{180}{100} = 1.0 \times 1.8 = 1.8$$

Now a European basket of goods and services costs only 1.8 baskets of Canadian goods and services.

That is all there is to calculating real exchange rates.

Data boxes apply real data to the concept.

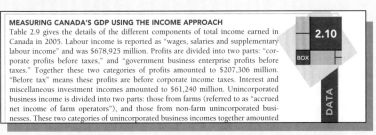

MEASURING CANADA'S GDP USING THE INCOME APPROACH

Table 2.9 gives the details of the different components of total income earned in Canada in 2005. Labour income is reported as "wages, salaries and supplementary labour income" and was $678,925 million. Profits are divided into two parts: "corporate profits before taxes," and "government business enterprise profits before taxes." Together these two categories of profits amounted to $207,306 million. "Before tax" means these profits are before corporate income taxes. Interest and miscellaneous investment incomes amounted to $61,240 million. Unincorporated business income is divided into two parts: those from farms (referred to as "accrued net income of farm operators"), and those from non-farm unincorporated businesses. These two categories of unincorporated business incomes together amounted

BOX 2.10 · DATA

To keep students focused on the forest as well as the trees, there are — at strategic points in each chapter — **Recap** boxes. These Recaps attempt to put the main ideas of the previous section into a nutshell. They are themselves recapitulated in the end-of-chapter summaries, which are also designed to review the most important concepts presented in the chapter.

RECAP **THE CURRENT MACROECONOMIC SITUATION**

The Canadian economy, like the U.S. economy, enjoyed a long period of expansion in the 1990s. Because of the decline in the information technology sector, the growth rate of GDP declined in 2001. This decline was exacerbated by the September 11 terrorist attacks in the U.S., which resulted in a loss of confidence in the travel and airline industries.

Following the 2001 global slowdown, Canada's output growth outpaced that of the U.S. and other G-7 countries. But, in 2003, Canada experienced a series of unfavourable shocks: SARS, a case of mad cow disease, and an unprecedented appreciation of the Canadian dollar. Following the mid-2003 slowdown, the Canadian economy has demonstrated remarkable resilience, rebounding sharply in terms of real GDP growth.

CHAPTER SUMMARY

1. Growth accounting attempts to measure the sources of growth. It decomposes the sources of growth into three parts: growth in labour; growth in capital; and growth in multifactor productivity.

2. One principal force driving long-run growth in output per worker is the set of improvements in the efficiency of labour springing from technological progress.

3. A second principal force driving long-run growth in output per worker is the increases in the capital stock which the average worker has at his or her disposal and which further multiplies productivity.

4. An economy undergoing long-run growth converges toward and settles onto an equilibrium steady-state growth

path, in which the economy's capital–output ratio is constant.

5. The steady-state level of the capital–output ratio is equal to the economy's savings rate divided by the sum of its labour-force growth rate, labour efficiency growth rate, and depreciation rate.

6. In endogenous growth models growth is driven by endogenous factors that can be influenced by government policies. Endogenous growth models predict a wider diversity of living standards among different countries than the neoclassical growth model.

The **Key Terms and Equations** are summarized at the end-of-chapter for easy reference.

KEY TERMS AND EQUATIONS

capital (p. 84)	efficiency of labour (p. 79)	savings rate (p. 87)
capital intensity (p. 79)	labour force (p. 86)	steady-state growth path
convergence (p. 108)	output per worker (p. 84)	
depreciation (p. 87)	production function (p. 83)	

Solow residuals:
$$\frac{\Delta A_t}{A_t} = \frac{\Delta Y_t}{Y_t} - \alpha \times \frac{\Delta K_t}{K_t} - (1 - \alpha) \times \frac{\Delta L_t}{L_t} \qquad (3.4)$$

Evolution of K/L:
$$\Delta\left(\frac{K_t}{L_t}\right) = s \times \frac{Y_t}{L_t} - (\delta + n) \times \frac{K_t}{L_t} \qquad (3.10)$$

Romer's production function:
$$\frac{Y_t}{L_t} = A \times \frac{K_t}{L} \quad \text{where} \quad A = (\rho \times L)^{1-\alpha} \qquad (3.13)$$

Barro's production function:
$$\frac{Y_t}{L} = A \times \tau^{1-\alpha} \times \frac{K_t}{L} \quad \text{where} \quad A = (\rho \times L)^{1-\alpha} \qquad (3.17)$$

The extensive end-of-chapter exercises are divided into two sets, one that is tied to the theoretical material in the book — **Analytical Exercises** — and a second that is tied to recent events — **Policy Exercises**. It is important to have policy exercises at the end of chapters, but since few things turn students off as much as exercises that are obsolete, we have tried to make them current in the book and we will add new ones to our dynamic website at **www.mcgrawhill.ca/olc/delong**.

ANALYTICAL EXERCISES

1. Would an increase in the saving and investment share of Canada's total output raise growth in productivity and living standards?

2. Many observers project that by the end of the twenty-first century the population of the industrialized countries will be stable. Using the Solow growth model, what would such a downward shift in the growth rate

3. What are the arguments for having a strong patent system to boost economic growth? What are the arguments for having a weak system of protections of intellectual property? Under what systems do you think that the first will outweigh the second? Under what circumstances do you think that the second will outweigh the first?

POLICY EXERCISES

1. Assume that the economy's production function is Cobb-Douglas:

$$Y = K^\alpha \times L^{1-\alpha}$$

the capital stock is 80, the total labour force $\bar{L}$ is 100, and $\alpha = 0.4$.
a. Derive the labour demand function.
b. Derive the equilibrium real wage.
c. What is the potential output for this economy?

2. Suppose an economy with the standard Cobb-Douglas production function

5. In recent years foreign exchange speculators have become much more confident in the long-run value of the dollar. What would you suspect has happened to net exports?

6. Consumers whose stock market wealth has multiplied over the past decade have recently started pulling money out of the stock market to enhance their standard of living. What kind of shift in which parameter of the consumption function could be used to model this phenomenon?

And finally, the **Glossary** provides fuller and deeper explanations of economics concepts than is typically found in other books. Once again, for some students such extended definitions are truly useful.

STRUCTURE

While the treatment of many if not all topics is unique, the structure of the book follows a standard pattern that has served macroeconomists well. **Part I** contains two chapters — Introduction to Macroeconomics, and Measuring the Macroeconomy. **Chapter 1** begins with an overview of what macroeconomics is and then covers a brief history of Canadian economic growth. The chapter closes with a quick tour of recent macroeconomic events and macroeconomic policy dilemmas in the world, included both to pique student interest and to give them a sense of the kinds of questions and issues that macroeconomics is supposed to help resolve.

Chapter 2 focuses on six key variables that together allow one to gain a firm hold on the state of the macroeconomy. These variables are (1) real GDP, (2) the unemployment rate, (3) the inflation rate, (4) the interest rate, (5) the level of the stock market, and (6) the exchange rate. The chapter explains how well we are able to measure these key variables and what the measurements mean, as well as giving some background on the historical behaviour of these variables.

Part II focuses on long-run growth and contains two chapters — The Theory of Economic Growth and The Reality of Economic Growth: History and Prospect. **Chapter 3** focuses on growth theory. It starts with a simple-to-understand neoclassical model, the "Solow growth model." We study how in the neoclassical model the economy converges to its steady-state equilibrium and the important factors that can affect this equilibrium — the level of technology, the saving rate, and the rate of growth of population. This chapter then proceeds to provide an extensive treatment of the endogenous growth models due to Paul Romer, Robert Barro, and Sergio Rebelo. Endogenous growth is a very important topic at more advanced macroeconomics courses, and it is unfortunate that it has not received sufficient coverage in intermediate textbooks. We provide a simplified treatment of these models and compare them to the neoclassical model.

Chapter 4 begins with a survey of very long-run economic growth before the industrial revolution and then moves on to the industrial revolution itself. This chapter also examines the performance of the Canadian economy relative to the U.S. economy. It then shifts its focus to patterns of growth and development the world over — including the East Asian miracle, stagnation in Africa, and the convergence of the Organisation for Economic Cooperation and Development (OECD) nations to common levels of productivity and industrial structure — before concluding with a discussion of economic policies and how they affect long-run growth. In a sense, Chapter 4 should be part of *everyone*'s general education. It is, in summary and compressed form, an inquiry into the nature and causes of the wealth of nations. In our view, intermediate macroeconomics is the most natural place to provide this overview of long-run economic growth.

Part III presents flexible-price, business-cycle macroeconomics with two real-side chapters — Building Blocks of the Flexible-Price Model and Equilibrium in the Flexible-Price Model — and one money and inflation chapter — Money, Prices, and Inflation. Since many of the functions are the same in the flexible-price, full-employment model of Part III and the sticky-price model of Part IV, the real-side chapters are written with an eye toward making it clear what changes and what doesn't when we move from flexible- to sticky-price models. **Chapter 5** covers the determination of potential output when wages and prices are flexible, the domestic components of aggregate demand — consumption, investment spending, and government purchases — and the determinants of the final component of aggregate demand — net exports.

Chapter 6 focuses first on how the demand and supply for loanable funds push the interest rate to the level at which investment demand equals saving supply and the economy is at full employment with real GDP equal to potential output. It then shows how to use the method of comparative statics to analyze the effects of changes in economic policy and the economic environment on the macroeconomy. It concludes with a section on supply shocks and on "real" business cycles, which are understood as fluctuations in current and expected future productivity and thus in the value of investment spending today.

Chapter 7 moves from the real to the monetary side in the flexible-price framework. It focuses first on the utility of money and on the simple interest-inelastic quantity theory, and it then moves on to consider the determinants of the price level and inflation when money demand is sensitive to the nominal interest rate.

Part IV's presentation of sticky-price macroeconomics is divided into four chapters — The Income-Expenditure Framework and the Multiplier; The IS-LM Model: Macroeconomic Equilibrium with Fixed Prices; The Aggregate Demand–Aggregate Supply Model; and The Phillips Curve and Expectations. This material not only rounds out the sticky-price, business-cycle framework but also reaches back to the previous section to explain under what circumstances flexible-price and under what circumstances sticky-price modelling is likely to be appropriate. **Chapter 8** provides the standard treatment of the sticky-price, income-expenditure inventory-adjustment model. Its innovative feature is that, because the model begins with the open-economy case, the calculated value of the multiplier is realistic, as opposed to the grossly inflated multiplier values calculated in closed economy models with lump-sum taxes, something students then have to unlearn.

Chapter 9 then builds on Chapter 8 to construct the IS and LM curves. It asks what determines the interest rate when the Bank of Canada is not following a policy of interest-rate targeting and then explains that the interest rate and aggregate demand are jointly determined by the money market equilibrium — as summarized in the LM curve — and by the goods market equilibrium — as summarized by the IS curve. It goes on to analyze the impact of changes in the economic environment and economic policy on the exchange rate and the trade balance.

Chapter 10 introduces the concepts of aggregate demand and aggregate supply. Then the chapter uses the aggregate demand and aggregate supply curves to help students understand macroeconomic fluctuations in Canada in the post–World War II period. It thus demonstrates that the models are actually useful and that they help us understand why the Canadian business cycle behaved as it did in the post–World War II period.

Chapter 11 puts in place the keystone for Parts III and IV. It analyzes not just the determination of real GDP in the sticky-price framework, but also how prices change — how inflation is generated — by the state of aggregate demand relative to potential output. It presents the Phillips curve and the key determinants of the location of the Phillips curve: the natural rate of unemployment on the one hand and the expected rate of inflation on the other. It then presents the three kinds of inflation expectations we expect to see — static, adaptive, and rational expectations of inflation — and the circumstances under which we expect to see each one. The chapter concludes by outlining the transition from the sticky-price short run to the flexible-price long run: It helps students consider under what circumstances the better answers are generated by using the flexible-price model of Part III and under what circumstances the better answers are generated by the sticky-price model of Part IV.

Part V, which provides the payoff to all of this model-building work, begins with economic policy in three chapters — Stabilization Policy; The Budget Balance, the National Debt, and Investment; and Changes in the Macroeconomy and Changes in Macroeconomic Policy. This material allows students to think through the issues and to understand the debates about proper macroeconomic management, both for stabilization and for enhancing economic growth.

Chapter 12 deals with the institutions of macroeconomic policy, the power and limits of stabilization policy, monetary versus fiscal policy, rules versus authorities, and extreme situations such as financial crises.

Chapter 13 covers the government's budget and the government debt, outlining both short-run stabilization and long-run growth implications of the government's budget.

Chapter 14, Changes in the Macroeconomy and Changes in Macroeconomic Policy, deals with the fact that because the macroeconomy changes over time, macroeconomists are always aiming at a moving target.

Part VI provides a more extensive treatment of the open economy, and discusses the international monetary arrangements in the world in historical perspective. **Chapter 15** provides a complete analysis of the balance of payments, exchange rate regimes, capital mobility, international interest parity conditions, and the well-known Mundell-Fleming model. The Mundell-Fleming model is then used to study the effects of fiscal, monetary, and other economic shocks on the equilibrium of the economy, in the short and the long run, under flexible and fixed exchange rates. The chapter ends with a discussion of the related issues of devaluation, balance of payments crises, imperfect asset substitutability, and imperfect capital mobility.

Chapter 16 deals with international monetary arrangements since the late nineteenth century. It starts with a study of the fixed exchange rate systems of the Gold

Standard, and the Bretton Woods system, and how they were replaced by the existing flexible exchange rate system. The Canadian experiences under these systems are discussed. The chapter also discusses the costs and benefits of fixed and flexible exchange rate systems, as well as the currency crises that beset the European, Mexican, and East Asian economies in recent years.

Part VII concludes the book. **Chapter 17,** The Future of Macroeconomics, focuses on where macroeconomists disagree and on how the science is evolving, even in the absence of structural change in the macroeconomy. Finally, the **Epilogue** sums up the lessons of the book and reminds readers of what we do not know.

FLEXIBILITY

There are several ways in which the book can be used as an intermediate macroeconomics textbook. Since instructors differ in the way they present the material, this text has been structured to provide maximum **flexibility**. It can accommodate a standard, two-semester course in intermediate macroeconomics, a macroeconomics course for non-specialists in the field, or even a course in international monetary economics.

For a **two-semester** course structure, one can follow the layout of the book and cover Parts I to III in the first semester and Parts IV to VII in the second semester. Alternatively, the first semester can cover Parts I, III, and IV of the book. This sequence will give students a complete treatment of macroeconomics with a special emphasis on the open economy. This would also be a good alternative, if some students were not expected to take intermediate macroeconomics in both semesters. The second semester can then include Parts V, VI, II and VII, in this order, which can be regarded as a more in-depth analysis of the macroeconomy.

Some instructors prefer to teach sticky-price macroeconomics before flexible-price models. These instructors can adopt the following alternative: In the first semester cover Part I first and then discuss sections 5.2 and 5.3 on the components of spending, Chapter 8 on the income expenditure model, Chapter 7 on the money market (ignoring analysis of price adjustments and inflation), Chapter 9 on the IS-LM model, followed by the aggregate supply–aggregate demand analysis of Chapter 10, and the Phillips curve analysis of Chapter 11. The flexible price chapters of Part III can be covered after these chapters, as a detailed examination of the long run. The second semester can consist of Parts V, VI, II, and VII, as outlined above.

The book has sufficient in-depth analysis and enough policy discussions that it can be used for a one-semester course for **non-specialists** in macroeconomics, especially as several economics departments and business schools require only introductory macroeconomics as a pre-requisite for such courses. To use the book in this manner, one can start with a detailed discussion of the IS and LM curves using the sections outlined above. The IS-LM framework can then be used to discuss policy issues and develop the monetary policy reaction function, using the Taylor rule, following Chapters 9 and 10. Finally, several institutional and policy issues can be discussed by following Chapters 11 and 13.

Finally, the monetary theory and open economy discussion of the textbook are sufficiently in-depth that it can also be used for a one-semester undergraduate course in **international monetary economics**. For this course, first discuss the balance of payments accounts and the important interest rate parity conditions, following the discussion in Sections 15.1 to 15.3 of Chapter 15. Next, derive the IS curve from

Sections 5.2 to 5.3 of Chapter 5, Section 8.2 of Chapter 8, and Sections 9.1 to 9.2 of Chapter 9. When discussing the IS curve for this course it is important to evade references to the subsection entitled "The Exchange Rate" on pages 164 to 166; and never regard the real exchange rate as being determined by equation (5.17) on page 164. After deriving the IS curve, discuss the money market and develop the LM curve by following pages 205 to 210, 215 to 217, 212 to 213, and Sections 9.3 to 9.4 of Chapter 9. Once the IS and LM curves have been developed, discuss the Mundell-Fleming model with flexible and fixed exchange rates from Sections 15.4 to 15.8. Finally, discuss the various international monetary arrangements and policy issues following Chapter 16.

SUPPLEMENTS

◆ For the Instructor

Instructor's Online Learning Centre   The OLC at **www.mcgrawhill.ca/olc/delong** includes a password-protected website for instructors. The site offers download-able supplements, including a new set of short answer problems, and **PageOut**, the McGraw-Hill Ryerson course website development centre.

Instructor's CD-ROM   This CD-ROM contains all the necessary Instructor Supplements, including:

- **Instructor's Manual** Written by the authors, this useful manual offers a number of general information elements — sample syllabi, web resources, print resources, and some mathematical background (with some homework problems/solutions) — along with the following elements for each chapter — Overview, Annotated Outline, Mathematical Tools, Teaching Tips, Answers to Textbook Exercises, Additional Exercises (and Answers), and Additional Readings.

- **Computerized Test Bank** Written by the author, this test bank contains almost 1,300 multiple-choice questions categorized by objective, level, type, and source. The test bank is available in the latest Diploma test-generating software, ensuring maximum flexibility in test preparation, including the reconfiguring of graphing exercises. This Brownstone program is the gold standard of testing programs.

- **Microsoft® PowerPoint® Presentation** Prepared by the authors, these slides contain all of the illustrations from the textbook, dynamic slides built in for key figures, along with a detailed, chapter-by-chapter review of the important ideas presented in the book.

◆ For the Students

iStudy   Open 24 hours a day so you can study when you want, how you want, and where you want.

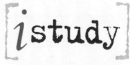

Many students find study guide materials to be indispensable in helping to understand the course material being learned. *iStudy* (the interactive study guide) will help students meet their goals by testing their cumulative understanding of the material they are studying; this will help students assess their mastery of the concepts they are learning.

Each chapter in *iStudy* contains an overview, a set of matching questions, and multiple-choice questions. These are followed by exercises, Manipulation of Concepts and Models, and Applying the Concepts and Models. The answers (and, in some cases, suggested answers) and grading are provided automatically when the student clicks the submit button. *iStudy* also contains "Interactive Graphs" which depict major graphs and instruct students to shift the curves, observe the outcomes, and derive relevant generalizations.

iStudy comprises a superb "tutor" for students. To see a free sample chapter, go to the Online Learning Centre at **www.mcgrawhill.ca/olc/delong**. Full access can be purchased at the textbook Online Learning Centre or by purchasing a pin code card through your campus bookstore. Please contact your *iLearning* Sales Specialist for additional information regarding packaging access to *iStudy* with the student text.

Student Online Learning Centre   This electronic learning aid, located at **www.mcgrawhill.ca/olc/delong**, offers a wealth of materials, including quizzes, Weblinks including access to Σ-STAT and the CANSIM II database, a link to Brad DeLong's extremely useful and diverse website, and much more.

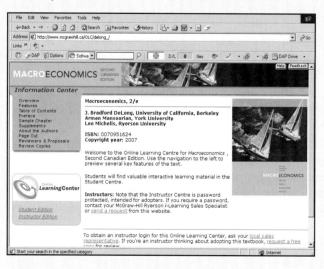

Σ-STAT   is Statistics Canada's education resource that allows you to view socio-economic and demographic data in charts, graphs, and maps. Access to Σ-STAT and the CANSIM II database is made available from this website by special agreement between McGraw-Hill Ryerson and Statistics Canada to purchasers of the DeLong textbook. Please visit the Online Learning Centre for additional information.

COURSE MANAGEMENT

PageOut   McGraw-Hill Ryerson's course management system, PageOut, is the easiest way to create a website for your economics course. There is no need for HTML coding, graphic design, or a thick how-to book. Just fill in a series of boxes in plain English and click on one of our professional designs. In no time, your course is online!

For the integrated instructor, we offer *Macroeconomics* content for complete online courses. Whatever your needs, you can customize the *Macroeconomics* Online Learning Centre content and author your own online course materials. It is entirely up to you. You can offer online discussion and message boards that will complement your office hours and reduce the lines outside your door. Content cartridges are also available for course management systems, such as **WebCT** and **Blackboard**. Ask your *iLearning* Sales Specialist for details.

SUPERIOR SERVICE

Service takes on a whole new meaning with McGraw-Hill Ryerson and *Macroeconomics*. More that just bringing you the textbook, we have consistently raised the bar in terms of innovation and educational research — both in economics and in education in general. These investments in learning and the education community have helped us to understand the needs of students and educators across the country and allowed us to foster the growth of truly innovative, integrated learning.

Integrated Learning   Your Integrated Learning Sales Specialist is a McGraw-Hill Ryerson representative who has the experience, product knowledge, training, and support to help you assess and integrate any of your products, technology, and services into your course for optimum teaching and learning performance. Whether it's helping your students improve their grades or putting your entire course online, your *i*Learning Sales Specialist is there to help you do it. Contact your *i*Learning Sales Specialist today to learn how to maximize all of McGraw-Hill Ryerson's resources!

iLearning Services   McGraw-Hill Ryerson offers a unique *i*Service package designed for Canadian faculty. Our mission is to equip providers of higher education with superior tools and resources required for excellence in teaching. For additional information, visit **www.mcgrawhill.ca/highereducation/iservices** or contact your local *i*Learning Sales Specialist.

Teaching, Learning & Technology Conference Series   The educational environment has changed tremendously in recent years, and McGraw-Hill Ryerson continues to be committed to helping you acquire the skills you need to succeed in this new milieu. Our innovative Teaching, Learning & Technology Conference Series brings faculty together from across Canada with 3M Teaching Excellence award winners to share teaching and learning best practices in a collaborative and stimulating environment. Preconference workshops on general topics, such as teaching large classes and technology integration, will also be offered. We will also work with you at your own institution to customize workshops that best suit the needs of your faculty.

ACKNOWLEDGEMENTS

This book evolved over the past year with the valuable contributions of several individuals. Our primary debts go to the McGraw-Hill Ryerson team that was involved in the project. Their expertise and professionalism have helped us immensely in shaping the book in its present form. We owe special thanks to the economics editor, Ron Doleman, Bruce McIntosh, Sponsoring Editor, the Senior Developmental Editor, Maria Chu, the Senior Supervising Editor, Anne Nellis, the Copy Editor, Trish O'Reilly, the Senior Production Coordinator, Andrée Davis, and the Publisher, Lynn Fisher. Their skill and judgement are reflected in this edition of the book.

We also owe a debt of gratitude to our research assistant, Brennan Thompson, for his skill and efficiency in collecting the Canadian data for the graphs and tables of the Second Canadian Edition of the book. His painstaking effort is greatly appreciated.

In addition, many colleagues and friends gave generously of their time to give advice and help us improve the manuscript in various ways. For their help, we are most grateful to our colleagues Tasso Adamopoulos, Constantine Angyridis, Thomas Barbiero, Ingrid Bryan, and Louis Christofides.

Likewise, we are most grateful to the following reviewers, whose recommendations and insights helped us to make significant improvements in the content and presentation of the book. Reviewers of the first and second editions include:

Tasso Adamopoulos, York University
Iris Au, University of Toronto
Glen Copplestone, University of Western Ontario
Doug Curtis, Trent University
Ajit Dayanandan, University of Northern British Columbia
Joseph DeJuan, University of Waterloo
Yolina Denchev, University of Victoria
Mohammed H.I. Dore, Brock University
Ida Ferrara, York University
Rashid Khan, McMaster University
Brian Krauth, Simon Fraser University
Leigh MacDonald, University of Western Ontario
James Nason, University of British Columbia
Dan Otchere, Concordia University
Alvaro Pereira, University of British Columbia
Nazmi Sari, University of Saskatchewan
Frank Strain, Mount Allison University
Javid Taheri, Saint Mary's University
Frank Trimnell, Ryerson University
Graham Voss, University of Victoria
Andrew Wong, University of Alberta
Ayoub Yousefi, University of Waterloo

PART

Preliminaries

Intermediate macroeconomics books usually begin with some preliminary information, and this one is no exception. It begins with an overview of the subject (Chapter 1) that is intended to provide an orientation to the discipline. You need to know, for example, that the field of macroeconomics studies total economic activity, the total number of people employed, and why the overall price level rises and falls.

This information is followed by an overview of the data used by macroeconomists (Chapter 2). Students and other readers need to know what these data are and how they fit together in the National Income and Expenditure Accounts before they can properly begin using the data to understand the state of the economy.

1

Introduction to Macroeconomics

QUESTIONS

What is macroeconomics?

How does macroeconomic policy affect living standards?

What are the prominent features of Canadian economic development?

What contributed to the productivity slowdown of 1970s?

What are the current macroeconomic conditions in Canada, the United States, and the rest of the world?

1.1 OVERVIEW

WHAT IS MACROECONOMICS?

What exactly is macroeconomics? **Macroeconomics** is the subdiscipline of economics that tries to answer the last four questions that begin this chapter. Answers to all these questions depend on what is happening to the economy as a whole, the economy in the large, the *macroeconomy*. "Macro" is, after all, nothing but a prefix for "large." Thus macroeconomics is the branch of economics related to the economy as a whole.

Macroeconomists' principal task is to try to figure out why overall economic activity rises and falls. Why are measures such as the total value of all production, the total income of workers and property owners, the total number of people employed, or the unemployment rate higher in some years than in others? Macroeconomists also attempt to understand what determines the level and rate of change of overall prices. The proportional rate of change in the price level has a name you have undoubtedly heard thousands of times: the *inflation rate*. Finally, along the way macroeconomists study other variables — such as interest rates, stock market values, and exchange rates — that play a major role in determining the overall levels of production, income, employment, and prices.

But there is more to macroeconomics! Macroeconomics is also concerned with policies that improve our living standards. In order to study these policies, macroeconomists have to incorporate microeconomic theory into their analyses and study the details of what determines, for example, the decisions of individual households on consumption and education, and what determines the investment decisions of individual firms. Once macroeconomists know what determines the decisions of households and firms, they can prescribe policies to promote people's welfare. These policies could involve subsidizing education in order to increase the productivity of workers or subsidizing investment in research and development in order to encourage inventions of new goods and services, production technologies, and production methods. Such policies will promote economic growth and raise the living standards of society.

MACROECONOMICS VERSUS MICROECONOMICS

By itself macroeconomics is only half of economics. For more than half a century economics has been divided into two branches, macroeconomics and microeconomics. Macroeconomists examine the economy in the large, focusing on feedback from one component of the economy to another and studying the total level of production and employment. In contrast, **microeconomics**, which was probably the subject of your last economics course, deals with the economy in the small. Microeconomists study the markets for single commodities, examining the behaviour of individual households and businesses. They focus on how competitive markets allocate resources to create producer and consumer surplus, as well as on how markets can go wrong.

The two groups of economists also differ in their views of how markets work. Microeconomists assume that imbalances between demand and supply are resolved by changes in prices. Rises in prices bring forth additional supply, and falls in prices bring forth additional demand, until supply and demand are once again in balance. Macroeconomists consider the possibility that imbalances between supply and demand can be resolved by changes in quantities rather than in prices. That is, businesses may be slow to change the prices they charge, preferring instead to expand or contract production until supply balances demand. Table 1.1 summarizes these differences in approach.

In every generation, economists attempt to integrate microeconomics and macroeconomics by providing "microfoundations" for the macroeconomic topics of inflation, the business cycle, and long-run growth. But no one believes that the bridge between microeconomics and macroeconomics has yet been soundly built. Economists are divided roughly evenly between those who think that the failure to successfully integrate microeconomics and macroeconomics is a flaw that urgently needs to be corrected and those who think it is a regrettable but minor annoyance. Thus less knowledge may carry over from microeconomics to macroeconomics than one might expect or hope. Be careful in trying to apply the principles and conclusions of microeconomics to macroeconomic questions — and vice versa.

TABLE 1.1
The Two Branches of Economics

Macroeconomists	Microeconomists
Focus on the economy as a whole.	Focus on the markets for individual commodities and on the decisions of single economic agents.
Spend much time analyzing how total income changes and how changes in income cause changes in other modes of economic behaviour.	Hold total income constant.
Spend a great deal of time and energy investigating how people form their expectations and change them over time.	Don't worry much about how decision makers form their expectations.
Consider the possibility that decision makers might change the quantities they produce before they change the prices they charge.	Assume that economic adjustment occurs first through prices that change to balance supply and demand and that only afterward do producers and consumers react to the changed prices by changing the quantities they make, buy, or sell.

MACROECONOMIC POLICY

GROWTH POLICY

The government's *growth policy* — what it does to accelerate or decelerate long-run economic growth — is surely the most important aspect of macroeconomic policy. Nothing matters more in the long run for the quality of life in an economy than its long-run rate of economic growth.

Consider Argentina, which was once one of the most prosperous nations in the world. In 1929, for example, it was fifth in the world in the number of automobiles per capita. Yet today Argentina is classified as a "developing" country, and as Figure 1.1 shows, it has fallen far behind rich developed industrial economies like Canada. Why? Destructive economic policies have retarded Argentina's economic growth. Today Argentines are richer than their predecessors were at the beginning of the twentieth century, but they are not nearly as well off as they might have been had Argentina's economic policies been as good and its economic growth as fast as those in Canada.

Destructive policies include irresponsible government policies involving, for example, high inflation, high budget deficits, low expenditures on law and order, little effort to control corruption, low expenditures on education and infrastructure, and little or no support for research and development. On the other hand, constructive policies involve low inflation and budget deficits, high expenditures on law and order, effective control of corruption, high expenditures on education and infrastructure, and sustained support of research and development.

In Canada, where throughout the twentieth century economic policies were supportive of growth, the past 100 years have led to extraordinary prosperity. Today economic output per person in Canada is among the highest in the world. According to semiofficial estimates, Canadians today are more than nine times as wealthy as their predecessors were at the start of the twentieth century.

In the long run, nothing a government can do does more good for the economy than adopting good policies for economic growth.

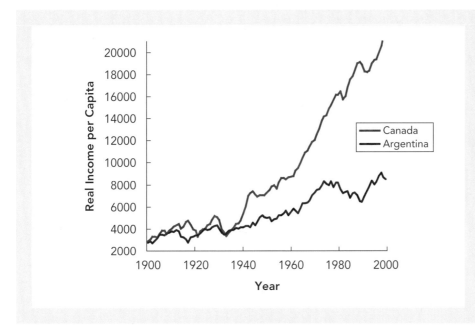

Source: Angus Maddison, *The World Economy: Historical Statistics* (Paris: OECD, 2003).

FIGURE 1.1

Long-Run Economic Growth: Canada and Argentina, 1900–2000

At the start of the twentieth century, Argentina was as rich — and seen as having as bright a future — as Canada. But economic policies that were mostly bad for long-run growth left Argentina far behind Canada.

STABILIZATION POLICY

The second major branch of macroeconomic policy is the government's *stabilization* policy. History does not show a steady, stable, smooth upward trend toward higher production and employment. Typically, levels of production and employment fluctuate above and below long-run growth trends. Production can easily rise several percentage points above the long-run trend or fall 5 percentage points or more below the trend (see Figure 1.2). Unemployment can fall so low that businesses become desperate for workers and will spend much time and money training them. Or it can rise to 12 percent of the labour force in a deep recession, as it did in 1982.

Such fluctuations in production and employment are commonly referred to as *business cycles*. Periods in which production grows and unemployment falls are called *booms*, or macroeconomic **expansion**s. Periods in which production falls and unemployment rises are called **recession**s or, worse, **depressions**. Booms are to be welcomed; recessions are to be feared.

Today's governments have powerful abilities to improve economic growth and to smooth out the business cycle by diminishing the depth of recessions and depressions. Good macroeconomic policy can make almost everyone's life better; bad macroeconomic policy can make almost everyone's life much worse (see Box 1.1). For example, policy makers' reliance on the gold standard as the international monetary system during the Great Depression was the source of macroeconomic catastrophe and resulting human misery. Thus the stakes that are at risk in the study of macroeconomics are high.

Business-cycle fluctuations are felt not only in production and employment but also in the overall level of prices. Booms usually bring inflation, or rising prices. Recessions bring either a slowdown in the rate of inflation, or *disinflation* as it is called, or an absolute decline in the price level, called **deflation**. Interest rates, the

FIGURE 1.2

The Canadian Business Cycle: Fluctuations in Total Production (Real GDP, 1997 Prices) Relative to the Long-Run Growth Trend, 1961–2005

Since 1960 business-cycle fluctuations have caused the level of production in Canada to fluctuate as much as 5 percent below or above the trend level of real GDP.

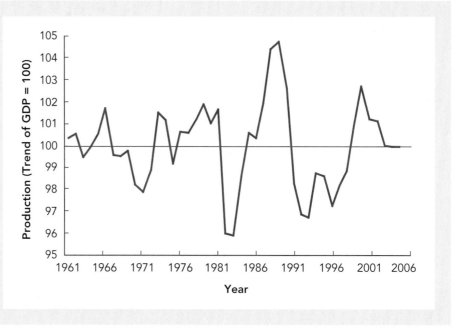

Source: Adapted from the Statistics Canada CANSIM II database, Series V1992067.

level of the stock market, and other economic variables also rise and fall with the principal fluctuations of the business cycle.

As we discuss in Chapter 14, business cycles in Canada have been shorter and less severe in the post-World War II era than in the first half of the twentieth century. The reason for this is that the Canadian government, like other governments in industrialized countries, has pursued more active stabilization policies in the post-World War II period. Nonetheless, some government polices have been the cause of recessions in Canada's recent economic history. Examples include the recessions of 1981–1982 and 1991–1992 that were the results of the anti-inflationary policies of the Bank of Canada.

BOX 1.1 — DATA

MACROECONOMIC POLICY AND YOUR QUALITY OF LIFE

At the end of 1993 Canada's macroeconomy was in the worst shape since the Great Depression. The unemployment rate was close to 12 percent. In an average week in 1993, some 1.5 million Canadians were unemployed — actively seeking work but unable to find a job that seemed worth taking. That year the average household income in Canada was close to 5 percent below its long-run trend.

By contrast, at the end of 2005 Canada's unemployment was less than 7 percent, and average household income was close to 3 percent above trend. In which year would you rather be trying to find a job?

Bad macroeconomic policy makes years like 1993 much more common than years like 2005. Although good macroeconomic policy cannot maintain the degree of relative prosperity seen in 2005 indefinitely, it can all but eliminate the prospect of years like 1993.

WHY MACROECONOMICS MATTERS

Why does macroeconomics matter? Why should we care about the questions at the heart of macroeconomics? There are at least three reasons.

CULTURAL LITERACY

First (but least important), macroeconomics is a matter of cultural literacy. Much discussion in newspapers, on television, and at parties concerns the macroeconomy. This should not be surprising: The twentieth-century Canadian economy was, all in all, extraordinarily successful. Today we are on average some 50 percent richer than our parents were when they were our age. If economic growth continues at its recent pace, our children may be five or more times as rich as our grandparents were.

Our modern industrial economy has delivered increases in material prosperity and living standards that no previous generation ever saw. (We discuss this topic at greater length in Chapter 4.) This increasing material prosperity means that the economy has a cultural salience today that it did not have in previous centuries, when productivity was stagnant and material standards of living improved only as fast as a glacier moves.

Thus, if you want to follow and participate in public debates and discussions, you need to know about macroeconomics. If you don't, you won't understand news reports on changes in the economy, such as those listed in Figure 1.3.

SELF-INTEREST

A second (and more important) reason to care about macroeconomics is that the macroeconomy matters to you personally. Each of us is interested in particular issues in *micro*economics. Farmers and bakers are interested in the price of wheat; computer manufacturers and users are interested in the price of microprocessors; and three of us are *very* interested in the price of economics professors. What happens in these individual markets — for wheat, for microprocessors, and for economics professors — shapes the lives of farmers, bakers, computer programmers, and economics professors.

Economic News
Fri, 19 May 2006, 4:41 pm EDT

CAE wins $48-million contract; Housing affordability deteriorates; Cross-border travel rebounds; Rivals battle over TV listings; Sorbara's name taken off search warrant; Centurion shuffles execs; CRTC backs Allarco bid for pay-TV licence; No oil supply shortage: OPEC; Italian eyewear firm buys Shoppers Optical; Dell switches chips; Nortel signs China deal; Syncrude shuts down Mildred Lake plant; Gold's high a low for Afghan brides; Labatt USA sells Rolling Rock to Anheuser; Commodities too rich by half: Merrill; The 96-cent daily grind; BMO looks to leverage China IPO win; Rothmans blames smugglers for falling profit; Sears swings to profit; Skype VoIP freebie could put Vonage on the ropes; Xandros seeks its niche as Linux hype wanes; Micron to unveil 8-megapixel image chip; U.S. jobless rate jumps

FIGURE 1.3
The Daily Flow of Economic News
Economic news flows past us constantly throughout the day. The total volume of information is overwhelming. Thus one of the major problems of macroeconomics is figuring out how to process all this information — how to make sense of it without drowning in information overload and without throwing valuable news away.

Source: www.globeandmail.com/business

What happens in the macroeconomy shapes *everyone's* life. A rise in inflation is sure to enrich debtors (people who have borrowed) and impoverish creditors (people who have lent money to others). An expanding economy will make real incomes rise. A deep recession will increase unemployment and make those who lose their jobs have a hard time finding others. Your bargaining power vis-à-vis your employer (or, on the other side of the table, your bargaining power vis-à-vis your employees) depends on the phase of the business cycle.

Though you cannot control the macroeconomy, you can understand how it affects your opportunities. To some degree, forewarned is forearmed: Whether or not you understand your opportunities may depend on how much attention you pay in this course. The macroeconomy is not destiny: Some people do very well in their jobs and businesses in a recession, and many do badly in a boom. Nevertheless, it is a powerful influence on individual well-being. To paraphrase Russian revolutionary Leon Trotsky, you may not be interested in the macroeconomy, but the macroeconomy is interested in you.

CIVIC RESPONSIBILITY

A third important reason to care about macroeconomics is that by working together we can improve the macroeconomy. We get to vote, one of the most precious rights human beings have ever had. In electing our government, we indirectly make macroeconomic policy. As we will see in the next section, the government's macroeconomic policy matters, because it can *accelerate* (or decelerate) long-run economic growth and *stabilize* (or destabilize) the short-run business cycle. In election after election, candidates will present themselves and seek your vote. Those who win will try to manage the macroeconomy. If you are not literate in macroeconomics, you won't be able to distinguish the candidates who might become effective macroeconomic managers from those who are clueless or cynical, promising more than they can deliver. As Box 1.2 describes, some politicians have tried to use macroeconomic policy for their own short-term political gain.

ECONOMICS: IS IT A SCIENCE?

If you are coming to economics from a background in the *natural* sciences, you probably expect economics to be something like a natural science, only less so: To the extent that it works, it works more or less like chemistry, though it does not work as well. Economic theories are unsettled and poorly described. Economists' predictions are often wrong.

If you hold these opinions, you are half-right. While economics is a science, it is not a *natural* science. It is a *social* science. Its subject is not electrons or elements but human beings: people and how they behave. This subject matter has several important consequences. Some of them make economics easier than a natural science, some of them make economics harder than a natural science, and some of them just make it different.

First, because economics is a social science, debates within economics last a lot longer and are *much* less likely to end in a clear consensus than are debates in the natural sciences. The major reason is that different people have different views of what makes a free, a good, a just, or a well-ordered society. They look for an economy that harmonizes with their vision of what a society should be. They ignore or explain away facts that turn out to be inconvenient for their particular political views. People are, after all, only human.

POLICY

ECONOMIC POLICY AND POLITICAL POPULARITY

Politicians believe strongly that their success at the polls depends on the state of the economy. They think that fairly *and* unfairly they get the credit when the economy does well and suffer the blame when the economy does badly. One of the most outspoken political leaders on this topic was mid-twentieth-century American politician Richard M. Nixon, who publicly blamed his defeat in the 1960 presidential election on the Eisenhower administration's unwillingness to take action against an economic slump:

"The matter was thoroughly discussed by the Cabinet. . . . [S]everal of the Administration's economic experts who attended the meeting did not share [the] bearish prognosis. . . . [T]here was strong sentiment against using the spending and credit powers of the Federal Government to affect the economy, unless and until conditions clearly indicated a major recession in prospect. . . . I must admit that I was more sensitive politically than some of the others around the cabinet table. I knew from bitter experience how, in both 1954 and 1958, slumps which hit bottom early in October contributed to substantial Republican losses in the House and Senate. . . . The bottom of the 1960 dip did come in October . . . the jobless roles increased by 452,000. All the speeches, television broadcasts, and precinct work in the world could not counteract that one hard fact."

Economic historians continue to dispute the causes of the "stagflation" — a combination of relatively high inflation and relatively high unemployment — that struck the American economy in the early 1970s, after Richard Nixon finally became president. Was it the result of his manipulation of economic policy for political goals so that during his 1972 reelection campaign the economy would look better than it had in 1960? The evidence is contradictory. But no matter how much Nixon's policy contributed to stagflation, all observers agree that his major goal was not to create a healthier economy over the long term but to make the economy look good in 1972.

Source: Richard M. Nixon, *Six Crises* (Garden City, NY: Doubleday, 1962), pp. 309–311.

Economists *try* to approach the objectivity that characterizes most work in the natural sciences. After all, what is is, and what is not is not. Even if wishful thinking or predispositions contaminate the results of a single study, later studies can correct the error. But economists never approach the unanimity with which physicists embraced the theory of relativity, chemists embraced the oxygen theory of combustion, and biologists rejected the Lamarckian inheritance of acquired characteristics. Biology departments do not have Lamarckians. Chemistry departments do not have phlogistonists. But economics departments do have a wide variety of points of view and schools of thought.

Second, the fact that economics is about people means that economists cannot ethically undertake large-scale experiments. Economists cannot set up special situations in which potential sources of disturbance are reduced to a minimum, then observe what happens, and generalize from the results of the experiment (where sources of disturbance are absent) to what happens in the world (where sources of disturbance are common). Thus the experimental method, the driver of rapid progress in many of the natural sciences, is lacking in economics. This flaw makes economics harder to analyze, and it makes economists' conclusions much more tentative and subject to dispute, than is the case with natural sciences.

Third, the subjects economists study — people — have minds of their own. They observe what is going on around them, plan for the future, and take steps to avoid future consequences that they foresee and fear will be unpleasant. At times they simply do what they want, just because they feel like doing it. Thus in economists' analyses the present often depends not just on the past but on the future as well — or on what people expect the future to be. Box 1.3 presents one example of this: how people's **expectations** of the future and particularly their fear that there might be a depression contributed to the coming of the Great Depression of the 1930s, and the recession of 2001.

This third wrinkle makes economics in some sense very hard. Natural scientists can always assume the arrow of causality points from the past to the future. In economics people's expectations of the future mean that the arrow of causality often points the other way, from the (anticipated) future back to the present.

RELIANCE OF MACROECONOMICS ON QUANTITATIVE MODELS AND THE ABSTRACT

In spite of the political complications, the nonexperimental nature, and the peculiar problems of cause and effect in economics, the discipline remains a *quantitative* science. Most of the relationships that economists study come quantified. Thus economics makes heavy use of arithmetic and algebra, while political science, sociology, and most of history do not. Economics makes heavy use of arithmetic to measure economic variables of interest. Moreover, economists use mathematical *models* to relate these variables.

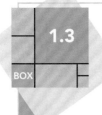

BOX 1.3 EXAMPLE

EXPECTATIONS AND THE COMING OF THE GREAT DEPRESSION

An important example of how people's expectations can change the course of economic events comes from the stock market crash of 1929. The crash changed what people in the industrialized countries expected about the future of the economy, and the shifts in spending caused by their changed expectations played a key role in causing the greatest economic depression in American history, the Great Depression.

On October 29, 1929, the price of shares traded on the New York Stock Exchange suffered their largest one-day percentage drop in history. Stock values bounced back a bit initially, but by the end of the week they were down by more than a quarter (see Figure 1.4). Gloom fell over Wall Street. Many people had lost a lot of money.

You can probably guess what happened in the months after the crash. Most people simply stopped buying big-ticket items like cars and furniture. This massive drop in demand reduced new orders for goods. The drop in output generated layoffs in many industries. Even though most people's incomes had not yet changed, their expectations of their future income had.

The drop in demand produced by this shift in expectations helped bring on what people feared; it put America and other industrialized countries on the path to the Great Depression. The Great Depression happened in large part because people expected something bad to happen. Without that pessimistic shift in expectations triggered by the crash of 1929, there would have been no Great Depression.

A more recent example of a stock market crash, and its ensuing recession, is the stock market crash of 2001, which was initially due to a change in general expectations regarding the performance of the information technology (IT) sector. It is generally believed that the public was over-optimistic about the future of the IT sector in the late 1990s, which had led to a bubble in their stock prices

FIGURE 1.4
The Stock Market, 1928–1932

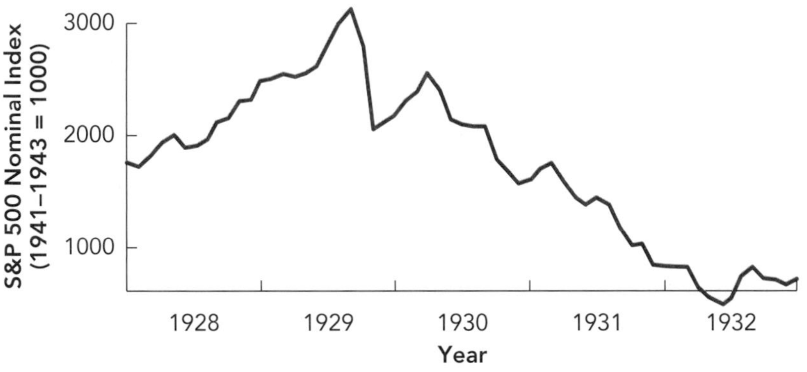

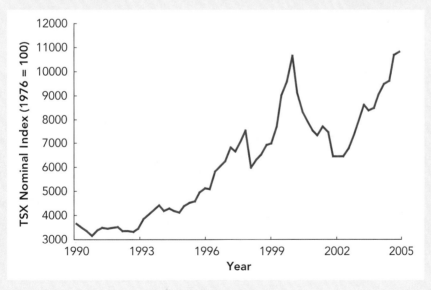

Source: J. Bradford DeLong and Andrei Shleifer, "Closed End Fund Discounts: A Yardstick of Small-Investor Sentiment," *Journal of Portfolio Management* 18:2 (Winter 1992), pp. 46–53.

FIGURE 1.5
The TSX Index, 1990–2005

It is generally believed that the public was over-optimistic about the future of the IT sector in the late 1990s, which led to a bubble in stock prices. The disillusionment about this sector in 2000 caused a sharp decline in that sector's stock prices in 2001. This was aggravated by the September 11 terrorist attacks, which had dire implications for the airline and travel industries.

Source: Adapted from the Statistics Canada CANSIM II database, Series V122620.

(see Figure 1.5). The disillusionment regarding this sector in late 2000 led to a sharp decline in that sector's stock prices in 2001. This was further aggravated by the September 11 terrorist attacks, which had dire implications for the airline and travel industries. These two events contributed to the recession of 2001.

http://cansim2.statcan.ca/

The economy is complex. Economists must simplify it. To understand this complex phenomenon, they restrict their attention to a few behavioural relationships — cause-and-effect links between economic quantities — and a handful of **equilibrium conditions** — conditions that must be satisfied for economic activity to be stable and for supply and demand to be in balance. They attempt to capture these behavioural relationships and equilibrium conditions in simple algebraic equations and geometric diagrams. Then they try to apply their equations and graphs to the real world, while hoping that their simplifications have not made the model a distorted and faulty guide to how the real-world economy works.

Among economists, the process of reducing the complexity and variation of the real-world economy to a handful of equations is known as "building a model." Using models to understand what is going on in the complex real-world economy has been a fruitful intellectual strategy. But model building tends to focus on the variables and relationships that fit easily into the algebraic model. It overlooks other factors.

Economics might have developed as a descriptive science, like sociology or political science. If so, courses in economics would concentrate on economic institutions and practices and the institutional structure of the economy as a whole. But it has not; it has instead become a more abstract science that emphasizes general principles applicable to a variety of situations. Thus a large part of economics involves a particular set of tools: a unique way of thinking about the world that is closely linked with the analytical tools economists use and that is couched in a particular technical language and a particular set of data. While one can get a lot out of sociology and political science courses without learning to think like a sociologist or a political scientist (because of their focus on institutional description), it is not possible to get much out of an economics course without learning to think like an economist.

> **RECAP   MACROECONOMICS**
>
> Macroeconomics is that branch of economics related to the economy as a whole. However, macroeconomics is not only the study of aggregate variables such as output, employment, the stock market, prices, interest rates, and exchange rates. It is also the study of how the behaviour of households and firms affect these aggregates, and thus what policy prescriptions are appropriate. The government's *growth policy* is an important aspect of macroeconomic policy. Nothing matters more in the long run for the quality of life in an economy than its long-run rate of economic growth. The government's *stabilization* policy is also important. Typically, levels of production and employment fluctuate above and below long-run growth trends; and the government tries to stabilize these fluctuations. While economics is a science, it is not a *natural* science. It is a *social* science. The subjects economists study — people — have minds of their own, and think ahead. Thus in economics it is common for the (expected) future to influence the past, and chains of causation can get very tangled. Economics has developed as an abstract, simplifying, model-oriented discipline.

1.2 CANADIAN ECONOMIC GROWTH

Canada has gone through various phases of economic growth and development since its European colonization in the sixteenth and seventeenth centuries. These phases include the period up to Canadian Confederation in 1867, the period between Confederation and World War I, the inter-war period, and the modern era from 1945 to the present. Canadian economic historians have used various economic theories to explain Canada's economic growth.[1] Two prominent and in many respects complementary theories are the neoclassical growth theory and the *staples theory* of Canadian economic growth.

The standard neoclassical growth model, which we will study in Chapter 3, explains economic growth in terms of growth of the factors of production, such as labour and capital, and improvements in technology over time, which are accounted for by changes in total factor productivity. The *staples theory* emphasizes the role of land and natural resources and primary products that have fuelled Canadian economic growth since early on in its history. *Staples* are commodities that are produced with a high content of natural resources and are exported to the rest of the world. In Canada the important staples include fish, fur, timber, wheat, and, in the twentieth century, minerals, newsprint, and hydroelectric power.

According to the staple thesis, the early staples provided the basis for Canada's economic growth and the main impetus for capital accumulation and the development of the country's industrial base to satisfy the flow of primary products and people from the Pacific to the Atlantic Oceans. Further, because of Canada's geography, government intervention was required to build transportation routes and railways to overcome natural barriers. In addition, to protect the development of the manufacturing sector in Canada, protectionist policies were often used in the form of high tariffs imposed on imports of manufactured commodities. Indeed, the construction of the Canadian Pacific Railway (1880–1885) and the imposition of high tariffs on imports were the main ingredients of the national policy implemented by the Macdonald government in 1879.

ECONOMIC ACTIVITY BEFORE 1867

Economic activity before Confederation concentrated on the production of the staples fish, fur, and timber in order to satisfy European demand for these products, mainly in France and Great Britain. Fur trade flourished in the St. Lawrence, Hudson Bay, and Great Lakes areas, and the city of Montreal was a main fur trade post in the seventeenth and eighteenth centuries.

Fur trade depended mainly on hunting and thus it was not very conducive to the development of settlements. On the other hand timber trade that replaced fur trade in the first half of the nineteenth century had economic characteristics that favoured settlements. Lumbering cleared the land for the commencement of agriculture and farming settlements. Also after leaving their Canadian timber in Europe the returning ships provided cheap voyage to immigrants from Great Britain and Ireland. This led to a huge increase of immigrants in (Upper) Canada that were involved more in agriculture than in lumbering. The agricultural sector in Canada grew rapidly in the early part of the nineteenth century.

THE NATIONAL ECONOMY DURING 1867–1913

Canada's economic performance from Confederation to World War I follows two distinct periods. First, the three decades after 1867 were an era of low economic growth and low settlement activity in the west. At the same time, the process of

---

[1] Two excellent references on the history of Canadian economic development are R. Pomfret, *The Economic Development of Canada*, 2nd ed. (Scarborough, ON: Nelson Canada Ltd., 1993) and K. Norrie, D. Owram, and J.C.H. Emery, *A History of the Canadian Economy*, 3rd ed. (Toronto: Thomson Nelson, 2002).

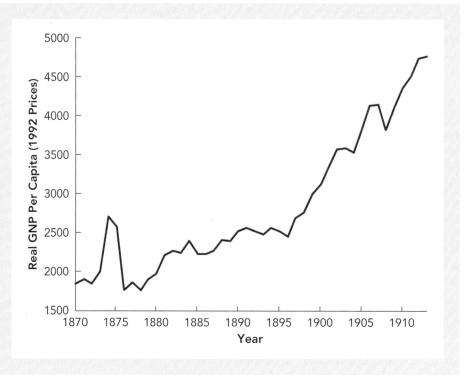

FIGURE 1.6

Real GNP Per Capita (1992 Prices) in Canada, 1870–1913

The Canadian economy grew much faster after 1890 than it did in the preceding quarter century. The difference in performance between the two periods is also reflected in real per capita GNP growth rates. Real per capita GNP grew at an annual rate of 1.06 percent between 1870 and 1896, and at a rate of 3.95 percent between 1896 and 1913.

Source: M.C. Urquhart, *Gross National Product, Canada 1870–1926* (Kingston & Montreal: McGill-Queen's University Press, 1993), Table 1.6, pp. 24–25.

industrialization in the central provinces of Ontario and Quebec was very slow compared to the industrialization activity in the United States. Second, beginning in 1896 and continuing until the outbreak of the War the population of the prairies increased at an accelerating rate, and wheat exports increased dramatically following the upturn in the world price of wheat in the same year. For this reason, this is called the period of the *wheat boom* in Canada. The wheat boom was made possible by the low transportation costs provided by the newly built CPR. Further, the national policy allowed the Canadian industry to grow during this period behind the protective wall of tariffs.

Figure 1.6 shows Canada's real per capita GNP[2] for the period 1870–1913. It is clear from the figure that the Canadian economy grew much faster after 1890 than it did in the preceding quarter century. The difference in performance between the two periods is also reflected in real per capita GNP growth rates. Real per capita GNP grew at an annual rate of 1.06 percent between 1870 and 1896, and at a rate of 3.95 percent between 1896 and 1913.

Another general feature of the Canadian economy during this period is rapid structural change and a shift in the distribution of real GDP by sector. Thus, there was a relative fall in the share of agriculture in the economy and a large increase in the service sector. In 1870 agriculture and services (including construction and utilities) accounted for 37.1 percent and 36 percent of real GDP respectively. By 1910, these shares were 21.6 percent and 50 percent respectively. The share of manufacturing fluctuated but remained unchanged in relative importance at about 22 percent over the four decades.

---

[2] As we discuss in Chapter 2, gross national product (GNP) is the value of all goods and services produced by a country's factors of production (located either at home or abroad) in a given year, whereas gross domestic product (GDP) is the value of all goods and services produced by the factors of production (either domestic or foreign owned) located within a country in a given year.

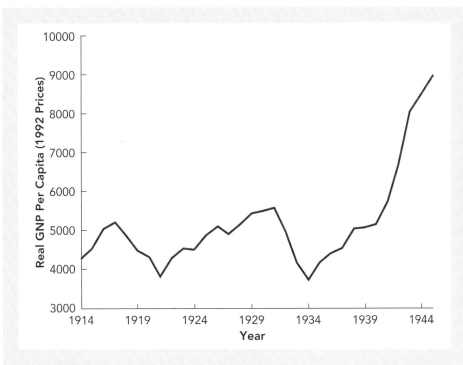

FIGURE 1.7

Real GNP Per Capita (1992 Prices) in Canada, 1914–1945

Canada's economic record in this period shows more than ever its dependence on international events. The main features of the Canadian economy in the period 1914–45 are volatility in economic activity and continuous adjustment to a series of major and prolonged shocks, beginning with World War I in 1914, the Great Depression of the 1930s, and World War II in 1939.

Sources:
1914–1926: Nominal GNP and Population: M.C. Urquhart, (1993). *Gross National Product, Canada 1870–1926.* McGill-Queen's University Press, Kingston & Montreal, Table 1.6, pp. 24–25.
1927–1945: Nominal GNP: From the Statistics Canada publication, "Historical Statistics of Canada," Catalogue 11–516, 1983, Series F13, Population and Series A1.
1914–1945: Price Level: Calculated from the Statistics Canada CANSIM I database, Series P100000.

THE TURBULENT YEARS 1914–1945

The main features of the Canadian economy in the period 1914–1945 are volatility in economic activity and continuous adjustment to a series of major and prolonged shocks, beginning with World War I in 1914, the Great Depression of the 1930s, and World War II in 1939. See Figure 1.7.

Canada's economic record in this period shows more than ever its dependence on international events. Real per capita GNP fell in 1914 and then rose every year until 1917. This pattern was followed by a prolonged decline until 1921 and thereafter a pronounced expansion that peaked in 1928. Because of the international depression real per capita GNP declined sharply during the period 1929–1933 back down to its 1921 level. However by 1940 it regained its 1928 value and continued expanding throughout World War II. During this period Canada's trade relations shifted. Total trade (exports plus imports) with the U.K. fell, in relative terms, throughout this period while trade with the U.S. increased.

http://www.statcan.ca/
http://www.statcan.ca/english/
freepub/11-516-XIE/sectiona/
toc.htm

THE POST-WAR ERA: SINCE 1945

The modern post-war era is characterized by significant economic growth. At the end of the 1990s the Canadian economy was larger, richer, and structurally different from that at the end of World War II. In real terms (1992 dollars), GDP increased from $109.9 billion in 1947 to $938.3 billion in 2001, or by more than 8.5 times. Over the same period Canada's population increased by almost 2.5 times, from 12.5 million to 31.0 million. This means that real per capita GDP increased by 3.4 times, so that, using this as a measure of well-being, the average Canadian was more than three times as well off in 2001 as at the end of World War II.

Another feature of the Canadian economy in the post-war era is the ongoing structural change. During this period, there was a continuing decline in the proportion of labour employed in the agricultural sector and a steady increase in the proportion of labour employed in the service sector. The manufacturing sector's share of employment peaked in the mid-1950s and has been declining slowly ever since. Resource industries, other than agriculture, have maintained their small share of total employment over more than a century.

In terms of overall macroeconomic performance, the post-war period divides naturally into two sub-periods. The first runs from 1946 to 1973, and the second from 1973 to the present. The dominant characteristic of the first sub-period is rapid growth and prosperity, while that of the second is a slowdown in growth and economic challenge. For instance, real per capita GDP grew at an average annual rate of 2.8 percent between 1947 and 1973, but at only 1.7 percent between 1973 and 1992.

The sub-period from the end of World War II to the early 1970s is one of the most prosperous in Canada's economic history. The nation benefited from the new fixed exchange rate regime of Bretton Woods in 1944, and the creation of institutions such as the World Bank and the International Monetary Fund (IMF) that provided much needed stability in the post-war international monetary system. Canada as a small open economy reaped the benefits of increased trade in goods, services, and primary commodities. The unrivalled U.S. expansion in the two decades following WWII increased Canadian exports to that country and created employment and economic growth at home. Added to these forces were other internal factors such as growing population and income, rising labour force participation rates, new infrastructure developments, more education and training, and new resource discoveries such as oil and natural gas.

With respect to the second sub-period from 1973 to the present, the decade 1973–1982 turned out to be a challenging one for Canada as well as for the global economy. Macroeconomic performance deteriorated and economic growth slowed, and the economy experienced the twin problems of inflation and unemployment or *stagflation* that seemed to defy standard macroeconomic theory, and was ultimately explained in terms of negative supply shocks hitting the economy, such as rising oil prices. Following the oil price increase in 1973–1974, real GDP growth fell to 4.4 percent in 1974 from 7.7 percent a year earlier, and then to 2.6 percent in 1975. It rose to 6.2 percent in 1976, but it declined thereafter, only to become negative in 1982, following the second oil price shock in 1981. At the same time unemployment and inflation increased to reach double-digit levels in 1982.

The period since 1982 has been one of a series of government policy actions designed to increase the efficiency and productivity of the Canadian economy. The major issue of freer trade with the United States was resolved by the signing of the Free Trade Agreement (FTA) with the U.S. under the Mulroney government in 1989. The FTA was expanded to the North America Free Trade Agreement (NAFTA) to include Mexico in 1994. Also, the large government budget deficits of the past two decades were reduced and turned into surpluses, following the Chretien government's commitment to do so starting in 1995. Further, on the monetary side, the zero inflation policy, introduced in 1988 by the then Bank of Canada Governor John Crow, has led to a dramatic reduction in the rate of inflation in the range of 1 to 3 percent from double-digit inflation. However, although these measures

http://www.bank-banque-canada.ca/

have promoted trade and growth in the country, aggregate productivity growth in Canada has fallen behind that of the U.S., especially after the mid-1990s, meaning that living standards in Canada have not kept up with those south of the border.

Figure 1.8 provides a snapshot of the Canadian economy for the period 1926–2005 in terms of movements of real (1971 dollars) GDP per worker. The figure shows clearly the downturns of economic activity due to the Great Depression in 1929–1933, the 1945–1946 aftermath of WWII that was associated with reduced military expenditures, the stagflation of 1981–1982, the 1991–1992 recession caused perhaps by tight monetary policy (zero inflation policy) and the slowdown of the U.S. economy, and the 2001–2002 slowdown due to the stock market crash of 2001. The figure also shows the sustained post-WWII expansion of the Canadian economy and the slowdown of economic growth since 1973. The average annual rate of growth of output per worker was 2.7 percent during the period 1950–1973, while for the period 1973–1995 it was only 1.6 percent. After 1995 this rate of growth has increased by a small amount, largely due to the adoption of computers in the production process. The post-1973 slowdown did not affect the Canadian economy

FIGURE 1.8
Real GDP per Worker (1971 Prices) in Canada, 1926–2005
The figure shows clearly the downturns of economic activity due to the Great Depression in 1929–1933, the 1945–1946 aftermath of WWII that was associated with reduced military expenditures, the stagflation of 1981–1982, the 1991–1992 recession caused perhaps by tight monetary policy (zero inflation policy) and the slowdown of the U.S. economy, and the 2001–2002 slowdown due to the stock market crash of 2001. The figure also shows the sustained post-WWII expansion of the Canadian economy and the slowdown of economic growth since 1973. After 1995 the rate of growth has increased by a small amount.

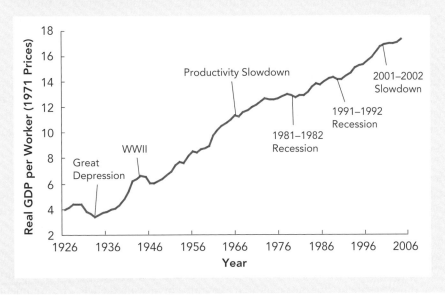

Source: Statistics Canada, Historical Statistics of Canada, Series F55 (real GNP, 1926–1960), D129 (employed persons, 1926–1945), D139 (employed persons, 1946–1975); and CANSIM II, Series V1992067 (real GDP, 1961–2005), V498086 (nominal GDP, 1961–2005), and V2064890 (employed persons, 1976–2005).

TABLE 1.2
The Magnitude of the Post-1973 Productivity Slowdown in the G-7 Economies

| | Output-per-worker in Manufacturing | |
Country	1961–1972	1973–2005
Canada	4.0	2.6
France	6.2	3.6
Germany*	4.7	2.4
Italy	5.3	2.7
Japan	9.1	3.9
U.K.	3.2	3.2
U.S.	3.5	3.7

Source: U.S. Department of Labor, Bureau of Labor Statistics
Note: *Includes only West Germany until 1990.

alone. It hit — to different degrees and with different effects — the other major economies of the world's industrial core of the U.S., Western Europe, and Japan as well (see Table 1.2). Box 1.4 below provides some possible explanations for this slowdown.

1.4

BOX

DETAILS

POSSIBLE CAUSES OF THE PRODUCTIVITY SLOWDOWN

Observers have pointed to four factors as possible causes of the productivity slowdown: oil prices, the baby boom, increased problems of economic measurement, and environmental protection expenditures — and there are no doubt others. In this Box we discuss each one of these explanations and point out their shortcomings.

The most prominent explanation is the tripling of world oil prices by the OPEC cartel in 1973, in the wake of the third Arab-Israeli war. Productivity growth slowed at almost exactly the same time that oil prices skyrocketed. Economists hypothesized that in response to the tripling of world oil prices firms began redirecting their capital expenditures from capital that produced more output to capital that used less energy; firms retired a large share of their most energy-intensive capital and began to substitute workers for energy use wherever possible. The problem with this explanation is twofold: First, since 1986 real oil prices have been *lower* than they were before 1973; hence the productivity slowdown should have ended a decade ago. Second, energy costs are not that large a share of the typical business's costs.

The argument that the productivity slowdown can be explained by expenditures on environmental protection is a branch of the "problems-of-measurement" argument. When the price of electricity goes up because power companies switch to burning higher-priced low-sulfur coal or install sulfur-removing scrubbers in their chimneys, they are producing not just electric power but electric power plus cleaner air. But the System of National Accounts does not count pollution reduction as a valued economic output. Industrialized economies have spent a fortune on environmental protection in the past generation, and have in gross received big benefits from this investment, but the gains aren't included in measured GDP. The argument that the productivity slowdown can be explained by problems of economic measurement is a bit subtle. Few doubt that these problems lead to understatements of the rate of economic growth. But to account for a slowdown in economic growth, the problems of measurement must have gotten worse. They must be worse now than they were three decades ago.

In the 1970s the large baby-boom generation began to enter the labour force. The relatively young labour force had many more workers with little experience than did the labour force of the 1960s and 1950s. Some economists argue that this fall in the average level of labour-force experience generated the productivity slowdown. Others point out that the baby-boom generation had little experience but a lot of education and that in the past education had been a powerful *booster of* productivity. The average level of education in the labour force increased quite rapidly as the baby-boom generation entered the economy.

The causes of the productivity slowdown remain uncertain, and the slowdown itself remains a mystery.

RECAP   CANADIAN ECONOMIC GROWTH

Economic historians have attempted to explain Canadian economic growth in terms of growth of its factors of production and technological improvements over time, as well as in terms of the *staples theory*, which emphasizes the role of land and natural resources in economic growth. Staples are commodities produced with a high content of natural resources and exported abroad. Canadian economic activity before confederation concentrated on the production of the staples fish, fur, and timber. The period 1867–1913 includes the *wheat boom* beginning in 1896 and rapid growth due to the development of agriculture. The period 1914–1945 was turbulent, including World War I, the Great Depression of the 1930s, and World War II. The post-war era since 1945 has been characterized by significant economic growth and increasing living standards for Canadians.

1.3 THE CURRENT MACROECONOMIC SITUATION

CANADA

The state of the Canadian economy is regularly reported by the Department of Finance in its quarterly publication *The Economy in Brief* and its annual Economic and Fiscal update. As with the U.S. economy, the Canadian economy enjoyed a long period of expansion in the 1990s. With 22 consecutive quarters of growth, this was Canada's longest period of expansion since the 1960s. The real GDP growth rate in 2000 was around 4.3 percent. Because of the decline in the information technology sector at the beginning of 2001, the growth rate of GDP declined in 2001. This decline was exacerbated by the September 11 terrorist attacks in the U.S., which resulted in a loss of confidence and decline in the travel and airline industries. In spite of this, the growth rate in 2001 was negative only in the third quarter (−0.6 percent). The growth rate in the fourth quarter of 2001 was 2 percent. As

www.fin.gc.ca

Canada's real GDP growth was not negative for two consecutive quarters, some economists argue that it did not suffer a recession in 2001.

One of the most important factors that reduced the severity of the slowdown was the strength of consumer confidence, which held up consumption expenditures despite the sharp declines in investment. The reason for the consumer confidence, despite the fall in stock prices, was the sharp rise in house prices. This was fuelled by the dramatic reductions in real interest rates by the U.S. Federal Reserve and the Bank of Canada. During 2001 the U.S. Federal Reserve lowered the Federal Funds Rate 11 times, by a total of 475 basis points (that is, 4.75 percentage points). The Bank of Canada followed suit, lowering its Bank Rate 10 times during 2001, by a total of 375 basis points. This led to lower mortgage rates, which in turn raised the demand for residential investment. Lower interest rates also led to dramatic increases in demand for automobiles and other consumer durables.

Following the 2001 global slowdown, Canada's output growth outpaced that of the U.S. and other Group of Seven (G-7) countries. But, in 2003, Canada experienced a series of unfavourable shocks. First, the outbreak of severe acute respiratory syndrome (SARS), which had a heavy toll on tourism, was soon followed by the discovery of a case of BSE (bovine spongiform encephalitis, known as mad cow disease) in Alberta that led to a sharp decline in the exports of beef. These unfavourable shocks were compounded by the unprecedented appreciation of the Canadian dollar in 2003, which made Canadian goods expensive relative to foreign produced goods, hurting the exports-oriented industries.

Following the mid-2003 slowdown, the Canadian economy has demonstrated remarkable resilience, rebounding sharply in terms of real GDP growth. In 2004 and 2005, GDP increased at the rate of 2.9 percent per year, largely due to strong increases in domestic demand and exports resulting from a global recovery — and above the rate recorded in the U.S. At the same time, the unemployment rate fell steadily, and stood at 6.4 percent in February 2006, its lowest level in over 30 years.

During the last three-quarters of 2001 corporate profits declined substantially, after 11 successive gains in previous quarters. In the last quarter of 2001 corporate profits declined by 20.5 percent. This was the main reason for the decline in business fixed investment, and reduction in inventories, which pulled down the growth rate. Because of the fall in the growth rate the unemployment rate had an upward trend, increasing from 6.7 percent in June 2000 to 7.2 percent in September 2001.

The decline in the value of the Canadian dollar in terms of other currencies, most notably the US dollar, in the 1990s was worrisome to many Canadians. There were two major reasons for this. First, because Canada has a relatively large primary goods sector, the fall in the world prices of commodities, which are quoted in US dollars, in the 1990s meant that Canada received a smaller number of Canadian dollars for its exports of primary commodities, for example, energy, forestry, mining and agricultural products. This, in effect, reduced the demand for the Canadian dollar in the foreign exchange market. Second, there has been an increase in the productivity gap between the U.S. and Canadian manufacturing sectors. This has reduced the competitiveness of the Canadian manufacturing sector, reducing their exports and the demand for the Canadian dollar that is associated with them. These two trends led to the decline in the value of the Canadian dollar in the 1990s by reducing the demand for it in the foreign exchange markets.

Nevertheless, since 2003, the Canadian dollar has appreciated more than 30 percent against the US dollar. Two major reasons for this are the rising commodity prices in recent years and, more important, the growing indebtedness of the U.S. against other countries. Given low private savings and high budget deficits, the U.S. has been borrowing heavily from other countries in order to finance its expenditures. Several economists believe that international investors are not willing to buy more U.S. bonds and equities as before, because their portfolios already contain a very large volume of U.S. assets. With the demand for U.S. assets saturated, the demand for the US dollar is not as buoyant as before, leading to a decline in its value relative to other currencies, or equivalently to an increase in the values of other currencies relative to the US dollar.

In much of the 1970s Canada's labour productivity (that is, output per worker) was strong relative to that of the U.S. However, since the mid-1980s Canada's relative labour productivity followed a sharp downward trend, mainly for the following two reasons: First, the primary goods sectors are a relatively large part of the Canadian economy; and these sectors, in general, experience less productivity growth than the manufacturing sector. Second, since the mid-1990s the U.S. economy has experienced a substantial gain in productivity from the information and communication technologies (ICT). The U.S. industries have been very fast in developing the ICT sector and in adopting computers in the manufacturing sector. It is hoped that this technology adoption will eventually take place in the Canadian manufacturing sector as well; and that free trade with the U.S. will contribute to this process.

The monetary and fiscal policies followed by the Bank of Canada and the Ministry of Finance have been very effective in recent years. The Bank of Canada continues its policy of maintaining the inflation rate between 1 and 3 percent. The inflation rate has been within this range since 1992. The target has been easier to maintain in recent years with the government's fiscal success of turning its budget deficits of the 1980s and early 1990s into surpluses. The government budget has been in a surplus since 1996. With these surpluses, as well as the good performance of the economy, the government has been able to reduce the federal debt-to-GDP ratio from its peak of 71 percent in 1995–1996 to 34.9 percent at the end of 2003. The federal budget is expected to balance or to be in a surplus in 2005 and in each of the two subsequent years. With the inflation rate and the federal budget under control, the important fundamentals of the economy appear to be promising, allowing the Bank of Canada to respond rapidly and effectively to unfavourable shocks.

THE UNITED STATES

In 1995, the U.S. macroeconomy was enjoying a moderately strong but uneven recovery. The collapse of the dot-com stock market bubble in 2000 and the September 11, 2001, terrorist destruction of the World Trade Center and attack on the Pentagon triggered a decline in economic activity — a recession — as businesses that were more pessimistic about the prospect of future profits and scared of the uncertainty produced by terrorism cut back their investment spending, and production and employment fell. Between the beginning of the recession and the end of 2001, the U.S. economy lost 0.9 million jobs. In response to these adverse shocks, the *Federal Reserve* reduced interest rates far and fast to try to encourage businesses to invest more: The three-month money-market nominal interest rate that had been 6.74 percent per year in the summer of 2000 had been cut to 1.75 percent per year by the late fall of 2001 and to 1 percent by the middle of 2003. And the Bush tax cuts directed more money into the hands of consumers, who increased their spending, which reduced the magnitude of the recession's spending shortfall.

Thus slowly in 2002 and more rapidly in 2003, the economy began to recover. Demand and production began to grow again. However, demand and production growth in 2003 and 2004 was, in everyone's estimation, insufficient. Because of rapid underlying productivity growth in the American economy, the renewed economic expansion did little to expand employment. With a relatively disappointing job market, wages did not rise by much. The recovery of 2003 and 2004 did an enormous amount to boost productivity and profits and a substantial amount to boost production but little to boost employment or wages.

By the end of 2004 there were renewed worries among economists. One set of worries was that the United States could not afford the large tax cuts of the Bush administration — that they would produce very large budget deficits that would retard economic growth in the future. The Bush tax cuts, in combination with the extra defense spending authorized after September 11, eliminated the government budget surplus that had been painfully created during the 1990s. Given Americans' low private saving rate, the elimination of public saving was likely in the medium run to reduce investment, and thus to slow growth. And the tax cuts were not designed in a way that would produce many significant supply-side production benefits. The principal long-run impact of the tax cuts would be a further reduction in America's already low national saving rate and a slowing of economic growth.

Moreover, by the end of 2004 there were worries that a forthcoming sharp decline in the value of the dollar would provide a further adverse and contractionary shock to the United States and to the world economy. Should foreign exchange speculators lose confidence in the dollar, the value of foreign currency could rise far and fast, possibly causing macroeconomic problems. Economists are very good at pointing out economic situations that are inconsistent with fundamental values — policies, imbalances, or balance sheet problems that cannot possibly last and are bound to end, perhaps in a crisis. But they are bad at forecasting when and how such imbalances will end.

The recession of 2001 had been preceded by a remarkable decade-long economic boom. Policy makers and economists advocating the Clinton administration's economic programs — deficit reduction and the lowering of trade barriers — had done so in the interest of accelerating long-run growth. Reduced trade barriers would allow for closer international integration, a finer international division of labour, and increased productivity. Deficit reduction would make possible high-investment economic expansion, which would then become high-productivity growth expansion.

EUROPE

In the early 2000s 11 western European countries adopted the euro as their common currency. The adoption of the euro was followed not by strong growth but by stagnation and recession. European unemployment rates mounted toward 10 percent between 2000 and 2004, and real GDP growth for the euro zone was rarely above 2 percent per year. There was certainly room for economic expansion in Europe: Consumer prices were rising at less than 2 percent per year. The challenge for European economic policy remained one of avoiding rises in inflation while attempting to reduce western Europe's distressingly high and stubborn rate of unemployment, yet interpreting the European Central Bank's actions as part of any policy intended to try to meet that challenge remains difficult.

However, for the first time in decades Europeans were hopeful that the next decade would bring a reduction, not an increase, in unemployment. Changes in policy were making the European labour market more flexible and in the long run should make it easier for firms to change the number of workers they employ, which should make it easier for workers to find jobs and thus lower unemployment. Most of western Europe is perhaps half a decade behind the United States in its adoption of data processing and data communications technology. Thus there is good reason to hope that the information-technology-driven productivity growth acceleration experienced by the United States in the late 1990s should be visible in western Europe in the late 2000s.

And in eastern Europe, economies continue to grow, as the long and slow process of "transition" away from communism has continued.

JAPAN

At the end of 2004, Japanese interest rates remained astonishingly low — 0.03 percent per year in the three-month money market — and were expected to remain low for the foreseeable future. Japan was still undergoing deflation, with consumer prices expected to fall by 1.0 percent in the next year. However, this trend soon reversed itself. As of May 2006, the Japanese inflation rate was positive and expected to continue to stay positive in the coming year.

Fortunately, Japan is no longer in recession: The country has experienced several straight quarters of positive growth in real GDP. Although unemployment in Japan remains above 5 percent — an astonishingly high level for Japan — it is no longer increasing. There is good reason to believe that Japan's decade-long experience with stagnation and recession is over, and that Japanese economic growth has resumed.

The start of the 1990s saw the collapse of the Japanese stock and real estate markets, the end of the so-called *bubble economy*. The 1990s as a whole saw the breakdown of the Japanese model of economic growth, as the economy stagnated for much of the decade. Now there is a general recognition that Japan faces a structural economic crisis. But there is no political consensus as to what is to be done, and the major political steps that need to be taken to restore growth — restructuring the Japanese financial system and deregulating transportation and distribution — have been long delayed.

The Bank of Japan is now pursuing a policy of making *short-term safe nominal interest rates* as close to zero as it can. But what matters for investment spending is not a low short-term safe nominal interest rate but a low long-term risky real interest rate, and that will remain high as long as bond traders fear that (1) the low–interest rate policy may be temporary, (2) many companies may go bankrupt and never repay the money they borrow, and (3) prices may decline more rapidly, turning low nominal interest rates into high inflation-adjusted real interest rates. For most of the 1990s and into the early 2000s, even interest rates near zero proved insufficient to boost investment.

EMERGING MARKETS

Elsewhere in the world, the big economic news is the enormous growth booms in China and in India. Together their populations make up 40 percent of the human race, and their economies were expected to grow at 8 percent and 6 percent in 2005, respectively. The pace of investment in China is blistering as its exports continue to expand: China consumes more than a quarter of the world's steel and cement. China's boom is driven by its manufacturing exports. India's boom is driven by investment for the internal market and by growing exports of business and other services to the world's industrial core.

In the case of China, the boom is further driven by an undervalued exchange rate. The Chinese government would rather sell its workers' products cheaply than watch the value of its currency rise and risk high unemployment in its major cities. The Bank of China (along with other Asian central banks) buys up huge amounts of dollar-denominated assets every month in order to keep the value of the US dollar from falling and the value of the Chinese yuan from rising. The U.S. government does not strongly object: Purchases by the Bank of China keep U.S. interest rates from rising and allow the funding of the U.S. government budget deficit and of much U.S. private investment that could not be covered by America's own small national saving.

As of the end of 2004, the financial crisis in East Asia of the past decade was only a distant memory. The panic that started in 1997 on the part of investors in New York, Frankfurt, London, and Tokyo, and the consequent withdrawal of their money from emerging market economies, imposed very high costs: massive bankruptcies, high interest rates, increases in unemployment, falls in production. But foreign investors appear to have regained confidence in East Asian economies.

However, the destabilizing factors in the world economy that made for the East Asian crisis of 1997–1998 are still present, as can be seen by the crash of the Argentinean economy at the end of 2001. Many argued that a critical cause of the East Asian crisis and, before it, the Mexican financial crisis was that the governments retained the ability to devalue and depreciate the currency and that that was a key source of the capital flight that rippled through their economies and set off the crises. Argentina, however, handed authority over its exchange rate to an independent organization — a "currency board." Yet that did not help. When in 2001 investors in New York, Frankfurt, London, Tokyo, and elsewhere became worried that the Argentine government's failure to balance its budget heralded a future of more rapid money printing and inflation, the same factors came into play. And the fact of Argentina's currency board only meant that the crisis became more convoluted and difficult to resolve — it was still not resolved three years after its beginning.

Elsewhere in Latin America as of 2005, growth continued to be positive but disappointing. The Mexican government continued to wrestle with the problem of fixing its still-insolvent banking system. Brazil struggled under the burden of its large national debt and attempted to fulfill the hopes of growth with equity raised by the election of left-of-centre president Luis Ignacio da Silva.

The most disappointing areas of the world as far as economic growth was concerned continued to be the Middle East and Africa.

RECAP THE CURRENT MACROECONOMIC SITUATION

The Canadian economy, like the U.S. economy, enjoyed a long period of expansion in the 1990s. Because of the decline in the information technology sector, the growth rate of GDP declined in 2001. This decline was exacerbated by the September 11 terrorist attacks in the U.S., which resulted in a loss of confidence in the travel and airline industries.

Following the 2001 global slowdown, Canada's output growth outpaced that of the U.S. and other G-7 countries. But, in 2003, Canada experienced a series of unfavourable shocks: SARS, a case of mad cow disease, and an unprecedented appreciation of the Canadian dollar. Following the mid-2003 slowdown, the Canadian economy has demonstrated remarkable resilience, rebounding sharply in terms of real GDP growth.

In the U.S., because of rapid underlying productivity growth, the recovery of 2003 and 2004 did enormous amounts to boost productivity and profits but little to boost employment or wages.

The adoption of the euro by 11 western European countries in the early 2000s was followed not by strong growth but by stagnation and recession. Nevertheless, changes in policy were making the European labour market more flexible, which would hopefully reduce unemployment in the long run.

At the end of 2004, the Japanese interest rates remained astonishingly low, as Japan was still undergoing deflation. In 2005 and 2006, however, the inflation rate was positive.

Elsewhere in the world, the big economic news is the enormous growth booms in China and in India, which were driven by their exports to the world's industrial core. The prospects for the rest of the emerging markets depend on how rapidly the industrial core would recover and how strong its demand for imports would be.

CHAPTER SUMMARY

1. Macroeconomics is the study of the economy in the large — the determination of the economywide levels of production, employment and unemployment, and inflation or deflation.

2. There are three key reasons to study macroeconomics: to gain cultural literacy, to understand how economic trends affect you personally, and to exercise your responsibility as a voter and citizen.

3. Canadian economic activity before Confederation concentrated on the production of the staples fish, fur, and timber.

4. The period 1867–1913 for Canada includes the *wheat boom* beginning in 1896 and rapid growth due to the development of agriculture.

5. The post-war era since 1945 has been characterized by significant economic growth and increasing living standards for Canadians.

6. Reasons for the widening gap between Canadian and U.S. productivity include (1) the relatively large agriculture and primary resources sectors in Canada and (2) the substantial gain in productivity from the information and communication technologies in the U.S. since the mid-1990s.

KEY TERMS

deflation (p. 5)

depression (p. 5)

equilibrium condition (p. 12)

expansion (p. 5)

expectations (p. 10)

macroeconomics (p. 2)

microeconomics (p. 3)

recession (p. 5)

ANALYTICAL EXERCISES

1. What are the key differences between microeconomics and macroeconomics?

2. How would a sharp increase in oil prices reduce productivity growth?

3. How would the entry of a large number of young people into the labour force reduce productivity growth?

4. How can changes in expectations lead to a stock market crash and a recession?

5. Roughly, how much higher is *measured* real GDP per worker in 2005 than it was in 1973?

POLICY EXERCISES

1. What have been the main factors that have contributed to Canadian economic growth since Confederation? Briefly outline Canada's economic development since Confederation.

2. Why do you think Canada did better than Argentina in the twentieth century?

3. What are some possible reasons for the increase in the value of the Canadian dollar in recent times?

4. What are the prominent features of monetary and fiscal policies in Canada in recent years?

5. Discuss some of the important macroeconomic events in the U.S. in recent years.

2 Measuring the Macroeconomy

QUESTIONS

What key data do macroeconomists look at?

How are key macroeconomic data estimated and calculated?

What is the difference between nominal and real values?

How are stock market values related to interest rates?

How are interest rates related to the price level and the inflation rate?

How is unemployment related to total production?

What is right — and what is wrong — with the key measure of economic activity, real GDP?

2.1 THE IMPORTANCE OF DATA

Economics is a *social* science: It is about us, about what we do. Thus it shares with other social sciences one important source of information: introspection. We can ask ourselves "Why did I do that?" or "If I had done that, what would I have been thinking?" We can ask other people and listen to their answers ("I did that because . . ."). In most of the other social sciences, the overwhelming source of information is introspection, either our own or other people's.

Economists are in a better position than most other social scientists as far as their sources of information are concerned. Everything that passes through the economy is priced and sold. Thus economists have quantitative data to work with: prices, quantities, and values. Having quantitative data allows economists to do more than many other social scientists. They can use theories to make not just qualitative but quantitative forecasts. With data they can test theories, comparing what was actually the case to what various theories would have predicted.

SIX KEY VARIABLES

You can get a good idea of the pulse of recent economic activity by simply looking at six key economic variables. Together they summarize the state of the macroeconomy. If you want to be able to say more than "the economy is good" or "the economy is not so good," you need to understand and be able to analyze these six variables:

- Real gross domestic product.
- The unemployment rate.
- The inflation rate.
- The interest rate.
- The level of the stock market.
- The exchange rate.

The first two are the most important: They are directly and immediately connected to people's material well-being. The other four are indicators and controls that are not directly and immediately connected to people's current material well-being, but they profoundly influence the economy's direction. Let's look at each of these indicators more closely.

REAL GDP

The first key variable is the level of real gross domestic product, called **real GDP** or often just GDP for short. "Real" GDP means GDP adjusted for changes in the overall level of prices. If total spending doubles, because the average level of prices doubles, but the total flow of commodities does not change, then real GDP does not change. Economic variables are either *real* — that is, they have been adjusted for changes in the price level and inflation — or *nominal* — that is, they have not been adjusted for changes in the price level and inflation.

"Gross" means that this measure includes the replacement of worn-out and obsolete equipment and structures as well as completely new investment. (Gross measures contrast with net measures, which include only investment that adds to the capital stock — not investment that merely replaces worn-out and obsolete capital stock. Net measures are better than gross measures, but the information needed to construct them is not as reliable.)

"Domestic" means that this measure counts economic activity that happens in Canada, whether or not the workers are legal residents and whether or not the factories are owned by Canadian residents.

Finally, "product" means that real GDP represents the production of *final goods and services*. It includes both consumption goods (things that consumers buy, take home or take out, and consume) and investment goods (things like machine tools, office equipment, and newly constructed houses and office buildings, which boost the country's capital stock and productive capacity). It also includes government purchases, things that the government (acting as our collective agent) buys and uses.

Real GDP divided by the number of workers in the economy is the most frequently used summary index of the economy. It is a measure of how well the economy produces goods and services that people find useful — the necessities, conveniences, and luxuries of life. It is, however, a flawed and imperfect index. It says nothing, for instance, about the relative distribution of the nation's economic product. And because it measures market prices not user satisfaction, it is an imperfect measure of material well-being. Nevertheless, **real GDP per worker** remains the best readily available economic index.

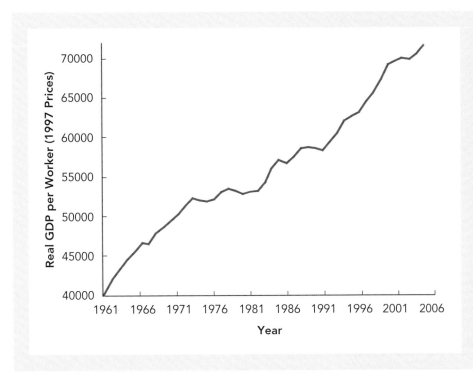

FIGURE 2.1

Real GDP per Worker (1997 Prices) in Canada, 1961–2005

Despite temporary setbacks in recessions and depressions — of which the Great Depression of the 1930s was by far the largest — the principal event of the twentieth century was the almost quintupling of measured real GDP per worker from the 1920s to the 2000s. Other, more recent, macroeconomic events include the 1974–1975 and 1980–1983 major recessions, the 1990–1991 minor recession, and the two-decade-long period of stagnation from the early 1970s to the early 1990s as well as the slowdown of 2000–2001.

Source: Statistics Canada, Historical Statistics of Canada, Series D129 (employed persons, 1961–1975); and CANSIM II database, Series V2064890 (employed persons, 1976–2005) and V1992067 (real GDP, 1961–2005).

Figure 2.1 shows real GDP per worker in Canada during the period 1961–2005, in constant 1997 prices. During this period real GDP had a positive trend. Despite temporary setbacks in recessions and depressions — of which the Great Depression of the 1930s was by far the largest — the principal event of the twentieth century was the almost quintupling of measured real GDP per worker from the 1920s to the 2000s. Other, more recent, macroeconomic events include the 1974–1975 and 1980–1983 major recessions, the 1990–1991 minor recession, and the two-decade-long period of stagnation from the early 1970s to the early 1990s as well as the slowdown of 2000–2001.

THE UNEMPLOYMENT RATE

The second key variable is the **unemployment rate**. The unemployed are people who want to work and are actively looking for jobs but have not yet found one (or have not yet found one that they consider attractive enough to take). The unemployment rate is equal to the number of unemployed people divided by the total labour force, which is the sum of the number of unemployed people and the number of people who have jobs.

Most people consider unemployment to be a bad thing, and it usually is. Yet it is important to notice that an economy with no unemployment at all would probably be a badly working economy. Just as an economy needs inventories of goods — goods in transit, goods in process, goods in warehouses or on store shelves — in order to function smoothly, it needs "inventories" of jobs looking for workers (vacancies) and workers looking for jobs (the unemployed). An economy in which

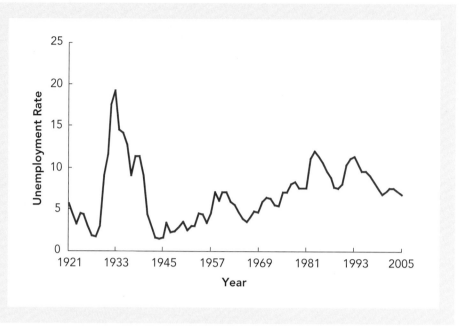

Source: Statistics Canada, Historical Statistics of Canada, Series D129 (labour force, 1921–1945), D132 (unemployed, 1921–1945), and D233 (unemployment rate, 1946–1975); and CANSIM II database, Series V2064894 (unemployment rate, 1976–2005).

FIGURE 2.2
The Canadian Unemployment Rate, 1921–2005

In the twentieth century Canada's unemployment rate dipped as low as 1.4 percent during World War II and rose as high as 19 percent during the Great Depression of the 1930s. Since World War II, Canada's unemployment rate has fluctuated between 3 and 12 percent, with the highest rates occurring in the decades of the 1980s and 1990s.

each business grabbed the first person who walked through the door to fill a newly open job and in which each worker took the first job offered would be a less productive economy. Workers should be somewhat choosy about what jobs they take. They should decline jobs when they think that "this job pays too little" or "this job would be too unpleasant." Likewise, employers should be choosy about which workers they hire. Such *frictional unemployment* is an inevitable part of the process that makes good matches between workers and firms — matches that pair qualified workers with jobs that use their qualifications.

During recessions and depressions, however, unemployment is definitely not frictional. In these downturns in the business cycle the unemployment rate can rise far above the level resulting from a normal and healthy process of job search. The market economy breaks down, failing to match workers willing and able to work with businesses that could put their skills and labour power to work making useful goods and services. Economists call this type of unemployment *cyclical unemployment*. When the unemployment rate is high, the market economy is not functioning well. The unemployment rate is the best indicator of how well the economy is doing relative to its productive potential.

As can be seen from Figure 2.2, in the twentieth century Canada's unemployment rate dipped as low as 1.4 percent during World War II and rose as high as 19 percent during the Great Depression of the 1930s, the principal macroeconomic catastrophe of the past century. No other recession or depression came close to having the Great Depression's devastating impact. During the Great Depression, the unemployment rate in the United States rose to 25 percent, and in Germany to 33 percent. Since World War II, Canada's unemployment rate has fluctuated between 3 and 12 percent, with the highest rates occurring in the decades of the 1980s and 1990s.

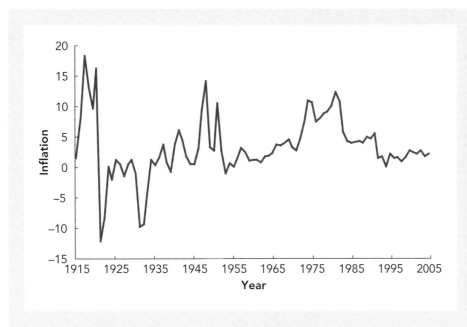

Source: Adapted from the Statistics Canada CANSIM II database, Series V735319 (CPI inflation).

FIGURE 2.3
Canadian Inflation Rates, 1915–2005
Significant peaks of inflation occurred during World Wars I and II. Before World War II, deep recessions, like the Great Depression of the 1930s, were accompanied by deflation: a decline in the level of overall prices. The accelerating inflation of the late 1970s and early 1980s led the Bank of Canada to raise interest rates in order to decrease aggregate demand. As a result, there was a steep decline in inflation in the mid-1980s. The inflation rate was further reduced in the 1990s.

THE INFLATION RATE

A third key economic indicator is the **inflation rate**, a measure of how fast the overall price level is rising. If the inflation rate is 5 percent this year, it means that in general things cost 5 percent more this year than they did last year in money terms, in terms of symbols printed on dollar bills. A very high inflation rate — more than 20 percent a month, say — can cause massive economic destruction, as the price system breaks down and the possibility of using profit-and-loss calculations to make rational business decisions vanishes. Such episodes of *hyperinflation* are among the worst economic disasters that can befall an economy. The most prominent hyperinflation in the twentieth century was that of Germany in the 1920s, when at times it was over 1000 percent *per month*. Fortunately, the Canadian economy has not experienced a hyperinflation in the twentieth century.

Figure 2.3 shows the Canadian inflation rates for the period 1915–2005. Significant peaks of inflation occurred during World Wars I and II. Before World War II, deep recessions, like the Great Depression of the 1930s, were accompanied by deflation: a decline in the level of overall prices that bankrupted businesses and banks, exacerbating the fall in output and employment. Strangely, since World War II, there has been only one single year — 1953 — during which the price level declined. Otherwise, there has been inflation; that is, the rate of change of the price level has been positive.

The accelerating inflation of the late 1970s and early 1980s led the bank of Canada to raise interest rates in order to decrease aggregate demand. As a result, there was a steep decline in inflation in the mid-1980s. The inflation rate was further reduced in the 1990s. The Bank of Canada's target now is to keep the inflation rate within the range of 1 to 3 percent.

THE INTEREST RATE

The fourth key economic indicator is the **interest rate**. Though economists speak of "the" interest rate, there are actually many different interest rates applying to loans of different durations and different degrees of risk. (After all, the person or business entity that you lend your money to may be unable to pay it back; that is a risk you accept when you make a loan). The different interest rates often move up or down together, so economists speak of "the" interest rate, referring to the entire complex of different rates. But interest rates do not move in concert all the time. The causes of variations in the *yield curve,* which describes the pattern of interest rates, are an important part of macroeconomics.

The interest rate is important because it governs the redistribution of purchasing power across time. Those people or business enterprises who think they can make good use of additional financial resources borrow, promising to return the purchasing power they use today with *interest* in the future. Those business enterprises or people who have no immediate use for their financial resources lend, hoping to profit when the borrower returns the borrowed sum — what financiers call the principal — with interest.

When economists think about interest rates, they almost always prefer to focus on the real interest rate rather than the nominal interest rate. The *nominal interest rate* is the interest rate in terms of money — for example, how many dollars' worth of interest a borrower must pay to borrow a given sum of money for one year. The *real interest rate* is the interest rate in terms of goods and services — for example, how much purchasing power over goods and services a borrower must pay in order to borrow a given amount of purchasing power for one year. The difference between the two is that nominal interest rates do not take proper account of the effect of inflation; real interest rates do.

Whenever interest rates are low — that is, when money is "cheap" — investment tends to be high, because businesses find that a wide range of possible investment projects will generate enough cash to pay the interest on borrowed money, repay the principal of the loan, and still produce a profit. Whenever interest rates are high — that is, when money is "dear" — investment tends to be low, because businesses find that most possible investment projects will not generate enough cash flow to repay the principal and the high interest.

Figure 2.4 shows the real interest rates on a 91-day Treasury Bill and on a long-term bond that matures in ten years or more, during the period 1946–2005. Clearly, interest rates have fluctuated widely in Canada since 1946. Real interest rates have even been negative at times. During the 1970s nominal interest rates were so low and inflation was so high that the interest and principal on a short-term loan bought fewer commodities when the loan was repaid than the original principal could have purchased when the loan was made. In the early 1980s real interest rates increased radically because the Bank of Canada was trying to reduce the inflation rate. Until 2000 they had remained higher than their levels in the 1950s and 1960s.

THE STOCK MARKET

The level of the **stock market** is the key economic indicator you hear about most often — you hear about it every single day unless you try hard to avoid the news. The level of the stock market is an index of expectations for the future. When the

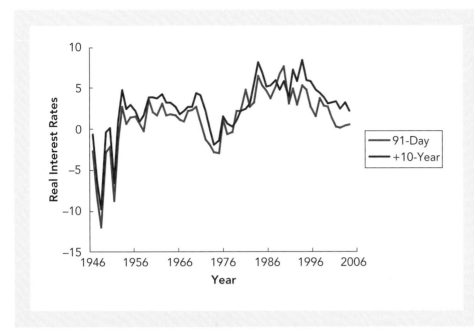

FIGURE 2.4
Canadian Real Interest Rates, 1946–2005
Interest rates have fluctuated widely in Canada since 1946. Real interest rates have even been negative at times — for example, in the 1970s. In the early 1980s real interest rates increased radically as the Bank of Canada was trying to reduce the inflation rate. Until 2000 they had remained higher than their levels in the 1950s and 1960s.

Source: Adapted from the Statistics Canada CANSIM II database, Series V122484 (91-day), V122487 (+10-year), and V735319 (CPI).
Note: Real interest rates calculated using Fisher equation.

stock market is high, investors expect economic growth to be rapid, profits to be high, and unemployment to be relatively low. (Note, however, that there is an element of tail chasing in the stock market. Perhaps it would be more accurate to say that the stock market is high when average opinion expects that average opinion will expect that future economic growth will be rapid.) Conversely, when the stock market is low, investors expect the economic future to be relatively gloomy.

One of the major indexes that tracks the performance of the stock market as a whole is the U.S. Standard and Poor's composite index, S&P 500. The Canadian counterpart to the S&P 500 is the Toronto Stock Exchange's TSX index. Figure 2.5 plots the real value — that is, the value adjusted for inflation — of this stock market index over time. At times, such as at the end of the 1960s or the end of the 1990s, the stock market appears significantly overvalued compared to its standard historical patterns. During such episodes investors are implicitly forecasting a major boom and continued rapid productivity growth. When their forecasts turn out to be wrong, these investors are severely disappointed with their stock market investments, as they were in the early 1970s and early 2000s.

THE EXCHANGE RATE

The sixth key economic quantity is the *exchange rate*. The **nominal exchange rate** is the rate at which the moneys of different countries can be exchanged for one another. The **real exchange rate** is the rate at which the goods and services produced in different countries can be exchanged for one another. The exchange rate governs the terms on which international trade and investment take place. When the domestic currency is appreciated, its value in terms of other currencies is high. Foreign

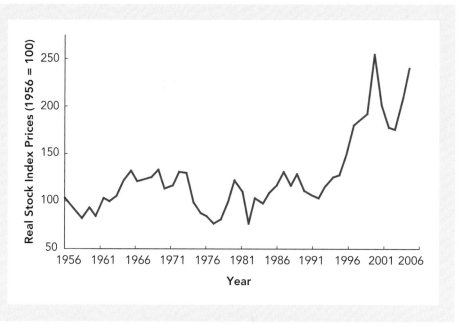

FIGURE 2.5

Real TSX Stock Index Prices, 1956–2005

At times, such as the end of the 1960s or the end of the 1990s, the stock market appears significantly overvalued compared to its standard historical patterns. During such episodes investors are implicitly forecasting a major boom and continued rapid productivity growth. When their forecasts turn out to be wrong, these investors are severely disappointed with their stock market investments, as they were in the early 1970s and early 2000s.

Source: Adapted from the Statistics Canada CANSIM II database, Series V122620 (TSX) and V735319 (CPI).

produced goods are relatively cheap for domestic buyers, but domestic-made goods are relatively expensive for foreigners. In these circumstances imports are likely to be high; exports are likely to be low. When the domestic currency is depreciated, the opposite is the case: Domestically made goods are cheap for foreign buyers. Thus exports are likely to be high. But domestic consumers' and investors' power to purchase foreign-made goods is limited. Thus imports are likely to be low.

The nominal exchange rate tells us how many units of domestic currency are needed to buy one unit of the foreign currency; it is the value of the foreign currency in terms of the domestic currency. The real exchange rate tells us how many units of domestically produced goods are needed in order to purchase one unit of foreign produced goods; it is the price of a foreign produced good in terms of the domestically produced good.

In the first half of the twentieth century, and also from 1962 until the early 1970s, the Canadian exchange rate was *fixed* vis-à-vis other major currencies in the Bretton Woods system. The Bank of Canada stood ready to buy or sell dollars in exchange for other currencies at fixed parities. During 1950–1962 and also since the early 1970s the Canadian exchange rate has been *floating* — free to move up or down in response to the market forces of supply and demand. Figure 2.6 shows the Canadian *real* exchange rate from 1951 to 2005. As seen in Figure 2.6, in the 1990s the dollar lost a lot of its value (the real exchange rate increased), while in recent years it has recovered to a very large extent (the real exchange rate decreased).

The real GDP, the unemployment rate, the inflation rate, the interest rate, the stock market, and the exchange rate — these are the six key economic indicators. Know the values of these key variables in context — both their relative levels today and their recent trends — and you have a remarkably complete picture of the current state of the macroeconomy. In studying these macroeconomic variables, we will

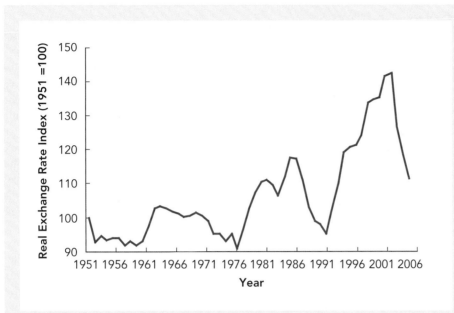

FIGURE 2.6
The Canadian Real Exchange Rate: The Canadian Dollar versus the US Dollar, 1951–2005
In the 1990s the Canadian dollar lost a lot of its value (the real exchange rate increased), while in recent years it has recovered to a very large extent (the real exchange rate has decreased).

Source: Adapted from the Statistics Canada CANSIM II database, Series V37426 (nominal USD/CAD exchange rate), V11123 (U.S. CPI), and V735319 (Canadian CPI).

start from the last, exchange rates, and go back to the first, GDP, because this way we will be discussing the least complicated concepts first.

FLOW VARIABLES AND STOCK VARIABLES

Notice some macroeconomic variables are *flow variables,* which are measured *per unit of time.* Examples of flow variables are the gross domestic product, the inflation rate, and the interest rate. Other macroeconomic variables are *stock variables,* which are measured *at a point in time.* Examples of stock variables are the unemployment rate, the level of the stock market, and the exchange rate. Box 2.1 explains more completely the distinction between stock variables and flow variables.

RECAP   **TRACKING THE MACROECONOMY**

Know and understand six key variables, and you understand most of what there is to know about the state of the macroeconomy. The first key variable is the level of real GDP — the real inflation-adjusted value of goods and services. The second key variable is the unemployment rate — the fraction of the labour force that is out of work. The third key variable is the inflation rate — a measure of how rapidly the overall price level is changing. The fourth key variable is the interest rate — the cost of borrowing. The fifth key variable is the level of the stock market — a good indicator of investor confidence and of the likely future pace of investment spending. The sixth and last key variable is the exchange rate — the price at which goods made here at home are exchanged for goods made abroad.

STOCKS AND FLOWS

In macroeconomics we make a distinction between stocks and flows when building models. *Flows* are variables that are measured *per unit of time.* Examples of flow variables are income, output, saving, investment, and government expenditures. We talk about income per month, per quarter, or per year. Specifying the length of time over which a flow variable is measured is crucial. Your monthly income has a different value than your annual income. Your monthly consumption is different from your annual consumption.

On the other hand, *stocks* are variables that are measured *at a point in time.* Stock variables include capital, wealth, government debt, etc. Notice we talk about the government debt having a specific value in dollars as of June 15, 2002, for example. We do *not* talk about the level of government debt in dollars *per year.* We talk about the value of the stock of capital in a firm in dollars at a point in time. We do *not* talk about the value of the capital stock in dollars per year.

Stock and flow variables are related to each other. A flow variable is the difference between the values of a stock variable at two different points in time. For example, the stock of capital at the beginning of year 2 minus the stock at the beginning of year 1 is called investment *per year* during period 1 (a flow). Your wealth (a stock) at the beginning of year 2 minus your wealth at the beginning of year 1 is called your saving *per year* during period 1 (a flow). The amount of government debt (a stock) at the beginning of year 2 minus its amount at the beginning of year 1 is called government budget deficit *per year* during year 1 (a flow).

2.2 THE EXCHANGE RATE

NOMINAL VERSUS REAL EXCHANGE RATES

The nominal exchange rate is the relative price of two different kinds of money, as set in the *foreign exchange market.* Domestic exporters earn foreign currency when they export — sell goods to people abroad. Foreign producers earn domestic currency when they sell us imports — sell their goods to people here. Both then have a problem. Domestic exporters can't pay domestic workers with foreign currency; foreign producers can't pay foreign workers with domestic currency. Foreign producers need to trade the dollars they have earned for money that is useful to them; domestic exporters need to trade the foreign currency they have earned for dollars they can use.

How do foreign producers and domestic exporters solve this problem? They turn to the foreign exchange market, where those who have foreign currency but want Canadian dollars exchange it for Canadian dollars and those who have dollars but want foreign currency exchange Canadian dollars for other currencies. Henceforth, we will use the term "dollar" and use the symbol $ to refer to the Canadian currency. We will use the term "US dollar" and use the symbol US$ to refer to the American currency. Those with foreign currency who want dollars include not only domestic exporters but also foreigners wishing to invest in Canada. Those with dollars who want foreign currency include not only foreigners who have sold Canadian imports but also Canadian residents who wish to invest abroad. The nominal exchange rate can be defined in two different but related ways: (a) the **domestic exchange rate** — call it e — which is the domestic currency price of one unit of foreign currency or (b) the **foreign exchange rate** — call it e^f — which is the foreign currency price of one unit of domestic currency. Clearly, by definition, e is the reciprocal of e^f and vice versa: $e = 1/e^f$. Consequently, which exchange rate is used in theory or practice is immaterial and the choice is only a matter of convenience. Throughout this text-book we will tend to emphasize the domestic exchange rate, which is a convenient way to translate foreign variables into Canadian currency.

If the nominal exchange rate between the dollar (the currency of Canada) and the euro (the currency of the European Union) is $1.40 = €1.00, then a single euro costs $1.40 in Canadian currency. It takes less than one euro — 0.71 euro and change — to buy a single dollar.

Economists, however, are more interested in the real exchange rate: the nominal rate adjusted for changes in the value of the currency. The nominal — the money — exchange rate can change without affecting the pattern of cross-national trade. When the real exchange rate — the rate in terms of goods and services — changes, the pattern of cross-national trade must change as well.

Suppose a burst of inflation doubled the price level in Canada, so everything that once cost $1 in Canada now costs $2, everything that used to cost $2 now costs $4, and so on. Suppose also that the nominal exchange rate changed from $1.40 = €1.00 to $2.80 = €1.00. Before the burst of inflation you could sell goods in Europe for €0.71 (and change), turn the euros into $1.00, and buy Canadian goods. After the burst of inflation you could sell goods in Europe for €0.71 (and change), turn the euros into approximately $2.00, and buy the exact same Canadian goods as before. The change in the nominal exchange rate has offset the change in the Canadian price level. In this case the real exchange rate — the rate at which goods trade for goods — has not changed. The terms at which the goods of one country are traded for the goods of another are the same.

Now suppose that a burst of inflation doubled the price level in Canada but that $1.40 still exchanges for €1.00 on the foreign exchange market. Has the exchange rate changed? The nominal exchange rate has not changed: 0.71 (plus change) euros will still get you a dollar; $1.40 will still get you a euro. However, that dollar will buy only as many goods in Canada as 50 cents would have bought before. The doubling of the Canadian price level, coupled with the unchanged nominal exchange rate, means that the same quantity of Canadian-made goods will buy twice as many European-made goods. Thus the real exchange rate has halved.

Of course, if the price levels in different countries do not change, then there is no distinction between a change in the nominal exchange rate and a change in the real exchange rate. If the nominal exchange rate doubled — changed from $1.40 = €1.00 to $2.80 = €1.00 — but the price levels in Canada and Europe remained the same, then investors would need twice as many dollars to buy the same amount of foreign currency. Thus it would cost twice as many Canadian-made goods to buy the same amount of foreign-made goods. The real exchange rate would have doubled as well.

THE REAL EXCHANGE RATE

CALCULATING THE REAL EXCHANGE RATE

To calculate the real exchange rate ε, you need to know three pieces of information. First, you need to know the price level in the home country — call it P, for price. Second, you need to know the price level abroad — call it by P^f. Third, you need to know the nominal exchange rate e. You can then calculate the value of the real exchange rate by multiplying the nominal exchange rate by the ratio of the foreign price level to the home price level:

$$\varepsilon = e \times \frac{P^f}{P} \tag{2.1}$$

Box 2.2 illustrates how the process works.

2.2

BOX

EXAMPLE

CALCULATING THE REAL EXCHANGE RATE

Suppose that the index of the Canadian price level is 50.00, the index of the foreign (the euro) price level is 110, and the nominal exchange rate (the price of the foreign currency in dollars) is $1.40 = €1. Then the real exchange rate would be:

$$\varepsilon = e \times \frac{P^f}{P} = 1.4 \times \frac{110}{50.00} = 1.4 \times 2.20 = 3.08$$

This means that one needs to pay 3.08 baskets of Canadian goods and services in order to buy one basket of European goods and services.

Now suppose the Canadian price level were to rise to 100, the foreign price level were to rise to 180, and the price of foreign currency were to fall to parity — i.e., $1.00 = €1. In that case the real exchange rate would be:

$$\varepsilon = e \times \frac{P^f}{P} = 1.0 \times \frac{180}{100} = 1.0 \times 1.8 = 1.8$$

Now a European basket of goods and services costs only 1.8 baskets of Canadian goods and services.

That is all there is to calculating real exchange rates.

CALCULATING THE OVERALL EXCHANGE RATE: INDEX NUMBERS

If you open up a newspaper in search of *the* exchange rate for the dollar, you will not find it. Instead, you will find a list of rates similar to the one in Table 2.1 but with many more entries — one line for almost every country on the globe.

There is an exchange rate for the dollar against each and every other currency — a dollar–Swiss franc exchange rate, a dollar–yen exchange rate, a dollar–euro exchange rate, a dollar–pound exchange rate, a dollar–US dollar exchange rate, a dollar–Mexican peso exchange rate, and more than 100 more for all the other currencies. Which of these is the exchange rate?

In this situation economists do what they usually do when they are confronted with too much variety. They take an average and hope that deviations from the average will cancel each other out. In other words, they construct an **index number** to stand in place of the more than 100 exchange rates of the Canadian dollar against other currencies. The usual approach is to take a trade-weighted average, in which each currency receives a weight equal to its share of total Canadian trade.

Let's go through the steps of calculating an index number for the exchange rate. To keep this example simple, we will restrict ourselves to the Canadian exchange rate vis-à-vis the six largest other industrial countries. First, we set the *base year* to be 1999, meaning that all exchange rates that we average will be relative to their value in 1999. They will all be of the form

$$\frac{\text{Exchange rate in this year}}{\text{Exchange rate in 1999}} \tag{2.2}$$

Furthermore, each exchange rate's weight in the index will be the share of Canada's trade with that particular country's economy in 1999. Thus the index number can be represented by the equation

$$\text{Index} = \sum_{\text{all countries}} \left(\frac{\text{exchange rate in this year}}{\text{exchange rate in 1999}} \times \text{share of trade in 1999} \right) \tag{2.3}$$

TABLE 2.1

Sample Nominal Exchange Rates vis-à-vis the Canadian Dollar as of May 5, 2006

http://www.bank-banque-canada.ca/

Currency	Value	Change from Previous Day
Argentine peso	0.362600	−0.000400
Australian dollar	0.853200	−0.001700
Brazilian real	0.538300	0.002300
Chinese renminbi	0.138200	0.000100
European euro	1.409700	0.005800
Indian rupee	0.024710	0.000020
Indonesian rupiah	0.000126	0.000000
Japanese yen	0.009846	0.000091
Mexican peso	0.101100	0.000200
Russian rouble	0.040890	0.000090
South African rand	0.183200	0.000000
South Korean won	0.001178	0.000000
New Turkish lira	0.840800	0.000700
U.K. pound sterling	2.058000	0.012000
U.S. dollar	1.107200	0.000400

Source: Bank of Canada.

where Σ — the Greek capital letter sigma — stands for "sum" or "add up," the parentheses to the right of sigma tell what is to be summed, and the notation beneath sigma tells the range over which the sum applies. The equation says, "For all of these countries, add up the products of their exchange rates this year divided by their exchange rates in 1999 and multiplied by their share of total trade with Canada in 1999."

By convention, economists usually set the value of an index number in its base year to 100. To do this, simply multiply the equation for the index by 100:

$$\text{Index} = 100 \times \sum_{\text{all countries}} \left(\frac{\text{exchange rate in this year}}{\text{exchange rate in 1999}} \times \text{share of trade in 1999} \right) \quad (2.4)$$

Table 2.2 shows the results of this calculation for the year 2001. Figure 2.7 presents the exchange rate index from 1997 to 2001

We have gone step-by-step through the process of defining the exchange rate, distinguishing between real and nominal exchange rates, calculating real exchange rates, and calculating a weighted average to arrive at *the* exchange rate. Both the calculation of index numbers and the distinction between real and nominal quantities will come up over and over again in this book. So pay attention.

TABLE 2.2
Calculating the Exchange Rate Index for 2005

Country	Exchange Rate (Value of Foreign Currency)		Rate in 2005/ Rate in 1999	Share of 1999 Trade	Contribution to Index
	1999	2005			
Japan	0.013	0.011	0.842	0.040	0.034
E.U. (excl. U.K.)	1.585	1.509	0.952	0.060	0.057
U.K.	2.404	2.207	0.918	0.022	0.020
U.S.	1.486	1.212	0.815	0.879	0.717
				Sum:	0.828
				× 100 =	
				Value of index	**82.778**

Source: Bank of Canada (exchange rates) and Industry Canada, Strategis (trade data).

FIGURE 2.7
The Exchange Rate Index, 1997–2005
The dollar experienced sharp depreciations in the late 1990s. In 2002 Canada's exchange rate index was over 30 percent higher than it was in 1997. Since then, however, the dollar has experienced a sharp appreciation.

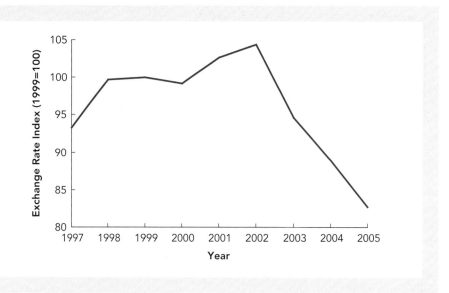

Source: Bank of Canada (exchange rates) and Industry Canada, Strategis (trade data).
Note: ECU (European Currency Unit) rate substituted for euro for the years 1997 and 1998.

http://www.census.gov/

RECAP THE EXCHANGE RATE

Domestic exporters earn foreign currency when they export — sell goods to people abroad. Foreign producers earn domestic currency when they sell us imports — sell their goods to people here. Both then have a problem. Domestic exporters can't pay domestic workers with foreign currency. Foreign producers can't pay foreign workers with domestic currency. Domestic producers need to trade the foreign currency they have earned for dollars they can use. They turn to the foreign exchange market, where those who have foreign currency but want dollars exchange it for dollars, and those who have dollars but want foreign currency exchange dollars for other currencies.

2.3 THE STOCK MARKET AND INTEREST RATES

THE STOCK MARKET

We don't have to calculate the value of an index for the stock market because news agencies perform that task for the public. As we have said, the best — the most representative — index of the U.S. stock market is probably Standard and Poor's composite index. The Canadian counterpart to the S&P 500 is the Toronto Stock Exchange (TSX) index.

Although we don't have to assemble and calculate a stock market index, we do have to divide the numbers reported in the news by some measure of the price level — usually either the *GDP deflator* or the *consumer price index (CPI)*. If both the price level and the (nominal) value of the stock market double, a representative share of stock is worth no more in real terms. To arrive at real magnitudes, economists *deflate* nominal magnitudes like a stock index by some measure of the price level in order to arrive at *real* magnitudes. In this case we are most interested in the real value of the stock market.

THE USEFULNESS OF KNOWLEDGE ABOUT THE STOCK MARKET

Current stock market indexes are the easiest economic statistics to get. But what good is knowing the real value of the stock market to a macroeconomist? The stock market is a sensitive indicator of the relative optimism or pessimism of investors, and therefore it is a good forecaster of future investment spending.

To see why, we need to think about the mechanisms underlying the stock market. Most investors in the stock market face a choice between holding stocks and holding bonds. *Stocks* are shares of ownership of a corporation, and give you ownership of that corporation's profits or earnings. *Bonds* are debts that the corporation owes you. A bond is a piece of paper that gives you periodic interest payments and, at the bond's maturity, returns to you the principal amount of the bond.

It is clear what the rate of return is on money invested in bonds. It is simply the interest payment the bond issuer makes divided by the price of the bond. Call this real rate of interest in the economy r. If you invest in shares of stock, what is your rate of return? You paid a price P^s (P for price, s for stock) for each share. The corporation reports earnings E^s per share. Some of those earnings will be paid out directly to shareholders in the form of dividends. Others will be retained and reinvested, boosting the corporation's fundamental value. Both components increase shareholder wealth, and together they are the return on the investment in stocks. Thus an investor in stocks gets a return on each dollar invested of

$$\frac{E^s}{P^s} \tag{2.5}$$

Which will the investor prefer to hold, stocks or bonds? Saying that investors will prefer stocks if E^s/P^s is greater than r is not quite right. Investments in stocks are risky. The company might go bankrupt, its reported earnings might be rigged, or the market might go down. As compensation for this risk, investors in stocks demand an extra return called the *risk premium*, or σ^s (the Greek lowercase letter sigma, with s for stocks as a superscript). So investors will want to hold only stocks if

$$\frac{E^s}{P^s} > r + \sigma^s \tag{2.6}$$

Investors will want to hold safer bonds if

$$\frac{E^s}{P^s} < r + \sigma^s \tag{2.7}$$

And investors will hold both stocks and bonds if

$$\frac{E^s}{P^s} = r + \sigma^s \tag{2.8}$$

Since in the world outside the classroom we see investors holding both stocks *and* bonds — some holding one, some holding the other, and some holding both — it is this last equation that must be true. If we turn this equation around, the value of stocks is equal to corporate earnings divided by the sum of the real interest rate on bonds and the risk premium:

$$P^s = \frac{E^s}{r + \sigma^s} \tag{2.9}$$

However, there is one more complication. The accounting earnings reported in the financial press — call them E^a — are not the earnings E^s that belong in the numerator of the stock valuation equation. The financial press reports what the firm's accountants have calculated, but investors are interested in some long-run average of expected future earnings. In order to apply the stock-price valuation formula, you also need an estimate of the relationship between the current earnings E^a that you see in the newspaper and "permanent" earnings E^s. (See Figure 2.8.)

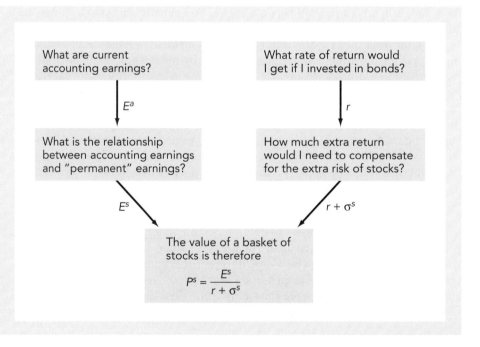

FIGURE 2.8
Calculating the Value of a Basket of Stocks

THE STOCK MARKET SUMMARIZES A LOT OF INFORMATION

The real value of the stock market sums up, in one number that is reported every day:

- The current level of earnings, or profits.
- Whether investors are optimistic (expecting long-run earnings to be above today's level) or pessimistic (expecting long-run earnings to be below today's level), and how optimistic or pessimistic they are.
- The current cost of capital — whether money is cheap and easy to borrow (in which case r is low) or expensive (in which case r is high).
- Attitudes toward risk — whether people are strongly averse to the risks involved in entrepreneurship (in which case σ^s is high) or willing to gamble on new industries and new businesses (in which case σ^s is low).

These are the factors that determine whether corporate managers are willing to undertake investments to boost their companies' capital stocks. Thus the stock market summarizes all the information relevant to the economy-wide level of investment spending. Its usefulness as a summary of all the information relevant to determining investment spending is the reason it is one of the six key variables of macroeconomics.

INTEREST RATES

The interest rate is the price at which purchasing power can be shifted from the future into the present — borrowed today with a promise to pay it back with interest in the future. Interest is not a single lump sum but an ongoing stream of payments made over time. Thus it is what economists call a *flow* variable. A flow variable cannot be measured simply as a quantity; it must be measured as a quantity per unit of time. In the case of the interest rate, it is measured not as a percentage of the amount borrowed, the principal, but as a *percentage per year*.

Economists like to talk about "the" interest rate in the same way that they like to talk about "the" exchange rate. But just as there are a large number of different exchange rates, there are a large number of interest rates. Loans of higher risk carry higher interest rates: Whomever you lent your money to might not pay it back — that is a risk you accepted when you lent in the first place. Loans of different duration carry different interest rates as well. Moreover, differences in tax treatment — whether and when you have to pay taxes on interest earned from bonds — also lead to differences in interest rates.

TERM STRUCTURE OF INTEREST RATES

Table 2.3 and Figure 2.9 show a small sample of the interest rates (or yields) as of May 22, 2002 quoted on Canadian securities with maturities between one month and ten years. This is an example of the *term structure* of interest rates, i.e., the yield to maturity of *all* securities of *all* maturities. In Figure 2.9 the interest rate is measured on the vertical axis and the term to maturity (in months) is measured on the horizontal axis. Clearly, as of May 22, 2002 the term structure of the Canadian interest rates was upward-sloping. Longer-term securities paid higher yields than shorter-term securities. For instance, on May 22, 2002 the yield on a three-month security was 2.5 percent, but it was 5.61 percent on a ten-year security.

Economists developed theories to explain the term structure of interest rates and hence the shape of the yield curve, which, in general, could be upward-sloping, flat,

TABLE 2.3
Government of Canada Securities Yield Curve, as of May 22, 2002

Term	Yield
1 month	2.19
2 month	2.39
3 month	2.59
6 month	2.87
1 year	3.40
2 year	4.17
3 year	4.28
5 year	5.00
10 year	5.61

Source: Bank of Canada.

FIGURE 2.9
Government of Canada Securities Yield Curve, May 22, 2002

The interest rate on a long-term security is an *average* of the current short rate and the *expected* future rates on securities of shorter maturity. If future short rates are expected to rise, then the yield curve will be upward sloping.

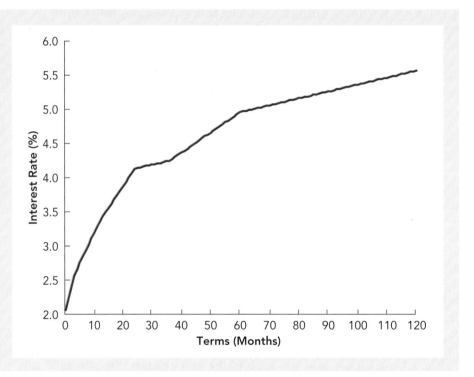

Source: Bank of Canada.

or even downward-sloping. According to the well-known *expectations theory of the term structure*, the interest rate on a long-term security is an *average* of the current short rate and the *expected* future rates on securities of shorter maturity. If future short rates are expected to be constant over time, then the yield curve will be flat or a horizontal line at the level of the current short rate. If on the other hand future short rates are expected to rise, then the yield curve will be upward sloping. Conversely, if the future short rates are expected to fall, the yield curve will be downward sloping.

Thus, if the expectations theory of the term structure is correct, the upward sloping Canadian yield curve shown in Figure 2.9 reflects expectations of rising future short rates. Such expectations could be caused by many factors, including increased uncertainty about future economic conditions, inflationary expectations, and uncertainty about government policies.

The term structure of interest rates has important policy implications. The term structure is a channel through which government policies can affect the long-term prospects of an economy. For instance, if the government can adopt policies that lower expected future short rates, then the long-term interest rates will be lower, thereby spurring an increase in investment and economic growth in the long-run.

Moreover, the interest rates published in the newspaper are nominal rates: They tell how much money you earn in interest per year if you lend out a sum of dollars now and collect the principal at the loan's maturity. You will not be surprised to learn that economists are interested instead in the real interest rate: how much purchasing power over goods and services you get in the future in return for trading away your purchasing power over goods and services today.

When we calculate real exchange rates, or real stock values, or real GDP, we divide the nominal exchange rate or stock index value or nominal GDP level by the price level, but that is not what we do to calculate real interest rates. Instead of dividing the nominal interest rate by the price level, we *subtract* the inflation rate — the percentage rate of change in the price level — from the nominal interest rate to get the real interest rate. Box 2.3 explains the reason for this procedure, and Box 2.4 generalizes by explaining a few more mathematical tricks that are useful when we are shifting between levels and growth rates.

CALCULATING REAL INTEREST RATES

Why subtract the inflation rate from the nominal interest rate? Suppose you borrow $10 million for one year at a nominal interest rate of 8 percent per year. Suppose further that the annual inflation rate is also 8 percent, so the price level will rise by 8 percent between now and next year. Thus whatever goods you want to buy will be more expensive. Let's say you want to buy cheap television sets priced at $200 a set this year; they will cost $216 a set by next year.

Right now when you borrow, you get $10 million. Next year you will have to pay back $10.8 million — $10 million principal and $800,000 interest. You borrow enough now to buy 50,000 TV sets. Next year, when you pay back your loan with interest, you will pay the lender $10.8 million, just enough money to buy 50,000 cheap TV sets. Thus you will return the same purchasing power over goods and services as what you borrowed, making a real interest rate of zero (see Figure 2.10).

Suppose the inflation rate had been 4 percent, so the price of a standard basket of goods and services, and of the cheap TV sets you are buying, will rise from $200 to $208 next year. You borrow $10 million, enough to buy 50,000 cheap TV sets. Next year, when you pay back your loan with its 8 percent annual interest, you will pay the lender $10.8 million, enough money to buy 51,923 TV sets. The extra 1,923 TV sets are a 3.846 percent increase in purchasing power over goods and services. Thus

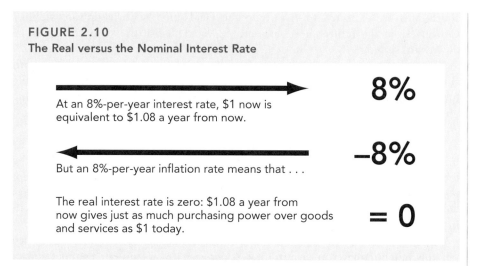

FIGURE 2.10
The Real versus the Nominal Interest Rate

At an 8%-per-year interest rate, $1 now is equivalent to $1.08 a year from now.   **8%**

But an 8%-per-year inflation rate means that . . .   **–8%**

The real interest rate is zero: $1.08 a year from now gives just as much purchasing power over goods and services as $1 today.   **= 0**

you will return 3.846 percent more purchasing power than you borrowed. However, to keep things simple, economists round the percentage off and call it a 4 percent real interest rate. (You will find that economists often round off numbers, drop small terms from equations, and generally do whatever they can to make things simpler.)

Thus the rule: To calculate a *real* interest rate, subtract the inflation rate from the *nominal* interest rate.

2.4

BOX

TOOLS

SOME USEFUL MATHEMATICAL TOOLS
In saying that the real interest rate is the nominal interest rate minus the inflation rate, we are using one of three mathematical tools that will make life a lot easier throughout this course. They are all *approximations*. But they are all close enough for our purposes, and they make life simpler. They are as follows:

1. *The growth-of-a-product rule:* The proportional change of a *product* is equal to the *sum* of the proportional changes of its components.

2. *The growth-of-a-quotient rule:* The proportional change of a *quotient* is equal to the *difference* between the proportional changes of its components.

3. *The growth-of-a-power rule:* The proportional change of a *quantity raised to a power* is equal to the *proportional change in the quantity times the power* to which it is raised.

As we just saw in calculating the real interest rate, these three rules are only approximations: An 8 percent increase in a nominal sum of money and a 4 percent increase in the price level produce not a 4 percent but a 3.846 percent increase in real purchasing power over goods and services. But that is close enough.

To illustrate the first, product, rule, suppose we have two variables, P (price) and Q (quantity) that together are multiplied to make up E (expenditure), $E = P \times Q$. Then,

Proportional change in E = proportional change in P + proportional change in Q

Thus if real production Q is growing at 5 percent per year, and the price level P is growing at 2 percent per year, then total nominal expenditure E will be growing at a proportional rate of 5 percent + 2 percent = 7 percent per year.

To illustrate the second, quotient, rule, start out with *E* (expenditure) and *Q* (quantity) so that when we divide them we get *P* (price), $E/Q = P$. Then,

Proportional change in *P* = proportional change in *E* − proportional change in *Q*

Thus if nominal expenditure *E* is growing at 7 percent per year and real production *Q* is growing at 5 percent per year, then the price level *P* must be growing at a proportional rate of 7 percent − 5 percent = 2 percent per year.

To illustrate the third, power, rule, suppose that real GDP *Y* is equal to the economy's capital stock *K* raised to a power — K^α, *K* raised to the power α. (Recall that $X^{0.5}$ is the square root of *X*, that $X^1 = X$, and that $X^2 = X \times X$.) Then,

Proportional change in $Y = \alpha \times$ proportional change in *K*

Thus if α equals 0.5, and thus $Y = K^{0.5}$, and if the capital stock *K* is growing at 6 percent per year, real GDP *Y* will be growing at 0.5×6 percent = 3 percent per year.

You may hear people say that a background in calculus is needed to understand intermediate macroeconomics. That is not true. In fact, 95 percent of what calculus is used for in intermediate macroeconomics is contained in these three mathematical tools. (Of course, calculus is needed if you want to understand just *why* they work.)

RECAP   THE STOCK MARKET AND INTEREST RATES

We don't have to calculate an index for the stock market because news agencies perform that task for the public already. We do, however, have to divide the numbers reported in the news by some measure of the price level in order to adjust for inflation and determine the real value of the stock market. To arrive at real magnitudes, economists *deflate* nominal magnitudes like a stock index by some measure of the price level in order to arrive at *real* magnitudes. In this case we are most interested in the real value of the stock market. Note that when we calculate real interest rates, we do not divide the nominal interest rate by the price level. Instead we *subtract* the inflation rate — the percentage rate of change in the price level — from the nominal interest rate to get the real interest rate.

2.4 THE PRICE LEVEL AND INFLATION

THE CONSUMER PRICE INDEX

The idea that economists need to measure the **price level** and to use it to calculate real quantities has come up several times already. Estimating the price level and its proportional rate of change — the inflation rate — is at the heart of macroeconomics.

The most frequently seen measure of the overall price level is the consumer price index, or CPI. (Other measures of prices include the producer price index of prices paid not by consumers but by companies, the economy-wide GDP deflator, and the domestic purchases deflator.) The CPI is calculated and reported once a month by **Statistics Canada**. It is an expenditure-weighted index, in which each good or service receives a weight equal to its share in total expenditure in the base year. (See Box 2.5 for a sample calculation.)

http://www.statcan.ca/

Statistics Canada changes the basket of goods and services used in constructing the CPI on a regular basis to keep the weighted "market basket" of goods and services used in calculating the index reasonably close to the goods and services consumers are currently buying. If it were not, the CPI would be of doubtful relevance. Who would care about the rate of change in the price of a statistical market basket that didn't represent what consumers were really buying?

BOX 2.5   EXAMPLE

CALCULATING PRICE INDEXES

One standard example economists use to illustrate how a price index is calculated is an index for consumers of fruit (perhaps because calculating indexes allows economists to really add apples and oranges). Suppose that in the base year a consumer buys $4.50 worth of oranges at a price of $0.75 a kilogram, $4.20 worth of apples at $1.20 a kilogram, $0.90 worth of pears at $0.90 a kilogram, and $0.40 worth of bananas at $0.40 a kilogram. Then, with a total of $10 spent on fruit in the base year, the price index for fruit will be given by

$$\text{Price index for fruit} = \frac{\text{price of oranges today}}{\text{price of oranges in base year}} \times \text{orange index weight}$$

$$+ \frac{\text{price of apples today}}{\text{price of apples in base year}} \times \text{apple index weight}$$

$$+ \frac{\text{price of pears today}}{\text{price of pears in base year}} \times \text{pear index weight}$$

$$+ \frac{\text{price of bananas today}}{\text{price of bananas in base year}} \times \text{banana index weight}$$

$$= \frac{\text{price of oranges today}}{\$0.75} \times 45 + \frac{\text{price of apples today}}{\$1.20} \times 42$$

$$+ \frac{\text{price of pears today}}{\$0.90} \times 09 + \frac{\text{price of bananas today}}{\$0.40} \times 04$$

We multiply the total annual expenditure on each fruit by 100 so that in the base year the price index will be equal to 100, as is customary for economists to do.

Now consider a year in which, as shown in Table 2.4, the price of oranges has risen to $1.50, the price of apples has fallen to $1.00, and the prices of pears and bananas have not changed. The overall fruit price index will be

$$\text{Price index for fruit} = \frac{\$1.50}{\$0.75} \times 45 + \frac{\$1.00}{\$1.20} \times 42 + \frac{\$0.90}{\$0.90} \times 09 + \frac{\$0.40}{\$0.40} \times 04 = 138$$

TABLE 2.4
Calculating a Price Index for Fruit: An Example

Fruit	Base-Year Expenditure	Base-Year Price (per Kilogram)	Subsequent-Year Price (per Kilogram)
Oranges	$4.50	$0.75	$1.50
Apples	4.20	1.20	1.00
Pears	0.90	0.90	0.90
Bananas	0.40	0.40	0.40

KINDS OF INDEX NUMBERS

Using relative expenditure levels in a fixed base year as the weights in a price index produces a kind of index that economists call a *Laspeyres index*. The CPI is a Laspeyres price index. Another type of index, a *Paasche index*, is in a sense the opposite of a Laspeyres index. A Laspeyres index of production or consumption counts up the current dollar value of what is produced or consumed and divides by what the value of what is produced or consumed would have been if all commodities had sold for their prices in the base year. The expenditure weights in a Paasche index are variable: If expenditures on a particular good rise this year and make it a large part of the current dollar value, then that good's weight in the price index will rise too. The second most-often-seen indicator of the price level is the GDP deflator, which will be discussed in detail below. At this stage it suffices to know that the GDP deflator was a Paasche index before Statistics Canada changed its calculations in May 2001. Box 2.6 compares the pluses and minuses of these two kinds of price indexes.

In general, a Laspeyres index overstates price increases. In the real world, when some items become expensive, consumers *substitute* and buy other items that remain cheap. But a Laspeyres index, because it is based on a fixed market basket of goods and services, does not take account of this substitution. Thus it suffers from what economists call *substitution bias,* and it tends to overstate changes. A Paasche index, on the other hand, understates the increase in fruit prices. It calculates the difference between the price today of the *fruit you bought* and the price back in the base year. The Paasche index takes account of substitution. But it doesn't take account of the fact that the substituted items are less valued than the items they replace. The Paasche index reports, in the example of Box 2.6, that the skyrocketing price of oranges has no effect on fruit prices. Yet it makes no sense to say that a frost that makes oranges completely unaffordable has no effect on the price of fruit.

So which is the "correct" price index? The answer is "neither." There is no final and definitive resolution to this "index number problem." All price indexes are imperfect. All try to summarize in a single number what is inherently a multidimensional reality of many prices changing in different directions and different proportions.

To strike a balance between the Laspeyres and Paasche indexes with their two types of biases, one should use the *Fisher index*, which is a geometric average of the Laspeyres and Paasche indexes. Hence, the Fisher index is the square root of the product of the Laspeyres and Paasche indexes:

$$\text{Fisher Index} = \sqrt{\text{Laspeyres Index} \times \text{Paasche Index}}$$

Box 2.6 compares the Fisher index with the Laspeyres and Paasche indexes. Statistics Canada started measuring the GDP deflator as a Fisher index in May 2001.

Another complication with constructing a series for a price index is the choice of the base period. In constructing a series for a price index one could choose a single period for the whole series as the base period. This may, however, cause complications because in an economy that experiences dramatic changes in the composition of goods and services produced or consumed one should change the base period in order to take into account such changes in the baskets of goods. One solution is to use a *chained index,* whereby for each period the previous period is treated as the base period. With a chained index the base period changes continuously, and it takes into account changes in the composition of the basket of goods and services produced or consumed. This way one can compute the Laspeyres, Paasche, or Fisher chained indexes.

LASPEYRES, PAASCHE, AND FISHER INDEX NUMBERS

To see the difference between a Laspeyres, a Paasche, and a Fisher index, return to our fruit example in Box 2.5. Suppose the prices of apples, pears, and bananas remain at their base-year levels, but surprise frosts destroy the orange crops in both Florida *and* California. The price of oranges skyrockets to $8.20 a kilogram (see Table 2.5), so no one buys any oranges — instead, consumers double their purchases of apples, pears, and bananas to 7 kilograms of apples, 2 kilograms of pears, and 2 kilograms of bananas.

The CPI for fruit, a Laspeyres index, would then be

$$\text{Price index for fruit} = \frac{\$8.20}{\$0.75} \times 45 + \frac{\$1.20}{\$1.20} \times 42 + \frac{\$0.90}{\$0.90} \times 09 + \frac{\$0.40}{\$0.40} \times 04 = 550$$

According to this index, the price of fruit is five and a half times as high as that in the base year.

The deflator for fruit, a Paasche index, would be

- Total nominal expenditure on fruit in the frost year: $11
- Cost of buying those pieces of fruit in the base year: $11
- Dividing the first number by the second, we discover that the price of fruit has not changed from its base-year value, 100.

Finally, the Fisher index for fruit is the geometric mean of the CPI and the deflator for fruit; that is,

$$\text{Fisher index} = \sqrt{550 \times 100} = 234.52$$

TABLE 2.5
Two Different Kinds of Indexes: An Index Number Example

Fruit	Base-Year Expenditure	Base-Year Price (per Kilogram)	Subsequent-Year Price (per Kilogram)
Oranges	$4.50	$0.75	$8.20
Apples	4.20	1.20	1.20
Pears	0.90	0.90	0.90
Bananas	0.40	0.40	0.40

THE INFLATION RATE

The CPI is reported once a month in the form of the percentage change in consumer prices over the preceding month. "Consumer prices in November rose 0.3 percent above their level in October," a newscaster will say. Eventually, 12 monthly changes in consumer prices over the course of the year are added up and become that year's **inflation** rate. (See Figure 2.3.) "The consumer price inflation rate in 1999 was 1.75 percent," the newscaster will say.

Because the inflation rate is a measure of the rate of change in prices over time, it is a *flow* variable (see Box 2.1). When we speak of the inflation rate, we speak of it as such-and-such percent *per year*. Speaking of the inflation rate without reference to a measure of time is incomplete. But people do, and we always assume that when the time measure is omitted, the inflation percentage is an annual rate.

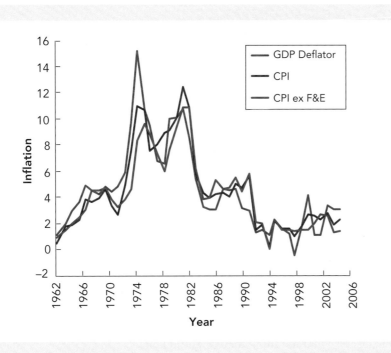

FIGURE 2.11

Different Measurements of Canada's Inflation, 1962–2005

Different measures of inflation tell slightly different stories about inflation. But all tell the same broad story: Differences are small relative to the large swings in the inflation rate from one decade to another.

Source: Adapted from the Statistics Canada CANSIM II database, Series V498086 (nominal GDP), V1992067 (real GDP), V735319 (CPI), and V735600 (CPI ex F&E).

What the inflation rate is at any moment depends on which price level it is based on. The CPI-based inflation rate will not be exactly the same as the GDP-deflator-based inflation rate. Figure 2.11 plots three different measures of inflation in Canada: the GDP deflator, the CPI, and the CPI that omits the volatile prices of food and energy, which can cause severe transitory fluctuations in the overall index (the CPI ex F&E). As is clear from Figure 2.11, in some years the CPI measure of inflation was higher than the GDP measure, while in other years the reverse was true. This seems to contradict our discussion that a measure of inflation based on a Laspeyres price index (the CPI) overestimates the true inflation rate, while a measure based on a Fischer index (the GDP deflator) is a less biased measure of inflation. It is important to note, however, that, as will be explained below, the CPI and GDP deflator are measured using two different baskets of goods. The prices of these two baskets may change differently in different time periods, which may then give rise to the two measures of inflation behaving differently relative to each other in different time periods.

RECAP   THE PRICE LEVEL AND INFLATION

Already the idea that economists need to measure the price level and to use it to calculate real quantities has come up several times. Estimating the price level and its proportional rate of change — the inflation rate — is at the heart of macroeconomics. The most frequently seen measure of the overall price level is the Consumer Price Index, or CPI. It is a fixed weight — a Laspeyres index of prices. Each good or service receives a weight equal to its share in total expenditure in the base year. And periodically the base year is moved forward in time.

2.5 UNEMPLOYMENT

CALCULATING THE UNEMPLOYMENT RATE

The unemployment rate is a key indicator of economic performance. An economy with persistent high unemployment is wasting its productive resources: Its level of output is below its productive potential. Such an economy surely has a lower level of social welfare than otherwise might easily be attained. Being unemployed is not pleasant, nor is fearing unemployment for no other reason than the turning of the wheel of the business cycle.

Keeping unemployment low is one of the chief goals of macroeconomic policy. Yet in the course of the business cycle unemployment rises and falls.

Every month Statistics Canada sends interviewers to talk to 60,000 households in a nationwide survey called the Labour Force Survey (LFS). Statistics Canada uses the LFS data to estimate the unemployment rate — the fraction of people who were between 15 and 65 years old and who (a) wanted a job, (b) looked for a job, but (c) could not find an acceptable job. Statisticians classify the people who are interviewed into four categories:

1. Those who were employed in some sort of job when interviewed.
2. Those who were out of the labour force and did not want a job immediately.
3. Those who did want a job immediately but had not been looking for one because they did not think they could find one.
4. Those who did want a job immediately, had been looking, but had not found a job they would take.

http://cansim2.statcan.ca/

According to the Statistics Canada definition of the unemployment rate, the *labour force* is group 1 plus group 4 — those who had jobs plus those who were looking for jobs:

$$\text{Labour force} = \text{employed} + \text{looking for work} \qquad (2.10)$$

The unemployment rate is the numer of unemployed — those in group 4 — divided by the total labour force:

$$\text{Unemployment rate} = \frac{\text{looking for work}}{\text{labour force}} = \frac{\text{looking for work}}{\text{employed} + \text{looking for work}} \qquad (2.11)$$

The unemployment rate is a *stock* variable. Saying that the current unemployment rate is 4 percent, with no reference to a measure of time, makes perfect sense.

The official unemployment rate may well underestimate the real experience of unemployment. Someone in group 3, who wants a job but has given up looking, certainly feels unemployed and may well feel as unemployed as someone in group 4. Perhaps these *discouraged workers* should be included in the unemployment rate. Furthermore, some people in group 1 have part-time jobs but want full-time jobs. Perhaps these *part-timers for economic reasons* should be counted as unemployed, or as half-unemployed.

Economists have noted striking and persistent variations in unemployment by demographic group and class. Teenagers age 16 to 19 have higher unemployment rates than adults, and high school dropouts have higher unemployment rates than those who have postgraduate degrees. For most of the post–World War II period (but not recently) women have had higher unemployment rates than men. Significantly, recessions don't just raise the unemployment rate; they disproportionately

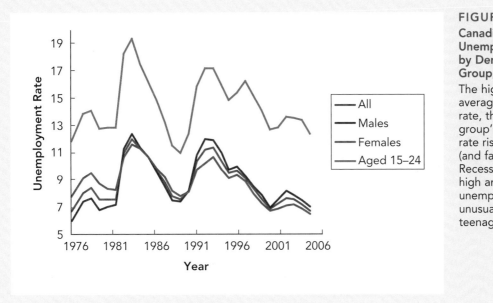

FIGURE 2.12

Canadian Unemployment Rates by Demographic Group, 1976–2005

The higher a group's average unemployment rate, the more the group's unemployment rate rises in recessions (and falls in booms). Recessions — times of high and rising unemployment — are unusually difficult for teenage workers.

Source: Adapted from the Statistics Canada CANSIM II database, Series V20464894 (All), V2064903 (males), V2064912 (females), and V2064921 (aged 15–24).

raise the unemployment rate among these high-unemployment groups. Figure 2.12 contrasts the unemployment rates of various groups of workers.

The question "How long is the typical person who loses his or her job unemployed?" is hard to answer because it is an ambiguous one. Most people who become unemployed on any one day — say, July 16, 2001 — remain unemployed for only a short time; more than half find a job within a month. Yet of all the people who are unemployed on July 16, 2001, some three-quarters of them will be unemployed for more than two months before they find another job.

Figure 2.13 plots the unemployment rates for the four regions of Canada for the period 1976–2005. The unemployment rates in the different regions exhibit similar patterns. Mainly due to their lack of natural resources or manufacturing industries, the Maritimes (i.e., Nova Scotia, Prince Edward Island, and New Brunswick) and Newfoundland have unemployment rates that are substantially higher than the national average. The unemployment rate in central Canada (i.e., Ontario and Quebec) is more volatile than in other regions. The reason is the relatively large manufacturing sector in central Canada, which is more exposed to business fluctuations. The unemployment rates in Western Canada (i.e., Alberta and British Columbia) and the Prairies (i.e., Manitoba and Saskatchewan) have by and large been below the national average. The reason for this is the large commodity sector in these regions, with large reserves of oil in Alberta, forestry in British Columbia, and large agricultural sectors in Manitoba and Saskatchewan.

OKUN'S LAW

Okun's law states that that there is an inverse relationship between the deviations of the unemployment rate, u, relative to the natural rate, u^*, and the deviations of the real GDP, Y, relative to potential GDP, Y^*. Potential GDP is the level of GDP attained

FIGURE 2.13

Canadian Unemployment Rates by Region, 1976–2005

Mainly due to their lack of natural resources or manufacturing industries, the Maritimes and Newfoundland have unemployment rates that are substantially higher than the national average. The unemployment rate in Central Canada is more variable than in other regions because of its relatively large manufacturing sector, which is more exposed to business fluctuations. The unemployment rates in Western Canada and the Prairies have by and large been below the national average, because of the large commodity sectors in these regions.

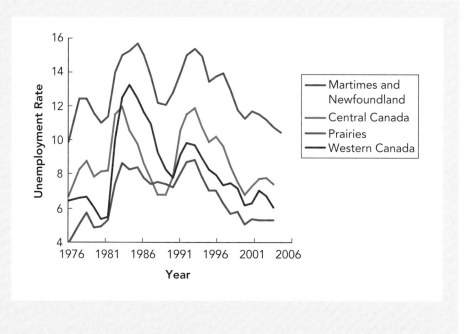

Source: Statistics Canada CANSIM II database, Series V2065083 (Newfoundland unemployment), V2065078 (Newfoundland labour force), V2065272 (P.E.I. unemployment), V2065267 (P.E.I. labour force), V2065461 (N.S. unemployment), V2065456 (N.S. labour force), V2065650 (N.B. unemployment), V2065645 (N.B. labour force), V2065839 (Quebec unemployment), V2065834 (Quebec labour force), V2066028 (Ontario unemployment), V2066023 (Ontario labour force), V2066217 (Manitoba unemployment), V2066212 (Manitoba labour force), V2066406 (Saskatchewan unemployment), V2066401 (Saskatchewan labour force), V2066595 (Alberta unemployment), V2066590 (Alberta labour force), V2066783 (B.C. unemployment), and V2066779 (B.C. labour force).

Note: Regional rate is a weighted (by size of labour force) average of provincial rates.

when the resources of the economy are fully employed, and the natural rate of unemployment is the rate of unemployment consistent with potential GDP. Okun's law can be expressed in different alternative ways as we will discuss in Chapter 11. The exact form of Okun's law is

$$\frac{Y - Y^*}{Y^*} = -\lambda(u - u^*)$$

where λ is a parameter that relates the deviations of the unemployment rate relative to its natural rate to the proportional deviations of the real GDP relative to its potential in a given economy. A convenient approximation to this equation is

$$\% \text{ change in real GDP} = a - b \times (\text{change in unemployment rate}) \qquad (2.12)$$

where a and b are constants that are different for different economies. The parameter a measures the percentage growth in full employment output, and the "slope" coefficient b measures the sensitivity of changes in the growth rate of real GDP to changes in the unemployment rate.

Figure 2.14 shows **Okun's law** for Canada using GDP growth and unemployment data for the period 1962–2005. It turns out that for this time period $b = 1.65$ in Canada. This means that a 1-percent reduction in the Canadian unemployment rate is associated with a 1.65-percent increase in the growth rate of real GDP in Canada.

Because of Okun's law, if you know what is happening to real GDP relative to potential output, you have a good idea of what is happening to the unemployment rate, and vice versa. Box 2.7 explains the details of Okun's law at greater length.

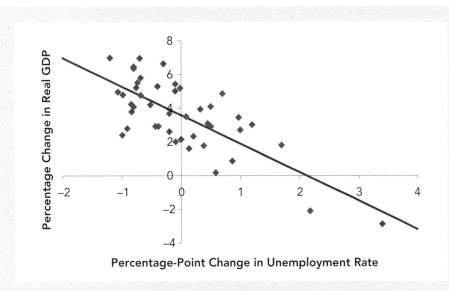

FIGURE 2.14

Okun's Law: Canada, 1962–2005

A 1-percent reduction in the Canadian unemployment rate is associated with a 1.65-percent increase in the growth rate of real GDP in Canada.

Source: Statistics Canada, Historical Statistics of Canada, Series D233 (unemployment, 1950–1975); CANSIM II database, Series V2064894 (unemployment, 1976–2005) and V1992067 (real GDP, 1961–2005).

WHY THE OKUN'S LAW COEFFICIENT IS SO LARGE

Okun's law posits not a 1-to-1 relation but a 1.65-to-1 relationship between real GDP growth and the unemployment rate. That is, a 1-percentage-point fall in the unemployment rate is associated not with a 1 but a 1.65 percent boost in the level of production.

Why is the Okun's law coefficient so large? Why isn't it the case that a 1-percentage-point fall in unemployment produces a 1 percent rise in output, or even less? One answer is that the unemployment rate, as officially measured, does not count discouraged workers. In a recession, the number of people at work falls, the number of people looking for work rises, and the number of people who are not looking for work because they doubt they could find jobs — but who would be working if business conditions were better — rises. Because the conventionally measured unemployment rate does not include these discouraged workers, more than a 1 percent rise in real GDP is needed to reduce the unemployment rate by 1 percentage point.

Moreover, when business returns to normal, firms' initial response is not to hire more employees but to ask existing employees to work longer hours. So average hours of work per week go up, and the unemployment rate falls by less than one would otherwise expect.

Finally, in some industries, employing more workers increases production by more than a proportional amount: Product design and setup need to be done only once, no matter how much is produced. Thus businesses that have *economies of scale* do not need twice as many workers to produce twice as much output.

2.7

BOX

DETAILS

For the U.S. economy the parameter b is roughly 2.5. Hence a 1-percent reduction in the U.S. unemployment rate is associated with a 2.5-percent increase in the real GDP growth rate in the U.S. Consequently, GDP growth in the U.S. is more sensitive to reductions in the unemployment rate than is GDP growth in Canada.

http://stats.bls.gov/opub/mlr/
mlrhome.htm

One important reason for the difference in the parameter *b* between Canada and the U.S. is the gap between labour productivity in the two countries. Labour productivity is measured as the ratio of real GDP to the number of hours worked. Clearly, if labour productivity is higher in the U.S. than in Canada, then a given reduction in the unemployment rate will lead to a larger increase in GDP in the U.S. than in Canada. Recent estimates show that labour productivity in Canada was about 81 percent of the productivity in the U.S. in 1998. (See, for example, the study by Eldridge and Sherwood in *Monthly Labour Review*, February 2001.)

> **RECAP   THE UNEMPLOYMENT RATE**
>
> The unemployment rate is a key indicator of economic performance. An economy with persistent high unemployment is wasting its productive resources: its level of output is below its productive potential. Moreover, the official unemployment rate may well underestimate the real experience of unemployment in the Canadian economy.

2.6 REAL GDP

Sixth and last of the key economic variables is real GDP, the most frequently used measure of economic performance. You will see other measures of total production and total income as well. All of them are close cousins of real GDP: GNP (gross national product), NNP (net national product), NDP (net domestic product), and NI (national income). And you will hear commentators refer to "total output," "total production," "national product," "total income," and "national income." Except when you are focusing explicitly on the details of the **National Income and Expenditure Accounts**, treat all these terms as synonyms for real GDP.

http://www.statcan.ca/english/
sdds/1901.htm

Real GDP is calculated by adding up the value of all final goods and services produced in the economy. Because it measures the rate at which goods and services are produced, real GDP is a flow variable; it is usually expressed as an annual amount. Often, however, you will not hear the phrase "per year." But when you hear that real GDP in the fourth quarter of 2002 was such and such, remember that such a statement means that the flow of production in the fourth quarter was such and such per year. And when you hear that real GDP in the fourth quarter of 2002 grew at so-and-so percent, remember that such a statement means that real GDP in the fourth quarter grew at so-and-so percent per year — the difference between real GDP in the third quarter and real GDP in the fourth quarter is only one-quarter of the reported annual growth rate.

What are the final goods and services that make up GDP? A *final good or service* is something that is not used further in production during the course of the year. Thus final goods and services include:

- Everything bought by consumers.
- Everything bought by businesses not as an input for further production but as an investment to increase the business's capital stock and expand its future production capacity.
- Everything bought by the government.

Because GDP measures *product* and not *spending,* it includes a balancing item, *exports minus imports.* Because imported goods bought by consumers, installed as pieces of investment, or bought by the government were not made in Canada, they are not part of gross domestic product, so imports need to be subtracted from GDP. Because exported goods bought by foreigners were made in Canada, they *are* part of GDP and need to be added to the total.

REAL AND NOMINAL GDP

When economists add up final goods and services produced in the year to calculate GDP, how do they weight each good or service? The answer is that they use market value — what people paid for a good or service — in the calculation of *nominal* GDP. Box 2.8 presents a stylized, hypothetical example of how this is done.

In 2005 nominal GDP (that is, GDP measured at 2005 prices) was $1.37 trillion; in 2004 nominal GDP (that is, measured at 2004 prices) was $1.29 trillion. Thus the growth rate of nominal GDP between 2004 and 2005 was 6.20 percent. But it is clear this *nominal* measure of GDP, in which current-year prices are used to weight the final goods and services produced and to calculate growth rates, is not a good measure of productivity or material output. It confuses changes in the overall price level — inflation or deflation — with changes in total production. Suppose production in the next year stayed unchanged but prices doubled; nominal GDP would double. Suppose production doubled but prices stayed the same; nominal GDP would also double. While nominal GDP does not distinguish between these two sources of increase in total expenditure, we need to distinguish between them. Hence economists favour real GDP — the value of final goods and services weighted by the prices

WEIGHTING GOODS AND SERVICES BY THEIR MARKET VALUES

2.8

BOX

EXAMPLE

How do economists weight goods and services by their market values? Recall the discussion of the CPI earlier in this chapter (see Box 2.5) in which the representative consumer bought 11.5 kilograms of fruit:

Fruit	Quantity (Kilograms)	Price (per Kilogram)
Oranges	6	$0.75
Apples	3.5	1.20
Pears	1	0.90
Bananas	1	0.40

If these quantities were the final goods and services produced in a particular year — let's call it year 1 — and we then wanted to measure the GDP of fruit, we simply multiply the quantities produced by their market prices:

$$GDP = 6 \text{ kgs oranges} \times \$0.75/\text{kg} + 3.5 \text{ kgs apples} \times \$1.20/\text{kg}$$
$$+ 1 \text{ kg pears} \times \$0.90/\text{kg} + 1 \text{ kg bananas} \times \$0.40/\text{kg}$$
$$= \$10.00$$

The nominal GDP of fruit in year 1 is $10.

BOX

EXAMPLE

2.9

Recall the hypothetical example in Box 2.8. Assume that in the year following year 1 — year 2 — the prices and quantities of fruit produced are as follows:

Fruit	Quantity (Kilograms)	Price (per Kilogram)
Oranges	8	$1.00
Apples	3.5	1.20
Pears	1	0.50
Bananas	1	0.40

Now we can calculate nominal GDP of fruit in both year 1 and year 2 and real GDP of fruit (at year 1 prices) in both year 1 and year 2:

- Nominal GDP of fruit in year 1: $10.00
- Real GDP of fruit in year 1 (at year 1 prices): $10.00
- Nominal GDP of fruit in year 2: $13.10
- Real GDP of fruit in year 2 (at year 1 prices): $11.50

The nominal quantity grows by 31 percent between year 1 and year 2. The real quantity grows by only 15 percent between year 1 and year 2. The difference is inflation, the change in the price level.

of some particular base year. Box 2.9 illustrates the weighting of goods and services in terms of base-year prices.

Whenever you hear a statement such as "Real GDP in 2004 was 1.12 trillion 1997 dollars," remember that "1997 dollars" means that 1997 is the base year of the calculation. When measured using 1997 prices, GDP in 2004 — real GDP — was not $1.29 trillion but only $1.12 trillion. The difference, the gap between $1.29 and $1.12, was due to price inflation between 1997 and 2004. Real GDP in 2005 was 1.16 trillion. Hence between 2004 and 2005 real GDP rose by only 3.57 percent, not 6.20 percent.

As has been noted above, economists construct an alternative index number for the rate of inflation, the GDP deflator, from nominal GDP and real GDP. The procedure is

1. Calculate nominal GDP.

2. Calculate real GDP.

3. Divide the first number by the second; the quotient is the GDP deflator.

The GDP deflator measured this way is a Paasche index — the kind of index that tends to understate the effect on the price level of a rise in the price of a particular good. While the GDP deflator takes account of purchasers' ability to substitute away from items that have increased prices, it does not take account of the reduction in utility — the implicit cost to consumers — of settling for second best. As stated earlier, Statistics Canada measures the GDP deflator as a Fisher index, which is more complicated to derive. We will not discuss the Fisher index beyond what was discussed earlier.

There are important differences between the CPI and the GDP deflator. First, as discussed in Section 2.4, the CPI is a *Laspeyres* price index whereas the GDP deflator, as currently measured by Statistics Canada, is a *Fisher* price index. Second, the

GDP deflator is an index for the price of all the final goods and services *produced* in the economy, while the CPI is an index for the price of goods and services *consumed*. There is no reason for the price of the basket of goods consumed to be the same as the price of basket of goods produced. Several goods consumed are imported, while several goods produced are exported. Also, several goods produced are purchased by the government or by firms, and not by consumers.

INTERMEDIATE GOODS, INVENTORIES, AND IMPUTATIONS

INTERMEDIATE GOODS

GDP is defined as the market value of final goods and services produced. Thus so-called *intermediate goods* — goods sold to another business for use in further production — are excluded from GDP. A product made by one business and sold to another will eventually show up in the national income and product accounts and be counted as part of GDP. It will show up when the second business sells its product (which will by then embody the value added by the first producer) to a consumer, an investor, a foreign purchaser, or the government. Meanwhile, because the value of an intermediate good is included in the price of the final good that the intermediate good is used to make, its value must be excluded from GDP.

For example, if a builder buys wood from a lumber mill to build a house, the value of the wood becomes part of the value of the house. To count the sale of the wood to the home builder as well as the sale of the newly built house to its purchaser would be to count the wood twice. And what would happen if the builder bought the lumber mill and thus no longer had to buy finished wood? GDP should not go down just because two businesses have merged.

One way to think about intermediate goods is that GDP represents the economic value added at every stage of production. The value added by any one business is equal to the total value of the firm's products minus the value of the materials and intermediate goods the firm purchases. In computing value added from start to finish, each intermediate good and service enters the calculation twice: once with a plus sign, when the value added of the business that made the good is calculated, and once with a minus sign, when the value added of the business that uses the good is calculated. Using this value-added approach, every good and service in the economy cancels out except those that are *not* sold to other businesses for use in the production process. The goods whose values do not cancel out are the *final goods and services* — consumption goods, goods purchased by the government, goods purchased as part of investment, and net exports.

INVENTORIES

What happens if the production process is not finished when the end of the year rolls around and Statistics Canada closes the books on that year's GDP calculation? Some intermediate goods will not have been used to produce goods for final sale. The value has already been added in making the intermediate good, but no final good that embodies that value has yet been sold. The National Income and Expenditure Accounts finesses this problem by treating inventories at the end of a period as a special kind of final good, a form of investment. A business that produces intermediate goods or final goods and doesn't sell them by the end of the year is treated as having "purchased" those goods for itself as part of its capital stock. The general rule is that whenever a business increases its end-of-period inventory, that increase is counted as a component of investment and of final demand.

What happens the next year when the final goods are finished and sold? The value of those final goods sold becomes part of the next period's GDP. But the intermediate goods that went into them are counted as a negative investment, a disinvestment, in inventory. Thus the intermediate goods left over from this year and used next year are *subtracted* from next year's GDP.

IMPUTATIONS

What about goods and services that are produced and consumed but not sold in the marketplace? Such goods and services lack prices and market values; how are they counted in GDP? In some cases national income accounts estimate — they guess, really — what goods or services would have sold for on the market if there had been a market.

The largest such "imputation" in the National Income and Expenditure Accounts is found in housing. When somebody rents an apartment or a house, the rent he or she pays to the landlord becomes part of GDP as the purchase of "housing services" by the renter. When a landlord rents a house to a tenant, the landlord is selling a service — the usefulness of having a roof over the renter's head — just as a barber is selling a service when a customer gets a haircut. Thus rent is one item in consumer spending on services. Accountants enter it as a component of expenditure in the FIRE (finance, insurance, and real estate) sector, a large component of consumer demand.

However, over 60 percent of Canadians own their own houses and are their own landlords. These homeowners do not write a monthly rent cheque to themselves. Counting renter-occupied housing as part of GDP but ignoring owner-occupied housing would not be consistent. Therefore GDP includes the *imputed* rent on owner-occupied dwellings — the amount Statistics Canada thinks that owner-occupied apartments and houses would rent for if they were rented out.

The inclusion of the cost of goods and services bought by the government may also be understood as an imputation. Since citizens do not directly pay firefighters, police officers, judges, and other government employees, the value of what the government spends on firefighting — in wages, insurance, materials, and so forth — is counted in GDP.

THE EXPENDITURE APPROACH

How does Statistics Canada construct its measure of real GDP? Statistics Canada includes in its measure of real GDP, which we will always denote by Y in equations and diagrams, the values of the following:

- Goods and services that are ultimately bought and used by households (except for newly constructed buildings); these goods and services are termed **consumption spending** (denoted C).
- Goods and services (including newly constructed buildings) that become part of society's business or residential capital stock; these goods and services are termed **investment spending** (denoted I). Gross investment spending is divided into two parts: the capital consumption allowance, or the depreciation of worn-out or obsolete capital; and net investment, which increases the total capital stock. Investment can be divided into four components: houses and apartments (residential structures), other buildings and infrastructure (nonresidential structures), machines (producers' durable equipment), and, as noted above, the change in business inventories (see Table 2.6).

TABLE 2.6
Components of Investment in 2005

Category of Investment	2005 (Millions)
Total private gross investment spending	$260,969
Residential structures	89,101
Nonresidential structures	69,606
Machinery and equipment	91,104
Business investment in inventories	11,158

Source: Statistics Canada CANSIM II database, Table 380-0017.

TABLE 2.7
Components of GDP in 2005

Category of GDP	2005 (Millions)
Total GDP	$1,371,425
Consumption spending	760,380
Investment spending	260,969
Government spending	298,506
Net exports	52,007
Statistical discrepancy	–437

Source: Statistics Canada CANSIM II database, Table 380-0017.

- **Government purchases** (denoted G). Note that government purchases do not include any payments the government makes that are not payment for a good or service provided to the government.
- **Net exports** (denoted NX) are a balancing item included in GDP: the GDP total needs to be adjusted for the difference between exports and imports to make the national income and product accounts consistent.

Accountants add up all these components to arrive at GDP (see Table 2.7). This definition of GDP, the national income identity, is one of the most fundamental bases of macroeconomics:

$$Y = C + I + G + NX \tag{2.13}$$

This is the equation that you will write down more than any other during any macroeconomics course.

Goods (and services) produced abroad but consumed or used in Canada are imports. Goods (and services) produced in Canada and shipped abroad to be consumed or used there are gross exports. The distinction between gross exports and net exports is similar to the distinction between gross investment and net investment. Gross exports are exports before the counterbalancing factor of imports has been subtracted. Most often gross exports are less important than net exports — the difference between gross exports and imports, the net flow of goods into or out of Canada.

OTHER MEASURES OF INCOME

GDP is the value of goods and services produced in the economy within a given time period (usually a year or a quarter). There are other measures of income that are as important. Economists refer to net domestic product (NDP) versus GDP, gross national product (GNP) versus GDP, and at market prices versus GDP at factor cost. It is important to be clear about different measures of income, and how they relate to each other.

GROSS VERSUS NET

So far we have discussed *gross* domestic product. It was *gross* because no account was made of depreciation when we arrived at this measure of income. Depreciation, which is also referred to as *capital consumption allowance*, is the fall in the value of capital because it wears out in the production process. If we deduct depreciation from GDP, we arrive at NDP:

$$NDP = GDP - Depreciation \qquad (2.14)$$

NATIONAL VERSUS DOMESTIC

Next, we may want to calculate gross *national* product (GNP), as opposed to GDP. Gross national product is the value of the gross output of all final goods and services produced by the factors of production *owned* by the residents of the country within a time period, while GDP is the value of the gross output of all final goods and services produced by all factors *located* within the borders of the country.

Some of the factors owned by the domestic residents may be located in other countries. Shares in firms located in other countries will reflect such ownerships. Also, foreigners may own some of the factors of production located in the domestic economy. Shares in domestic firms located in the economy but held by foreigners will reflect such ownerships. Income earned by the factors of production owned by the domestic residents but located abroad is called *income from abroad*. Income earned by the factors of production located in the economy but owned by foreign residents is called *income paid to foreigners*. Net income from abroad is defined as income from abroad minus income paid to foreigners:

$$GNP = GDP + net\ income\ from\ abroad. \qquad (2.15)$$

Of course, one can also calculate net national product (NNP). This measure of national product takes into account the fact that capital depreciates in the production process. Net national product (NNP) is net domestic product (NDP) plus net property income from abroad:

$$NNP = NDP + net\ income\ from\ abroad. \qquad (2.16)$$

MARKET PRICES VERSUS FACTOR COST

The distinction between *market prices* and *factor costs* is important if there are indirect taxes or subsidies involved in the economy. The government collects indirect taxes on sales of goods and services, such as the goods and services tax (GST) or the provincial sales tax (PST). Indirect subsidies are subsidies on sales of goods and services. Some governments pay such subsidies on the sale of certain important goods (such as milk) in order to encourage their consumption.

In deriving GDP usually we use market prices, that is, prices paid by the purchasers, in order to evaluate different components of aggregate expenditures (consumption, investment, government expenditures, and net exports). Hence, the GDP we derive is GDP *at market prices*. However, these market prices will include indirect taxes and will exclude indirect subsidies. In order to arrive at the prices received by the producers (also referred to as factor costs) we must deduct indirect taxes and add indirect subsidies to the market prices. Hence, to obtain GDP at factor cost, we should deduct indirect taxes, and add indirect subsidies to GDP at market prices:

$$\text{GDP at factor cost} = \\ \text{GDP at market prices} - \text{indirect taxes} + \text{indirect subsidies.} \quad (2.17)$$

Of course, one will have NDP at factor cost versus NDP at market prices, GNP at factor cost versus GNP at market prices, NNP at factor cost versus NNP at market prices, and so on.

WHAT MEASURE OF INCOME TO USE?

In practice, it is very hard to calculate the loss in the value of capital used in the production process (depreciation). Hence, "gross" measures involve smaller measurement errors than "net" measures.

If we are interested in the value of output produced in the economy we should use a "domestic" measure. On the other hand, if we are interested in measuring the well-being of the residents of the country, we should use a "national" measure, as this will measure the income earned by the factors of production *owned* by the residents of the economy.

In measuring the value of output produced we are ultimately interested in measuring income earned by the factors of production. The producers pay income to the workers, landlords, owners of the shares in firms, etc. Hence, in measuring income we are interested in measuring the total revenue made by the producers. To calculate this, we must use the value of output sold using the prices received by the producers. Thus, to measure income we must use a "factor cost" as opposed to a "market price" measure.

In Table 2.8 we calculate different measures of income for Canada in 2005. In the Appendix to this chapter we discuss the *circular flow of income*, which is used to show that adding up the values of GDP at factor cost measured as explained above

TABLE 2.8
Measures of Income for Canada in Current Dollars, 2005

GDP at market prices	$1,368,726 million
Minus: Capital consumption allowances	181,427
NDP at market prices	1,187,299
Minus: Taxes less subsidies on products	94,750
Minus: Taxes less subsidies on factors of production	59,961
NDP at factor cost	1,032,588
Plus: Net income from abroad	−24,518
NNP at factor cost	1,008,070

Source: Statistics Canada CANSIM II database, Tables 380-0001 and 380-0015.

is equal to total income earned in the economy. Total income earned in the economy is wages, rents, profits, interest on loans, and other incomes earned in the economy. Due to measurement errors, these two different measures of GDP at factor cost are usually not exactly equal to each other. As a result, an entry called *statistical discrepancy* is included in national income accounting tables in order to make the two measures exactly equal.

WHAT IS AND IS NOT IN GDP

DEPRECIATION AND NET OUTPUT

Real GDP is a very imperfect measure of total economic activity, or material well-being. Some things that are included in GDP should not be, and some things that are not included in GDP should be. For example, every year a portion of the nation's capital stock loses value. It wears out or becomes obsolete, so it is no longer worth keeping it operating because the cost of doing so is higher than the value of the goods the capital produces. Replacing such worn-out or obsolete capital is as much a cost of production to a business (or a government) as is meeting the business's payroll. Such replacement is surely not an *increase* in the nation's capital stock. Yet GDP counts *all* investment — including this replacement investment — in its measure of total economic activity, for the measure of investment included in real GDP is gross investment.

Why is replacement investment included in real GDP? Why is it seen not as a cost of doing business but as the near-equivalent of building a new factory to expand the business's productive capacity? Depreciation expenditures, which are also referred to as "capital consumption allowances," are counted in real GDP because the statisticians who compile the National Income and Expenditure Accounts have no confidence in their estimates of economy-wide depreciation. A better measure of economic activity is net domestic product (NDP) which, as we saw above, includes only net investment and excludes depreciation. However, the national income accountants prefer to focus attention on measures that they think are reasonably accurate, and so they downplay the (poorly measured) NDP and play up the GDP estimate.

GOVERNMENT PURCHASES

Government purchases of goods and services are also counted in GDP. The government uses the goods and services it purchases: It builds roads, provides police protection and courts, runs schools, issues weather reports, maintains the national parks, maintains the armed services, and so on.

Many of these services, if they were provided by private businesses, would be counted as intermediate goods — things that are not of final value themselves but are aids to private-sector production. As such, they would be excluded from the GDP. Think about it. Suppose two companies made a contract that a certain arbitrator would be the judge of any disputes that arose between them, and suppose they paid the arbitrator a retainer. The services of the private judge that they hired would be classified in the National Income and Expenditure Accounts as an intermediate good and would not be included in the final goods and services added up to calculate GDP.

Nevertheless, *all* government purchases of goods and services are counted as part of GDP, including the money the government collects in taxes and then pays to its own judges, bailiffs, and clerks, many of whom decide business-to-business disputes. A large number of government purchases fall into this category. They are counted as part of GDP, but they would not be counted had they been made for analogous substantive purposes by private businesses.

WHAT ISN'T IN GDP BUT SHOULD BE

Moreover, many expenditures excluded from the National Income and Expenditure Accounts, and thus from GDP, probably should not be. Production that takes place within the household is excluded from GDP. That is, the work family members do to keep their own households going, for which they are not paid, is excluded from GDP.

Thus many Canadians—most of them adult women—spend long hours performing services, such as cooking, cleaning, shopping, and chauffeuring, that would count as employment and would count in GDP if they were receiving pay for them rather than doing them for their own families. As Figure 2.15 shows, only a little more than 45 percent of Canadian women were counted in the labour force in 1976, even though most of them would have said that they worked full days. Within-the-household production has never been counted as part of GDP. When the National Income and Expenditure Accounts was set up, economists believed that it would be difficult or impossible to obtain reasonable, credible, defensible estimates of the economic value of within-the-household production.

Yet the exclusion of within-the-household production makes a difference not just for the level of national product but for its rate of growth. Over time the border between paid market and unpaid nonmarket, within-the-household work has shifted. Be suspicious of economic growth rates based on total GDP, GDP per capita, or GDP per adult, because they are distorted by the shifting dividing line between what people do and how they arrange their work. A meal cooked is a meal cooked

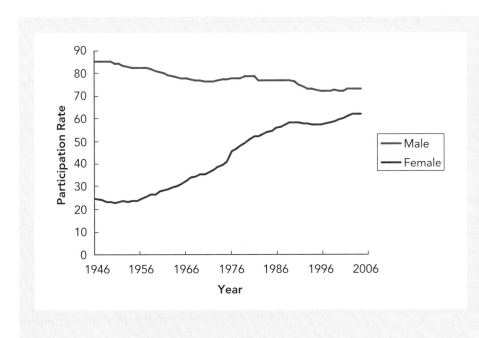

FIGURE 2.15

Labour-Force Participation Rates by Gender, 1946–2005

The paid-labour-force participation rates of men and women have been converging for a generation, as male labour-force participation has fallen slightly and female participation has grown rapidly. What were the counterparts of the women who worked for wages in 2005 doing back in 1946? They were working, but not for wages. And their work then wasn't counted as part of GDP.

Source: Statistics Canada CANSIM II database, Series V2064904 (male) and V2064913 (female).

whether it is part of the market paid work of a restaurant chef or part of the unpaid work of a homemaker. Over time the share of meals prepared in the first way has grown, while the share of meals prepared in the second way has shrunk. This shift in the dividing line between home cooking and dining out has raised measured GDP, but the shift by itself is not an increase in society's wealth.

http://www.statcan.ca/english/ freepub/11-516-XIE/sectiona/ toc.htm

DEPLETION, POLLUTION, AND "BADS"

The National Income and Expenditure Accounts makes no allowance for the depletion of scarce natural resources. To the extent that an economy produces a high income in the act of using up valuable natural resources, that income is not true GDP at all but the depletion of natural resources. Kuwait, Qatar, and Saudi Arabia have high levels of measured real GDP per worker, but much of their income arises not out of sustainable production but out of the sale of limited and depletable natural resources. A better system would have a category for the depletion of natural resources.

Moreover, the National Income and Expenditure Accounts contains no category for the production of "**bads**" — things that you would rather *not* have. Producing more smog does not diminish GDP. The extra cases of lung cancer produced by cigarette smoking do not diminish GDP (indeed, they raise the medical care sector's contribution to GDP). If the demand for locks and alarm systems rises because crime increases, GDP increases. As noted before, GDP is a measure of only the economy's level of productive effort, not of well-being.

THE INCOME APPROACH

The total value of output produced is equal to the income earned by the workers, owners of the firms, bondholders, landowners, and all others who are involved in producing the goods and services in the economy. This gives us the *income approach* to measuring domestic product. In this approach, domestic product is equal to the sum of all incomes earned in the economy. The income earned by the employees of companies and institutions is referred to as *labour income*. The income earned by the bondholders and other lenders is called *interest income*. The income earned by the owners and equity holders of companies is referred to as *corporate profits*. Some income is also earned by the self-employed people, including landlords, and is referred to as *unincorporated business income*, which includes rents. Hence, according to the income approach,

$$\text{Domestic product} = \text{labour income} + \text{interest income} + \text{corporate profits}$$
$$\text{before taxes} + \text{unincorporated business income} \qquad (2.18)$$

There are two important points about this equation that should be noted. First, since this measure of domestic product sums all incomes earned by all the factors of production in the economy, it is a measure of domestic product at *factor cost*. The reason is that in order to arrive at profits we use goods prices that firms and corporations receive, which exclude indirect taxes and include indirect subsidies.

Second, when reporting profits, firms take account of depreciation and obsolescence. Hence, profits reported are net of depreciation, making the above measure of output *net* domestic product.

Thus, equation (2.18) gives us net domestic product (NDP) at factor cost. Box 2.10 calculates Canada's GDP for 2005 using the income approach, and gives more details about the income approach.

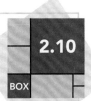

MEASURING CANADA'S GDP USING THE INCOME APPROACH

Table 2.9 gives the details of the different components of total income earned in Canada in 2005. Labour income is reported as "wages, salaries and supplementary labour income" and was $678,925 million. Profits are divided into two parts: "corporate profits before taxes," and "government business enterprise profits before taxes." Together these two categories of profits amounted to $207,306 million. "Before tax" means these profits are before corporate income taxes. Interest and miscellaneous investment incomes amounted to $61,240 million. Unincorporated business income is divided into two parts: those from farms (referred to as "accrued net income of farm operators"), and those from non-farm unincorporated businesses. These two categories of unincorporated business incomes together amounted to $86,217 million. Finally, firms and corporations often adjust the values of their inventories; and this is referred to as "inventory valuation adjustment," which was $−442 million. Summing the amounts for the first seven entries in Table 2.9, we obtain net domestic product at factor cost: $1.033 trillion.

Finally, notice that the last entry in Table 2.9, referred to as a statistical discrepancy, reconciles the value of NDP at factor cost as measured by the income approach with the value of NDP at factor cost as measured by the expenditure approach in Table 2.8.

TABLE 2.9
Income Approach to Measuring Domestic Product, 2005

Wages, salaries and supplementary labour income	$ 678,925 million
Corporation profits before taxes	193,936
Government business enterprise profits before taxes	13,370
Interest and miscellaneous investment income	61,240
Accrued net income of farm operators from farm production	1,551
Net income of non-farm unincorporated business, including rent	84,666
Inventory valuation adjustment	−442
Net domestic product at factor cost	1,033,246
Statistical discrepancy	−658

Source: Statistics Canada CANSIM II database, Table 380-0001.

RECAP REAL GDP

Real GDP is calculated by adding up the value of all final goods and services produced in the economy. Because it measures the rate at which goods and services are produced, real GDP is a flow variable: Remember that real GDP is measured as the value of goods and services produced *per year*. Real GDP has four components: (i) everything bought by consumers, (ii) everything bought by firms to increase their capital stock, (iii) everything bought by the government (including the time of bureaucrats), and (iv) net exports.

CHAPTER SUMMARY

1. Because economics studies goods and services that flow through the market and are bought and sold with prices attached, economists have a lot of quantitative data to work with.

2. The real exchange rate is the relative price at which two countries' goods exchange for each other. You calculate it by adjusting the nominal exchange rate for changes in the price levels in the two countries.

3. The level of the stock market is a valuable summary index of a range of factors that affect investment: the current level of profits, investors' optimism or pessimism, the real rate of interest, and attitudes toward risk.

4. Real interest rates are much more important variables to keep track of than are nominal interest rates. You calculate the real interest rate by subtracting the rate of inflation from nominal interest rates.

5. The most commonly seen measure of the price level is the consumer price index (CPI). The proportional rate of change of the price level is called the inflation rate.

6. Unemployment and total output are linked through Okun's law: a 1-percentage-point change in the unemployment rate comes with a 1.65 percent change in the level of output in the opposite direction.

7. Real GDP is the most commonly seen measure of the overall level of economic activity. It is the value — calculated using market prices in some chosen base year — of all final goods and services produced in a year.

8. The line between GDP and not GDP is principally the result of economists' beliefs in the 1940s and 1950s about what it would be possible to measure easily. It is not the result of a set of principled decisions about what kinds of activities should and should not be included in a measure of material welfare.

KEY TERMS AND EQUATIONS

"bads" (p. 66)

consumption spending (p. 60)

domestic exchange rate (p. 36)

foreign exchange rate (p. 36)

government purchases (p. 61)

index number (p. 38)

inflation (p. 50)

inflation rate (p. 31)

interest rate (p. 32)

investment spending (p. 60)

National Income and Expenditure Accounts (p. 56)

net exports (p. 61)

nominal exchange rate (p. 33)

Okun's law (p. 54)

price level (p. 47)

real exchange rate (p. 33)

real GDP (p. 28)

real GDP per worker (p. 28)

Statistics Canada (p. 47)

stock market (p. 32)

unemployment rate (p. 29)

Real exchange rate: $\qquad \varepsilon = e \times \dfrac{P^*}{P}$ (2.1)

Exchange rate index $= 100 \times \displaystyle\sum_{\text{all countries}} \left(\dfrac{\text{exchange rate in this year}}{\text{exchange rate in the base year}} \times \text{share of trade in the base year} \right)$ (2.4)

Labour force = employed + looking for work (2.10)

Unemployment rate $= \dfrac{\text{looking for work}}{\text{labour force}} = \dfrac{\text{looking for work}}{\text{employed + looking for work}}$ (2.11)

Okun's law: $\qquad$ % change in real GDP $= a - b \times$ (change in unemployment rate) (2.12)

Income identity: $\qquad Y = C + I + G + NX$ (2.13)

Net domestic product: $\quad$ NDP = GDP − Depreciation (2.14)

Gross national product: $\quad$ GNP = GDP + net income from abroad (2.15)

Net national product: NNP = NDP + net income from abroad   (2.16)

Gross domestic product (GDP) at factor cost = GDP at market prices – indirect taxes + indirect subsidies   (2.17)

Domestic product =   labour income + interest income + corporate profits + unincorporated business income   (2.18)

ANALYTICAL EXERCISES

1. Are capital goods — large turbine generators, jet airliners, bay-spanning bridges — intermediate goods or final goods? How are they included in GDP?

2. How do the labour and other factors of production that go into producing intermediate goods ultimately get counted in GDP?

3. Explain whether or not and why the following items are included in the calculation of GDP:
   a. Increases in business inventories.
   b. Sales of existing homes.
   c. Fees earned by real estate agents on selling existing homes.
   d. Income earned by Canadians living and working abroad.
   e. Purchases of IBM stock by your brother.
   f. Purchase of a new tank by the Defence Ministry.
   g. Rent that you pay to your landlord.

4. Which interest rate concept — the nominal interest rate or the real interest rate — do lenders and borrowers care more about? Why?

5. Which is the more important measure for assessing an economy's performance, real GDP or nominal GDP?

6. Consider the two definitions of the nominal exchange rate, e and e^f in Section 2.2.

   a. Write down the real exchange rates ε and ε^f corresponding to e and e^f and interpret them.
   b. Using the definitions ε and ε^f in (a) show that:
   $$\Delta\varepsilon/\varepsilon = \Delta e/e + \Delta P^f/P^f - \Delta P/P$$
   and
   $$\Delta\varepsilon^f/\varepsilon^f = \Delta e^f/e^f + \Delta P/P - \Delta P^f/P^f$$

   Interpret these relations.
   c. As we will discuss in Chapter 15, the theory of relative purchasing power asserts that the real exchange rate is constant over time. If this is true, how would you simplify the two expressions in part (b) of the question? Interpret your results.

7. Suppose the nominal GDP grows at the rate of 2 percent per year, while at the same time prices increase at the rate of 1 percent per year. What is the growth rate of real GDP?

8. Suppose the price level in the U.S. increases at the rate of 1 percent per year, the price level in Canada increases at the rate of 2 percent per year and the value of the US dollar relative to the Canadian dollar increases at the rate of 1 percent per year. What is the rate of change in the real exchange rate?

POLICY EXERCISES

1. In a particular year the (short-term) nominal interest rate on three-month Treasury bills averaged 10 percent, and the GDP deflator rose from 50.88 to 55.22. What was the annual rate of inflation? What was the real interest rate? Were real interest rates higher in year A described above or in year B, when the (short-term) nominal interest rate on three-month Treasury bills was 4.8 percent and the inflation rate was 2.6 percent?

2. Suppose in a particular year the GDP deflator rose at an annual rate of 2.6 percent, and the short-term interest rate on three-month Treasury bills averaged 4.8 percent.

What was the (short-term) nominal interest rate? What was the (short-term) real interest rate?

3. In 1992 the implicit GDP deflator (in 1992 dollars) was equal to 100; in 1993 it was equal to 101.54. What was the annual rate of inflation between 1992 and 1993? In 1994 the implicit GDP deflator (in 1992 dollars) was equal to 102.70. What was the annual rate of inflation between 1993 and 1994?

4. In 1992 both nominal GDP and real GDP (measured in 1992 dollars) were equal to $702,393 billion. By 1997 nominal GDP had risen to $885,022 billion, and the

implicit GDP deflator had risen to 108.59. What was real GDP in 1997? What was the average rate of real GDP growth between 1992 and 1997?

5. Use the data in the following table to answer the questions below:

	Real GDP* (billions)	Labour Force (millions)
1981	$551.30	12.22
1991	692.25	14.33
2001	1,011.09	16.25

* In 1992 dollars.

What was real GDP per worker in 1981, 1991, and 2001? How fast did real GDP per worker grow between 1981 and 1991? Between 1991 and 2001?

6. Consider the following data for 2000 in millions of dollars.

Consumption spending	594,089
Investment spending	194,177
Government purchases	219,816
Net exports	55,397
Capital consumption allowances	135,781
Indirect taxes less subsidies	127,745

a. Using this data calculate gross domestic product (GDP) at market prices.

b. Calculate GDP at factor cost.

c. Calculate net domestic product (NDP) at factor cost.

7. Consider the following data for 2000 in millions of dollars.

Wages, salaries & supplementary labour income	545,110
Corporation profits before taxes	129,821
Government business enterprise profits before taxes	11,832
Interest & miscellaneous investment income	53,933
Accrued net income of farm operators from production	1,758
Net income of non-farm unincorporated businesses, including rents	63,962
Inventory valuation adjustment	−3,431
Capital consumption allowances	135,781
Indirect taxes less subsidies	127,745
Net income from abroad	−22,368

a. Using this data calculate net domestic product (NDP) at factor cost.

b. Calculate GDP at market prices.

c. Calculate net national product (NNP) at factor cost.

8. How does the level of the stock market today compare with what it was in 1999? What were the reasons for the decline in stock prices in 2001?

2A

The Circular Flow of Economic Activity

When economists speak of the "circular flow" of economic activity, they have a definite picture in mind. They see patterns of spending, income, and production as liquid flowing through various sets of pipes. In this extended metaphor, categories of agents in the economy — all businesses, the government, all households — are the pools into and out of which the fluid of purchasing power (i.e., money) flows.

Thus economists think of economic activity — the pattern of production and spending in the economy — as a circular flow of purchasing power through the economy. The circular flow metaphor allows them confidently to predict that changes in one part of the economy will affect the whole and to explain what the likely effects will be. It allows them to simplify economic behaviour, to understand the entire set of decisions made by different agents in different parts of the economy by thinking of a few typical decisions made by abstract representative agents.

THE CIRCULAR FLOW DIAGRAM

Figure 2A.1 shows a simplified diagram of the circular flow. It omits the government and international trade. Nevertheless, it is a good starting point for our discussion. In this figure, money payments flow from firms to households as businesses pay their workers and their owners for their labour and capital. This is the "income side" of the circular flow: Firms buy the *factors of production,* capital and labour, from the households that own them. Money payments then flow from households to firms as households buy goods. This is the "expenditure side" of the circular flow: Households buy *final goods and services* from businesses. Note that these flows balance: The purchasing power that firms earn by selling their goods is the same as the purchasing power that firms spend by buying factors of production, and the incomes of households are equal to their total expenditures.

This simplified diagram is expanded in Figure 2A.2 to take account of the roles of the government, financial markets, and international trade and investment. But the core idea of a balanced circular flow of purchasing power is still present. Along the top of the diagram there is still the flow of incomes to households from businesses as they purchase labour and other factors of production from the households

FIGURE 2A.1

The Circular Flow Diagram

Households spend money buying the products made by businesses, and businesses turn around and spend the same money buying *factors of production* — workers' time and attention, finance, the use of land and other property — from households.

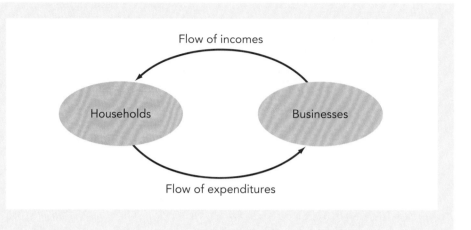

that own them. All these components of business expenditure — rent, wages, salaries, benefits, interest, and profits — become the components of household income. Toward the bottom left of the diagram are the uses of household incomes — consumption spending, savings, and taxes. Consumption spending flows directly to businesses as households purchase consumption goods. Total taxes flow to the government, which uses some of this revenue to make transfer payments — classified here as negative taxes — back to households, uses most of them for government purchases, and sends the remaining government budget surplus into financial markets as the government uses its budget surplus to buy back bonds.

Households save the portion of their incomes that is left over after taxes and consumption spending. These savings flow into financial markets as they are put into banks and mutual funds. Businesses seeking to invest draw on the pool of savings to gain financing for purchasing capital goods to expand their productive capacity. Exports serve as an addition to (and imports a subtraction from) total demand for domestically made products.

Thus at the bottom right we have the components of *aggregate demand:* consumption spending, investment spending, government purchases, and net exports (which are, in Canada today, net imports, a subtraction from GDP, because imports are greater than gross exports).

Within the *business sector,* businesses buy and sell intermediate goods from each other as they strive to produce goods and services and make profits. Within the *household sector,* households buy and sell assets from and to one another. These within-the-business-sector and within-the-household-sector transactions are important components of the economy. But because they net out to zero within the business sector or within the household sector, they are not counted as part of the circular flow of economic activity.

To better grasp the circular flow of economic activity, look at one particular part of the circular flow, a dollar paid out by a business as a dividend to a shareholder. The dollar is payment for use of a factor of production, the capital invested in the business by the shareholder. When the dividend cheque is deposited, it becomes part of the shareholder's household income. Suppose the household doesn't spend it but simply keeps the money in the bank, thus saving it. The bank will notice that it has an extra dollar on deposit and will loan that dollar out to a business in need of

FIGURE 2A.2

The Circular Flow of Economic Activity

This version of the circular flow is complicated by the addition of the government and financial markets to the diagram. Not all final goods and services are bought by households. Some are bought by the government, which imposes taxes to raise resources to finance itself. Some are bought by businesses seeking to invest, which raise the needed resources by issuing stock, issuing bonds, and borrowing — all of which take place in *financial markets*. This version is also complicated by its recognizing that there is a world outside, a world that buys the products of domestic businesses and that invests through domestic financial markets.

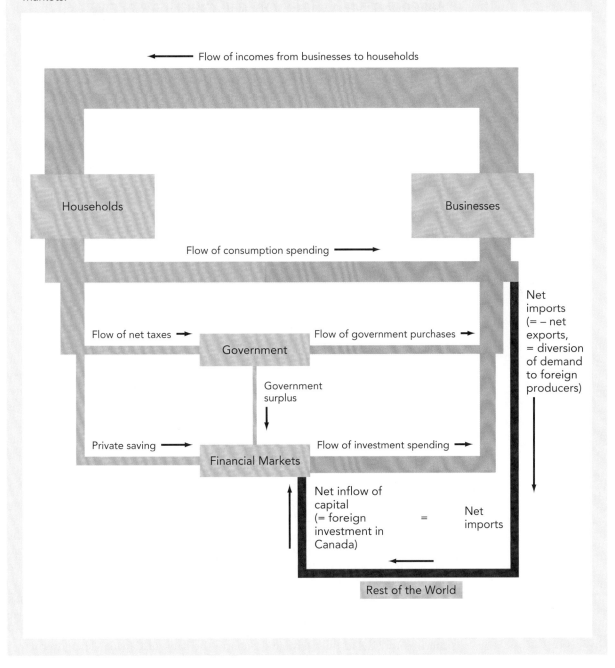

cash to build up its inventory. That business will then spend the dollar buying goods and services as it builds up its inventory. As soon as the dollar shows up as a component of business investment spending, the circular flow is complete. The dollar's worth of purchasing power has flowed from the business sector to the household sector, then flowed as part of the flow of savings into the financial markets, and finally flowed out of the financial markets and back to the business sector as part of business investment spending.

DIFFERENT MEASURES OF THE CIRCULAR FLOW

Income, production, and expenditure can be measured at three different points in the circular flow:

1. At the point where consumers, exporters, the government, and firms that are making investments purchase goods and services from businesses. This measurement is real GDP, or total output. It is the total production of goods and services. It is the expenditure-side measure of the circular flow.

2. At the point in the circular flow where businesses pay households for the factors of production. Businesses need labour, capital, and natural resources, all factors of production owned directly or indirectly by households. When businesses buy them, they provide households with incomes. This measurement is called *total income* or *national income*. It is the income-side measure of the circular flow.

3. At the point where households decide how to use their income. How much do they save? How much do they pay in taxes? How much do they spend on consumption goods? This measure of the circular flow of economic activity is the "uses-of-income" measure.

The measure used most often is the expenditure-side measure: the gross domestic product produced by firms and demanded by purchasers. It is estimated by summing the four components of spending (and sales) — consumption, government purchases, investment, and net exports. If we compare the expenditure-side measure of GDP with the income-side or uses-of-income-side measure, we will find that, aside from differences created by different accounting conventions, they are equal. They are equal because the circular flow principle is designed into the National Income and Expenditure Accounts. Every expenditure on a final good or service is accounted for as a payment to a business. Every dollar payment that flows into a business is then accounted for as paid out to somebody. It can be paid out as income — wages, fringe benefits, profits, interest, or rent — or as an expenditure on goods or services of another business that then, in turn, purchases factors of production.

What if you want to withdraw your income from the circular flow? Suppose, for instance, that you simply take the dollar bills you receive and use them to buy something old and precious from another household — a bar of gold, say. And suppose you keep the bar of gold in your basement. Doesn't that break the circular flow? The answer is that it does not. You no longer have your income, but the household that you bought the gold bar from does. That household will then either spend it on consumption goods, save it, or have it taxed away.

What if you decided to hide the dollar bills in your basement? Doesn't that break the circular flow? The answer, again, is that it does not. The Royal Mint will notice that the total number of dollar bills circulating in the economy has dropped. It will print up more dollar bills and hand them to the Bank of Canada. The government will spend these extra dollar bills, and thus replace the ones you have hidden. The net effect is the same as it would be if you had saved the dollar bills by lending them out to the government through the purchase of a Treasury bond. There are only two differences between buying a Treasury bond and your basement storage scheme: (1) You have a stack of dollar bills in your basement rather than a piece of paper with the words "Treasury bond" written on it. (2) The government does not pay interest on the dollar bills stacked in your basement, but it does pay interest on its bonds. In the circular flow diagram, you have saved your income, but you have saved it in a relatively pointless way by making the government an interest-free loan.

RECAP   **THE CIRCULAR FLOW OF ECONOMIC ACTIVITY**

Money flows from households to firms as households buy goods. This is the "expenditure side" of the circular flow: Households buy *final goods and ser vices* from businesses. Businesses then turn around and buy factors of production from households. These payments make up household income. This is the "income side" of the circular flow. The circular flow principle is that the two flows must match: In the economy as a whole, expenditure must equal income.

Long-Run Economic Growth

Long-run economic growth is the subject of this two-chapter part. Chapter 3 covers the theory of growth, and Chapter 4 covers the worldwide pattern of economic growth. Long-run economic growth is the most important topic in macroeconomics. Standards of living in Canada today are substantially better than they were at the end of the nineteenth century. Successful economic growth has meant that almost all citizens of Canada today live better, and we hope happier, lives than even the rich elite of a century ago. The study of long-run economic growth aims at understanding its sources and causes and at determining what government policies will promote or retard long-run economic growth.

The study of long-run growth is also a separate module that is not very closely connected to the study of business cycles, recessions, unemployment, inflation, and stabilization policy that make up the bulk of the subject matter of macroeconomics courses and of this book. Any discussion of economic policy has to refer to long-run economic growth: The effect of a policy on long-run growth is its most important element. But the models used and the conclusions reached in Part II will by and large not be used in subsequent parts. Starting in Chapter 5, our attention turns from growth to business cycles.

Why, then, include this two-chapter part on long-run growth? The principal reason is that long-run economic growth is such an important topic that it must be covered.

3

The Theory of Economic Growth

QUESTIONS

What are the principal determinants of long-run economic growth?

What equilibrium condition is useful in analyzing long-run growth?

How quickly does an economy head for its steady-state growth path?

What effect does faster population growth have on long-run growth?

What effect does a higher savings rate have on long-run growth?

What government policies can enhance growth?

3.1 SOURCES OF LONG-RUN GROWTH

Ultimately, long-run economic growth is *the* most important aspect of how the economy performs. Material standards of living and levels of economic productivity in Canada today are about four times what they are today in, say, Mexico because of favourable initial conditions and successful growth-promoting economic policies over the past two centuries. Material standards of living and levels of economic productivity in Canada today are at least five times what they were at the end of the nineteenth century and more than ten times what they were at the founding of the country. Successful economic growth has meant that most citizens of Canada today live better, along almost every dimension of material life, than did even the rich elite in preindustrial times.

It is definitely possible for good and bad policies to accelerate or retard long-run economic growth. Argentines were as rich as Canadians in the late nineteenth century, but Canadians today have perhaps four times the material standard of living and the economic productivity level of Argentines. Almost all this difference is due to differences in growth policies — good policies in the case of Canada, bad policies in the case of Argentina — for there were few important differences in initial conditions at the start of the twentieth century to give Canada an edge.

Policies and initial conditions work to accelerate or retard growth through two principal channels. The first is their impact on the available level of *technology* that multiplies the efficiency of labour. The second is their impact on the **capital intensity** of the economy — the stock of machines, equipment, and buildings that the average worker has at his or her disposal.

BETTER TECHNOLOGY

The overwhelming part of the answer to the question of why Canadians today are more productive and better off than their predecessors of a century or two ago is "better technology." We now know how to make electric motors, dope semiconductors, transmit signals over fibre optics, fly jet airplanes, machine internal combustion engines, build tall and durable structures out of concrete and steel, record entertainment programs on optical discs, make hybrid seeds, fertilize crops with better mixtures of nutrients, organize an assembly line for mass production, and do a host of other things that our predecessors did not know how to do a century or so ago. Perhaps more important, the Canadian economy is equipped to make use of all these technological discoveries.

Better technology leads to a higher level of **efficiency of labour** — the skills and education of the labour force, the ability of the labour force to handle modern machine technologies, and the efficiency with which the economy's businesses and markets function. An economy in which the efficiency of labour is higher will be a richer and a more productive economy. This technology-driven overwhelming increase in the efficiency with which we work today is the major component of our current relative prosperity.

Thus it is somewhat awkward to admit that economists know relatively little about better technology. Economists are good at analyzing the consequences of advanced technology, but they have less to say than they should about the sources of such technology. (We shall return to what economists do have to say about the sources of better technology toward the end of Chapter 4.)

CAPITAL INTENSITY

The second major factor determining the prosperity and growth of an economy — and the second channel through which changes in economic policies can affect long-run growth — is the *capital intensity* of the economy. How much does the average worker have at his or her disposal in the way of capital goods — buildings, highways, docks, cranes, dynamos, numerically controlled machine tools, computers, molders, and all the others? The larger the answer to this question, the more prosperous an economy will be: A more capital-intensive economy will be a richer and a more productive economy.

There are, in turn, two principal determinants of capital intensity. The first is the *investment effort* being made in the economy: the share of total production — real

GDP — saved and invested in order to increase the capital stock of machines, buildings, infrastructure, and other human-made tools that amplify the productivity of workers. Policies that create a higher level of investment effort lead to a faster rate of long-run economic growth.

The second determinant is the *investment requirements* of the economy: the amount of new investment that goes to simply equipping new workers with the economy's standard level of capital or to replacing worn-out and obsolete machines and buildings. The ratio between the investment effort and the investment requirements of the economy determines the economy's capital intensity.

This chapter focuses on the intellectual tools that economists use to analyze long-run growth. It outlines a relatively simple framework for thinking about the key growth issues. Thus, this chapter looks at the theory. The following chapter looks at the facts of economic growth.

Note that, as mentioned above, the tools have relatively little to say about the determinants of technological progress. They do, however, have a lot to say about the determinants of the capital intensity of the economy. And they have a lot to say about how evolving technology and the determinants of capital intensity together shape the economy's long-run growth.

RECAP   SOURCES OF LONG-RUN GROWTH

Ultimately, long-run economic growth is *the* most important aspect of how the economy performs. Two major factors determine the prosperity and growth of an economy: the pace of technological advance and the capital intensity of the economy. Policies that accelerate innovation or that boost investment to raise capital intensity accelerate economic growth.

3.2 GROWTH ACCOUNTING

In 1956 Robert Solow of MIT developed a general framework for measuring the contributions of factors of production to the growth of output. Soon after, Edward Denison of the Brookings Institution used this framework to measure the sources of growth for the U.S. economy. Since then Solow's growth accounting formula has been successfully applied to data for different countries.

Solow proposed using a neoclassical production function for growth accounting. The production function tells us how much the economy can produce given the economy's resources and the level of technology. We can write the production function as

$$Y_t = A_t \times F(K_t, L_t) \tag{3.1}$$

where Y_t denotes real GDP, L_t denotes total labour used in the production process, K_t is total capital, and A_t denotes the current level of technology, more commonly referred to as multi-factor productivity (MFP) or total factor productivity. $F(\cdot)$ is the production function, which shows how output is systematically related to capital, labour and the current level of technology. Often in economic modelling we assume that the production function has a particularly simple form, referred to as the Cobb-Douglas function. With the Cobb-Douglas production function we have

$$Y_t = A_t \times K_t^{\alpha} \times L_t^{1-\alpha} \tag{3.2}$$

ON THE PROPERTIES OF COBB-DOUGLAS PRODUCTION FUNCTION

With the Cobb-Douglas production function (3.2) the parameter α measures the fraction of total income earned by capital, while $1 - \alpha$ measures the fraction of total income earned by labour. To see this, consider a change in output ΔY_t brought about by a change in capital ΔK_t. From equation (3.2), it is clear that ΔY_t and ΔK_t will be related to each other as follows:

$$\Delta Y_t = \alpha \times \frac{A_t \times K_t^{\alpha} \times L_t^{1-\alpha}}{K_t} \times \Delta K_t = \alpha \times \frac{Y_t}{K_t} \times \Delta K_t$$

Next, notice that we can re-write this equation as

$$\alpha = \frac{(\Delta Y_t / \Delta K_t) \times K_t}{Y_t} \tag{B3.1}$$

Finally, note that $\Delta Y_t / \Delta K_t$ is the marginal productivity of capital. It measures the change in output due to a one unit increase in capital. With perfect competition, the rental rate of capital is equal to its marginal productivity. Hence, $\Delta Y_t / \Delta K_t$ is income earned by each unit of capital, and the numerator of the right-hand side of equation (B3.1) is the income earned by capital. Clearly, then α measures the fraction of total income earned by capital. Similarly, it can be shown that $1 - \alpha$ is the fraction of total income earned by labour.

BOX 3.1

TOOLS

The properties of the Cobb-Douglas production function will be further discussed in the next section. At this stage, however, it will suffice to note that α is a parameter between 0 and 1 that measures the share of total income earned by capital, while $1 - \alpha$ measures the share of total income earned by labour. These important results are shown in Box 3.1, and are used very effectively in growth accounting.

Using the rules for deriving proportional changes discussed in Box 2.4 of Chapter 2, it follows from equation (3.2) that a percentage change in output $\Delta Y_t / Y_t$ will be the sum of a percentage change in multi-factor productivity $\Delta A_t / A_t$, a fraction α of a percentage change in capital $\Delta K_t / K_t$, and a fraction $1 - \alpha$ of the percentage change in labour $\Delta L_t / L_t$. Thus, we will have

$$\frac{\Delta Y_t}{Y_t} = \alpha \times \frac{\Delta K_t}{K_t} + (1 - \alpha) \times \frac{\Delta L_t}{L_t} + \frac{\Delta A_t}{A_t} \tag{3.3}$$

This is the key equation in growth accounting. It states that the growth rate of output $\Delta Y/Y$ can be decomposed into three components: (i) the contribution from the growth of capital $\alpha \times \Delta K/K$, (ii) the contribution from the growth of labour $(1 - \alpha) \times \Delta L/L$, and (iii) the contribution from the growth of multi-factor productivity $\Delta A/A$.

http://www.statcan.ca/

Notice changes in multi-factor productivity can come about for many reasons — from new ways of constructing buildings, new invented machines, and new sources of power, but also from changes in work organization, in the efficiency of government regulations, in the literacy and skills of the workforce, and many other factors.

TABLE 3.1

Average Annual Rates of Growth of Output and Contributions by Type of Input, 1961–1999

Source of Growth	Input Shares	Input Growth	Components	Contributions to Output Growth (%)
Capital	$\alpha = 0.37$	$\Delta K/K = 3.77$	$\alpha \times \Delta K/K$	1.4
Labour	$(1 - \alpha) = 0.63$	$\Delta L/L = 1.93$	$(1 - \alpha) \times \Delta L/L$	1.2
Multi-factor productivity			$\Delta Y/Y - \alpha \times \Delta K/K - (1 - \alpha) \times \Delta L/L$	1.2
Total (Output)			$\Delta Y/Y$	3.8

Source: Adapted from the Statistics Canada publication, "Productivity Growth in Canada," Catalogue 15–204, 2001.

Note that if we know the growth rates of output, the capital stock, and the labour force as well as the parameter α then we can use equation (3.3) to calculate the growth of multi-factor productivity as the residual

$$\frac{\Delta A_t}{A_t} = \frac{\Delta Y_t}{Y_t} - \alpha \times \frac{\Delta K_t}{K_t} - (1 - \alpha) \times \frac{\Delta L_t}{L_t} \tag{3.4}$$

Robert Solow suggested this method of estimating the growth of multi-factor productivity, known as the *Solow residual*.

Table 3.1 reports such a decomposition for Canada for the period 1961–1999. For this period the average annual rate of growth of output is $\Delta Y/Y = 3.8$ percent. The second column of the table reports the average shares of total income earned by capital and labour, which are $\alpha = 0.37$ and $1 - \alpha = 0.63$, respectively. The third column reports the average annual rates of growth of capital and labour, which are, respectively, $\Delta K/K = 3.77$ percent and $\Delta L/L = 1.93$ percent. Solving for these figures in equation (3.4), one derives the average annual rate of growth of multi-factor productivity as 1.2 percent.

Figure 3.1 shows recent estimates for growth in multi-factor productivity for 17 OECD countries for the 1980s and 1990s. The rate of growth of multi-factor productivity in Canada during the 1980s was lower than its 1.2 percent average for the 1961–1999 period. Notice also that the rate of growth of multi-factor productivity in Canada has been substantially lower than in the U.S., our most important trading partner; and it has been moderate relative to other countries.

RECAP GROWTH ACCOUNTING

Using the neoclassical production function, one can decompose the growth rate of output into three components: (i) the contribution from the growth of capital, (ii) the contribution from the growth of labour, and (iii) the contribution from the growth of multi-factor productivity. The rate of growth of multi-factor productivity in Canada during the 1980s and 1990s was lower than in the U.S., and it was moderate relative to other countries

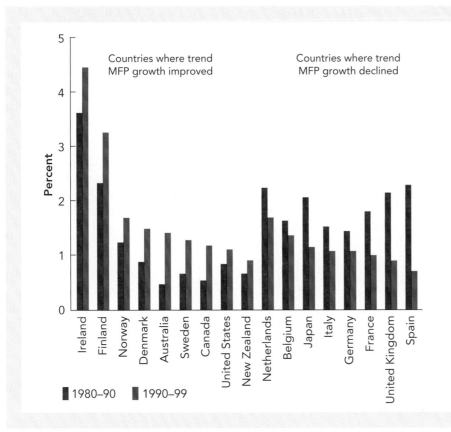

FIGURE 3.1

Multi-factor Growth for OECD Countries in 1980s and 1990s

The rate of growth of multi-factor productivity in Canada during the 1980s was lower than its 1.2 percent average for the 1961–1999 period. It was also substantially lower than in the U.S., and moderate relative to other countries.

Source: Adapted from *The New Economy: Beyond the Hype*, page 15. OECD copyright, 2001. The OECD Growth Project.

3.3 THE NEOCLASSICAL GROWTH MODEL

Economists begin to analyze long-run growth by building a simple, standard model of economic growth — a *growth model*. This standard model is also called the Solow model, after Nobel Prize–winning MIT economist Robert Solow. Economists then use the model to look for an *equilibrium* — a point of balance, a condition of rest, a state of the system toward which the model will converge over time. Once you have found the equilibrium position toward which the economy tends to move, you can use it to understand how the model will behave. If you have built the right model, it will tell you in broad strokes how the economy will behave.

In economic growth economists look for the *steady-state balanced-growth equilibrium*. In a steady-state balanced-growth equilibrium the capital intensity of the economy is stable. The economy's capital stock and its level of real GDP are growing at the same proportional rate. And the capital–output ratio — the ratio of the economy's capital stock to annual real GDP — is constant.

THE PRODUCTION FUNCTION

The first component of the model is a technological relationship described by the **production function**. As discussed earlier, this relationship tells us how the productive resources of the economy — the labour force, the **capital** stock, and the level of technology — can be used to determine the level of output in the economy.

In growth theory, economists have used different specifications for the level of technology. We have already seen one specification in equation (3.1). Box 3.2 offers a detailed discussion of different specifications for the levels of technology. Here, to simplify the analysis, we assume that technological progress takes the form of increasing the level of labour efficiency. Hence, the production function we use has the form:

$$Y = F(K, E, \times L)$$

where capital K and labour L are defined as before, while E measures the level of labour efficiency or labour productivity, which is determined by the current level of technology and the efficiency of business and market organization.

We assume that $F(\cdot)$ is a constant returns to scale production function. Hence, if K and $E \times L$ are increased by a factor of, say, $1/L$ then output Y will also increase by the same factor. Thus, we can write

$$\frac{Y}{L} = F\left(\frac{K}{L}, E\right) \qquad (3.5)$$

Moreover, with constant returns to scale, the production function exhibits diminishing marginal productivity in both its arguments. Hence, if one of the factors of production is fixed, successive increments in the other factor will lead to successively smaller increases in output. With this property, we say the production function is concave in both its arguments.

It is often convenient to use the Cobb-Douglas specification for the production function $F(\cdot)$:

$$Y = K^\alpha \times (E \times L)^{1-\alpha}$$

or in per worker terms

$$\frac{Y}{L} = \left(\frac{K}{L}\right)^\alpha \times E^{1-\alpha} \qquad (3.6)$$

Hence, the economy's **output per worker** Y/L is equal to the capital stock per worker K/L raised to the exponential power of some number α and then multiplied by the current efficiency of labour E raised to the exponential power $1 - \alpha$.

The efficiency of labour E and the number α are *parameters* of the model. The parameter α is always a number between 0 and 1. The best way to think of it is as the parameter that governs how fast diminishing returns to capital set in. We will refer to it as the diminishing-returns-to-capital parameter. Figure 3.2 plots a typical Cobb-Douglas production function. So long as $0 < \alpha < 1$ the production function exhibits diminishing returns to capital. That is, for given amounts of E and L, increases in K lead to less than proportional increases in output per worker Y/L. As will be seen below, this property of the production function has important consequences for the long-run growth properties of the neoclassical growth model.

No economist believes that there is, buried somewhere in the earth, a big machine that forces the level of output per worker to behave exactly as calculated by the algebraic production function above. Instead, economists think that the Cobb-Douglas production function is a simple and useful approximation. The process that does determine the level of output per worker is an immensely complex one: Everyone in the economy is part of it, and it is too complicated to work with. Using the

DETAILS

3.2

BOX

CLASSIFICATION OF TECHNOLOGICAL PROGRESS

Exogenous technological growth is the main engine for **steady-state growth** in the neoclassical model. Without technological progress all variables per worker will be constant in the steady state. This is clearly an unrealistic feature of the model. In most industrialized counties the growth rates of consumption and output per worker have been positive over long periods of time. In Canada, for example, during the historical period 1961 to 1999, the growth rate of output was 3.8 percent, of which 1.2 percent was due to exogenous productivity growth or technological progress.

Economists John Hicks, Roy Harrod, and Robert Solow have used three alternative means of introducing technological progress into the neoclassical growth model. We state each definition in turn using a general production function with two inputs, capital, K, and labour, L. As we shall see, each definition is "neutral" with respect to a specific economic variable (i.e., it leaves that economic variable unaffected).

(a) Hick's Neutral Technological Change

A technological innovation is "Hicks neutral" if it does not affect the ratio of the marginal product of labour ($\Delta Y_t/\Delta L_t$) to the marginal product of capital ($\Delta Y_t/\Delta K_t$) for a given capital–labour ratio. This property is satisfied if the production function takes the form

$$Y_t = A_t \times F(K_t, L_t)$$

where A_t is an index of the economy's state of the technology.

(b) Harrod Neutral Technological Change

A technological innovation is "Harrod neutral" if it leaves unaffected the ratio of the total income earned by capital to total income earned by labour. This definition is consistent with a production function of the form

$$Y_t = F(K_t, E_t \times L_t)$$

where E_t is the technology index. This form of technological change is called *labour-augmenting* technological change because it increases output the same way as an increase in the stock of labour, L.

(c) Solow Neutral Technological Change

A technological innovation is "Solow neutral" if it leaves unaffected the ratio of the total income earned by labour to total income earned by capital. It can be shown that this definition implies a production function of the form

$$Y_t = F(B_t \times K_t, L_t)$$

where B_t is the technology index. This type of technological change is called *capital augmenting* because it raises production the same way as an increase in the stock of capital, K.

It is important to note that in the neoclassical growth model only labour-augmenting technological change turns out to be consistent with the existence of a steady state, where, as defined below, all relevant quantities grow at constant rates in the long run. For this reason, we adopt this form of technological improvement in this book in order to analyze the effects of technological growth on the economy.

FIGURE 3.2

The Cobb-Douglas Production Function

When the parameter α is close to 0, there are sharply declining marginal returns to increasing capital per worker: An increase in capital per worker produces much less in increased output than the last increase in capital per worker. Diminishing returns to capital accumulation set in rapidly and ferociously. The converse holds when α is close to 1.

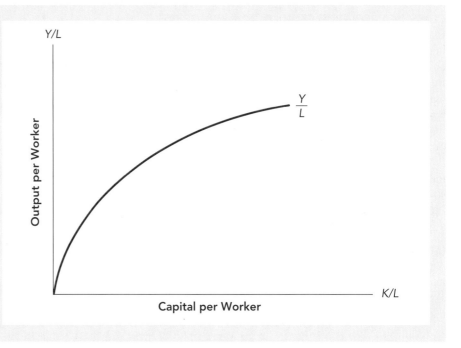

Cobb-Douglas production function involves a large leap of abstraction. Yet it is a useful leap, for using this approximation to analyze the economy will lead us to approximately correct conclusions.

LABOUR FORCE OR POPULATION GROWTH

We assume — once again making a simplifying leap of abstraction — that the **labour force** L of the economy is growing at a constant proportional rate given by the value of a parameter n. (Note that n does not have to be the same across countries and can shift over time in any one country.) Thus we can calculate the growth of the labour force between this year and the next with the formula

$$L_{t+1} = (1 + n) \times L_t \tag{3.7}$$

Next year's labour force will be n percent higher than this year's labour force. Thus if this year's labour force is 10 million and the growth rate parameter n is 2 percent per year, then next year's labour force will be

$$
\begin{aligned}
L_{t+1} &= (1 + n) \times L_t \\
&= (1 + 2\%) \times L_t \\
&= (1 + 0.02) \times 10 \\
&= 10.2 \text{ million}
\end{aligned}
$$

We assume that the rate of growth of the labour force is constant not because we believe that labour-force growth is unchanging but because the assumption makes the analysis of the model simpler. The trade-off between realism in the model's description of the world and simplicity as a way to make the model easier to analyze is one that economists always face. They usually resolve it in favour of simplicity.

USING THE PRODUCTION FUNCTION

For given values of E (say, 10,000) and α (say, 0.3), this production function tells us how the capital stock per worker is related to output per worker. If the capital stock per worker is $250,000, then output per worker will be

$$\frac{Y}{L} = \$250{,}000^{0.3} \times 10{,}000^{0.7}$$
$$= \$41.628 \times 630.958$$
$$= \$26{,}265$$

And if the capital stock per worker is $125,000, then output per worker will be

$$\frac{Y}{L} = \$125{,}000^{0.3} \times 10{,}000^{0.7}$$
$$= \$33.812 \times 630.958$$
$$= \$21{,}334$$

Note that the first $125,000 of capital boosted production from $0 to $21,334, and that the second $125,000 of capital boosted production from $21,334 to $26,265, less than one-quarter as much. These substantial diminishing returns should not be a surprise: The value of α in this example — 0.3 — is low, and low values are supposed to produce rapidly diminishing returns to capital accumulation.

Nobody expects anyone to raise $250,000 to the 0.3 power in her or his head and come up with 41.628. That is what calculators are for! This Cobb-Douglas form of the production function, with its fractional exponents, carries the drawback that we cannot expect students (or professors) to do problems in their heads or with just pencil and paper. However, this form of the production function also carries substantial benefits: By varying just two numbers — the efficiency of labour E and the diminishing-returns-to-capital parameter α — we can consider and analyze a very broad set of relationships between resources and the economy's productive power.

In fact, this particular Cobb-Douglas form of the production function was developed by Cobb and Douglas for precisely this purpose: By judicious choice of different values of E and α, it is simple to "tune" the function so that it can capture a large range of different kinds of behaviour.

SAVINGS AND INVESTMENT

Last, assume that a constant proportional share, equal to a parameter s, of real GDP is saved each year and invested. S is thus the economy's **savings rate**. Such gross investments add to the capital stock, so a higher amount of savings and investment means faster growth for the capital stock. But the capital stock does not grow by the full amount of *gross* investment. A fraction δ (the Greek lowercase letter *delta*, for "**depreciation**") of the capital stock wears out or is scrapped each period. Thus the actual relationship between the capital stock now and the capital stock next year is

$$K_{t+1} = K_t + (s \times Y_t) - (\delta \times K_t) \tag{3.8}$$

The level of the capital stock next year will be equal to the capital stock this year plus the savings rate s times this year's level of real GDP minus the depreciation rate δ times this year's capital stock, as Figure 3.3 shows.

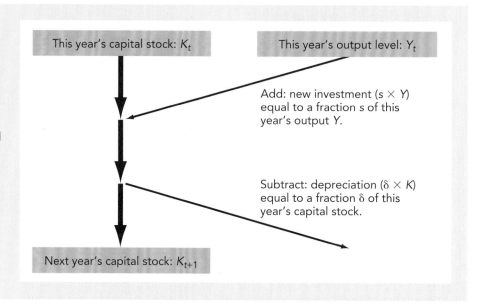

FIGURE 3.3

Changes in the Capital Stock

Gross investment adds to and depreciation subtracts from the capital stock. Depreciation is a share α of the current capital stock. Investment is a share s of current production.

This year's capital stock: K_t

This year's output level: Y_t

Add: new investment $(s \times Y)$ equal to a fraction s of this year's output Y.

Subtract: depreciation $(\delta \times K)$ equal to a fraction δ of this year's capital stock.

Next year's capital stock: K_{t+1}

THE MECHANICS OF THE NEOCLASSICAL GROWTH MODEL

In growth theory the focus is on the determinants of output per worker Y/L, consumption per worker C/L, and capital per worker K/L, as these variables reflect the well-being of the population. Let us first derive expressions for these variables. We will assume that the level of labour efficiency E is either fixed or it grows at an exogenous rate. Hence, the level and its rate of growth will be assumed to have been determined outside the model. From the production function (3.5) it is clear that to derive output per worker one should first derive the capital–labour ratio. Once output per worker is known one can then derive consumption per worker, as $C/L = (1 - s) \times Y/L$.

We first derive the evolution of the capital per worker, which is given by

$$\Delta \left(\frac{K_t}{L_t} \right) = \frac{\Delta K_t}{L_t} - \frac{K_t}{L_t^2} \times \Delta L_t \tag{3.9}$$

where $\Delta K_t = K_{t+1} - K_t$ and $\Delta L_t = L_{t+1} - L_t$.

Next note that from equation (3.7) $\Delta L_t = n \times L_t$ while from equation (3.8) $\Delta K_t = s \times Y_t - \delta K_t$. Substituting these results into equation (3.9) and simplifying, we obtain

$$\Delta \left(\frac{K_t}{L_t} \right) = s \times \frac{Y_t}{L_t} - (n + \delta) \times \frac{K_t}{L_t} \tag{3.10}$$

Equation (3.10) has a straightforward interpretation. $s \times Y_t/L_t$ is total saving per worker in year t, which will be equal to *actual* gross investment per worker in year t. On the other hand, $(n + \delta) \times K_t/L_t$ is total gross investment per worker that is needed in year t in order to maintain the capital per worker at a constant level. With a fraction δ of K being worn out in any year, $\delta \times K_t/L_t$ is the total investment per worker required to replace depreciated capital. With the population growing at the rate of n, $n \times K_t/L_t$ is the amount by which capital per worker alive in year t should increase in order for the capital per worker next year to be the same as it is this year. Thus, according to equation (3.10), if actual gross investment per worker $s \times K_t/L_t$ is larger (conversely, smaller) than the investment per worker needed to keep capital per worker at a constant level, then the capital per worker next year will be larger (conversely, smaller) than the capital per worker this year.

THE STEADY STATE

The long-run equilibrium or steady state of the economy is determined by the requirement that all the *endogenous* variables in the model like output Y, capital K, and consumption C grow at constant rates over time, with their per worker counterparts, Y/L, K/L, and C/L either constant or growing at constant rates over time. The economic condition that must be satisfied at the steady state is that total saving per worker must equal total required investment per worker.

Analytically, we define the steady state by the condition $\Delta(K/L) = 0$ and we use equation (3.10) to solve for the steady-state capital–labour ratio $(K/L)^*$ after substituting the production function (3.5) for Y/L for a given level of labour efficiency E:

$$s \times F((K/L)^*, E) = (n + \delta) \times (K/L)^*$$

Having computed $(K/L)^*$, equation (3.1) can be used to find the steady-state level of output per worker as $(Y/L)^* = F((K/L)^*, E)$. The steady-state level of consumption per worker can then be obtained from the relation $(C/L)^* = (1 - s) \times (Y/L)^*$.

Figure 3.4 depicts the steady-state equilibrium as well as the adjustment of the capital per worker to its steady-state level. Using the production function, saving per worker is $s \times F(K_t/L_t, E)$, which is the concave schedule $s \times (Y_t/L_t)$ in Figure 3.4. This is the production function per worker multiplied by the marginal propensity to save s. The schedule representing the investment per worker required to keep capital per worker constant is, on the other hand, a straight line through the origin with slope $(n + \delta)$. Henceforth, this schedule will be referred to as the *required investment* schedule.

Point SS gives the economy's steady state, because at that point all the variables grow at constant rates. At point SS saving per worker is exactly equal to the investment per worker that is required in order to keep capital per worker constant over time. With $(K/L)^*$ constant, it is clear from the production function (3.5) that output per worker will also be constant over time. With $(Y/L)^*$ constant over time, saving per worker $s \times (Y/L)^*$ and consumption per worker $(1 - s) \times (Y/L)^*$ will also be constant over time. It then follows that at point SS aggregate capital K, output Y, and consumption C will be growing at the same rate as the labour force, at rate n.

THE ADJUSTMENT PROCESS TO THE STEADY STATE

Referring to Figure 3.4, if capital per worker is initially at level $(K/L)^0$ then saving per worker at point B, (i.e., gross actual investment per worker) will be larger than the required investment per worker at point D. As a result, capital per worker will be increasing over time until the economy reaches the steady-state point SS. Similarly, if capital per worker is initially at level $(K/L)^1$ then required investment

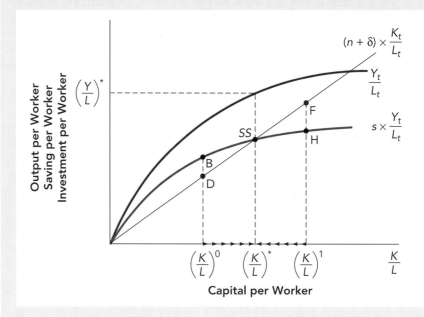

FIGURE 3.4

Steady-State Output, Savings, and Investment in the Neoclassical Growth Model

The saving per worker schedule is s times the output per worker schedule. The "required investment schedule" is a straight line. The steady state of the economy is at point SS. If capital per worker is initially below its steady-state level, then savings per worker will be larger than required investment per worker. As a result, K/L will be increasing over time until the economy reaches the steady-state point SS. Similarly, if capital per worker is initially larger than its steady-state level, then K/L will be decreasing over time toward the point SS.

per worker at point F is larger than saving per worker at point G and hence capital per worker will be decreasing over time until we reach point SS. Clearly, these arguments show that the neoclassical growth model possesses a unique and stable steady state.

An important implication of the adjustment process in the neoclassical growth model is that different economies with the same rates of saving, population growth, and technology will tend to converge over time to the same steady-state level of per capita income. This prediction has received a lot of attention in recent literature on empirical growth, under the title of economic convergence across different economies. We will discuss the hypothesis of income convergence among different groups of countries in the next chapter.

It is important to note that income convergence is consistent only with the predictions of the neoclassical growth model. Other growth theories, including the endogenous growth models of the next section or the Harrod-Domar model in Box 3.4, do not, in general, predict income convergence across different states or regions.

THE HARROD-DOMAR GROWTH MODEL

The Harrod-Domar growth model was one of the earlier attempts to incorporate equilibrium growth theory into modern economic analysis. It was developed by the two British economists Roy Harrod and Evsey Domar in the early 1940s and focused on positive economic growth under conditions of full employment of resources. Harrod and Domar showed that under certain conditions a growing economy may be associated with underutilized resources, such as labour and capital. In the growth literature this has come to be known as the Harrod-Domar controversy.

Like all models of exogenous economic growth, the Harrod-Domar model is based on three underlying relationships: a production function, an exogenous supply of labour growth, and a saving/investment relationship. The latter two relationships are the same as in the neoclassical growth model, namely $\Delta L_t/L_t = n$ and $\Delta K_t = s \times Y_t - \delta \times K_t$ respectively. However, on the production side, Harrod and Domar assumed the following fixed proportions or Leontief production function:

$$Y_t = F(K_t,\ L_t) = \min(A \times K_t,\ B \times L_t)$$

where A and B are positive constants.

This production function states that output is equal to the minimum of the quantities inside the parentheses. Three cases arise with this production function: (a) if $A \times K_t < B \times L_t$, then capital will be fully used, but a portion of the labour force will be unemployed, (b) if $A \times K_t > B \times L_t$, then labour will be fully employed, but a portion of the existing capital will be idle, and (c) if $A \times K_t = B \times L_t$, then all labour and capital will be fully employed.

We can now see the main ingredients of the Harrod-Domar controversy. Consider the first case (a), where $Y_t = A \times K_t$. In this case, the growth rate output must be equal to the growth rate of capital in the long-run equilibrium. Given the assumptions of the model, it can be easily shown that this requires:

$$\Delta Y_t/Y_t = \Delta K_t/K_t = s \times A - \delta$$

Next, consider case (b) where $Y_t = B \times L_t$. In this case, in equilibrium, the growth rate of output must be equal to the growth rate of labour:

$$\Delta Y_t/Y_t = \Delta L_t/L_t = n$$

Now, it is clear from the last two equations that if *both* capital and labour are to be fully employed, as in case (c), the following equality must hold:

$$s \times A = n + \delta$$

Since both sides of this equation involve fixed parameters, the chances of this equality holding are almost nil. For this reason it is called a "knife edge" case. This has given rise to the following controversy: If $s \times A > n + \delta$, the long-run equilibrium of the economy will be characterized by full employment of workers but with a portion of the capital stock being idle. On the other hand, if $s \times A < n + \delta$, the long-run equilibrium of the economy will be associated with no idle capital but increasing unemployment of labour.

The source of the Harrod-Domar controversy derives from the rigidity of their model's assumptions. For one, the model assumes a fixed-coefficients production function, which does not allow for any substitution between capital and labour when the economic environment changes. For example, the parameters A and B in the production function are fixed and independent of factor prices or the level of inputs employed. Another assumption is that the saving rate s is also exogenous and does not change with the state of the economy. For example, in the case of idle capital above, the households still save the same amount out of their income! Obviously this is quite an unrealistic situation, which points to the implausibility of the Harrod-Domar assumptions.

There are several ways to avoid the Harrod-Domar controversy and guarantee that $s \times A = n + \delta$ holds in the long-run equilibrium. One way is to endogenize the saving rate s by using a more complete model, in which households change their saving behaviour in a way to maximize their welfare over their lifetime. The so-called Ramsey model of optimizing behaviour achieves exactly this objective. Another way is to leave s fixed, but specify a production function with an elasticity of substitution between capital and labour different from zero. This would make the production parameters A and B endogenous and dependent on the capital–labour ratio. This way, changes in the capital–labour ratio can help establish the above equality. The neoclassical growth model, in fact, adopts the latter approach.

THE EFFECTS OF AN INCREASE IN THE SAVING RATE

Suppose that, starting from an initial steady point SS_0, with corresponding capital–labour ratio $(K/L)^*$ and output per person $(Y/L)^*$, there is an increase in the saving rate s, from s_0 to s_1. As shown in Figure 3.5, this will shift up the saving schedule to the new position $s_1 \times (Y_t/L_t)$. Hence, at the original capital per worker ratio $(K/L)^*$ there will be an increase in saving per worker above that which is required to keep K/L constant. As a result, K/L will start to increase over time. The process will continue until a new steady state is reached at point SS_1, with higher levels of capital–labour ratio $(K/L)^{**}$ and output per person $(Y/L)^{**}$.

FIGURE 3.5

An Increase in the Saving Rate in the Neoclassical Growth Model

An increase in the saving rate from s_0 to s_1 will shift up the saving schedule. Hence, at the original capital per worker ratio $(K/L)^*$ there will be an increase in savings per worker above that which is required to keep K/L constant. As a result, K/L will increase until a new steady state is reached at point SS_1.

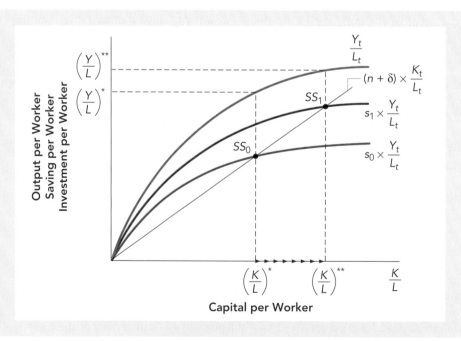

Notice that during the adjustment period from point SS_0 to point SS_1, K/L increases because capital will be growing at a rate which is greater than the rate of growth of population. With K/L growing during the adjustment period, it is clear from the production function (3.5) that Y/L will also be growing until point SS_1 is reached. Hence, during the adjustment period aggregate output Y will be growing at a higher rate than n.

Once the new steady state is reached, Y and K will be growing once again at the rate of population growth n, and Y/L and K/L will be constant with a zero growth rate. Consequently, a key prediction of the neoclassical growth model is that an economy's growth rate is *independent* of the saving rate in the steady state. Further, changes in the saving rate can have only a transitory effect on the growth rate of output per worker during the adjustment process to the new steady state. And the only permanent effect of an increase of the saving rate is to increase the steady state levels of the capital–labour ratio and the output per worker.

THE EFFECTS OF AN INCREASE IN THE RATE OF POPULATION GROWTH

It is not difficult to analyze the steady-state effects of population growth in the neoclassical growth model. In this model population growth has the same effect on the economy as does an increase in the depreciation rate of capital. The reason for this is that population growth *depreciates* the existing capital in the sense that it requires new investment in order to provide the new workers with the necessary capital and keep the capital–labour ratio constant. With saving per worker fixed this implies a reduction in K/L and Y/L in the new steady state.

THE GOLDEN RULE LEVEL OF CONSUMPTION

The ultimate purpose of saving, investment, and growth is to increase the level of income per worker and to promote the living standards of a country's residents. One indicator of well-being that economists have used routinely is the level of consumption per worker. The higher the level of consumption per worker the higher the standard of living that the residents of a country can enjoy.

In the neoclassical growth model the steady-state level of consumption will depend on the savings rate s; and there is a savings rate that will maximize the steady-state level of consumption per worker. This maximum *steady-state* level of consumption per worker is known as the *golden rule* level of consumption per worker. Corresponding to the golden rule level of consumption per worker there is a golden rule level of capital per worker. This is the *steady-state* level of capital per worker that maximizes the steady-state level of consumption per worker. It can be shown that the condition that guarantees the golden rule is given by the equation

$$MPK(K/L) = n + \delta \tag{B3.4}$$

where $MPK(K/L) = \Delta F(K/L, E)/\Delta K$ is the marginal product of capital as a function of capital per worker, for a given level technology E.* The steady-state capital per worker

BOX 3.5

DETAILS

---

*Note that $MPK(K/L)$ gives us the additional output the country can have if K/L increases by one unit. On the other hand, $n + \delta$ gives us the additional "required investment" that will be needed if K/L increases by one unit. Hence, $MPK(K/L) - (n + \delta)$ gives us the increase in consumption resulting from a one unit increase in K/L. As long as $MPK(K/L) > (n + \delta)$ consumption can be increased by increasing K/L. Similary, as long as $MPK(K/L) < (n + \delta)$ consumption can be increased by decreasing K/L.

ratio $(K/L)_{gr}$, say, that satisfies this equation is the golden rule level of capital per worker. Note that $\Delta F(K/L, E)/\Delta K$ is the slope of the production function in Figure 3.6. Condition (B3.4) then says that at $(K/L)_{gr}$ the slope of the production function is equal to the sum of the population growth rate, n, and the rate of capital depreciation, δ.

Once $(K/L)_{gr}$ is computed, we can use the production function to obtain the golden rule level of income per worker, $(Y/L)_{gr} = F[(K/L)_{gr}, E]$. Further, denoting the corresponding saving rate by s_{gr}, we can obtain the golden rule level of consumption per worker as $(C/L)_{gr} = (1 - s_{gr})(Y/L)_{gr}$.

The golden rule steady-state analysis is useful in practice because it can be viewed as a benchmark against which different government policies can be compared and evaluated. For instance, if the government follows policies that lead to a saving rate s_1 that is considerably less than s_{gr}, then the economy will settle down to a steady state at which capital per worker will be less than $(K/L)_{gr}$, as shown in Figure 3.6. Consequently, the steady-state consumption per worker will not be maximized and the country's steady-state standard of living will not be as high. In this case, government policies that induce people to increase their saving rate toward s_{gr} will be desirable. Similar but opposite arguments apply when the saving rate is greater than s_{gr}.

FIGURE 3.6

The Golden Rule Levels of Captial and Consumption

The steady golden rule level of capital per worker $(K/L)_{gr}$ is determined by the condition $MPK(K/L) = n + \delta$. The golden rule level of consumption per worker is given by $(1 - s_{gr}) \times (Y/L)_{gr}$. If the saving rate is at s_1, less than s_{gr}, then the steady-state consumption per worker is not maximized. In that case, policies that increase the saving rate towards s_{gr} would be desirable.

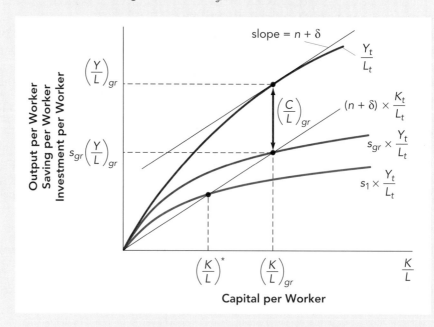

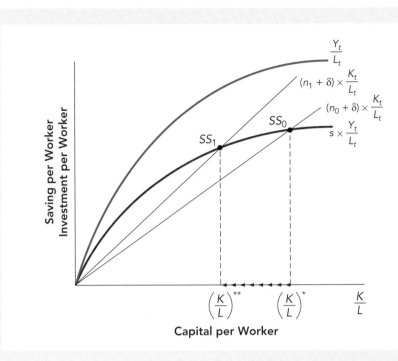

FIGURE 3.7

An Increase in Population Growth in the Neoclassical Growth Model

An increase in the population growth rate from n_0 to n_1 will shift up the required investment per worker schedule. As more people enter the economy and with saving per worker the same, there will be a reduction in capital per worker. Over time, K/L will be falling until a new steady state is reached at point SS_1.

To see this clearly, suppose that we start in a steady state at point SS_0 in Figure 3.7 and there is an increase in the population growth rate n, from n_0 to n_1. This will shift up the schedule representing required investment per worker. With more people entering the economy but with saving per worker the same, this will start to reduce capital per worker. Over time, K/L will be falling until a new steady state is reached at point SS_1, with a lower steady-state capital per worker $(K/L)^{**}$. From the production function (not shown), it also follows that Y/L will fall to a new steady-state level $(Y/L)^{**}$.

Notice that during the adjustment period from point SS_0 to point SS_1, K/L falls because capital will be growing at a rate that is smaller than the rate of growth of population. With capital per worker K/L falling during the adjustment period, it is clear from the production function (3.5) that output per worker Y/L will also be falling until point SS_1 is reached. However, the growth rate of Y itself will be permanently higher at the new level n_1.

THE EFFECTS OF AN EXOGENOUS TECHNOLOGICAL IMPROVEMENT

Now we examine the effects of a *once and for all* improvement in the level of technology. As discussed above, we have assumed that it is *labour-augmenting*, that is it comes about through improvements in the efficiency of labour, which is represented by the letter E in the production function (3.5). Because we do not specify what determines E, we call it *exogenous* technological change. Indeed, this is a major weakness of the neoclassical growth model.

An increase in E causes the production function (3.5) to shift upward to a new position, so that now more output per worker can be produced at each level of capital per worker. As a result, saving per worker will also increase. Consequently,

FIGURE 3.8
An Increase in Labour
Efficiency in the
Neoclassical Growth
Model

A *once and for all*
increase in labour
efficiency from E_0 to E_1
will shift up the saving
schedule. Hence, at
the original capital per
worker ratio $(K/L)^*$
there will be an
increase in saving per
worker above that
which is required to
keep K/L constant.
Thus, K/L will be
increasing over time
toward the new
steady-state point SS_1.

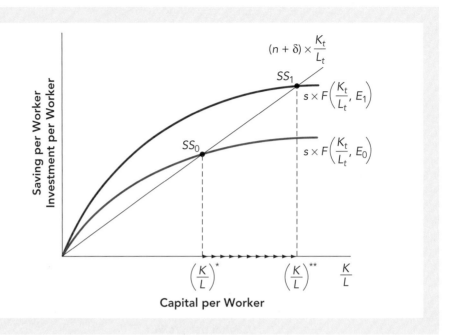

the steady-state effects of exogenous technological change are similar to those that
we studied above in the context of an increase in the economy's saving rate.

Suppose that we start in a steady state at point SS_0 in Figure 3.8, and there is an
increase in labour efficiency E, from E_0 to E_1. This will shift up the saving schedule,
because it will increase output corresponding to each level of capital per worker.
Hence, at the original capital per worker ratio $(K/L)^*$ there will be an increased
saving per worker above that which is required to keep K/L constant. As a result, K/L
will start to increase over time. The process will continue until a new steady state is
reached at point SS_1, with steady state capital–labour ratio $(K/L)^{**}$.

Notice during the adjustment period the K/L increases because capital will be
growing at a rate that is greater than the rate of growth of population. With K/L
growing during the adjustment period, it is clear from the production function (3.5)
that Y/L will also be growing until point SS_1 is reached. Hence, during the adjustment period aggregate output Y will be growing at a higher rate than n.

What is the effect of the increase in labour efficiency on the rate of growth of output per worker Y/L? Using the tools discussed in Box 2.4 of Chapter 2, the rate of
growth of Y/L is equal to the rate of growth of Y minus the rate of growth of L. Since
during the adjustment process the rate of growth of Y is larger than n, it follows that
Y/L will be growing at a rate that is larger than zero. Nevertheless, the growth rate
of Y/L will be declining over time until it reaches zero once the new steady is
reached. Hence, the growth of Y/L eventually comes to a halt.

It is also important to keep in mind that here we analyzed only the effects of a
one time increase in E. Our results would be quite different if we had assumed
instead that the exogenous technological improvement was occurring continuously
every time period at some given rate g. In the neoclassical growth model presented
in this chapter continuous growth in output per capita requires continuous growth
in E at the exogenous rate g. We discuss this case below in Section 3.5, Steady-State

Growth and Dynamics of the Growth Models. First, however, we will look at endogenous growth models, which are alternative ways in which economists have attempted to account for technological change in modern growth theory.

RECAP THE NEOCLASSICAL GROWTH MODEL

In growth theory the focus is on the determinants of output per worker Y/L, consumption per worker C/L, and capital per worker K/L, as these variables reflect the well-being of the population. In the neoclassical growth model the state of technology is exogenous. In the steady-state aggregate capital, output, and consumption will be growing at the same rate as the labour force. An increase in the savings rate will increase the steady-state level of K/L, Y/L, and C/L. An increase in the rate of growth of population (the labour force) will reduce the steady-state levels of K/L, Y/L, and C/L. An exogenous increase in the level of labour efficiency will increase the steady-state levels of K/L, Y/L, and C/L.

3.4 ENDOGENOUS GROWTH MODELS

Paul Romer of Stanford University and Robert Lucas of the University of Chicago pointed out in the 1980s that there were some empirical regularities that contradict the predictions of the neoclassical growth model. First, the model suggests that countries with similar rates of growth of population should eventually converge to the same steady-state point in Figure 3.4. This cannot account for the disparities we observe in standards of living around the world, where poor countries seem to have standards of living that are permanently below those of the rich countries.

Another empirical regularity that contradicts the predictions of the neoclassical growth model is with regard to the growth rate of output per worker. Recall in the neoclassical model that after a technological improvement there will be an increase in the growth rate of output per worker, but this growth rate will gradually decline to its original level in the new steady state, which is zero (see also Section 3.6 below for more details). Romer, considering growth rates over centuries, discovered that over such long periods growth seems to have accelerated over time, and in recent decades it has been relatively stable.

Another shortcoming of the neoclassical growth model is that it relies on exogenous factors to generate ongoing growth in the economy (see Box 3.6 below). Ideally, economists would like to explain the effects of policy changes on growth, and recommend policies that would foster growth. We would like to explain, for example, whether free trade and economic integration would have any effect on growth.

These empirical considerations and theoretical issues have led to a new wave of research in growth theory that aims at constructing models in which growth is generated by *endogenous* factors that could be influenced by government policies. In this section we will present simplified versions of three popular endogenous growth models.

ROMER'S GROWTH MODEL

Romer argued that capital K should not be regarded as physical capital alone, but it should also include knowledge. Hence, when measuring the amount of capital available in a company we are interested in the amount of knowledge that is incorporated in, for example, the computer software as much as the machinery that is available to them.

Once K incorporates physical capital and knowledge, then one can extend the model to incorporate *learning-by-doing*. The idea here is that the employees of the company can learn and improve upon the knowledge (e.g., the software) that is incorporated in the machineries used in the company. With the knowledge available to them the employees are better able to foresee the next steps involved in improving the machinery or the production process. This idea of learning-by-doing and how it can be related to K can be captured by assuming that labour efficiency E is proportional to capital:

$$E_t = \rho \times K_t \quad \text{where} \quad 0 \leq \rho \leq 1 \tag{3.11}$$

Substituting for E_t from equation (3.11) into the Cobb-Douglas production function (3.6), we obtain a simple expression for the production function:

$$\frac{Y_t}{L_t} = \left(\frac{K_t}{L_t}\right)^\alpha \times \left(\rho \times K_t\right)^{1-\alpha}$$

Now multiplying the right-hand side of this equation by L_t/L_t (i.e., unity), we can re-write it as

$$\frac{Y_t}{L_t} = (\rho \times L_t)^{1-\alpha} \times \frac{K_t}{L_t} \tag{3.12}$$

Assume there is no labour force growth, and $L_t = L$ for all t. Then we can re-write the production function (3.12) as

$$\frac{Y_t}{L_t} = A \times \frac{K_t}{L} \quad \text{where} \quad A = (\rho \times L)^{1-\alpha} \tag{3.13}$$

In Figure 3.9 the production function (3.13) will be a straight line through the origin with slope A, and saving per worker will be a straight line through the origin with slope $s \times A$. With no population growth ($n = 0$), the *required investment* schedule will have a slope of δ.

As should be clear from Figure 3.9, in this model saving per worker will always be above the investment per worker that is needed in order to keep K/L at a constant level. Hence, growth will never come to a halt. The amount by which K/L will increase over time will be saving per worker ($s \times A \times K_t/L$) minus the investment per worker that is needed to keep K/L at a constant level ($\delta \times K_t/L$). Hence, capital per worker will grow regardless of how rich the country is; and its growth rate will be constant. As a result, a poor country will never be able to catch up with a rich country in terms of its capital per worker.

What is the prediction of this model regarding the effects of free trade and economic integration on growth? Free trade and market integration will give people in the country access to knowledge in other countries. Hence, with free trade labour efficiency will increase. Thus, by increasing labour efficiency, free trade will foster growth.

BARRO'S GROWTH MODEL

Robert Barro of Harvard University has proposed an endogenous growth model that explicitly incorporates government expenditures and can be used to discuss the issue of the optimum size of government. Barro regards government expenditures on

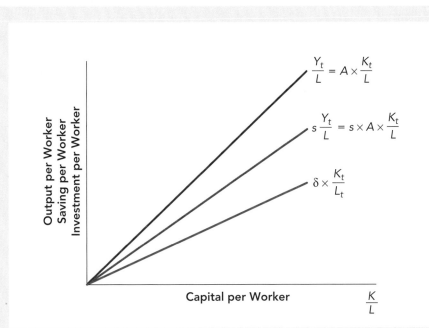

FIGURE 3.9
Output, Savings, and Investment in Romer's Growth Model
In Romer's model the production function per worker and the savings function per worker are straight lines through the origin. As a result, saving per worker will always be above the investment per worker that is needed in order to keep *K/L* at a constant level. Hence, growth will never come to a halt.

the economy's infrastructure as entering the production function as another factor of production. This is a very reasonable assumption to make, since government expenditures on health services, education, law and order, communication systems, and other infrastructures do increase productivity in the private sector.

In terms of the model we have developed above, in Barro's growth model labour efficiency in period *t* can be regarded as depending on government expenditures G_t. Let us assume

$$E_t = \rho \times G_t \quad \text{where} \quad 0 \le \rho \le 1 \tag{3.14}$$

Substituting for E_t from equation (3.14) into the Cobb-Douglas production function (3.6), we obtain the production function proposed by Barro:

$$\frac{Y_t}{L_t} = \left(\frac{K_t}{L_t}\right)^{\alpha} \times (\rho \times G_t)^{1-\alpha} \tag{3.15}$$

To simplify the analysis, we assume that government expenditures are financed by proportional taxes on capital. Hence, for simplicity let us assume that

$$G_t = \tau \times K_t \tag{3.16}$$

where τ is the tax rate.[1]

Substituting for G_t from equation (3.16) into (3.15), and assuming that population growth is zero (i.e., $L_t = L$ for all *t*), we obtain

$$\frac{Y_t}{L} = \left(\frac{K_t}{L}\right)^{\alpha} \times (\rho \times \tau \times K_t)^{1-\alpha}$$

---

[1]In fact, Barro assumes that government expenditures are financed by a proportional tax on income: $G_t = \tau \times Y_t$. It can be shown that the essence of Barro's results remains unchanged with the alternative assumption that government expenditures are financed with proportional taxes on capital.

FIGURE 3.10

Output, Savings, and Investment in Barro's Growth Model

In Barro's growth model the schedules representing production per worker and saving per worker are straight lines through the origin. Hence, as in Romer's model, growth does not come to a halt. In Barro's model labour efficiency depends on government expenditures. Hence, government expenditures can affect the slopes of these schedules.

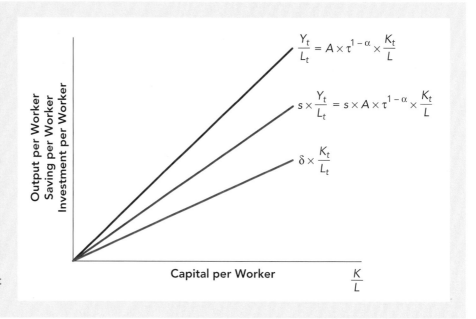

Now multiplying the right-hand side of this equation by L/L (i.e., unity), we can re-write it as

$$\frac{Y_t}{L} = A \times \tau^{1-\alpha} \times \frac{K_t}{L} \quad \text{where} \quad A = (\rho \times L)^{1-\alpha} \tag{3.17}$$

Equation (3.17) implies that in Figure 3.10 the production function will be a straight line through the origin with slope $A \times \tau^{1-\alpha}$.

Because households pay a tax to the government, disposable income per worker is $(Y_t/L) - \tau \times (K_t/L)$ or, upon using equation (3.17), $A \times \tau^{1-\alpha} \times (K_t/L) - \tau \times (K_t/L)$. Saving per worker is a fraction s of disposable income. Hence, saving per worker is $s \times (A \times \tau^{1-\alpha} - \tau) \times (K_t/L)$. The saving per worker schedule will be a straight line through the origin with slope $s \times (A \times \tau^{1-\alpha} - \tau)$. The slope of the saving function will also be equal to saving per K/L. Let us call this average saving or average *actual* investment.

On the other hand, the required investment schedule will be as before. It will be a straight line through the origin with slope δ. The slope of the required investment schedule will also be equal to required investment per K/L. Let us call it *average required investment*. In order to maximize growth the government should maximize the difference between average saving (or average *actual* investment) and average required investment. As average required investment $n + \delta$ cannot be affected by the government, to maximize growth the government should choose a tax that will maximize average saving.

In Figure 3.11 we plot average saving $s \times (A \times \tau^{1-\alpha} - \tau)$ for different values of τ. Average saving is increasing in τ when τ is small. It reaches a maximum at $\bar{\tau}$, and then it is decreasing for values of τ above $\bar{\tau}$. The reason for this result is that an increase in τ has two competing influences on income and saving. First, an increase in τ has the direct effect of reducing the disposable income of households, which tends to reduce saving. Second, the taxes that are collected by the

FIGURE 3.11

The Growth-Maximizing Tax Rate in Barro's Growth Model

An increase in τ has two competing effects on income and savings. First, it reduces disposable income directly. Second, the taxes collected by the government provide productive government expenditures on infrastructure, which tends to increase production. The growth-maximizing tax rate is $\bar{\tau}$. For values of τ smaller than $\bar{\tau}$ the second effect dominates, while for values of τ larger than $\bar{\tau}$ the first effect dominates.

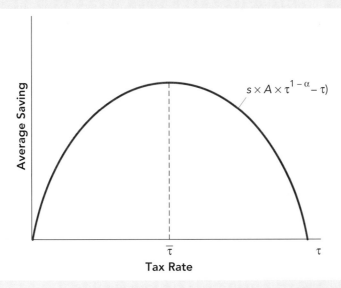

government are used to provide productive government expenditures on infrastructure, which tends to increase production, income, and saving. For values of τ smaller than $\bar{\tau}$ the second effect dominates, while for values of τ larger than $\bar{\tau}$ the first effect dominates.

Average saving is maximized when $\tau = \bar{\tau}$. This then maximizes average *actual* investment over required investment in any period, which in turn maximizes the growth rate. Barro's model, then, is a useful model for studying the optimum size of government, and it has received attention in policy discussions.

REBELO'S GROWTH MODEL

As can be seen from equations (3.13) and (3.17) in the Romer and Barro models output is a linear function of capital. This implies that with these models there is no diminishing marginal productivity of capital. As we shall see shortly, this is the main ingredient of endogenous growth models that distinguishes them from the neoclassical model. Recognizing this, Sergio Rebelo of Northwestern University has suggested using the production function

$$Y_t = A \times K_t$$

where A is treated as a fixed parameter. Rebelo's *AK* model is particularly simple, and is often used to discuss issues when other endogenous growth models are cumbersome.

3.5 STEADY-STATE GROWTH AND DYNAMICS OF THE GROWTH MODELS

In this section we study in more detail the steady-state growth properties of the neo-classical and endogenous growth models, and compare and contrast their properties. As the subsequent analysis will make clear, without exogenous technological growth there will be no steady-state growth in *per worker* variables in the neoclassical growth model. Growth comes to a halt in the steady state due to diminishing returns to capital. On the other hand, in the endogenous growth model returns to capital are constant and thus positive growth can go on forever in the steady state.

STEADY-STATE GROWTH AND DYNAMICS IN THE NEOCLASSICAL GROWTH MODEL

In Figures 3.4 to 3.8 the intersection of the saving schedule and the required investment schedule is the steady state of the economy. At this point all variables grow at constant rates. Hence, sometimes the steady state is also referred to as the balanced growth equilibrium. It turns out that a substantial amount can be said about the properties of the steady state. In Box 3.6 we derive the detailed properties of the steady state when labour efficiency grows at an exogenous rate of g. Here we treat the level of labour efficiency as constant, and show that in that case there will be no steady-state growth in per worker variables in the neoclassical model.

In order to gain more insight into the source of the last result it is useful to analyze the transition dynamics of the neoclassical growth model, that is, the model's adjustment path to its steady-state equilibrium. To this end, consider again equation (3.10) divided through by K/L so that the left-hand variable is the growth rate of capital per worker, g_k say:

$$g_k = \frac{s \times F(K/L, E)}{K/L} - (n + \delta) \tag{3.18}$$

where $g_k = \frac{\Delta(K/L)}{K/L}$.

Equation (3.18) shows that g_k is the difference of two terms, the first being the product of the saving rate s multiplied by the average product of capital per worker $\frac{s \times F(K/L, E)}{K/L}$ and the second is $(n + \delta)$. Figure 3.12 plots both terms against K/L.

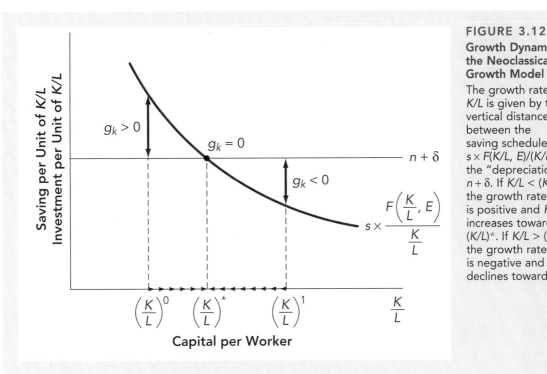

FIGURE 3.12
Growth Dynamics in the Neoclassical Growth Model
The growth rate, g_k, of K/L is given by the vertical distance between the saving schedule $s \times F(K/L, E)/(K/L)$ and the "depreciation" line $n + \delta$. If $K/L < (K/L)^*$ the growth rate of K/L is positive and K/L increases toward $(K/L)^*$. If $K/L > (K/L)^*$ the growth rate of K/L is negative and K/L declines toward $(K/L)^*$.

The first term is downward sloping and approaches zero as K/L tends to infinity, and the second term is a horizontal line at $(n + \delta)$. The vertical distance between the two schedules is g_k, the growth rate of capital per worker. The intersection of the two schedules determines the steady-state value of K/L where $g_k = 0$. To the left of the steady state g_k is positive and thus K/L rises over time. But as K/L rises the distance between the two schedules decreases and hence g_k approaches zero as K/L approaches $(K/L)^*$. Similar but opposite arguments can be made for levels of K/L to the right of the steady state. These arguments show formally that the neoclassical growth model has a unique steady-state equilibrium, and that steady-state growth of capital per worker comes to an end in an economy with no technological change (i.e., $g = 0$).

The source of these findings is the *diminishing returns to capital* per worker. Due to the concavity of the production function, as K/L increases the average product of capital per worker $\dfrac{F(K/L, E)}{K/L}$ falls causing a reduction in the saving per worker and in the growth rate of the economy. Eventually, growth of K/L comes to a halt, when saving per worker is just equal to required investment per worker. With K/L not growing in the steady state, and with E fixed, it is clear from the production function (3.5) that output per worker Y/L will also not be growing in the steady state. With consumption per worker C/L equal to $(1 - s)Y/L$, it is clear that C/L will also not be growing in the steady state.

Obviously, if diminishing returns to capital could be avoided, we could have an economy with perpetual positive growth in K/L even in the steady state. This is indeed the case with the endogenous growth models that we study next.

3.6

BOX

DETAILS

STEADY-STATE GROWTH

In the neoclassical growth model the intersection of the savings and required investment schedules is the steady state of the economy. At this point all variables grow at constant rates. A substantial amount can be said about the properties of the steady state. This is important because in extensions of the neoclassical model the focus is sometimes on the properties of the steady state, as the model is sometimes so complicated that not much can be said about the properties of the model outside the steady state.

Here we derive the growth rates of output and capital when population L grows at the rate of n and labour efficiency E grows at the rate of g. To this end, first note that the equality of savings and investment, equation (3.8), implies

$$s \times Y_t = \Delta K_t - \delta \times K_t$$

Dividing both sides of this equation by K_t, we obtain

$$s \times \frac{Y_t}{K_t} = \frac{\Delta K_t}{K_t} - \delta \tag{B3.5.1}$$

Next, note that by definition all variables grow at constant rates in the steady state. Hence, in equation (B3.5.1) $\frac{\Delta K_t}{K_t}$ must be a constant in the steady state. With $\frac{\Delta K_t}{K_t}$ constant, it follows from (B3.5.1) that in the steady state the ratio of output to capital must also be constant. Hence, in the steady state, output and capital must be growing at the same rate. That is, in the steady state

$$\frac{\Delta Y_t}{\Delta Y_t} = \frac{\Delta K_t}{K_t} \tag{B3.5.2}$$

Furthermore, note that we can substitute for Y_t from the production function (3.4) into (B3.5.1) to obtain

$$s \times \frac{F(K_t, E_t \times L_t)}{K_t} = \frac{\Delta K_t}{K_t} - \delta \tag{B3.5.3}$$

Upon using the fact that the production function is homogeneous of degree one in K_t and $E_t \times L_t$, equation (B3.5.3) reduces to

$$s \times F(1, E_t \times L_t / K_t) = \frac{\Delta K_t}{K_t} - \delta \tag{B3.5.4}$$

Since in the steady state $\frac{\Delta K_t}{K_t}$ is constant, it follows from (B3.5.4) that in the steady state $\frac{E_t \times L_t}{K_t}$ must also be constant. Hence, in the steady state the rate of growth of labour efficiency E_t (that is, $\frac{\Delta E_t}{E_t}$ or g) plus the rate of growth of population (that is, $\frac{\Delta L_t}{L_t}$ or n) must be equal to the rate of growth of capital. Thus, in the steady state the rates of growth of output and capital must be equal to $g + n$:

$$\frac{\Delta Y_t}{Y_t} = \frac{\Delta K_t}{K_t} = g + n$$

The rate of growth of output per person Y/L or capital per person K/L will be g. This is the rate of growth of output or capital (that is, $g + n$) minus the rate of growth of population (that is, n).

STEADY-STATE GROWTH AND DYNAMICS IN THE ENDOGENOUS GROWTH MODEL

To simplify the analysis we consider Rebelo's *AK* model:

$$Y = A \times K \tag{3.19}$$

SOLVING FOR THE STEADY STATE

Here is a numerical example to show how to solve for the steady state in the neoclassical model and in Rebelo's endogenous growth model. For simplicity, we consider an economy with no exogenous technological growth and assume that the economy's saving rate s is 10 percent (i.e., $s = .10$), the capital's depreciation rate d equals 4 percent per year (i.e., $\delta = .04$), and the labour force grows at the rate n equal to 1 percent per year (i.e., $n = .01$).

(a) Neoclassical Growth Model

Assume that the production function is Cobb-Douglas and has the form

$$Y = F(K, E \times L) = K^{1/2} \times L^{1/2}$$

where we have set $E = 1$ without loss of generality. Dividing both sides of this equation with L, we can write production function as

$$Y/L = (K/L)^{1/2}$$

Using this information, the steady-state condition (SS) in the text becomes

$$.10(K/L)^{1/2} = (.01 + .04) \times (K/L)$$

Solving this equation we obtain the steady-state level of capital per worker for this economy $(K/L)^* = 4$. Substituting this into the production function gives us the steady-state output per worker $(Y/L)^* = 2$. Steady-state consumption per worker is $(C/L)^* = (1 - .10) \times (Y/L)^* = 1.8$.

Since, there is no exogenous technological growth in this economy, the steady-state growth rate of output per worker is zero, while output itself grows at the rate of growth of population n, which we have assumed to be 1 percent per year.

(b) The Rebelo Endogenous Growth Model

Now assume that the production function is

$$Y = A \times K = 1 \times K$$

where we set A equal to 1 for simplicity. In per worker terms, the production function has the form

$$Y/L = 1 \times (K/L)$$

Recall that there is no unique steady-state capital–labour ratio in this model. There is an infinity of K/L ratios that are consistent with this economy's steady growth rate. This steady-state growth rate is

$$g_k = s \times A - (n + \delta) = .10 \times (1) - (.01 + .04) = .05$$

Thus, in contrast to the neoclassical economy, the endogenous growth economy grows at the rate of 6 percent per year, even though we have assumed that there is no exogenous technological growth. As an exercise, we encourage the reader to provide the graphical representation of these results.

Also, assume that labour L grows at rate n and that capital K depreciates at rate δ.

In order to analyze the growth properties of this economy, notice first that equation (3.19) implies that Y and K grow at the same rate. It is easy to derive this rate. Using equation (3.8), which equates saving to investment, together with equation (3.19) we get

$$\Delta K = s \times Y - \delta \times K = s \times A \times K - \delta \times K \qquad (3.20)$$

which when divided through by K gives

$$\frac{\Delta K}{K} = s \times A - \delta \qquad (3.21)$$

Therefore output and capital grow at the rate $s \times A - \delta$ over time. Similarly with labour growing at rate n, it follows immediately that output per worker Y/L and capital per worker K/L grow at the rate given by

$$g_k = s \times A - \delta - n \qquad (3.22)$$

The growth rate of K/L is now the difference between the two terms sA and $(n + \delta)$, both of which are straight lines as shown in Figure 3.13. The figure is drawn under the assumption that $s \times A$ is greater than $(n - \delta)$. As long as this is the case, g_k will be positive for all values of K/L. The economy will be growing at the steady-state rate forever, without having to rely on exogenous technological progress. With $Y/L = A \times K/L$ and $C/L = (1 - s) \times K/L$, it is clear that output per worker and consumption per worker will also be growing at the rate of g_k.

This startling result is a direct consequence of the nature of the production function (3.19), which is associated with a constant average and marginal product of capital equal to the positive parameter A for any level of K. Hence, with non-diminishing returns to capital economic growth can go on forever.

FIGURE 3.13
Growth Dynamics with Endogenous Growth

If the production function is AK then the saving schedule is a straight line at $s \times A$, while the required investment schedule is a straight line at $n + \delta$. Given that $s \times A$ exceeds $n + \delta$, there is continuous growth in the steady state, even without exogenous technological change.

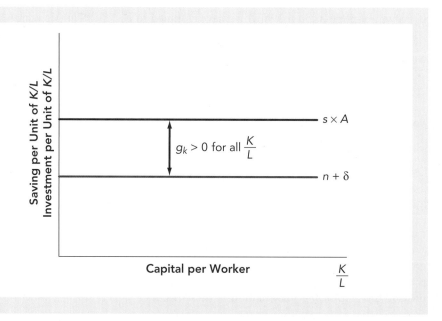

COMPARISON OF THE NEOCLASSICAL AND ENDOGENOUS GROWTH MODELS

We are now in a position to summarize and compare the findings of the neoclassical and endogenous growth models.

1. In the neoclassical growth model with no exogenous technological growth, the steady-state growth rate output per worker is zero and independent of the economy's saving rate. An increase in the saving rate can have only a temporary effect on the economy steady-state growth rate of capital per worker, output per worker, or consumption per worker. Under the same conditions, the endogenous growth model predicts a positive steady-state growth of capital per worker, output per worker, and consumption per worker. Moreover, with endogenous growth these growth rates are greater the larger is the economy's saving rate (see equation (3.22)).

2. Population growth does not affect long-run growth of capital per worker, output per worker, and consumption per worker in the neoclassical growth model, but it reduces steady-state growth of these variables in the endogenous growth model. The same comments apply for an increase in the depreciation rate δ.

3. In the neoclassical growth model, positive steady-state growth of capital per worker, output per worker, and consumption per worker can occur only at the rate of exogenous technological change g. In the endogenous growth model, steady-state growth can occur even when $g = 0$.

4. The reason for the result in (3) above is that without exogenous technical progress (i.e., with $g = 0$) growth in the neoclassical model comes to an end due to the diminishing returns to capital given the concavity of the neoclassical production function. In the endogenous growth model returns to capital are constant and this is the fundamental cause for continuous steady-state growth in that model.

RECAP   **STEADY-STATE GROWTH AND DYNAMICS OF THE GROWTH MODELS**

In the steady state, *per worker* variables such as capital per worker or output per worker are either constant or grow at constant rates. In the neoclassical model with no technological change there is no steady-state growth in the economy. Growth comes to a halt due to diminishing returns to capital. With positive technological progress, output per worker in the steady state grows at the rate of growth of the exogenous technological progress. On the other hand, in the endogenous growth model returns to capital are constant and thus positive growth can go on forever in the steady state, even without any exogenous technological progress.

3.6 ECONOMIC CONVERGENCE AND DIVERGENCE

An important issue in the recent literature on empirical growth is whether different countries across the globe tend to converge or diverge over time in terms of their per capita income levels and therefore their standards of living. If growth rates in real per capita output converge over time, then poor countries tend to grow faster than rich ones and catch up with them eventually. This has given rise to the *convergence hypothesis* of whether poor regions or countries have the tendency to grow faster than rich ones.

Two types of **convergence** have been analyzed in the literature, *absolute* convergence and *conditional* convergence. The hypothesis of *absolute convergence* states that poor economies tend to grow faster per capita than rich ones. This concept assumes that countries are similar in other characteristics regarding saving rates, population growth rates, production technologies, education and human capital, government policies and the like. On the other hand, *conditional convergence* takes into account the fact that countries may differ in these important characteristics. Hence, conditional convergence states that poor economies tend to grow faster in terms of per capita income than rich ones, provided that we take into account differences in country characteristics.

Economic theory is not entirely supportive of either type of convergence. Whereas the standard neoclassical growth model predicts economic convergence, the more recent endogenous growth models reject convergence and predict economic divergence across countries in general. We now use the earlier analysis to gain more insight on these ideas.

Consider first a situation where all countries have identical preferences and technologies, but they differ only in terms of their initial capital–labour ratios, or equivalently, their initial levels of per capita incomes, with poor countries having lower initial per capita incomes than rich ones. Under these conditions, the growth dynamics of the neoclassical growth model in Figure 3.12 make it clear both that all the economies will have the same steady-state capital–labour ratio or per capita income, and that the poor economies will grow faster than the rich ones (i.e., given that $(K/L)^0_{poor} < (K/L)^0_{rich}$ it follows that $g_{k,poor} > g_{k,rich}$). Hence, if all the economies are similar in terms of their saving rates, population growth, depreciation rates, and production technologies, but differ only in their starting per capita incomes (because of, say, exogenous events such as wars or transitory shocks to their production functions), then poor countries will catch up to the rich ones eventually, and in the long run living standards around the world will be more or less equalized. That is, in this case the neoclassical model predicts absolute convergence.

Alternatively assume that, in addition, two or more economies differ in terms of some important characteristic such as saving rates. Specifically, suppose that a group of economies have a low saving rate, and another group a high saving rate. Then, using Figure 3.12, it is easy to see that the first group of economies will have a steady-state capital–labour ratio or per capita income that is less than that of the second group of economies. Further, within each group, the poor countries will tend to grow faster than the rich ones and thus converge over time to their common steady state. However, across the two groups, the economies will converge to two different steady states. That is, in this case the neoclassical model predicts conditional convergence. This means that living standards will converge only within each group of similar economies, not across all the economies. For example, under conditional convergence, a poor country with a low saving rate will catch up in the future to a rich country with also a low saving rate, but it will never achieve the living standards of a rich country with a high saving rate.

Considering the endogenous growth models it is easy to see that they predict economic divergence. Consider for simplicity Rebelo's *AK* model and assume again there are two groups of countries, one group with a low saving rate and the other with a high saving rate. Suppose also that all the other parameters are the same across all the countries. Then, it is clear from Figure 3.13 that the low-saving countries will have a growth rate that is permanently lower than that of the high-saving countries, regardless of initial conditions. Hence, the two groups of economies will never converge in their per capita incomes, and living standards will be permanently different across the world. Thus, this endogenous growth model predicts economic divergence among different groups of countries.

Notice that for convergence to hold we must observe an *inverse* relationship between per capita growth rates and initial per capita incomes in a cross section of countries. This is the same thing as saying that countries with low starting per capita incomes have a higher growth rate than countries with high starting per capita incomes. Also, the speed of convergence to the steady state depends on the gap between initial per capita income and steady-state per capita income. The larger is this gap, the faster will be the convergence to the steady state.

To examine the hypothesis of convergence empirically we collected annual data on 17 countries in the Asia-Pacific region[2], and computed their real per capita GDP growth rates for the period 1965–2004. Figure 3.14 plots the average annual growth rate of real per capita GDP against the log of real per capita GDP at the start of the period, 1965, for the 17 countries. It is evident from this figure that the initially poorer East Asian economies experienced significantly higher per capita growth rates than the more developed economies of Australia, Canada, New Zealand, and the U.S. Clearly, the "best fitting" line through these data points is one with a

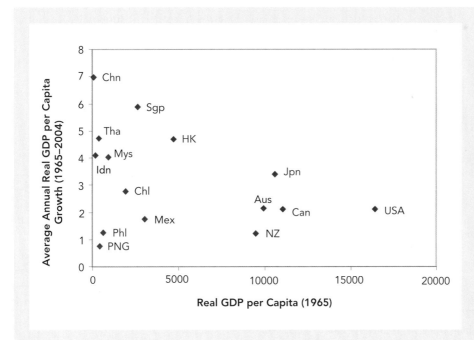

FIGURE 3.14

Asia-Pacific Region: GDP Growth versus Initial GDP

The average annual growth rate of real per capita GDP for the period 1965–2004 is plotted against the log of real per capita GDP in 1965 for 17 countries of the Asia-Pacific region. Initially the poorer East Asian economies grew faster than the developed economies of Australia, Canada, New Zealand, and the U.S. This evidence supports the hypothesis of absolute convergence among these countries.

Source: World Bank, World Development Indicators.

---

[2]The countries are Australia, Canada, Chile, China, Hong Kong, Indonesia, Japan, Korea, Malaysia, Mexico, New Zealand, Papua New Guinea, Philippines, Singapore, Taiwan, Thailand, and the U.S.

negative slope that highlights the inverse relationship between growth rates and initial per capita incomes (draw this line as an exercise). In other words, this sample supports the hypothesis of absolute convergence among these countries.

A large number of recent studies have used actual economic data to analyze the hypothesis of economic convergence across different countries, and also different provinces/states within countries.[3] The empirical findings have been mixed with some studies supporting convergence and other studies rejecting convergence in favour of divergence. Serge Coulombe of the University of Ottawa and Frank Lee of the Department of Finance analyzed economic convergence among the Canadian provinces.[4] These authors found evidence in favour of convergence among the Canadian provinces for different measurements of per capita income and output for the period 1961–1991. We examine the issue of convergence and other issues of empirical growth in greater detail in the next chapter.

RECAP ECONOMIC CONVERGENCE AND DIVERGENCE

Economic convergence among a set of countries or regions exists if their growth rates of real per capita output converge over time. Otherwise the economies are said to diverge. Two notions of convergence have been analyzed in the literature: *absolute convergence* and *conditional convergence*. Absolute convergence states that poor economies tend to grow faster than rich ones and eventually catch up with them. Conditional convergence states that poor economies tend to grow faster than rich ones, provided that we take into account differences in country characteristics. The neoclassical growth model is supportive of both types of convergence, whereas the endogenous growth model predicts economic divergence in general. The empirical evidence is mixed. Some studies support convergence and some indicate divergence.

CHAPTER SUMMARY

1. Growth accounting attempts to measure the sources of growth. It decomposes the sources of growth into three parts: growth in labour; growth in capital; and growth in multifactor productivity.

2. One principal force driving long-run growth in output per worker is the set of improvements in the efficiency of labour springing from technological progress.

3. A second principal force driving long-run growth in output per worker is the increases in the capital stock which the average worker has at his or her disposal and which further multiplies productivity.

4. An economy undergoing long-run growth converges toward and settles onto an equilibrium steady-state growth path, in which the economy's capital–output ratio is constant.

5. The steady-state level of the capital–output ratio is equal to the economy's savings rate divided by the sum of its labour-force growth rate, labour efficiency growth rate, and depreciation rate.

6. In endogenous growth models growth is driven by endogenous factors that can be influenced by government policies. Endogenous growth models predict a wider diversity of living standards among different countries than the neoclassical growth model.

---

[3]For a summary of this literature see Barro and Sala-i-Martin, *Economic Growth*, McGraw-Hill (1995).
[4]See Serge Coulombe and Frank Lee, "Convergence across Canadian Provinces, 1961 to 1991," *Canadian Journal of Economics*, 1991, pp. 886–98.

KEY TERMS AND EQUATIONS

capital (p. 84)

capital intensity (p. 79)

convergence (p. 108)

depreciation (p. 87)

efficiency of labour (p. 79)

labour force (p. 86)

output per worker (p. 84)

production function (p. 83)

savings rate (p. 87)

steady-state growth path (p. 85)

Solow residuals:
$$\frac{\Delta A_t}{A_t} = \frac{\Delta Y_t}{Y_t} - \alpha \times \frac{\Delta K_t}{K_t} - (1 - \alpha) \times \frac{\Delta L_t}{L_t} \qquad (3.4)$$

Evolution of K/L:
$$\Delta \left(\frac{K_t}{L_t} \right) = s \times \frac{Y_t}{L_t} - (\delta + n) \times \frac{K_t}{L_t} \qquad (3.10)$$

Romer's production function:
$$\frac{Y_t}{L_t} = A \times \frac{K_t}{L} \quad \text{where} \quad A = (\rho \times L)^{1-\alpha} \qquad (3.13)$$

Barro's production function:
$$\frac{Y_t}{L} = A \times \tau^{1-\alpha} \times \frac{K_t}{L} \quad \text{where} \quad A = (\rho \times L)^{1-\alpha} \qquad (3.17)$$

Steady-state growth rate of K/L in the neoclassical model:
$$g_k = \frac{s \times F(K/L, E)}{K/L} - (n + \delta) \qquad (3.18)$$

Rebelo's production function:
$$Y = A \times K \qquad (3.19)$$

Growth rate of K/L in the endogenous growth model:
$$g_k = s \times A - \delta - n \qquad (3.22)$$

ANALYTICAL EXERCISES

1. Explain the effects of an increase in the rate of depreciation of capital in the neoclassical growth model, and in Romer's model.

2. Suppose the economy's aggregate production function is given by

$$Y_t = (K_t)^{0.5} \times (E \times L_t)^{0.5}$$

   where Y_t is aggregate output, K_t is capital, L_t is labour, and E is the efficiency of labour. Assume that the capital's depreciation rate is 3 percent per year, the rate of population growth is 1 percent per year, and the efficiency of labour is $E = 1$.

   a. Suppose that the saving rate is 10 percent of GDP. What is the steady-state capital–labour ratio? What is the value of output per worker in the steady state?

   b. Suppose that the saving rate is 15 percent of GDP. What is the steady-state capital–output ratio? What is the value of output per worker along the economy's steady-state growth path?

3. What happens to the steady-state capital–output ratio if the rate of technological progress increases? Would the steady-state growth rate of output per worker increase, decrease, or remain in the same position?

4. According to the marginal productivity theory of distribution, in a competitive economy the rate of return on a dollar's worth of capital — its profits or interest — is equal to capital's marginal productivity. If this theory holds and the marginal productivity of capital is indeed

$$\frac{dY}{dK} = \alpha \times \frac{Y}{K}$$

   how large are the total earnings received by capital? What share of total output will be received by the owners of capital as their income?

5. What is meant by convergence in growth theory? What is the evidence regarding convergence?

6. What are some of the possible shortcomings in the predictions of the neoclassical growth model? How do endogenous growth models attempt to overcome these possible shortcomings?

POLICY EXERCISES

1. Suppose because of the elimination of the federal budget deficit the national saving rate is boosted from 16 percent to 20 percent of real GDP. Suppose further that the rate of labour force growth is 1 percent per year, the depreciation rate is 3 percent per year, the level of the efficiency of labour E is 30,000, and that the diminishing-returns-to-capital parameter α is 1/3. Suppose that these rates continue into the indefinite future. What would be the steady-state level of output per worker before the budget deficit was eliminated? What would be the steady-state level of output per worker after the budget deficit is eliminated?

2. What are the long-run costs as far as economic growth is concerned of a policy of taking money that could reduce the national debt — and thus add to national savings — and distributing it as tax cuts instead? What are the long-run benefits of such a policy? How can we decide whether such a policy is a good thing or not?

3. Suppose because of the computer revolution the efficiency of labor E increases from 30,000 to 40,000. Suppose the rate of labour force growth were to remain constant at 1 percent per year, the depreciation rate were to remain constant at 3 percent per year, and the saving rate were to remain constant at 20 percent per year. Assume that the diminishing-returns-to-capital parameter α is 1/3. What is the change in the steady-state output per worker?

4. Suppose that a sudden disaster — an epidemic, say — reduces a country's population and labour force, but does not affect its capital stock. What is the immediate effect of the epidemic on output per worker and on the economy-wide level of output? What happens subsequently?

5. Suppose that environmental regulations lead to a slowdown in the rate of growth of the efficiency of labour in the production function, but also lead to better environmental quality. Should we think of this as a "slowdown" in economic growth?

6. Consider the Barro growth model, where the production function is $\dfrac{Y_t}{L_t} = \left(\dfrac{K_t}{L_t}\right)^{\alpha} \times G_t^{1-\alpha}$, and $G_t = \tau \times K_t$. Assume there is no depreciation or population growth.
   a. For this model, derive the steady-state growth rate.
   b. Derive the growth-maximizing level of taxes.

7. Consider an economy with a labour-force growth rate of 2 percent per year, a depreciation rate of 4 percent per year, a rate of growth of the efficiency of labour of 2 percent per year, and a saving rate of 16 percent of GDP. If the saving rate increases from 16 to 17 percent, what is the proportional increase in the steady-state level of output per worker if the diminishing-returns-to-capital parameter α is $^1/_3$? $^1/_2$? $^2/_3$? $^3/_4$?

4

The Reality of Economic Growth: History and Prospect

QUESTIONS

What is modern economic growth?

What was the post-1973 productivity slowdown? What were its causes? Is the productivity slowdown now over?

Why are some nations so (relatively) rich and other nations so (relatively) poor?

What policies can speed up economic growth?

What are the prospects for successful and rapid economic development in tomorrow's world?

4.1 AN OVERVIEW OF ECONOMIC GROWTH

BEFORE THE INDUSTRIAL REVOLUTION

If we take the scattered and imperfect information we have about the global economy from the distant past to today, we see a pattern like that depicted in Table 4.1.

Until 1800 the growth rates of human populations were glacial. Population growth between 5000 BC and AD 1800 averaged less than one-tenth of a percent per year. (Nevertheless, the cumulative magnitude of population growth was impressive, carrying the number of human beings alive on the planet from perhaps 5 million in 5000 BC to 900 million in 1800 — 7000 years is a long time.) Until 1500, as best we can tell, there had been next to *no* growth in output per worker for the average human for millennia. Even in 1800 the average human had a material standard of living (and an economic productivity level) at best twice that of the average human in the year 1. The problem was not that there was no technological progress. There was. Humans have long been ingenious. Warrior, priestly, and bureaucratic elites in 1800 lived much better than their counterparts in previous

TABLE 4.1
Economic Growth through Deep Time

Year	Population*	GDP per Capita†
–5000	5	$ 130
–1000	50	160
1	170	135
1000	265	165
1500	425	175
1800	900	250
1900	1,625	850
1950	2,515	2,030
1975	4,080	4,640
2000	6,120	8,175

* Millions.
† In year-2000 international dollars.
Source: Joel Cohen, *How Many People Can the Earth Support?* (New York: Norton, 1995).

millennia had lived. But just because the ruling elite lived better does not mean that other people lived any better.

Only after 1800 do we see large sustained increases in worldwide standards of living. After 1800 human numbers grew as the population explosion took hold. It carried the total population to 6 billion in October 1999. Population growth on a world scale accelerated from a rate of 0.2 percent per year between 1500 and 1800 to 0.6 percent per year between 1800 and 1900, 0.9 percent per year between 1900 and 1950, and 1.9 percent per year between 1950 and 1975 before the first slowing of the global rate of population growth — 1.6 percent per year from 1975 to 2000.

Average rates of material output per capita, which grew at perhaps 0.15 percent per year between 1500 and 1800, grew at roughly 1 percent per year worldwide between 1800 and 1900 and at an average pace of about 2 percent per year world-wide between 1900 and 2000, as Figure 4.1 shows.

PREMODERN ECONOMIC "GROWTH"

Why were there no sustained increases in the material productivity of human labour before 1500? Because improved technology quickly ran aground on resource scarcity. As human populations grew, the stocks of known natural resources had to be divided among more and more people: Miners had to exploit lower-quality metal ores, farmers had to farm lesser-quality agricultural land, and forests vanished. Who alive today has ever seen one of the cedars of Lebanon? In spite of technological progress, resource scarcity meant that the efficiency of labour was little, if any, greater in AD 1500 than in 1500 BC.

One of the oldest ideas in economics is that increases in technology inevitably run into natural-resource scarcity and so lead to increases in the numbers of people but not in their standard of living or productivity. This idea was introduced late into economics by Thomas R. Malthus, who was to become the first academic professor of economics (Adam Smith had been a professor of moral philosophy) at the East India Company's Haileybury College.

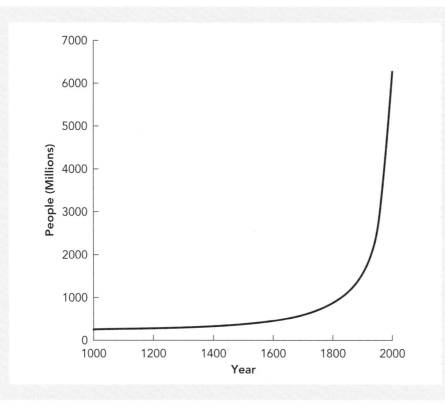

Source: Joel Cohen, *How Many People Can the Earth Support?* (New York: Norton, 1995); United Nations and Michael Kremer of MIT.

Malthus saw a world in which inventions and higher living standards led to increases in the rate of population growth. With higher living standards women ovulated more frequently, and more pregnancies were successfully carried to term. Better-nourished children (and adults) had a better chance of resisting diseases. Moreover, when incomes were high, new farmsteads were relatively plentiful, and getting the permission of one's father or elder brother to marry was easier. For these reasons, both social and biological, a higher standard of living before 1800 led to a faster rate of population increase. And the faster rate of population growth increased natural-resource scarcity and lowered productivity until once again people were so poor and malnourished that population growth was roughly zero.

THE END OF THE MALTHUSIAN AGE

TECHNOLOGY

We clearly no longer live in a **Malthusian age**. For at least 200 years improvements in the efficiency of labour made possible by new technologies and better organizations have *not* been neutralized by natural-resource scarcity. (But a Malthusian age may return: Project twentieth-century population growth rates forward and calculate that the year 2200 population of the earth will be 93 billion; it requires skill and ingenuity to argue today that resource scarcity will not be a dominant feature of such a world.)

What caused the end of the Malthusian age? How did humanity escape from the trap in which invention and ingenuity increased the numbers but not the material well-being of humans?

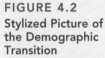

FIGURE 4.2
Stylized Picture of the Demographic Transition

The demographic transition sees, first, a rise in birth rates and a sharp fall in death rates as material standards of living increase above subsistence levels. But after a while birth rates start to decline rapidly too. The end of the demographic transition sees both birth and death rates at a relatively low level and the population nearly stable.

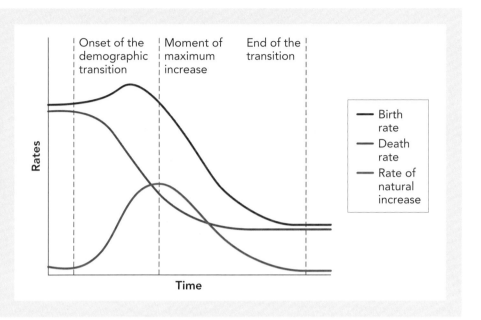

The key is that even in the Malthusian age the pace at which inventions occurred increased steadily. First of all, the population grew. Inventions made communication easier; especially after the invention of printing, knowledge could spread widely and quickly. More people meant more inventions: Two heads are greater than one. The rate of technological progress slowly increased over the millennia. By about 1500 it passed the point at which **natural-resource scarcity** could fully offset it. Sustained increases not just in population but in the productivity of labour followed.

THE DEMOGRAPHIC TRANSITION

At first the rise in material standards of living brought sharp increases in the rate of population growth: the population explosion. But as material standards of living rose far above subsistence, countries began to undergo the **demographic transition**, sketched out in Figure 4.2.

Birth control meant that those who did not wish to have more children could exercise their choice. Parents began to find more satisfaction in having a few children and paying a great deal of attention to each. The resources of the average household continued to increase, but the number of children born fell. The long-run relationship between levels of productivity and population growth rates was not — as Malthus thought — a spiral of ever-faster population growth rates as material standards of living increased. Instead, population growth rates peaked and began to decline.

In the world today not all countries have gone through their demographic transitions. Many countries are not rich enough to have begun the population growth declines seen in the second half of the demographic transition. Countries such as Nigeria, Iraq, Pakistan, and the Congo are currently projected to have population growth rates in excess of 2 percent per year over the next generation, as Figure 4.3 shows. But there is also a large group of developing countries like Thailand, China, Korea, and South Africa in which population growth over the next generation is projected to be less than 1 percent per year. And in the industrialized countries — like Japan, Italy, and Germany — populations are projected to stay nearly the same over the next generation.

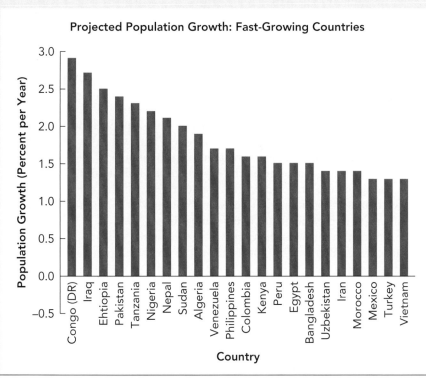

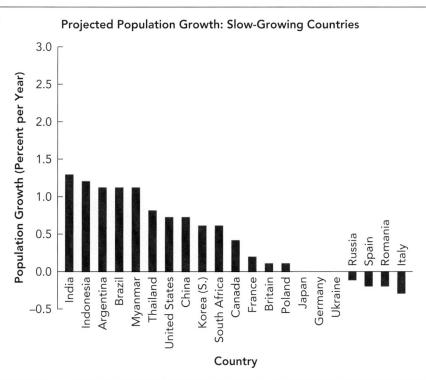

FIGURE 4.3
Expected Population Growth Rates, 1997–2002
The population of India is projected to grow at 1.3 percent and that of China at 0.7 percent per year over the next generation. Demographers today believe that the world population has at most one more doubling to undergo before the demographic transition will have taken hold throughout the world.

Source: United Nations.

THE INDUSTRIAL REVOLUTION

The century after 1750 saw the **Industrial Revolution** proper: the invention of the steam engine, the spinning jenny, the power loom, the hydraulic press, the railroad locomotive, the water turbine, and the electric motor, as well as the hot-air balloon, gas lighting, photography, and the sewing machine. But the Industrial Revolution was not just a burst of inventions. It was an economic transformation that revolutionized the *process* of invention as well. Since 1850 the pace of invention and innovation has further accelerated: steel making, the internal combustion engine, pasteurization, the typewriter, the cash register, the telephone, the automobile, the radio, the airplane, the tank, the limited-access highway, the photocopier, the computer, the pacemaker, nuclear weapons, superconductivity, genetic fingerprinting, and the human genome map. The coming of the Industrial Revolution marked the beginning of the era of modern economic growth: the era in which it was expected that new technological leaps would routinely revolutionize industries and generate major improvements in living standards.

The fact that Britain was the centre of the Industrial Revolution meant that for a century, from 1800 to 1900, British levels of industrial productivity and British standards of living were the highest in the world. It also meant that English (rather than Hindi, Mandarin, French, or Spanish) became the world's de facto second language. But the technologies of the Industrial Revolution did not remain narrowly confined to Britain. Their spread was rapid to western Europe and the United States. It was less rapid — but still relatively thorough and complete — to southern and eastern Europe and, most interesting perhaps, Japan, as shown in Figure 4.4.

FIGURE 4.4
Industrializing Areas of the World, 1900

Perhaps the most important lesson to draw from this short look at economic history is that economists' standard growth models apply to a relatively narrow slice of time. For instance, the growth model discussed in Chapter 3 does not illuminate very much regarding the period before 1800, yet it is very useful in analyzing what has happened over the past two centuries, as well as what is going on today with respect to the growth of different national economies.

■ Industrializing areas

Source: Steven Dowrick and J. Bradford DeLong, "Globalization and Convergence," in Jeffrey Williamson et al., eds. *Globalization in Historical Perspective* (Chicago: University of Chicago Press, 2005).

THE TWENTIETH CENTURY

Between approximately 1890 and 1930, or perhaps 1890 and 1950, a host of innovative technologies and business practices were adopted in the United States. Europeans speak of "Fordism": taking the part — Henry Ford's assembly lines in Detroit and his mass production of the Model-T Ford — for the whole. The fact that other industrial economies were unable to fully adopt American technologies of mass production and mass distribution in the first half of the twentieth century gave the United States a unique level of industrial dominance and technological leadership in the years after 1950.

RECAP   AN OVERVIEW OF ECONOMIC GROWTH

Up until 1800 human populations grew very slowly, and human living standards were stagnant. After 1800 we see sustained rises in living standards, and human numbers grew as the population explosion took hold and carried our total population to 6 billion in 2005. At first the rise in material standards of living brought sharp increases in the rate of population growth: The population explosion. But as material standards of living rose far above subsistence, countries began to undergo the *demographic transition*; population growth rates peaked and began to decline toward stability.

The century after 1750 saw the Industrial Revolution, which substantially accelerated the process of invention and growth. Since Britain was at the centre of the Industrial Revolution, for the period 1800–1900 its industrial productivity and living standards were the highest in the world. In the twentieth century the United States became the centre of invention and innovations.

4.2 ECONOMIC GROWTH IN CANADA AND THE U.S.

In this section we highlight the history of economic growth in the U.S. and then we compare it to the history of economic growth in Canada, which we discussed in Chapter 1. The discussion centres on the important issues of productivity slowdown and the productivity gap between the two economies. We close the section with a discussion of recent trends in income inequality in the two countries.

U.S. ECONOMIC GROWTH

Figure 4.5 depicts movements of real (1958 US dollars) GNP per worker for the U.S. Throughout the nineteenth century and the first three-quarters of the twentieth century the pace of labour productivity growth in the U.S. continued to accelerate. The growth rate of output per worker rose from about 0.5 percent per year between 1800 and 1870 to about 1.6 percent per year between 1870 and 1929. Growth slowed slightly during the Great Depression and World War II decades — a measured growth rate of 1.4 percent per year from 1929 to 1950. But then growth accelerated. The growth rate of output per worker between 1950 and 1973 in the United States was 2.1 percent per year. In 1973 the upward trend in **productivity growth** stopped. Between 1973 and 1995 output per worker in the U.S. economy grew at only 0.6 percent per year. This is the growth slowdown discussed in the previous section.

http://www.statcan.ca/english/
IPS/Data/15-204-XIE.htm

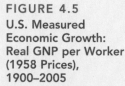

FIGURE 4.5

U.S. Measured Economic Growth: Real GNP per Worker (1958 Prices), 1900–2005

With the exception of the Great Depression of the 1930s and the productivity slowdown period of the 1970s and 1980s, measured real GNP per worker in the United States has grown steadily with only minor interruptions.

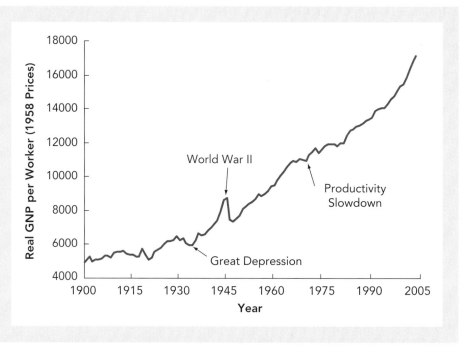

Source: U.S. Census Bureau, Historical Statistics of the United States, Series D5 (employed persons, 1900–1938) and F1 (real GNP, 1900–1946); and U.S. Department of Labor, Bureau of Labor Statistics, Series CEU0000000001 (employed persons, 1939–2005); and U.S. Federal Reserve, FRED, Series gnp (nominal GNP, 1947–2005) and gnpc96 (real GNP, 1947–2005).

Since 1995, however, productivity growth in the American economy has accelerated once again to a pace of 2.1 percent per year. The recent acceleration in productivity growth is largely attributed to a sustained investment boom, a large share of which is believed by some economists to be driven by the rapidly falling price of computers.

Comparing Figures 1.8 and 4.5, one could discern very similar patterns in growth of GDP per worker in Canada and the U.S. Both countries experienced economic downturns due to the Great Depression in 1929–1933, the 1945–1946 aftermath of WWII, the stagflation of 1981–1982, and the 1991–1992 recession. Both countries also experienced a slowdown in growth of GDP per worker after 1973. A noticeable difference is that the U.S. economy seems to have reversed this slowdown in growth since the early 1980s, whereas in Canada such a reversal took place a decade later. We next turn to this issue in the broader context of the Canada versus U.S. productivity gap.

THE CANADA–U.S. PRODUCTIVITY GAP

One of the worrisome trends for the Canadian economy in recent years has been the widening productivity gap relative to the U.S. If Canadian industries are less productive than their U.S. counterparts, then their average costs will also be higher, making them less competitive. Allan Crawford of the Bank of Canada has provided a recent discussion of this issue.[1]

---

[1] See "Trends in Productivity Growth in Canada," by Allan Crawford, published in *Bank of Canada Review*, Spring 2002, pp. 19–32. Also see "Productivity Levels between Canadian and U.S. Industries," by Someshwar Rao, Jianmin Tang, and Wemin Wang, published in *International Productivity Monitor* (no. 9, Fall 2004), available online at: http://www.csls.ca/ipm/ipm9asp.

The most popular measure of productivity used by economists is *labour productivity*, which is output produced per each labour hour. The reason this is a popular measure of productivity is that labour is the largest input in the production process. It is, moreover, relatively easy to measure labour input without substantial measurement error. Because of the substantial diversity in capital equipment, it is hard to collect data on capital equipment and discern from the data how much capital is actually used in the production process.

Lower labour productivity in Canada implies that the same amount of labour produces less output in Canada than in the U.S. This means that the cost of producing each unit of the good will be higher, making Canadian industries less competitive.

From Figures 1.8 and 4.5 one can see that both countries experienced a slowdown in labour productivity starting in the mid-1970s, but the persistence of this slowdown was quite different. The U.S. **productivity slowdown** was reversed in the early 1980s and, with the exception of a small decline in 1991, strong productivity growth continued until the end of the 1990s. This is the period of the *long boom* in the U.S. economy according to leading U.S. economists. In Canada, productivity growth did not recover until about 1992, about ten years later than in the U.S., and even then it was only briefly strong enough to reverse the decline relative to the U.S. Figure 4.6 provides confirmation. Part of this Canadian experience has been labelled the *great slump.*

Figure 4.6 shows the *relative* labour productivity in Canada versus the U.S. (that is, labour productivity in Canada divided by labour productivity in the U.S.). As seen from this figure, in much of the 1970s Canada's labour productivity was strong relative to that of the U.S. However, from the mid-1980s until early 1990s Canada's relative labour productivity followed a sharp downward trend. Although this trend was reversed in the 1990s, the sharp negative trend reappeared after 2000.

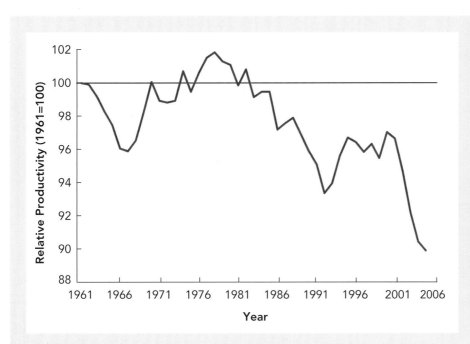

FIGURE 4.6
Relative Labour Productivity in Canada versus the U.S.

In much of the 1970s Canada's labour productivity was strong relative to that of the U.S. However, from the mid-1980s until early 1990s Canada's relative labour productivity followed a sharp downward trend. Although this trend was reversed in the 1990s, it reappeared in the 2000s.

Source: *International Productivity Monitor,* Centre for the Study of Living Standards.

One can identify a number of reasons for the decline in Canada's relative labour productivity in recent years. First, the agriculture and primary resources (e.g., mining and energy) sectors are a relatively large part of the Canadian economy. These sectors, in general, experience less productivity growth than the manufacturing sector. Second, since the mid-1990s the U.S. economy has experienced a substantial gain in productivity from the information and communication technologies (ICT). The U.S. industries have been very fast in developing the ICT sector and in adopting computers in the manufacturing sector, with the U.S. manufacturing sector spending substantially more on new machinery and equipment. This has led to substantial gains in labour productivity in the U.S.

What are the prospects for Canada's relative labour productivity? Although the U.S. has been very fast in adopting computers in the manufacturing sector, this technology adoption will eventually take place in the Canadian manufacturing sector as well. Once this is done, Canada's relative labour productivity will improve. Continued free trade with the U.S. will contribute to this process by confronting Canadian firms with competition from the U.S. In the 1990s some economists advocated fixing the value of the Canadian dollar in term of the US dollar, or even adopting a currency union with the U.S. as a means of increasing technology adoption. The argument was that the fall in the value of the Canadian dollar in the 1990s had been the result of a loss in competitiveness by Canadian industries. This fall in the value of the dollar had shielded Canadian industries from foreign competition; and, therefore, they had not been forced to adopt new technologies. The fall in the value of the dollar had also delayed technology adoption by Canadian industries by making imports of technology intensive capital goods more expensive.

It is, nevertheless, important to note that the argument that the fall in the value of the Canadian dollar in the 1990s delayed technology adoption is controversial. Some economists believe that the fall in the value of the dollar encouraged exports, and allowed export-oriented industries to reap the benefits of increasing returns to scale.

http://www.bankofcanada.ca/en/review/index.html

RECAP   ECONOMIC GROWTH IN CANADA AND THE U.S.

One could discern very similar patterns in growth of GDP per worker in Canada and the U.S. A noticeable difference is the fact that the U.S. economy seems to have reversed its post-1973 slowdown in growth since the early 1980s, whereas in Canada such a reversal took place a decade later. Reasons for the widening gap between Canadian and U.S. productivity include (1) the relatively large agriculture and primary resources sectors in Canada and (2) the substantial gain in productivity from the information and communication technologies in the U.S. since the mid-1990s.

4.3 INCOME INEQUALITY AND STANDARDS OF LIVING

The growth of output per worker does not necessarily reflect an increase in living standards for everyone in the economy. Therefore, it is also important to consider changes in the degree of income inequality in the economy. An index of income inequality that is most widely used in economics is called the Gini coefficient. In this section we define the Gini coefficient and report how it has changed over time in Canada and some other countries.

Before defining the Gini coefficient, however, we should discuss the Lorenz curve, which tells us the percentage of total income earned by different groups of individuals in a country starting with the poorest and going up to the richest. Figure 4.7 shows two hypothetical Lorenz curves. The vertical axis in the figure measures *income shares* and the horizontal axis measures *percentages* of the population, from the poorest to the richest. The Lorenz curve along the 45° line represents perfect equality, in the sense that income shares and population percentages coincide: for instance, income earned by the poorest 20 percent of the population accounts for 20 percent of the total income generated in the economy and so on. Lorenz curves below the diagonal represent income inequality. The further away from the diagonal a Lorenz curve is the greater the income inequality in a country.

The shaded area between the Lorenz curve and the 45° line is an indication of income inequality in a country. The Gini coefficient measures this area as a percentage of the total area under the 45° line. The larger the Gini coefficient the larger is the degree of inequality in the country.

In Figure 4.8 we show the Lorenz curves for Canada and the U.S. for two points in time that are approximately two decades apart: for Canada 1981 versus 2000, and for the U.S. 1979 versus 2000. Notice, there has not been a noticeable shift in the Lorenz curve for Canada between these dates, while the Lorenz curve for the U.S.

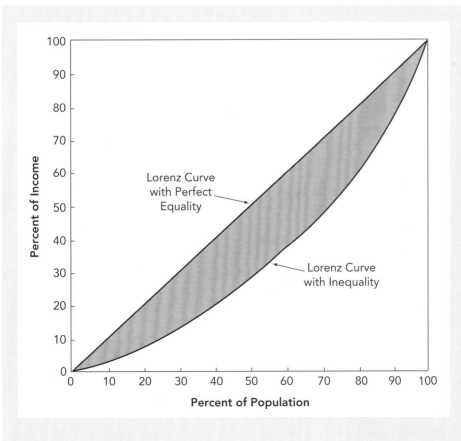

FIGURE 4.7
Lorenz Curves and Gini Coefficient

The vertical axis in the figure measures *income shares* and the horizontal axis measures *percentages* of the population, from the poorest to the richest. The Lorenz curve along the 45° line represents perfect equality. The further away from the diagonal a Lorenz curve is the greater the income inequality in a country. The shaded area between the Lorenz curve and the 45° line is an indication of income inequality in a country. The Gini coefficient measures this area as a percentage of the total area under the 45° line. The larger the Gini coefficient the larger is the degree of inequality in the country.

FIGURE 4.8
The Lorenz Curves for Canada and the U.S.

Here are Lorenz curves for Canada and the U.S. for two points in time that are approximately two decades apart: for Canada 1981 versus 2000, and for the U.S. 1979 versus 2000. Notice, there has not been a noticeable shift in the Lorenz curve for Canada between these dates, while the Lorenz curve for the U.S. has shifted down significantly. Hence, while income inequality did not change much in Canada, it changed significantly in the U.S.

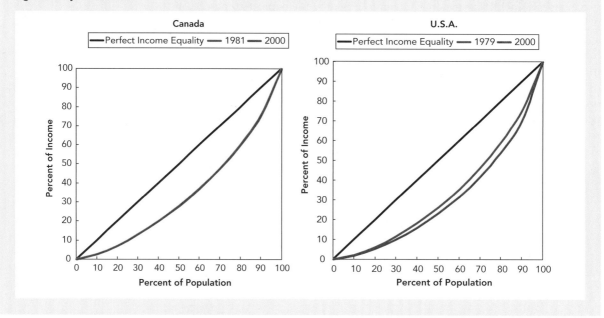

Source: World Income Inequality Database, http://www.wider.unu.edu/wiid/wiid.htm.

has shifted down significantly. Hence, while income inequality did not change much in Canada, it changed significantly in the U.S.

To further illustrate the changes in income distribution in Canada and the U.S. in these years, Table 4.2 reports the proportions of total incomes in Canada and in the U.S. earned by different quintiles of the population in these years. The first quintile is the 10 percent of the labour force with the lowest income, the second quintile is the 20 percent of the labour force with the lowest income and so on. Notice, in Canada, between 1981 and 2000, the total income earned by the poorest 10 percent of the labour force increased from 2.62 percent to 2.71 percent of total earnings. On the other hand, the earnings of the *richest* 10 percent of the Canadian labour force (i.e., the difference between the last two quintiles) increased from 24.21 percent to 24.75 percent of total income. These changes in income distribution are not very large compared to the changes in the U.S. In the U.S., between 1979 and 2000, income earned by the poorest 10 percent of the labour force *fell* from 2.04 percent to 1.79 percent of total income, while the income earned by the richest 10 percent increased from 24.75 percent to 29.92 percent of total income.

Table 4.3 reports the Gini coefficients for several countries at two points in time, one in the early 1980s or late 1970s (except for Russia in 1992) and another in the early 2000s. Clearly Canada's income inequality has remained roughly constant over this time period, as has been the case with France, Germany, Japan, and Italy. Income inequality has increased moderately in Brazil, Mexico, and Russia, and it has increased the most in Argentina, the U.K., and the U.S. On the other hand, income inequality

TABLE 4.2

Income Distribution in Canada and the U.S.

In Canada, between 1981 and 2000, the total income earned by the poorest 10% of the labour force increased from 2.62% to 2.71% of total earnings, while the earnings of the *richest* 10% of the Canadian labour force (i.e., the difference between the last two quintiles) increased from 24.21% to 24.75% of total income. In the U.S., between 1979 and 2000, income earned by the poorest 10% of the labour force *fell* from 2.04% to 1.79% of total income, while the income earned by the richest 10% increased from 24.75% to 29.92%.

Quintiles	Canada		U.S.	
	1981	2000	1979	2000
10.00	2.62	2.71	2.04	1.79
20.00	7.26	7.29	6.12	5.32
30.00	13.16	13.11	11.62	10.05
40.00	20	20.01	18.37	15.97
50.00	27.94	28.03	26.31	23.14
60.00	37.05	37.17	35.53	31.64
70.00	47.62	47.72	46.4	41.76
80.00	60.21	60.11	59.23	54.08
90.00	75.79	75.25	75.25	70.08
100.00	100	100	100	100

Source: World Income Inequality Database, http://www.wider.unu.edu/wiid/wiid.htm.

TABLE 4.3

Gini Coefficients for Selected Countries in the Early 1980s and 2000s

Canada's income inequality has remained roughly constant over this time period, as has been the case with France, Germany, Japan, and Italy. Income inequality has increased moderately in Brazil, Mexico, and Russia, and it has increased the most in Argentina, the U.K., and the U.S. On the other hand, income inequality has been reduced significantly in India. Also, judging from the magnitude of the Gini coefficients across countries, Canada has a more unequal distribution of income than all of the European countries on this table, with the exception of the U.K., and a more equal income distribution relative to its NAFTA partners, Mexico and the U.S.

Country	Gini Coefficient around 1980	Gini Coefficient around 2000	
Canada	32.29*	32.45**	*Gini 1981, **Gini 2000
U.S.	34.47*	40.19**	*Gini 1979, **Gini 2000
India	43.00*	31.70**	*Gini 1975, **Gini 1999
Russia	43.84*	45.64**	*Gini 1992, **Gini 2000
U.K.	25.28*	34.84**	*Gini 1980, **Gini 2000
France	31.56*	28.00**	*Gini 1981, **Gini 2000
Germany	28.12*	29.04**	*Gini 1981, **Gini 2000
Japan	33.40*	31.88**	*Gini 1980, **Gini 1998
Italy	37.00*	35.87**	*Gini 1980, **Gini 2000
Argentina	40.50*	52.20**	*Gini 1980, **Gini 2001
Brazil	57.40*	59.93**	*Gini 1981, **Gini 2001
Mexico	48.58*	51.19**	*Gini 1984, **Gini 2002

Source: United Nations University, World Institute for Development Economics Research (WIDER) Data Base at: www.wider.unu.edu/wiid/wiid.htm.

has been reduced significantly in India. Also, judging from the magnitude of the Gini coefficients across countries, Canada has a more unequal distribution of income than all of the European countries on this table, with the exception of the U.K., and a more equal income distribution relative to its NAFTA partners, Mexico and the U.S.

> **RECAP** **INCOME INEQUALITY AND STANDARDS OF LIVING**
>
> The growth of output per worker does not necessarily reflect an increase in living standards for everyone in the economy. Therefore, it is also important to consider changes in the degree of income inequality in the economy. In recent decades income inequality has not changed much in Canada, but it has increased significantly in the U.S. Canada has a more unequal distribution of income than several European countries but more equal income distribution relative to its NAFTA partners, Mexico and the U.S.

4.4 MODERN ECONOMIC GROWTH AROUND THE WORLD

DIVERGENCE, BIG TIME

The industrial core of the world economy saw its level of material productivity and standard of living explode in the nineteenth and twentieth centuries. Elsewhere the growth of productivity levels and standards of living and the spread of industrial technologies were slower. As the industrialized economies grew while industrial technologies spread slowly elsewhere, the world became a more and more unequal place. As development economist Lant Pritchett puts it, the dominant feature of world economic history is "**divergence**, big time." In terms of relative incomes and productivity levels, the world today is more unequal and more *divergent* than ever before, as Figure 4.9 shows.

Those who live in relatively poor regions of the world today have higher material living standards than did their predecessors who lived in those regions a century ago. But the relative gap vis-à-vis the industrial core has grown extraordinarily and extravagantly. In the first half of the nineteenth century the average inhabitant of an average country had perhaps one-half the material standard of living of a citizen of the world's leading industrial economy. Today the average inhabitant of an average country has only one-sixth the material standard of living and productivity level of the leading nation. (Box 4.1 provides some insight into the difficulties of making such comparisons.)

THE EXCEPTION: OECD ECONOMIES

It is not inevitable that there be such divergence. The United States — with its 14- to 25-fold increase in output per worker over the years since 1870 — has not been the fastest-growing economy in the world. A number of other economies at different levels of industrialization, development, and material productivity a century ago have now *converged*, and their levels of productivity, economic structures, and standards of living today are very close to those of the United States (see Box 4.2). The six largest of these converging economies and the United States make up the so-called Group of Seven, or G-7, economies, whose leaders gather for annual

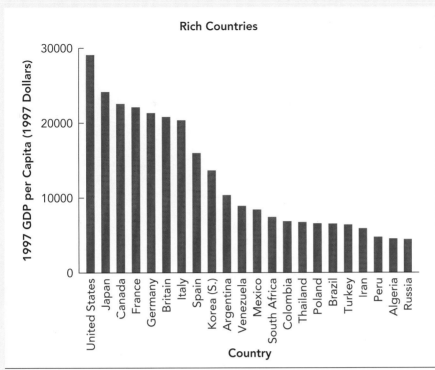

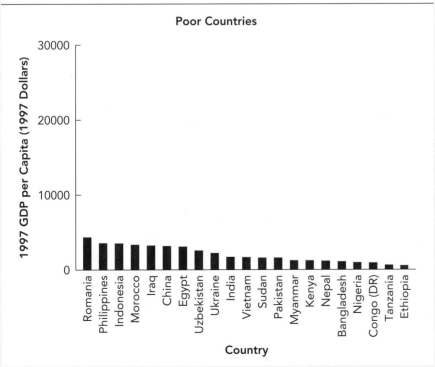

FIGURE 4.9

World Distribution of Income, Selected Countries

In some places modern economic growth has taken hold and propelled levels of productivity and living standards upward. In other places people on average live little, if any, better than their ancestors did. The world is a more unequal place, in relative income terms, than it has been since there were some human tribes that had fire and others that did not.

Source: Authors' calculations from Alan Heston's and Robert Summer's Penn World Table, www.nber.org.

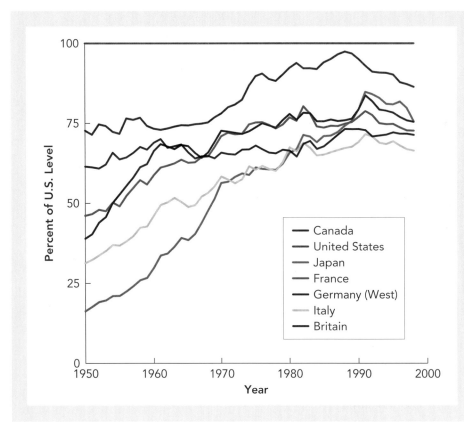

FIGURE 4.10

Convergence among the G-7 Economies: Output per Capita as a Share of U.S. Level

In 1950 GDP per capita levels in the six nations that now are America's partners in the G-7 varied from 20 percent of the U.S. level (Japan) to 70 percent of the U.S. level (Canada). Today estimates of GDP per capita place levels in all six at more than 65 percent of the U.S. level — and they would be even closer to the U.S. level if the measurements took account of the shorter average work year abroad.

Source: Authors' calculations.

summit meetings. The six non-U.S. members' steady process of convergence to the U.S. level from 1950 until 1990 is shown in Figure 4.10.

Most of these economies were significantly poorer than the United States in 1870 and even in 1950. The Japanese economy, for example, went from a level of output per capita equal to 16 percent of the U.S. level in 1950 to 84 percent of the U.S. level in 1992 — before falling steeply backward during Japan's recent recession. Italian

4.1

BOX

TOOLS

PURCHASING-POWER-PARITY AND REAL EXCHANGE RATE COMPARISONS

When our focus is on comparing standards of living, either across time or across countries, we get much more meaningful figures by correcting current (and even average trend) exchange rates for differences in *purchasing power parity (PPP)*. The differences between estimates of relative income levels based on current exchange rates and estimates based on PPP calculations can be very large. On a purchasing-power-parity basis the GDP per worker in Canada today is some 13 times the GDP per worker in India; by contrast, on an average exchange rate basis the GDP per worker in Canada today is more than 70 times the level in India.

PPP-based calculations attempt (as the name applies) to translate one currency into another at a rate that preserves average purchasing power. But current exchange rates do not preserve purchasing power. If you exchange your dollars in Canada for rupees in India you will find that your rupees in India will buy about the same amount of internationally traded manufactured goods as your dollars would have bought in Canada. (Unless, of course, you try to buy something that the Indian government has decided to put up a trade barrier against.) But your rupees in India will buy you vastly more in the way of personal services, the products of skilled craftspeople, and any other labour-intensive goods and services.

Why? International arbitrage keeps the exchange rate at the level that makes easily traded manufactured goods roughly equally expensive. If they weren't, someone could make an easy fortune by shipping them from where they were cheap to where they were dear. But how — in this world of stringent immigration restrictions — can a cook in Bangalore take advantage of the fact that there is fierce demand in Toronto for caterers who can prepare a good curry? Because relative productivity levels in labour services are much more equal than relative productivity levels in manufacturing, living standards throughout the world are more equal than exchange rate–based calculations suggest.

WHY HAVE THESE ECONOMIES CONVERGED?

By and large the economies that have converged are those that belong to the Organisation for Economic Cooperation and Development (OECD), which was started shortly after World War II, in the days of the Marshall Plan, as a group of countries that received (or gave) Marshall Plan aid to help rebuild and reconstruct after the war. Countries that received Marshall Plan aid adopted a common set of economic policies: large private sectors freed of government regulation of prices, investment with its direction determined by profit-seeking businesses, large social insurance systems to redistribute income, and governments committed to avoiding mass unemployment.

The original OECD members all wound up with mixed economies. In these, markets direct the flow of resources, while governments stabilize the economy, provide social insurance safety nets, and encourage entrepreneurship and enterprise. The member nations arrived at this setup largely due to good luck, partly due to the Cold War, and partly as a result of post–World War II institutional reforms.

This configuration was essentially the price countries had to pay for receiving Marshall Plan aid. The U.S. executive was unwilling to send much aid to countries that it thought were likely to engage in destructive economic policies, largely because it did not believe that it could win funding from the Republican-dominated Congress for a Marshall Plan that did not impose such strict *conditionality* upon recipients. By contrast, countries that were relatively rich after World War II but did not adopt OECD-style institutional arrangements — such as Argentina and Venezuela — lost relative ground.

As the OECD economies became richer, they completed their demographic transitions: Population growth rates fell. The policy emphasis on entrepreneurship and enterprise boosted national investment rates, so the OECD economies all had healthy investment rates as well. These factors boosted their steady-state capital–output ratios. And the diffusion of technology from the United States did the rest of the job in bringing OECD standards of economic productivity close to the U.S. level.

4.2

BOX

POLICY

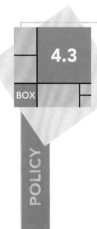

POLICY

BOX

4.3

THE EAST ASIAN MIRACLE

The story of extraordinarily successful economies goes beyond the original OECD nations. The economies of the "East Asian miracle" have over the past two generations exhibited stronger growth than has ever before been seen anywhere in the world. They have not yet converged to the standards of living and levels of economic productivity found in the world economy's industrial core, but they are converging.

Immediately before World War II the regions that are now South Korea, Hong Kong and Singapore, and Taiwan had output-per-worker levels less than one-tenth the level of the United States. Today Singapore's GDP per capita is 90 percent, Hong Kong's is 70 percent, Taiwan's is 50 percent, and South Korea's is 45 percent of the U.S. level. A second wave of East Asian economies — Malaysia and Thailand — now average more than one-quarter of the U.S. level of GDP per capita.

The successful East Asian economies share a number of similarities with the OECD economies in terms of economic policy and structure. Resource allocation decisions are by and large left to the market. Governments regard the encouragement of entrepreneurship and enterprise as a major goal. And high savings and investment rates are encouraged by a number of different government policies.

Yet there are also a number of differences vis-à-vis the OECD. Governments in East Asia have been more aggressive in pursuing *industrial policy* and somewhat less aggressive in establishing social insurance systems than have the OECD economies. However, they have also had more egalitarian income distributions and hence less need for redistribution and social insurance. They have subsidized corporations that they believe are strategic for economic development, thinking that their bureaucrats know better than the market — heresy to economists. (However, it is worth noting that they have focused subsidies on the companies that have proved successful at exporting goods to other countries, so their bureaucrats have in a sense been rewarding the judgment of *foreign* markets.) The examples of successful catching up suggest that growth could have been faster in the world economy. Economies — even very poor ones — can rapidly adopt modern machine technologies and move their productivity levels close to first-world leading-edge standards.

levels of GDP per capita have gone from 30 to 65 percent of the U.S. level; German levels, from 40 to 75 percent; Canadian levels, from 70 to 85 percent; and British levels, from 60 to 70 percent in the past half-century. Moreover, as Box 4.3 shows, the East Asian economies have also "converged."

THE RULE: DIVERGENCE BEHIND THE IRON CURTAIN

But convergence is the exception. Divergence is the rule. And perhaps the most important driving force behind divergence is communism: Being unlucky enough to have been ruled by communists in the twentieth century is a virtual guarantee of relative poverty.

There used to be a snaky geographic line across Eurasia that Winston Churchill had once called the "Iron Curtain." On one side were regimes that owed their allegiance to Karl Marx and to Marx's viceroys on earth. On the other side were regimes that claimed, in the 1946–1989 Cold War, to be of the "free world" — regimes that were, if not good, at least less worse. Walk this geographic line, shown in Figure 4.11, from Poland to Korea and then hop over to the only Western

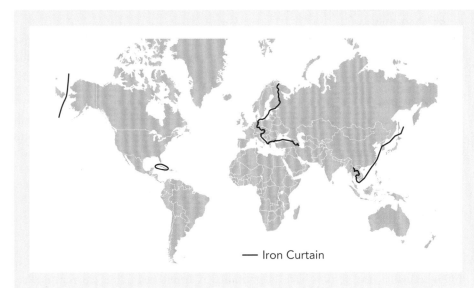

FIGURE 4.11
The Iron Curtain

hemisphere communist satellite — Cuba — looking first left at the level of material welfare in the communist countries and then right at the level of material welfare in the noncommunist countries. The location of the Iron Curtain is a historical accident: It is where Stalin's Russian armies stopped after World War II, where Mao's Chinese armies stopped in the early 1950s, and where Giap's Vietnamese armies stopped in the mid-1970s.

Notice as you walk that to your right, outside the Iron Curtain, the countries are far better off in terms of GDP per capita (see Table 4.4). They are not necessarily better off in education, health care, or the degree of income inequality. If you were in

TABLE 4.4
The Iron Curtain: GDP-per-Capita Levels of Matched Pairs of Countries

East-Bloc Country	GDP per Capita	Matched West-Bloc Country	GDP per Capita	Relative Gap (%)
North Korea	$ 700	South Korea	$13,590	94
China	3,130	Taiwan	14,170	78
Vietnam	1,630	Philippines	3,520	54
Cambodia	1,290	Thailand	6,690	81
FSR Georgia	1,960	Turkey	6,350	69
Russia	4,370	Finland	20,150	78
Bulgaria	4,010	Greece	12,769	69
Slovenia	11,800	Italy	20,290	42
Hungary	7,200	Austria	22,070	67
Czech Republic	10,510	Germany	21,260	51
Poland	6,520	Sweden	19,790	67
Cuba	3,100	Mexico	8,370	63

http://www.nber.org

Source: Authors' calculations from Alan Heston's and Robert Summer's Penn World Table, www.nber.org.

4.4

BOX

POLICY

POSTCOMMUNISM

The demolition of the Berlin Wall and the elimination of the Iron Curtain have not significantly improved the situation in what are euphemistically and optimistically called "economies in transition" (from socialism to capitalism, that is). Figuring out how to move from a stagnant, ex-communist economy to a dynamic, growing one is very difficult, and no one has ever done it before.

A few of the economies in transition appear to be on the path toward rapid convergence with western Europe: Slovenia, Hungary, the Czech Republic, and Poland have already successfully maneuvered through enough of the transition phase to have advanced their economies beyond the point reached before 1989. It seems clear that their economic destiny is to become, effectively, part of western Europe. Slovakia, Lithuania, Latvia, and Estonia appear to have good prospects of following their example.

Elsewhere, however, the news is bad. Whether reforms have taken place step-by-step or all at once, whether ex-communists have been excluded from or have dominated the government, and whether governments have been nationalist or internationalist, the results have been similar. Output has fallen, corruption has been rife, and growth has not resumed. Material standards of living in the Ukraine today are less than half of what they were when General Secretary Gorbachev ruled from Moscow.

Economists debate ferociously the appropriate economic strategy for unwinding the inefficient centrally planned Soviet-style economy. The fact that such a transition has never been undertaken before should make advice givers cautious. And one other observation should make advice givers depressed: The best predictor of whether an eastern European country's transition will be rapid and successful or not appears to be its distance from western European political and financial capitals like Vienna, Frankfurt, and Stockholm.

---

the poorer half of the population, you probably received a better education and had access to better medical care in Cuba than in Mexico. But the countries fortunate enough to lie outside what was the Iron Curtain were and are vastly more prosperous. Depending on how you count and how unlucky you are, 40 and 94 percent of the potential material prosperity of a country was annihilated if it happened to fall under communist rule in the twentieth century. The fact that a large part of the globe was under communist rule in the twentieth century is one major reason for the world's *divergence*. A failure to successfully aid post-communist economies in their transition would be a further blow, and as Box 4.4 discusses, "transition" is not going well.

THE RULE: DIVERGENCE IN GENERAL

Even if attention is confined to noncommunist-ruled economies, there still has been enormous divergence in relative output-per-worker levels over the past 100 years. Since 1870, the ratio of richest to poorest economies has increased sixfold. In 1870 two-thirds of all countries had GDP per capita levels between 60 and 160 percent of the average. Today the range that includes two-thirds of all countries extends from 35 to 280 percent of the average.

SOURCES OF DIVERGENCE

The principal cause of the extraordinary variation in output per worker between countries today is differences in their respective steady-state capital–output ratios. Two secondary causes are, first, openness to creating and adapting the technologies that enhance the efficiency of labour as measured by levels of development two generations ago and, second, the level of education today.

Productivity two generations ago is a good indicator of the level of technological knowledge that had been acquired as of a half-century ago. The level of education today captures the country's ability to invent and acquire further technological expertise today. Without education, inventing new and adopting foreign technological knowledge are simply not possible.

GLOBAL PATTERNS

Together these factors — the determinants of capital–output ratios and the two determinants of access to technology — account for the bulk of the differences between countries in their relative productivity levels.

The determinants of the steady-state balanced-growth capital–output ratio play a very powerful role. A higher share of investment in national product is powerfully correlated with relative levels of output per worker. No country with an investment rate of less than 10 percent has an output-per-worker level even 20 percent of that of the United States. No country with an investment share of less than 20 percent has an output-per-worker level greater than 75 percent of the U.S. level.

A high level of labour-force growth is correlated, albeit less powerfully, with a low level of output per worker. The average country with a labour-force growth rate of more than 3 percent per year has an output-per-worker level of less than 20 percent of the U.S. level. The average country with a labour-force growth rate of less than 1 percent has an output-per-worker level that is greater than 60 percent of the U.S. level.

Together these determinants of the steady-state capital–output ratio can, statistically, account for up to half of the variation in national economies' levels of productivity per worker in the world today. The power of these factors is central to the theoretical model of economic growth presented in Chapter 3 and should not be underestimated. Indeed, their power is the reason we spent so much space on the standard growth model in Chapter 3.

But the factors stressed in Chapter 3 are not the only major determinants of relative wealth and poverty in the world today. Differences in the efficiency of labour are as important as differences in steady-state capital–output ratios. Differences in the efficiency of labour arise from the differential ability of workers to handle and utilize modern technologies. The efficiency of labour is high where education levels are high — so workers can use the modern technologies they are exposed to — and where economic contact with the industrial core is high — so workers and managers are exposed to the modern technologies invented in the world's R&D laboratories.

Schooling is the variable that has the strongest correlation with output per worker. Countries that have an average of four to six years of schooling have output-per-worker levels that average 20 percent of the U.S. level. Those with an average level of schooling of more than ten years have output-per-worker levels of 65 percent of the U.S. level, as Figure 4.12 shows.

FIGURE 4.12

GDP-per-Worker Levels and Average Years of Schooling

Countries with a high number of average years of schooling have a better chance of being relatively well off. Education opens the door to acquiring the technologies of the Industrial Revolution.

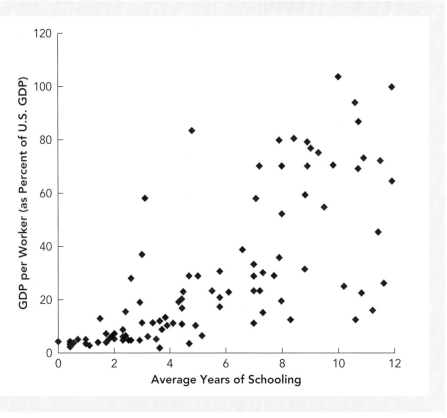

Source: Authors' calculations from Penn World Table data constructed by Alan Heston and Robert Summers, www.nber.org/.

There is no single best indicator of a country's exposure to — and thus ability to adopt and adapt — the technologies invented in the industrial core that amplify the efficiency of labour. Some economists like Jeffrey Sachs and Andrew Warner of Harvard focus on trade and foreign investment as the main sources of increased efficiency and technological capability. Others like Charles Jones and Robert Hall of Stanford focus on geographic and climatic factors that have influenced migration and still influence trade and intellectual exchange. Still others like Ken Sokoloff and Stan Engerman or Andrei Shleifer, Rafael La Porta, Florencio Lopez-di-Silanes, and Robert Vishny focus on institutions of governance and their effect on entrepreneurship as the key variable. But as much as economists dispute which variables are most important as determinants of technology transfer and the efficiency of labour, all agree that all these variables are important indeed to understanding why our world today is the way it is.

CAUSE AND EFFECT, EFFECT AND CAUSE

All the factors discussed above are both causes and effects. High population growth and low levels of output per worker go together both because rapid population growth reduces the steady-state capital–output ratio and because poor countries have not yet undergone their demographic transitions. This interaction — in which a high rate of population growth reduces the steady-state capital–output ratio and a low steady-state capital–output ratio means that the demographic transition is not far advanced — creates a vicious spiral that reinforces relative poverty.

Moreover, demography is not the only vicious spiral potentially present. A poor country must pay a high relative price for the capital equipment it needs to acquire in order to turn its savings into productive additions to its capital stock. This should come as no surprise. The world's most industrialized and prosperous economies are the most industrialized and prosperous because they have attained very high levels of manufacturing productivity: Their productivity advantage in unskilled service industries is much lower than that in capital- and technology-intensive manufactured goods. The higher relative price of machinery in developing countries means that poor countries get less investment — a smaller share of total investment in real GDP — out of any given effort at saving some fixed share of their incomes.

Moreover, to the extent that education is an important kind of investment, a good education is much harder to provide in a poorer country. Even primary education requires at its base a teacher, some books, and a classroom — things that are relatively cheap and easy for a rich country to provide but expensive for a poor country. In western Kenya today the average primary school classroom has 0.4 book per pupil.

But there is also the possibility for virtuous circles. Anything that increases productivity and sets the demographic transition in motion will reduce the rate of growth of the labour force, increase the amount of investment bought by any given amount of savings, and make education easier.

How important are these vicious spirals and virtuous circles? It is hard to look at the cross-country pattern of growth over the past century without thinking that such vicious spirals and virtuous circles *must* have been very important. Otherwise, the massive divergence in relative productivity levels seems inexplicable.

RECAP   **MODERN ECONOMIC GROWTH AROUND THE WORLD**

The industrial core of the world economy saw its level of material productivity and standards of living explode in the nineteenth and twentieth centuries. Elsewhere the growth of productivity levels and standards of living and the spread of industrial technologies were slower, and consequently the gap between rich and poor countries has widened enormously over the past century.

High population growth and low levels of output per worker go together both because rapid population growth reduces the steady-state capital–output ratio, and because poor countries have not yet undergone their demographic transitions, which lower population growth. Low investment rates and low levels of output per worker go together both because low investment reduces the steady-state capital–output ratio, and because poor countries face adverse terms of trade and high prices for capital goods that make investment difficult and expensive. Thus the obstacles to rapid growth in many poor countries in the world today are overwhelming.

4.5 POLICIES AND LONG-RUN GROWTH

HOPES FOR CONVERGENCE

RELATIVE AND ABSOLUTE STAGNATION

Always keep in mind that in the context of economic growth "stagnation" and "failure" are relative terms. Consider Argentina once again, for it has been one of the world's most disappointing performers in terms of economic growth in the twentieth century. Argentina has experienced substantial economic growth. *Officially measured* labour productivity or national product per capita in Argentina today is perhaps three times what it was in 1900. True productivity, taking adequate account of the value of new commodities, is higher. But the much more smoothly running engine of capitalist development in Norway — no more, and probably less, rich and productive than Argentina in 1900 — has multiplied *measured* national product per capita there by a factor of nine.

A pattern of productivity growth like Argentina's is heartbreakingly slow when compared to what, reasonably, might have been and was achieved by the world's industrial leaders. What is bad about falling behind, or falling further behind, is not that second place is a bad place to be — it is false to think that the only thing that matters is to be top nation and that it is better to be poor but first than rich but second. What is bad about falling behind is that the world's industrial leaders provide an easily viewable benchmark of how things might have been different and of how much better things might have been. There was no destiny keeping Buenos Aires today from looking like and having its people as rich as those of Paris, Toronto, or Sydney.

HALF EMPTY AND HALF FULL

In many respects, it is decidedly odd that the world distribution of output per worker is as unequal as it is. World trade, migration, and flows of capital should all work to move resources and consumption goods from where they are cheap to where they are dear. As they travel with increasing speed and increasing volume as transportation and communication costs fall, these commodity and factor-of-production flows should erode differences in productivity and living standards between national economies. Moreover, most of the edge in standards of living and productivity levels held by the industrial core is no one's private property but, instead, is the common intellectual and scientific heritage of humankind. Hence every poor economy has an excellent opportunity to catch up with the rich by adopting and adapting from this open storehouse of modern machine technology.

We can view this particular glass either as half empty or as half full. Half full is that much of the world has already made the transition to sustained economic growth. Most people today live in economies that, while far poorer than the leading-edge postindustrial nations of the world's economic core, have successfully climbed onto the escalator of economic growth and thus the escalator to modernity. The economic transformation of most of the world is less than a century behind that of the leading-edge economies — only an eyeblink behind from the perspective of the six millennia since the spread of agriculture out of the Middle East's fertile crescent.

Moreover, perhaps we can look forward to a future in which convergence of relative income levels will finally begin to take place. The bulk of humanity is now achieving material standards of living at which the demographic transition takes hold. As population growth rates in developing countries fall, their capital–output ratios will begin to rise quickly. With tolerable government, reasonable security of property, and better ways of achieving an education, their output-per-worker levels and material standards of living will converge to the world's leading edge.

Half empty is that we live today in the most unequal age — in terms of the divergence in the life prospects of children born into different economies — that the world has ever seen. One and a half billion people today live in economies that have *not* made the transition to intensive economic growth and have *not* climbed onto the escalator to modernity. It is very hard to argue that the median inhabitant of Africa is *any* better off in material terms than his or her counterpart of a generation ago.

POLICIES FOR SAVING, INVESTMENT, AND EDUCATION

It is certainly possible for a government to adopt policies that boost national savings, improve the ability to translate savings into productive investment, and accelerate the demographic transition.

SAVINGS AND INVESTMENT

Policies that ensure savers get reasonable rates of return on their savings have the potential to boost the savings rate. By contrast, systems of economic governance in which profits are diverted into the hands of the politically powerful through restrictions on entrepreneurship tend over time to diminish savings, as do economic policies that divert the real returns to savings into the hands of financiers or the government through inflation. Government deficits also have the potential to reduce the savings rate: Unless consumers and investors are farsighted enough to recognize that a government deficit now means a tax increase later, a government that spends more than it raises in revenue must borrow — and the amount borrowed is not a contribution to total national savings because it is not available to fund investment.

A number of potential policies work to boost investment for a given amount of savings. Policies that welcome foreign investors' money have the potential to cut a decade or a generation off the time needed to industrialize — if the foreign-funded capital is used wisely. Free-trade policies that allow businesses to freely earn and spend the foreign exchange they need to purchase new generations of machinery and equipment are an effective way of boosting investment. Policies that impose heavy tariffs or require scarce import licences in order to purchase foreign-made capital equipment are a sure sign that a country will not get its money's worth out of a given nominal savings share but will, instead, find that real investment remains low. Indeed, many of the most successful *developmental states* have done the opposite. They have provided large subsidies to fund investment and expansion by businesses that have demonstrated their competence and productivity by successfully exporting and thus competing in the world market.

EDUCATION

Universal education, especially of girls, pays a twofold benefit. Investments are more likely to be productive with a better-educated workforce to draw on; hence investments are more likely to be made. Educated women are likely to want at least as much education for their children as they had, and they are likely to have relatively attractive opportunities outside the home — so the birthrate is likely to fall.

It is certainly the case that the developing countries of the world appear, for the most part, to be going through the demographic transition faster than the economies of today's industrial core did in the past three centuries. Thus current estimates of the world's population in 2050 are markedly lower than the estimates of a decade ago. Ten years ago the projected global population in 2050 was 16 billion or more; today it is 12 billion or less. This is due, in part at least, to rapid expansions in educational attainment in today's developing economies.

A high level of educational attainment also raises the efficiency of labour both by teaching skills directly and by making it easier to advance the general level of technological expertise. A leading-edge economy with a high level of educational attainment is likely to have more inventions. A follower economy with a high level of educational attainment is likely to have a more successful time at adapting to local conditions the inventions and innovations from the industrial core of the world economy. How large these effects are at the macroeconomic level is uncertain, but that they are there nobody doubts.

The East Asian economies, especially, provide examples of how uncorrupt and well-managed developmental states can follow macroeconomic policies that accelerate economic growth and convergence. These economies, which have provided incentives to accelerate the demographic transition and boost savings and investment, have managed to close the gap vis-à-vis the world economy's industrial core faster than anyone would have believed possible.

POLICIES FOR TECHNOLOGICAL ADVANCE

Without better technology, increases in capital stock produced by investment rapidly run into diminishing returns. And without improvements in the "technologies" of organization, government, and education, productivity stagnates.

Somewhat surprisingly, economists have relatively little to say about what governs technological progress. Why did better technology raise living standards by 2 percent annually a generation ago but by less than 1 percent today? Why did technology progress by only 0.25 percent per year in the early 1800s? Improving literacy, communications, and research and development may help explain faster progress since the Industrial Revolution than before it and faster progress in the twentieth than in the nineteenth century. Yet, as noted above, as important a feature of recent economic history as the post-1973 productivity slowdown remains largely a mystery.

INVENTION AND INNOVATION

Economists note that technological progress has two components: science (solid-state physics and the invention of the transistor, the mapping of the human genome, the discovery that potassium nitrate, sulfur, and charcoal when mixed together and exposed to heat have interesting properties) and research and development that leads to successful innovation. About pure science economists have almost nothing to say. About research and development, and the innovations it generates, economists have rather more to say.

Economists note that perhaps 75 percent of all scientists and engineers in the U.S. and other industrialized countries work on research and development for private firms. R&D spending amounts to about 3 percent of GDP in the United States and other advanced industrial economies. One-fifth of total gross investment is research and development. More than half of net investment is research and development — investments in knowledge, as opposed to investments in machinery, equipment, structures, and infrastructure.

Businesses conduct investments in R&D to increase their profits. Firms spend money on R&D for reasons analogous to those that lead them to expand their capacity or improve their factories. If the expected present value of profits from an R&D project at the prevailing rate are greater than the costs of the project, then the business will spend money on the project. If not, then it will not.

RIVALRY AND EXCLUDABILITY

But there are features of technology that make thinking about the R&D process more complicated than thinking about other types of investment. First and most important, research and development is a public good. A firm that has discovered something — a new and more profitable process, a new and better way of organizing the factory, a new type of commodity that can be produced — will not reap the entire social benefit from its discovery. Other businesses can examine the innovation — the product, the process, the method of organization — and copy it. They can probably do so for a much lower cost than it took to research and develop the innovation in the first place.

By contrast, a firm that has just spent a large sum to buy and move into a new building does not have to worry that any firm will use that building as well. As a commodity, a building — or a machine, or even the skills and experience inside a worker's head — is both rival and excludable. To say that a commodity is *rival* means that if one firm is using it, another firm cannot do so: I cannot use that hammer to pound this nail if you are now using it to pound that other nail. To say that a commodity is *excludable* means that the "owner" of the commodity can easily monitor who is using it and can easily keep those whom he or she does not authorize from using it.

Most physical commodities are (or, with the assistance of the legal system, can easily be made) both rival and excludable. But by their nature ideas are not. Ideas are definitely not rival — there is nothing in the physical universe that makes it impossible for me to use the same idea you are using. And ideas are hard to make excludable as well: How can you keep me from thinking what I want to think?

PATENTS AND COPYRIGHTS

To protect ideas and **intellectual property** in general, countries have **patent laws and copyrights.** *Patents* give a firm that has discovered something new the right to exclude anyone else from using that discovery for a period of years. But even the strictest patent and copyright laws are incomplete. Often the most valuable part of the R&D process is figuring out not how to do something but whether or not it (or something very close to it) can be done at all. Once a patent has been granted, other firms can and do search for alternative ways of making it or ways of making something close to it that are not covered by the patent.

Governments seeking to establish patent laws face a difficult dilemma. If their patent laws are strong, then much of the modern technology in the economy will be restricted in use: either restricted to being used only by the inventor or restricted because the inventor is charging other firms high licensing fees to use the technology (or not letting them use it at all). There is no social cost involved in letting everyone use the idea or the process or the innovation, once it is discovered. Information, after all, wants to be free. Thus a government that enacts strict patent laws is pushing the average level of technology used in its factories and businesses at some particular moment far below the level that could be achieved at that particular moment.

On the other hand, if the patent laws are weak and thus provide little protection to inventors and innovators, then the profits that inventors and innovators earn will be low. Why then should businesses devote money and resources to research and development? They will not. And the pace of innovation, and thus of technological improvement, will slow to a crawl.

This dilemma cannot be evaded. The profits from innovation come because the innovator has a monopoly right to the innovation — and hence the rest of the economy is excluded from using that item of technology. Reduce the degree of exclusion to lower the deadweight loss from using less-than-best-practice technology, and you will find that you have reduced the rewards to research and development (and thus presumably the pace of R&D as well). Increase the strength of the patent system to raise the rewards to research and development, and you will find that you have increased the gap between the average technology used in the economy and the feasible best practice.

Moreover, technological progress depends on more than the *appropriability* of research — the extent to which the increased productivity made possible by innovation boosts the profits of the innovating firm. It also depends on the productivity of research: how much in the way of new productivity-enhancing inventions is produced by a given investment in R&D? Economists don't know much about the interactions among product development, applied research, and basic research, so they have little to say about how to improve the productivity of research and the pace of productivity growth.

WILL GOVERNMENTS FOLLOW GOOD POLICIES?

That governments *can* assist in growth and development does not mean that governments *will*. The broad experience of growth in developing economies — outside the East Asian Pacific Rim, outside the OECD — has been that governments often *won't*. Over the past two decades many have argued that typical systems of regulation in developing countries have retarded development by

- Embarking on "prestige" industrialization programs that keep resources from shifting to activities in which the country had a long-run comparative advantage.
- Inducing firms and entrepreneurs to devote their energies to seeking rents by lobbying governments, instead of seeking profits by lowering costs.
- Creating systems of regulation and project approval that have degenerated into extortion machines for manufacturing bribes for the bureaucrats.

Many governments — particularly unelected governments — are not *that* interested in economic development. Giving valuable industrial franchises to the nephews of the dictator; making sure that members of your ethnic group are in key places to extort bribes; or taking the foreign exchange that would have been spent importing productive machinery and equipment and using it instead to buy more modern weapons for the army — these can seem more attractive options. In the absence of political democracy, the checks on a government that does not seek economic development are few.

Moreover, checks on government that do exist may not be helpful. In a non-democracy, or a shaky semidemocracy, there are two possible sources of pressure on the government: riots in the capital and coups by the soldiers. Even a government that seeks only the best for its people in terms of economic growth will have to deal with these sources of pressure and will have to avoid riots in the capital and coups by the soldiers.

Coups by the soldiers are best avoided by spending money on the military. Riots in the capital are best avoided by making sure that the price of food is low and that influential opinion leaders in the capital are relatively happy with their material standards of living. Thus governments find themselves driven to policies that redistribute income from the farms to the cities, from exporting businesses to urban consumers of imported goods, from those who have the power to invest and make the economy grow to those who have the power to overthrow the government.

If the rulers have the worst of motives, government degenerates into *kleptocracy*: rule by the thieves. If government has the best of motives, it is still hard to avoid policies that diminish saving and retard the ability to translate savings into productive investment. W. W. Rostow recounts a visit by President Kennedy to Indonesia in the early 1960s; Kennedy talked about economic development and a South Asian Development Bank to provide capital for Indonesia's economic growth. Indonesia's then-dictator Sukarno responded, "Mr. President, development takes too long. Give me West Irian [province, the western half of the island of New Guinea, to annex] instead."

Taken as a group, the poor countries of the world have *not* closed any of the gap relative to the world's industrial leaders since World War II.

NEOLIBERALISM

Much thinking about the proper role of government in economic growth over the past two decades has led to conclusions that are today called *neoliberal*. The government has a sphere of core competencies — administration of justice, maintenance of macroeconomic stability, avoidance of deep recessions, some infrastructure development, provision of social insurance — at which it is effective. But there is a large area of potential activities in which governments (or, at least, governments that do not have the bureaucratic honesty and efficiency needed for a successful *developmental state*) are more likely to be destructive than constructive — hence the neoliberal recommendation that governments attempt to shrink their role back to their core competencies and thus to deregulate industries and privatize public enterprises. Whether such policies will in fact lead to convergence rather than continued divergence is still an open question.

RECAP   POLICIES AND LONG-RUN GROWTH

Most people today live in economies that, while far poorer than the leading-edge post-industrial nations of the world's economic core, have successfully climbed onto the escalator of economic growth and thus the escalator to modernity. A follower economy with a higher level of educational attainment is likely to have a much more successful time at adapting to local conditions inventions and innovations from the industrial core of the world economy. Thus education appears to be a key policy for successful economic growth outside the industrial core. Inside the industrial core, without better technology increases in the capital stock produced by investment rapidly run into diminishing returns. One-fifth of total gross investment is research and development. More than half of net investment is research and development — investments in knowledge, as opposed to investments in machinery, equipment, structures, and infrastructure.

That governments *can* assist in growth and development does not mean that governments *will*. Many governments — particularly unelected governments — are not *that* interested in economic development. In the absence of political democracy, the checks on a government that does not seek economic development are few.

CHAPTER SUMMARY

1. Before the commercial revolution — before 1500 or so — economic growth was very slow. Populations grew at a glacial pace. And as best we can tell there were no significant increases in standards of living for millennia before 1500: Humanity was caught in a Malthusian trap.

2. The way out of the Malthusian trap opened about 1500. Thereafter populations grew, and standards of living and levels of material productivity grew as well.

3. The Industrial Revolution was the start of the current epoch: the epoch of modern economic growth. Beginning in the mid-eighteenth century the pace of invention and innovation ratcheted up. Key inventions replaced muscle with machine power, and material productivity levels boomed.

4. Modern economic growth is well-described by the growth model in Chapter 3, which is why we spent so much time on it. Output per worker and capital per worker increase at a pace measured in percent per year, a pace that is extraordinarily rapid in long-term historical perspective.

5. Looking across nations, the world today is an astonishingly unequal place in relative terms. The relative gap between rich and poor nations in material productivity is much greater than it has ever been before.

6. Combining the determinants of the steady-state capital–output ratio with the proximate determinants — the level of technological knowledge in a country after World War II and its average level of educational attainment — accounts for the overwhelming bulk of variation in the relative wealth and poverty of nations today.

7. Macro policies to increase economic growth are policies to accelerate the demographic transition (through education), to boost savings rates, to boost the amount of real investment that a country gets for a given savings effort, and (again through education) to boost the rate of invention or of technology transfer.

8. The U.S. economy seems to have reversed its post-1973 slowdown in growth since the early 1980s whereas in Canada such a reversal took place a decade later.

9. What are the prospects for successful rapid development in tomorrow's world? Do you see the glass as half empty or half full?

KEY TERMS

demographic transition (p. 116)

divergence (p. 126)

Industrial Revolution (p. 118)

intellectual property (p. 139)

Malthusian age (p. 115)

natural-resource scarcity (p. 116)

patent laws and copyrights (p. 139)

productivity growth (p. 119)

productivity slowdown (p. 121)

ANALYTICAL EXERCISES

1. Would an increase in the saving and investment share of Canada's total output raise growth in productivity and living standards?

2. Many observers project that by the end of the twenty-first century the population of the industralized countries will be stable. Using the Solow growth model, what would such a downward shift in the growth rate of the labour force do to the growth of output per worker and to the growth of total output (consider both the effect on the steady-state growth path and the transition from the "old" positive population growth to the "new" zero population growth steady-state growth path)?

3. What are the arguments for having a strong patent system to boost economic growth? What are the arguments for having a weak system of protections of intellectual property? Under what systems do you think that the first will outweigh the second? Under what circumstances do you think that the second will outweigh the first?

4. What steps do you think that international organizations — the UN, the World Bank, or the IMF — could take to improve political leaders' incentives to follow growth-promoting policies?

5. Suppose somebody who hasn't taken any economics courses asks you why humanity escaped from the

Malthusian trap — of very low standards of living and slow population growth rates that nevertheless put pressure on available natural resources and kept output per worker from rising — in which humanity found itself between 8000 BC and AD 1800. What answer would you give?

6. Suppose somebody who hasn't taken any economics courses asks you why some countries are so very, very much poorer than others in the world today. What answer would you give?

7. The *endogenous growth theorists,* led by Stanford's Paul Romer, argue that it is a mistake to separate the determinants of the efficiency of labour from investment — that investments both raise the capital–worker ratio and increase the efficiency of labour as workers learn about the new technology installed with the purchase of new, modern capital goods. If the endogenous growth theorists are correct, is the case for government policies to boost national savings and investment rates strengthened or weakened? Why?

8. Suppose that population growth depends on the level of output per worker, so

$$n = 0.0001 \times \left[\left(\frac{Y}{L} \right) - \$200 \right] \qquad (1)$$

The population growth rate n is zero if output per worker equals $200, and each $100 increase in output per worker raises the population growth rate by 1 percent per year. Suppose also that the economy is in its Malthusian regime, so the rate of increase of the efficiency of labour E is zero and output per worker is given by

$$\frac{Y_t}{L_t} = \left(\frac{s}{n + \delta} \right)^{\frac{\alpha}{1-\alpha}} E_0 \qquad (2)$$

with the diminishing-returns-to-investment parameter $\alpha = 0.5$, the depreciation rate $\delta = 0.04$, and the efficiency of labour $E_0 = \$100$.

a. Suppose that the savings rate s is equal to 8 percent per year. Graph (on the same set of axes) steady-state output-per-worker (Y/L) as a function of the population growth rate n from equation (2) and the population growth rate n as a function of output per worker (Y/L) from equation (1).

b. Where do the curves cross? For what levels of output per worker Y/L and population growth n is the economy (i) on its steady-state path and (ii) at its Malthusian rate of population growth?

c. Suppose that the savings rate rises by an infinitesimal amount — say, by one-hundredth of 1 percentage point, from 0.08 to 0.0801. Calculate approximately how the equilibrium position of the economy will change. By how much, and in which direction, will steady-state output per worker change? By how much, and in which direction, will the population growth rate change?

9. Suppose we have our standard growth model with s = 20 percent, n = 1 percent, g = 1 percent, and α = 3 percent. Suppose also that the current level of the efficiency of labour E is $10,000 per year and the current level of capital per worker is $50,000. Suppose further that the parameter α in the production function

$$\frac{Y_t}{L_t} = \left(\frac{K_t}{L_t} \right)^{\alpha} \times E_t^{1-\alpha}$$

is equal to 1: α = 1.

a. What can you say about the future growth of output per worker in this economy? Can you write down an equation for what output per worker will be at any date in the future?

b. Suppose that the savings rate s is not 20 but 15 percent. How will the future growth of output per worker be different?

c. Why aren't the normal tools of analysis and rules of thumb of the growth model of much use when α = 1? (Consider the shape of the production function and what that says about diminishing returns to investment.)

POLICY EXERCISES

1. Take a look in the back of this book at the rate of growth of real GDP per worker in Canada over the period 1991 to 2001. How large was the "trend" component of growth per year? How large was the "cycle" component of growth per year?

2. Take a look at the first three columns of the "Canadian Macroeconomic Data" table at the back of the book. Identify the years that are business cycle

peaks — years that are followed by a decline in real GDP or real GDP per worker. Are the two possible sets of business cycle peaks the same? Calculate economic growth rates between business cycle peaks, and make a table of these annual peak-to-peak growth rates. Is this a good way of looking for and estimating changes in long-run economic growth trends in Canada? Why or why not?

3. Look at the relative purchasing-power-parity levels of GDP per worker for the G-7 economies — Germany, France, Britain, Italy, Canada, Japan, and the United States. Have the nations drawn closer together in levels of GDP per worker in the past five years?

4. What items of news have you read about in the past week that you would classify as shifts in macro policies that encourage growth?

5. What items of news have you read about in the past week that you would classify as shifts in macro policies that discourage growth?

6. What items of news have you read about in the past week that you would classify as shifts in micro policies that encourage growth?

7. What items of news have you read about in the past week that you would classify as shifts in micro policies that discourage growth?

8. Do you believe that over the next three decades the lower-income countries of the world will catch up to — or at least draw nearer in relative terms to — the high-income countries? Why or why not?

9. Discuss the possible explanations for the productivity gap between Canada and the U.S. What kind of government policies would help in reducing the productivity gap?

Flexible-Price Macroeconomics

This part looks from a direction opposite to the long-run view of the economy presented in Part II. The chapters in this part take a "snapshot" of the economy, looking at the economy over such a short period of time that its productive resources are effectively fixed. They examine not growth but levels. The key questions are:

1. What determines the equilibrium level of real GDP (Y)?

2. What economic forces keep real GDP (Y) at its equilibrium level?

3. What determines the composition of real GDP — the division of production and spending between consumption goods (C), investment goods (I), government purchases (G), and net exports (NX)?

Part III answers these questions in the flexible-price case, in which markets clear — every buyer finds a willing seller and every seller finds a willing buyer. This assumption means, most importantly, that labour supply equals demand: No firms wanting to hire workers are left unsatisfied, and no workers willing to work are left permanently unemployed. (In Part IV, we analyze the case in which prices are sticky, real GDP is not always equal to potential output, and unemployment can rise high above frictional levels.)

Chapter 5 assembles the building blocks of what will become the flexible-price model of the macroeconomy. Chapter 6 puts these building blocks together and assembles the model. It also demonstrates how to use the model to analyze the level and components of real GDP. Chapter 7 turns the focus of attention from production to the price level and shows how to analyze the determinants of the price level and inflation in the flexible-price case.

5

Building Blocks of the Flexible-Price Model

QUESTIONS

What is a full-employment analysis?

What keeps the economy at full employment when wages and prices are flexible?

What determines the level of consumption spending?

What determines the level of investment spending?

What determines the level of net exports?

What determines the level of the exchange rate?

I n the previous two chapters we have looked at long-run growth — at how the economy develops and evolves over periods as long as generations. In this chapter we shift our point of view and take a "snapshot" of the economy, looking at it over such a short period that its productive resources are fixed.

In this short-period analysis, the key questions are three: What determines the equilibrium level of real GDP (Y)? What are the economic forces that keep real GDP (Y) at its equilibrium value? And what determines the division of real GDP between consumption spending (C), investment spending (I), government purchases (G), and net exports (NX)? This chapter provides one answer to the first two questions, working under the assumption that prices and wages are fully flexible — also known as the classical model. If wages and prices are sufficiently flexible (as we assume they are here in Part III), then markets clear: Quantities demanded are equal to quantities supplied. In particular, the labour market clears: Employment is equal to the labour force (save for some "frictional" unemployment), and production is equal to potential output. Should production not be equal to potential output, rising or falling real wages will quickly lower or raise firms' demands for labour and bring the economy back to equilibrium.

The third question cannot be fully answered in this chapter. What this chapter does is assemble the building blocks needed to answer it. The full answer, however, comes only in Chapter 6.

Whereas in the classical model all prices and wages are fully flexible, there is another school of thought that focuses on a shorter time horizon over which workers and firms sign contracts that fix wages in the short run. According to this theory, with wages fixed in this manner, prices will also be sticky in the short run; and with sticky prices the equilibrium of the economy will, in general, not involve full employment. This model, also known as the Keynesian model, will be discussed in Chapters 8 to 10.

We should also be clear about the flexible-price model of this chapter and the growth models of chapters 3 and 4. In the flexible-price model capital is fixed, whereas in the growth models capital was allowed to adjust. In that sense, the growth models focus on a longer time horizon than the flexible-price model.

5.1 POTENTIAL OUTPUT AND REAL WAGES

In the flexible-price model of the macroeconomy, two sets of factors determine the levels of potential (and actual) output and of real wages: the production function and the balance of supply and demand in the labour market.

THE PRODUCTION FUNCTION

Chapter 3 introduced the **production function**, the rule that tells us how much the economy can produce given its available productive resources. Output (Y) is determined by the labour force (L), the economy's capital stock (K), and the efficiency of labour (E). The production function tells us that output is

$$Y = F(K, E \times L) \tag{5.1}$$

The graph in Figure 5.1 shows one slice of this production function — the relationship between the capital stock K and output Y, holding labour L and the efficiency of labour E fixed.

In Chapter 3 all the variables in the production function had the subscript t, indicating the year they referred to. Because we were looking at changes over time, keeping track of which year we were talking about was important. In this chapter we are looking at the economy at one instant, not over time, and so we do not have to keep track of the year. To reduce clutter in the equations, we will drop the subscripts and speak simply of the labour force L, the capital stock K, the efficiency of labour E, and the level of output Y.

The assumption that wages and prices are flexible was commonly made by the so-called classical economists, who wrote before World War II. Thus this assumption is also called the *classical assumption*. The classical assumption guarantees that markets work — that prices adjust rapidly to eliminate gaps between the quantities demanded and the quantities supplied. Thus no businesses find their inventories of unsold goods piling up, and there is full employment: Everyone who wants a job (at the market-clearing level of wages) can get a job, and every business that wants to hire a worker (at the market-clearing level of wages) can hire a worker. Because

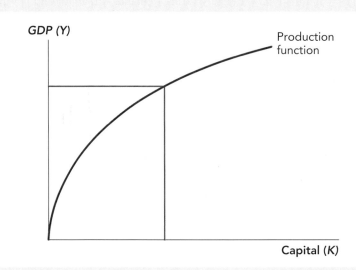

FIGURE 5.1
The Production Function
Holding the labour force and the efficiency of labour constant, real GDP increases as the capital stock increases. Because each successive addition to the capital stock produces a smaller increase in output, the production function is curved. The higher the level of α, the greater the curvature and the more rapidly the returns to investment diminish.

of full employment, actual output is equal to potential output: There is no gap between the economy's productive potential and the level of output the economy produces.

The classical assumption made in Chapters 5, 6, and 7 means that Part III is devoted to full-employment flexible-price macroeconomics. The flexible-price assumption is not always a good one, however. Experience has shown that a market economy does not always work well and does not always produce full employment. So in Part IV we will drop this assumption and make instead the "Keynesian" assumption that wages and prices are sticky (see Table 5.1).

If the classical flexible-price assumption is not always a good one to make, why make it at all? It *is* a good assumption if wages and prices are relatively flexible and have enough time to adjust in order to balance supply and demand. The classical assumption simplifies the analysis of several issues, making it easier to grasp how

TABLE 5.1
Classical Flexible-Price versus Keynesian Sticky-Price Analyses

Issue	Classical	Keynesian
Wages and prices	Fully flexible	Can be "sticky" or fixed
Expectations	Consistent with full employment	Volatile — can take a number of forms
Labour market	Always in equilibrium with full employment	Can be out of equilibrium, causing involuntary unemployment
Effect of shocks to aggregate demand	Change in the composition but not the level of GDP	Change in the composition and the level of GDP

the macroeconomy works. In general it is better to start with the simpler cases before looking at more complicated ones. Moreover, the way an economy functions under the flexible-price assumption provides a useful baseline against which to assess economic performance. Nevertheless, we must remember that Part III presents only one model of the economy: the classical model. The Keynesian sticky-price model behaves very differently in a number of ways.

THE LABOUR MARKET

When markets work well, what keeps the economy at full employment and actual production equal to potential output? One way to look at this issue is that the answer lies in the adjustment of prices and supply and demand in the labour market. When the supply of and demand for labour balance, real GDP will equal potential output.

LABOUR DEMAND

Economists try to suppress every detail and difference that does not matter to the overall result in order to simplify the analysis and focus it on the important factors that count. Because differences between businesses will not matter, let's think about an economy with a large number of competitive firms, each of which owns K units of capital. Each of these firms hires L workers and pays each worker the same wage W. Each firm sells Y units of its product at a per-unit price P. The typical firm does not control either the wages it must pay or the prices it receives; those are determined by the market. The firm tries to make as much money as it can. The firm's profits are simply its revenues minus its costs, and its only costs are the wages it pays to workers. Therefore

$$\text{Profits} = \text{revenues} - \text{costs}$$
$$= (P \times Y) - (W \times L) \qquad (5.2)$$

To figure out how many workers to hire, the firm follows two simple rules:

1. Hire workers to boost output.
2. Stop hiring when the extra revenue from the output produced by the last worker hired just equals his or her wage.

The value of the output produced by the last worker hired is the product price P times the **marginal product of labour** (**MPL**). The cost of hiring the last worker is his or her wage W. The firm will keep hiring until

$$(P \times MPL) - W = 0$$

What is the marginal product of labour? For simplicity, suppose labour efficiency E is fixed at unity. The typical firm owns K units of capital, and its output is what can be made by that capital and the firm's workers according to the production function

$$Y = F(K, L)$$

The marginal product of labour is the difference between what the firm can produce with its current labour force L and what it would produce if it hired one more worker (see Figure 5.2):

$$MPL = F(K, L + 1) - F(K, L)$$

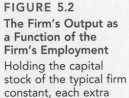

FIGURE 5.2
The Firm's Output as a Function of the Firm's Employment
Holding the capital stock of the typical firm constant, each extra worker the firm employs produces smaller and smaller increases in total output. As the level of employment increases, this marginal product of labour (*MPL*) decreases.

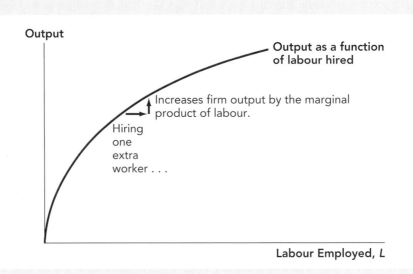

FIGURE 5.3
The Typical Firm's Hiring Policy
The typical firm chooses to hire the number of workers that make marginal revenue — the *MPL* times the product price *P* — equal to the wage *W*. At that point the revenue and cost curves are parallel, and profit is maximized.

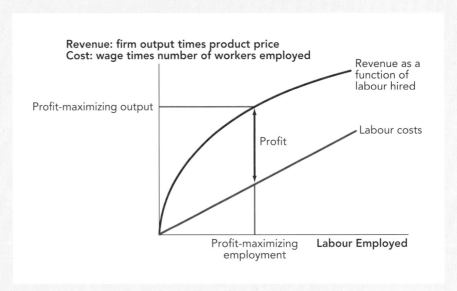

Notice the *MPL* is simply the slope of the production function in Figure 5.2. Further, the slope of the production function becomes smaller as *L* increases, which means that the *MPL* falls as *L* increases.

As Figure 5.3 shows, the firm hires workers up to the point where the product price times the marginal product of labour equals the wage:

$$(P \times MPL) - W = 0$$

or where the *MPL* is equal to the **real wage** *W/P*:

$$MPL = W/P \tag{5.3}$$

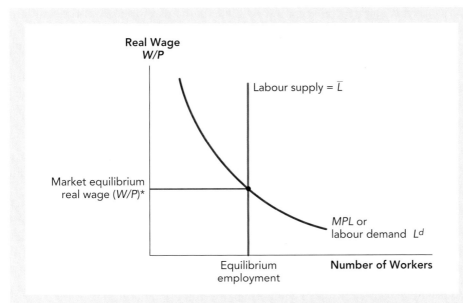

FIGURE 5.4
Equilibrium in the Labour Market
The equilibrium level of employment is equal to the labour force. At the equilibrium level of the real wage, there is neither excess demand for nor excess supply of labour.

In Figure 5.4 we plot the *MPL* as a function of the amount of labour (or number of workers) employed. As we have noted above, the *MPL* falls as the number of workers hired increases. Hence, the *MPL* schedule is downward sloping. Next note, that if we were to measure the real wage on the vertical axis in Figure 5.4, then for any given real wage *W/P* the *MPL* schedule will give us the amount of labour (or number of workers) that the firm would like to employ. Hence, the *MPL* schedule is the **labour demand** L^d schedule.

The *MPL* schedule in Figure 5.4 is the labour demand schedule for a single firm. Strictly speaking, in order to derive the economy-wide labour demand schedule we should aggregate the labour demand schedules of all the firms in the economy. Recall that for simplicity we have assumed that all firms are identical, which means that the aggregate labour demand schedule is the number of firms in the economy multiplied by *MPL*. In macroeconomics we simplify matters, and bypass this aggregation, by assuming that there is a single representative firm in the economy; that is, the *MPL* schedule is assumed to be the schedule for the economy-wide labour demand.

LABOUR MARKET EQUILIBRIUM

In the section above we calculated economy-wide labour demand. But what is the labour supply? The answer is simple: It is the number of workers who want to work. The labour market will be in equilibrium when firms' total demand for workers is equal to the labour force.

Can the labour market not be in equilibrium if wages and prices are flexible? Think about what would happen if **labour supply** were not equal to demand. Suppose there are more workers than firms want to hire at current wages and prices. Then some of the unemployed will underbid the employed workers, offering to take their jobs and work for less. The workers who are employed will respond by offering to accept lower wages to keep their jobs. The wage *W* will decline relative to the price level P, and the real wage W/P will fall. As the real wage falls, firms will hire more workers.

Suppose firms want to hire more workers than there are people in the labour force. Some firms will try to bid workers away from other firms by offering higher wages. The real wage W/P will rise. As the real wage rises, employers will reduce the quantity of labour they demand. Thus, in **labour market equilibrium**, labour demand L^d will equal total labour force $\overline{L}$ (see Figure 5.4):

$$L^d = \overline{L} \tag{5.4}$$

Labour demand is equal to the labour force when the real wage WP is $(W/P)^*$. As long as wages and prices are flexible enough for this adjustment process to work, the economy will remain at full employment.

Note that a full-employment economy is not necessarily the best or even a good economy. The real incomes of people who don't own chunks of the capital stock are their real wages. If real wages are low, their real incomes will be small, and social welfare may be low.

EMPLOYMENT AND OUTPUT

When the labour market is in equilibrium, the output produced is equal to

$$Y^* = F(K, \overline{L}) \tag{5.5}$$

where Y^* is called potential output.

The conclusion is clear: If markets work well — if wages and prices are flexible and adjust to balance supply and demand, and if markets are competitive — then the actual level of production in the economy Y will equal the economy's **potential output** Y^*, as Figure 5.5 shows. Box 5.1 derives the equilibrium full-employment real wage and potential output when the production function is Cobb-Douglas.

FIGURE 5.5

In a Full-Employment Economy, Real GDP Equals Potential Output

When the economy is at full employment, the level of employment is equal to the labour force and real GDP is equal to potential output.

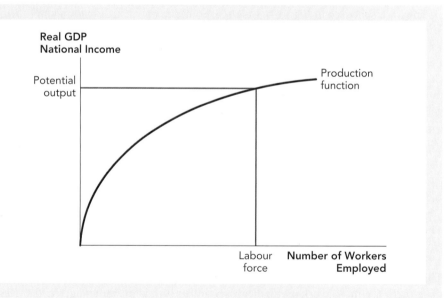

LABOUR MARKET EQUILIBRIUM WITH COBB-DOUGLAS PRODUCTION FUNCTION

Assume that the economy's production function is Cobb-Douglas:

$$Y = K^{\alpha} \times L^{(1-\alpha)}$$

Then the marginal product of labour is

$$MPL = (1-\alpha) \times K^{\alpha} \times L^{-\alpha}$$

Hence, using equation (5.3), we can derive the demand for labour L^d as

$$L^d = \left(\frac{1}{1-\alpha} \times \frac{W}{P} \times K^{-\alpha} \right)^{\frac{1}{\alpha}} = K \times \left(\frac{(1-\alpha)}{W/P} \right)^{\frac{1}{\alpha}}$$

If the total labour force is $\bar{L}$ then the equilibrium real wage can be determined from the labour market equilibrium condition (5.4):

$$\bar{L} = K \times \left(\frac{1-\alpha}{W/P} \right)^{\frac{1}{\alpha}}$$

which can be solved for W/P to give us the equilibrium real wage:

$$\left(\frac{W}{P} \right)^{*} = (1-\alpha) \times \left(\frac{K}{L} \right)^{\alpha}$$

Assuming that $K = 70$, $\alpha = 0.3$, and $\bar{L} = 100$, the equilibrium real wage is

$$\left(\frac{W}{P} \right)^{*} = 0.7 \times \left(\frac{70}{100} \right)^{0.3} = 0.63$$

and potential output is

$$Y^* = 70^{0.3} \times 100^{0.7} = 89.85$$

RECAP   POTENTIAL OUTPUT AND REAL WAGES

A flexible-price economy is a full-employment economy: Wages are flexible enough to keep supply and demand in balance in the labour market. Because there are enough jobs for all the workers who want to work at the prevailing market-clearing wage, real GDP in a flexible-price economy is always equal to potential output and unemployment is not a problem. This classical model of the macroeconomy is the polar opposite of the Keynesian model, where prices and wages are sticky, markets do not always clear with supply and demand in balance, high unemployment is possible, and there are gaps between real GDP and potential output.

5.2 DOMESTIC SPENDING

In Chapter 2 we saw via the national income identity that total spending is divided into four components:

- Consumption spending (C)
- Investment spending (I)
- Government purchases (G)
- Net exports, the balancing item (NX)

These four components add up to national income, which according to the circular flow principle, is the same as aggregate demand (E) and real GDP, Y;

$$C + I + G + NX = Y \qquad (5.6)$$

In this section we look at the determinants of the three domestic components of spending, C, I, and G. We discuss international trade in a later section.

CONSUMPTION SPENDING

Individual households make the spending and saving decisions that ultimately determine the flow of consumption spending. In this section we first examine how households divide their income up among taxes, saving, and consumption spending. Then we will see how consumption spending varies in response to changes in income and in other aspects of the economic environment.

THE HOUSEHOLD'S DECISIONS

The wages of workers plus the profits of property owners (rent, interest, dividends, and retained earnings) add up to national income. Because at this level of analysis we are uninterested in any accounting distinctions between national income and real GDP, we use the letter Y to represent both. (Recall that the circular flow principle guarantees that whatever businesses produce and sell must show up as income for households.)

Households pay some of their income to the government in net taxes — taxes less transfer payments from the government — which we write as T. To keep the analysis simple, throughout this book we will assume that net taxes are equal to the constant average tax rate t multiplied by national income:

$$T = t \times Y \qquad (5.7)$$

In the real world taxes are not proportional to income. Our tax system is some-what progressive, which means that richer taxpayers on average pay more of their income in taxes than do the relatively poor. Once again, however, the complications induced by the fact that our tax system is not proportional to income are not central to the analysis, so we follow economists' standard practice of simplifying wherever possible.

The amount left after households pay their taxes is their **disposable income**, written Y^D:

$$Y^D = Y - T = (1 - t)Y \qquad (5.8)$$

Households also save some of their income to boost their wealth and future spending. We represent private household savings by S^H — S for "savings" and H for "household." (Note that household savings include the retained earnings of corporations: The National Income and Expenditure Accounts treats undistributed corporate earnings that are retained by the corporation as if they were distributed to the shareholding households and then immediately reinvested back into the corporation.) Households spend the rest of their income — everything that is not saved or paid to the government in taxes — buying consumption goods:

$$C = Y^D - S^H = Y - T - S^H \qquad (5.9)$$

In Canada today, consumption spending C — purchases by households for their own use, from pine nuts and flour to washing machines and automobiles — accounts for roughly 57 percent of GDP. We will break consumption spending down into a baseline level of consumption (defined as the value of a parameter C_0) and a fraction (a parameter C_y) of disposable income Y^D, or a fraction $C_y \times (1 - t)$ of total income Y:

$$C = C_0 + C_y \times Y^D = C_0 + C_y \times (1 - t)Y \qquad (5.10)$$

Thus we assume that consumption spending C is a linear function of real GDP Y.

Notice that in writing this particular **consumption function**, we have once again followed the economists' principle (or vice) of ruthless simplification. In this complicated world, consumption spending does not depend on disposable income alone. Other factors affecting it include changes in the real interest rate, household total stock market and real estate wealth, the demographic structure of the population, income distribution, consumers' relative optimism, expected future income growth, tolerance for risk, and whether consumers see changes in disposable income as transitory or permanent. (If consumers expect an income increase to be transitory, they will save most of it and spend only a little; if they expect an income increase to be permanent, they will spend most of it.) But here and throughout the book we will sweep these complications under the rug. We will think about only baseline consumption C_0, the marginal propensity to consume C_y, and disposable income Y^D as the determinants of consumption spending (although we will occasionally sneak in other factors by saying that they change baseline consumption C_0).

THE MARGINAL PROPENSITY TO CONSUME

The baseline level of consumption, the parameter C_0, is the amount households would spend on consumption goods if they had no income at all. That is, it is the amount by which they would draw down their wealth in the absence of income in order to keep body and soul together.

The **marginal propensity to consume (MPC)**, the same parameter C_y in the consumption function, is the amount by which consumption spending rises in response to a \$1 increase in disposable income (see Figure 5.6). We are sure that C_y is greater than zero: If incomes rise, households will use some of their extra income to boost their consumption spending. We are also sure that C_y is less than 1: As incomes rise, households will increase their savings as well; they will not spend all their extra income on consumption goods.

The value of the marginal propensity to consume also depends on how long people expect the change in income to last. As discussed in Appendix 5A, if people expect the change in income to be *permanent*, then the MPC is likely to be relatively large. If they expect the change in income to be *transitory* — and think their income next year will revert back to its normal pattern — the MPC is likely to be relatively small. With these two parameters, C_0 and C_y, we can calculate what the total level of consumption spending will be for each possible level of disposable income Y^D (see Box 5.2).

FIGURE 5.6

The Consumption Function

Consumption spending depends on the level of disposable income and two parameters: C_y (the marginal propensity to consume, or MPC) and C_0 (the baseline level of consumption). If we know both these parameters and the value of disposable income Y^D, we can plot the level of consumption spending at each possible level of disposable income.

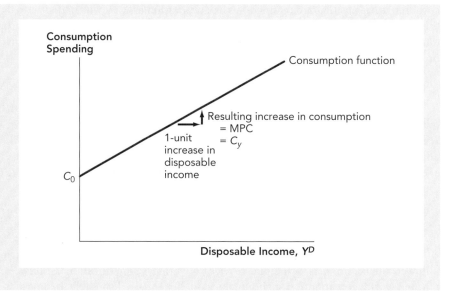

BOX 5.2

EXAMPLE

CALCULATING CONSUMPTION FROM INCOME

If we know the parameters C_0 (the baseline level of consumption), C_y (the marginal propensity to consume, or MPC), and t (the tax rate), we can calculate the level of consumption spending C for any level of total national income Y using the equation

$$C = C_0 + C_y \times Y^D = C_0 + C_y \times (1 - t)Y$$

Suppose the tax rate t is 25 percent, the total national income Y is \$1 trillion, the baseline level of consumption C_0 is \$200 billion, and the marginal propensity to consume C_y is 0.6. We first calculate disposable income — how much households have left after paying their taxes. Disposable income is equal to $(1 - t)Y$, which for these parameter values and this level of national income is

$$(1 - 0.25) \times \$1 \text{ trillion} = \$750 \text{ billion}$$

We can then calculate consumption:

$$\begin{aligned} C &= C_0 + C_y \times \$750 \text{ billion} \\ &= \$200 \text{ billion} + 0.6 \times \$750 \text{ billion} \\ &= \$650 \text{ billion} \end{aligned}$$

What will happen if disposable income rises from \$750 billion to \$800 billion? Consumption spending will rise from \$650 billion to \$680 billion, that is, by an amount equal to the marginal propensity to consume, 0.6, times the change in disposable income, \$50 billion.

INVESTMENT SPENDING

In Canada today investment spending averages roughly 20 percent of GDP. But investment spending is the most volatile and variable component of GDP.

(*Note:* Economists' definition of "investment spending" is probably not what you think it is; Boxes 5.3 and 5.4 explain how economists define and calculate investment spending.)

Fluctuations in economy-wide investment spending have two sources. First is the interest rate: The higher the real interest rate, the lower is investment spending. A higher real interest rate makes investment projects more expensive for firms to undertake, so they undertake fewer of them. Second is business managers' and investors' confidence — what John Maynard Keynes called their "animal spirits." The higher their confidence, the higher is investment spending. Optimistic managers and investors are more willing to bet their careers and fortunes on the belief that an expansion of productive capacity or some other investment will pay off.

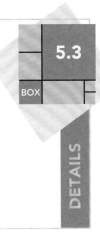

WHAT IS INVESTMENT?

When economists use the term "investment," they mean something different from what most people mean by the word. Most people use it to mean activity such as buying a stock or bond, a certificate of deposit, or commodity futures. But such purchases do not directly increase the economy's capital stock or have any place in the national income and product accounts.

When economists use the term "investment" or "investment spending," they are talking about transactions that add to the capital stock and increase potential output. Such transactions include the purchase and installation of new business machinery and equipment, the construction and purchase of a new building (or the repair of an old one), and a change in business inventories.

KINDS OF INVESTMENT

Economists categorize investment in two different ways. The first distinction they draw is between gross investment and net investment. *Gross investment* is the total sum of spending on machines, construction (houses, factories, office buildings, roads, dams, and bridges), and additions to inventories.

Some of gross investment adds to the capital stock of machines, goods in process, buildings, and other structures that amplify productivity. The rest of gross investment replaces worn-out and obsolete pieces of capital. The amount of gross investment spending that increases the capital stock is called *net investment*. The amount of investment spending that replaces obsolete and worn-out capital is called *depreciation* or capital *consumption*.

Economists also categorize investment according to use, as follows:

1. Residential construction
2. Nonresidential construction
3. Equipment investment
4. Inventory investment

To some degree, these four subcategories of investment have different determinants and different consequences. But in order to simplify and construct a useful model, we ignore those differences.

WHY FIRMS INVEST

A business invests because its managers believe that the investment project will be profitable: The appropriately discounted return on the investment must be greater than the investment's cost. The higher the interest rate, the lower is the appropriately discounted return on the investment project. The higher the interest rate, the smaller is the number of potential investment projects that will be profitable. Thus a lower interest rate leads to higher investment spending.

How many investment projects will a higher interest rate discourage? How much lower will investment be if the interest rate is higher? Analyzing these questions is beyond the scope of this book. (Appendix 5B, however, presents the key concept of *present value,* a tool used in finance to assess whether an investment project is worth undertaking at the prevailing interest rate.)

The interest rate most relevant to determining investment is the long-term, real, risky interest rate. The relevant interest rate is long-term because investment projects affect the business's profits and costs for a long time to come. The relevant interest rate is real — that is, inflation-adjusted — because an investment project gives the business that undertakes it a real, physical asset, not a financial claim denominated in dollars. The relevant interest rate is risky because investment projects are risky. In calculating whether investment projects are worthwhile, be sure to compare apples to apples. Discount the long-term, real, risky profits anticipated from undertaking an investment project by the long-term, real, risky interest rate.

THE INVESTMENT FUNCTION

To model the inverse relationship between the level of investment spending and the long-term, real, risky interest rate, set investment spending I equal to the baseline level of investment (the value of the parameter I_0) minus the **real interest rate r** times the slope of the investment function parameter I_r (see Figure 5.7):

$$I = I_0 - I_r \times r \qquad\qquad (5.11)$$

In the real world, the investment function is very volatile, mainly because it depends so much on the confidence of the firms about the future level of economic activities.

FIGURE 5.7
The Investment Function

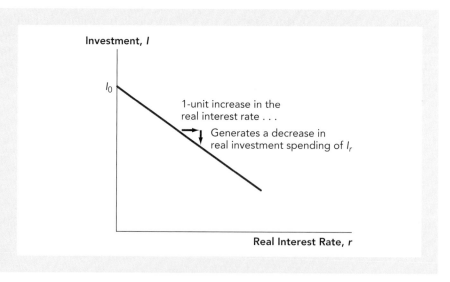

HOW INVESTMENT RESPONDS TO A CHANGE IN INTEREST RATES

From the parameters I_0 (the baseline level of investment) and I_r (the responsiveness of investment to a change in real interest rates) we can calculate the level of investment spending for each possible value of the real interest rate r.

For example, suppose that I_0 is $200 billion and that I_r is $1,000 billion. Then we can use the equation

$$I = I_0 - I_r \times r$$

to calculate that if the real interest rate is 5 percent, then the level of investment spending is $150 billion:

$$I = \$200 \text{ billion} - \$1,000 \text{ billion} \times 0.05 = \$150 \text{ billion}$$

If the real interest rate is 10 percent, the level of investment spending is $100 billion:

$$I = \$200 \text{ billion} - \$1,000 \text{ billion} \times 0.10 = \$100 \text{ billion}$$

And if the real interest rate is 0 percent, the level of investment spending is $200 billion:

$$I = \$200 \text{ billion} - \$1,000 \text{ billion} \times 0 = \$200 \text{ billion}$$

Fluctuations in the confidence of the firms lead to fluctuations in I_0, and hence the investment function. Box 5.5 shows how to use this **investment function** equation to calculate the level of investment spending at a particular interest rate. Box 5.6 presents an alternative way of thinking about the investment function — one that focuses on the stock market, not on interest rates.

Notice the pattern used for parameters so far: C_0, C_y, I_0, I_r. This should make the symbols used in algebraic equations clearer and easier to remember. The capital letter in the name of each parameter tells you what variable is on the left-hand side of the equation in which the parameter appears. A C means that the parameter is part of an equation determining the level of consumption spending C; an I means that the parameter is part of an equation determining the level of investment spending I; and so forth. The subscript tells you the variable by which the parameter is multiplied in that equation. For example, I_r is the amount by which investment spending I changes in response to a change in the real interest rate r.

Like the consumption function, the investment function is an enormous simplification of real-world investment patterns. In the real world, firms' investment decisions depend not only on the real interest rate but also on how much money the firms have available. Total profits are also an important determinant of investment. In the real world, some components of investment — construction, for example — are very sensitive to changes in the real interest rate. Other components of investment — for example, inventory investments by small firms with little access to outside sources of funding — are not. Box 5.7 discusses two tools government policy makers sometimes have at their disposal to change the level of investment.

GOVERNMENT PURCHASES

The federal, provincial, and local governments buy the labour of government employees — judges, teachers, health employees, air traffic controllers, customs

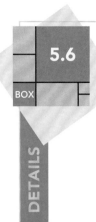

5.6

BOX

DETAILS

THE STOCK MARKET

An alternative way of looking at investment — one that would complicate our models too much for us to use it here — sees the level of investment spending as a function of the level of the stock market. Think about what determines stock market values. Most investors in the stock market face a choice between holding *stocks* — shares of ownership of a corporation that also give you ownership of that corporation's profits or earnings — or holding *bonds:* pieces of paper that represent loans that pay interest. If you invest your money in bonds, you earn the real interest rate *r*. If you invest in shares of stock, your return is equal to your share of the profits of the companies in which you have invested.

When expected future profits are high, investors find stocks more attractive than bonds and thus bid up stock prices. When the real interest rate falls, investors also find stocks more attractive than bonds and bid up stock prices. In either case, the stock market will rise. However, when expected future profits are high, businesses invest more. When the real interest rate falls, businesses find investment projects cheaper and also invest more. The same things that determine the value of the stock market also determine the level of investment spending. The stock market and investment move together: What raises or lowers one raises or lowers the other.

The only significant difference is that causes of fluctuations in investment affect the stock market first and investment spending second. The stock market is thus a very useful leading indicator of investment spending. Keep a close watch on the stock market if you want to forecast the level of investment spending.

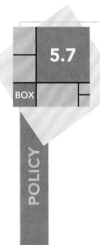

5.7

BOX

POLICY

HOW TO BOOST INVESTMENT

As we saw in Chapters 3 and 4, a high level of saving and investment is one of the keys to a prosperous economy. The higher the share of GDP devoted to investment spending, the higher is the steady-state capital–output ratio and the richer is the economy.

Governments seeking to boost investment have two major tools at their disposal. First, they can lower real interest rates (or induce the central bank to lower them). If real interest rates are lowered, more investment projects will be undertaken and investment spending will rise. Second, governments can try to raise the baseline level of investment by encouraging private decision makers. They can exhort and reassure them. More important, policy makers can try to reduce or eliminate sources of risk. Instilling confidence that the economy will be stable and risks will be managed is perhaps the best way to boost investment by encouraging optimism.

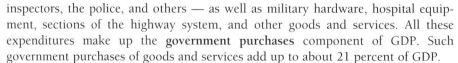

inspectors, the police, and others — as well as military hardware, hospital equipment, sections of the highway system, and other goods and services. All these expenditures make up the **government purchases** component of GDP. Such government purchases of goods and services add up to about 21 percent of GDP.

Note that government *spending* is larger than government *purchases*. In addition to buying goods and services (including the work-time of its employees), the government also spends by transferring money to citizens through welfare and other programs, Employment Insurance benefits, disability benefits, Canada Pensions, interest payments on the public debt, and other **transfer payments**. Because transfer payments do not themselves represent demand for final goods and services, they do not show up directly as a portion of GDP in the government purchases total G. Rather, transfer payments show up in the National Income and Expenditure Accounts as negative taxes. The variable T — taxes — represents **net taxes**, taxes less transfer payments. It is the net amount by which the government's tax and transfer system reduces disposable income.

RECAP   DOMESTIC SPENDING

Consumption spending C depends on four factors: the baseline level of consumption C_0, the marginal propensity to consume (MPC) C_y, the tax rate t, and the level of real GDP (or national income) Y:

$$C = C_0 + C_y \times (1 - t)Y$$

Investment spending I depends on three things: the baseline level of investment I_0, the interest sensitivity of investment I_r, and the real interest rate r:

$$I = I_0 - I_r \times r$$

We leave the determinants of government purchases G to the political scientists.

As noted above, in this book we assume net taxes T, taxes less transfers, are equal to the average tax rate t times GDP Y:

$$T = tY$$

We do not inquire into what determines either government purchases G or the average tax rate t. We leave that for the political scientists. We do look at what happens when government spending G or the tax rate t changes.

5.3 INTERNATIONAL TRADE

The final component of GDP is net exports — the difference between **gross exports** and **imports**. Gross exports are made up of goods and services that are produced in the home country and then sold abroad. GDP is a measure of production, and since gross exports are part of production, they need to be counted in GDP. But first imports need to be subtracted from GDP. Not all the goods and services that make up consumption, investment, and government purchases are produced domestically. Consumption, for instance, includes spending on Chinese toys, U.S. computers, Brazilian coffee, and Scottish tweeds as well as on domestically made goods. So adding up C, I, and G overestimates domestic demand for Canadian-made products. By adding *net* rather than *gross* exports to $C + I + G$, economists (a) take account of goods made domestically that are sold to foreigners and don't show up in $C + I + G$ and (b) correct $C + I + G$ for the amount of foreign-made goods it counts.

GROSS EXPORTS

The volume of gross exports from Canada depends on two variables. The first is the real GDP of our trading partners — call it Y^f, for "foreign GDP." The second is the real exchange rate — call it ε. The higher the value of the real exchange rate — the more expensive the foreign currency — the cheaper are Canadian-made goods to foreigners, and the more of them they buy.

Thus the function for gross exports GX is

$$GX = (X_f \times Y^f) + (X_\varepsilon \times \varepsilon) \tag{5.12}$$

Here, just as in the investment and consumption equations, X_ε and X_f are parameters that help determine gross exports. X_f is the increase in exports generated by an increase in foreign GDP. It is the proportion of foreign income spent on our exports. X_ε is the increase in exports produced by a rise in the real exchange rate ε.

IMPORTS AND NET EXPORTS

The value of demand for imports — for products produced abroad — depends on domestic real GDP: The higher the real GDP, the more money consumers and investors spend on imports.

The *quantity* of imports demanded depends as well on the real exchange rate ε. The higher the real exchange rate — the higher the value of foreign currency — the more expensive are foreign-made goods and the fewer of them are bought by domestic consumers and investors.

Let IM be the *volume* of foreign goods imported. Then IM will decrease if there is an increase in ε and it will increase if there is an increase in domestic income Y. We can, thus, write

$$IM = (IM_Y \times Y) - (IM_\varepsilon \times \varepsilon) \tag{5.13}$$

where IM_ε measures the sensitivity of the volume of imports to changes in the real exchange rate ε, and IM_Y measures the marginal propensity to import.

Notice, however, that IM is the volume of *foreign* goods. In order to compare this with gross exports GX, which are in terms of *domestic* goods, we should multiply IM with ε. Hence, $\varepsilon \times IM$ is imports measured in terms of units of domestic goods, which can now be compared with GX, as both are in the same units.

We can then define **net exports, NX**, as the excess of gross exports over imports:

$$NX = GX - \varepsilon \times IM \tag{5.14}$$

Net exports then depend on the real exchange rate, ε, on real GDP abroad, Y^f, and on real GDP here at home, Y. More precisely, after substituting for GX and IM from equations (5.1) and (5.13) into (5.14), we obtain

$$NX = [(X_f \times Y^f) + (X_\varepsilon \times \varepsilon)] - \varepsilon \times [(IM_y \times Y) - (IM_\varepsilon \times \varepsilon)] \tag{5.15}$$

This equation is rather long and messy looking. To simplify it we will make the assumption that when there is a change in ε the value of imports in terms of domestic goods does not change; that is, $\varepsilon \times IM = IM_y \times Y$. Using this assumption and the definition of gross exports in equation (5.12), we can write the expression for net exports from equation (5.14) as

$$NX = [(X_f \times Y^f) + (X_\varepsilon \times \varepsilon)] - IM_y \times Y \tag{5.16}$$

In the real world, the relationship between the real exchange rate, domestic and foreign outputs, and net exports is not as simple. Many determinants of net exports are suppressed in order to keep the model simple. In particular, substantial lags are involved in processing export and import orders, which gives rise to what is known as the J-Curve phenomenon, as Box 5.8 explains.

THE J-CURVE

Trade links across countries take time to create, modify, and terminate. In the real world there are institutional rigidities that make the volumes of imports IM and gross exports GX fixed in the short run. For example, there are long time lags between orders that are placed and the delivery of the goods, and payments for them that are due upon delivery.

Hence, if we treat IM and GX as fixed in the short run, then it is clear from equation (5.14) that after an increase in ε there will be a fall in net exports NX. This happens because even though the volume of imports IM is unaffected, the increase in ε increases their values $\varepsilon \times IM$ in terms of the domestic good. Over time, however, when GX and IM adjust net exports will increase. The adjustment of NX will follow a path that is like a J, as in Figure 5.8, and for this reason, this phenomenon is referred to as the J-Curve.

The J-Curve has been discussed extensively in relation to developing countries; but this phenomenon is also present in the data for several developed countries including Canada and the United States. Such empirical evidence is provided by David Backus of New York University and Patrick Kehoe and Finn Kydland of the University of Minnesota.*

FIGURE 5.8

The J-Curve

An increase in ε at time t_0 will not affect the volumes of exports and imports instantly. Therefore, at time t_0 net exports will fall. Net exports will only gradually increase over time when the volumes of imports and exports are allowed to adjust.

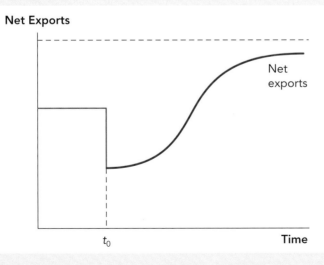

*The paper by Backus, Kehoe, and Kydland was published in the *American Economic Review* in 1994 (volume 84, pp. 84–103), with the title "Dynamics of the Trade Balance and the Terms of Trade: The J-Curve?"

THE EXCHANGE RATE

We have seen that the exchange rate is an important determinant of net exports. But what determines the exchange rate?

Consider foreign exchange speculators whose job it is to trade currencies and make money. They spend their days glued to computer terminals, watching the prices of bonds denominated in different currencies flash across the screen. They buy and sell bonds and stocks of different countries and governments denominated in different currencies — dollars, euros, pounds, yen, pesos, ringgit, and more than 100 others. Their lives are ruled by greed and fear, as sketched out in Figure 5.9:

- *Greed:* Suppose a trader sees higher interest rates paid on the bonds of Canadian companies denominated in dollars than on those of German companies denominated in euros. In this case, there is money to be made by selling ("going short") German companies' bonds, buying ("going long") Canadian companies' bonds, and pocketing the extra interest.

- *Fear:* Suppose that the trader is long on dollar-denominated bonds and short on euro-denominated bonds and the Canadian exchange rate rises. At a higher real exchange rate, each dollar is worth fewer euros; whatever profits were expected from the interest rate spread are wiped out by the capital loss caused by the exchange rate movement. If today's value of the exchange rate is different from long-run historical trends, the fear that exchange rates will return to their normal relationships and impose large foreign exchange losses will be immense.

The greater the difference in interest rates in favour of dollar-denominated securities, the higher is the greed factor. And the higher the greed factor, the lower must be the value of the exchange rate in order for fear to offset greed. The enormously liquid, enormously high-volume, enormously volatile foreign exchange markets settle at the point where greed and fear balance. Thus the real exchange rate ε is equal to the average foreign exchange trader's opinion ε_0 of what the exchange rate should be if there were no interest rate differentials minus a parameter ε_r times the interest rate differential between domestic real interest rates r and foreign real interest rates r^f:

$$\varepsilon = \varepsilon_0 - \varepsilon_r \times (r - r^f) \tag{5.17}$$

The longer that interest rate differentials are expected to continue, and the more slowly that real exchange rates are expected to revert to trend, the higher ε_r will be and the larger will be the effect of a given interest rate differential on the exchange rate.

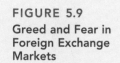

FIGURE 5.9
Greed and Fear in Foreign Exchange Markets

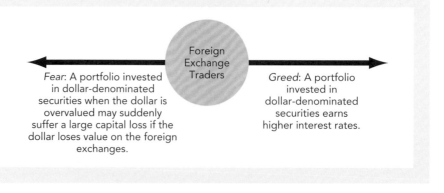

Fear: A portfolio invested in dollar-denominated securities when the dollar is overvalued may suddenly suffer a large capital loss if the dollar loses value on the foreign exchanges.

Foreign Exchange Traders

Greed: A portfolio invested in dollar-denominated securities earns higher interest rates.

AN ALTERNATIVE EXPLANATION FOR EQUATION (5.17)

An alternative explanation for the fundamental equation for the determination of the real exchange rate (5.17) focuses on the portfolio choices of the individual household, which buys domestic and foreign bonds in order to transfer purchasing consumption goods from the present to the future. With imperfect international capital mobility and imperfect international asset substitutability, the household will be holding a portfolio of domestic and foreign bonds whose composition will depend on the real rates of return on domestic versus foreign bonds $(r - r^f)$.

Suppose for whatever reason there is an increase in the real rate of return on Canadian bonds r relative to European bonds r^f. Then the household will re-shuffle its portfolio of assets, substituting some Canadian bonds for some European bonds. To do this, the household will sell some European bonds in exchange for euros, take the euros to the foreign exchange market, convert them into Canadian dollars, and use these dollars to buy Canadian bonds. All households will want to make such a portfolio substitution, increasing the demand for the dollar on the foreign exchange market. This increased demand for the dollar on the foreign exchange market will then put downward pressure on the price of the dollar relative to euros. As a result, to buy one euro investors will now need fewer dollars; that is, the nominal exchange rate e will fall. The fall in the nominal exchange rate will also reduce the real exchange rate $\varepsilon = e \times P^f/P$. This is an alternative explanation for why an increase in the interest rate differential $(r - r^f)$ reduces the real exchange rate.

Notice the size of the parameter ε_r in equation (5.17) depends on the degrees of international capital mobility and international asset substitutability. With higher degrees of international capital mobility and international asset substitutability, an increase in the interest rate differential $(r - r^f)$ will lead to a larger substitution of Canadian for European bonds, and therefore a larger fall in the real exchange rate. Hence, with higher degrees of international capital mobility and international asset substitutability the parameter ε_r will be larger.

We will refer to equation (5.17) as the *fundamental equation for the determination of the real exchange rate*. An alternative explanation for this equation that some may find more appealing is presented in Box 5.9.

Remember: The exchange rate is the value of foreign currency. If foreign currency becomes more valuable, the exchange rate rises; if domestic currency becomes more valuable, the exchange rate falls. Often you will hear people talk of an appreciation or revaluation of the dollar or of a depreciation or devaluation of the dollar. An *appreciation* or *revaluation* of the dollar is a reduction in the value of the exchange rate. A *depreciation* or *devaluation* of the dollar is an increase in the value of the exchange rate.

If we take the equation for net exports

$$NX = GX - IM = (X_f \times Y^f) + (X_\varepsilon \times \varepsilon) - (IM_y \times Y) \tag{5.18}$$

and substitute into it the equation for the value of the exchange rate, the result is the relatively unappetizing

$$NX = GX - IM = (X_f \times Y^f) + (X_\varepsilon \times \varepsilon_0) - (X_\varepsilon \times \varepsilon_r \times r) + (X_\varepsilon \times \varepsilon_r \times r^f) - (IM_y \times Y) \tag{5.19}$$

This equation is unappetizing because it is complex. It is nevertheless valuable because it contains a lot of information. It tells us directly how domestic and foreign

interest rates affect net exports, without requiring that we go through the intermediate step of calculating the real exchange rate. This direct equation is sometimes
valuable because removing the exchange rate means that (for the moment at least)
we have one less thing to keep track of. Tweaking a model to rid it of complicating
variables is a standard technique of economists.

RECAP   **INTERNATIONAL TRADE**

Gross exports depend positively on foreign real GDP and on the exchange rate. Imports depend positively on domestic real GDP. The difference between gross exports and imports is net exports, which is the fourth and last component of aggregate demand.

In turn, the exchange rate depends on a number of factors, the most important
of which is the domestic real interest rate. The higher the domestic real interest
rate, the lower the exchange rate. The most important of the other factors
that affect the real exchange rate are interest rates abroad and foreign exchange
speculators' confidence.

5.4 CONCLUSION

Needless to say, the short-run flexible-price analysis begun in this chapter is not
complete. The chapter has focused only on the building blocks of the analysis. What
determines the division of real GDP between its four components is explained in
Chapter 6. Moreover, recall that this chapter has presented only a short-run, snapshot view of the economy. It has not discussed the impact of changes in policy and
in the economic environment on economic growth. That was done in Chapters 3
and 4 (refer to them to analyze how changes in investment spending ultimately
affect productivity).

Moreover, this chapter has ignored the nominal financial side of the economy —
money, prices, and inflation — entirely. That topic will be covered in Chapter 7.

Last, but not least, the flexible-price analysis of this part, Part III, is itself not a
complete analysis of even the short-run real side of the economy. It needs to be sup-
plemented by the analysis of what happens when prices are sticky. That analysis is
carried out in Part IV.

CHAPTER SUMMARY

1. This chapter has begun the analysis of a flexible-price,
full-employment economy in the short run — a period
short enough that potential output is fixed, but long
enough for flexible wages and prices to bring supply and
demand into balance and thus markets into equilibrium.

2. When the economy is at full employment, the level of
real GDP is equal to potential output, which is the
level of output generated by the production function of

Chapter 3 from the current stocks of labour and capital
and the current efficiency of labour.

3. When wages and prices are flexible, the working of the
labour market keeps the economy at full employment.
If labour demand is less than the size of the labour
force, falling wages raise employment; if labour demand
is greater than the size of the labour force, rising wages
lower employment.

4. The level of consumption spending is determined by many things, but the most important of them are four: Real GDP (or national income) Y, the average tax rate t, the baseline level of consumption C_0, and households' marginal propensity to consume (MPC) C_y. National income and the tax rate together determine disposable income Y^D:

$$Y^D = (1 - t)Y$$

Disposable income, the baseline level of consumption, and the MPC together determine the level of consumption according to the consumption function:

$$C = C_0 + C_y \times Y^D$$

or

$$C = C_0 + C_y \times (1 - t)Y$$

5. The level of investment spending is primarily determined by two factors: Business managers' degree of optimism, which powerfully affects the baseline level of investment spending I_0, and the real interest rate r, for the higher is the real interest rate the lower is investment spending. The simple investment function is:

$$I = I_0 - I_r \times r$$

6. The stock market is a useful indicator of the future value of investment spending. Its value depends on the same factors — the degree of optimism about future profits and the real interest rate.

7. The exchange rate is determined by foreign exchange traders' view of the long-run equilibrium value of the exchange rate and the interest rate differential between investments at home and investments abroad.

8. Net exports are determined by the level of the exchange rate, the level of real GDP (which determines the level of imports), and the level of real GDP abroad (which affects the level of exports).

KEY TERMS AND EQUATIONS

consumption function (p. 155)

disposable income (p. 154)

government purchases (p. 160)

gross exports (p. 161)

imports (p. 161)

investment function (p. 159)

labour demand (p. 151)

labour market equilibrium (p. 152)

labour supply (p. 151)

marginal product of labour (MPL) (p. 149)

marginal propensity to consume (MPC) (p. 155)

net exports (NX) (p. 162)

net taxes (p. 161)

potential output (p. 152)

production function (p. 147)

real interest rate (p. 158)

real wage (p. 150)

transfer payments (p. 161)

Labour demand:	$MPL = W/P$	(5.3)
Potential output:	$Y^* = F(K, \overline{L})$	(5.5)
Consumption function:	$C = C_0 + C_y \times Y^D = C_0 + C_y \times (1 - t)Y$	(5.10)
Investment function:	$I = I_0 - I_r \times r$	(5.11)
Equilibrium real exchange rate:	$\varepsilon = \varepsilon_0 - \varepsilon_r \times (r - r^f)$	(5.17)
Net exports function:	$NX = GX - IM = (X_f \times Y^f) + (X_\varepsilon \times \varepsilon) - (IM_y \times Y)$	(5.18)

ANALYTICAL EXERCISES

1. In the full-employment model, what determines the level of real GDP?

2. In the economy as a whole, what makes labour demand equal to the labour force?

3. What happens if the parameter C_0 in the consumption function rises?

4. What happens to net exports if foreign exchange speculators become more optimistic about the long-run real value of the domestic currency?

5. What happens to net exports if interest rates abroad rise?

POLICY EXERCISES

1. Assume that the economy's production function is Cobb-Douglas:

$$Y = K^\alpha \times L^{1-\alpha}$$

the capital stock is 80, the total labour force $\bar{L}$ is 100, and $\alpha = 0.4$.

a. Derive the labour demand function.

b. Derive the equilibrium real wage.

c. What is the potential output for this economy?

2. Suppose an economy with the standard Cobb-Douglas production function

$$Y^* = K^\alpha \times (\bar{L} \times E)^{1-\alpha}$$

has a diminishing-returns parameter α equal to $\frac{1}{3}$, a total labour force $\bar{L}$ equal to 100 workers, capital stock K equal to 40 million, and an efficiency of the labour force E equal to 2. What is the value of potential output Y^*? What is the value of potential output per worker $Y^*/\bar{L}$? What is the market-clearing real wage (in dollars per year) at which the economy is at full employment, with neither unemployed workers nor excess demand for labour?

3. In an economy at full employment with an unchanging diminishing-returns parameter α and output per worker growing at 3 percent per year, at what rate must the real wage be growing in order to maintain full employment?

4. What would you expect to happen to real investment if the real value of the stock market increases substantially?

5. In recent years foreign exchange speculators have become much more confident in the long-run value of the dollar. What would you suspect has happened to net exports?

6. Consumers whose stock market wealth has multiplied over the past decade have recently started pulling money out of the stock market to enhance their standard of living. What kind of shift in which parameter of the consumption function could be used to model this phenomenon?

7. Consider the consumption model presented in Appendix 5A. Suppose future period is five times longer than the present ($\theta = 5$), the real interest rate is 2 percent, and the utility function is

$$U = C^{0.5}_{now} \times C^{0.5}_{future}$$

a. What is the consumer's budget constraint?

b. What is C_{now}?

c. Suppose the government has some unexpected expenditure of $100 and decides to finance it by raising taxes on Y_{now} by $100. What would be the effect on the budget constraint and on C_{now}?

d. Now suppose instead of raising taxes on Y_{now} by $100 to finance its unexpected expenditure, the government borrows $100 now and raises taxes on Y_{future} by $102/5 dollars (i.e., $100 \times (1 + r)/\theta$). What would be the effect on the budget constraint and on C_{now}? Would the effect on consumption be different from that in part c? Discuss.

5A

A Closer Look at Consumption

5A.1 PERMANENT AND TRANSITORY INCOME

One of the most important factors omitted from our consumption function is the distinction between permanent and transitory income. Your *permanent income* is the average level that you expect your level of income to be in the future. Your *transitory income* is the difference between your income now and your permanent income. Milton Friedman was the very first to point out that not this year's income but permanent income is likely to be the main determinant of consumption.

THE BUDGET CONSTRAINT

Think of a consumer trying to decide how much to spend in two periods only — now and the future. Suppose that he or she can save (or borrow) in the present for the future at a real interest rate r. And suppose that the now and the future are not necessarily the same length of time: The future period is some parameter θ times the length of the present period. In the present the typical consumer decides how much to spend and how much to save. Income Y_{now}, consumption C_{now}, and saving S are linked by

$$S = Y_{now} - C_{now} \tag{5.20}$$

In the future, the consumer adds his or her future income to savings — which have in the meantime grown because they have earned real interest at rate r — and spends the total (you can't take it with you, after all!):

$$\theta \times C_{future} = \theta \times Y_{future} + (1 + r)S \tag{5.21}$$

Combining these two equations produces what economists call the *present value* form of the *consumer's budget constraint:*

$$C_{now} + [\theta C_{future}/(1 + r)] = Y_{now} + [\theta Y_{future}/(1 + r)] \tag{5.22}$$

Total consumption spending now and in the future must equal total income in the two periods. Future income and consumption count a little bit less — are "discounted" by the real interest rate — in order to turn them into "present values"

FIGURE 5A.1

The Budget Constraint

You can read off income in the present and the future from the circle showing the consumer's income in both periods. By borrowing and lending, the consumer is free to choose levels of consumption in the present and the future corresponding to any point along the budget-constraint line. The slope of the budget line corresponds to the real interest rate. The higher the real interest rate, the steeper is the line — the more you can boost consumption in the future by cutting back and saving today.

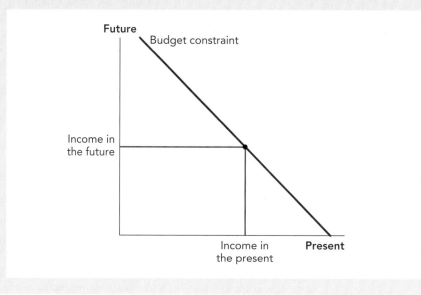

before adding them to current consumption. Because savings earn interest, you must put aside only $1/(1 + r)$ dollars today in order to be able to spend 1 dollar on consumption in the future. Hence 1 dollar of consumption — or income — in the future has a "present value" of only $1/(1 + r)$ dollars today.

We can show this budget constraint on a diagram that plots the present on the horizontal axis and the future on the vertical axis (see Figure 5A.1). By borrowing or saving the consumer can redistribute consumption across time.

THE MARGINAL UTILITY OF CONSUMPTION

A representative consumer modelled by an economist will try to arrange his or her consumption now and in the future to maximize his or her utility. And any representative consumer in a model built by an economist will have a very simple utility function to maximize, such as

$$U = C_{now}{}^{\gamma} \times C_{future}{}^{(1-\gamma)} \tag{5.23}$$

Where γ — the Greek letter *gamma* — is the parameter of the utility function. It governs how much the consumer values consumption now as opposed to consumption in the future.

If the marginal utility of per unit of time consumption (MUC) today is more than $(1 + r)/\theta$ times the MUC in the future, the consumer can increase his or her total utility a bit by cutting consumption in the future by an average of $(1 + r)/\theta$ dollars, reducing savings now by 1 dollar and increasing consumption now by 1 dollar. If the marginal utility of consumption today is less than $(1 + r)/\theta$ times the MUC in the future, the consumer can increase his or her total utility a bit by boosting consumption in the future by $(1 + r)/\theta$ dollars, increasing savings now by 1 dollar and cutting consumption now by 1 dollar. Thus if the consumer is behaving like a proper agent in an economist's model, it must be that

$$\frac{\text{MUC}_{\text{now}}}{\text{MUC}_{\text{future}}} = \frac{1 + r}{\theta} \qquad (5.24)$$

What is the marginal utility of consumption now? Just as with the marginal product of labour, it is the change in utility produced by adding 1 more unit of consumption now:

$$\text{MUC}_{\text{now}} = [(C_{\text{now}} + 1)^{\gamma} \times C_{\text{future}}^{1-\gamma}] - (C_{\text{now}}^{\gamma} \times C_{\text{future}}^{1-\gamma})$$

which can be simplified to

$$\text{MUC}_{\text{now}} = [(C_{\text{now}} \times 1)^{\gamma} - C_{\text{now}}^{\gamma}] \times C_{\text{future}}^{1-\gamma} \qquad (5.25)$$

Once again we can use our rule for the growth rate of a quantity raised to a power — in this case C_{now} growing at the proportional rate of $1/C_{\text{now}}$ — and thus evaluate the marginal utility of consumption. It is

$$\text{MUC}_{\text{now}} = \gamma(C_{\text{now}})^{\gamma-1} \times C_{\text{future}}^{1-\gamma} \qquad (5.26)$$

Similarly, the marginal utility of consumption in the future is

$$\text{MUC}_{\text{future}} = (1 - \gamma) C_{\text{now}}^{\gamma} \times C_{\text{future}}^{-\gamma} \qquad (5.27)$$

Thus if the consumer is behaving as expected,

$$\frac{1 + r}{\theta} = \frac{\gamma(C_{\text{now}})^{\gamma-1} \times C_{\text{future}}^{1-\gamma}}{(1 - \gamma)C_{\text{now}}^{\gamma} \times C_{\text{future}}^{-\gamma}} = \frac{\gamma C_{\text{future}}}{(1 - \gamma)C_{\text{now}}} \qquad (5.28)$$

or

$$C_{\text{future}} = \frac{(1 + r) \times (1 - \gamma)}{\theta\gamma} \times C_{\text{now}} \qquad (5.29)$$

This equation tells us that the consumer spends a fraction γ of the present value of his or her total income on current consumption:

$$C_{\text{now}} = \gamma \times \left(Y_{\text{now}} + \frac{\theta Y_{\text{future}}}{1 + r}\right) \qquad (5.30)$$

He or she spends the rest on future consumption. Once again, there is nothing especially "deep" in this simple result. Economists use this particular utility function often because it produces simple results.

Note that using this equation, a \$1 increase in transitory income — in Y_{now} but not in Y_{future} — would lead to a γ dollar increase in consumption today. But a \$1 increase in permanent income — in both Y_{now} and Y_{future} — would generate an increase in consumption in the present of

$$\Delta C_{\text{now}} = \gamma \times \left(1 + \frac{\theta}{1 + r}\right) \qquad (5.31)$$

Thus the marginal propensity to consume is much larger if a change in income is permanent than if it is transitory. When an increase is transitory, consumers tend to smooth out their consumption over time by saving the bulk of the windfall, as shown in Figures 5A.2 and 5A.3. If consumers do not believe a change in income will be permanent, they will not adjust their spending now by very much.

For example, consider the U.S. experience in the late 1960s when President Lyndon Johnson proposed and Congress passed the Vietnam War income surtax. The surtax, a 10 percent increase in federal taxes, was imposed in an attempt to

FIGURE 5A.2

Consumption Smoothing

Consumers try to smooth consumption over time. If their income is unusually high in the present, they will spend little of the excess and save most of it.

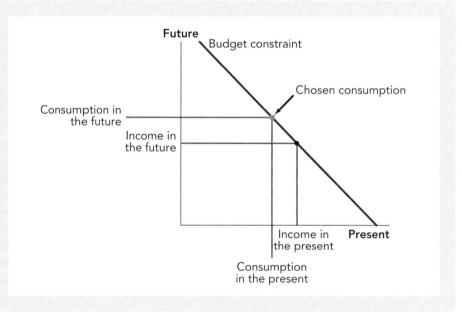

FIGURE 5A.3

The Effect of an Increase in Transitory Income

A change in transitory income — a change in income in the present but not the future — leads to a change in consumption in the present that is only a small fraction of the change in today's income.

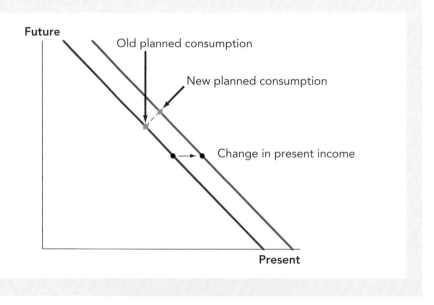

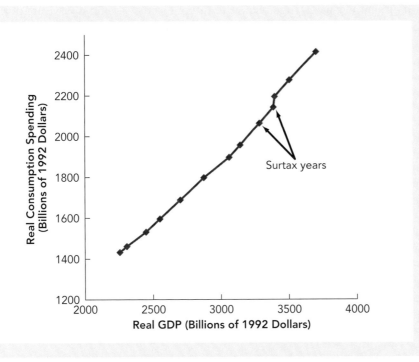

FIGURE 5A.4

Effects of the Vietnam War Surtax on Consumption

The Vietnam War surtax had next to no effect on consumption because it was broadly seen as a *transitory* change in tax policy.

Source: The 1999 edition of *Economic Report of the President* (Washington, DC: Government Printing Office).

reduce consumption spending and so reduce inflationary pressures during the Vietnam War. But President Johnson sold the surtax to Congress (and to the public) by promising that it would be a short-term, temporary measure with no permanent effects. He was convincing. Because everyone believed that the tax increase was short-term and temporary, it had no effect on consumers' beliefs about their permanent income. Everyone saw it as a change in transitory income only. And so it had next to no effect on consumption spending, as you can see in Figure 5A.4.

5A.2 CONSUMPTION AND THE REAL INTEREST RATE

An increase in the real interest rate makes saving more profitable: It means a higher rate of return earned on wealth saved and invested. Consumer saving is equal to after-tax income minus consumption. Does this mean that consumption spending is powerfully affected by the real interest rate and that an increase in the real interest rate decreases consumption spending? Probably not. An increase in the real interest rate does increase the rate of return on savings, and this induces a consumer to *substitute* saving for consumption in the present. But return to the expression for consumption spending now — C_{now} — derived earlier in this appendix:

$$C_{\text{now}} = \gamma \times \left(Y_{\text{now}} + \frac{\theta Y_{\text{future}}}{1 + r} \right)$$

If current income is large relative to future income — as it is if we are thinking of people saving for their retirement — then a change in the real interest rate r has no effect on current consumption spending. Thus it has no effect on current saving — the difference between current income and current consumption.

Why not? Because an increase in saving doesn't just make it more attractive to substitute saving for consumption today. An increase in the real interest rate also increases consumers' total lifetime wealth: Their permanent income is boosted because they earn higher returns on the money that they do save. This higher *permanent income* increases consumption in the present — and so reduces current saving. Which effect dominates? Is the income effect stronger, or is the substitution effect stronger? For consumers with low future incomes, the two effects almost cancel out. For consumers with high future incomes, they do indeed save more. But consumers with high future incomes had little reason to save to begin with, so even a large proportional increase in their saving has little effect on total economy-wide saving.

As a result, most economists think that these two effects roughly balance each other. They believe that changes in real interest rates have a small negative effect on consumption spending and a small positive effect on savings. But the effect of the real interest rate on consumption spending is not large enough to be worth the extra complication it would add to our models here.

5B

Present Value and Investment

How should you decide whether an investment is worth making? Suppose that you are on the investment committee of a business and that brought before you is a proposal to make a $100 million investment this year that will pay off by creating $130 million worth of real inflation-adjusted value five years hence.

If the real interest rate is 5 percent and if you take the $100 million and invest it in the bond market, after one year you will have $100 × (1 + 5 percent) = $105 million. After two years, you will have $105 × (1 + 5 percent) = $110.25 million; after three years, $110.25 × (1 + 5 percent) = $115.76 million; and after five years, $127.63 million of real inflation-adjusted purchasing power. Thus you will make more money in risk-adjusted, inflation-adjusted expected-value terms by undertaking the investment project than by undertaking the next-best alternative, so the investment project is worthwhile.

If the real interest rate is 6 percent, however, the answer will be different. At 6 percent, after five years you will have $100 × (1.06)^5 = $133.8 million in inflation-adjusted purchasing power. The investment project will lose money compared to the next-best alternative, so it should not be undertaken.

Such comparisons are easier if you use an economists' concept called *present value*. The present value is the amount of wealth that you would have to set aside today and invest at the real interest rate to generate some particular amount of purchasing power in the future. If the real interest rate is 5 percent per year, to have $130 million of inflation-adjusted purchasing power in five years you would have to take $101.85 million today, put it aside, and let it compound in the bond market: $101.85 × (1.05)^5 = $130 million. Thus the *present value* of $130 million in five years at an interest rate of 5 percent is $101.85 million.

To calculate the present value $PV of a sum of inflation-adjusted purchasing power $SUM to be received n years in the future at an interest rate of r percent per year, you *discount* the future sum back to the present at the rate r using the formula

$$\$PV = \frac{\$SUM}{(1 + r)^n} \tag{5.32}$$

because $PV in the bond market at an interest rate of r for n years will compound to $SUM. (If whether or not the $SUM will actually be paid in the future is subject to more than the usual amount of risk found in the bond market, the present value will be lower: you can either risk-adjust the $SUM to a lower value or risk-adjust the discount rate r by adding a risk premium σ, and discounting at $r + \sigma$.)

With present value, the decisions of business investment committees become easier. One investment project will be a better use of resources than another only if the first has a higher present value than the second.

Most investment projects don't yield returns in the shape of a single, lump-sum payment n years into the future. Most yield a stream of profits each year for a prolonged period. Thus more useful than the formula for the present value of a $SUM n years in the future is the $STREAM formula for the present value of a stream of payments each year from now into the indefinite future:

$$\$PV = \frac{\$STREAM}{r} \tag{5.33}$$

Think of how much a flow of real purchasing power of $1 million per year each year into the indefinite future is worth. If you wanted to receive such an annual flow, how much would you have to put into the bond market today? $1/r$ million invested in the bond market yields an annual flow of real purchasing power of $1 million per year. Thus an investment project that you expect to yield a cash flow of $STREAM in real purchasing power per year each year has a present value of $STREAM/$r$.

You can see from these financial formulas how important the real interest rate is for determining whether investments are worthwhile or not. If an investment project promises a long-running stream of returns — as in the example above — a small change in the real interest rate can have an enormous impact on present value.

These topics are pursued further in finance courses, but not in intermediate macroeconomics.

6

Equilibrium in the Flexible-Price Model

QUESTIONS

When wages and prices are flexible, what economic forces keep total production equal to aggregate demand?

Why does the flow of funds through financial markets have to balance?

What are the components of savings flowing into financial markets?

What is a comparative-statics analysis?

What are supply shocks?

What are real business cycles?

In Chapter 5 we considered the building blocks of the flexible-price model and the conditions that lead to equilibrium in the labour and goods markets of the economy. The key assumption in the analysis was wage and price flexibility. With complete wage and price flexibility, the labour and goods markets are always in equilibrium, such that total employment is equal to the available labour supply (save for frictional unemployment) and total production is at the potential level of output, Y^*.

The full employment equilibrium of the economy requires also that aggregate demand is equal to aggregate supply at the potential level of output. In this chapter, we establish the full employment equilibrium by completing the flexible-price model of Chapter 5 with the flow-of-funds market, which determines the equilibrium real interest rate by equating total saving to total investment at the potential level of output. The equilibrium real interest rate guarantees that aggregate demand is exactly equal to aggregate supply, and thus the economy is at the full employment equilibrium.

The rest of Chapter 6 uses the complete model to predict how the full employment equilibrium is affected by economic shocks, emanating both from aggregate demand and aggregate supply. On the demand side, we examine the effects of fiscal, investment, and foreign shocks. On the supply side, we consider the effects of oil shocks and technological shocks that underlie recent theories of *real business cycles*.

6.1 FULL-EMPLOYMENT EQUILIBRIUM

EQUILIBRIUM AND THE REAL INTEREST RATE

The first section of Chapter 5 showed that, under the flexible-price full-employment classical assumptions, GDP and national income Y equal potential output Y^*:

$$Y = Y^* \tag{6.1}$$

Briefly, as shown in the upper panel of Figure 6.1, the labour market is in equilibrium at point A, where the demand for labour is equal to the labour force, $\bar{L}$, at the equilibrium real wage $(W/P)^*$. Note, for the moment, that flexibility of wages and prices is essential in attaining point A. If, for example, wages and prices were fixed in such a way that their ratio was different from $(W/P)^*$, then, obviously, there would be either excess demand or excess supply of labour and the labour market would not be in equilibrium. Given full employment of labour, it is easy to determine the potential level of output from the production function as shown at point B in the lower panel of Figure 6.1.

The rest of Chapter 5 set out the determinants of each of the components of total spending. We saw that the exchange rate is a function of (a) the real interest rate differential between home and abroad and (b) foreign exchange traders' opinions:

$$\varepsilon = \varepsilon_0 - \varepsilon_r \times (r - r^f) \tag{6.2}$$

We saw the determinants of consumption spending:

$$C = C_0 + C_y \times (1 - t) \times Y \tag{6.3}$$

of investment spending:

$$I = I_0 - I_y \times r \tag{6.4}$$

and of net exports:

$$NX = (X_f \times Y^f) + (X_\varepsilon \times \varepsilon_0) - (X_\varepsilon \times \varepsilon_r \times r) + (X_\varepsilon \times \varepsilon_r \times r^f) - (IM_y \times Y) \tag{6.5}$$

We left the determination of government purchases to the political scientists:

$$G = \bar{G} \tag{6.6}$$

These four components add up to aggregate demand, or total expenditure, which we can write E if we want to emphasize that, conceptually, demand is not quite the same as real GDP Y. However, in equilibrium aggregate demand E will add up to real GDP Y:

$$C + I + G + NX = E = Y \tag{6.7}$$

But the determinants of each of the components of total spending E seem to have nothing at all to do with the production function that determines the level of real GDP Y. How does aggregate demand add up to potential output? Can we be sure that all the output businesses think they can sell when they hire more workers is in fact sold? The answer is that in the flexible-price full-employment classical model of this

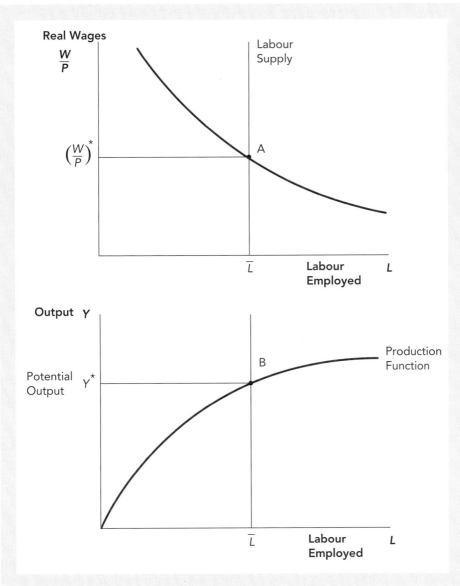

FIGURE 6.1
Equilibrium in the Labour Market and Goods Market
With complete wage and price flexibility, the labour market is in equilibrium at point A and the goods market is in equilibrium at point B.

section, the real interest rate r plays the key balancing role in making sure that the economy reaches and stays at equilibrium.

If we look at all the determinants of all the components of total spending, we see that the components depend on four sets of factors:

- *Factors that are part of the domestic economic environment* (such as consumers' and investors' baseline spending C_0 and I_0 and government purchases G).
- *Factors that are determined abroad* (such as foreign real GDP Y^f and exchange speculators' view of the long-run "fundamental" value of the exchange rate ε_0).
- *The level of real GDP Y itself* (which is a determinant of consumption spending and imports).
- *The real interest rate.*

Of all these factors, only one — the real interest rate — is a price determined by supply and demand here at home. So if market forces are to cause the components of total spending to add up to real GDP, those market forces must work through the interest rate.

To understand what makes aggregate demand equal to potential output, we need to look at the market in which the interest rate functions as the price: the market for loanable funds. When you lend money, the interest rate is the price you charge and the price the borrower pays. Thus we need to look at the flow of loanable funds through the financial markets, the places where household savings and other inflows into financial markets are balanced by outflows to firms seeking capital to expand their productive capacity. The equilibrium we are looking for is one in which supply equals demand in the financial markets. According to the circular flow principle, if financial markets are in equilibrium, then the sum of all the components of spending is equal to real GDP.

THE FLOW OF FUNDS THROUGH FINANCIAL MARKETS

The circular flow principle ensures that if supply equals demand in the flow of funds through **financial markets**, then aggregate supply (real GDP Y, equal to potential output Y^*) is equal to aggregate demand (the sum of all the components of total spending: $C + I + G + NX$). To see this, begin by assuming that real GDP is equal to potential output Y^* and that the circular flow principle holds — real GDP is equal to aggregate demand:

$$Y^* = Y = C + I + G + NX \tag{6.8}$$

Then rewrite this expression by moving everything except for investment spending I to the left-hand side:

$$Y^* - C - G - NX = I$$

Now include taxes T in the left-hand side by adding and subtracting it:

$$(Y^* - C - T) + (T - G) - NX = I \tag{6.9}$$

Note that the right-hand side is simply investment, the net flow of purchasing power out of the financial markets as firms raise money to build factories and structures and boost their productive capacity. The left-hand side is equal to **total savings**: the flow of purchasing power into financial markets as households, the government, and foreigners seek to save by committing their money to buy valuable financial assets here at home. Thus we see that whenever the circular flow principle holds, the supply and demand in the flow of funds through financial markets balances as well. (Although, as Box 6.1 points out, the relationship is not direct.)

The $Y^* - C - T$ inside the first set of parentheses is private savings. Because national income is equal to potential output, Y^* is just total household income. Take income, subtract consumption spending, subtract taxes, and what is left is **private savings**: the flow of purchasing power from households into the financial markets.

The $T - G$ inside the second set of parentheses is **public savings**: the government's budget surplus (or government dissaving, the government's budget deficit, if G happens to be larger than T). It is the flow of funds from the government into the financial markets.

The last term — minus net exports, $-NX$ — is the **capital inflow**, the net flow of purchasing power that foreigners channel into domestic financial markets. To see this, notice $-NX$ is the excess of our imports over our exports. For us to be able to

6.1

BOX

DETAILS

FINANCIAL TRANSACTIONS AND THE FLOW OF FUNDS

Notice that the relationship between the flows of funds into and out of financial markets is indirect. When the government runs a surplus, the government does not directly lend money to a business that wants to build a new factory. Instead, it uses the surplus to buy back some of the bonds that it previously issued. The bank that owned those bonds then takes the cash and uses it to buy some other financial asset — perhaps bonds issued by a corporation. The chain of transactions within financial markets comes to an end only when some participant makes a loan to an investing company or buys a newly issued bond or stock and so transfers purchasing power to the company actually undertaking an investment.

Similarly households or foreigners using financial markets to save rarely buy newly issued corporate bonds or shares of stock that are part of an initial public offering that transfer purchasing power directly to a company undertaking investment. Instead, they usually purchase already-existing securities or simply deposit their wealth in a bank. The relationship between the flows of funds into and out of financial markets is indirect, but it is very real.

pay for our excess imports, we must be borrowing from foreigners. This is called capital inflow. Since we borrow from foreigners –*NX* is also called **international savings**. As Figure 6.2 illustrates, minus net exports are the excess of dollars earned by foreigners selling imports into the home country over and above the amount of dollars foreigners need to buy our exports. If net exports are less than zero, foreigners have some dollars left over. They then have to do something with these extra dollars. Foreigners find dollars useful in only two ways: for buying our exports

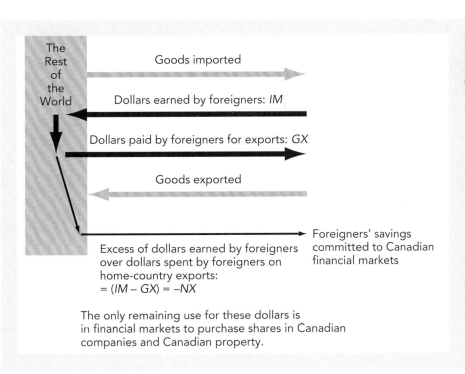

FIGURE 6.2
Imports Minus Gross Exports Equal the Capital Inflow

(but if net exports are less than zero, there aren't enough exports to soak up all the dollars they earn) and for buying property here — land, stocks, buildings, bonds. So this last term is the net flow of purchasing power into domestic financial markets by foreigners wishing to park some of their savings here. (When net exports are positive, this term is the net amount of domestic savings diverted into overseas financial markets).

FLOW-OF-FUNDS EQUILIBRIUM

We have established that the three terms on the left-hand side of the equation

$$(Y^* - C - T) + (T - G) - NX = I$$

are the three flows of purchasing power into the financial markets: private savings, government savings, and international savings. Added together they make up the supply of loanable funds. The demand for loanable funds is simply investment spending. And the price of loanable funds is the real interest rate, as Figure 6.3 illustrates.

What happens if the flow of funds does not balance — if at the current long-term real interest rate r the flow of savings into the financial markets exceeds the demand by corporations and others for purchasing power to finance investments? If the left-hand side is greater than the right, some financial institutions — banks, mutual funds, venture capitalists, insurance companies, whatever — will find purchasing power piling up as more money flows into their accounts than they can find good securities and other investment vehicles to commit it to. They will try to underbid their competitors for the privilege of lending money or buying equity in some particular set of investment projects. How do they underbid? They underbid by saying that they will accept a lower interest rate than the market interest rate r.

FIGURE 6.3
Equilibrium in the Flow of Funds

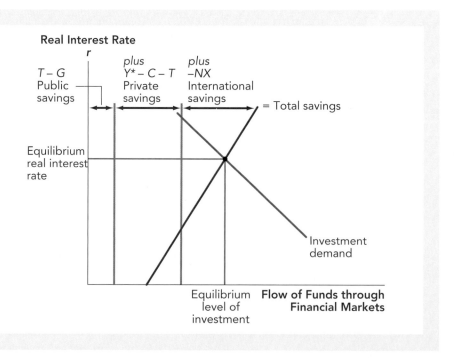

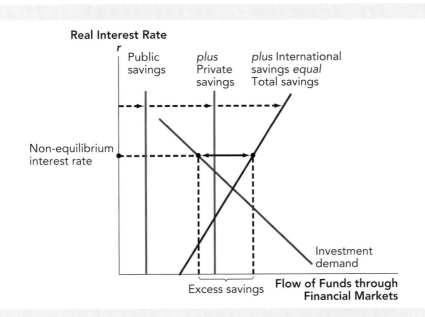

Real Interest Rate

Public savings

plus Private savings

plus International savings *equal* Total savings

Non-equilibrium interest rate

Investment demand

Excess savings

Flow of Funds through Financial Markets

FIGURE 6.4
Excess Supply of Savings in the Flow of Funds
When the interest rate is such that there is an excess supply of savings, some savers will offer to accept a lower interest rate and the interest rate will drop.

Thus if the flow of savings exceeds investment, the interest rate r falls. As r falls, the number and value of investment projects that firms and entrepreneurs find it worthwhile to undertake rises. (See Figure 6.4.)

The process will stop when the interest rate r adjusts to bring about equilibrium in the loanable funds market. The flow of savings into the financial markets will then be just equal to the flow of purchasing power out of financial markets and into the hands of firms and entrepreneurs using it to finance investment.

RECAP   FULL-EMPLOYMENT EQUILIBRIUM

In the flexible-price model real GDP is equal to potential output. But real GDP is also equal to aggregate demand, the sum of consumption, investment, government purchases, and net exports. The determinants of aggregate demand seem to have nothing to do with potential output. What makes aggregate demand add up to the economy's productive potential? The key is that in the flexible-price model the real interest rate is the price that adjusts in order to keep real GDP equal to aggregate demand and potential output. The real interest rate is the price that equilibrates the market for loanable funds — the place where savings flow into and investment financing flows out of financial markets.

6.2 USING THE MODEL

COMPARATIVE STATICS AS A METHOD OF ANALYSIS

The flexible-price full-employment model we have built gives us the capability to determine the level and composition of real GDP and national income. If we know the economic environment and economic policy, we can use the model to determine the equilibrium real interest rate, either by solving the algebraic equations or by drawing the flow-of-funds diagram and looking for the point where supply balances demand, or by doing both. We can then calculate the equilibrium values of a large number of economic variables — real GDP, consumption spending and investment spending, imports and exports, the real exchange rate, and more. In fact, three of the six key economic variables — real GDP, the exchange rate, and the real interest rate — come directly from the model. (We will see how to calculate the price level and the inflation rate in Chapter 7.) In a flexible-price model like this one the unemployment rate is not interesting, for the economy is always at full employment. And we have seen that the stock market is proportional to and a leading indicator of investment spending.

However, the model so far gives us the capability to calculate not just the current equilibrium position of the economy but also how that equilibrium will change in response to changes in the economic environment or in economic policy. To do so, we use a method of analysis economists call **comparative statics.** We determine the response of the economy to some particular shift in the environment or policy in three steps. We first look at the initial equilibrium position of the economy without the shift. We then look at the equilibrium position of the economy with the shift. We then identify the difference in the two equilibrium positions as the change in the economy in response to the shift.

Let's see how the model can be used to analyze the consequences of three disturbances to the economy: (a) changes in fiscal policy, in the government's tax and spending plans, (b) changes in investors' relative optimism, and (c) changes in the international economic environment.

CHANGES IN FISCAL POLICY

Suppose the economy is in equilibrium when policy makers decide to increase annual government purchases by the amount ΔG. (As before, Δ, the Greek capital letter *delta*, stands for "change.") Let's look at what happens to the components of aggregate demand one by one.

The change in government purchases has no effect on consumption. Because potential output does not change, national income does not change. Neither national income, baseline consumption, the tax rate, nor the marginal propensity to consume shifts, so there is no effect on the consumption function (6.3).

Thus

$$\Delta C = 0$$

While the shift in government purchases has no *direct* effect on investment, there will be an indirect effect. Investment depends on the interest rate, and the interest rate will change as a result of the change in government purchases. So from the investment function (6.4) we can conclude that the level of investment spending will change by

$$\Delta I = -I_r \Delta r$$

That is, the shift in investment spending will be equal to the sensitivity of investment to the interest rate times the shift in the equilibrium real interest rate.

Nothing in the international economic environment changes. Nor does the level of potential output change. So looking at the net exports function (6.5), it is clear that here, as well, the only shift will be a proportional change in response to the shift in the equilibrium real interest rate:

$$\Delta NX = -(X_\varepsilon \varepsilon_r \Delta r)$$

Finally, real GDP Y does not change because potential output does not change, and this is a full-employment model with real GDP always equal to potential output:

$$\Delta Y = \Delta Y^* = 0$$

Putting all these pieces together, we have assembled the relevant components of aggregate demand in "change" form. We can see that as government purchases shift, the other components of aggregate demand will have to shift with it:

$$\Delta Y = \Delta I + \Delta G + \Delta NX$$

$$0 = -I_r \Delta r + \Delta G - X_\varepsilon \varepsilon_r \Delta r$$

By putting the change in the real interest rate on the left-hand side of the equation and everything else on the right, we discover that the shift in government purchases means that the equilibrium real interest rate must change by

$$\Delta r = \frac{\Delta G}{I_r + X_\varepsilon \varepsilon_r}$$

To understand this answer, look at the flow-of-funds diagram in Figure 6.5. More government purchases mean less government savings. This shortfall in savings creates a gap between investment demand and savings supply: The interest rate rises. The rising interest rate lowers the quantity of funds demanded for investment financing and increases international savings flowing into domestic financial

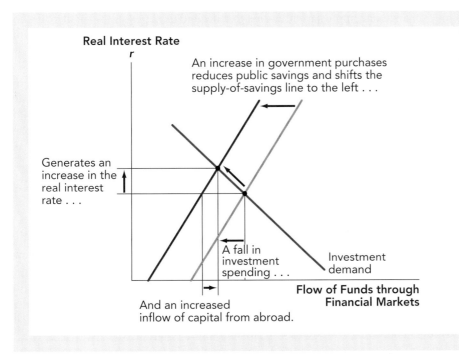

Real Interest Rate
r

An increase in government purchases reduces public savings and shifts the supply-of-savings line to the left . . .

Generates an increase in the real interest rate . . .

A fall in investment spending . . .

Investment demand

Flow of Funds through Financial Markets

And an increased inflow of capital from abroad.

FIGURE 6.5
Flow of Funds:
An Increase in
Government
Purchases

markets. The flow-of-funds market settles down to equilibrium at a new, higher equilibrium interest rate r with a new, lower level of investment. On the flow-of-funds diagram, the increase in government purchases and the consequent reduction in government savings have shifted the flow-of-funds supply curve to the left. The equilibrium position in the diagram has moved up and to the left along the investment curve.

Once the change in the equilibrium interest rate has been calculated, determining what happens to the rest of the economy is straightforward. Simply substitute the change in the equilibrium interest rate into the model's behavioural relationships and calculate the changes in the equilibrium levels of the components of GDP and in the equilibrium level of the real exchange rate.

The change in investment spending is the interest sensitivity of investment I_r times the change in the equilibrium real interest rate, which we already calculated above:

$$\Delta I = -I_r \times \Delta r = \frac{-I_r}{I_r + X_\varepsilon \varepsilon_r} \Delta G \tag{6.10}$$

The changes in net exports and in the exchange rate are also equal to their sensitivities to the real interest rate times the change in the equilibrium real interest rate:

$$\Delta NX = \frac{-X_\varepsilon \varepsilon_r}{I_r + X_\varepsilon \varepsilon_r} \Delta G \tag{6.11}$$

$$\Delta \varepsilon = \frac{-\varepsilon_r}{I_r + X_\varepsilon \varepsilon_r} \Delta G \tag{6.12}$$

The overall picture of the changes generated by the increase in government purchases is clear. The increase in government purchases has led to a shortfall in savings and a rise in real interest rates. The higher real interest rates have led to lower investment and to an appreciation in the home currency: a lower level of ε. This exchange rate appreciation has led to a decline in net exports. The declines in net exports and in investment spending just add up to the increase in government purchases, so the level of GDP is unchanged and still equal to potential output — as we assumed it would be.

Note that the fall in investment is not as large as the rise in government purchases. The increase in government purchases reduced the flow of domestic savings into financial markets, but the increased flow of foreign-owned capital into the market partially offset this reduction. The extra savings from abroad kept the decline in investment from being as large as the rise in government purchases, as Figure 6.6 shows.

INVESTMENT SHOCKS: CHANGES IN INVESTORS' OPTIMISM

Suppose the economy is in equilibrium, when domestic businesses become more optimistic about the future and increase the amount they wish to spend on new plant and equipment. What would be the effect of this shift on the economy? It would produce a domestic investment boom — a rise ΔI_0 in the value of I_0 in the investment equation, (6.4). While the increased optimism of investors increases investment, it is going to be associated with an increase in interest rates, so total investment spending will increase by an amount less than the rise in I_0:

$$\Delta I = \Delta I_0 - I_r \times \Delta r$$

FIGURE 6.6

The Interest Rate, the Exchange Rate, and the Capital Inflow

Why does a rise in the domestic interest rate increase the flow of savings into the loanable funds market? Start in the upper left panel of the figure, where the total savings and investment demand curves cross to determine the equilibrium level of investment spending and the real interest rate. That real interest rate then helps determine the real exchange rate, as shown in the upper right panel: The higher the real interest rate, the lower is the real exchange rate. That real exchange rate then helps determine net exports, as shown in the lower right panel. And the value of net exports is the inverse of international savings, the capital inflow into the flow of funds. Thus the total savings curve slopes upward: The higher the interest rate, the lower the exchange rate, the lower net exports, and the more international savings flow into domestic financial markets.

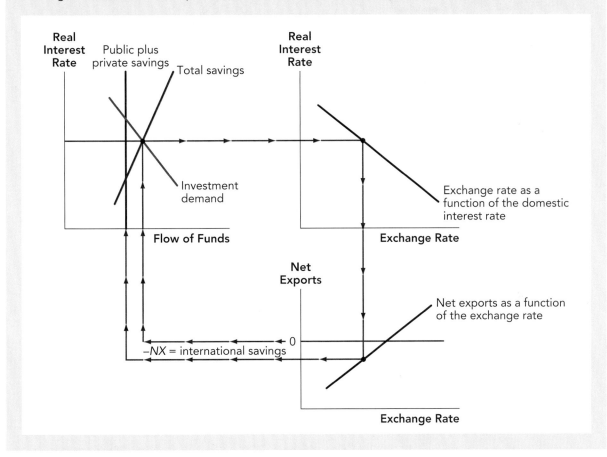

The increase in the domestic interest rate will change the exchange rate and net exports, but the other variables in the model will be unaffected. Government spending and consumption spending are unchanged; foreign income, foreign interest rates, and foreign exchange traders' long-run expectations are unchanged.

As Figure 6.7 shows, the investment boom has shifted the demand-for-loanable-funds curve to the right and increased the equilibrium real interest rate. The increased equilibrium interest rate leads to no change in consumption spending or in government purchases; it leads to a fall in the exchange rate and in net exports, as Figure 6.8 shows.

FIGURE 6.7
Flow of Funds: An Investment Boom

An investment boom shifts the investment demand curve to the right. The new equilibrium in the flow-of-funds market has a higher real interest rate and a higher level of investment spending. Note that investment spending does not rise by the full amount of the shift in the investment demand curve. Higher interest rates "crowd out" some of the increase in investment spending.

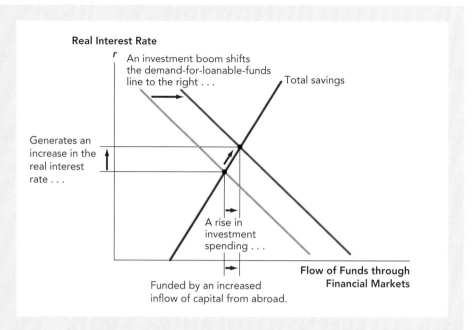

FIGURE 6.8
The International Consequences of an Investment Boom

A change in business managers' optimism that shifts the investment demand curve to the right triggers a rise in the real interest rate, a fall in the exchange rate, a fall in net exports, and an increase in foreigners' funding of domestic investment. Thus the higher domestic interest rate pulls foreign funds into the country to finance higher desired domestic investment.

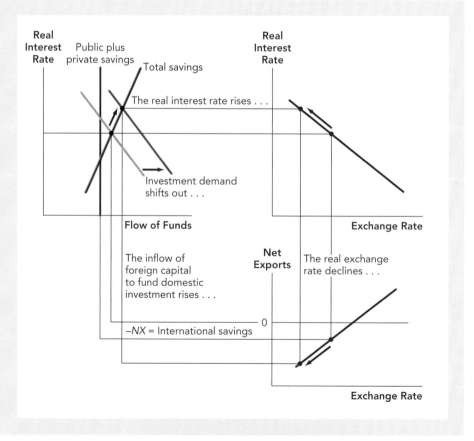

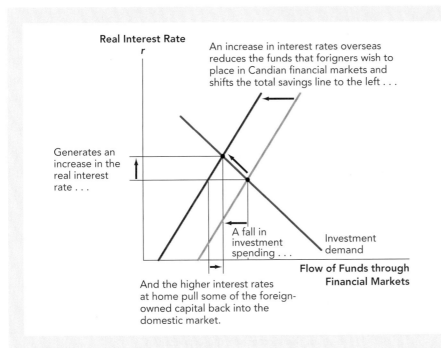

FIGURE 6.9

Flow of Funds: An Increase in Interest Rates Abroad

A rise in foreign interest rates diminishes foreigners' willingness to finance domestic investment and shifts the flow-of-funds savings supply curve to the left. The economy's equilibrium moves up and to the left along the investment demand curve. The new equilibrium has a higher real interest rate and lower investment spending.

INTERNATIONAL DISTURBANCES

AN INCREASE IN FOREIGN INTEREST RATES

Now consider a disturbance from abroad: an upward jump in the foreign real interest rate r^f. This increases the exhange rate, and as a result, net exports rise. As net exports rise, the inflow of foreign funds to finance domestic investment falls. The supply of savings in the flow-of-funds diagram shifts to the left, and the domestic interest rate rises.

Consumption spending and government purchases will not be affected by the rise in overseas interest rates, the fall in the exchange rate, and the rise in the domestic interest rate that it triggers. Nothing has happened to affect any of the determinants of consumption spending or government purchases. Investment spending, however, will fall by the shift in the equilibrium domestic interest rate. As the economy responds to this shift, the changes in the national income will be zero, as the economy is at full employment.

Again, the quickest way to understand the shift in the economy's equilibrium is to use the flow-of-funds diagram. The rise in the foreign interest rate reduces the amount of capital that foreigners want to devote to domestic investments. It shifts the flow-of-funds supply curve to the left, as Figure 6.9 shows. As a result, the economy's equilibrium moves up and to the left along the investment demand curve. The new equilibrium has a higher domestic interest rate and a lower value for investment.

GDP remains equal to potential output. The domestic interest rate rises less than the change in the foreign interest rate, raising the real exchange rate as shown in Figure 6.10. Thus the economy's level of net exports grows by as much as the level of domestic investment shrinks.

A DECLINE IN CONFIDENCE IN THE CURRENCY

Suppose the economy is in equilibrium when there is a decline in foreign exchange speculators' confidence in the currency and thus in the long-run value of the

FIGURE 6.10

The Real Exchange Rate and Domestic Interest Rates

A rise in foreign real interest rates raises the value of the exchange rate, but not by as much as one would expect from the change in foreign interest rates alone. Domestic interest rates rise as well and partially offset the effect of changing foreign interest rates on the exchange rate.

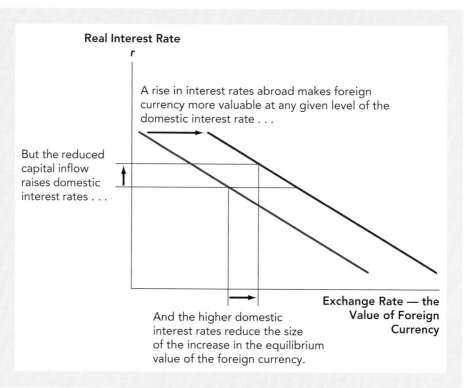

Real Interest Rate
r

A rise in interest rates abroad makes foreign currency more valuable at any given level of the domestic interest rate . . .

But the reduced capital inflow raises domestic interest rates . . .

And the higher domestic interest rates reduce the size of the increase in the equilibrium value of the foreign currency.

Exchange Rate — the Value of Foreign Currency

exchange rate ε_0. What will happen? The exchange rate will fall more than the decline in ε_0, because the exchange rate is affected not just by foreign exchange speculators' beliefs but also by the domestic real interest rate, and the domestic interest rate will change because the change in the exchange rate will alter the flow of funds through financial markets. The change in net exports, and thus in the inflow of capital, will be proportional to the change in the exchange rate. The changing domestic interest rate will shift the level of domestic investment spending as well.

Why does a decrease in foreign exchange speculators' long-run confidence — for an increase in ε_0 is a belief that the long-run value of the currency will be lower — have these effects? The shift in confidence means that at current exchange and interest rates, foreign exchange speculators wish to pull their money out of the home currency; they are not happy using their money to finance domestic investment. Thus on the flow-of-funds diagram in Figure 6.11 the savings supply curve shifts to the left. Once again, the equilibrium point moves up and to the left along the investment demand curve. Once again, the economy comes to rest at a point with a higher domestic interest rate and a lower value for investment. The equilibrium value of the exchange rate is higher, and so is the value of net exports. Box 6.2 provides a numerical example of this process. Box 6.3 discusses the Mexican and East Asian financial crises.

The four cases we have analyzed here are not exhaustive. There are many other changes in the economic environment or in economic policy that the flexible-price model is useful for analyzing. Think of these four as examples of how to proceed: identify the components of real GDP that are going to change, determine the change in the equilibrium real interest rate, and then use the change in that rate and the triggering shift in the economic environment to calculate the postchange state of the economy.

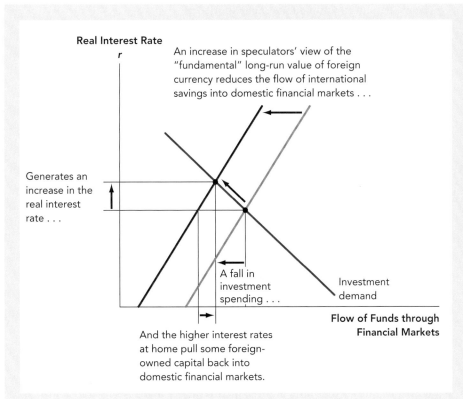

Real Interest Rate
r

An increase in speculators' view of the "fundamental" long-run value of foreign currency reduces the flow of international savings into domestic financial markets . . .

Generates an increase in the real interest rate . . .

A fall in investment spending . . .

Investment demand

Flow of Funds through Financial Markets

And the higher interest rates at home pull some foreign-owned capital back into domestic financial markets.

FIGURE 6.11
Flow of Funds: A Decline in Exchange Rate Confidence

If foreign exchange traders lose confidence in the long-run value of the domestic currency, the effects on the domestic economy are very similar to the effects of a rise in foreign interest rates: The value of the exchange rate rises, and the savings supply curve shifts to the left.

6.2

BOX

EXAMPLE

THE EFFECT OF A FALL IN CONFIDENCE IN THE CURRENCY

Suppose the parameters describing the economy are

$t = 0.33$ — A tax rate of one-third.

$I_r = 900$ — A 1-percentage-point fall — a decline by 0.01 — in the annual interest rate raises investment spending by $9 billion a year (i.e., $900 \times 0.01 = 9$).

$C_y = 0.75$ — A marginal propensity to consume of three-quarters.

$\varepsilon_0 = 100$ — When interest rates at home and abroad are equal, the initial value of the exchange rate is 100.

$\varepsilon_r = 1{,}000$ — A 1-percentage-point change — a change by 0.01 — in the interest rate difference between home and abroad generates a 10-unit shift in the exchange rate (i.e., $1{,}000 \times 0.01 = 10$).

$X_\varepsilon = 0.6$ — A 1-unit change in the exchange rate (i.e., a change in ε by 1) leads to a $0.6 billion-a-year change in exports.

Suppose that, initially, home interest rates are equal to foreign interest rates. What happens if this economy is hit by a sudden loss in confidence in the long-run value of its currency, a rise in ε_0 from 100 to 120?

Consumption and government purchases do not change, so the relevant changes in the national income identity are

$$\Delta Y^* = 0 = \Delta I + \Delta NX$$

The changes in investment and net exports are

$$\Delta I = -I_r \times \Delta r$$
$$\Delta NX = X_\varepsilon \times \Delta\varepsilon = X_\varepsilon \times (\Delta\varepsilon_0 - \varepsilon_r \Delta r)$$

With these particular parameter values, these three equations become

$$\Delta I = -900 \times \Delta r$$
$$\Delta NX = 0.6 \times (20 - 1,000 \times \Delta r)$$
$$0 = \Delta I + \Delta NX$$

Substituting the values from the first two into the third

$$0 = -900\Delta r + 12 - 600\Delta r$$
$$1,500\Delta r = 12$$
$$\Delta r = 0.008 = 0.8\%$$

The real interest rate rises by eight-tenths of a percentage point. Thus investment falls by \$7.2 billion and net exports rise by \$7.2 billion

$$\Delta I = -900 \times 0.8\% = -7.2$$
$$\Delta NX = 6 \times 2 - 0.6 \times 1,000 \times 0.8\% = 12 - 4.8 = 7.2$$

and the change in the equilibrium value of the real exchange rate, the value of foreign currency, is

$$\Delta\varepsilon = \Delta\varepsilon_0 - \varepsilon_r \Delta r = 20 - 1,000 \times 0.8\% = 12$$

Higher interest rates partially offset the loss of confidence in the currency, and so the exchange rate — the value of foreign currency — increases by only a little more than half the magnitude of currency traders' loss of confidence.

RECAP   USING THE MODEL

To use the flexible-price model to understand the economy, begin by drawing the flow-of-funds diagram and calculating the equilibrium real interest rate. You can then use the equilibrium real interest rate and your knowledge of the economic environment to calculate the equilibrium values of a large number of economic variables — real GDP, consumption spending and investment spending, imports and exports, the real exchange rate, and more. You can also use the model to calculate how the economy's equilibrium will change in response to changes in the environment or in policy. Doing so involves using a method called comparative statics: Look first at the initial equilibrium position of the economy without the shift. Look second at the equilibrium position of the economy with the shift. Then identify the difference in the two equilibrium positions as the dynamic change in the economy in response to the shift.

6.3 SUPPLY SHOCKS

So far we have assumed that the level of potential output is fixed. Whatever shocks have affected the economy, they have had no effect on *aggregate supply,* no effect on potential output. But there are shocks to a flexible-price full-employment economy

6.3

BOX

POLICY

THE MEXICAN AND EAST ASIAN FINANCIAL CRISES

At the end of 1994, currency traders and international investors lost confidence in the Mexican peso. In the middle of 1997, they lost confidence in virtually all the currencies of the rapidly growing developing economies of East Asia.

Sharp rises in real interest rates, falls in domestic investment, and declines in the value of the affected domestic currencies followed in both crises. Some commentators railed against these changes. From the right, the editorial page of the *Wall Street Journal,* for example, denounced the International Monetary Fund (IMF) and the U.S. Treasury for advising the affected countries that the values of their domestic currencies should depreciate and the home-currency value of foreign currencies, the exchange rate, should rise. From the left, other economists denounced the IMF and the U.S. Treasury for advising countries to allow the real interest rate to rise.

There are complicated and delicate issues involved in crisis management. But our analysis above of the consequences of a collapse in foreign exchange trader confidence in the currency should make us skeptical of both positions. Our analysis strongly suggests that both the *Wall Street Journal,* which attacked the IMF from the right, and the economists who attacked the IMF from the left were wrong. In our flexible-price model the fall in exchange rate confidence and the resulting decline in international investment *must* lead to a rise in domestic interest rates and a fall in investment. There is no alternative equilibrium in which this does not happen. The fall in exchange rate confidence and the decline in international investment *must* also lead to a rise in the exchange rate and a rise in net exports. There is no alternative equilibrium in which this doesn't happen.

There is a legend that King Canute's advisers told him that he was so powerful that he could command the tides to stop. Our analysis of the consequences of a collapse of exchange rate confidence suggests that — unless confidence can be restored — those who demand that such a crisis be resolved without a rise in the exchange rate and a rise in domestic interest rates are giving advice as good as that given to King Canute.

that change aggregate supply. **Supply shocks** like the 1973 tripling of world oil prices reduce potential output. Inventions and innovations can be positive productivity shocks that increase the level of potential output.

We can use the full-employment model to analyze the effects of a supply shock on the economy. However, the effects of a supply shock are different in one important respect from the effects of the demand or international shocks we analyzed above. In response to a supply shock the level of GDP *does* change — even in this full-employment chapter — because the level of potential GDP has changed. In each case, call the resulting supply-shock-driven change in potential output ΔY^*.

OIL AND OTHER SUPPLY SHOCKS

In 1973 the world price of oil tripled. In response to the 1973 Arab–Israeli War, the Organization of Petroleum Exporting Countries exerted its market power to restrict the worldwide supply of oil and raise the price. Capital- and energy-intensive production processes that had made economic sense and been profitable with oil costing less than US$3 a barrel became unproductive and unprofitable with oil costing US$10 a barrel. Thus potential output fell because it was now more profitable to use technologies that economized on oil by intensively using other factors of production such as labour, and so the efficiency of labour E in the production function fell.

Looking at the changes in the national income identity,

$$\Delta C + \Delta I + \Delta G + \Delta NX = \Delta Y^* \tag{6.13}$$

we find them more complex than those in the case of the demand shocks because the change in real GDP is not zero. If we expand the changes of the national income identity by substituting for each component of GDP the equation for its determinants, we produce

$$[C_y(1 - t)\Delta Y^*] - I_r\Delta r + (-X_\varepsilon\varepsilon_r\Delta r - IM_y\Delta Y^*) = \Delta Y^* \tag{6.14}$$

We can regroup and solve this equation for the change Δr in the equilibrium interest rate:

$$\Delta r = -\left[\frac{1 - C_y(1 - t) + IM_y}{I_r + X_\varepsilon\varepsilon_r}\Delta Y^*\right] \tag{6.15}$$

A negative value for ΔY^* — an adverse supply shock, one that lowers the level of potential output and GDP — generates an *increase* in the domestic real interest rate. Why? Because a fall in GDP due to an oil price increase or some other adverse supply shock reduces incomes and so reduces the flow of private savings into financial markets. (Although a decline in incomes carries with it a decline in consumption, and in net exports, but these declines do not match the decline in income, so domestic savings fall.)

As Figure 6.12 shows, the fall in domestic savings shifts the savings supply curve to the left, raising the real interest rate and reducing investment. As before, the increase in the domestic real interest rate makes foreigners more willing to invest in

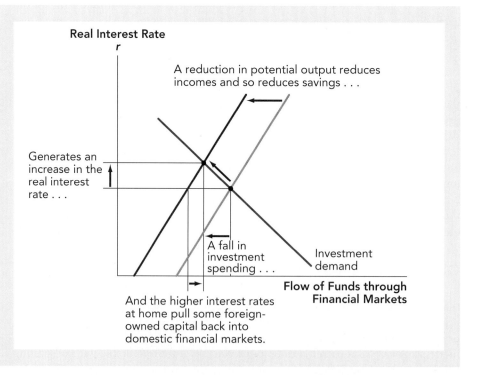

FIGURE 6.12

Flow of Funds: An Adverse Supply Shock

An adverse supply shock will diminish savings, raise the real interest rate, and lower investment.

Real Interest Rate
r

A reduction in potential output reduces incomes and so reduces savings . . .

Generates an increase in the real interest rate . . .

A fall in investment spending . . .

Investment demand

Flow of Funds through Financial Markets

And the higher interest rates at home pull some foreign-owned capital back into domestic financial markets.

the home country. It increases the flow of foreign savings (which partly offsets the leftward shift in the savings supply curve), reduces net exports, and lowers the exchange rate (lowers the value of foreign currency).

By now it must seem as though every shock that affects a full-employment economy does one of four things:

- Shifts the savings supply curve to the left (raising domestic interest rates and lowering investment).
- Shifts the savings supply curve to the right (lowering domestic interest rates and raising investment).
- Shifts the investment demand curve to the left (lowering investment and lowering domestic interest rates).
- Or shifts the investment demand curve to the right (raising investment and raising domestic interest rates).

If you think this, you are right. Every shock to the economy will affect the flow of funds in one of the above four ways. Analyzing the effect of a shock on savings and investment is key to understanding its economy-wide impact.

Outside the flow of funds, however, different kinds of shocks have other, less similar effects. From the change in the level of GDP and the change in the interest rate, it is straightforward to calculate the effect of the supply shock on the other economic variables: consumption, investment, and net exports.

We encourage the reader to show that an adverse supply shock — a negative value for ΔY^* — leads to declines in consumption, investment, and net exports; it leads to an appreciation of the home currency and thus to a reduction in the value of foreign currency — in the exchange rate. It also leads to a rise in the price level and an acceleration of inflation (topics covered in the next chapter).

REAL BUSINESS CYCLES

The mid-twentieth century economist Joseph Schumpeter was the most powerful exponent of the belief that changes in technology are the principal force driving business cycles. Schumpeter saw technological progress as inherently lumpy: There were five-year periods during which a great deal of new technology diffused rapidly throughout the economy. These were booms. There were five-year periods during which the pace of technological innovation and diffusion was much slower. These were periods of relative stagnation. Schumpeter saw the key feature of the business cycle as the comovements of output, employment, investment, and interest rates: All were high together in a boom; all were low together (relative to trend) in a recession.

It is easy to see how uneven invention and innovation patterns could generate such **real business cycle**s — business cycles driven by the fundamental technological dynamic of the economy. Suppose that the most common shift in technology involves (a) a sudden step up in the efficiency of labour, accompanied by (b) a sudden rise in investment demand as it becomes more profitable for a business to enlarge its capital stock. Such a shock has a supply component — an increase ΔY^* in this year's potential output — and an investment demand component — an increase ΔI_0 in this year's investment demand.

How does the economy's full-employment equilibrium shift in response to such a combined shock? We simply add together the effects of a supply shock, outlined immediately above, and the effects of an investment boom driven by investors' increasing optimism, outlined in the previous section. The change in the equilibrium domestic real interest rate from a supply shock is

$$\Delta r = -\left[\frac{1 - C_y(1 - t) + IM_y}{I_r + X_\varepsilon \varepsilon_r} \Delta Y^*\right] \tag{6.16}$$

The change from an investment demand shock is

$$\Delta r = \frac{\Delta I_0}{I_r + X_\varepsilon \varepsilon_r} \tag{6.17}$$

Adding them together, the change in the equilibrium interest rate from this Schumpeterian technology shift is

$$\Delta r = -\frac{[1 - C_y(1 - t) + IM_y]}{I_r + X_\varepsilon \varepsilon_r} \Delta Y^* + \frac{\Delta I_0}{I_r + X_\varepsilon \varepsilon_r} \tag{6.18}$$

The increased profitability of investment expands investment demand, shifting the investment demand curve to the right. But the positive technology shock does more than just make investment more profitable: It boosts the current efficiency of labour as well. Higher productivity means higher incomes, which mean more savings, which shift the total savings line to the right as well. The increase in investment demand tends to raise the interest rate; the increase in savings caused by higher incomes tends to lower it. Which dominates? Suppose that the investment demand condition dominates. Then the domestic real interest rate will rise, as Figure 6.13 shows.

As long as the shock shifts the investment demand curve in Figure 6.13 to the right by more than it shifts the total savings line, the value of the exchange rate will fall, and net exports will decrease.

Thus this positive-technology shock to both the efficiency of labour and the profitability of investment has produced:

- A rise in output.
- A sharp rise in investment.
- A decline in the exchange rate: a decrease in the value of foreign currency and an increase in the value of domestic currency.
- A decrease in net exports: an increase in the flow of foreign capital into the country to finance domestic investment.

These shifts in the economy are typically found in a business-cycle boom. Perhaps these Schumpeterian forces are the principal cause of the booms and recessions that we see in our economy.

Most economists, however, would be skeptical of the claim that most of our business cycles are such *real business cycles*. There is one characteristic feature of the boom phase of the business cycle as defined by Schumpeter that the model cannot produce: a fall in unemployment. This chapter's model, after all, is one in which the economy is always at full employment, so how could the model produce an increase in employment correlated with its technology-driven boom?

Some economists speculate that the pattern of unemployment found in the business cycle is due to movements in the level of real wages. When real wages are higher than expected or than average, more people are willing to work for wages. When real wages are temporarily lower than their average trend, some workers

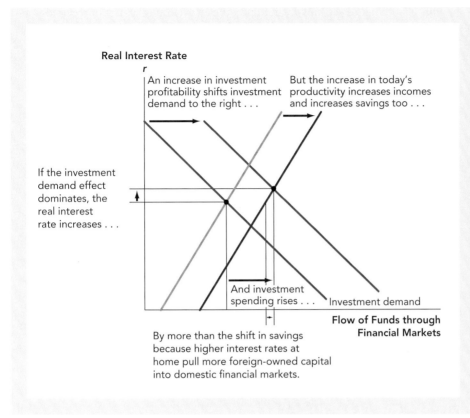

Real Interest Rate

An increase in investment profitability shifts investment demand to the right . . .

But the increase in today's productivity increases incomes and increases savings too . . .

If the investment demand effect dominates, the real interest rate increases . . .

And investment spending rises . . .

Investment demand

Flow of Funds through Financial Markets

By more than the shift in savings because higher interest rates at home pull more foreign-owned capital into domestic financial markets.

FIGURE 6.13
Flow of Funds: A Schumpeterian Combined Productivity-and-Investment Shock
Higher productivity today and optimism about future technological developments affect both the supply and the demand curves in the market for loanable funds. It is plausible to conclude that the economy will boom, with real GDP and investment rising, domestic real interest rates rising, the exchange rate falling, and capital flowing in to finance domestic investment. This pattern is the standard pattern seen in a business-cycle boom.

choose to forgo working for a month or a season or a year. According to this approach, unemployment is high whenever a significant fraction of labour-force members have looked at their employment opportunities, found that they were being offered unusually low wages, and decided to do something other than work for a while.

There is, however, a serious problem with this approach. Few of the cyclically unemployed in a business-cycle slump choose to describe themselves as "voluntarily unemployed." They see themselves not as people making a rational economic decision to spend a lot more time being leisurely but as people who want to work — who would be eager to work if only someone would hire them at the wages others are being paid — but who can't find work because there is excess supply in the labour market.

A second problem is that real-business-cycle theory explains booms — rapid rises in output — as the result of the rapid diffusion of technology and a sharp increase in the efficiency of labour. But how can it describe recessions or depressions, during which production does not grow at all but declines? Does the efficiency of labour decline because of technological regress? Are we supposed to believe that production was lower in 1991 than in 1990 because businesses had forgotten how to use their most productive modes of operation? This seems unlikely. Thus the Schumpeterian approach may well provide a correct theory of booms — or at least some booms. It is harder to see how it could provide an accurate account of recessions and depressions or of the high levels of cyclical unemployment found in times of recession and depression.

RECAP   **SUPPLY SHOCKS**

There are shocks to a flexible-price macroeconomy that change the level of potential output. For example, in 1973 the world price of oil tripled, and capital- and energy-intensive production processes that had made economic sense and been profitable with oil costing less than US$3 a barrel became unproductive and unprofitable with oil costing US$10 a barrel. Thus potential output fell. An adverse supply shock will reduce potential output, will in all likelihood raise real interest rates, and is likely to lead to a rise in the price level as well.

Another type of shock that changes the level of potential output is a technology shock. The economist Joseph Schumpeter was the most powerful exponent of the belief that changes in technology are the principal force driving business cycles. It is easy to see how uneven invention and innovation patterns could generate such real business cycles as producers and investors respond to changing technology and investment opportunities. It is harder to see how changes in technology could cause large-scale unemployment or the production declines that occur in recessions and depressions.

6.4 CONCLUSION

This chapter has analyzed a flexible-price macroeconomy in the *short run* — a time in which neither labour nor capital stocks have an opportunity to change. It has taken a snapshot of the economy in equilibrium at a point in time. It has asked how the equilibrium would be different if the economic environment or economic policy were different. It has at times implicitly talked about the dynamic evolution of the economy in the short run by describing the economy as shifting from one equilibrium to another in response to a change in policy or in the environment.

The flexible-price model presented here is very powerful. It allows us to say a great deal about the way various kinds of shocks will affect the economy and the composition of total spending and output as long as full employment is maintained. It has even, in its discussions of supply shocks and of Schumpeterian real business cycles, dipped into analyzing not just changes in the composition of demand but changes in the level of production.

Nevertheless, it is worth stressing what this chapter has not done:

- It has not discussed the impact of changes in policy and the economic environment on economic growth — that was done in Part II, Chapters 3 and 4. Refer to those chapters to analyze how changes in savings ultimately affect productivity and material standards of living in the long run.
- It has ignored the nominal financial side of the economy — money, prices, and inflation — completely. That topic will be covered in Chapter 7.
- It has maintained the full-employment assumption — that notion will be relaxed in Part IV, the chapters starting with Chapter 8.

CHAPTER SUMMARY

1. When the economy is at full employment, real GDP is equal to potential output.

2. In a flexible-price full-employment economy, the real interest rate shifts in response to changes in policy or the economic environment to keep real GDP equal to potential output.

3. The real interest rate balances the supply of loanable funds committed to financial markets by savers with the demand for funds to finance investments. The circular flow principle guarantees that when the savings supply equals investment, aggregate demand and real GDP will equal potential output.

4. Supply shocks are sharp, sudden changes in costs — like the world oil price increase of 1973 — that shift the efficiency of labour as changed prices cause businesses to economize on or intensively use labour.

5. Real-business-cycle theory attempts to use this chapter's model to account for changes not just in the short-run composition of real GDP but in the short-run level of real GDP as well. It may be (and it may not be) a good theory for booms, or for some booms, but it is hard to see how it could ever be a good explanation of recessions or depressions.

KEY TERMS AND EQUATIONS

capital inflow (p. 180)

comparative statics (p. 184)

financial markets (p. 180)

international savings (p. 181)

private savings (p. 180)

public savings (p. 180)

real business cycle (p. 195)

supply shocks (p. 193)

total savings (p. 180)

Flow-of-funds identity: $(Y^* - C - T) + (T - G) - NX = I$ (6.9)

ANALYTICAL EXERCISES

1. Suppose that in the flexible-price full-employment model the government increases taxes and government purchases by equal amounts. The tax increase reduces consumption spending. What happens qualitatively (tell the direction of change only) to investment, net exports, the exchange rate, the real interest rate, and potential output?

2. What happens according to the flexible-price full-employment model if the intercept C_0 of the consumption function rises. Explain qualitatively (tell the direction of change only) what happens to consumption, investment, net exports, the exchange rate, the real interest rate, and potential output.

3. Explain qualitatively the direction in which consumption, investment, government purchases, net exports, the exchange rate, the real interest rate, and potential output move in the flexible-price full-employment model if the government raises taxes.

4. Give three examples of changes in economic policy or in the economic environment that would shift the total savings curve on the flow-of-funds diagram to the left.

5. Give three examples of changes in the economic environment or in economic policy that would increase the equilibrium real exchange rate.

POLICY EXERCISES

1. Suppose that the relevant parameters of the economy are:

   $t = 0.33$ Tax rate of one-third.

   $I_r = 900$ A 1-percentage-point fall in the interest rate (i.e., a 0.01 unit fall in r) raises investment spending by \$9 billion a year (i.e., $900 \times 0.01 = 9$).

   $C_y = 0.75$ A marginal propensity to consume of three-quarters.

   $\varepsilon_r = 10$ A 1-percentage-point change in the interest rate difference vis-à-vis abroad generates a 10 unit shift in the exchange rate.

$X_\varepsilon = 0.6$ A 1 unit change in the exchange rate leads to a $0.6-billion-a-year change in exports.

And suppose that an irrational exuberance causes a stock market boom that leads consumers to increase their spending by $20 billion at a constant level of disposable income. What would be the increase in interest rates in response to such an exuberance-driven consumption boom?

2. In the economy presented in question 1, suppose that total GDP is $1 trillion and that the government does not want real interest rates to rise and investment to fall in response to the stock market-generated consumption boom. What kinds of policies can the government undertake? How successful will they be?

3. In the economy presented in question 1 suppose that total GDP is $1 trillion, and the government raises taxes and cuts spending by $300 million. What, qualitatively and quantitatively, does the flexible-price full-employment model say should be the consequences of these policies if the relevant parameters of the economy are those given in question 1?

4. Consider two economies. In one, the relevant parameters are:

$Y^* = \$1,000$ In billions; potential output equals $1 trillion.

$t = 0.33$ Tax rate of one-third.

$I_r = 900$ A 1-percentage-point fall in the interest rate (i.e., a 0.01 unit fall in r) raises investment spending by $9 billion a year (i.e., $900 \times 0.01 = 9$).

$C_y = 0.75$ A marginal propensity to consume of three-quarters.

$\varepsilon_r = 10$ A 1-percentage-point change in the interest rate difference vis-à-vis abroad generates a 10 unit shift in the exchange rate.

$X_\varepsilon = 0.6$ A 1 unit change in the exchange rate leads to a $0.6 billion-a-year change in exports.

In the other, the relevant parameters are:

$Y^* = \$1,000$ In billions; potential output equals $1 trillion.

$t = 0.33$ Tax rate of one-third.

$I_r = 900$ A 1-percentage-point fall in the interest rate (i.e., a 0.01 unit fall in r) raises investment spending by $9 billion a year.

$C_y = 0.5$ A marginal propensity to consume of one-half.

$\varepsilon_r = 10$ A 1-percentage-point change in the interest rate difference vis-à-vis abroad generates a 10 unit shift in the exchange rate.

$X_\varepsilon = 0.6$ A 1 unit change in the exchange rate leads to a $0.6 billion-a-year change in exports.

Compare the effects of a $10 billion increase in government purchases on these two economies. In which economy do interest rates go up by more? In which economy does investment go down by more?

5. One of the current debates in Canadian politics is what to do with the federal government budget surplus. Consider the following two alternative policies:
   a. Use the government budget surplus to reduce taxes.
   b. Use the government budget surplus to reduce the government debt.

Which one of these policies seems likely to lead to lower interest rates? To lead to higher investment spending? To lead to a lower value of the exchange rate?

6A
Solving the Model

FLOW-OF-FUNDS EQUILIBRIUM

At what level of the real interest rate will the flow of funds through financial markets be in equilibrium? At what level will the real interest rate be stable? To determine the flow-of-funds equilibrium, look more closely at the supply of and demand for funds. First, let's look at the determinants of the supply of private savings:

$$Y^* - C - T = [1 - t - (1 - t)C_y]Y^* - C_0 \qquad (6.19)$$

Second, let's look at the determinants of public savings:

$$T - G = tY^* - \bar{G} \qquad (6.20)$$

Third, let's look at the determinants of international savings:

$$-NX = IM_y Y^* + X_\varepsilon \varepsilon_r r - X_f Y^f - X_\varepsilon \varepsilon_0 - X_\varepsilon \varepsilon_r r^f \qquad (6.21)$$

These three added together make up the flow-of-funds supply of savings. Note that in Figures 6.3 and 6.4 the supply of savings is upward-sloping: When the interest rate r rises, the total savings flow increases. An increase in the real interest rate attracts foreign capital into domestic financial markets.

The flow-of-funds demand is simply the investment function:

$$I = I_0 - I_r r \qquad (6.22)$$

Equilibrium is, of course, where the supply and demand curves cross — where the supply of savings is equal to investment demand. What is the equilibrium interest rate? It is the level at which the supply of savings is equal to investment demand. To get an explicit expression for the interest rate, begin by writing out the determinants of all the pieces of savings:

$$\{[1 - t - (1 - t)C_y]Y^* - C_0\} + (tY^* - \bar{G}) + (IM_y Y^* + X_\varepsilon \varepsilon_r r - X_f Y^f - X_\varepsilon \varepsilon_0 - X_\varepsilon \varepsilon_r r^f) = I_0 - I_r r \qquad (6.23)$$

Group all the terms that depend on Y^* on the left of the left-hand side, all the terms that are constant in the middle of the left-hand side, and all the terms that depend on international factors on the right of the left-hand side, and move all the terms with the real interest rate r over to the right-hand side:

$$\{1 - [(1 - t)C_y - IM_y]\}Y^* - (C_0 + I_0 + \overline{G}) - (X_f Y^f + X_\varepsilon \varepsilon_0 + X_\varepsilon \varepsilon_r r^f) = -(I_r + X_\varepsilon \varepsilon_r)r$$

And divide by $-(I_r + X_\varepsilon \varepsilon_r)$ to determine the equilibrium real interest rate r:

$$r = \frac{(C_0 + I_0 + \overline{G}) + (X_f Y^f + X_\varepsilon \varepsilon_0 + X_\varepsilon \varepsilon_r r^f) - \{1 - [(1 - t)C_y - IM_y]\}Y^*}{I_r + X_\varepsilon \varepsilon_r} \quad (6.24)$$

Given the parameters of the flexible-price model and the value of potential GDP, it is straightforward to calculate the equilibrium real interest rate r by substituting the parameters into the formula for r.

For example, when parameter values are:
Potential output $Y^* = \$1{,}000$ billion
Baseline consumption $C_0 = \$300$ billion
Baseline investment $I_0 = \$100$ billion
Government purchases $\overline{G} = \$200$ billion
Tax rate $t = 25$ percent
MPC $C_y = 0.67$
Propensity to import $IM_y = 0.2$
Abroad, $X_f = 0.01$ and $Y^f = \$10{,}000$ billion
Foreign exchange speculators' long-run view $\varepsilon_0 = 100$
Foreign interest rates $r^f = 0$
Sensitivity of exports to the exchange rate $X_\varepsilon = 1$
Sensitivity of investment to the interest rate $I_r = 900$
Sensitivity of the exchange rate to the interest rate $\varepsilon_r = 600$
Then replacing each of the parameters with its value produces

$$r = \frac{(300 + 100 + 200) + (0.01 \times 10{,}000 + 1 \times 100 + 1 \times 600 \times 0) - \{1 - [(1 - 0.25) \times 0.67 - 0.2]\} \times 1{,}000}{900 + 1 \times 600}$$

$$= \frac{600 + 200 - 0.7 \times 1{,}000}{1{,}500}$$

$$= \frac{100}{1{,}500} = 0.0667$$

Thus we have an equilibrium real interest rate of 6.67 percent per year.

Is the economy in fact in equilibrium when the real interest rate is 6.67 percent per year? Yes. At that level of the interest rate:

- Private savings equal –$50 billion (yes, they are less than zero — households are drawing down their wealth in order to finance high current consumption), as you can see by substituting the parameters into the equation that determines private saving.

$$Y^* - C - T = [1 - t - (1 - t)C_y]Y^* - C_0$$

- Government savings equal $50 billion, as you can see by subtracting government purchases from taxes.

- The capital inflow from abroad — minus net exports — equals $40 billion, as you can see by substituting the parameter values and a real interest rate of 6.67 percent into the equation:

$$-NX = IM_y Y^* + X_\varepsilon \varepsilon_r r - X_f Y^f - X_\varepsilon \varepsilon_0 - X_\varepsilon \varepsilon_r r^f$$

that determines minus net exports.

- These three components of saving add up to $40 billion.

- Investment is equal to $40 billion.

Thus the flow of funds through financial markets balances.

Looking at the components of real GDP:
- Consumption spending equals $800 billion.
- Investment spending equals $40 billion.
- Government purchases equal $200 billion.
- Net exports equal –$40 billion.
- All these add up to $1,000 billion: the level of potential output

Total spending — aggregate demand — is indeed equal to real GDP.

A GOVERNMENT PURCHASES BOOM

Assume that the parameters of the model are:

$t = 0.33$ — Tax rate of one-third of income.

$I_r = 900$ — A 1-percentage-point fall in the interest rate (i.e., a fall of 0.01 in r) raises investment spending by $9 billion a year (i.e., 900 $\times$ 0.01 = 9).

$C_y = 0.75$ — A marginal propensity to consume of three-quarters.

$\varepsilon_r = 10$ — A 1 percentage point change (i.e., a change of 0.01) in the interest rate difference vis-à-vis abroad generates a 10 unit change in the exchange rate.

$X_\varepsilon = 60$ — A 1 unit change in the exchange rate (i.e., a change in ε by 1) leads to a $60 billion-a-year change in exports.

Suppose that there is a sudden increase in government purchases of $600 million a year. This boom in spending increases the equilibrium real interest rate by 1 percentage point:

$$\Delta r = \frac{\Delta G}{I_r + X_\varepsilon \varepsilon_r} = \frac{\$15}{900 + 60 \times 10} = \frac{15}{1,500} = 0.01 = 1\%$$

As a result, the equilibrium values of the other variables in the economy will change by

$$\Delta G = \Delta G = +\$15 \text{ billion}$$

$$\Delta I = \frac{-I_r}{I_r + X_\varepsilon \varepsilon_r} \Delta G = \frac{-900}{900 + 60 \times 10} \$15 = -\$9 \text{ billion}$$

$$\Delta C = 0$$

$$\Delta NX = \frac{-X_\varepsilon \varepsilon_r}{I_r + X_\varepsilon \varepsilon_r} \Delta G = \frac{-(60 \times 10)}{900 + 60 \times 10} \$15 = -\$6 \text{ billion}$$

$$\Delta \varepsilon = \frac{-\varepsilon_r}{I_r + X_\varepsilon \varepsilon_r} \Delta G = \frac{-10}{900 + 60 \times 10} \$15 = -0.1 = -10\% \text{ change}$$

In sum, the $15-billion increase in annual government purchases shifts the economy's equilibrium by raising the real interest rates by 1 percent. Such an increase in the real interest rate carries with it a 10-percent fall in the exchange rate. The interest rate increase reduces investment spending by $9 billion a year. The exchange rate decline reduces net exports by $6 billion a year.

Some additional insight into this example can be gained by looking at the flow-of-funds diagram in Figure 6A.1. The increase in government spending shifts the supply-of-loanable-funds curve to the left by $15 billion. Given the slopes of the loanable funds supply and the investment demand curves, the result of this leftward shift is a $9-billion fall in annual investment — and a 1-percentage-point rise in the real interest rate.

FIGURE 6A.1
Flow-of-Funds:
A $15-Billion Increase
in Government
Purchases

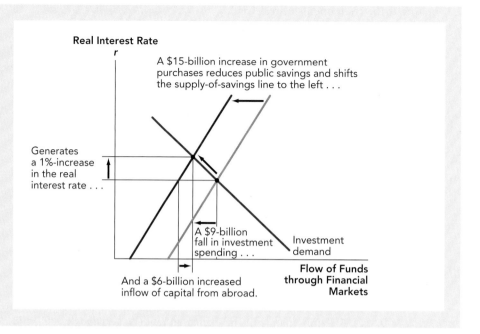

Real Interest Rate
r

A $15-billion increase in government purchases reduces public savings and shifts the supply-of-savings line to the left . . .

Generates a 1%-increase in the real interest rate . . .

A $9-billion fall in investment spending . . .

Investment demand

Flow of Funds through Financial Markets

And a $6-billion increased inflow of capital from abroad.

FIGURE 6A.2
The Impact of a
Change in the
Domestic Interest
Rate on the Exchange
Rate

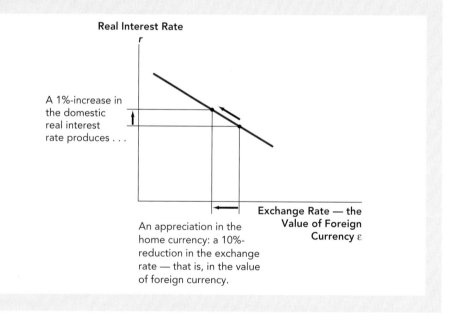

Real Interest Rate
r

A 1%-increase in the domestic real interest rate produces . . .

Exchange Rate — the Value of Foreign Currency ε

An appreciation in the home currency: a 10%-reduction in the exchange rate — that is, in the value of foreign currency.

Given this 1-percentage-point rise in the real interest rate, it is straightforward to determine the resulting change in the exchange rate, as shown in Figure 6A.2, and thus the change in net exports.

What if this model economy had experienced a change not in government spending but in tax rates? A hint: The effects of a cut in tax rates are very similar but not quite identical to an increase in government spending. A tax cut increases household incomes, and households then divide their increased disposable incomes, spending some of the increase on consumption and saving the rest.

7

Money, Prices, and Inflation

QUESTIONS

What do economists mean by "money"?

Why is money useful?

What do economists mean when they say that money is a unit of account?

What determines the price level and the inflation rate?

Why would a government ever generate hyperinflation — a condition in which prices rise by more than 20 percent a *month*?

What determines the level of money demand?

What determines the level of the money supply?

Why is inflation seen as something to be avoided?

7.1 MONEY

Newspaper and television commentators devote a lot of attention to **inflation**. Inflation disrupts the economy in a number of different ways. Moreover, even when inflation is absent, fear that it will emerge has a powerful effect on the economy. The actions of economic policy-making agencies like the Bank of Canada are tightly constrained by fear that certain courses of action will lead to inflation.

As Figure 7.1 shows, in the 1970s Canada experienced episodes of mild (1 to 3%), creeping (4 to 7%) and galloping (7 to 15%) inflation. Although relatively mild, that inflation was large enough to cause significant economic and political trauma. Avoiding a repeat of the inflation of the 1970s remains a major goal of economic policy even today, a quarter of a century later.

Many countries have experienced inflations that are *not* mild. In Russia in 1998 the price level rose at a rate of 60 percent. In Germany in 1923 prices rose at a rate

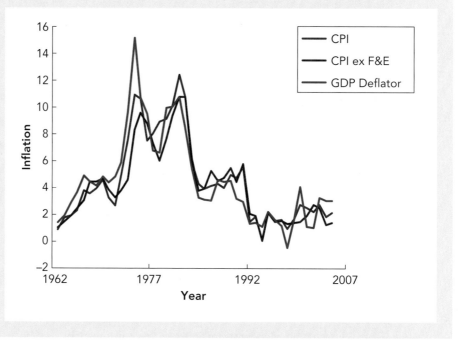

FIGURE 7.1
Different Measures of Canadian Inflation, 1962–2005
All measures of price changes show a burst of inflation in Canada in the 1970s.

Source: Adapted from the Statistics Canada CANSIM II database, Series V735319 (CPI), V735600 (CPI ex F&E), V498086 (nominal GDP), and V1992067 (real GDP).

http://www.statcan.ca/
http://cansim2.statcan.ca/

of 60 percent per *week*. So-called **hyperinflation**s have been seen in many other countries in this century, from Argentina to Ukraine, from Hungary to China. They are extremely destructive, inflicting severe damage on the ability of **money** to grease the wheels of the social mechanism of exchange that is the market economy. The system of prices and market exchange breaks down, and production can fall to a small fraction of potential output.

Chapters 5 and 6 did not discuss the determination of the level of prices and the inflation rate. They did not have to. It was perfectly possible to figure out what the real interest and exchange rates, the level of real GDP, and the division of real GDP into its components were without mentioning the overall price level or the rate of inflation. And there was no feedback from production and output back to the price level.

The power to analyze real variables without referring to the price level is a special feature of the flexible-price full-employment model of the economy. Economists call it the *classical dichotomy*: Real variables (such as real GDP, real investment spending, or the real exchange rate) can be analyzed and calculated without thinking of nominal variables such as the price level. Economists also speak of it as the property whereby money is **neutral** or is a *veil* — a covering that does not affect the shape of the face underneath.

Starting in Chapter 8 the classical dichotomy will not hold. Money will not be neutral: The determination of the price level and its changes will be intimately tied up with fluctuations in production and employment. This is because Chapter 8 introduces prices that are sluggish, or sticky, or that are fixed. Hence they cannot adjust smoothly and instantaneously to changes in nominal variables like the **money stock** and the **price level**. But here in Part III prices are flexible, and the **classical dichotomy** holds.

This chapter explores what determines the overall level of prices and the rate of inflation (or deflation) in our flexible-price full-employment model of the macroeconomy. This topic is worth examining for two reasons. First, it provides a useful baseline analysis against which to contrast the conclusions of future chapters. Second, whenever we look over relatively long spans of time — decades, perhaps — wages and prices *are* effectively flexible, they *do* have time to move in response to shocks, and the flexible-price assumption is a fruitful and useful one.

MONEY: LIQUID WEALTH THAT CAN BE SPENT

When noneconomists use the word "money," they may mean a number of things. "She has a lot of money" usually means that she is wealthy; wealth is the value of all assets (money, real estate, bonds, and stocks) she owns. "He makes a lot of money" usually means that he has a high income; income is what he earns every year from his work and his assets. When economists use the word "money," however, they mean something different. To economists, *money* is wealth that is held in a readily spendable form. Money is that kind of wealth that you can use immediately to buy things because others will accept it as payment. Today the economy's stock of money is made up of:

- Coins and currency that are transferred by handing the cash over to a seller (almost everyone will accept cash as payment for goods and services).
- Chequing account balances that are transferred by writing a cheque (which most people will accept as payment for goods and services).
- Other assets — like savings account balances — that can be turned into cash or demand deposits nearly instantaneously, risklessly, and costlessly.

Why do economists adopt this special definition of money? Giving household words special definitions is probably a bad thing to do, since it can cause confusion and misunderstanding. Yet economists do so not only for "money" but also for terms such as "investment" and "utility."

Whether assets that can be quickly and cheaply turned into cash (savings account balances, money market mutual funds, liquid Treasury securities, and so on) are included in the money stock is a matter of taste and judgment. At what level of cost and inconvenience is an asset no longer "readily spendable"? There is no clear answer. Thus economists have a number of different measures of the money stock — identified by symbols like H, M1, M2, M2+, and M2++ — each of which draws the line around a different set of assets that it counts as wealth readily *enough* spent to be "money."

THE USEFULNESS OF MONEY

In our world all you need to carry out a market transaction — whether you want to buy or sell some good or service — is either to have money yourself (if you want to buy) or to deal with a purchaser who has money (if you want to sell). In a barter economy, an economy without the social convention of money, market exchange would require the so-called *coincidence of wants*: You would have to have physically in your possession some good or service that another person wants, and that person would have to have in his or her possession some good or service that you want. As Figure 7.2 shows, finding consumption goods to satisfy the coincidence of wants would get remarkably complicated very quickly. Without money, an extraordinary amount of time and energy would be spent simply arranging the goods one needed to trade. Money eliminates a double coincidence of wants, reduces transaction costs and promotes market efficiency.

UNITS OF ACCOUNT

There is one other feature worth noting. The same assets that serve as the most common form of readily spendable purchasing power also serve as *units of account*. Dollars or euros or yen are not only what we use to settle transactions but also what

FIGURE 7.2

Coincidence of Wants

Without money, how is the carpenter to persuade the farmer to give him corn when the farmer wants a haircut but doesn't need furniture — which the cook wants? How is the mover going to persuade the cook to feed him when the cook doesn't need the moving truck — the writer does? With money, all can sell what they have for cash and have confidence that they can then turn around and use the cash to buy what they need.

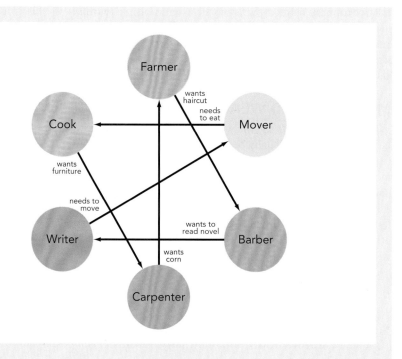

we use to quote prices to one another. At some times and places the functions of money as a **medium of exchange** and as a **unit of account** have been separated, but today they almost invariably go together.

This is a potential cause of trouble. Anything that alters the real value of the domestic money in terms of its purchasing power over goods and services will also alter the real terms of existing contracts that use money as the unit of account. The effect of changes in the price level on contracts that have used the domestic money as a unit of account is a principal source of the social costs of inflation and deflation. The effect of changes in the exchange rate on contracts that have used foreign monies as units of account is a principal source of the social costs of currency crises.

RECAP MONEY

To an economist, "money" is wealth that is held in a readily spendable form. Money is that kind of wealth that you can use immediately to buy things because others will accept it as payment. Money is useful because in its absence we would have a barter economy and market exchange would require the so-called *coincidence of wants*. Without money, an extraordinary amount of time and energy would be spent simply arranging the goods one needed to trade.

The same assets that serve as the most common form of readily spendable purchasing power also serve as *units of account*. Dollars or euros or yen are not only what we use to settle transactions but also what we use to quote prices to one another. This is a potential cause of trouble. The effect of changes in the price level on contracts that have used the domestic money as a unit of account is a principal source of the social costs of inflation and deflation. The effect of changes in the exchange rate on contracts that have used foreign monies as units of account is a principal source of the social costs of currency crises.

7.2 THE QUANTITY THEORY OF MONEY

THE DEMAND FOR MONEY

People have a *demand* for money just as they have a demand for any other good. They want to hold a certain amount of wealth in the form of readily spendable purchasing power because the stuff is useful. The more money in your portfolio, the easier it is to buy things. Too little money makes life pointlessly difficult. You have to waste time running to the bank for extra cash or waste energy and time liquidating pieces of your portfolio before you can carry out your normal daily transactions.

Nevertheless, you don't want to have too much of your wealth in the form of readily spendable purchasing power. Cash sitting in your pocket is not earning interest at the bank. Wealth you do not want to spend for five years could earn a higher return as a certificate of deposit or as an investment in the stock market than as cash in your chequing account.

Figure 7.3 summarizes the reasons for and opportunity cost of holding money. The higher the flow of spending, the more money the households and businesses in the economy will want to hold. How much more? That depends on the transactions technology of the economy: what businesses will take credit cards, how easy it is to get cheques approved, the nominal interest rate, and so forth. In this section of the chapter, however, we ignore all other determinants of money demand and focus on the flow of spending as *the* principal determinant of money demand.

THE QUANTITY EQUATION

The theory that the only important determinant of the demand for money is the flow of spending gives rise to the **quantity theory of money demand**. This theory is derived from the quantity theory (North American) equation of exchange

$$M \times V = (P \times Y)$$

rewritten in the Cambridge (England) form

$$M = \frac{1}{V} \times (P \times Y) \tag{7.1}$$

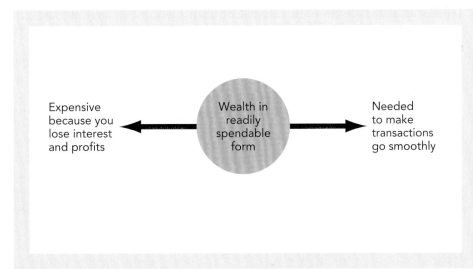

Expensive because you lose interest and profits ← Wealth in readily spendable form → Needed to make transactions go smoothly

FIGURE 7.3

Reasons for and Opportunity Cost of Holding Money

As with every other economic decision, the amount of wealth households and businesses want to hold in the readily spendable form of money depends on the benefits of holding money and the opportunity cost — the lost interest and profits — of doing so.

In either of the equations on the previous page, M is the money stock in the economy, $P \times Y$ represents the total nominal flow of spending. For each dollar of spending on goods and services, households want to hold $1/V$ dollars' worth of money. The parameter V — a constant, or perhaps growing slowly and predictably (in this section of the chapter only — later on things become more complicated!) — is the **velocity of money**. The velocity of money is a measure of how "fast" money moves through the economy: how many times a year the average unit of money shows up in someone's income and is then used to buy a final good or service that counts in GDP.

MONEY AND PRICES

THE PRICE LEVEL

Together, the quantity theory of money and the full-employment assumption allow us to determine the price level in the flexible-price model of the macroeconomy. Real GDP Y is equal to potential output (Y^*) and $Y = Y^*$. The velocity of money V is determined by the sophistication of the banking system and the social conventions that govern payment and settlement. For the "M1" concept of money — currency plus chequing account deposits — the current velocity V is about 7.5: Businesses and households want to hold about \$1 of their wealth in the form of M1 for every \$7.5 of real GDP produced. Velocity has not been constant over time. In the years immediately after World War II, the M1 velocity of money was only 6 and it was 17 in 1991 (see Figure 7.4). It is important to note that, in making these calculations, we use the fact that the money market always clears: money supply is equal to money demand. This will be further discussed in Section 7.3.

Thus if we know real GDP Y, the velocity of money V, and the money stock M, we can calculate that the price level is

$$P = \left(\frac{V}{Y}\right) \times M \tag{7.2}$$

Box 7.1 presents an example of such a quantity-theory calculation.

Should the price level be momentarily higher than the quantity equation predicts, households and businesses will notice that they have less wealth in the form of readily spendable purchasing power than they want. They will cut back on purchases for a little while to build up their liquidity. As they cut back on purchases, sellers will note that demand is weak and will cut their prices, so the price level will fall.

Should the price level be momentarily lower than the quantity equation value, households and businesses will note that they have more wealth in the form of money than they want, so they will accelerate their purchases to reduce their money balances. Sellers will note that demand is strong and will raise their prices, so the price level will rise. As long as prices are flexible, the economy's price level will remain at its quantity-theory equilibrium. Transitory fluctuations in the velocity of money mean that day-to-day or even year-to-year changes in the money stock are not mirrored in equivalent proportional changes in the price level. But on a decade-to-decade time scale the quantity theory of money is a very reliable guide to and predictor of large movements in prices. However, using the quantity theory in this way requires that we know the level of the money stock. What determines the level of the money stock?

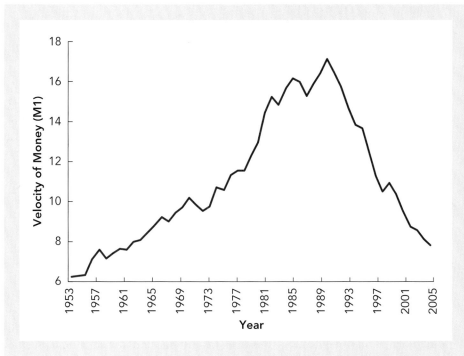

FIGURE 7.4
The Velocity of Money M1, 1953–2005
Between 1960 and 1990 it looked as though the velocity of money was slowly and steadily increasing as the banking system improved its efficiency and the technology available for conducting transactions. But in the 1990s and 2000s the velocity of money fell far short of its pre-1990 trend. Economists attribute this to lower inflation rates in the 1990s and 2000s, which diminished incentives to economize on cash and chequing account balances.

Source: Adapted from the Statistics Canada CANSIM II database, Series V37200 (M1), V500633 (nominal GDP, 1953–1960), and V498086 (nominal GDP, 1961–2005).

CALCULATING THE PRICE LEVEL FROM THE QUANTITY EQUATION

It is straightforward to use the quantity theory of money

$$P = \left(\frac{V}{Y}\right) \times M$$

to calculate the price level. For example, in the year 2000 real GDP (in 1992 dollars) was equal to $921.485 billion, the M1 measure of the money stock was equal to $106.572 billion, and the velocity of money was equal to 9.993. Therefore:

$$P = \left(\frac{9.993}{\$921.485}\right) \times \$106.572 = 1.156$$

In the third quarter of 2000 the price level was equal to 15.6 percent of its 1992 level, which works out to an average rate of inflation of about 2 percent per year from 1992 to 2000.

Had velocity grown an additional 10 percent between 1992 and 2000, the price level would have grown an additional 10 percent as well if the money stock and real GDP were unchanged from their historical values. Had the money stock grown by an additional 10 percent between 1992 and 2000, the price level would have grown by an additional 10 percent as well if velocity and real GDP were unchanged from their historical values. And had real GDP grown by an additional 10 percent between 1992 and 2000, this would have reduced the 2000 price level by 10 percent relative to its historical value if velocity and the money stock were unchanged from their historical values.

7.1

BOX

EXAMPLE

http://www.bank-banque-canada.ca/

THE MONEY STOCK

Determination of the money stock is the basic task of *monetary policy*. In Canada the **Bank of Canada**, the country's central bank, determines the money stock, through its control over the **monetary base**, the sum of currency in circulation and of deposits of the chartered banks at the Bank of Canada. When the central bank wants to reduce the monetary base, it sells short-term government bonds and accepts currency or deposits at its regional branches as payment. The currency is then removed from circulation and stored in a basement somewhere; the deposits the central bank receives as payment are then erased from its books. Thus the monetary base declines. When the Bank of Canada wants to increase the monetary base, it buys short-term government bonds, paying for them with currency or by crediting the seller with a deposit at the Bank of Canada. These transactions are called **open-market operations**, because the Bank of Canada buys or sells bonds on the open market. (See Figure 7.5.)

Although the Bank of Canada directly controls the monetary base, the other measures of the money stock that we discuss in Box 7.2 are determined by the interaction of the monetary base with the banking sector. Banks accept chequing and savings account deposits. They lend out the purchasing power deposited in the bank, earn interest, and provide the depositor with a claim to wealth in readily spendable form. But the central bank limits commercial banks' ability to accept deposits. It requires that commercial banks redeposit at the Bank of Canada a certain proportion of their total deposits. Financial institutions find it prudent to hold extra liquid reserves in case an unexpectedly large number of depositors seek to withdraw their money. There is nothing worse for a financial institution than to be unable to meet its depositors' demands for money. Thus, as Box 7.2 shows, broader measures of the money stock are larger than but limited in their growth by the size of the monetary base, the **reserve requirements** of the chartered banks and other financial institutions, and financial institutions' extremely powerful incentive never to get caught without enough cash to satisfy depositors' demands.

In this chapter (and later chapters too) we sweep these complications under the rug. We assume that the central bank can easily set the money stock at whatever level it wishes. (Although these subjects are given short shrift in this book, they are explored in great depth in money and banking textbooks and are discussed in Section 7.6 below).

FIGURE 7.5
Open-Market Operations
The Bank of Canada controls the money supply through open-market operations: purchases and sales of bonds on the open market. A purchase of bonds increases the economy's money stock. A sale of bonds sucks cash out of the economy and reduces the money stock.

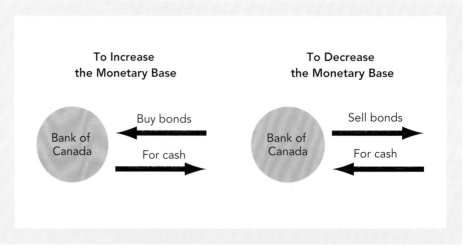

CANADIAN MONETARY AGGREGATES

Counting the quantity of money in an economy is a challenging exercise because it is often difficult to know what to include. Because the possibilities are so numerous, most countries have several definitions. Those used in Canada, from the narrowest to the broadest, include

- *currency outside banks:* the notes and coins issued by the Bank of Canada and the Royal Canadian Mint that are outside the banking system;
- *M1:* currency outside banks (held by households and firms) plus Canadian-dollar demand deposits (chequing accounts) at Canadian banks net of the private sector float (a balancing amount related to transactions that are not yet complete);
- *M2:* M1 plus the chartered banks' holdings of personal saving deposits (these may have chequable features) and nonpersonal (firms') notice deposits;
- *M2+:* M2 plus personal and nonpersonal deposits at the near banks (trust companies, credit unions, caisses populaires, and so on) plus funds invested in certain money market mutual funds; and
- *M2++:* M2 plus Canada Saving Bonds and non–money market mutual funds.

Source: "Rapid Money Growth May Bring Higher Inflation," by William Robson and Shay Aba, *C.D. Howe Institute Commentary*, Number 114, September 2000, www.cdhowe.org.

Table 7.1 summarizes the definitions of the money stock.

TABLE 7.1
Measure of the Money Stock

Concept of Money	Assets Included in the Concept	Amount, 2005 (in Millions)
C	Currency	45,321
H	Monetary Base: Assets that can serve as reserves for banks	48,320
M1	Currency plus demand deposits	161,241
M2	M1 plus savings account deposits and small time deposits	651,167
M2+	M2 plus desposits at trust and mortgage loan companies, caisses populaires, and credit unions	907,482
M2++	M2+ plus Canada Savings Bonds and non–money market mututal funds	1,326,219

Source: Adapted from the Statistics Canada CANSIM II database, Series V37173 (C), V37145 (H), V37200 (M1), V37198 (M2), V37131 (M2+), and V37150 (M2++).

INFLATION

The quantity equation

$$P = \left(\frac{V}{Y}\right) \times M$$

leads immediately to an equation for the inflation rate π — the proportional rate of change of the price level — if you recall our rule from Chapter 2 about how to calculate the proportional growth rates of products or quotients. Put simply, the proportional growth rate of a product is the sum of the growth rates of the terms multiplied together; the proportional growth rate of a quotient is the difference between the growth rates of the individual terms. Thus

inflation = velocity growth rate + money growth rate − real GDP growth rate

To write this relationship in more compact form, use a lowercase m and v for the proportional growth rates of the money stock and velocity and use a lowercase y for the growth rate of real GDP. Then

$$\pi = m + v - y \qquad (7.3)$$

If the proportional growth rate of real GDP is 4 percent per year, the velocity of money V increases at a proportional rate of 2 percent per year, and the money stock M grows at 5 percent per year, then

$$\pi = 5\% + 2\% - 4\% = 3\%$$

The inflation rate is 3 percent per year.

Most changes in the rate of inflation are due to changes in the rate of growth of the money stock. It is rare that there are substantial and persistent changes in y, the rate of growth of real GDP. The variable v, the rate of growth of velocity, is determined by the slow pace of institutional and technological change in the banking system. But m, the rate of growth of the money stock, can change quickly and substantially. Thus if you see a large and persistent change in inflation, odds are that it is due to a change in the rate of growth of the money stock. When one looks across countries, some of which have astonishingly high rates of money growth, the correlations between money growth and inflation are very strong indeed, as Figure 7.6 shows: The higher the rate of money growth, the higher the rate of inflation.

If the Bank of Canada keeps the money stock relatively stable, prices will be relatively stable and inflation will be low. If the Bank of Canada lets the money stock grow more quickly, then prices will be unstable and inflation will be relatively high. But at a short term, year-to-year time scale the relationship is not very close.

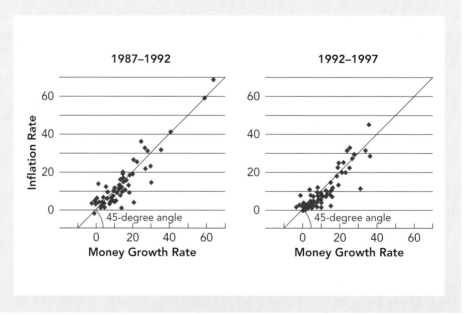

FIGURE 7.6
Money Growth and Inflation across Countries

For each country, one point shows the growth rate of money and the inflation rate for five-year periods, 1987–1992 (left) and 1992–1997 (right). Points on the 45-degree angle line have money growth rate equal to the inflation rate. Almost all countries are clustered close to that 45-degree line; the higher the money growth rate, the higher the inflation rate.

Source: Gerald P. Dwyer and R.W. Hafer "Are Money Growth and Inflation Still Related?" *Federal Reserve Bank of Atlanta Monthly Review*, Second Quarter 1999, pp. 32–43.

7.3 THE INTEREST RATE AND MONEY DEMAND

Up until now we have not made a distinction between money supply and money demand. The reason for this is that until now we have assumed that the money market always clears, that is, money supply is always equal to money demand. As we have used algebra in analyzing the model, this was a useful assumption we made without compromising any rigour. At this stage, however, it is important to be more specific by distinguishing money demand from money supply. We should also consider how they interact in order to determine the equilibrium in the money market.

MONEY DEMAND

In this section we think more systematically about the determinants of money demand. Because the real world is more complicated than the simplest quantity theory implies, representing the velocity of money as a constant or slowly moving steady trend is misleading. In the real world, inflation is not always proportional to money growth. Hence, V is not fixed, but is influenced by other factors such as the nominal interest rate.

As Figure 7.7 shows, M1 growth has been much more volatile than inflation in Canada over the period 1953–2006. Notice that in the early 1970s M1 growth fell sharply in order to reduce the inflationary pressures brought about by the oil price shock of 1973–74. Also, up to the mid-1970s inflation and M1 growth had upward trends and were positively correlated. However, since the early 1980s the association between the two variables is rather weak with inflation falling and M1 growth exceeding inflation and being more volatile on average.

Economic theory suggests that money demand should be *inversely* related to the nominal interest rate, which is the sum of the real interest rate and the current inflation rate. The cash in your purse or wallet does not earn interest. Your chequing account balances earn little or no interest as well. As a result, their purchasing power

FIGURE 7.7

Money Growth and Inflation Are Not Always Parallel

Up to the mid-1970s the correlation between M1 growth and inflation were positive. After the mid-1970s, this correlation broke down.

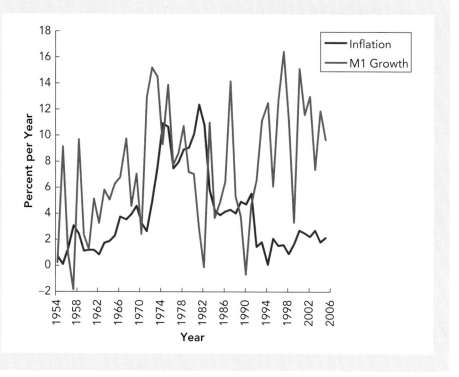

Source: Adapted from the Statistics Canada CANSIM II database, Series V735319 (CPI) and V73200 (M1).

over real goods and services erodes at the rate of inflation. The expected real return on keeping your money in readily spendable form is $-\pi^e$, the negative of the expected inflation rate π^e.

By contrast, were you to take a dollar out of your chequing account and invest it, its real return would be the real interest rate r. The difference between the rate of return on money balances and the rate of return on other assets is the *opportunity cost* of holding money. This opportunity cost is the sum of the inflation rate π^e and the real interest rate r, that is, the nominal interest rate i. The higher the opportunity cost of holding money, the lower is the demand for money balances. Economic theory thus tells us that the velocity of money will be a function like

$$V = V^L \times [V_0 + V_i \times (r \times \pi^e)] \tag{7.4}$$

where V^L is the financial technology-driven trend in the velocity of money, and $V_0 + V_i \times (r + \pi^e)$ captures the dependence of the demand for money on the nominal interest rate. The higher the nominal interest rate $i = r + \pi^e$, the higher is the velocity function V and the lower is the demand for money (see equation (7.1) above).

Such a function for velocity means that the demand for nominal money balances, denoted by M^d, is

$$M^d = \frac{P \times Y}{V^L \times [V_0 + V_i \times (r + \pi^e)]}$$

Most of the time, however, we are interested in quantities expressed in terms of goods (i.e., in real terms). Dividing nominal money demand by the price level, we obtain the real demand for money

$$\frac{M^d}{P} = \frac{Y}{V^L \times [V_0 + V_i \times (r + \pi^e)]} \tag{7.5}$$

The demand for real money balances is also known as liquidity preference, L. Notice the demand for real money balances falls when the nominal interest rate increases, while it increases when output increases. Hence, to simplify the analysis usually we assume that liquidity preference takes a simple linear form:

$$L = L_0 - L_i \times (r + \pi^e) + L_y \times Y \tag{7.6}$$

In equation (7.6) L_0 is the autonomous part of demand for real money balances; that is, the part of real money balances that does not depend on the nominal interest rate or output. The value of L_0 depends on the preferences of households and firms and on the technology level in the financial sector.

The sensitivity of the demand for real money balances to changes in the nominal interest rate is given by the parameter L_i. This parameter tells by how much households and businesses shrink the amount of wealth they want to hold in the liquid form of money when the nominal interest rate i goes up. The more sensitive is the liquidity preference to changes in the nominal interest rate, the larger will be L_i.

The sensitivity of the demand for real money balances to changes in output is given by L_y. This parameter tells how much in the way of extra real money balances people demand when total Y goes up. Thus, the more sensitive is the liquidity preference to changes in Y, the larger will be L_y.

The liquidity preference schedule is drawn in Figure 7.8 as an inverse function of the nominal interest rate as explained above, for a given value of Y. However, if Y changes so will the demand for real money balances. For instance, in Figure 7.8, if Y increases the demand for real money will increase and the liquidity preference schedule will shift out and to the right, and if Y falls it will shift down and to the left (show these shifts as an exercise). The reason for these changes is the transactions demand for money. The real income, Y, is a proxy for the aggregate volume of transactions in the economy. Thus, the more transactions that individuals and firms undertake in the economy, the more liquidity they require and the greater is their demand for real money. Notice if the parameter L_y is larger, then for a given increase in income Y, there will be a larger increase in the demand for real money balances, and therefore a larger outward shift in the liquidity preference curve.

Notice also that an increase in the general price level, P, increases the demand for *nominal* money, M^d, in the same proportion, as people need more dollars to carry out their transactions. However, the demand for real money, M^d/P, is independent of the price level P. This makes sense, since the amount of money demanded by people in terms of the goods it can buy should not depend on P.

EQUILIBRIUM IN THE MONEY MARKET

We have now learned about the money stock (i.e., the money supply), and its control by the Bank of Canada. We have also learned about money demand, and how

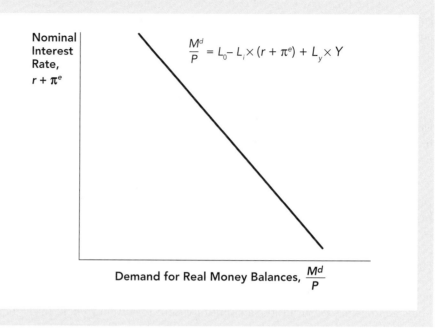

it is affected by the level of real interest rates, expected inflation, GDP, the price level, and financial technology. Now, we bring money supply and money demand together to determine the equilibrium in the money market.

The liquidity preference schedule shown in Figure 7.8 is the demand for real money balances. This demand schedule will have to interact with the schedule for the supply of real money balances in order to give us the equilibrium in the money market. The supply (or stock) of nominal money balances is determined by the Bank of Canada, and is denoted by M^s. At this stage, for simplicity, let us assume that the supply of nominal money balances is independent of the nominal interest rates. The supply of real money balances will then be M^s/P, which will also be independent of the nominal interest rate. Thus, the schedule representing the supply of real money balances will be a vertical line, as shown in Figure 7.9.

The equilibrium in the money market will be given by the equality of real money supply to real money demand. This is at point B in Figure 7.9, where we have

$$\frac{M^s}{P} = \frac{M^d}{P} = \frac{M}{P} \tag{7.7}$$

where M is the equilibrium quantity of the money stock. Hence, in **money market equilibrium** the following relation holds,

$$\frac{M}{P} = L_0 - L_i \times (r + \pi^e) + L_y \times Y \tag{7.8}$$

This is the reason why in previous sections we used M to denote the money stock, without making a distinction between money demand and money supply.

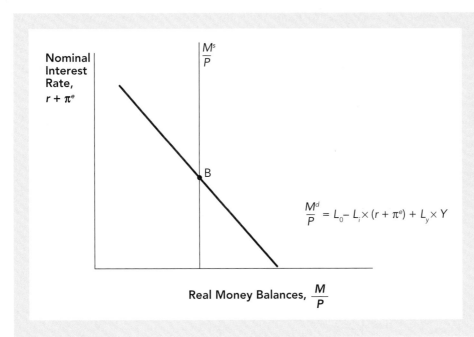

FIGURE 7.9
Money Market Equilibrium
The interaction of real money demand M^d/P and real money supply M^s/P determines the equilibrium in the money market.

MONEY, PRICES, AND INFLATION

Because liquidity preference depends on the expected rate of inflation, we need to keep track of two equations to determine the behaviour of money, prices, and inflation. The first comes directly from the money-demand function and is the equation for the price level, equation (7.2):

$$P = \frac{M \times V}{Y} \qquad (7.9)$$

The second comes from taking the proportional rate of change on both sides of equation (7.9). If expected inflation is equal to actual inflation and the proportional rate of change of the velocity trend is v, then as before

$$\pi = m + v - y \qquad (7.10)$$

Thus if the rate of growth of the money stock is +6 percent per year, the velocity trend is +1 percent per year, and real GDP growth is +4 percent per year, inflation is 3 percent per year.

Suppose that the rate of growth of the money stock suddenly increases permanently from 6 to 10 percent per year. When the economy settles down, the new inflation rate will be 4 percent per year higher — 7 percent instead of 3 percent per year. But at an inflation rate of 7 percent per year, the opportunity cost of holding money is higher. If the real interest rate is stable at 3 percent per year, then the opportunity cost of holding money has just jumped from 6 to 10 percent per year.

A higher opportunity cost of holding money will raise the velocity of money. If the money stock and real GDP remain fixed, this increase in the velocity of money will cause the price level to jump suddenly and discontinuously, as is shown in Figure 7.10! By how much will the price level jump? That depends on how sensitive money demand is to changes in the nominal interest rate. The more sensitive is money demand to the nominal interest rate, the larger will be the sudden jump in the price level.

Thus in the flexible-price macroeconomy, a change in the rate of growth of the money stock not only changes the long-run inflation rate, but also causes an

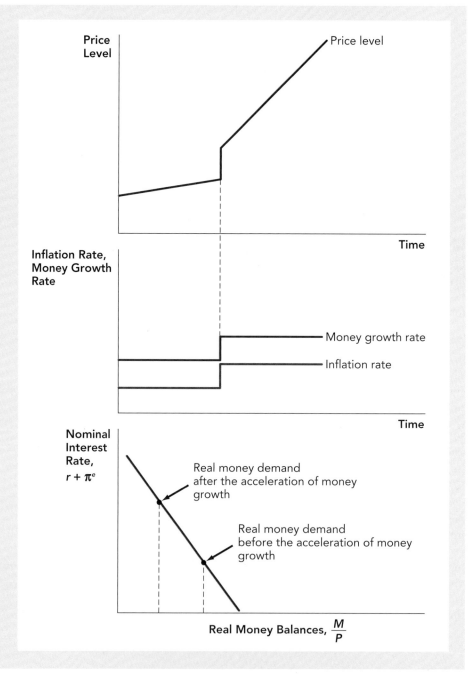

FIGURE 7.10

Effects of an Increase in Money Growth

An increase in the rate of growth of the money stock leads to an immediate jump in the price level, a step-up of the inflation rate, and a fall in the quantity of real money demanded.

immediate jump in the price level at the moment that households and businesses become aware that the rate of money growth has changed.

RECAP INTEREST RATES AND MONEY DEMAND

The real world is more complicated than the quantity theory implies. The velocity of money is not a constant or a trend but depends on the nominal interest rate and other factors. The higher the nominal interest rate, the higher is the velocity of money.

Because the nominal interest rate depends on the inflation rate, an increase in the growth rate of the money stock will have an amplified effect on the price level. First, the price level will rise because there is more money. Second, the velocity of money will increase because inflation rates and nominal interest rates are higher — and this increase in the velocity of money will generate a further increase in the price level.

7.4 INNOVATIONS IN FINANCIAL TECHNOLOGY

The demand for money is very much affected by innovations in banking technology. In this section we will discuss the effects of three financial innovations that have received a lot of attention in recent decades; an increase in the acceptability of credit cards, an increase in the use of automated banking machines (ATMs), and an increase in the use of *Interac* or debit cards.

AN INCREASE IN THE USE OF CREDIT CARDS

First, consider the effect of an increase in the use of credit cards. With this innovation the demand for money will fall, as credit cards will be used to carry out transactions instead of money. This reduces the autonomous part of liquidity preference L_0, and in terms of Figure 7.11 it shifts the liquidity preference schedule to the left, as there will be lower demand for money corresponding to each nominal interest rate.

How would the money market equilibrium be restored after this fall in liquidity preference? With output Y, real interest rates r, and the expected inflation rate π^e the same, for the money market to clear there must be a fall in real money supply M^s/P. With the nominal money supply M^s fixed, the fall in M^s/P is brought about by an increase in the price level P. This will shift the money supply schedule to the left, until it intersects the new liquidity preference schedule at the original nominal interest rate. Thus, in Figure 7.11 the equilibrium will shift from point A to point B. Notice the change from point A to point B does not affect the nominal interest rate. The reason for this is that the financial innovation happens once and for all and it does not affect expected inflation, π^e, which depends essentially on the *rates of growth* of money and output.

What is the economic intuition for this increase in the price level? When credit cards are more widely accepted workers and firms try to reduce their real money holdings and spend their real money holdings on goods and services, which

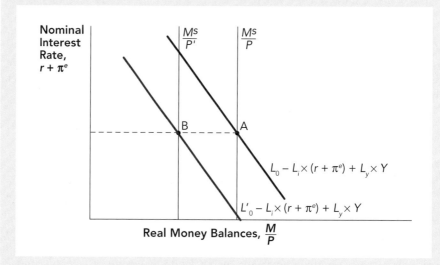

FIGURE 7.11
The Effects of a Fall in Real Money Demand
Increased use of credit cards, ATM machines, and Internet and telephone banking will shift the real money demand schedule to $L'_0 - L_i \times (r + \pi^e) + L_y \times Y$. With output Y, real interest rates r, and the expected inflation rate π^e the same, for the money market to clear there must be a fall in real money supply M^s/P. With the nominal money supply M^s fixed, the fall in M^s/P is brought about by an increase in the price level to P'. Thus, the equilibrium will shift from point A to point B.

increases the demand for goods and services. Since with flexible prices the output supplied is always at its full employment level, the increased demand for goods and services will result in an increase in the price level P.

MORE WIDESPREAD USE OF AUTOMATED BANKING MACHINES

Next, consider the effects of more widespread use of automatic teller machines (ATMs) and telephone and Internet banking. These innovations will also reduce the demand for money and reduce L_0. The reason is that with ATMs and telephone and Internet banking it will be easier to transfer funds between accounts and between different assets. In particular, it will be easier to convert less liquid assets into money. As a result, at any instant people will hold less money, knowing that they can convert other assets into money on short notice at relatively low cost and with little inconvenience. The adjustment of the money market equilibrium will again be as portrayed in Figure 7.11.

MORE WIDESPREAD USE OF *INTERAC* (DEBIT CARDS)

Finally, consider the effect of an increase in the acceptability of *Interac* payments. When you pay for a purchase with *Interac* the amount of the transaction is directly deducted from your bank account (either savings or checking account). Clearly,

Interac reduces demand for coins and notes. Nevertheless, notice that for an *Interac* payment to be processed you will need enough balances in your bank accounts. Thus, *Interac* increases the demand for bank accounts held by households and firms. In fact, the increase in the demand for bank accounts by households and firms will completely offset the fall in the demand for notes and coins, and therefore there will be no effect on the M2 definition of the demand for money.

On the other hand, the demand for the M1 definition of money may fall or stay the same. If households and firms decide to use their chequing accounts for *Interac* payments then the demand for the M1 definition of money will be unchanged; the balances on the chequing accounts will increase by the same amount that the demand for notes and coins falls. On the other hand, if the households and firms decide to use their savings accounts for *Interac* payments then the demand for the M1 definition of money will fall, as savings accounts are not part of the definition of M1.

> **RECAP INNOVATIONS IN THE FINANCIAL MARKETS**
>
> The demand for money is very much affected by innovations in the financial markets. For example, an increase in the acceptability of credit cards or an increase in the use of ATMs reduces real money demand. An increase in the use of *Interac* has no effect on the demand for M2, but may reduce or leave unchanged the demand for M1.

7.5 THE COSTS OF INFLATION

Why should we care whether the central bank controls the money supply so that inflation is low and stable or lets the money supply expand rapidly and produce high and unpredictable inflation? One reason *not* to care about inflation is the fear that inflation makes us directly and significantly poorer. Any claim by a politician that inflation is the "cruelest tax" because its higher prices rob Canadians of the benefits of their wages is not coherent. Inflation raises all nominal prices and wages in the economy. The higher nominal prices that a worker has to pay because of inflation are, on average (but only on average), offset by the higher nominal wages that his or her employer can pay because of inflation. Higher living standards come from better technology and more capital-intensive production processes, not from reduced inflation.

Inflation does have costs, but they are subtle. For the most part, the costs of moderate inflation appear to be relatively small, smaller than one would guess given the strength of today's political consensus that price stability is a very desirable goal.

THE COSTS OF MODERATE EXPECTED INFLATION

The costs of *expected inflation* are especially small. Expected inflation raises the nominal interest rate, which you will recall is equal to the real interest rate plus the rate of inflation. Since the nominal interest rate is the opportunity cost of holding money balances, when the rate is high, you devote more time and energy to managing your cash balances. From the viewpoint of the economy as a whole, this extra time and energy is just wasted. Nothing useful is produced, and valuable resources that could be used to add to output or be simply spent on enjoying yourself are used up.

Expected inflation wastes time and energy in other ways as well. Firms find that they must spend resources changing their prices not because of any change in their business but simply because of inflation. Households find that it is harder to figure out what is a good buy and what is a bad one as inflation pushes prices away from what they had perceived normal prices to be. The most serious costs of expected inflation surely come from the fact that our tax laws are not designed to deal well with inflation. Lots of productive activities are penalized, and lots of unproductive ones rewarded, simply because of the interaction of inflation with the tax system. The fact that debt interest is treated as a cost means that in times of high inflation it is artificially cheap to finance businesses by issuing bonds or borrowing at the bank, and so businesses adopt debt-heavy capital structures that may make the economy more vulnerable to financial crises and that certainly increase the amount of resources wasted paying bankruptcy lawyers, as businesses with lots of debt tend to go bankrupt relatively easily.

Nevertheless when the rate of inflation is low — perhaps less than 10 percent per year, probably less than 5 percent per year, and certainly less than 2 percent per year — these costs are too small to worry about because they are counterbalanced by benefits. Suppose the central bank wants to push the real interest rate below zero in some economic crisis? It cannot do so unless there is some inflation in the economy, because nominal interest rates cannot be less than zero and the real interest rate is the difference between the nominal interest rate and the inflation rate. Many economists and psychologists have speculated that worker morale is greatly harmed if worker wages are clearly and unambiguously cut. A small amount of inflation may then grease the wheels of the labour market, allowing for wage adjustment without the damaging effect on morale of explicit wage cuts.

THE COSTS OF MODERATE UNEXPECTED INFLATION

Unexpected inflation does have significant and worrisome costs, for unexpected inflation redistributes wealth from creditors to debtors. Creditors receive much less purchasing power than they had anticipated if a loan falls due during a time of significant inflation. Debtors find the payments they must make much less burdensome if they borrow over a period of significant inflation. The process works in reverse as well: If inflation is less than had been expected, creditors receive a windfall and debtors go bankrupt. Most people are averse to risk. We buy insurance, after all. People who are averse to risk dislike uncertainty and unpredictability — and unexpected inflation certainly creates uncertainty and unpredictability.

Yet perhaps the economic costs of moderate unexpected inflation are relatively low. Why don't debtors and creditors want to insure themselves against inflation risk by *indexing* their contracts and using some alternative, more stable unit of account? In economies with high and variable inflation, we do see such indexation. The fact that we do not see it in countries with moderate and low inflation suggests that the costs of inflation to individual debtors and creditors (though perhaps not to society as a whole) must be relatively low.

Nevertheless, there is a powerful political argument that the costs of moderate inflation are high. Voters do not like moderate inflation. The 1970s saw government after government in the industrialized world voted out of office. Polls showed that voters interpreted the rising rates of inflation as signs that the political parties in power were incompetent at managing the economy. Since the end of the 1970s, no major political party in the industrialized world has dared run on a platform of less price stability and more inflation.

HYPERINFLATION AND ITS COSTS

The costs of inflation mount to economy-destroying levels during episodes of *hyperinflation,* when inflation rises by more than 20 percent *per month.* Hyperinflations arise when governments attempt to obtain extra revenue by printing money but overestimate how much they can raise. For some governments, printing money is an important source of revenue. Most governments tax their citizens or borrow from people who think that the government will pay them back. But if a government finds that it does not have the administrative reach to increase its explicit tax take and that no one will lend to it, it can simply print money and use the bills hot off the press to purchase goods and services.

Where do the resources — the power to buy goods and services — that the government acquires by printing money come from? A government that finances its spending by printing money is actually financing its spending by levying a tax on holdings of cash. Suppose I have $500 in cash in my pocket when the government suddenly announces it has printed up enough extra dollar bills to double the economy's cash supply. With Y and V unchanged, doubling the money supply doubles the price level. The $500 in my pocket will buy only as much after the government's money-printing spree as $250 would have bought before. The situation is as if the government levied a special one-time 50 percent tax on cash holdings.

Where did the 250 real dollars in my pocket go? The government has them: It now has 500 newly printed dollars, even if each of them is worth half a preinflation dollar in real terms. Clearly, printing money can be easier than imposing a 50 percent explicit tax. To collect an explicit tax, a government needs an entire wealth-tracking, money-collecting, compliance-monitoring bureaucracy. To print money, all the government needs is a printing press, some ink, some paper, and a working connection to the electric power grid.

Almost everyone agrees that this **inflation tax** — also called **seigniorage** because the right to coin money was originally a right reserved to certain feudal lords, certain *seigneurs* — is a bad policy. One of the first principles of public finance is that taxes should be broad-based and lie relatively lightly on economic activity. The inflation tax is a heavy tax on a narrow base of economic activity, the activity of holding money. Moreover, the inflation tax is a heavy tax on one small slice of money holding: cash, deposits held by households and firms, and chartered bank deposits at the central bank (see Figure 7.12). Box 7.3 provides more details on the inflation tax.

For these reasons, the inflation tax is resorted to only by a government that is falling apart and lacks the administrative capacity to raise money in any other way. Even so, such a government usually finds out afterward that the costs of the inflation tax and hyperinflation outweigh the benefits. Eventually prices rise so rapidly that the monetary system breaks down. People would rather deal with each other in barter terms than use a form of cash whose value is shrinking measurably every day. GDP starts to fall as the economy begins to lose the benefits of the division of labour. In the end the government finds that its currency is next to worthless. It runs the

FIGURE 7.12
The Inflation Tax
The "inflation tax" is a way for the government to get command over goods and services just as much as is any other tax. Those who pay the inflation tax are those who hold assets that lose value in the event of inflation.

Households and businesses have $500 billion in cash and reserves.

The government prints an extra $500 billion in cash.

The price doubles, and so household and business cash and reserves lose half their real value: They're now worth only $250 billion in preinflation terms.

Where did the other $250 billion in real purchasing power go? The government now has it, having raised it through the "inflation tax."

7.3

BOX

DETAILS

MORE ON THE INFLATION TAX

The total revenue collected by the government in the form of the inflation tax is given by the value of real money the balances M/P multiplied by the inflation rate π on these balances. Hence, the total government revenue from the inflation tax is $\pi \times M/P$. Once this formula for the revenue from the inflation tax is established it is easy to see why in countries with governments that rely heavily on the inflation tax as a source of revenue inflation gets out of control and the country soon experiences hyperinflation.

Suppose households and firms realize that the government is going to tax their money holdings by keeping on printing money to raise revenue through the inflation tax. They will then respond by holding a smaller amount of real money balances, which will reduce the tax base M/P for the government. When M/P falls the government realizes it has to increase the inflation rate further in order to be able to raise the same amount of revenue. But when the inflation rate rises, then M/P falls further. This vicious circle soon gets out of control and the country then experiences hyperinflation.

printing presses faster and faster and yet finds that the money it prints buys less and less. At the end of the German hyperinflation of the 1920s, 1 trillion marks were needed to buy what 1 mark had bought less than 10 years before.

In recent times, seigniorage is a small part of the total government revenues of developed countries with well-established tax collecting institutions. For example, for Canada seigniorage is around 2 percent of government revenues and around 0.43 percent of total GDP. For the U.S. these figures are also very similar to Canada. On the other hand, for less developed countries with less developed tax collecting institutions, seigniorage forms a larger part of total government revenues. For example, for India and Pakistan, seigniorage is over 10 percent of total government revenues and around 2 percent of GDP.

RECAP   THE COSTS OF INFLATION

The economic costs of expected moderate inflation are small. They are largely the costs of extra trips to the bank and of time and resources wasted in the socially unproductive activity of keeping one's money balance near its target level. The economic costs of moderate unexpected inflation are larger. It redistributes wealth unexpectedly between debtors and creditors and increases risk. Largest, however, are the political costs of moderate inflation: Voters seem to use inflation as a sign that the government's economic policy is not sound.

If you look for high economic costs of inflation, you must turn your attention to episodes of hyperinflation. In a hyperinflation a government without the ability to tax or borrow resorts to printing money to buy goods and services. The inflation rate rises to 20 percent per month or more. The price mechanism breaks down as people resort to barter. And production falls.

7.6 THE MONEY SUPPLY PROCESS: DETAILS

Until now we have had a very simple view of the money supply process. In fact, the money supply process is quite intricate, and it involves the activities of the commercial banks as well as the central bank. In this section we will analyze the money creation process in detail in the context of the assets and liabilities of the chartered banks and the central bank. First, we study how the activities of the central bank impinge upon the assets and liabilities of the chartered banks. Then, we look at the role of the chartered banks in the money supply process; and why a one unit increase in the monetary base will lead to a more than one unit increase in the money supply.

We assume that money (M) is currency held by households and firms (CU) plus bank deposits held by household and firms (D),

$$M = CU + D \qquad (7.11)$$

M will be M1, M2, M2+, or M2++, depending on how we define deposits D, following the definitions in Table 7.1.

THE BALANCE SHEETS OF THE CHARTERED BANKS AND THE CENTRAL BANK

The balance sheet of an institution records all the assets and liabilities of that institution. Assets are the things the institution owns, while liabilities are the things the institution owes others. There are two institutions that are relevant for us in the money supply process: the central bank and the chartered banks. Here we study the parts of the balance sheets of these institutions that are relevant for the money supply process.

Table 7.2 shows the relevant parts of the balance sheet of the central bank. There are three assets of the central bank that are relevant for the money supply process. First are the central bank's holdings of domestic bonds. Second are the central bank's holdings of foreign currencies and foreign denominated bonds, which are referred to as the central bank's foreign exchange reserves and are denoted by FX. Third are the central bank's loans to the chartered banks.

There are also two liabilities of the central bank that are relevant for the money supply process. First is the currency held by households and firms, which is denoted by CU. Second are the reserves of the chartered banks, which are denoted by RE. These reserves are the liquid assets the chartered banks hold in order to be able to provide currency to households and firms on demand should households and firms wish to convert their deposits into cash. The reserves of the chartered banks are equal to the currency they hold in their vaults *plus* the deposits they hold at the central bank.

Now let us consider the consolidated balance sheet of the chartered banks, the relevant parts of which are given in Table 7.3. There are two major assets that the chartered banks have that are relevant to the discussion of the money supply process. First, the chartered banks hold reserves, RE, which consists of currency in their vaults and the deposits they have at the central bank. Second, the chartered banks have made loans in the amount of L to households and firms. These loans are

TABLE 7.2
The Balance Sheet of the Central Bank

Assets	Liabilities
Bonds	Currency held by households and firms (CU)
Foreign exchange reserves (FX)	Reserves of the chartered banks (RE)
Loans to the chartered banks	

TABLE 7.3
The Consolidated Balance Sheet of the Chartered Banks

Assets	Liabilities
Reserves (RE)	Deposits held by households and firms (D)
Loans made to households and firms (L)	Loans from the central bank

owed to the chartered banks by the households and firms; and therefore they constitute assets for the chartered banks.[1]

Two liabilities of the chartered banks are relevant for our discussion of the money supply process. These are the *deposits* held by households and firms, D, and the *loans* that the chartered banks obtain from the central bank.

CHARTERED BANK RESERVES, THE MONETARY BASE, AND THE MONEY SUPPLY

We can now define two important variables in the money supply process: *chartered bank reserves* and the *monetary base*. As discussed below, these variables have very important bearings on the money supply process.

Chartered bank reserves are important in the money supply process because they are directly related to the chartered banks' ability to create deposits. When chartered banks make loans to households and firms they increase L in their assets. At the same time, when the chartered banks make loans to households and firms they make funds available to them by increasing the balance on their deposit accounts, D. The chartered banks can create deposits in this manner because at any point in time only a fraction r_D of total deposits D are converted into currency by the households and firms. Hence, chartered banks can always honour their obligation to convert deposits into currency by holding reserves that are equal to a fraction r_D of the deposits held by households and firms:

$$RE = r_D \times D \tag{7.12}$$

The monetary base or high-powered money (henceforth, denoted by H) is the sum of currency held by households and firms and the reserves of the chartered banks:

$$H = CU + RE \tag{7.13}$$

An important point to notice is that all the elements of the monetary base appear in the liabilities column of the central bank; and the central bank has direct control over it. Notice that the central bank does *not* have direct control over the money supply, as defined by equation (7.11), because it does not have direct control over the deposits created by the chartered banks, D. It is, therefore, important in the study of the money supply process to derive a relationship between the monetary base and the money supply.

The equations (7.11), (7.12), and (7.13) can be used to derive the relationship between the monetary base and the money supply. To do this, we also assume that households and firms hold a fraction c of their deposits in the form of currency. Hence,

$$CU = c \times D \tag{7.14}$$

In general, c will depend on the interest rate on deposits and on the banking technology. The higher this interest rate the less attractive CU will be relative to D, and hence the smaller will be c.

---

[1] Chartered banks own other assets such as government bonds, securities, and real estate; but these assets are not relevant for our discussion of the money supply process.

FIGURE 7.13

Changes in the Currency-to-Deposits Ratio, 1953–2005

The currency-to-deposits ratio has decreased over time since 1953. Its sharp decline means that changes in the money stock are not highly correlated with changes in the monetary base produced by Bank of Canada's open-market operations.

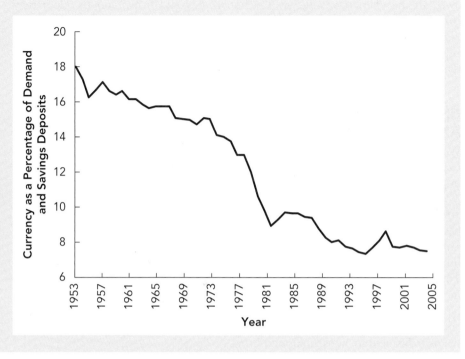

Source: Adapted from the Statistics Canada CANSIM II database, Series V37173 (currency), V37195 (demand deposits), and V3718 (savings deposits).

Substituting for CU and RE from equations (7.12) and (7.14) into equations (7.11) and (7.13) we obtain, respectively,

$$M = (c + 1) \times D \tag{7.15}$$

and

$$H = (c + r_D) \times D \tag{7.16}$$

Equations (7.15) and (7.16) give us the following relationship between the monetary base and the money supply:

$$M = \frac{1 + c}{c + r_D} \times H = m \times H \tag{7.17}$$

where m is called the **money multiplier**. The money multiplier gives the amount by which the money supply will increase if the monetary base increases by one unit. The money multiplier is larger than unity as $r_D < 1$. For instance, for values of r_D and c equal to 0.1 and 0.2, respectively, m is equal to 4. Nevertheless, the factors that determine the money multiplier do change over time. Figure 7.13 shows how one of the factors, the currency-to-deposits ratio, has varied since 1953. One striking feature of this figure is the sharp decline in the currency-to-deposit ratio since the 1970s, which was due to financial innovations that made deposits close substitutes for currency.

CENTRAL BANK'S CONTROL OF THE MONEY SUPPLY

Now we study three specific policies of the central bank that may affect the money supply. First is an open market operation, whereby the central bank buys or sells bonds on the stock market. Second are the effects of a change in the interest on the loans the central bank has made to the chartered banks. Finally, we consider the effects of a mandatory change in r_D, the ratio of chartered bank reserves to deposits.

OPEN MARKET OPERATION

Consider an open market operation in which the central bank buys $1 million worth of bonds from households and firms in exchange for money. This increases the currency held by households and firms CU by $1 million. Hence, by equation (7.13) the monetary base also increases by $1 million. This increase in the monetary base will increase the money supply by m times $1 million.

The process by which the money supply increases by m times $1 million is as follows. The initial increases in currency held by households and firms, CU, from equation (7.14), will result in an increase in the ratio CU/D in excess of the optimal ratio given by c. Hence, part of the increase in CU will be placed in deposits D. As households and firms place part of their extra currencies in bank deposits, there will be an increase in the amount of currency that is held by the chartered banks. The increase in currency held by the chartered banks will mean an increase in the chartered banks' reserves RE. With more reserves available to them, the chartered banks will be more willing to make loans, and hence create deposits, according to equation (7.12). Therefore, the increase in the money supply as defined by equation (7.11) will be m times the initial increase in CU, in accordance with equation (7.17).

CHANGE IN THE INTEREST ON LOANS TO CHARTERED BANKS

In our discussion of equation (7.12) we stated that the deposit to reserve ratio, r_D, will depend on short-term interest rates. More precisely, r_D depends on the rate the central bank charges on the short-term loans it makes to the chartered banks, which in Canada is called the **bank rate**. The reason for r_D depending on the bank rate is as follows: If the chartered banks are short of cash they will have to take emergency short-term loans from the central bank. If the interest on these loans is higher, the chartered banks will be more cautious in their holdings of reserves, thus increasing r_D in equation (7.12). This means that the chartered banks will have to reduce the deposits they make available to households and firms. Hence, the chartered banks will not make new loans, and they will not renew some of the loans that mature, until the newly desired level of r_D is achieved. This way, the money multiplier m falls and the money supply is reduced.

At this point it is important to mention that when the central bank increases the interest it charges on its short-term loans, the chartered banks automatically increase the interest they charge on the loans they make to households and firms. The reason for this is that by increasing the interest on the loans they make, the chartered banks send the signal that they are less willing to make loans.

CHANGE IN THE RESERVE-TO-DEPOSITS RATIO

Finally, suppose the central bank sets a reserve-to-deposits ratio for the chartered banks that is above what this ratio would have been without any intervention. This will increase r_D in equation (7.12), and it will reduce the money multiplier m in equation (7.17). For the same level of the monetary base H, this policy will reduce the money supply, because it will make banks more reluctant to create deposits by making loans to the households and firms.

In reality, in recent years the central banks in industrialized countries have stopped the practice of setting reserve requirements for chartered banks. The Bank of Canada stopped the practice of setting reserve requirements in 1994. Although the chartered banks have no legal reserve requirements, they are still required to clear all their daily transactions through reserve accounts at the Bank of Canada; otherwise they are penalized. This provides them with an incentive to set their own non-zero, reserve-to-deposit ratio, r_D.

RECAP THE MONEY SUPPLY PROCESS: DETAILS

The central bank has direct control over the monetary base; it does *not* have direct control over all the elements of the money supply. The money multiplier gives the amount by which the money supply will increase if the monetary base increases by one unit. An open market operation in which the central bank buys bonds worth $1 million from households and firms in exchange for money increases the monetary base by $1 million and the money supply by $1 million times the money multiplier. An increase in the interest rate on the short-term loans the central bank makes to the chartered banks will reduce the reserve-to-deposits ratio of the chartered banks, which will increase the money multiplier.

CHAPTER SUMMARY

1. By "money" economists mean something special: wealth in the form of readily spendable purchasing power.

2. Without money it is hard to imagine how our economy could successfully function. The fact that everyone will accept money as payment for goods and services is necessary for the market economy to function.

3. Money is not only a medium of exchange, but also a unit of account — a yardstick that we use to measure values and to specify contracts.

4. Money demand is determined by (a) businesses' and households' desire to hold wealth in the form of readily spendable purchasing power in order to carry out transactions, and (b) businesses' and households' recognition that there is a cost to holding money — wealth in the form of readily spendable purchasing power pays little or no interest.

5. The velocity of money is how many transactions a given piece of money manages to facilitate in a year. The principal determinant of the velocity of money is the economy's "transactions technology": the organization of its financial system.

6. The stock of money is determined by the central bank.

7. The price level is equal to the money stock times the velocity of money divided by the level of real GDP.

8. The inflation rate is equal to the proportional growth rate of the money stock plus the proportional growth rate of velocity minus the proportional growth rate of real GDP.

9. Governments cause hyperinflations because printing money is a way of taxing the public, and a government that cannot tax any other way will be strongly tempted to resort to it.

10. The money multiplier gives the amount by which the money supply will increase if the monetary base increases by one unit. The money multiplier is larger than unity.

11. An open market operation in which the central bank buys bonds worth $1 million from households and firms in exchange for money increases the monetary base by $1 million and the money supply by $1 million times the money multiplier.

12. An increase in the interest rate on the short-term loans the central bank makes to the chartered banks will reduce the reserve-to-deposits ratio of the chartered banks, which will increase the money multiplier.

KEY TERMS AND EQUATIONS

Bank of Canada (p. 212)

bank rate (p. 231)

central bank (p. 212)

classical dichotomy (p. 206)

hyperinflation (p. 206)

inflation (p. 205)

inflation tax (p. 225)

medium of exchange (p. 208)

monetary base (p. 212)

money (p. 206)

money market equilibrium (p. 218)

money multiplier (p. 230)

money stock (p. 206)

neutral (p. 206)

open-market operations (p. 212)

price level (p. 206)

quantity theory of money (p. 209)

reserve requirements (p. 212)

seigniorage (p. 225)

unit of account (p. 208)

velocity of money (p. 210)

Quantity equation:	$M = \dfrac{1}{V} \times (P \times Y)$	(7.1)
Equilibrium inflation rate:	$\pi = m + v - y$	(7.3)
Real money demand:	$\dfrac{M^d}{P} = \dfrac{Y}{V^L \times [V_0 + V_i \times (r \times \pi^e)]}$	(7.5)
Liquidity preference:	$L = L_0 - L_i \times (r + \pi^e) + L_y \times Y$	(7.6)
Definition of money:	$M = CU + D$	(7.11)
Money supply vs the monetary base:	$M = \dfrac{1 + c}{c + r_D} \times H = m \times H$	(7.17)

ANALYTICAL EXERCISES

1. Economists say that a government can raise real revenue — real power to buy goods and services — through the "inflation tax." Who is it that pays this tax? How is it that the government collects it?

2. Suppose that real GDP is $1,000 billion, the velocity of money is 5, and the money stock is $250 billion. What is the price level?

3. Suppose that the rate of labour-force growth is 1 percent per year, the rate of growth of the efficiency of labour is 3 percent per year, the economy is on its steady-state growth path, and the velocity of money is increasing at 1 percent per year. Suppose also that the Governor of the Bank of Canada calls you into his or her office and asks how fast money growth should be to achieve a stable price level. What answer do you give?

4. Suppose that the rate of labour-force growth is 3 percent per year, but the efficiency of labour is stable and the economy is on its steady-state growth path. Suppose also that the rate of growth of the nominal money stock is 10 percent per year. Do you think that it is likely that the inflation rate is less than 5 percent per year? Why or why not?

5. What would the Bank of Canada have to do if it wanted to raise the monetary base today by $10 million? What do you guess would happen to the price of short-term government bonds if the Bank of Canada did this?

6. Explain the difference between the foreign exchange reserves of the central bank, the reserves of the chartered banks, and the monetary base.

POLICY EXERCISES

1. In early September 1998 the monetary base was $34.6 billion. Suppose that the Canadian government decided to raise $17.3 billion in real purchasing power (in the dollars of September 1998) through the inflation tax. What would happen to the price level?

2. In the third quarter of 1998 nominal GDP was $236 billion. The monetary base H was $34 billion; M1 was $91 billion; and M2 was $446 billion. Calculate the velocities of the monetary base, M1, and M2.

3. Between 1990 and 1998 M1 increased from $41.3 billion to $89.5 billion, while nominal GDP increased from $680 billion to $915 billion. What was the average annual rate of increase of the M1 money stock? Of nominal GDP? Of M1 velocity?

4. Between 1980 and 1990, and between 1990 and 1998 M1 increased from $25 billion to $41 billion to $90 billion; and M2 rose from $134 billion to $359 billion to $446 billion, while nominal GDP rose from $315 billion to $680 billion to $915 billion. Calculate the average annual rates of increase of M1, M2, and nominal GDP $P \times Y$ between 1980 and 1990 and between 1990 and 1998. Calculate the average annual rates of increase of the velocity of Ml and M2 between 1980 and 1990 and between 1990 and 1998. How constant do these velocity trends appear to be both across time and across different measures of the money stock?

5. Suppose that you were told that the rate of inflation was about to decline significantly over the next decade. Would you expect the velocity of money to rise unusually fast, behave normally, or fall over the course of the decade?

6. Consider an economy in which the currency-to-deposits ratio is 0.3, and the reserve-to-deposits ratio is 0.1. Suppose the central bank purchases $10 million worth of bonds from households and firms in exchange for cash. Explain by how much the money supply will increase.

PART IV

Sticky-Price Macroeconomics

Chapters 3 through 7 do not give a complete picture of the macroeconomy. In Chapters 3 through 7, growth is smooth from year to year. But in the real world growth is not. In Chapters 3 through 7, supply and demand in the labour market are always in balance. But in the real world the labour market is not always in equilibrium.

To understand these business-cycle fluctuations in economic growth and unemployment, we need a model that does not require that employment be full and real GDP equal to potential output. The full-employment model of Part III is not of help because its flexible-price assumption guarantees full employment. Here in Part IV, therefore, we need to break this flexible-price assumption to build a useful model of the business cycle.

From this point forward prices will be "sticky": They will not move freely and instantaneously in response to changes in demand and supply. We will use this sticky-price model to account for business-cycle fluctuations.

Building this sticky-price model of the macroeconomy is the task of Part IV. Chapter 8 focuses on how, when prices are sticky, the inventory adjustment process is the key to understanding how GDP can fall below or rise above potential output. Chapter 9 analyzes how changes in the interest rate affect investment, exports, and GDP. Chapter 10 focuses on equilibrium in the money market and the balance of aggregate demand and aggregate supply. Chapter 11 focuses on expectations and inflation. It links the sticky-price model of Part IV back to the flexible-price model of Part III by analyzing which model is most useful in what sets of circumstances.

8

The Income-Expenditure Framework and the Multiplier

QUESTIONS

What are "sticky" prices?

What factors might make prices sticky?

When prices are sticky, what determines the level of real GDP in the short run?

When prices are sticky, what happens to real GDP if some component of aggregate demand falls?

When prices are sticky, what happens to real GDP if some component of aggregate demand rises?

What determines the size of the spending multiplier?

Over the past decade real GDP in the Canadian economy has grown at an average rate of 3.1 percent per year. At the same time, the Canadian unemployment rate has fluctuated around an average level consistent with stable inflation — a **natural rate of unemployment** — of about 7.5 percent. (Note, however, that this natural rate of unemployment is not a constant: It moves slowly over time.) And the inflation rate in Canada has averaged about 1.6 percent per year.

If Chapters 3 through 7 gave a complete picture of the macroeconomy, economic growth would be smooth. Real GDP would grow 3.1 percent — the current rate of growth of potential GDP — year after year, not just on average. The unemployment rate would remain steady at its *natural rate* of approximately 7.5 percent. And inflation would be steady as well, determined by the rates of growth of potential output and the money stock and on the velocity of money.

If such were the case, the analysis in Chapters 3 and 4 would provide a complete picture of how potential output grew over time. The analysis in Chapters 5 and 6 would explain why real GDP equals potential output and how national income is divided

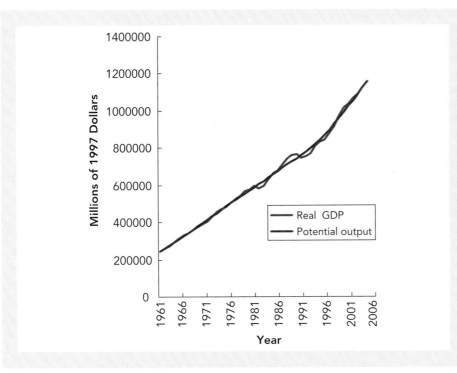

FIGURE 8.1
Real GDP and Potential Output, 1961–2005 (millions of 1997 dollars)
From year to year real GDP fluctuates around potential output. The flexible-price full-employment classical model of Chapters 5 and 6 cannot account for these fluctuations in real GDP relative to potential output.

Source: Adapted from the Statistics Canada CANSIM II database, Series V1992067 (real GDP).

among the different components of aggregate demand. The analysis in Chapter 7 would detail how the price level and the inflation rate are determined. It would be the last chapter in this textbook. Your survey of macroeconomics would be finished.

But Chapters 3 through 7 do not give a complete picture of the macroeconomy. Growth is not at all smooth; on a year-to-year time scale, it is not even guaranteed. In 1982 real GDP was not 3.1 percent more but 6 percent less than it was in 1981 (see Figure 8.1). Between 1979 and 1982 the unemployment rate rose by 3.6 percentage points, and it rose again by 3.7 percentage points between 1989 and 1992. Unemployment was only 6.4 percent in 2006, but it was 11.2 percent in 1992. Inflation in 2006 was only 2.4 percent per year, but in 1981 it was 12.4 percent.

http://cansim2.statcan.ca/
http://www.statcan.ca/

These fluctuations in growth are called *business cycles*. A business cycle has two phases: an exciting expansion or boom phase as production, employment, and prices all grow rapidly, and a subsequent recession or depression phase during which inflation falls or prices slump, unemployment rises, and production falls. During booms, output grows faster than trend, investment spending amounts to a higher-than-average share of GDP, unemployment falls, and inflation usually accelerates. During recessions, output falls, investment spending is a low share of real GDP, unemployment rises, and inflation usually decelerates.

8.1 STICKY PRICES

BUSINESS CYCLES

To understand business cycles, we need a model that does not guarantee always-full employment and in which real GDP does not always equal potential output. Business cycles, after all, are not fluctuations in potential output but fluctuations of actual production around potential output. Thus the full-employment model of Chapters 5 through 7 is of no help because its assumption that **prices are flexible** guarantees full employment. The flexible-price assumption allowed us to start our analysis by noting that the labour market would clear with the supply of workers equal to the demand for labour and that as a result firms would fully employ the labour force and thus real GDP and household income would be equal to potential output.

From this point forward, however, we need to break this flexible-price assumption in order to build a more useful model of the business cycle. Thus prices will be "sticky": They will not move freely and instantaneously in response to changes in demand and supply. Instead, prices will remain fixed at predetermined levels as businesses expand or contract production in response to changes in demand and costs. As you will see, such sticky prices make a big difference in economic analysis; they will drive a wedge between real GDP and potential output and between the supply of workers and the demand for labour. We will then be able to use this sticky-price model to account for business-cycle fluctuations.

Building this **sticky-price** model of the macroeconomy will take up all of Part IV. In this chapter, we will focus on how, when prices are sticky, firms hire or fire workers and expand or cut back production on the basis of whether their inventories are falling or rising. Inventory adjustment is the key to understanding how the level of real GDP can fall below and fluctuate around potential output. Chapter 9 focuses on the macroeconomic equilibrium with fixed prices in the context of the IS-LM model, and on how the equilibrium is affected by IS-LM and other shocks.

Chapter 10 deals with the determinants of aggregate demand and aggregate supply and analyzes how the equilibrium price and inflation are determined. The last chapter of Part IV, Chapter 11, focuses on expectations and inflation. By the end of Chapter 11 we will have linked up the sticky-price model of Part IV with the flexible-price model of Part III. We will understand the sorts of situations for which the sticky-price model is appropriate. And we will understand under what sets of circumstances wages and prices are flexible enough and have enough time to adjust for the flexible-price model to be the most useful way of analyzing the macroeconomy.

Up to this point this book has not been *cumulative*. You could understand the long-run growth analysis in Chapters 3 and 4 without a firm grasp of the introductory material in Chapters 1 and 2. You could understand the flexible-price analysis in Chapters 5 and 6 without a firm grasp of either the introductory or the long-run growth chapters. And you could understand Chapter 7 without having read anything earlier in the book. But from this point on, this book becomes very cumulative indeed: Chapter 9 is incomprehensible without a firm grasp of Chapter 8; Chapter 10 is incomprehensible without a firm grasp of Chapter 9; Chapter 11 is incomprehensible without a firm grasp of Chapter 10; and the chapters that follow 11 require it as well.

THE CONSEQUENCES OF STICKY PRICES

FLEXIBLE-PRICE LOGIC

To preview the difference between the flexible-price and the sticky-price models, let us analyze a decline in consumers' propensity to spend under both sets of assumptions. Suppose there is a sudden fall in the parameter C_0 that determines the baseline level of consumption in the consumption function

$$C = C_0 + C_y \times Y^D \tag{8.1}$$

At any given level of national income Y, consumers wish to save more and spend less. In the full-employment model of Chapters 5 through 7, a fall in annual consumption spending would have no impact on *real* GDP. No matter what the flow of aggregate demand, because nominal wages and prices are flexible, the labour market would still reach its full-employment equilibrium. And because the economy remains at full employment, real GDP would equal potential output.

The fall in consumption spending would have an effect on the economy — just not on the level of real GDP. As we saw in Chapters 5 and 6, a fall in consumption spending means an increase in savings. As consumption falls, the savings supply curve shifts rightward on the flow-of-funds diagram. Thus a fall in consumption spending reduces the equilibrium interest rate in the flow-of-funds market. It also increases the equilibrium level of investment and net exports by the amount necessary to keep GDP equal to potential output.

Moreover, as we saw in Chapter 7, such a fall in the real rate has consequences for money demand. Changes in households' and businesses' total demand for money M can be triggered by a change in the price level P, real GDP Y, the banking system structure-driven trend in the velocity of money V^t, or the dependence of velocity on the nominal interest rate. The higher the nominal interest rate i — which equals the real interest rate r plus the expected future inflation rate π^e — the lower are households' and businesses' demand to hold their wealth in the readily spendable and liquid form of money:

$$M = \frac{P \times Y}{[V_0 + V_i \times (r + \pi^e)]}$$

If we rearrange this equation to solve for the equilibrium price level P,

$$P = \left(\frac{M}{Y}\right) [V_0 + V_i \times (r + \pi^e)] \tag{8.2}$$

we see that a fall in the nominal interest rate means a fall in velocity and carries with it a fall in the price level. As households and businesses try to divert some of their spending to build up their stocks of liquid money, their actions put downward pressure on prices, restoring equilibrium in the money market.

Thus these are the flexible-price-model consequences of a fall in consumers' desired baseline spending:

- Consumption falls.
- Savings rise.
- The real interest rate falls.
- Investment rises.
- The value of the exchange rate rises.
- The price level declines.

STICKY-PRICE LOGIC

If wages and prices are sticky, the analysis is different. The first consequence of consumers' cutting back their spending will be a fall in the aggregate demand for goods. Consumer spending has fallen, yet nothing has happened to change the flow of spending on investment goods, the flow of net exports, or the flow of government purchases.

As businesses see spending on their products begin to fall, they will not cut their nominal prices (remember, prices are sticky). Instead, they will respond to the fall in the quantity of their products demanded by reducing their production, They want to avoid accumulating unsold and unsellable inventory. As they reduce production, they will fire some of their workers, and the incomes of the fired workers will drop. By how much will total national income drop? It will fall by the amount of the fall in consumption spending. (Moreover, because the decline in incomes leads to a further decline in consumption as households that have lost income cut back on their spending, national income and real GDP will fall by more than the decline in C_0. This *multiplier* process is discussed later on in the chapter.)

In sum, the consequences of a fall in consumption spending under the sticky-price assumption are:

- Consumption falls.
- Production and employment decline.
- National income declines.

In the flexible-price model, when consumption falls, investment and net exports rise. Why doesn't the same thing happen in the sticky-price model? Why doesn't a rise in investment spending keep GDP equal to potential output and keep employment full? What goes wrong with the flexible-price logic, according to which a fall in consumption spending generates an increase in savings that then boosts both investment spending and net exports?

The answer is that as firms cut back production and employment, total income falls. A fall in total income reduces savings (if consumption is held constant) just as a fall in consumption raises savings (if income is held constant). Under the sticky-price assumption the effects on savings of the fall in consumption and the fall in income cancel each other out, there is no change in the flow of savings. Thus there is no rightward shift in the position of the savings supply curve on the flow-of-funds diagram in Figure 8.2. There is no fall in interest rates to trigger higher investment (and a higher value of the exchange rate and expanded net exports). There is nothing to offset the fall in consumption spending and keep GDP from falling below potential output.

Why doesn't this sticky-price unemployment-generating logic work when prices are flexible? The answer is that when flexible-price firms see a fall in aggregate demand spending, they respond not by cutting production and employment but by cutting the nominal prices they charge and the nominal wages they pay. Since prices and wages both fall, the real incomes households earn remain constant. Thus a fall in consumption spending does induce a rise in savings — hence a fall in the real interest rate, a rise in investment spending, an increase in the value of the exchange rate, and a rise in net exports.

EXPECTATIONS AND PRICE STICKINESS

Note that price stickiness causes problems only in the short run. If managers, workers, consumers, and investors had time to foresee a fall in consumption and gradually adjust their wages and prices to it, even considerable stickiness in prices would not be a problem. With sufficient advance notice unions and businesses would strike wage bargains, and businesses could adjust their selling prices to make sure demand matches productive capacity. Both the stickiness of prices and the failure to accurately foresee changes far enough in advance are needed to create business cycles.

Thus one way to think about it is that the analysis in Part IV is a short-run analysis and the analysis in Part III is a longer-run analysis although still not as long-run

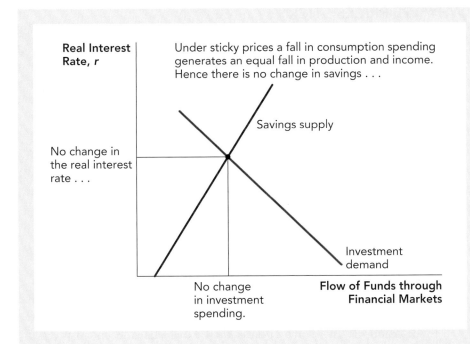

Real Interest Rate, r

Under sticky prices a fall in consumption spending generates an equal fall in production and income. Hence there is no change in savings . . .

Savings supply

No change in the real interest rate . . .

Investment demand

No change in investment spending.

Flow of Funds through Financial Markets

FIGURE 8.2

The Effect on Savings of a Fall in Consumption Spending in the Sticky-Price Model

With sticky prices, a fall in consumption spending carries with it a fall in incomes. Because consumption spending and incomes decline by the same amount, there is no change in the supply of savings through financial markets. Thus the real interest rate remains unchanged. There is no change in investment spending.

as the analysis of Part II. In the short run, prices are sticky; shifts in policy or in the economic environment that affect the components of aggregate demand will affect real GDP and employment. In the long run, prices are flexible and workers, bosses, and consumers have time to react and adjust to changes in policy or the economic environment. Thus in the long run, such shifts do not affect real GDP or employment.

Why do we need a sticky-price short-run model as well as the flexible-price model? Why isn't it good enough to say that once wages and prices have fully adjusted (however long that takes), unemployment will be back at its natural rate and real GDP will be equal to potential output? The most famous and effective criticism of such let's-look-only-at-the-long-run analyses was made by John Maynard Keynes on page 88 of his 1924 *Tract on Monetary Reform*. Criticizing one such long-run-only analysis, Keynes wrote: "In the long run [it] is probably true. . . . But this *long run* is a misleading guide to current affairs. *In the long run* we are all dead. Economists set themselves too easy, too useless a task if in tempestuous seasons they can only tell us that when the storm is long past the ocean will be flat once more."

Where is the line that divides the short run from the long run? Do we switch from living in the short run of Part IV to the long run of Part III on June 19, 2006? No, we do not. The long run is an analytical construct. A change can be considered "long run" if enough people see it coming far enough in advance and have had time to adjust to it — to renegotiate their contracts and change their standard operating procedures accordingly. The length of the long run, and thus how many of us will be dead before it comes, depends in turn on the degree of price stickiness and the process by which people form their expectations — both key topics for research in modern macroeconomics.

WHY ARE PRICES STICKY?

Why don't prices adjust quickly and smoothly to maintain full employment? Why do businesses respond to fluctuations in demand first by hiring or firing workers and accelerating or shutting down their production lines? Why don't they respond first by raising or lowering their prices.

Economists have identified any number of reasons that prices could be sticky, but they are uncertain which are most important. Some likely explanations are:

- Managers and workers find that changing prices or renegotiating wages is costly and hence best delayed as long as possible.
- Managers and workers lack information and so confuse changes in total economy-wide spending with changes in demand for their specific products.
- The level of prices is as much a sociological as an economic variable — determined as much by what values people think are "fair" as by the balance of supply and demand. Workers take a cut in their wages as an indication that their employer does not value them — hence managers avoid wage cuts because they fear the consequences for worker morale.
- Managers and workers suffer from simple "money illusion"; they overlook the effect of price-level changes when assessing the impact of changes in wages or prices on their real incomes or sales.

Let's look more closely at each of these likely explanations. Economists call the costs associated with changing prices "**menu costs,**" a shorthand reference to the fact that when a restaurant changes its prices, it must print up a new menu. In general, changing prices or wages may be costly for any of a large number of reasons. Perhaps people want to stabilize their commercial relationships by signing long-term contracts. Perhaps reprinting a catalogue is expensive. Perhaps customers find frequent price changes annoying. Perhaps other firms are not changing their prices and what matters most to a firm is its price relative to the prices of competitors. Hence managers and workers prefer to keep their prices and wages stable as long as the shocks that affect the economy are relatively small — or, rather, as long as the change they might want to make in their prices and wages is small.

A second source of price stickiness is misperception of real and nominal price changes. If managers and workers lack full information about the state of the economy, they may be unsure whether a change in the flow of spending on *their* products reflects a change in overall aggregate demand or a change in demand for their particular products. If it is the latter, they *should* respond by changing how much they produce, not necessarily by changing the price. If it is the former, they should respond by changing their price in accord with overall inflation, not by changing how much they produce.

If managers are uncertain which it is, they will split the difference. Hence firms will lower their prices less in response to a downward shift in total nominal demand than the flexible-price macroeconomic model would predict. If they keep their prices too high, they will have to fire workers and cut back production. Imperfect information is a possible source of sticky prices.

Yet a third reason why prices and wages are sticky is that workers and managers are really not the flinty-eyed rational maximizers of economic theories. In real life, work effort and work intensity depend on whether workers believe they are being treated fairly. A cut in nominal wages is almost universally perceived as unfair; wages depend on social norms that evolve slowly. Thus wages are by nature sticky. And if wages are sticky, firms will find that their best response to shifts in demand is to hire and fire workers rather than to change prices.

Last, workers, consumers, and managers confuse changes in nominal prices with changes in real (that is, inflation-adjusted) prices. Firms react to higher nominal prices by thinking falsely that it is more profitable to produce more — even though it isn't because their costs have risen in proportion. Workers react to higher nominal wages by searching more intensively for jobs and working more overtime hours, even though rises in prices have erased any increase in the real purchasing power of the wage paid for an hour's work. Such **money illusion** is a powerful generator of price stickiness and business-cycle fluctuations.

All these factors are potential sources of price stickiness. Your professor may have strong views about which is most important, but we believe that our knowledge is more limited. We are not sure the evidence is strong enough to provide clear and convincing support for any particular single explanation as the most important one. A safer position is to remain agnostic about the causes of sticky wages and prices, and so we will focus on analyzing their effects.

RECAP **STICKY PRICES**

The full-employment model of Chapters 5 through 7 does not help explain business cycles because its assumption that prices are flexible guarantees that real GDP is always equal to potential output. In order to build a more useful model of the business cycle, we need to assume that prices are sticky. If prices are sticky, the first consequence of a shock like consumers cutting back their spending will be a fall in the aggregate demand for goods. As businesses see spending on their products begin to fall, they will not cut their nominal prices but will reduce production and fire workers to avoid accumulating unsold and unsellable inventory. Thus output can fall below potential output, and unemployment can rise above its natural rate.

8.2 INCOME AND EXPENDITURE

If prices are sticky, higher aggregate demand boosts production, and this boosts incomes. Higher incomes give a further boost to consumption, and this in turn boosts aggregate demand some more. Thus any shift in a component of aggregate demand upward or downward leads to an *amplified* shift in total production because of the induced shift in consumption, as Figure 8.3 shows. The early-twentieth-century British economist John Maynard Keynes was one of the first to stress the importance of this *multiplier* process.

While in booms the multiplier process induces an upward spiral in production, in bad times it is a source of misery. The downward shock is amplified as those who have been thrown out of work cut back on their consumption spending in turn. Because consumption spending is more than two-thirds of aggregate demand, this multiplier effect can be significant because the positive-feedback loop is so large.

BUILDING UP AGGREGATE DEMAND

In the remainder of this chapter we will see how the level of aggregate demand is determined in the sticky-price macroeconomic model. We will use a bottom-up approach, building aggregate demand or planned expenditure *E* on domestically produced products up from the determinants of each of its components,

FIGURE 8.3
The Multiplier Process
In the multiplier
process, an increase in
spending causes an
increase in production
and incomes, which
leads to a further
increase in spending.
This positive-feedback
loop amplifies the
effect of any initial shift.

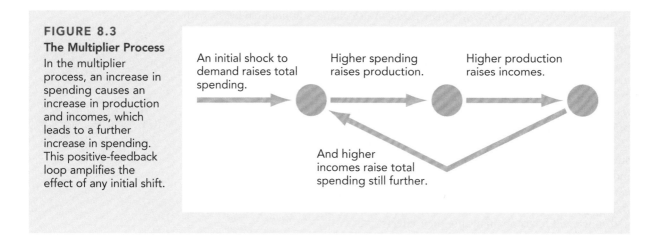

An initial shock to demand raises total spending.

Higher spending raises production.

Higher production raises incomes.

And higher incomes raise total spending still further.

consumption spending C, gross investment spending I, government purchases G, and net exports NX:

$$E = C + I + G + NX \tag{8.3}$$

As long as prices are sticky, the level of real GDP is determined by the level of aggregate demand

$$Y = E \tag{8.4}$$

and *not* by the level of potential output; that is,

$$Y \neq Y^* \tag{8.5}$$

THE CONSUMPTION FUNCTION

The two-thirds of GDP that is consumption spending is spending by households on things they find useful: services such as haircuts, nondurable goods such as food, and durable goods such as washing machines. As incomes rise, consumption spending rises with them, increasing demand and setting the multiplier process in motion. As we saw in Chapter 5, consumption spending does not rise dollar for dollar with total incomes. The share of an extra dollar of disposable income that is added to consumption spending is the **marginal propensity to consume (MPC)**, as shown in Figure 8.4, the parameter C_y in the consumption function equation. The share of an extra dollar of national income that shows up as additional consumption spending is equal to the marginal propensity to consume times the share of income that escapes taxes: $(1 - t)C_y$ in the **consumption function** equation:

$$C = C_0 + C_y (1 - t)Y \tag{8.6}$$

If changes in incomes are considered permanent, the MPC will be high: A $1 increase in incomes will lead to an increase in consumption of as much as 80 cents. But if changes in income are considered transitory, the MPC will be low: A $1 increase in incomes will lead to an increase in consumption of only 30 cents or so. Transitory increases in income have only a small effect on consumption because people seek to smooth out their consumption spending over time.

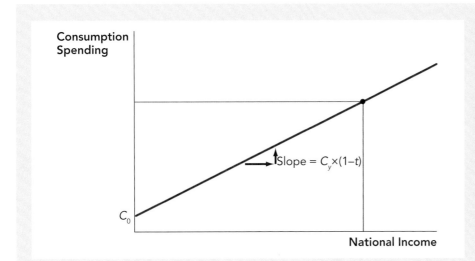

FIGURE 8.4

The Consumption Function and the Marginal Propensity to Consume

When drawn on a graph with economy-wide income on the horizontal axis and consumption spending on the vertical axis, the slope of the consumption function is the marginal propensity to consume.

For reasonably long-lasting shifts in the level of income, the MPC, C_y, is roughly 0.6. That is, 60 cents of every extra dollar of disposable income shows up as higher consumption. But remember that, as shown in Figure 8.4, the slope of the consumption function is smaller than the parameter C_y because the tax system means that a $1 increase in national income is a less-than-$1 increase in disposable income.

Box 8.1 shows how to use the consumption function and its parameters — the MPC and the tax rate — to calculate what consumption spending is.

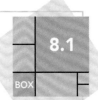

CALCULATING THE CONSUMPTION FUNCTION

Suppose statistical evidence tells us that the marginal propensity to consume out of disposable income C_y is 0.75. Suppose further that taxes amount to 40 percent of national income and that when real GDP — total national income — equals $800 billion, consumption equals $550 billion.

The fact that C_y is 0.6 and that the average tax rate t is 0.4 allows us to fill in some of the parameters in the consumption function:

$$\begin{aligned} C &= C_0 + C_y \times (1 - t) \times Y \\ &= C_0 + 0.75 \times (1 - 0.4) \times Y \\ &= C_0 + 0.45 \times Y \end{aligned}$$

We also know that when national income Y equals $800 billion, consumption C equals $550 billion:

$$\begin{aligned} \$550 &= C_0 + 0.45 \times \$800 \\ &= C_0 + \$360 \\ \$190 &= C_0 \end{aligned}$$

So the numerical form of the consumption function is

$$C = \$190 + 0.45 \times Y$$

EXAMPLE

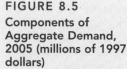

FIGURE 8.5

Components of Aggregate Demand, 2005 (millions of 1997 dollars)

By far the largest component of GDP is made up of consumption spending. Government purchases come second, gross investment comes third, and net exports come fourth.

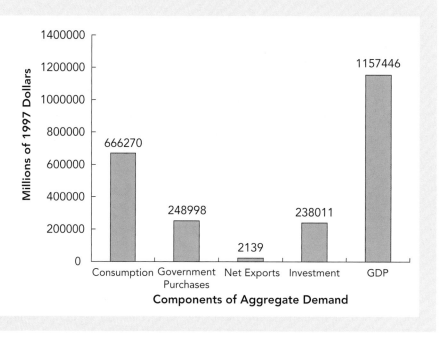

Source: Adapted from the Statistics Canada CANSIM II database, Table 380-0002.

Note: Does not sum due to statistical discrepancy.

THE OTHER COMPONENTS OF AGGREGATE DEMAND

The determinants of the other components of aggregate demand — investment spending, government purchases, and net exports — are familiar from Chapter 5.

The level of investment spending, I, is determined by the real interest rate and assessments of profitability made by business investment committees. The level of government purchases G is set by politicians. Net exports are equal to gross exports (a function of the real exchange rate ε and the level of foreign real GDP Y^f) minus imports. Figure 8.5 shows the relative sizes of these four components of aggregate demand for 2005.

THE IMPORTANCE OF INVESTMENT

The changes in investment spending shown in Figure 8.6 are the principal driving force behind the business cycle. Without exception, reductions in investment have played a powerful role in every single recession and depression. Increases in investment have spurred every single boom. Thus if we can understand the causes and consequences of changes in investment spending, we will understand most of what we need to know about business cycles.

THE ROLE OF INVESTMENT

From this point forward our analysis of investment spending will differ from the analysis in the flexible-price model of Chapters 5 and 6. The investment function looks the same in both models, but the process by which the economy reaches equilibrium is different. Hence the investment function plays a very different role in the two models.

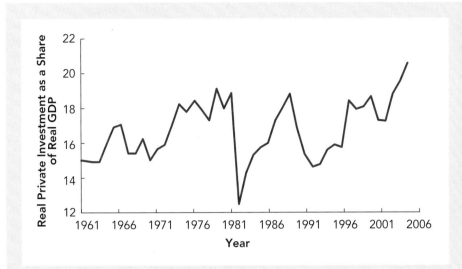

FIGURE 8.6

Investment as a Share of Real GDP, 1961–2005 (in 1997 dollars)
The substantial year-to-year swings in investment are one of the principal drivers of the business cycle. When investment booms, the economy as a whole booms too.

Source: Adapted from the Statistics Canada CANSIM II database, Series V1992053 (residential structures), V1992055 (non-residential structures), V1992056 (machinery and equipment), V1992057 (business inventories), and V1992067 (real GDP).

In the flexible-price model in Chapters 5 and 6, the real interest rate was a market-clearing price. It was pushed up or down by supply and demand to equate the flow of savings into financial markets (from households and businesses, the government, and foreigners) to the flow of investment funding out of financial markets (to finance increases in the capital stock). Supply and demand in the loanable funds market determined the interest rate. In the flexible-price model, the level of savings determined the level of investment, and the strength of investment demand determined the interest rate.

In the sticky-price model, the interest rate is not set in the loanable funds market. Instead, it is set directly by the central bank or indirectly by the combination of the stock of money and the liquidity preferences of households and businesses. The interest rate then determines the level of investment, which then plays a key role in **autonomous spending**. Together, autonomous spending and the multiplier determine the level of output.

What happened to the equilibrium in the loanable funds market? In the flexible-price model of Chapter 6, output was always at its full employment level Y^*, which made the aggregate savings a function of real interest rate r alone. Since investment demand is also a function of real interest rates, we could draw the figure for the loanable funds market and determine the equilibrium real interest rate from the total savings to investment relation:

$$(Y^* - T - C) + (T - G) - NX = I$$

On the other hand, in the fixed price model of the present chapter, interest rates are treated as fixed while output Y is variable and is determined by aggregate demand. Changes in output then result in adjustments in aggregate savings in order to achieve equilibrium in the loanable funds market consistent with the equality

$$(Y - T - C) + (T - G) - NX = I$$

http://cansim2.statcan.ca/
http://www.statcan.ca/

Notice the important difference in the two equations, corresponding to the flexible- and fixed-price models. In the flexible-price model, output is exogenously fixed at the full employment level Y^* and the real interest rate adjusts endogenously to bring about equilibrium in the loanable funds market. In the fixed-price model, the real interest rate is exogenously determined, but output Y adjusts endogenously to attain equilibrium in the same market. Thus, the equilibrium adjustment process involves adjustment in the real interest rate in the flexible-price model and adjustment in output in the fixed-price model. Yet in both cases, in the final equilibrium total savings equals total investment, or equivalently total *injections*, $G + I + GX$, equal total *withdrawals*, $S + T + IM$ where, in addition, $S = (Y - T - C)$ is private savings, GX is gross exports, and IM is gross imports.

SOURCES OF FLUCTUATIONS IN INVESTMENT

Fluctuations in investment have two sources. Some are triggered by changes in the real interest rate r. A lower real interest rate means higher investment spending, and a higher interest rate means lower investment spending. Other fluctuations are triggered by shifts in investors' expectations about future growth, profits, and risk. These two sources of fluctuations in investment correspond, respectively, to (1) changes in investment spending I produced by the interest sensitivity of investment parameter I_r times changes in r, and (2) changes in the baseline level of investment I_0 in the **investment function**

$$I = I_0 - I_r \times r \tag{8.7}$$

Both sources of fluctuations are important, but neither is clearly more important than the other.

INVESTMENT AND THE REAL INTEREST RATE

A business that undertakes an investment project always has alternative uses for the money. One alternative would be to take the money that would have been spent building the factory or buying the machines and place it instead in the financial markets — that is, lending it out at the market real rate of interest. Thus the *opportunity cost* of an investment project is the **real interest rate**. The higher the interest rate, the fewer the number and value of investment projects that will return more than their current cost, and the lower the level of investment spending. But which interest rate is the relevant one? There are many different interest rates.

THE LONG-TERM INTEREST RATE

The interest rate that is relevant for determining investment spending is a long-term interest rate. Investments are durable and long-lasting. Whenever a manager considers undertaking an investment project, he or she must compare the potential profits from the project to the opportunity to make money from a *long-term* alternative commitment of the funds elsewhere. The interest rate that is the opportunity cost of undertaking an investment project is the interest rate on a long-term loan for a period of a decade or more: the **long-term interest rate**.

This distinction matters, because long- and short-term interest rates are different and do not always move in step. Figure 8.7 shows a standard chart that plots the interest rate on bonds of different durations at three different years: 1995, 2000, and 2005. Looking at the shifts over time in such a yield curve chart shows that different interest rates do not always fluctuate together. It also shows that the long-term

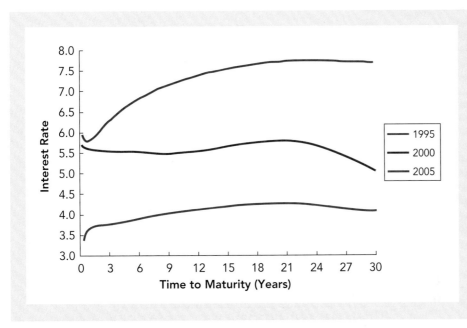

FIGURE 8.7
Bond Yield Curves
What interest rate the Candian government must pay to borrow money depends on how long it wants to borrow the money for. The same applies to private borrowers as well: Usually, the longer the term for which one wishes to borrow, the higher the interest rate one must pay.

Source: Bank of Canada.
Note: Yield curve data is as of Dec. 1 of each year.

interest rates are usually, but not always, higher than the short-term ones. For example, in 1995 and 2005 the **yield curve** is upward sloping for the long term and relatively flat for the short term, whereas in 2000 the yield curve is relatively flat for shorter terms to maturity, and downward sloping for longer terms to maturity. Equivalently, long-term loans carried much higher interest rates than short-term loans in 1995 than they did in 2005. However, long-term loans carried a lower interest rate than did short-term loans in 2000. The premium in the interest rate that the market charges on long-term loans vis-à-vis short-term loans is called the **term premium**.

As this chapter's appendix explains, when bond traders expect short-term interest rates to rise in the future, the term premium is large. When they expect **short-term interest rate**s to fall steeply, the term premium is negative. Financiers call such a rare happening an *inverted term structure*.

THE REAL INTEREST RATE
The interest rate that is relevant for investment spending decisions is not the nominal but the real interest rate. The nominal prices a business charges rise with inflation. If a business is willing to invest when the interest rate is 5 percent and inflation is 2 percent per year (and so the real interest rate is 3 percent per year), then the business should also be willing to invest when the interest rate is 10 percent and inflation is 7 percent per year (and so the real interest rate is still 3 percent per year). Figure 8.8 shows both nominal and real interest rates in Canada. There is a big difference between the two.

http://www.bank-banque-canada.ca/

THE RISKY INTEREST RATE
Lending money to a business always carries an element of risk. Perhaps the borrower will go bankrupt before the loan is due. Perhaps the creditors will find themselves

FIGURE 8.8

Gaps between Real and Nominal Interest Rates, 1961–2005

Most borrowers and lenders care not about the nominal interest rate — the interest rate in terms of money — but about the real interest rate on loans — the interest rate in terms of goods. The difference between the nominal and the real interest rates is the inflation rate.

Source: Adapted from the Statistics Canada CANSIM II database, Series V121758 (+10-year government bond yield) and V735319 (CPI).

last, or nearly last, in line as a small amount of leftover postbankruptcy assets are divided up. Financial institutions lending money are keenly interested in the financial health of those to whom they lend. The riskier they believe the loan is — the larger the possibility of a bankruptcy or a debt rescheduling appears to be — the higher is the interest rate that lenders will demand to compensate them for risk.

The interest rate that a firm faces is the interest rate charged to risky borrowers, not the interest rate charged to safe borrowers (like the Canadian government) to whom people lend when they want to sleep easily at night. The premium that lenders charge for loans to companies rather than to safe government borrowers is called the **risk premium**. (See Figure 8.9.) Financial and economic disturbances — like the default of the Russian government in August 1998 — can cause large and swift moves in the risk premium. The **risky interest rate** does not move in step with the **safe interest rate**.

Thus to determine the level of investment spending, take the baseline level of investment I_0 (determined by businesses' optimism, expected economic growth, and a bunch of other factors for which the level of the stock market serves as a convenient thermometer). Subtract from this baseline level the interest sensitivity of investment parameter I_r times the relevant interest rate r. The relevant interest rate must be *long-term* because most investments are long-term. The relevant interest rate must be *real* because investment projects are real assets: Their value rises with inflation. And the relevant interest rate must be *risky* because businesses borrowing to invest may go bankrupt. In the investment function

$$I = I_0 - I_r \times r$$

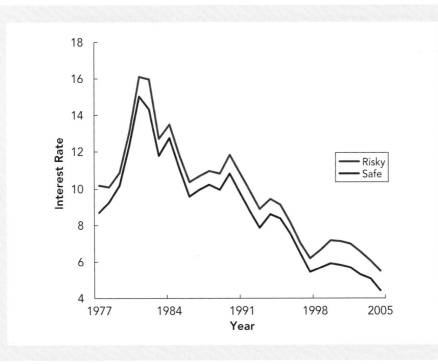

FIGURE 8.9

The Risk Premium: Safe and Risky Interest Rates, 1997–2005

Loans that are not made to the Canadian government are risky: lenders charge a risk premium that depends both on their tolerance for risk and on the amount of risk involved when they lend to other organizations. This risk premium is not constant but varies over time.

Source: Adapted from the Statistics Canada CANSIM II database, Series V121758 (+10-year government bond yield) and V121761 (long-term corporate bond yield).

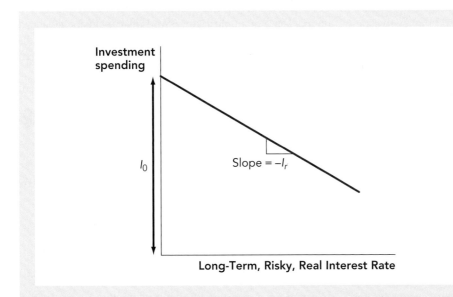

FIGURE 8.10

Investment as a Decreasing Function of the Long-Term, Real, Risky Interest Rate

The baseline level of investment I_0 tells us what the level of investment would be if the real interest rate were zero. The interest rate sensitivity parameter I_r tells us how much investment is discouraged by a 1-unit increase in the long-term, real, risky interest rate.

the relevant interest rate r is the long-term, real, risky interest rate, as is plotted in Figure 8.10.

The interest rate can be directly observed: It is what the newspapers print every day in their analyses of the bond market. But is there any easy way to observe the

THE STOCK MARKET AS AN INDICATOR OF FUTURE INVESTMENT

Recall from Chapter 2 that if investors in the stock market are acting rationally, the level of the stock market P^s will be equal to

$$P^s = E^a \times \left(\frac{E^s}{E^a} \right) \times \left(\frac{1}{r + \sigma^s} \right)$$

where

- E^a is the accounting earnings corporations report.
- E^s/E^a is the ratio of the long-run "permanent" earnings investors expect to today's accounting earnings. It is a measure of optimism, of expected future growth.
- r is the long-term real interest rate on bonds.
- σ^s is the risk premium investors require to invest in stocks rather than in less risky assets.

Thus the stock market sums up — in one easy-to-find number, reported daily — the real interest rate r plus the same important influences — profitability, expected growth, and attitudes toward risk — that determine the baseline level of investment I_0.

Think of it this way: An investor deciding whether or not to commit his or her portfolio to stocks (rather than bonds) is making more or less the same decision as that made by a business's investment committee deciding whether to build a factory. The purchase of a share of stock gives you title to a share in the ownership of past investments — factories, buildings, inventories, and organizations — that have been undertaken by one company. The same things that determine whether it is a good idea to undertake the construction of a new factory also determine whether it is a good idea to spend money to acquire title to a share of an old factory. And the conclusions reached by investors in the stock market that we observe every day in stock price fluctuations are likely to be much the same as the conclusions reached by businesses' investment committees.

The higher the stock market, the higher is the likely future level of investment spending.

rest of the determinants of investment spending — all of those that are packed into the baseline level of investment spending I_0? Box 8.2 tells us how.

NET EXPORTS

Net exports are equal to the difference between gross exports and gross imports:

$$NX = GX - IM = (X_f Y^f + X_\varepsilon \varepsilon) - IM_y Y \tag{8.8}$$

As we saw in Chapter 5, gross exports depend on foreign total income Y^f and the real exchange rate ε. An increase in foreign income increases the purchasing power of foreigners allowing them to buy more domestic exports. Similarly, an increase in the real exchange rate (a real depreciation of the domestic currency) makes domestically produced goods and services more competitive in international markets, and thus increases gross exports. Gross imports depend on the level of domestic income Y. An increase in domestic income increases the volume of imports from abroad.

GOVERNMENT EXPENDITURES

The level of government purchases of goods and services G is set by politicians. For our present purposes we will treat G as exogenously set by the government, although in practice G depends on several factors including the government's policies towards stabilizing business cycles.

PLANNED EXPENDITURE

AUTONOMOUS SPENDING AND THE MARGINAL PROPENSITY TO EXPEND

Let's take the equation for aggregate demand

$$E = C + I + G + NX \qquad (8.9)$$

We can now classify the components of aggregate demand into two groups. The first group is so-called autonomous spending, which we will call A. Autonomous spending is made up of the components of aggregate demand that do *not* depend directly on national income Y. The second group includes all other components of aggregate demand that depend directly on Y. Using this distinction, we can derive the form of A and the **planned-expenditure function** by substituting into equation (8.8) the determinants of C, I, G, and NX:

$$E = [C_0 + C_y (1 - t)Y] + (I_0 - I_r r) + G + (X_f Y^f + X_\varepsilon \varepsilon) + IM_y Y \qquad (8.10)$$

Further, as we saw in Chapter 5, the real exchange rate ε depends on the domestic real interest rate r (as well as on the foreign exchange speculators' opinions of fundamentals and foreign interest rates):

$$\varepsilon = \varepsilon_0 - \varepsilon_r(r - r^f) \qquad (8.11)$$

Substituting for the real exchange rate from equation (8.11) into (8.10) and rearranging the resulting expression, we can rewrite aggregate demand or planned expenditure in the more compact form

$$E = A + MPE \times Y \qquad (8.12)$$

where

$$A = C_0 + (I_0 - I_r r) + G + (X_f Y^f + X_\varepsilon \varepsilon_0 + X_\varepsilon \varepsilon_r r^f - X_\varepsilon \varepsilon_r r) \qquad (8.13)$$

and

$$MPE = C_y(1 - t) - IM_y \qquad (8.14)$$

is the **marginal propensity to expend** out of gross domestic income.

It becomes clear from equation (8.13) that autonomous spending depends on purely **exogenous** components, like C_0, I_0, or ε_0, as well as on the real interest rate r. Unlike the flexible price model of Part III, in Chapter 8 the real interest rate is also an exogenous variable, under the direct control of the central bank. For this reason, A will be treated as given in the analysis of this chapter, and will be affected only if any of its components changes. For instance, if the central bank raises r, A will be reduced due to the induced decline in both investment ($I_r r$) and exports ($X_\varepsilon \varepsilon_r r$). Besides the standard investment reduction, exports fall because the higher interest rate increases the demand for home-currency-denominated assets by foreign speculators, thereby driving down the real exchange rate and making home exports more expensive to foreigners.

FIGURE 8.11

An Increase in Autonomous Spending

An increase in autonomous spending shifts the planned-expenditure line upward.

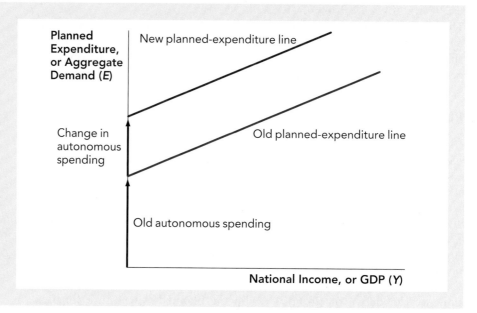

FIGURE 8.12

The Income-Expenditure Diagram

On the income-expenditure diagram, the line showing the relationship between total economy-wide income and total aggregate demand — the planned-expenditure line — is determined by two things: Autonomous spending is the level at which the planned-expenditure line intercepts the y axis. The marginal propensity to expend is the slope of the planned-expenditure line.

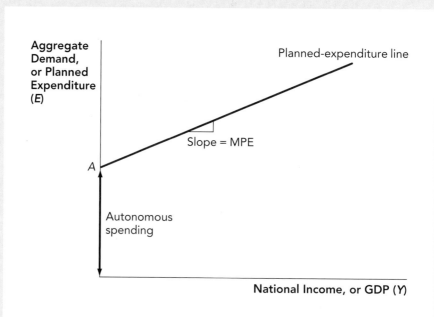

Figure 8.11 shows a typical graph of planned expenditure. Aggregate demand or planned expenditure is plotted on the vertical axis, and national income or real GDP is plotted on the horizontal axis of this **income-expenditure diagram**. In Figure 8.12, the intercept of the planned-expenditure or aggregate demand line is the level of autonomous spending *A*; the slope of the planned-expenditure or aggregate demand line is the marginal propensity to expend *MPE*.

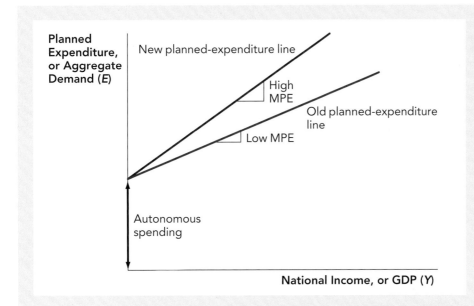

FIGURE 8.13

An Increase in the Marginal Propensity to Expend

A change in the marginal propensity to expend changes the slope of the planned-expenditure line.

A change in the value of any determinant of any component of autonomous spending — the baseline levels of consumption C_0, investment I_0, or government purchases G; the real interest rate r; and foreign-determined variables like foreign interest rates r^f, foreign levels of real income Y^f, or speculators' view of exchange rate fundamentals ε_0 — will shift the planned-expenditure line up or down. The higher the autonomous spending, the further from the x axis the planned-expenditure line will be (see Figure 8.11).

Changes in the marginal propensity to consume C_y, the tax rate t, or the propensity to spend on imports IM_y will change the MPE and the slope of the planned-expenditure line. The higher the MPE, the steeper is the slope of the planned-expenditure line (see Figure 8.13). Box 8.3 provides an example of how to calculate the MPE.

CALCULATING THE MPE

In the planned-expenditure function

$$E = A + MPE \times Y$$

the marginal propensity to expend (MPE) will be less than the slope of the consumption function $C_y(1 - t)$ because of the effect on the economy of imports. The MPE is

$$E = A + MPE \times Y$$

Thus if the marginal propensity to consume C_y is 0.75 and the tax rate is 40 percent, the 0.45 slope of the consumption function is an upper bound to the MPE. If imports are 15 percent of real GDP, then

$$MPE = [C_y(1 - t) - IM_y]$$
$$= [0.75 \times (1 - 0.4) - 0.15]$$

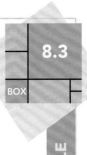

8.3

BOX

EXAMPLE

$$= 0.45 - 0.15 = 0.30$$

Such relatively small values of the MPE are typical for modern industrialized economies, which have substantial amounts of international trade (that is, relatively high values for IM_y), large social-democratic social-insurance states (that is, relatively high values for t), and deep and well-developed financial systems that provide ample room for household borrowing and lending to smooth out consumption (that is, relatively small values for C_y as well). However, in the past, in relatively closed economies, or in economies with undeveloped financial systems, the MPE can be significantly higher.

STICKY-PRICE EQUILIBRIUM

The economy will be in equilibrium when planned expenditure equals real GDP — which is, according to the circular flow principle, the same as national income. Under these conditions there will be no short-run forces pushing for an immediate expansion or contraction of national income, real GDP, and aggregate demand.

On the income-expenditure diagram, the points at which planned expenditure equals national income are a line running up and to the right at a 45-degree angle with respect to the x axis, as Figure 8.14 shows. This line covers all the possible points of equilibrium. The actual equilibrium will be that point at which planned expenditure is equal to national income. The point where this planned-expenditure line intersects the 45-degree equilibrium-condition line is the economy's equilibrium.

FIGURE 8.14

Equilibrium on the Income-Expenditure Diagram

On the income-expenditure diagram, the equilibrium point of the economy is that point where aggregate demand (as a function of total product) is equal to total product.

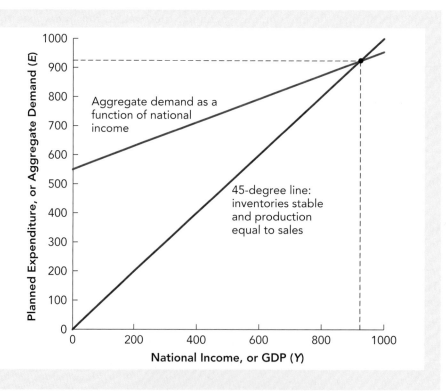

In algebra, the equilibrium values of aggregate demand E and real GDP or national income Y must satisfy both

$$E = A + MPE \times Y$$

and

$$E = Y$$

Substituting Y for E in the first of these equations and regrouping, the solution is

$$Y = E = \frac{A}{1 - MPE} \qquad (8.15)$$

If the numerical values of the parameters of the planned expenditure function

$$E = A + MPE \times Y$$

are A = \$560 billion and MPE = 0.3, then planned expenditure as a function of real GDP is

$$E = 560 + 0.3 \times Y$$

The equilibrium level of real GDP and aggregate demand is then

$$Y = \$800 \text{ billion}$$

If the economy is not on the 45-degree line, then aggregate demand E does not equal real GDP Y. If Y is greater than E, there is excess supply of goods. If E is greater than Y, there is excess demand for goods. In neither case is the economy in equilibrium.

In the first case, in which production exceeds demand, inventories are rising rapidly and firms unwilling to accumulate unsold and unsellable inventories are about to cut production and fire workers (see Figure 8.15). In the second case, in which demand

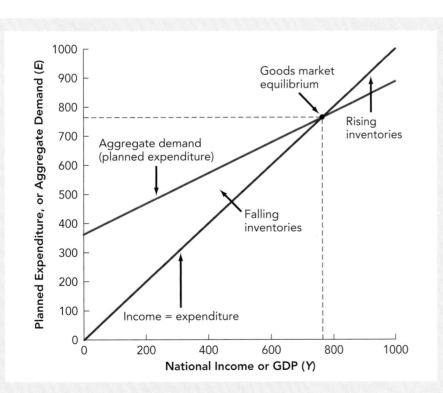

FIGURE 8.15

Inventory Adjustment and Equilibrium: Goods Market Equilibrium and the Income-Expenditure Diagram

If the economy is not at its equilibrium point, then either total production exceeds aggregate demand (in which case inventories are rising) or aggregate demand exceeds total production (in which case inventories are falling).

exceeds production, inventories are falling rapidly. Businesses are selling more than they are making. Some businesses will respond to the fall in inventories by boosting prices, trying to earn more profit per good sold. But the bulk of businesses will respond to the fall in inventories by expanding production to match demand. They are about to hire more workers. Real GDP and national income are about to expand.

Now suppose that businesses see their inventories falling and respond by boosting their production to equal last month's planned expenditure. Will such an increase bring the economy into goods market equilibrium, with planned expenditure equal to total income and real GDP? The answer is that it will not. To boost production, firms must hire workers, paying more in wages and causing household incomes to rise. When income rises, total spending rises as well. Thus the increase in production and income generates a further expansion in aggregate demand.

Even after production has increased to close the initial gap between aggregate demand and national income, the economy will still not be in equilibrium, as Figure 8.16 shows. Inventories will be falling even though hiring more workers has increased production. Because hiring more workers has also boosted total income and further increased aggregate demand, production will have to expand by a *multiple* of the initial gap in order to stabilize inventories. The process will come to an end, with aggregate demand equal to national income, only when both have risen to the level at which the planned-expenditure line crosses the 45-degree income-equals-expenditure line. And the process works in reverse if planned expenditure is below national income.

FIGURE 8.16

The Inventory Adjustment Process: An Income-Expenditure Diagram

If planned expenditure is greater than total production and inventories are falling, businesses will hire more workers and increase production.

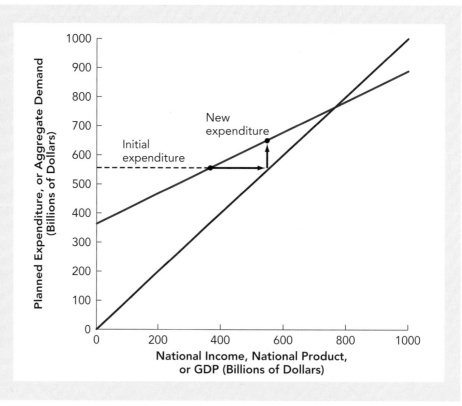

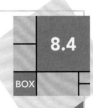

DETAILS

HOW FAST DOES THE ECONOMY MOVE TO EQUILIBRIUM?

At any one particular moment the economy does not have to be in short-run equilibrium. Aggregate demand can exceed real GDP, and national income and inventories can fall, for periods as long as a year. There *are* strong forces pushing the economy toward short-run equilibrium. Businesses do not like to lose money by producing things that they cannot sell or by not having things on hand that they could sell. But it takes at least months, usually quarters, and possibly more time for businesses to expand or cut back production.

For example, between 1990 and 1994 inventories fell. Real GDP was less than aggregate demand as businesses decided that their high levels of inventories were too large given the economic uncertainties created by the recession of the early 1990s. After 1994 inventories rose. For this period, GDP was greater than aggregate demand. (See Figure 8.17.)

FIGURE 8.17

Inventories as the Balancing Item: Inventory Investment 1961–2005 (millions of 1997 dollars)

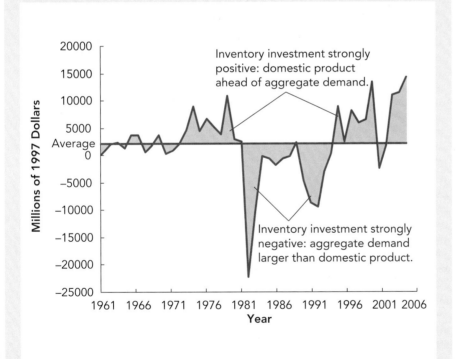

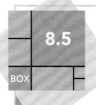

8.5

BOX

EXAMPLE

THE SEPTEMBER 11 TERRORIST ATTACK ON THE WORLD TRADE CENTER

The U.S. economy was already on the edge of recession in the summer of 2001 when the terrorist attack on New York's World Trade Center sent it over the edge (Figure 8.18). The attack on September 11, 2001, reduced autonomous spending through two different channels. First, the attack shook consumer confidence. The Conference Board's index of consumer confidence fell from 114 in August 2001 to 85 in November. Baseline consumption spending, the parameter C_0 in the consumption function, is closely linked to consumer confidence. Second, the attack on September 11 increased uncertainty. Would there be further attacks? What would the U.S. military response be? How would U.S. government spending shift in response to the attack? The first rule of planning for the future is that whenever uncertainty is unusually high, you are better off delaying whatever decisions you can until some of this uncertainty is resolved. Thus businesses undertaking investment projects adopted a wait-and-see approach. The result was that autonomous spending fell.

Had the terrorist attack been the only major shock to the U.S. economy, the recession would have been much deeper and longer than turned out to be the case. However, three *countervailing* forces produced boosts to autonomous spending in the

FIGURE 8.18

Month-to-Month Changes in U.S. Industrial Production, 2000–2002
Industrial production in the United States had been declining since late 2000 but was showing signs of recovery when the attack on the World Trade Center on September 11, 2001, shook consumer and business confidence. As consumers cut back on spending and as businesses adopted a wait-and-see attitude, U.S. industrial production dropped an additional 2.2 percent in the four months before recovery began.

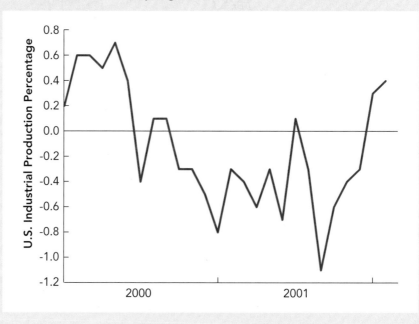

Source: Adapted from the Statistics Canada CANSIM II database, Series 19650248.

months after September 11, 2001. First, businesses took advantage of the interest rate reductions the Federal Reserve had been making since the start of 2001 to borrow money, and some of this borrowed money showed up as additional investment spending to boost autonomous spending. Second, the Bush tax cut of 2001 boosted consumers' incomes by early 2002 by an amount equal to some $80 billion of extra income a year, and this reduction in tax collections boosted total spending. Third, increased military and security spending raised government purchases G, which also boosted autonomous demand. Thus the economy reached at least a temporary low point at the end of 2001, and began a rebound of uncertain duration as aggregate demand began to rise once again.

CALCULATING THE DIFFERENCE BETWEEN AGGREGATE DEMAND AND REAL GDP

Suppose that our planned-expenditure function has numerical values for its coefficients, so that in billions

$$E = A + MPE \times Y$$
$$= \$560 + 0.3 \times Y$$

Suppose first that the current level of real GDP Y is $750 billion. Then aggregate demand — total *planned* expenditure — is

$$E = \$560 + 0.3 \times \$750$$
$$= \$785$$

and business inventories are being drawn down at a rate

$$\frac{\Delta inventories}{\Delta time} = Y - E = -\$350 \; billion \text{ per year}$$

Suppose, second, that the current level of total real GDP Y is $850 billion. Then total planned expenditure is

$$E = \$560 + 0.3 \times \$850$$
$$= \$815 \; billion \text{ per year}$$

and business inventories are being added to at a rate

$$\frac{\Delta inventories}{\Delta time} = \$350 \; billion \text{ per year}$$

However, if the current level of total national income (and of real GDP) Y is $800 billion, then total planned expenditure is

$$E = \$560 + 0.3 \times \$800$$
$$= \$800$$

and business inventories are stable

$$\frac{\Delta inventories}{\Delta time} = \$0$$

> **RECAP   INCOME AND EXPENDITURE**
>
> The force that pushes real GDP Y to equal aggregate demand E is the inventory-adjustment process. If real GDP exceeds aggregate demand, inventories are rising rapidly. Firms are unwilling to accumulate unsold and unsellable inventories, so they are about to cut production and fire workers to reduce real GDP. If real GDP is less than aggregate demand, inventories are falling rapidly as businesses are selling more than they are making. Businesses are about to expand production, hire more workers, and thus raise real GDP.

8.3 THE MULTIPLIER

DETERMINING THE SIZE OF THE MULTIPLIER

Suppose something happens to change the level of planned-expenditure at every possible level of total income. Anything that affects the level of autonomous spending will do. What would happen to the equilibrium level of total income and real GDP?

An upward shift in the planned-expenditure line would increase the equilibrium level of total income. At the prevailing level of national income, planned expenditure would be larger than real GDP. Businesses would find themselves selling more than they were making, and their inventories would fall. In response, businesses would boost production to try to keep inventories from being exhausted, and production would expand. How much production would expand depends on the magnitude of the change in autonomous spending and the value of the spending **multiplier**.

The value of the multiplier depends on the slope of the planned-expenditure line, the marginal propensity to expend (MPE). The higher the MPE, the MPE steeper is the planned expenditure line and the greater is the multiplier. A large multiplier can amplify small shocks to spending patterns into large changes in total production and income, as Figure 8.19 shows.

To calculate the multiplier, recall the simplified equation for planned expenditure

$$E = A + MPE \times Y$$

and the equilibrium condition

$$Y = E$$

Substitute the second into the first, and solve for Y:

$$Y = \frac{A}{1 - MPE}$$

Thus if autonomous spending changes by an amount ΔA, equilibrium real GDP changes by

$$\Delta Y = \frac{1}{1 - MPE} \times \Delta A \tag{8.16}$$

And if we want to express the denominator of this fraction in terms of the basic parameters of the model, it is

$$\Delta Y = \frac{1}{1 - [C_y(1 - t) - IM_y]} \times \Delta A \tag{8.17}$$

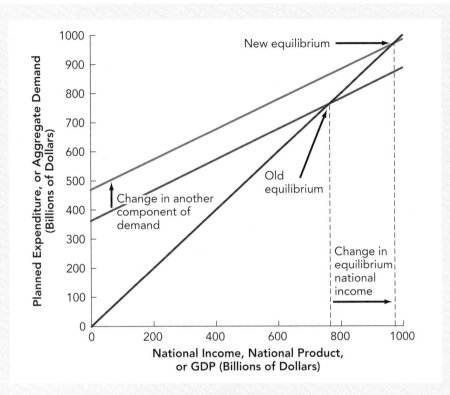

FIGURE 8.19
The Multiplier Effect
An increase in autonomous spending will generate an amplified increase in the equilibrium level of national income. Why? Because planned expenditure will rise not just by the increase in autonomous spending but by the increase in autonomous spending plus the marginal propensity to expend times the increase in the equilibrium level of national income.

This factor, $1/(1 - MPE) = 1/\{1 - [C_y(1 - t) - IM_y]\}$ is the *multiplier*: It multiplies the upward shift in the planned-expenditure line as a result of the increase in autonomous spending into a change in the equilibrium level of real GDP, total income, and aggregate demand.

Why the factor $1/(1 - MPE)$? Think of it this way: The *MPE* — the marginal propensity to expend — is the slope of the planned-expenditure line. A $1 increase in national income raises the equilibrium level of planned expenditure by $1, because expenditure has to go $1 higher to balance income and production. As Figure 8.20 shows, it also raises the level of planned expenditure by $*MPE*. Thus a $1 increase in the level of total income closes $(1 - *MPE*) of the gap between planned expenditure and total income. To close a full initial gap of $ΔA between planned expenditure and national income, the equilibrium level of national income must increase by $ΔA/(1 - *MPE*).

Because autonomous spending is influenced by a great many factors,

$$A = C_0 + (I_0 - I_r r) + G + (X_f Y^f + X_\varepsilon \varepsilon_0 - X_\varepsilon \varepsilon_r r + X_\varepsilon \varepsilon_r r^f)$$

almost every change in economic policy or the economic environment will set the multiplier process in motion.

CHANGING THE SIZE OF THE MULTIPLIER

One factor that tends to minimize the multiplier is the government's *fiscal automatic stabilizers*. The government doesn't levy a total lump-sum tax. Instead the

FIGURE 8.20
Determining the Size of the Multiplier

An increase ΔA in national income and total production raises the level of aggregate demand consistent with equilibrium by ΔA, but it also raises the level of planned expenditure by the $MPE \times \Delta A$. A ΔA dollar increase in national income and total production reduces the gap between total production and planned expenditure by only $(1 - MPE)\Delta A$. Hence the increase in the equilibrium level of national income produced by a change ΔA in autonomous spending is not ΔA but $\Delta A/(1 - MPE)$ — ΔA times the value of the multiplier.

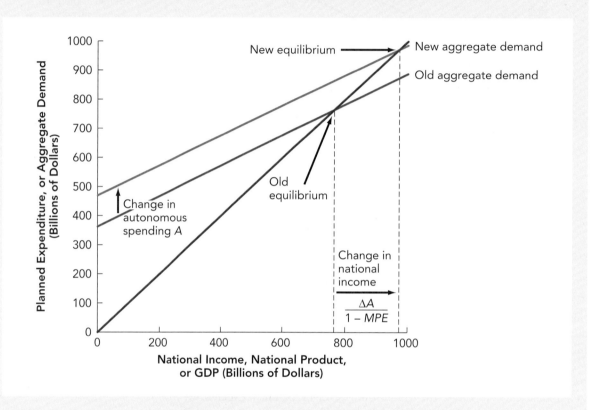

government imposes roughly proportional (actually slightly progressive) taxes on the economy, so government tax collections are equal to a tax rate t times the level of GDP Y: the total tax take equals $t \times Y$.

This means that the government collects more in tax revenue when GDP is relatively high. The collection of extra revenue dampens swings in after-tax income and thus reduces consumption. Similarly, the government collects less in tax revenue when GDP is relatively low; thus after-tax income is higher than that under lump-sum taxes, and this higher income boosts consumption. Because the fall in consumption is smaller, the multiplier is smaller. Disturbances to spending are not amplified as much as they used to be, and so shocks to the economy tend to cause smaller business cycles.

The automatic working of the government's tax system (and, to a lesser extent, its social welfare programs) function as an *automatic stabilizer*, reducing the

8.7

BOX

EXAMPLE

THE VALUE OF THE MULTIPLIER

Suppose that the planned-expenditure function has values for its parameters of $A = \$560$ billion and $MPE = 0.3$, so that

$$E = A + MPE \times Y$$
$$= \$560 + 0.3 \times Y$$

Then the equilibrium value of total income (and of real GDP) Y is $800 billion, for only at $Y = \$800$ billion is planned expenditure equal to real GDP.

Now suppose that autonomous spending A increases by an amount of $10 billion:

$$\Delta A = \$10$$

Then the planned-expenditure function is

$$E = \$570 + 0.3 \times Y$$

and the equilibrium value of total income (and real GDP) Y is $814.3 billion.

The change in Y divided by the change in autonomous spending is

$$\frac{\Delta Y}{\Delta A} = 1.43$$

This is equal to

$$1.43 = \frac{1}{1 - 0.3} = \frac{1}{1 - MPE}$$

which we saw above is the definition of the multiplier

magnitude of fluctuations in real GDP and unemployment. With a proportional tax system the multiplier is

$$\frac{\Delta Y}{\Delta A} = \frac{1}{1 - MPE} = \frac{1}{1 - [C_y(1 - t) - IM_y]} \tag{8.18}$$

If the government levied lump-sum taxes, the multiplier would be

$$\frac{\Delta Y}{\Delta A} = \frac{1}{1 - MPE} = \frac{1}{1 - (C_y - IM_y)} \tag{8.19}$$

How large are fiscal automatic stabilizers in Canada today? When national product and national income drop by a dollar, income tax and social security tax collections fall automatically by at least one-third of a dollar. Thus, the fall in consumers' disposable income is only two-thirds as great as the fall in national income, and the fall in consumption is only two-thirds as large as it would be without fiscal automatic stabilizers.

An economy that is more open to world trade will also have a smaller multiplier than will a less open economy. The more open the economy, the greater is the marginal propensity to expend on imports. The more of every extra dollar of income spent on imports, the less is left to be devoted to planned expenditure on *domestic products* — and therefore the smaller is the multiplier. If the share of imports in GDP is large, the potential change in the multiplier from an open economy

$$\frac{\Delta Y}{\Delta A} = \frac{1}{1 - MPE} = \frac{1}{1 - [C_y(1 - t) - IM_y]} \tag{8.20}$$

to that from a closed economy

$$\frac{\Delta Y}{\Delta A} = \frac{1}{1 - MPE} = \frac{1}{1 - [C_y(1 - t)]} \tag{8.21}$$

can be considerable. In modern industrialized economies where the share of imports in real GDP is certainly more than 10 percent, any calculation of the multiplier must take into account the effects of world trade.

RECAP   THE MULTIPLIER

If prices are sticky, higher aggregate demand boosts production, and this boosts incomes. Higher incomes give a further boost to consumption, and this in turn boosts aggregate demand some more. Thus any shift in a component of aggregate demand upward or downward leads to a multiplied shift in total production. The early-twentieth-century British economist John Maynard Keynes was one of the first to stress the importance of this multiplier process. The multiplier arises because aggregate demand E is equal to autonomous spending E times the marginal propensity to expend MPE times national income Y: $E = A + MPE \times Y$.

In equilibrium aggregate demand E equals national income Y, which is true if and only if $Y = [1/(1 - MPE)] \times A$. The term $1/(1 - MPE)$ is the value of the multiplier.

CHAPTER SUMMARY

1. Business-cycle fluctuations can push real GDP away from potential output and push unemployment far away from its average rate.

2. If prices were perfectly and instantaneously flexible, there would be no such thing as business-cycle fluctuations. Hence macroeconomics must consist in large part of models in which prices are sticky.

3. There are a number of reasons that prices might be sticky: menu costs, imperfect information, concerns of fairness, or simple money illusion. All seem plausible. None has overwhelming evidence of importance vis-à-vis the others.

4. In the short run, while prices are sticky, the level of real GDP is determined by the level of aggregate demand.

5. The short-run equilibrium level of real GDP is that level at which aggregate demand as a function of national income is equal to the level of national income, or real GDP.

6. Two quantities summarize planned expenditure as a function of total income: the level of autonomous spending and the marginal propensity to expend (*MPE*).

7. The level of autonomous spending is the intercept of the planned-expenditure function on the income-expenditure diagram. It tells us what the level of planned expenditure would be if national income were zero.

8. The *MPE* is the slope of the planned-expenditure function on the income-expenditure diagram. It tells us

how much planned expenditure increases for each $1 increase in national income.

9. The value of the MPE depends on the tax rate t, the marginal propensity to consume (MPC), and the share of spending on imports IM_y. In algebra, $MPE = C_y(1 - t) - IM_y$.

10. In the simple macro models, an increase in any component of autonomous spending causes a more-than-proportional increase in real GDP. This is the result of the multiplier process.

11. The size of the multiplier depends on the marginal propensity to expend (MPE): the higher the MPE, the higher is the multiplier. The value of the multiplier is

$$\frac{\Delta Y}{\Delta A} = \frac{1}{1 - MPE}$$

KEY TERMS AND EQUATIONS

autonomous spending (p. 247)

consumption function (p. 244)

exogenous (p. 253)

flexible prices (p. 238)

income-expenditure diagram (p. 254)

investment function (p. 248)

long-term interest rate (p. 248)

marginal propensity to consume (MPC) (p. 244)

marginal propensity to expend (MPE) (p. 253)

menu costs (p. 242)

money illusion (p. 243)

multiplier (p. 262)

natural rate of unemployment (p. 236)

planned-expenditure function (p. 253)

real interest rate (p. 248)

risk premium (p. 250)

risky interest rate (p. 250)

safe interest rate (p. 250)

short-term interest rate (p. 249)

sticky prices (p. 238)

term premium (p. 249)

yield curve (p. 249)

Aggregate demand:	$E = A + MPE \times Y$	(8.12)
Marginal propensity to expend:	$MPE = C_y(1 - t) - IM_y$	(8.14)
Equilibrium E and Y:	$Y = E = \dfrac{A}{1 - MPE}$	(8.15)
The multiplier:	$\dfrac{\Delta Y}{\Delta A} = \dfrac{1}{1 - MPE} = \dfrac{1}{1 - [C_y(1 - t) - IM_y]}$	(8.18)

ANALYTICAL EXERCISES

1. Describe, in your own words, the factors that determine the slope of the planned-expenditure curve.

2. Suppose that government purchases increase by $10 billion but there are no other changes in economic policy or the economic environment.
   a. What effect does this increase in government purchases have on the location of the planned-expenditure line?
   b. What effect does this increase in government purchases have on the planned-expenditure function?

   c. What effect does this increase in government purchases have on the equilibrium level of aggregate demand, national income, and real GDP?

3. Consider an economy in which prices are sticky, the marginal propensity to consume out of disposable income C_y is 0.6, the tax rate t is 0.25, and the share of national income spent on imports IM_y is 20 percent.
   a. Suppose that total autonomous spending is $600 billion. Graph planned expenditure as a function of total national income.

b. Determine the equilibrium level of national income and real GDP.

c. What is the value of the multiplier?

d. Suppose that total autonomous spending increases by $10 billion to $610 billion. What happens to the equilibrium level of national income and real GDP, Y?

4. Suppose that prices are sticky; the marginal propensity to consume out of disposable income C_y is 0.9. Suppose further that the economy is closed — the share of national income spent on imports is zero — and that the tax rate is 12.5 percent.

a. What is the marginal propensity to expend?

b. What is the value of the multiplier?

c. What level of autonomous spending would be needed to attain a level of equilibrium aggregate demand equal to $1 trillion?

5. Classify the following changes into two groups: those that increase equilibrium real GDP and those that decrease real GDP.

An increase in consumers' desire to spend today.

An increase in interest rates overseas.

A decline in foreign exchange speculators' confidence in the value of the home currency.

A fall in real GDP overseas.

An increase in government purchases.

An increase in managers' expectations of the future profitability of investments.

An increase in the tax rate.

6. (Appendix 8A). Consider the situation where an investor has two investment options over two years: Invest either in (a) one 2-year bond with return r or (b) one 1-year bond in each of the two years with annual returns: r_n^s in the first year, and expected return Er_j^s in the second year.

a. Derive the relationship between the long rate (r) and the two short rates (r_n^s and Er_j^s) and explain your results.

b. Derive the equation for the term premium and explain.

7. (Appendix 8A). In Exercise 6, assume that $r_n^s = 0.04$ and Er_j^s is either 0.05, or 0.04 or 0.03.

a. Compute the yield curve in each case, plot it on a graph, and comment.

b. Compute the term premium in each case and comment.

POLICY EXERCISES

1. Suppose that the economy is at its full-employment level of output of $1 trillion, with government purchases equal to $200 billion, the net tax rate equal to 30 percent, and the budget in balance.

a. Suppose that adverse shocks to consumption and investment lead real GDP to fall to $950 billion. What is the level of taxes collected? What is the government's budget deficit?

b. Suppose that favourable shocks to consumption and investment lead real GDP to rise to $1.2 trillion. What is the level of taxes collected? What is the government's budget balance?

c. Most economists like to calculate a "full-employment budget balance," equal to government purchases minus what tax collections would be if the economy were at full employment, and to take that balance as their summary measure of the short-run effect of government taxes and spending on the level of real GDP. What advantages does such a full-employment budget measure have over the actual budget as a measure of economic policy? What disadvantages does it have?

2. Suppose that the economy is short of its full-employment level of GDP, $900 billion, by $50 billion, with the MPC out of disposable income equal to 0.6, the import share IM_y equal to 0.25, and the tax rate t equal to 25 percent.

a. Suppose the government wants to boost real GDP up to full employment by cutting taxes. How large a cut in

the tax rate is required to do so? How large a cut in total tax collections is produced by this cut in the tax rate?

b. Suppose the government wants to boost real GDP up to full employment by increasing government spending. How large an increase in government spending is required to do so?

c. Can you account for any asymmetry between the answers to *a* and *b*?

3. Think about the four possible sources of price stickiness mentioned in this chapter: money illusion, "fairness" considerations, misperceptions of price changes, and menu costs. What have you read or seen in the past two months that strike you as examples of any of these four phenomena? In your opinion, which of the four sources seems likely to be the most important?

4. What changes in the economy's institutions can you think of that would diminish price stickiness and increase price flexibility? What advantage in terms of the size of the business cycle would you expect to follow from such changes in institutions? What disadvantages do you think that such institutional changes might have?

5. Suppose the government wants to increase real GDP by $50 billion. How would you suggest the government go about accomplishing this goal?

8A

The Term Premium and Expected Future Interest Rates

What determines the value of the *term premium* — the gap between short-term and long-term interest rates? To start thinking about this question, consider once again a simple two-period model in which the periods are "now" and the "future." Bankers make long-term loans that fall due in two periods. Bond traders buy and sell long-term bonds that fall due in two periods. The real interest rate paid on these long-term loans and bonds is the long-term real interest rate r. Bankers also make short-term loans (and bond traders also buy and sell short-term bonds) that mature in just one period.

Someone thinking about buying a long-term bond (or making a long-term loan) knows that for each real dollar invested in such financial instruments today, he or she will after two periods have

$$\text{Gross return} = 1 + r + r$$

Each period they will receive the long-term real interest rate, r, on their investment.

Someone thinking about buying a short-term bond today (or making a short-term loan) knows that for each real dollar invested in such financial instruments today, he or she will after the end of the first period (the one that is going on "now") have $1 + r_n^s$: r for the real interest rate, s because it is the rate paid on a short-term loan, and n because it is the interest rate paid in the now period. But the person's capital will then, at the start of the second period (the one that will happen in the future), be lying idle. The natural thing to do then will be to invest it again in another short-term bond (or make another short-term loan — this time at the short-term interest rate that will prevail in the future, r_f^s.

So after two periods someone who chooses today to invest money in short-term securities will have

$$\text{Gross return} = 1 + r_n^s + r_f^s$$

for each real dollar that he or she invested at the start of the first period.

What will a flint-eyed money-maximizing rational bond trader do? The first complication is that he or she doesn't know today what the future short-term real interest rate r_f^s will be when the time to reinvest the principal arrives. The best he or she can do is form an expectation now — E_n — of what the future short-term real interest rate will be: $E_n(r_f^s)$.

Thus the bond trader has to decide whether to invest for the long-term or for the short-term (and then, later, to reinvest). The returns from investing for the long-term will be greater if

$$\text{Long-term gross return} = 1 + 2r > 1 + r_n^s + E_n(r_f^s) = \text{short-term return}$$

Or, defining $E_n(\Delta r)$, the expected change in the short-term real interest rate, as the difference between expected future short rates $E_n(r_f^s)$ and current short rates r_f^s

$$\text{Expected change in short rates} = E_n(\Delta r^s) = E_n(r_f^s) - r_n^s$$

The returns from investing for the long-term will be greater if

$$r - r_n^s > \frac{E_n(\Delta r^s)}{2}$$

And the bond trader will probably decide to invest for the long-term. If

$$r - r_n^s < \frac{E_n(\Delta r^s)}{2}$$

then the returns from investing for the short-term will be greater, and the trader will probably decide to invest for the short-term.

In equilibrium there are *both* short-term and long-term bonds held and short-term and long-term loans made. So in equilibrium the typical bond trader and bank loan officer must think that the expected returns from long-term and short-term financial investments are roughly equal. In equilibrium,

$$r - r_n^s = \frac{E_n(\Delta r^s)}{2}$$

The term premium $r - r^s$ is equal to the expected change in short-term interest rates over the life span of the loan, weighted by the proportion of the loan's time span over which the changed short-term interest rate will apply. In other words, *the term premium tells you how bond traders expect short-term interest rates to move in the future.*

If financiers are buying two-year bonds at, say, 5.75 percent — when they could instead buy three-month T-bills every quarter for two years — then they must believe that either portfolio strategy will average out to about 5.75 percent over two years, or else they would all be crowding into one security or the other. Demand for the one would rise; demand for the other would fall. And the interest rates on them and on loans of that duration would change until once more it looked to bond traders that the two strategies were equally attractive. Similarly, if bond traders are buying three-month T-bills at, say, 4 percent when they could instead buy two-year bonds at 5.75 percent, then they must expect that higher short-term rates a year and a half in the future — say, 7.5 percent — will balance out today's low rates to average out to 5.75 percent.

This is the *expectations theory of the term structure*: The long-term interest rate is the average of what bond traders expect future short-term rates to be for the duration of the long-term loan. The term premium tells us how much bond traders are expecting the average short-term interest rate to rise (or fall) over the duration of the long-term loan.

From the standpoint of governments that seek to control interest rates, this dependence of today's long-term interest rate on expectations of what the short-term interest rate will be tomorrow is very inconvenient. All the changes in today's interest rate that the central bank can undertake today will have only a limited effect on long-term interest rates unless bond traders are convinced that policies once adopted will be continued. Thus central banks guard their reputation for *credibility* and *consistency* above everything else. They can preserve their ability to affect the economy by changing interest rates only if bond traders' expectations of the future, and thus today's long-term interest rates, react predictably to changes in interest rate policy. We deal with this issue in the next chapter.

9

The IS-LM Model: Macroeconomic Equilibrium with Fixed Prices

QUESTIONS

What is the IS curve? What use is it?

What determines the equilibrium level of real GDP when the central bank's policy is to keep the real interest rate constant?

What is the LM curve?

What is the IS-LM framework?

What is an IS shock?

What is an LM shock?

What is an international shock?

This chapter analyzes the macroeconomic equilibrium with sticky prices in the context of the IS-LM model. The IS curve is a combination of real interest rates and real GDPs such that the goods market is in equilibrium, holding all the other determinants of aggregate expenditure fixed.

The IS curve enables us to think about business cycles, as long as the central bank uses open market operations to set the real interest rate. Not all central banks that peg interest rates today pegged them in the past. So the analysis based on the IS curve alone is not complete, because it lacks a theory of what determines the real interest rate when it is not the interest rate but the money stock that is fixed. Moreover, even when central banks do peg interest rates, they usually peg not real but nominal interest rates. To think through the relationship between nominal and real interest rates, we need to understand the determinants of inflation.

Thus this chapter adds more analytical tools to extend the sticky-price model. To this end, after exploring the IS curve, we derive the LM curve to serve as its sibling. The **LM curve** is a combination of real interest rates and real GDPs such that the money market is in equilibrium, holding all other determinants of money demand and the real money supply fixed. It tells us how interest rates are determined when the stock of money is fixed. The LM curve joins the IS curve in the IS-LM framework and diagram, which provides our analysis of the determinants of real GDP and the interest rate when the money stock is fixed.

Then, we examine in more detail the international side. We examine the effects of changes in the economy's equilibrium on international economic variables, and the effects of changes abroad on the domestic economy's equilibrium.

9.1 THE IS CURVE

AUTONOMOUS SPENDING AND THE REAL INTEREST RATE

If we put the two interest rate terms in the equation for autonomous spending (equation (8.13)) together

$$A = [C_0 + I_0 + G + (X_f Y^f + X_\varepsilon \varepsilon_0 + X_\varepsilon \varepsilon_r r^f)] - (I_r + X_\varepsilon \varepsilon_r) \times r \qquad (9.1)$$

we see that a 1-percentage-point increase in interest rates reduces autonomous spending by an amount $(I_r + X_\varepsilon \varepsilon_r)$, as Figure 9.1 shows.

Think back to the **income-expenditure diagram** of Chapter 8. Recall that the equilibrium level of real GDP depended on the level of autonomous spending. Because a change in the real interest rate changes autonomous spending, it will change the equilibrium level of real GDP.

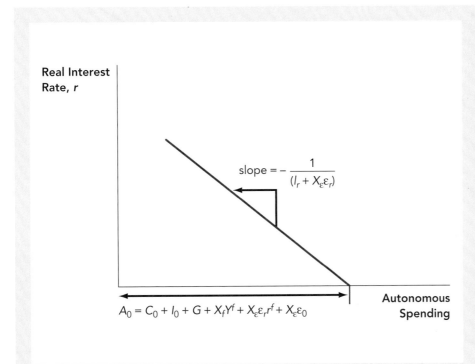

FIGURE 9.1

Autonomous Spending as a Function of the Real Interest Rate

The level of autonomous spending defined in Chapter 8 depends on the real interest rate: The higher the real interest rate, the lower is autonomous spending. The slope of the line depends not just on the interest sensitivity of investment spending but also on the interest rate sensitivity of exports — the sensitivity of exports to changes in the exchange rate times the sensitivity of the exchange rate to changes in the interest rate.

FROM THE INTEREST RATE TO INVESTMENT TO AGGREGATE DEMAND

By how much does a change in the interest rate change equilibrium real GDP? The effect will be equal to the interest sensitivity of autonomous spending ($I_r + X_\varepsilon\varepsilon_r$) times the multiplier of Chapter 8. This relationship between the level of the real interest rate and the equilibrium level of real GDP has a name that was coined by economist John Hicks more than 60 years ago: the "**IS curve**," where *IS* stands for "investment-saving." The IS curve is a workhorse tool that macroeconomists and macroeconomics courses use very, very frequently.

To construct the IS curve, we must first draw a diagram with equilibrium real GDP on the horizontal axis and the real interest rate on the vertical axis, as in Figure 9.2. We begin by picking a value for the real interest rate and then determine the level of autonomous spending at that real interest rate. Then we plug the corresponding level of autonomous spending into an income-expenditure diagram and draw the resulting planned-expenditure line. The point where the planned-expenditure line crosses the 45-degree line is the point at which aggregate demand equals national income. That is the value of equilibrium real GDP corresponding to our initial choice of the real interest rate.

FIGURE 9.2
The IS Curve
For each possible value of the real interest rate, there is a different level of autonomous spending. For each level of autonomous spending, the income-expenditure process generates a different equilibrium level of real GDP. The IS curve tells us what equilibrium level of real GDP corresponds to each possible value of the real interest rate.

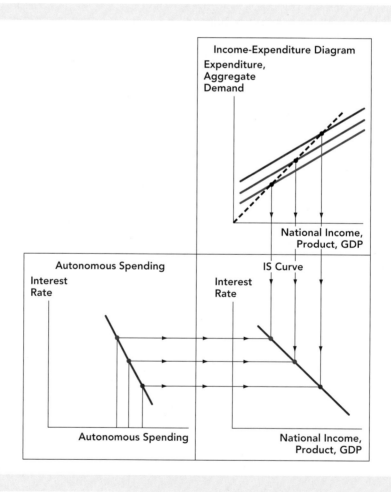

The interest rate we started with and the real GDP level we ended with make up a single point on the IS curve. We repeat the process for as many different possible interest rates as we need. Plotting the points on the IS diagram and connecting them produces the IS curve.

The algebra of the IS curve is straightforward, if a little crowded and complicated. We start from the formula for autonomous spending (9.1) and we divide the determinants of autonomous spending into those that don't depend on the interest rate and those that do, calling the first set of determinants "baseline autonomous spending," or A_0:

$$A_0 = [C_0 + I_0 + G + (X_f Y^f + X_\varepsilon \varepsilon_0 + X_\varepsilon \varepsilon_r r^f)] \tag{9.2}$$

$$A = A_0 - (I_r + X_\varepsilon \varepsilon_r) \times r \tag{9.3}$$

Next recall from the income-expenditure analysis in Chapter 8 that real GDP is equal to autonomous spending A divided by 1 minus the MPE:

$$Y = \frac{A}{1 - MPE} \tag{9.4}$$

Replacing A with its components, we see that real GDP Y is

$$Y = \frac{A_0}{1 - MPE} - \frac{I_r + X_\varepsilon \varepsilon_r}{1 - MPE} \times r \tag{9.5}$$

This equation can be expanded if we want to express the MPE and the baseline level of autonomous spending A_0 in terms of the underlying model parameters and policy variables:

$$Y = \frac{[C_0 + I_0 + G + (X_f Y^f + X_\varepsilon \varepsilon_0 + X_\varepsilon \varepsilon_r r^f)]}{1 - [C_y(1 - t) - IM_y]} - \frac{I_r + X_\varepsilon \varepsilon_r}{1 - [C_y(1 - t) - IM_y]} \times r \tag{9.6}$$

In this IS curve equation, the first set of terms is the value that real GDP would attain if the real interest rate were zero. The second set of terms determines the *slope* of the IS curve: the responsiveness of equilibrium real GDP to changes in the long-term, risky, real interest rate.

THE SLOPE AND POSITION OF THE IS CURVE

THE SLOPE OF THE IS CURVE

Notice that, in keeping with convention, when drawing the IS curve, we put the interest rate on the vertical axis and real GDP on the horizontal axis (see Figure 9.3). Therefore, in (r, Y)-space the steepness of the IS curve is determined by the slope of the IS curve:

$$\text{IS slope} = \frac{\Delta r}{\Delta Y} = -\frac{1 - [C_Y(1 - t) - IM_Y]}{I_r + X_\varepsilon \varepsilon_r} = -\frac{1 - MPE}{I_r + X_\varepsilon \varepsilon_r} \tag{9.7}$$

The slope of the IS curve depends on three factors, all clearly visible in the algebraic expression, equation (9.7). The first term is simply the inverse of the multiplier: $(1 - MPE)$. The smaller is $(1 - MPE)$ (and the larger, therefore, is the multiplier), the larger is the impact on aggregate demand set in motion by a given change in investment spending. The slope of the IS curve also depends on how large a change in

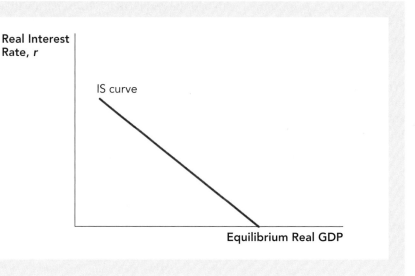

investment is generated by a change in interest rates (the I_r term) and on how large a change in exports is generated by a change in the real interest rate (the product of the interest rate sensitivity of the exchange rate and the exchange rate sensitivity of exports $X_\varepsilon \times \varepsilon_r$). Thus anything that affects the multiplier will change the slope of the IS curve as well. Anything that affects the responsiveness of investment to a change in real interest rates will change the slope of the IS curve. Anything that changes how large a swing in real exchange rates is induced by a change in interest rates will change the slope of the IS curve. And anything that affects how sensitive exports are to the exchange rate will change the slope of the IS curve. Box 9.1 shows how to combine these to calculate the slope of the IS curve.

THE POSITION OF THE IS CURVE

The position of the IS curve depends on the baseline level of autonomous spending A_0 times the multiplier $1/(1 - MPE)$.

$$\frac{A_0}{1 - MPE} = \frac{[C_0 + I_0 + G + (X_f Y^f + X_\varepsilon \varepsilon_0 + X_\varepsilon \varepsilon_r r^f)]}{1 - [C_y(1 - t) - IM_y]} \tag{9.8}$$

Anything that changes any of the non-interest-dependent components of autonomous spending will shift the position of the IS curve. An increase in government spending G will shift the IS curve to the right and raise the equilibrium level of real GDP for any fixed value of the real interest rate, as Figure 9.4 shows. An increase in the baseline level of investment spending I_0 or consumption spending C_0 will do the same. Other events that shift the IS curve to the right include increases in income overseas Y^f, increases in foreign exchange speculators' expectations ε_0, and increases in foreign interest rates r^f.

MOVING THE ECONOMY TO THE IS CURVE

What happens if the current level of real GDP and the interest rate is not on the IS curve? If the economy is above the IS curve on the diagram, then real GDP is

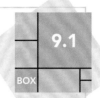

CALCULATING THE DEPENDENCE OF AGGREGATE DEMAND ON THE INTEREST RATE

To calculate how much a change in the interest rate will shift the equilibrium level of aggregate demand, you need to know four things:

- The marginal propensity to spend (MPE), and thus the multiplier ($1/(1 - MPE)$)
- The interest sensitivity of investment (I_r)
- How much a change in the interest rate will affect the exchange rate (ε_r)
- How much a change in the exchange rate will affect exports (X_ε)

Suppose that you know that the marginal propensity to expend is 0.5 and the interest sensitivity of investment is 1000: that is, a 1-percentage-point rise in the annual interest rate — an increase of 0.01 — decreases annual investment by $10 billion. Then the direct effects of interest rates on investment coupled with the multiplier would lead you to conclude that a 1-percentage-point increase in the interest rate would decrease equilibrium aggregate demand by $20 billion, acting through the investment channel alone.

However, there is another channel through which interest rates affect aggregate demand: the export channel. If a 1-percentage-point change in the interest rate reduces the value of the exchange rate by 10 units, and if each 1-unit reduction in the exchange rate reduces exports by $0.5 billion, then there would be an additional decrease of $2 \times 0.5 \times 10 = \$10$ billion in aggregate demand through the exports channel.

Thus, the total decline in equilibrium annual aggregate demand from a 1-percentage-point increase in the interest rate would be $30 billion. That would be the inverse of the slope of the IS curve.

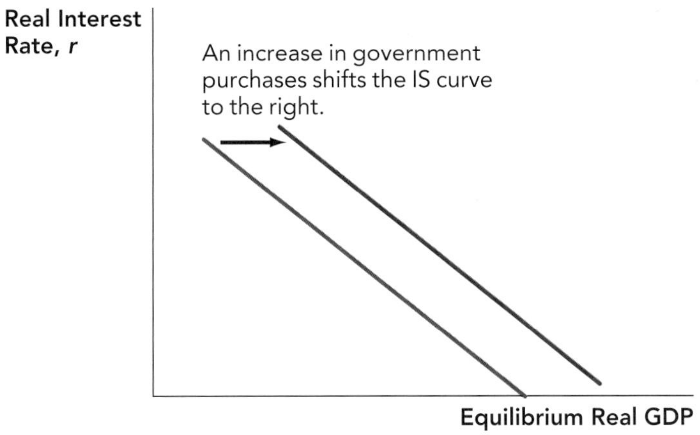

9.1
BOX
EXAMPLE

Real Interest Rate, r

An increase in government purchases shifts the IS curve to the right.

Equilibrium Real GDP

FIGURE 9.4

A Change in Fiscal Policy and the Position of the IS Curve

Practically any shift in policy or in the economic environment will change the position of the IS curve. In this case an increase in government purchases shifts the IS curve to the right.

FIGURE 9.5
Off of the IS Curve
The economy's position does not have to correspond to a point on the IS curve. But if the economy is not on the IS curve, then there are powerful forces that will push it toward the IS curve.

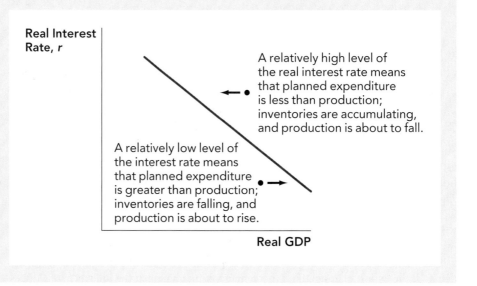

higher than planned expenditure. Inventories are rising rapidly and unexpectedly. So businesses cut back production. Employment, real GDP, and national income fall. If the economy is below the IS curve, aggregate demand is higher than total production. Inventories fall. Firms try to expand production in order to meet unexpectedly high demand. As they do, real GDP, employment, and national income rise, as Figure 9.5 shows.

The process that pulls the economy back to the IS curve works relatively slowly, over months, quarters, or possibly even years. Firms respond to increases in inventories by contracting (and to decreases in inventories by raising) production. As was noted in Chapter 8, the economy can stay away from its equilibrium on the income-expenditure diagram for a substantial time, all the while with inventories building up or falling. And if the economy is away from its equilibrium level of real GDP on the income-expenditure diagram, it is not on the IS curve either.

RECAP   **THE IS CURVE**

The higher the real interest rate, the lower are the investment spending and net exports components of autonomous spending and the lower is real GDP in the sticky-price model. The relationship between the real interest rate and real GDP is called the IS relationship. When plotted on a graph with real GDP on the horizontal axis and the real interest rate on the vertical axis, it is called the IS curve. The IS curve is downward-sloping. Its horizontal intercept is equal to baseline autonomous spending — what autonomous spending A would be if the interest rate were zero — times the multiplier. Its slope depends on the multiplier $(1/(1 - MPE))$ and the sum of two terms: (a) the interest sensitivity of investment spending I_r, and (b) the product of the exchange rate sensitivity of gross exports and the interest sensitivity of the exchange rate $X_\varepsilon \times \varepsilon_r$.

9.2 USING THE IS CURVE TO UNDERSTAND THE ECONOMY

SHIFTING THE IS CURVE

We have seen that anything that affects the non-interest-dependent components of autonomous spending shifts the position of the IS curve. Changes that increase baseline autonomous spending shift the IS curve to the right and raise equilibrium real GDP (if interest rates are constant). Changes that reduce baseline autonomous spending shift the IS curve to the left and reduce equilibrium real GDP (if interest rates are held constant).

For example, two kinds of changes in government policy directly affect the position of the IS curve. A shift in tax rates changes both the position and the slope of the IS curve. And a change in the level of government purchases shifts the IS curve to the right or the left. It thus increases or decreases the equilibrium level of real GDP associated with each possible level of the real interest rate. (See Box 9.2.)

MOVING ALONG THE IS CURVE

Changes in the level of the real interest rate r will move the economy either left and upward or right and downward along the IS curve: A higher real interest rate will produce a lower level of aggregate demand. A lower real interest rate will produce a higher level of aggregate demand and equilibrium real GDP. The Bank of Canada can control — target — interest rates to a considerable degree. Such an **interest rate targeting** central bank can stimulate the economy by cutting interest

A GOVERNMENT SPENDING INCREASE AND THE IS CURVE

It is straightforward to calculate the effect on equilibrium aggregate demand of an increase in a component of baseline autonomous spending such as government purchases. For example, suppose that in the economy the initial MPE is equal to 0.5, the baseline level of autonomous spending is $500 billion, a 1-percentage-point decline in the real interest rate (i.e., a decrease of 0.01 in r) raises investment spending by $11 billion (i.e., $I_r = 1100$, and thus $1100 \times 0.01 = 11$) and exports by $1.5 billion (i.e., $X_\varepsilon \varepsilon_r = 150$ and thus $150 \times 0.01 = 1.5$), and the real interest rate is fixed at 4 percent. Then the initial equilibrium level of annual real GDP is

$$Y = \frac{A_0}{1 - MPE} - \frac{I_r + X_\varepsilon \varepsilon_r}{1 - MPE} \times r = \frac{\$500}{1 - 0.5} - \frac{\$1100 + \$150}{1 - 0.5} \times 0.04$$

$$= \$1,000 - \$2,500 \times 0.04 = \$900 \text{ billion}$$

And suppose that annual government purchases are then raised by $\Delta G = \$20$ billion.

Since government purchases are a component of baseline autonomous spending A_0, the increase in equilibrium aggregate demand is straightforward to calculate as long as the central bank does not change the real interest rate r:

$$\Delta Y = \frac{\Delta A_0}{1 - MPE} - \frac{I_r + X_\varepsilon \varepsilon_r}{1 - MPE} \times \Delta r = \frac{\$20}{1 - 0.5} - \frac{\$1,100 + \$150}{1 - 0.5} \times 0 = \$40 \text{ billion}$$

Real equilibrium aggregate demand rises by $40 billion.

BOX 9.2

EXAMPLE

9.3

BOX

EXAMPLE

MOVING ALONG THE IS CURVE

Suppose that the staff projections of the Bank of Canada predict that if current poli-cies are continued, real GDP will be only $900 billion at a time for which estimates of potential output are $1.5 trillion. The Bank of Canada might well decide that it is time to lower interest rates to close such a "deflationary gap."

Suppose further that the staff estimates that the marginal propensity to spend is 0.5, that a 1-percentage-point fall in the real interest rate (i.e., a fall of 0.01 in r) gen-erates an extra $11 billion in annual investment spending (i.e., $I_r = 1100$, so that $1100 \times 0.01 = 11$), that a 1-percentage-point fall in the real interest rate (i.e., a fall of 0.01 in r) produces a 5 point rise in the real exchange rate (i.e., $\varepsilon_r = 500$, so that $500 \times 0.01 = 5$) and that each 1 point rise in the real exchange rate raises exports by $0.3 billion (i.e., $X_\varepsilon = 0.3$).

Such estimates of the structure of the economy imply that the inverse slope of the IS curve is

$$\text{Inverse IS slope} = -\frac{I_r + X_\varepsilon\varepsilon_r}{1 - MPE} = -\frac{\$1,100 + (500 \times \$0.3)}{1 - 0.5} = -\$2,500$$

So to boost equilibrium real GDP by $50 billion by moving the economy along the IS curve, the real interest rate has to be reduced by 0.02 — by 2 percentage points.

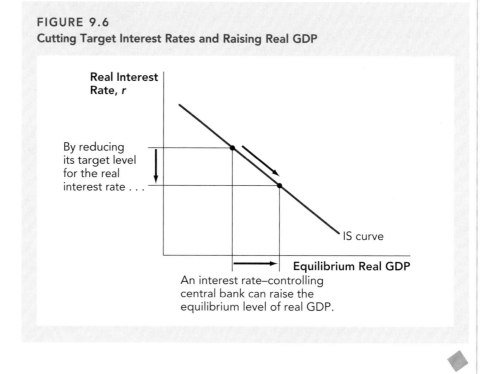

FIGURE 9.6
Cutting Target Interest Rates and Raising Real GDP

rates (see Box 9.3 and Figure 9.6) and can contract the economy by raising interest rates.

How does the Bank of Canada control interest rates? It does so by buying and selling short-term government bonds for cash in *open-market operations*, so-called because they are carried out in the "open market" and the Bank of Canada really does not care who it buys from or sells to. Whenever the Bank of Canada buys government bonds in return for cash, it increases the total amount of cash in the hands of the public and reserves in the hands of the banking system, as Figure 9.7 shows. Banks with the extra reserves use them to try to increase their deposits. Thus such an expansionary open-market operation increases the economy's stock of money: It increases the quantity of assets — chequing account deposits and cash — that are readily spendable purchasing power.

Banks, businesses, and households take a look at the larger quantity of money — wealth in the form of readily spendable purchasing power — that they hold. At the previous level of interest rates this is more money than they want to hold in their

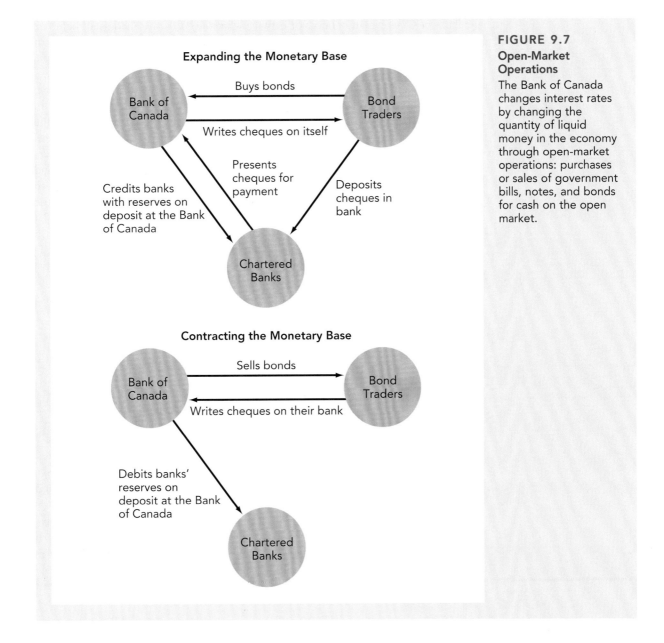

FIGURE 9.7
Open-Market Operations
The Bank of Canada changes interest rates by changing the quantity of liquid money in the economy through open-market operations: purchases or sales of government bills, notes, and bonds for cash on the open market.

portfolios. So households, businesses, and banks try to use this money to buy assets, such as bonds, that pay higher yields than cash. As they do so, they push the price of bonds up and the interest rate down. Thus an expansionary open-market operation reduces interest rates in the economy. The same process works in reverse to push interest rates up when the Bank of Canada sells bonds for cash on the open market. Box 9.3 shows how central bankers would go about trying to calculate the size of the change in interest rates needed to properly manage the economy.

DIFFICULTIES

There are, however, some difficulties in attempting to control aggregate demand by manipulating interest rates. First, our knowledge of the structure of the economy is imperfect. Perhaps at any particular moment the slope of the IS curve is half what the Bank of Canada staff believes or is twice what the Bank of Canada staff believes. Second, even when policies do have their expected effects, these effects do not necessarily arrive on schedule. As economist Milton Friedman often says, economic policy works with long *and* variable lags.

Moreover, the interest rates that the Bank of Canada can control are *short-term, nominal, safe* interest rates. The interest rate that determines where the economy in equilibrium is along the IS curve is the long-term, real, risky interest rate. Even if the government and central bank attain their target interest rate and even if the effects of changes in the interest rate are exactly as predicted and arrive exactly on schedule, there is a lot of potential slippage: Changes in the term premium between short and long interest rates, changes in the rate of inflation, and changes in the risk premium will each carry the economy to a point on the IS curve other than the point that the Bank of Canada wanted.

What determines the value of the *term premium* — the gap between short-term and long-term interest rates? Appendix 8A showed that the major determinant is expectations of future monetary policy. Long-term interest rates will be high relative to short-term interest rates if people expect short-term interest rates to be raised in the future; long-term interest rates will be lower relative to short-term interest rates if people expect short-term rates to be lowered in the future.

RECAP   USING THE IS CURVE TO UNDERSTAND THE ECONOMY

We have seen that anything that affects the non-interest-dependent components of autonomous spending shifts the position of the IS curve. Changes that increase baseline autonomous spending shift the IS curve to the right and raise equilibrium real GDP. Changes that reduce baseline autonomous spending shift the IS curve to the left and reduce real GDP. Changes in the level of the real interest rate r will move the economy either left and upward or right and downward along the IS curve: A higher real interest rate will produce a lower level of aggregate demand. A lower real interest rate will produce a higher level of aggregate demand and equilibrium real GDP. The Bank of Canada can control — target — interest rates to a considerable degree. Such an interest rate–targeting central bank can stimulate the economy by cutting interest rates and can contract the economy by raising interest rates.

9.3 THE MONEY MARKET WITH FIXED PRICES

In our earlier discussion of the goods market equilibrium with fixed prices, output adjusts in order to equilibrate aggregate savings and investment, or equivalently to achieve equilibrium in the loanable funds market at a given real interest rate. The next step in our study is to understand how the interest rate is determined in the fixed price model. To this end, we will consider, first, the money market equilibrium and then analyze the simultaneous equilibrium in the goods and money markets, which gives us the general equilibrium levels of output and interest rates.

WEALTH, BONDS, AND THE DEMAND FOR MONEY

Recall our discussion of money demand in Chapter 7. Think about a household or a business trying to figure out in what form to hold its wealth. The household can hold its wealth in the form of bonds, and other interest-bearing assets, or in the form of "money," which we call M — where money is shorthand for assets that are liquid, can be readily spent, or can be easily used to buy goods and services. Households and businesses can and do move their wealth back and forth between these two forms of assets.

Wealth held in the form of money earns little or no interest, whereas wealth held in the form of bonds earns interest at the nominal interest rate i. However, bonds cannot be readily spent: To transform them into a form that can be used to buy things takes time, and so if a large proportion of wealth is held in bonds, one may miss opportunities to buy goods and services. On the other hand, wealth held in the form of money is liquid, and it can be easily spent; that is the defining characteristic of money.

There are two important facts about the quantity of money that businesses and households wish to hold. First, real money demand is increasing in total income or real GDP. Second, real money demand is inversely related to the nominal interest rate: When nominal interest rates go up, demand for real money goes down.

The quantity of money demanded increases with total income or real GDP, Y, for the following reason. How much wealth you wish to hold in liquid form depends on how large are the purchases you typically make. And the higher the flow of total income, the greater the flow of purchases an average household or business wants to make.

Why does money demand decrease when the nominal interest rate increases? Think of it this way: You want to hold money because not having liquid assets to buy commodities is very inconvenient. But holding wealth in the form of money means that you are giving up the interest income you could have earned if you held bonds instead. Hence, the quantity of money demanded falls when the nominal interest rate rises. Notice that money demand depends *not* on the real interest rate r but on the nominal interest rate i. The part of your wealth that you hold as money — in the form of deposits in your checking account or cash in your pocket — earns zero nominal interest. By contrast, if you were to shift the wealth you hold as money into less liquid but more lucrative assets like bonds, it would earn the prevailing market nominal interest rate i. The difference between the expected return on holding wealth in the liquid form of money and on holding wealth in bonds is thus the nominal interest rate. The nominal interest rate i is thus the opportunity cost of holding money.

Economists try to fit these insights into their model by writing down a demand for real money, or liquidity preference function:

$$L = L_0 - L_i \times (r + \pi^e) + L_Y \times Y \tag{9.9}$$

In this equation, L_0 is the autonomous part of demand for real money balances; that is, the part of real money balances that does not depend on the nominal interest rate or real GDP. The value of L_0 depends on the preferences of households and firms and on the state of the technology in the financial sector.

The parameter L_Y tells how much extra real money balances people demand when real GDP, Y, increases by one unit. The parameter L_i tells how much households and businesses reduce their money holdings when the nominal interest rate i goes up by one percent. Note that, with Y fixed, an increase in the nominal interest rate reduces the quantity of money demanded by way of moving along the money demand curve. On the other hand, a change in Y shifts the entire curve, to the left if Y falls and to the right if Y increases.

MONEY SUPPLY AND MONEY DEMAND

Recall that in the flexible-price model analyzed in Chapter 7, the price level P would adjust instantly, in the face of an economic disturbance, in order to maintain **money market equilibrium**, where real money supply is equal to real money demand at the prevailing nominal interest rate. In the present chapter, however, the price level is fixed and cannot move instantly to keep the money market in equilibrium. In that case, what variable must adjust to make money supply equal to money demand? The answer is that the nominal interest rate must adjust instead to re-establish monetary equilibrium.

ADJUSTMENT TO EQUILIBRIUM

To understand the process by which the nominal interest rate adjusts in order to equate real money supply to real money demand in this model with fixed prices, first notice that government bonds are the closest substitute for money. Moreover, a government bond promises to pay a fixed number of dollars, called the *coupon*, each time period until maturity. Hence, if the market value of a government bond increases then the value of the coupon as a percentage of the value of the bond falls. The nominal interest rate is defined as coupon value as a percentage of the value of the bond, since coupons are fixed in nominal terms. Consequently, there is a fundamental inverse relationship between the market price of a bond and the nominal interest rate: When the price of the bond increases, the nominal interest rate falls — and vice versa. When the money market is out of equilibrium, the activities of households and firms result in changes in the market values of bonds and, hence, in the nominal interest rate.

Next, suppose the nominal interest rate is at level i_1 say, in Figure 9.8, such that the quantity of real money demanded is smaller than the quantity of real money supplied, relative to the equilibrium point A. That is, households and firms have more real money holdings than they desire at that interest rate. In that case, they will try to convert part of their excess real money holdings into government bonds. This raises the demand for bonds, and as a result the price of bonds rises and the nominal interest rate falls. As the nominal interest rate falls, the quantity of real money demanded rises because the opportunity cost of holding money is decreasing. When the nominal interest rate has fallen enough (to i_0) so that the quantity of real money demanded is equal to the real money supply, there is no more downward pressure on the nominal interest rate.

Finally, suppose the nominal interest rate is at the level i_2 in Figure 9.8, such that the quantity of real money demanded is larger than the quantity of real money supplied. Businesses and households will then sell bonds to boost their cash holdings.

FIGURE 9.8

The Money Market with Fixed Prices

If the nominal interest rate is at i_1 the real money demand is smaller than the real money supply. In that case, households and firms will try to convert part of their excess real money holdings into government bonds. This raises bond prices, and reduces interest rates. Similarly, if the nominal interest rate is at i_2 the real money demand is larger than the real money supply, and interest rates increase. The money market is in equilibrium when interest rates are at i_0.

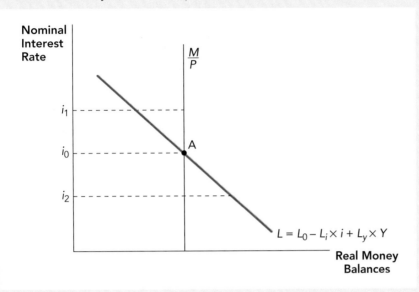

The price of bonds falls and the nominal interest rate rises. As the nominal interest rate rises, the quantity of real money demanded falls as well, because the opportunity cost of holding money has risen. When the nominal interest rate has risen far enough (to i_0), households and businesses are no longer trying to increase their liquid money balances, and there is no more upward pressure on the nominal interest rate. At that point the money market is again in equilibrium.

EFFECTS OF SHOCKS IN THE MONEY MARKET

Now we discuss the effects of some shocks in the money market, given fixed prices. We will discuss sequentially the effects of an increase in the nominal money supply and a fall in real money demand due to an increase in the use of credit cards or automated banking machines, as we did in Chapter 7. As mentioned earlier, with the price level assumed fixed, the burden of the adjustment falls on the nominal interest rate.

EFFECTS OF AN INCREASE IN THE MONEY SUPPLY

Suppose the central bank increases the nominal money supply through an open market operation; that is, it buys bonds from households and firms in the bond market in exchange for money. This action by the central bank will increase the total demand for bonds (by households, firms, and the central bank) in the bonds market, thereby raising bond prices and lowering the nominal interest rate.

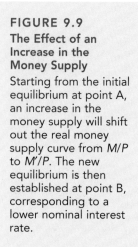

FIGURE 9.9

The Effect of an Increase in the Money Supply

Starting from the initial equilibrium at point A, an increase in the money supply will shift out the real money supply curve from M/P to M′/P. The new equilibrium is then established at point B, corresponding to a lower nominal interest rate.

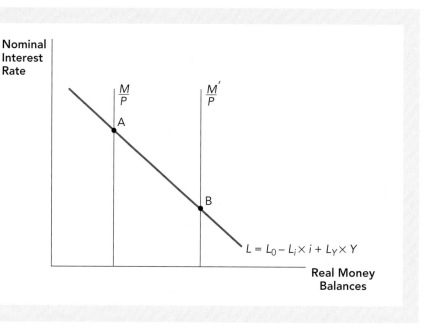

The effects of an increase in the money supply can also be discussed in terms of the money market equilibrium in Figure 9.9. Start from the initial equilibrium point at A. An increase in the money supply will shift out the real money supply curve from M/P to M'/P. The new equilibrium is then established at point B, with a lower nominal interest rate. In other words, for the households and firms to be induced to hold the additional money supplied by the central bank, the opportunity cost of holding money must fall.

EFFECTS OF A FALL IN REAL MONEY DEMAND

As was discussed at length in Chapter 7, the demand for real money balances can fall due to certain financial innovations. For example, if credit cards are more widely used then people will be holding less money in order to finance their transactions. The introduction of automated banking machines (ATMs), telephone banking, and Internet banking are other examples of financial innovations that reduce the demand for real balances. With such innovations, it is easier and cheaper to transfer funds between accounts, or to buy and sell stocks and bonds. As a result, people hold a relatively small amount of their wealth in terms of money, knowing that they can easily convert other assets into money on short notice relatively cheaply.

Consider the money market equilibrium in Figure 9.10, with the initial equilibrium at point A. A fall in the demand for real money balances that is brought about by financial innovations means that, at any interest rate and real GDP, less real money balances will be demanded. This shifts the liquidity preference curve to the left, and results in a new equilibrium at point B, with a lower nominal interest rate.

When the demand for real money balances falls as a result of a financial innovation, households and firms will have excess holdings of real balances, at the initial interest rate. In order to reduce their excess money balances, they will buy bonds, thereby increasing their demand. As a result, bond prices will increase, and the nominal interest rate will fall.

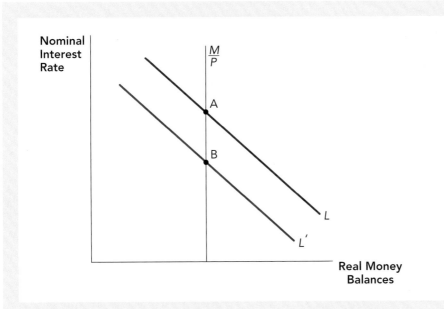

FIGURE 9.10

The Effects of a Fall in Real Money Demand

Starting from the initial equilibrium at point A, a financial innovation that reduces the demand for real money balances will shift the liquidity preference curve to the left. The new equilibrium at point B is associated with a lower nominal interest rate.

RECAP   THE MONEY MARKET WITH FIXED PRICES

In the fixed price model, the nominal interest rate adjusts instead to establish monetary equilibrium. An increase in the money supply will shift out the real money supply curve and lower nominal interest rates. A fall in the demand for real money balances that is brought about by financial innovations shifts the liquidity preference curve to the left, and results in a new equilibrium with a lower nominal interest rate.

9.4 THE LM CURVE

INTEREST RATES AND REAL GDP

With fixed prices, real GDP can be affected by many factors, including changes in government expenditures and the money supply. But as real GDP changes, the demand for real money also changes, and so does the money market equilibrium and hence the equilibrium nominal interest rate. It is then possible to trace out the relationship between the nominal interest rate and real GDP such that the money market is in equilibrium. This relationship is called the LM curve; (LM is shorthand for "liquidity preference–money supply").

To derive the LM curve consider first the left hand diagram in Figure 9.11, where the money market is in equilibrium at point A, with nominal interest rate at i_0, corresponding to an initial real GDP level Y_0, which determines the position of the real money demand curve. When real GDP rises to Y_1, the demand for real money increases and shifts the liquidity preference curve out and to the right. With higher incomes, households and firms wish to hold more real money balances. But if the

FIGURE 9.11

Deriving the LM Curve

In the left hand diagram, the money market is in equilibrium at point A, with nominal interest rate at i_0, corresponding to an initial real GDP level Y_0. When real GDP rises to Y_1, the demand for money curve shifts to the right, establishing a new equilibrium at point B. The LM curve in the right hand diagram is simply the combinations of interest rates and real GDPs like (i_0, Y_0) and (i_1, Y_1) such that the money market is in equilibrium.

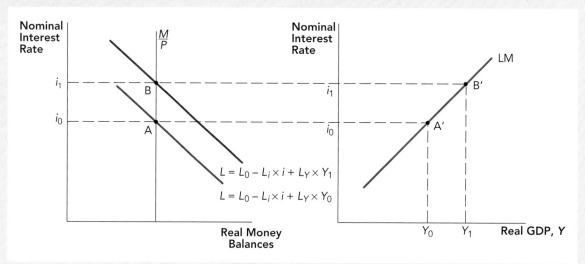

money supply does not increase, then, in aggregate, their real money holdings cannot grow. Households and businesses will then sell bonds as they try to increase their real money holdings — efforts that are futile in the aggregate but successful for individual households and firms — and these bond sales push down the price of bonds, which is the same thing as pushing up the nominal interest rate. As the interest rate rises, the opportunity cost of holding money increases, so real money demand falls. The nominal interest rate will rise until the resulting drop in real money demand has fully offset the increase in real money demand that resulted from the higher income and spending. The new money market equilibrium is established at point B, with nominal interest rate at i_1, corresponding to the new real GDP level Y_1.

Next, consider the right hand diagram in Figure 9.11, which measures the nominal interest rate i on the vertical axis and total income Y on the horizontal axis. The LM curve is simply combinations of interest rates and real GDPs such that the money market is in equilibrium. Thus, in Figure 9.11, the two combinations (i_0, Y_0) and (i_1, Y_1) at points A' and B' in the right hand diagram correspond to points A and B in the left hand diagram. The LM curve slopes upward: At a higher level of Y, the equilibrium nominal interest rate is higher.

The equation for the LM curve can be derived easily using the money market equilibrium condition: real money demand equals real money supply. Hence, at the equilibrium point of the money market, we have

$$L_0 - L_i \times (r + \pi^e) + L_Y \times Y = \frac{M}{P} \tag{9.10}$$

Treating the real money supply M/P as fixed, this equation gives, for each level of the nominal interest rate $(r + \pi^e)$ the level of Y such that the money market is in equilibrium. In particular, the equilibrium level of Y is given by

$$Y = \frac{M/P - L_0}{L_Y} + \frac{L_i}{L_Y} \times (r + \pi^e) \qquad (9.11)$$

This last equation is the equation of the LM curve.

SLOPE OF THE LM CURVE

As was the case with the IS curve, when drawing the LM curve the convention is to measure the nominal interest rate $i \equiv r + \pi^e$ on the vertical axis and real GDP Y on the horizontal axis, as in Figure 9.12. With this convention, the slope of the LM curve tells us the amount by which i must increase for each unit increase in Y in order to maintain equilibrium in the money market. Now, from equation (9.12) it is clear that the slope of the LM curve is

$$\text{LM slope} = \frac{\Delta i}{\Delta Y} = \frac{L_Y}{L_i} \qquad (9.12)$$

Clearly, the slope of the LM curve depends on two things: the sensitivity of liquidity preference to changes in real GDP and the sensitivity of liquidity preference to changes in the nominal interest rate.

Consider, first, the importance of the sensitivity of liquidity preference to changes in real GDP, which is measured by the parameter L_Y. If liquidity preference is relatively sensitive to changes in real GDP, then one unit increase in real GDP will lead to a large increase in real money demand. As a result, there will be a large outward shift in the liquidity preference curve, in the left hand diagram in Figure 9.11. With a large increase in real money demand there must be a large increase in interest rates in order to bring the money market back to equilibrium and to reduce the amount of real balances demanded back to the fixed real money supply. This, in turn, means that the LM curve will be relatively steep when L_Y is large.

Next, consider the importance of the sensitivity of liquidity preference to changes in the nominal interest rate, which is measured by the parameter L_i. Suppose that liquidity preference is more sensitive to changes in interest rates, so that L_i is larger. Then when output rises and the demand for real money balances increases, the nominal interest rate will have to increase by a relatively small amount in order to bring the money market back to equilibrium. Hence, if L_i is relatively large, then we will need a smaller increase in the nominal interest rate in order to bring the money market in equilibrium after one unit increase in Y. In this case the LM curve will be flatter.

SHIFTS OF THE LM CURVE

The LM curve gives us, for each level of output, the level of the nominal interest rate in order to attain equilibrium in the money market. As we have seen above, financial innovations and changes in the money supply affect the equilibrium in the goods market for any given level of output, and will shift the LM curve.

Consider first the effect of an increase in the money supply on the LM curve. Referring to Figure 9.9, notice that the liquidity preference curve is drawn for a given level of output Y. Hence, when the money supply increases, and the equilibrium shifts from point A to point B, a lower interest rate is required for the money market to clear. Hence, in Figure 9.12, after an increase in the money supply, the LM curve

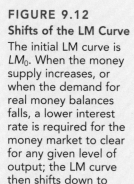

FIGURE 9.12

Shifts of the LM Curve

The initial LM curve is LM_0. When the money supply increases, or when the demand for real money balances falls, a lower interest rate is required for the money market to clear for any given level of output; the LM curve then shifts down to LM_1.

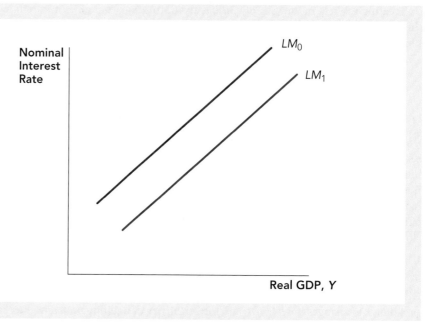

shifts down and to the right; for every level of output, a lower nominal interest rate will be required to clear the money market.

Next, consider the effect of a fall in the real money demand. Referring to Figure 9.10, the liquidity preference curve is drawn for a given level of output Y. A financial innovation reduces L_0 and shifts the liquidity preference curve down for the same level of output. Hence, when the real money demand falls due to a financial innovation, and the equilibrium shifts from point A to point B, a lower interest rate is required for the money market to clear. Hence, in Figure 9.12, after a fall in real money demand the LM curve shifts down and to the right; again, for every level of output, a lower nominal interest rate will be required to clear the money market.

RECAP   THE LM CURVE

The LM curve gives for each level of income the nominal interest rate that is consistent with equilibrium in the money market with fixed prices. As income increases the liquidity preference curve shifts to the right, giving rise to a new higher nominal interest rate. Hence, the LM curve is upward sloping. An increase in the money supply or a fall in real money demand due to financial innovations shifts the LM curve to the right.

9.5 THE IS-LM FRAMEWORK

In the rest of this chapter, we will combine the IS and LM curves in order to determine the general equilibrium interest rate and real GDP with fixed prices, in different situations. Notice, however, that, since investment demand depends on the real rate, in drawing the IS curve we measured the *real* interest rate on the vertical axis, while in drawing the LM curve we measured the *nominal* interest rate on the vertical axis.

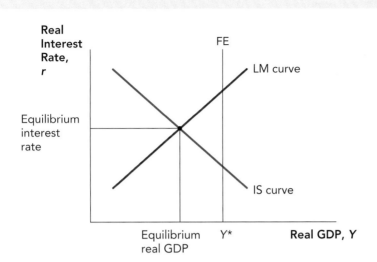

FIGURE 9.13

The IS-LM Diagram

What is the economy's equilibrium? It is the point at which the IS and LM curves cross. Along the IS curve, total production is equal to aggregate demand. Along the LM curve, the quantity of money demanded by house-holds and businesses is equal to the money stock. Where the curves cross, both the goods market and the money market are in balance.

In order to be able to draw both the IS and LM curves on the same diagram, we will assume that the **expected inflation** rate π^e is constant and will treat it as a fixed parameter in the LM equation. With this assumption, we can draw the LM curve as an increasing function of the *real* interest rate, as in Figure 9.13. Notice that even under the present assumption of fixed prices, expected inflation π^e may be fixed but different from zero, since it reflects expectations of price changes between the short run and the long run; the assumption of fixed prices is tenable only in the short run but not in the long run. In this sense, it helps to keep in mind that the IS-LM model is useful for short-run analysis rather than for long-run analysis.

In Figure 9.13, the equilibrium level of real GDP and of the interest rate is at the point where the IS curve and the LM curve cross. At that level of real GDP and total income Y and the real interest rate r, the economy is in equilibrium in both the goods market and the money market. Aggregate demand is equal to total production, so inventories are stable (that's what the IS curve indicates); and money demand is equal to money supply (that's what the LM curve indicates). Box 9.4 shows how to calculate the economy's equilibrium position for some specific parameter values of the sticky-price model.

It is important to keep in mind that the equilibrium level of real GDP in the IS-LM model is different, in general, from full employment or potential GDP, Y^*. As shown in Figure 9.13, the equilibrium real GDP is more likely to be below Y^*. The reason for this is that the IS-LM model assumes fixed prices, whereas Y^* is attained with fully flexible prices, which guarantees full employment (FE).

IS SHOCKS

Any change in economic policy or the economic environment that increases autonomous spending, such as an increase in government purchases, shifts the IS curve to the right. If the money stock is constant, it moves the economy up and to the right along the LM curve on the IS-LM diagram, as Figure 9.15 shows. The new equilibrium will have both a higher level of real interest rates and a higher equilibrium level of real GDP.

EXAMPLE

IS-LM EQUILIBRIUM

Suppose that the economy's marginal propensity to expend (MPE) is 0.5, that the initial level of baseline autonomous spending A_0 is $500 billion, and that a 1-percentage-point increase in the real interest rate (i.e., an increase of 0.01 in r) will reduce the sum of investment and net exports by $10 billion (i.e., $I_r + X_\varepsilon \varepsilon_r = 1,000$, so that $1,000 \times 0.01 = 10$). Suppose further that the expected inflation rate π^e is constant at 3 percent per year, and that the initial LM curve is

$$Y = \$100 + \$10,000 \times (r + \pi^e)$$

Then the economy's initial IS curve will be

$$Y = \frac{A_0}{1 - MPE} - \frac{I_r + X_\varepsilon \varepsilon_r}{1 - MPE} \times r = \frac{\$500}{1 - 0.5} - \frac{\$1,000}{1 - 0.5} \times r = \$1,000 - \$2,000 \times r$$

The initial equilibrium of the economy is at the one point that is on both the IS and the LM curves. Where is that point? Find it by substituting the LM-curve expression for Y into the IS curve:

$$Y = \$1,000 - \$2,000 \times r = \$100 + \$10,000 \times (r + 0.03)$$
$$\$600 = (\$2,000 + \$10,000) \times r$$
$$r = 0.05 = 5\%$$

If r equals 5 percent per year, then the equilibrium point for real GDP Y is $900 billion, as Figure 9.14 shows.

FIGURE 9.14
IS-LM Equilibrium Example

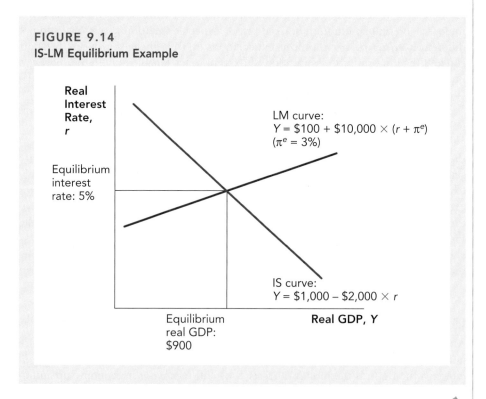

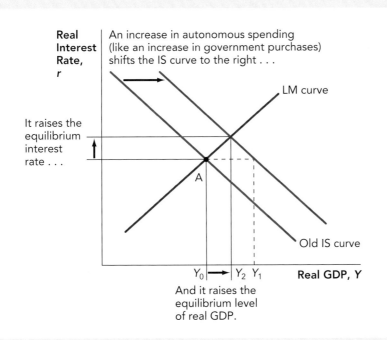

FIGURE 9.15
Effect of a Positive IS Shock
An expansionary shift in the IS curve raises both real GDP Y and the real interest rate r.

Exactly how the total effect of an expansionary shift in the IS curve is divided between increased interest rates and increased real GDP depends on the slope of the LM curve. Box 9.5 provides an example of how to calculate exactly what the effects are. If the LM curve is nearly horizontal (or if the central bank is targeting the interest rate — in which case there is no LM curve as such) there will be little or no increase in interest rates. The increase in equilibrium real GDP will be the same magnitude as the outward shift in the IS curve. If the LM curve is very steeply

AN IS SHOCK
Suppose that, as in Box 9.4, the economy's IS curve is

$$Y = \frac{A_0}{1 - MPE} - \frac{I_r + X_\varepsilon\varepsilon_r}{1 - MPE} \times r = \frac{\$500}{1 - 0.5} - \frac{\$1,000}{1 - 0.5} \times r = \$1,000 - \$2,000 \times r$$

and its LM curve is

$$Y = \$100 + \$10,000 \times (r + \pi^e)$$

with the expected inflation rate π^e constant at 3 percent per year. Thus the initial equilibrium is as in Box 9.4, with real GDP Y at $900 billion and the real interest rate r at 5 percent.

Now suppose that there is a positive real shock to the economy: There is no immediate increase in potenial GDP, yet new technological breakthroughs lead businesses to become more optimistic and generate an increase in baseline investment I_0 (and thus in baseline autonomous spending A_0) of $15 billion. What happens to the economy's equilibrium level of output and interest rates?

The new IS curve is

$$Y = \frac{A_0 + \Delta I_0}{1 - MPE} - \frac{I_r + X_\varepsilon \varepsilon_r}{1 - MPE} \times r = \frac{\$500 + \$15}{1 - 0.5} - \frac{\$1,000}{1 - 0.5} \times r = \$1,030 - \$2,000 \times r$$

Thus the IS curve shifts out and to the right by $30 billion — the magnitude of the shift in baseline autonomous spending times the multiplier.

The LM curve remains unchanged at

$$Y = \$100 + \$10,000 \times (r + \pi^e)$$

So, with expected inflation constant at 3 percent per year, the new equilibrium can be found by setting the values of Y produced by the IS and LM curves to be equal to each other:

$$Y = \$1,030 - \$2,000 \times r = \$100 + \$10,000 \times (r + 0.03)$$
$$\$630 = (\$2,000 + \$10,000) \times r$$
$$r = 5.25\%$$

With the real interest rate r equal to 5.25 percent per year, the annual equilibrium for real GDP Y equals $925 billion. A $30 billion outward shift in the IS curve has led to an increase of 0.25 percent in the real interest rate and a $25 billion increase in real GDP. The higher interest rate has "crowded out" one-sixth of the shift in autonomous spending, as Figure 9.16 shows.

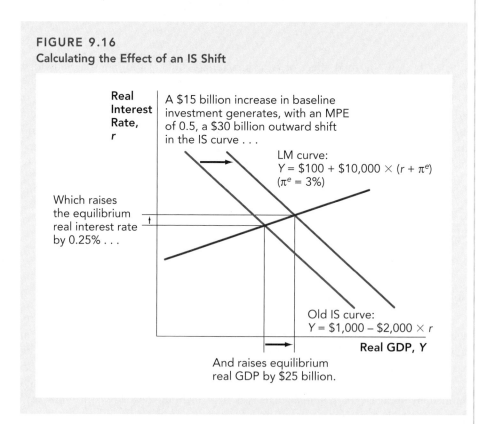

FIGURE 9.16
Calculating the Effect of an IS Shift

Real Interest Rate, r

A $15 billion increase in baseline investment generates, with an MPE of 0.5, a $30 billion outward shift in the IS curve . . .

LM curve:
$Y = \$100 + \$10,000 \times (r + \pi^e)$
($\pi^e = 3\%$)

Which raises the equilibrium real interest rate by 0.25% . . .

Old IS curve:
$Y = \$1,000 - \$2,000 \times r$

Real GDP, Y

And raises equilibrium real GDP by $25 billion.

sloped, there will be a big effect on interest rates and little effect on real GDP. The LM curve will be steeply sloped if demand for money is extremely interest *inelastic*, and it takes a large change in interest rates to cause a small change in households' and businesses' desired holdings of money.

LM SHOCKS

An increase in the nominal money stock (or a decrease in the price level, *P*) will shift the LM curve to the right. The larger money supply means that any given level of real GDP will be associated with a lower equilibrium nominal interest rate. Such an outward LM shift will shift the equilibrium position of the economy down and to the right along the IS curve, as Figure 9.17 shows. The new equilibrium position will have a higher level of equilibrium real GDP and a lower interest rate. Box 9.6 provides an illustrative example of such an expansionary LM shift. Conversely, a decrease in the nominal money supply or any other contractionary LM shock that shifts the LM curve in and to the left will shift the economy up and to the left along the IS curve, resulting in higher equilibrium interest rates and a lower equilibrium value of real GDP.

Note the difference between how the money market works in this sticky-price model and in the flexible-price model presented in Part III. In the flexible-price model, the real interest rate balanced the supply and demand for loanable funds flowing through the financial markets. Changes in the money stock had no effect on either the real interest rate or real GDP. Instead, the price level adjusted upward or downward to keep the quantity of money demanded equal to the money supply.

Here in the sticky-price model the price level is sticky; it cannot adjust instantly upward or downward. So an imbalance in money demand and money supply does not cause an immediate change in the price level. Instead, it causes an immediate change in the nominal interest rate.

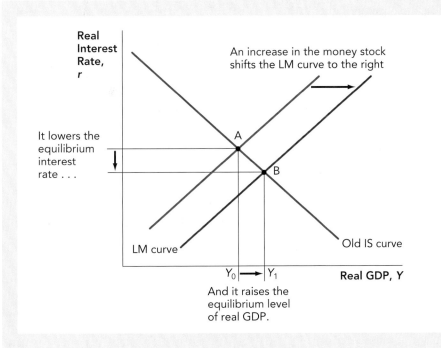

FIGURE 9.17
Effect of an Expansionary LM Shock

An expansionary shift in the LM curve raises real GDP *Y* and lowers the equilibrium interest rate *r*.

CALCULATING THE EFFECT OF AN LM SHOCK

Suppose that, as in Boxes 9.4 and 9.5, the economy's marginal propensity to expend (MPE) is 0.5, the initial level of baseline autonomous spending A_0 is $500 billion, and a 1-percentage-point increase in the real interest rate (i.e., an increase of 0.01 in r) reduces the sum of investment and net exports by $10 billion (i.e., $I_r + X_\varepsilon \varepsilon_r = 1,000$). Then the economy's initial IS curve is the same:

$$Y = \frac{A_0}{1 - MPE} - \frac{I_r + X_\varepsilon \varepsilon_r}{1 - MPE} \times r = \frac{\$500}{1 - 0.5} - \frac{\$1,000}{1 - 0.5} \times r = \$1,000 - \$2,000 \times r$$

Suppose further that the economy's initial LM curve is represented by the equation

$$Y = \$100 + \$10,000 \times (r + \pi^e)$$

and that the expected inflation rate π^e is constant at 3 percent per year. Thus the initial equilibrium of the economy is with real GDP Y at $900 billion and the real interest rate r at 5 percent.

Now suppose the central bank conducts an expansionary open market operation. It buys bonds for cash and increases the supply of money in the economy, shifting the LM curve to

$$Y = \$220 + \$10,000 \times (r + \pi^e)$$

So, with expected inflation constant at 3 percent per year, the new equilibrium can be found by setting the values of Y produced by the IS and LM curves to be equal to each other:

$$Y = \$1,000 - \$2,000 \times r = \$220 + \$10,000 \times (r + 0.03)$$
$$\$480 = (\$2,000 + \$10,000) \times r$$
$$r = 0.04 = 4\%$$

With the real interest rate r equal to 4 percent per year, annual equilibrium real GDP Y equals $920 billion — a $20 billion increase in the equilibrium level of annual real GDP, as shown in Figure 9.18.

FIGURE 9.18
An Expansionary Shift in the LM Curve

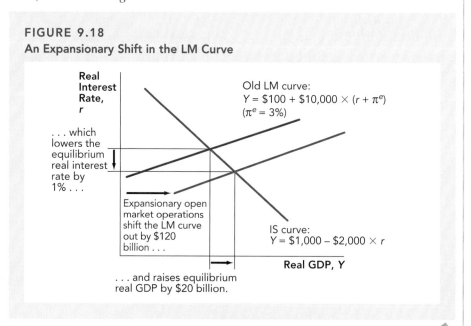

THE MULTIPLIERS AGAIN

Recall in Chapter 8 we derived the **government expenditure multiplier**, which gave us the increase in equilibrium output corresponding to one unit increase in government expenditures with fixed prices *and fixed real interest rates*. In the present chapter we can derive similar multipliers in a more complete model where the real interest rate is not fixed but is determined as part of the equilibrating process. They are, thus, general equilibrium multipliers, as opposed to the partial equilibrium multipliers of the previous chapter.

To this end, recall the equations of the IS and LM curves:

IS: $$Y = \frac{C_0 + I_0 + G + X_f \times Y^f + X_\varepsilon \times \varepsilon_0 + X_\varepsilon \times \varepsilon_r \times r^f}{1 - MPE} - \frac{I_r + X_\varepsilon \times \varepsilon_r}{1 - MPE} \times r$$

LM: $$Y = \frac{M/P - L_0}{L_Y} + \frac{L_i}{L_Y} \times (r + \pi^e)$$

Solving the LM equation for the real interest rate, r, and substituting the resultant expression into the IS equation, we obtain the equilibrium level of output, as given by the point of intersection of the IS and LM curves:

$$Y = Y_A + Y_G \times G + Y_M \times \frac{M}{P} \tag{9.13}$$

where

$$Y_A = \frac{C_0 + I_0 + X_f \times Y^f + X_\varepsilon \times \varepsilon_0 + X_\varepsilon \times \varepsilon_r \times r^f + (I_r + X_\varepsilon \times \varepsilon_r) \times \left(-\dfrac{L_0}{L_i} + \pi^e\right)}{(1 - MPE) + (I_r + X_\varepsilon \times \varepsilon_r) \times \dfrac{L_Y}{L_i}}$$

$$Y_G \equiv \Delta Y/\Delta G = \frac{1}{(1 - MPE) + (I_r + X_\varepsilon \times \varepsilon_r) \times \dfrac{L_Y}{L_i}} \tag{9.14}$$

and

$$Y_M \equiv \Delta Y/\Delta M = \frac{1/L_i}{(1 - MPE) + (I_r + X_\varepsilon \times \varepsilon_r) \times \dfrac{L_Y}{L_i}} \tag{9.15}$$

Although the expressions for Y_A, Y_G, and Y_M are rather complicated, they do convey important information. First, the coefficients Y_G and Y_M are the government expenditure and the **money supply multipliers** when interest rates are determined as part of the equilibrium process. Hence, Y_G tells us by how much output will increase if government expenditures increase by one unit, while Y_M tells us by how much output will increase if the money supply increases by one unit, allowing for adjustment in the equilibrium real interest rate.

Consider the government expenditures multiplier Y_G. Notice this multiplier is smaller than the multiplier we derived in Chapter 8 with fixed interest rates; that is, $Y_G < \dfrac{1}{1 - MPE}$. The reason for this is that in the IS-LM model, when government expenditures increase interest rates increase, which reduces investment and net exports. The fall in investment and net exports mitigates the effects on output, reducing the value of the government expenditures multiplier relative to what it would have been if interest rates were fixed. In terms of Figure 9.15, start from the initial equilibrium at point A, and suppose government expenditures increase by

ΔG units. Then if interest rates were fixed, output would increase by $\dfrac{\Delta G}{1 - MPE}$ units, which is given by the horizontal shift of the IS curve. But because interest rates are not fixed, output does not increase from Y_0 to Y_1, but from Y_0 to Y_2, giving us an increase in output equal to $Y_G \times \Delta G = Y_2 - Y_0$.

Next, consider the money supply multiplier. In Figure 9.17 start from the initial equilibrium point at A. If the money supply increases by ΔM units, then the equilibrium will shift to point B, and output will increase from Y_0 to Y_1; that is, $Y_M \times \Delta M = Y_1 - Y_0$. As seen from equations (9.14) and (9.15) above, the sizes of Y_G and Y_M depend on the slopes of the IS and LM curves, the discussion of which is given as an Analytical Exercise at the end of this chapter.

Finally, any shock that increases the value of Y_A will also increase the equilibrium output in the IS-LM model. Examples of such shocks are increases in autonomous consumption C_0, increases in autonomous investment, increases in foreign income, and so on.

INTEREST RATE TARGETS

The intersection of the IS and LM curves determines short-run equilibrium values of real GDP when the money stock is fixed. It provides a flexible and useful framework for analyzing the expenditure-driven determination of output, money market equilibrium, and interest rates. Even the case in which the central bank is targeting the interest rate can be viewed in the IS-LM framework, as in Figure 9.19. An interest rate target can be seen as simply a flat, horizontal LM curve at the target level of the interest rate.

CLASSIFYING ECONOMIC DISTURBANCES

The IS-LM framework allows economists to classify shifts in the economic environment and changes in economic policy into four basic categories, two that affect the LM curve and two that affect the IS curve. A surprisingly large number of **economic disturbances** affect aggregate demand and can be fitted into the IS-LM framework.

FIGURE 9.19
IS-LM Framework with an Interest Rate Target
When the central bank targets and fixes the interest rate, we can think of the LM curve as a horizontal line.

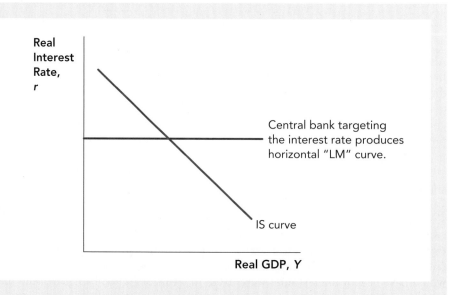

CHANGES THAT AFFECT THE LM CURVE

First, any change in the nominal money stock, in the price level, or in the trend velocity of money will shift the LM curve's location. Second, any change in the interest sensitivity of money demand — in how easy households and businesses find it to economize on their holdings of real money balances — will change the slope of the LM curve. Moreover, the fact that the IS-LM diagram is drawn with the *real* interest rate — the *long-term, risky, real* interest rate — on the vertical axis has important consequences. The LM curve is a relationship between the short-run nominal interest rate and the level of real GDP at a given, fixed level of the real money supply. As long as the spread between the short-term, safe, nominal interest rate i in the LM equation and the long-term, risky, real interest rate r in the IS equation is constant, there are no complications in drawing the LM curve on the same diagram as the IS curve.

But what if the expected rate of inflation π^e, the risk premium, or the term premium between short- and long-term interest rates changes? Then the position of the LM curve on the IS-LM diagram shifts either upward (if expected inflation falls, or if the risk premium rises, or if the term premium rises) or downward (if expected inflation rises, or if the risk premium falls, or if the term premium falls). Figure 9.20 illustrates what happens to the position of the LM curve if the expected inflation rate rises.

Thus changes in financial market expectations of future Bank of Canada policy, future inflation rates, or simply changes in the risk tolerance of bond traders shifts the LM curve. The IS-LM equilibrium is affected not only by disturbances in the money market but by broader shifts in the financial markets that alter the relationship between the nominal interest rates on short-term safe bonds and the real interest rate paid by corporations undertaking long-term risky investments.

http://www.bank-banque-canada.ca/

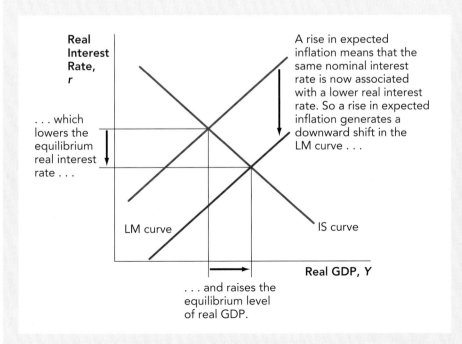

FIGURE 9.20

An Increase in Expected Inflation Moves the LM Curve Downward

The fact that the interest rate relevant to the IS curve is a real rate and the interest rate relevant to the LM curve is a nominal rate is a source of complications: A change in expected inflation lowers the real interest rate that corresponds to any given nominal interest rate, and so shifts the LM curve down on the IS-LM diagram.

CHANGES THAT AFFECT THE IS CURVE

Shifts in the IS curve are probably more frequent than shifts in the LM curve, for more types of shifts in the economic environment and economic policy affect planned expenditure than affect the supply and demand for money. Any change in the effect of a shift in interest rates on investment spending will change the slope of the IS curve. So will any change in either the sensitivity of exports to the exchange rate or the sensitivity of the level of the exchange rate to the level of domestic interest rates.

Furthermore, anything that affects the marginal propensity to spend — the MPE — will change the slope of the IS curve and the position of the IS curve as well. Any shift in the marginal propensity to consume C_y will change the MPE. Thus if households decide that income changes are more likely to be permanent (raising the marginal propensity to consume) or more likely to be transitory (lowering the marginal propensity to consume), they will raise or lower the MPE. Changes in tax rates have a direct effect on the MPE. So do changes in the propensity to import. Thus, for example, the imposition or removal of a tariff on imports to discourage them will affect the position and the slope of the IS curve.

Finally, changes in the economic environment and in economic policy that shift the level of autonomous spending shift the IS curve. Anything that affects the baseline level of consumption C_0 affects autonomous spending — whether it is a change in demography that changes desired savings behaviour, a change in optimism about future levels of income, or any other cause of a shift in consumer behaviour. Anything that affects the baseline level of investment I_0 affects autonomous spending — whether it is a wave of innovation that increases expected future profits and desired investment, a wave of irrational overoptimism or overpessimism, a change in tax policy that affects not the level of revenue collected but the incentives to invest, or any other cause. Changes in government purchases affect autonomous spending.

In sum, almost anything can affect the equilibrium level of aggregate demand on the IS-LM diagram. Pretty much everything *does* affect it at one time or another. One of the principal merits of the IS-LM is its use in sorting and classifying the determinants of equilibrium output and interest rates.

RECAP   THE IS-LM FRAMEWORK

The IS-LM framework determines the equilibrium interest rate and real GDP with fixed prices. Any change in economic policy or the economic environment that increases autonomous spending, such as an increase in government purchases, shifts the IS curve to the right. The new equilibrium will have both a higher level of real interest rates and a higher equilibrium level of real GDP. An increase in the money stock or a fall in real money demand will shift the LM curve to the right. The new equilibrium position will have a higher equilibrium level of real GDP and a lower level of real interest rates.

9.6 THE EXCHANGE RATE AND THE TRADE BALANCE

THE IS-LM FRAMEWORK AND THE INTERNATIONAL SECTOR

THE IS-LM FRAMEWORK AND THE EXCHANGE RATE

In our sticky-price model, the real exchange rate ε is equal to speculators' opinion of its baseline fundamental value, ε_0, minus a parameter ε_r times the difference between the real domestic interest rate (r) and the foreign interest rate abroad (r^f):

$$\varepsilon = \varepsilon_0 - \varepsilon_r(r - r^f) \tag{9.16}$$

Thus the effects of changes in domestic conditions on the value of the real exchange rate are easy to predict. As long as the domestic real interest rate does not change, domestic conditions will have no impact on the exchange rate. If the exchange rate shifts, it will do so for other, external reasons.

Changes in the IS and LM curves that *do* change the domestic real interest rate will change the real exchange rate, however, by an amount equal to the parameter ε_r times the shift in the domestic interest rate. A rightward expansionary shift in the IS curve and a leftward contractionary shift in the LM curve both lower the value of the exchange rate. A leftward contractionary shift in the IS curve and a rightward expansionary shift in the LM curve will both raise the value of the exchange rate. Figure 9.21 shows the latter case.

The effects of a change in domestic conditions on the real exchange rate are straightforward. The change in the exchange rate is proportional to the change in the real interest rate:

$$\Delta\varepsilon = -\varepsilon_r \times \Delta r \tag{9.17}$$

FIGURE 9.21

IS-LM and the Exchange Rate

A rightward shift in the LM curve will raise the exchange rate and the value of foreign currency and increase net exports.

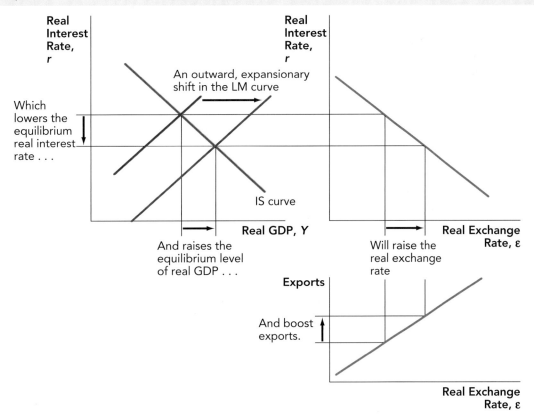

What determines the size of the proportionality factor ε_r, and thus the interest sensitivity of the exchange rate? It is a function of foreign exchange speculators' willingness to bear risk and their assessment of how long differentials between domestic and foreign interest rates will persist. If speculators think differences in interest rates will last a long time, the interest sensitivity of the exchange rate will be high. If speculators fear bearing risk, the interest sensitivity will be small.

THE IS-LM FRAMEWORK AND THE BALANCE OF TRADE

The effects in the IS-LM framework of changes in domestic conditions on the balance of trade are a little more complicated. Changes in r affect the exchange rate, which affects gross exports. Changes in total income Y affect imports. Figure 9.22 sketches out the chief causal links.

The effect on net exports is the difference between the effect of a change in the interest rate on gross exports (remember: the higher the domestic interest rate, the lower the value of the exchange rate and the lower the value of gross exports) and the effect of a change in real GDP on imports:

$$\Delta NX = \Delta GX - \Delta IM = -X_\varepsilon \times (\varepsilon_r \times \Delta r) - (IM_y \times \Delta Y) \qquad (9.18)$$

FIGURE 9.22
Effect of Change in Domestic Conditions on the Exchange Rate and the Balance of Trade

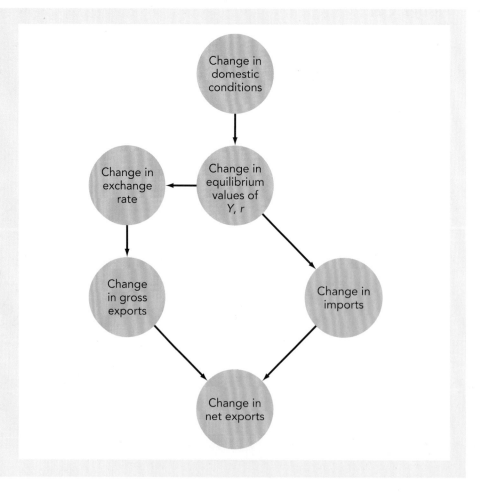

As the economy moves up or to the right (or both) on the IS-LM diagram, net exports fall.

INTERNATIONAL SHOCKS AND THE DOMESTIC ECONOMY

Three different types of international shocks will affect the IS-LM equilibrium. The first is a shift in foreign demand for domestic exports — the result, usually, of changes in foreign real GDP. The second is a shift in the foreign real interest rate, and the third is a change in foreign exchange speculators' view about the fundamental value of the exchange rate.

An increase in foreign demand for home-country exports will affect the domestic economy in the same way as any other expansionary IS shock. The increase in export demand is an increase in baseline autonomous spending A_0. It shifts the IS curve rightward by an amount $\Delta A_0/(1 - MPE)$. This rightward IS shift raises the equilibrium level of real GDP and, to the extent that the LM curve is upward-sloping, raises the real interest rate. The increase in the real interest rate would make exports more expensive to foreigners, and put some countervailing downward pressure on exports. The increase in the equilibrium level of real GDP would raise demand for imports. Figure 9.23 shows the major links in the causal chain.

FIGURE 9.23
Effect of an Increase in Foreign Demand for Exports

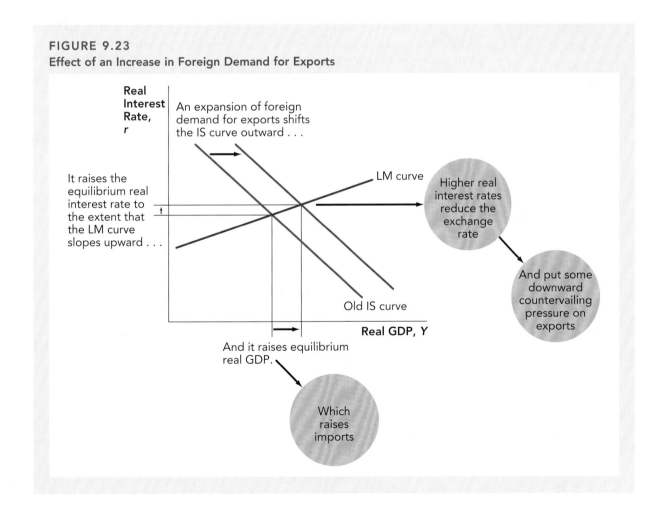

The second type of international shock, an increase in the foreign interest rate r^f, also has an immediate impact on the domestic economy but through different channels. An increase in the foreign interest rate raises the value of the exchange rate, and so boosts exports. The increase in exports shifts the IS curve to the right, leading to a higher level of equilibrium real GDP and — to the extent that the LM curve is upward-sloping — to higher real interest rates. The consequences of such a shift are similar to those of an increase in foreign incomes save for the direction in which the exchange rate moves.

The third type of international shock is a sudden change in speculators' expectations ε_0 of the long-run fundamental exchange rate. Consider an upward shock to ε_0. It would have effects identical to an increase in interest rates overseas: The exchange rate would rise, the IS curve would shift outward, equilibrium real GDP would increase, and — to the extent that the LM curve is upward-sloping — the domestic real interest rate would increase as well. Box 9.7 works through an example of such a change in exchange market speculators' expectations.

BOX
9.7
EXAMPLE

A SHOCK TO INTERNATIONAL INVESTORS' EXPECTATIONS

Suppose that the economy's LM curve is represented by the equation

$$Y = \$100 + \$10{,}000 \times (r + \pi^e)$$

and that the expected inflation rate π^e is constant at 3 percent per year. Suppose further that the economy's marginal propensity to expend [MPE] is 0.5, that the marginal propensity to import IM_y is 0.15, that the initial level of baseline autonomous spending A_0 is \$500 billion, that a 1-percentage-point increase in the real interest rate (i.e., an increase of 0.01 in r) reduces investment spending by \$4 billion (i.e., $I_r = 400$, so that $400 \times 0.01 = 4$), reduces the value of the exchange rate by 10 units (i.e., $\varepsilon_r = 1{,}000$, so that $1{,}000 \times 0.01 = 10$), and that each 1-unit increase in the exchange rate increases gross exports by \$0.6 billion (i.e., $X_\varepsilon = .06$). Then the economy's initial IS curve is

$$Y = \frac{A_0}{1 - MPE} - \frac{I_r + X_\varepsilon \varepsilon_r}{1 - MPE} \times r = \frac{\$500}{1 - 0.5} - \frac{\$400 + 1{,}000 \times \$0.6}{1 - 0.5} \times r$$

$$= \$1{,}000 - \$2{,}000 \times r$$

The initial equilibrium has annual real GDP at \$900 billion and a real interest rate of 5 percent.

Consider a sudden upward shock of 10 units to the exchange rate long-run fundamental, as foreign exchange speculators lose confidence in the value of the domestic currency and mark up their opinions ε_0 of the long-run fundamental value of the real exchange rate by an amount $\Delta\varepsilon_0 = 10$ units. Such a shock shifts the IS curve to the right, raising the level of real GDP on the IS curve for a given, fixed level of the real interest rate by an amount

$$\frac{X_\varepsilon \times \Delta\varepsilon_0}{1 - MPE}$$

The shifted IS curve is then

$$Y = \frac{A_0 + \Delta A_0}{1 - MPE} - \frac{I_r + X_\varepsilon \varepsilon_r}{1 - MPE} \times r = \frac{A_0 + X_\varepsilon \times \Delta\varepsilon_0}{1 - MPE} - \frac{I_r + X_\varepsilon \varepsilon_r}{1 - MPE} \times r$$

$$= \frac{\$500 + \$0.6 \times 10}{1 - 0.5} - \frac{\$400 + \$0.6 \times 1{,}000}{1 - 0.5} \times r = \$1{,}012 - \$2{,}000 \times r$$

The new equilibrium can be found by setting the values of Y produced by the IS and LM curve to be equal to each other

$$\$100 + \$10,000 \times (r + \pi) = Y = \$1,012 - \$2,000 \times r$$
$$\$612 = \$12,000 \times r$$
$$r = .051 = 5.1\%$$
$$Y = \$910$$

Equilibrium annual real GDP increases by $10 billion as the raised exchange rate boosts exports, and the domestic real interest rate rises by 0.1 percentage points from 5 percent per year to 5.1 percent per year.

The increase in the domestic real interest rate means that the total change in the real exchange rate

$$\Delta\varepsilon = \Delta\varepsilon_0 - \varepsilon_r \times \Delta r$$
$$= 10 - 1,000 \times 0.1\% = 9$$

is less than the 10-point magnitude of the initial shock to confidence in the currency: higher domestic real interest rates have offset some of the effect of the change in foreign exchange speculators' opinions. The increase in the domestic real interest rate also means that some domestic investment has been "crowded out" by the interest rate effects of the export boom

$$\Delta I = -I_r \times \Delta r = -\$400 \times 0.1\% = -\$4$$

The total effect on gross exports from the net change in the exchange rate is

$$\Delta GX = X_\varepsilon \times \Delta\varepsilon = \$0.6 \times 9 = \$5.4$$

Since the total change in imports is

$$\Delta IM = IM_Y \times \Delta Y = 0.15 \times \$10 = \$1.5$$

The total change in net exports from the shift in exchange speculator confidence is $3.9 billion.

RECAP   THE EXCHANGE RATE AND THE TRADE BALANCE

The effects of a change in domestic conditions on the real exchange rate are straightforward. The change in the exchange rate is proportional to the change in the real interest rate. What determines the size of the proportionality factor? It is a function of foreign exchange speculators' willingness to bear risk, and their assessment of how long differentials between domestic and foreign interest rates will persist. If speculators think differences in interest rates will last for a long time, the interest sensitivity of the exchange rate will be high. If speculators fear bearing risk, the interest sensitivity of the exchange rate will be small.

CHAPTER SUMMARY

1. The income-expenditure diagram takes autonomous spending as given and then determines the equilibrium level of real GDP, aggregate demand, and national income as functions of autonomous spending and the marginal propensity to spend.

2. The IS curve incorporates the effect of changing interest rates on autonomous spending and adds this effect to the income-expenditure diagram.

3. The IS curve slopes downward because a higher interest rate lowers both investment and exports, and these reductions in autonomous spending in turn lower aggregate demand and equilibrium real GDP.

4. When the central bank's policy involves targeting the real interest rate, then the position of the IS curve and the central bank's interest rate–target together determine the equilibrium level of aggregate demand and real GDP.

5. The money market is in equilibrium when the level of total incomes and of the short-term nominal interest rate is just right to make households and businesses want to hold all the real money balances that exist in the economy.

6. When the central bank's policy keeps the money stock fixed — or when there is no central bank — the LM curve consists of those combinations of interest rates and real GDP levels at which money demand equals money supply.

7. When the central bank's policy keeps the money stock fixed — or when there is no central bank — the point at which the IS and LM curves cross determines the equilibrium level of real GDP and the interest rate.

8. The IS-LM framework consists of two equilibrium conditions: The IS curve shows those combinations of interest rates and real GDP levels at which aggregate demand is equal to total production; the LM curve shows those combinations of interest rates and real GDP levels at which money demand is equal to money supply. Both equilibrium conditions must be satisfied.

9. An IS shock is any shock to the level of total spending as a function of the domestic real interest rate. An IS shock shifts the position of the IS curve. An expansionary IS shock raises real GDP and the real interest rate.

10. An LM shock is a shock to money demand or money supply. An LM shock shifts the position of the LM curve. An expansionary LM shock raises real GDP and lowers the interest rate.

11. Anything that affects the level of the real interest rate on the IS-LM diagram affects the real exchange rate. Increases in the real interest rate reduce the value of the real exchange rate, holding other things constant.

12. However, a number of different international shocks affect the real exchange rate as well as and in addition to changes in the domestic real interest rate. A collapse in foreign exchange speculators' confidence in the currency raises the real exchange rate. So does an increase in the real interest rate abroad.

KEY TERMS AND EQUATIONS

economic disturbances (p. 298)

expected inflation (p. 291)

government expenditure multiplier (p. 297)

income-expenditure diagram (p. 273)

interest rate targeting (p. 279)

IS curve (p. 274)

LM curve (p. 272)

money market equilibrium (p. 284)

money supply multiplier (p. 297)

Autonomous spending:
$$A = [C_0 + I_0 + G + (X_f Y^f + X_\varepsilon \varepsilon_0 + X_\varepsilon \varepsilon_r r^f)] - (I_r + X_\varepsilon \varepsilon_r) \times r \tag{9.1}$$

The IS curve:
$$Y = \frac{[C_0 + I_0 + G + (X_f Y^f + X_\varepsilon \varepsilon_0 + X_\varepsilon \varepsilon_r r^f)]}{1 - [C_y(1-t) - IM_y]} - \frac{I_r + X_\varepsilon \varepsilon_r}{1 - [C_y(1-t) - IM_y]} \times r \tag{9.6}$$

The LM curve:
$$Y = \frac{M/P - L_0}{L_Y} + \frac{L_i}{L_Y} \times (r + \pi^e) \tag{9.11}$$

Government expenditures multiplier:

$$Y_G \equiv \Delta Y/\Delta G = \cfrac{1}{(1 - MPE) + (I_r + X_\varepsilon \times \varepsilon_r) \times \cfrac{L_Y}{L_i}} \qquad (9.14)$$

Money supply multiplier:

$$Y_M \equiv \Delta Y/\Delta M = \cfrac{1/L_i}{(1 - MPE) + (I_r + X_\varepsilon \times \varepsilon_r) \times \cfrac{L_Y}{L_i}} \qquad (9.15)$$

ANALYTICAL EXERCISES

1. Why does an expansion of government purchases have an amplified impact on the equilibrium level of real GDP? Suppose that the central bank does not target interest rates but instead keeps the money stock constant. Is it still the case that an expansion of government purchases will cause a greater than one-for-one increase in the equilibrium level of real GDP?

2. Explain why the IS curve slopes downward. Is its slope steeper in a closed economy, with no international trade, or in an open economy?

3. For each of the following, decide whether the IS curve shifts in and to the left, shifts out and to the right, or stays unchanged:
   The tax rate decreases.
   Foreign interest rates rise.
   Businesses become more optimistic about future demand.
   Consumers desire to save a greater proportion of their income for the future.
   The central bank lowers the short-term nominal interest rate it controls.
   The term premium rises.
   Foreign exchange speculators become more pessimistic about the long-run value of domestic currency.

4. Suppose that the government and central bank together want to keep GDP constant but raise the rate of investment. What policies can they follow to achieve this?

5. Suppose that the level of investment spending does not depend at all on the interest rate. Does this mean that the IS curve is vertical? If not, how can it be that central-bank changes in the real interest rate affect the equilibrium level of real GDP?

6. What are the *qualitative* effects, in the IS-LM model, of each of the following changes?
   a. An increase in firms' optimism about future profits.
   b. A sudden improvement in banking technology that makes cheques clear two days faster.
   c. A wave of credit card fraud that leads people to use cash for purchases more often.
   d. A banking crisis that diminishes banks' willingness to accept deposits.
   e. A sudden military spending program.

7. What are the qualitative effects of an increase in real GDP on the rate of inflation?

8. Suppose that the expected rate of inflation suddenly jumped. What would happen — with no other changes in the economic environment — to the IS-LM equilibrium? Would equilibrium real GDP go up or down? Would the equilibrium real interest rate go up or down?

9. Suppose that the *term premium* — the gap between short-term and long-term interest rates — suddenly went up. With no other changes in the economic environment, what would happen to the IS-LM equilibrium? Would equilibrium real GDP go up or down? Would the equilibrium real interest rate in the IS curve go up or down?

10. Recall the expression for the government expenditure and money supply multipliers, Y_G and Y_M. Discuss how the sizes of these multipliers depend on the slopes of the IS and LM curves.

11. Re-solve the equations of the IS and LM curves, equations (9.6) and (9.11), for r in terms of y, and state the slopes of the IS and LM curves.

POLICY EXERCISES

1. Suppose that the consumption, investment, net exports, and exchange rate functions are:

   $$Y = C + I + G + NX$$
   $$C = C_0 + C_y(1 - t)Y = \$300 + 0.5(1 - 0.4)Y$$
   $$I = I_0 - I_r r = \$120 - \$1,000r$$

   $$GX = X_f Y^f + X_\varepsilon \varepsilon = 0.01Y^f + \$0.4\varepsilon$$
   $$IM = IM_y Y = .2Y$$
   $$NX = GX - IM$$
   $$\varepsilon = 100 + 1,000(r^f - r)$$

Derive the IS curve for this economy: real GDP as a function of all the unspecified variables in the economy. Suppose that the foreign interest rate r^f is 5 percent, that total foreign income Y^f is $10,000 billion, and that government spending G is $300 billion. What then is equilibrium annual real GDP if the central bank sets the real interest rate at 3 percent? At 5 percent? At 7 percent?

2. Suppose that the economy is the same as in problem 1 except for the fact that it is a closed economy. There are no imports and no exports: $IM_y = 0$, $X_f = 0$, and $X_\varepsilon = 0$. Derive the IS curve for this economy. What is equilibrium annual real GDP if the central bank sets the interest rate at 3 percent? At 5 percent? At 7 percent?

3. In which of the two economies — the open economy of problem 1 or the closed economy of problem 2 — do you think that changes in interest rates have larger effects on the equilibrium level of real GDP? Explain your answer.

4. Suppose that the short-term nominal interest rate — the one the central bank actually controls — is 3 percent. But also suppose that the inflation rate is zero, that the term premium is 4 percent, and that the risk premium is 3 percent.
   a. What is the real interest rate relevant for the IS curve?
   b. Suppose that the IS equation of the economy is $Y = $1,000 - 3,000 \times r$. What is the equilibrium level of real GDP?
   c. Suppose that the central bank wants to use monetary policy to raise Y to $900 billion. Can it do so by open-market operations that lower the short-term nominal interest rate? Explain why or why not. What other policy steps can you think of that the government and central bank could take to raise equilibrium real GDP to $900 billion?

5. Suppose that the consumption, investment, net exports, and exchange rate functions are:

   $Y = C + I + G + NX$
   $C = C_0 + C_y(1 - t)Y = $300 + 0.5(1 - 0.4)Y$
   $I = I_0 - I_r r = $120 - $1,000r$
   $GX = X_f Y^f + X_\varepsilon \varepsilon = 0.01Y^f + 0.4ε
   $IM = IM_y Y = .2Y$
   $NX = GX - IM$
   $\varepsilon = 100 + 1,000(r^f - r)$

   Suppose further that the government follows a balanced-budget rule: Government purchases G are equal to government tax collections tY. Derive the IS for this economy: real GDP as a function of all the unspecified variables in the economy. Is the level of real GDP along the IS curve more or less sensitive to changes in interest rates than it was in problem 1? Why?

6. Consider the economy presented in Box 9.4. The economy's marginal propensity to expend (MPE) is 0.5, the initial level of autonomous spending A_0 is $500 billion, and a 1-percentage-point increase in the real interest rate reduces the sum of investment and net exports by $10 billion. Suppose further that the expected inflation rate is constant at 3 percent per year, and that the LM curve is

$$Y = $100 + $10,000(r + \pi^e). \qquad (i)$$

The economy's initial IS curve is

$$Y = \frac{A_0}{1 - MPE} - \frac{I_r + X_\varepsilon \varepsilon_r}{1 - MPE} \times r$$

$$= \frac{$500}{1 - 0.5} - \frac{$1,000}{1 - 0.5} \times r \qquad (ii)$$

$$= $1,000 - $2,000 \times r$$

The initial equilibrium output is $900 billion and the initial equilibrium real interest rate is 5 percent.
   a. Suppose there is a recession abroad that results in a fall in gross exports. As a result autonomous spending A_0 falls to $470 billion. What is the effect on the equilibrium output and the interest rates?
   b. Consider again the initial equilibrium before the foreign recession. Suppose there is an increase in the demand for real money balances in this economy that shift the LM curve to

$$Y = $88 + $10,000(r + \pi^e) \qquad (iii)$$

   while the IS curve is given by (ii). Using a diagram show how this will shift the LM curve. What will be the new equilibrium interest rate and output?

7. Suppose that the Bank of Canada is wondering whether it should follow a policy of stabilizing the money stock or one of stabilizing the real interest rate. First, suppose that all shocks to the economy are shocks in autonomous spending: Which policy leads to smaller shifts in real GDP in response to shocks? Second, suppose that all of the shocks to the economy are shocks in the real money demand and in the LM equation.

   Which policy is now best in terms of leading to smaller shifts in real GDP? Third, suppose that the only shocks to the economy are changes in assessments of expected inflation π^e. Now what is your answer?

8. Suppose that money demand is interest insensitive, so that the money demand function does not depend on the interest rate at all. What, then, is the LM curve for this economy? What effect does an increase in government purchases have on the level of real interest rates and the equilibrium level of annual real GDP?

9. Suppose that the economy's LM curve is given by the equation

$$Y = \$100 + \$10,000 \times (r + \pi^e)$$

and that the expected inflation rate π^e is constant at 3 percent per year. Suppose further that the economy's marginal propensity to expend (MPE) is 0.6, that the marginal propensity to import IM_y is 0.25, that the initial level of baseline autonomous spending A_0 is $500 billion, that a 1-percentage-point increase in the real interest rate reduces investment spending by $4 billion and reduces the value of the exchange rate by 10 percent, and that a 1-unit increase in the exchange rate increases net exports by $0.6 billion.

What is the effect on the domestic economy's equilibrium of a sudden 30 percent increase in the exchange rate as foreign exchange speculators lose confidence in the economy?

10 The Aggregate Demand– Aggregate Supply Model

QUESTIONS

What is the relationship between prices, inflation, and aggregate expenditures?

What is the relationship between prices, inflation, and aggregate supply?

What is the difference between non-overlapping and overlapping labour contracts?

What is the Taylor rule?

How is the inflation rate determined in the short run?

What are the effects of anticipated and unanticipated policy changes?

What is the "Great Canadian Slump"?

In the aggregate expenditure framework of Chapter 8 and the IS-LM model of Chapter 9 we assumed that prices were fixed and firms responded to changes in aggregate expenditures by changing output. Hence, we say in these models output is "demand determined." In fact, the equilibrium point in these models gives us the *aggregate demand* for goods and services.

Although assuming that prices are fixed and output responds to changes in demand conditions is a relatively good approximation to how the economy operates in the short run, it is an assumption that should be relaxed in our model-building process in order to obtain a more complete picture of the macroeconomy in the long run.

In fact, even in the short run firms can respond to any disturbance not only by changing output, but also by changing prices. Of course, the price changes may be small in the short run, since labour costs are fixed by wage contracts. Further, allowing for price as well as output changes is essential for studying the adjustment of the economy from the short run to the long run, as discussed in Chapter 5.

The purpose of the present chapter, therefore, is first to study how output demanded, as given by the IS-LM model, is affected by changes in the price level. Using the IS-LM framework, we derive for each price level the amount of output demanded. This relationship is called the *aggregate demand curve*.

We then study how firms respond to changes in the price level, by deriving the *aggregate supply curve*, which gives us for each price level the amount of output that will be supplied by the firms. As we will see, the expectations of workers and firms about the price level and the inflation rate in the future play an important role in their negotiations regarding wage increases, and, thus, in the position of the aggregate supply curve.

Once the aggregate demand and aggregate supply curves are derived, it is relatively easy to discuss the adjustment of the economy from the short run (with sticky prices) to the long run (with flexible prices). We will see that this adjustment mechanism depends critically on whether labour contracts are signed at the same time across the economy or are staggered. In the latter case, the adjustment of the economy to its new long-run equilibrium will be protracted through time.

10.1 AGGREGATE DEMAND

THE PRICE LEVEL AND AGGREGATE DEMAND

In the S-LM model what happens to the level of real GDP as the price level rises? If the nominal money supply is fixed, then an increase in the price level reduces real money balances and shifts the LM curve back and to the left. The equilibrium real interest rate rises, and the equilibrium level of real GDP falls, as Figure 10.1 shows.

Suppose we draw another diagram, this time with the price level on the vertical axis and the level of real GDP on the horizontal axis. We use this new diagram to

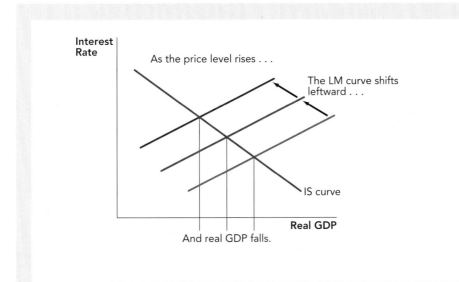

FIGURE 10.1

An Increase in the Price Level Shifts the LM Curve Left (If the Nominal Money Supply Is Fixed)

For a fixed level of the nominal money stock, an increase in the price level is a contractionary shift in the economy. The higher the price level, the lower the real money stock. The lower the real money stock, the further left the LM curve moves. The further left the LM curve, the lower real GDP is.

plot what the equilibrium level of real GDP is for each possible value of the price level. For each value of the price level, we calculate the LM curve and use the IS-LM diagram to calculate the equilibrium level of real GDP. As Figure 10.2 shows, we find — if the nominal money supply is fixed — a downward-sloping relationship between the price level and real GDP. With the nominal money stock held fixed, a rise in the price level decreases the real money stock, and shifts the LM curve to the left because the position of the LM curve depends on the value of the real money stock. A leftward shift in the LM curve reduces the equilibrium level of real GDP and increases the interest rate. The lower the price level, the higher real money balances are, the lower the interest rate is, the higher aggregate demand is, and the higher the equilibrium level of real GDP is. Economists call this curve — according to which a lower price *level* means higher aggregate demand — the **aggregate demand curve**.

FIGURE 10.2
From the IS-LM Diagram to the Aggregate Demand Curve

For a fixed value of the nominal money stock, each possible value for the price level produces a different LM curve. Plot the equilibrium value of real GDP for that LM curve on the horizontal axis and the price level on the vertical axis. The result is the aggregate demand curve.

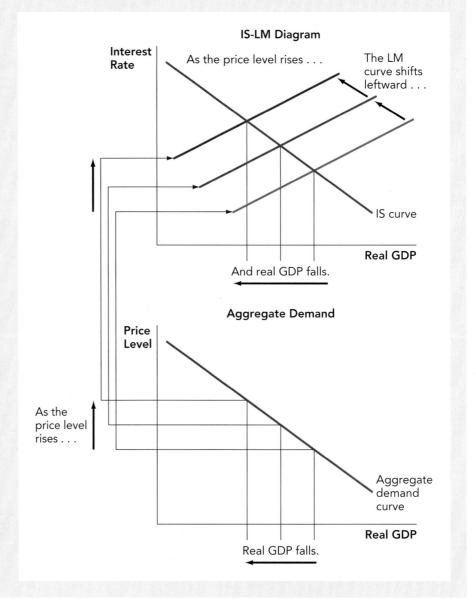

In this aggregate demand curve we can see how, over time, adjustments in prices and wages might carry the economy from the sticky-price model equilibrium back to the flexible-price equilibrium in which real GDP is equal to potential output. If real GDP is less than potential output, prices might fall over time, and falling prices would carry the economy down and to the right along the aggregate demand curve, increasing real GDP. If real GDP is greater than potential output, prices might rise over time, and rising prices would carry the economy up and to the left along the aggregate demand curve, reducing real GDP.

AD CURVE

Our treatment of aggregate demand, AD, so far has been verbal and graphical. However, we can derive the equation of the AD curve analytically by combining the IS and LM equations of Chapter 9. To this end, recall that, by definition, the AD curve gives the equilibrium real GDP demanded at different price levels. In view of this and the discussion leading to Figure 10.2, we can use the IS and LM equations in order to derive analytically the equation of the AD curve. Recall from Chapter 9, the point of intersection of the IS and LM curves gave us the equilibrium output for a given price level:

$$Y = Y_A + Y_G \times G + Y_M \times \frac{M}{P}$$

where the exact expressions for Y_A, Y_G, and Y_M were reported in Chapter 9. The important point to note is that in Chapter 9 prices were treated as fixed, and the focus was on the effects of changes in government expenditures, the money supply, etc. on the equilibrium with fixed prices.

At this stage, however, we concentrate on the determination of the price level, and as such we treat this equation as a relationship between output demanded at different price levels for given levels of Y_A, G, and M. Viewed this way, the above expression is the aggregate demand curve, AD. As is clear from this expression, for given values of Y_A, Y_G, Y_M, G, and M, an increase in the price level reduces output demanded. Thus, the AD curve is downward sloping. Using the above equation, the exact expression for the slope of the AD curve is $-Y_M \times \frac{M}{P^2}$, which is negative, given that Y_M and M are positive.

Clearly, the position of the AD curve depends on the levels of G, M, and Y_A. Hence, an increase in government expenditures G, or an increase in the money supply M, will increase output demanded, for any given price level, and the AD curve will shift to the right. Similarly, any shock that changes Y_A will shift the AD curve. Examples of shocks that increase Y_A and shift the AD curve to the right include, among other things, increases in autonomous consumption C_0, increases in autonomous investment, and increases in foreign income. In summary, given that the AD curve is derived from the IS and LM curves, any factor that shifts the IS or the LM curve — other than the price level — will shift the AD curve.

RECAP   **AGGREGATE DEMAND**

What happens to the level of real GDP demanded as the price level rises? Consider the IS-LM model: if the nominal money supply is fixed, then an increase in the price level reduces real money balances and shifts the LM curve back and to the left. The equilibrium real interest rate rises, and the equilibrium level of real GDP demanded falls. Economists call this relationship the aggregate demand relationship.

10.2 AGGREGATE SUPPLY

The aggregate supply gives the total output supplied by firms at any given price level. There are a number of ways in which one can view and derive the **aggregate supply curve**, depending on what assumptions we are prepared to make about wage and price flexibility in the economy. One method is based on the *misperceptions model* first proposed by Milton Friedman in 1968 and then formalized by Robert Lucas in the 1970s. This classic model assumes complete wage and price flexibility. The only *friction* in the economy is lack of information at the local production level of the general price level of the economy as a whole. Alternatively, a *Keynesian* aggregate supply can be derived by assuming explicitly that, in the face of economic disturbances, wages adjust much slower than prices because of the presence of institutions, e.g., labour unions, that fix the wage rate over the period of a labour contract. During that period, an economic shock that increases the price level and causes a fall in real wages and an increase in employment and output generates a positive relationship between output and price. In this section we discuss the two models sequentially.

THE MISPERCEPTIONS MODEL

The misperceptions model assumes first, that there are a large number of sectors in the economy, each producing a different good that is an imperfect substitute for other goods. Because goods are imperfect substitutes for each other, the supply of each good will depend on the price of that good relative to all others. Hence, the supply of each good will depend on the price of that good relative to the general price level.

Second, it is assumed that because there are a large number of sectors in the economy, people working in a sector will know exactly the current price of the good in their own sector; but they will not know the current price of the goods produced in other sectors. This is a realistic assumption, since it is costly to gather information about other sectors; and, therefore, it is natural to assume that information about the prices in other sectors will be available but with a delay. Hence, it is assumed that in each period people have to form expectations about the general price level, based on the information that is available to them.

Based on these assumptions, we can write the supply function for sector i as

$$\frac{Y_i - Y^*_i}{Y^*_i} = \theta \times \frac{P_i - P^e}{P^e} \tag{10.1}$$

where Y_i is output in sector i, Y^*_i is potential output in sector i, P_i is the price of the good produced in sector i, and P^e is the *expectation* about the general price level based on information available to the producers in any given sector.

According to equation (10.1), the proportional deviations of output in sector i from its potential level is equal to the parameter θ (the Greek letter "theta"), which represents the slope of the supply function, times the proportional deviations of the price in sector i from the expected general price. If the actual price in sector i is higher than the expected general price then output in sector i will be higher than its potential level. Conversely, if the actual price in sector i is lower than the expected general price then output in sector i will be lower than its potential level. For simplicity, we assume that the expected general price P^e is the same in all sectors.

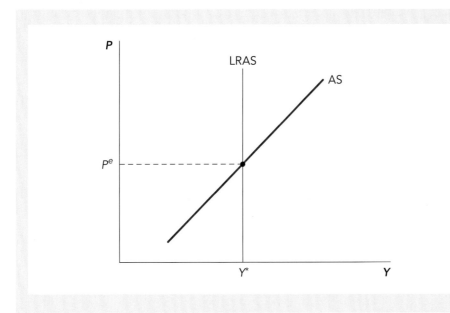

FIGURE 10.3

The Aggregate Supply Curve

The AS curve is upward sloping and its position depends on P^e. It intersects the long-run aggregate supply (LRAS) curve when $P = P^e$.

The next step in deriving the aggregate supply curve is to take the average of equation (10.1) over all sectors. This gives

$$\frac{Y - Y^*}{Y^*} = \theta \times \frac{P - P^e}{P^e} \tag{10.2}$$

where Y is aggregate actual output produced, Y^* is the aggregate potential output, P is the average actual price, and, as before, P^e is the expected price.

Equation (10.2) has very important implications. If for whatever reason the general price P is higher than what was expected P^e, then aggregate output Y will be higher than its potential level Y^*. The reason is that when P exceeds P^e then on average producers in a typical sector believe that their price is higher than the general price level. They will, therefore, increase output above its potential level. As this happens in the typical sector, aggregate output will increase above its potential level.

Equation (10.2) is the short-run aggregate supply curve, denoted by AS, and is shown in Figure 10.3. The AS curve is upward sloping and its position depends on P^e; AS shifts up when there is an increase in P^e, and it shifts down when there is a decrease in P^e. Also, it intersects the vertical line at Y^* when $P = P^e$. The vertical line through Y^* is the long-run aggregate supply curve, denoted by LRAS, because the long-run equilibrium lies along LRAS where $Y = Y^*$.

THE GENERAL EQUILIBRIUM OUTPUT AND PRICE

There are three *endogenous* variables that determine the long-run equilibrium in this economy: P, P^e, and Y. Consider first the determination of the expected price, P^e. There are a number of alternative approaches that we can use and we will discuss them in detail in the next chapter. Here, we consider the most popular approach; that P^e is determined assuming that people have **rational expectations**. With *rational expectations*, people use the model *and* all the information available to them when forming their expectations. Note that they have an expectation about the position of the aggregate demand curve. Suppose they expect it to be at AD^e in Figure 10.4.

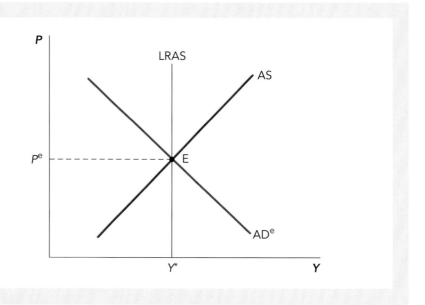

They also know that if expectations turn out to be correct (i.e., if $P^e = P$) then we will be at full-employment output Y^*. Hence, P^e is given by the intersection of the expected aggregate demand AD^e and long-run aggregate supply LRAS curves. As noted above, this is also the intersection point with the short-run aggregate supply curve, AS. Figure 10.4 shows that the economy is in general equilibrium at point E where $P = P^e$ and $Y = Y^*$.

Next, we study how the economy adjusts to its new general equilibrium point following an *economy-wide* shock. Economic shocks can be generated from changes in monetary and fiscal policy or from international disturbances such as an increase in the price of crude oil. The adjustment process depends crucially on whether the shock is *unanticipated* or *anticipated*.

UNANTICIPATED SHOCKS

Suppose the economy is initially in general equilibrium at point A on the AD-AS diagram in Figure 10.5 where AD_0 intersects AS_0 and LRAS. At this point there is full employment at Y^* and actual and expected prices are equal to P_0 (i.e., $P = P_0^e = P_0$). Suppose that everyone expects aggregate demand to be at AD_0 and the price to remain constant at P_0^e. However, suppose now there is an *unanticipated* increase in aggregate demand, maybe due to an unexpected increase in the money supply or exports or some other component of aggregate demand. Hence, actual aggregate demand turns out to be at AD_1. As a result of this unexpected increase in aggregate demand, the new short-run equilibrium will be at point B, where actual aggregate output rises to Y_B and the actual price level to P_B. The reason for this is that when aggregate demand increases, prices in all sectors increase. Because the increase in aggregate demand is *unanticipated* people in all sectors think that the relative price in their sector has increased. Thus, output in all sectors is increased, which in turn increases aggregate output.

How long will the economy stay at the short-run equilibrium? Not indefinitely, because at point B the actual price level P_B exceeds the expected price P_0^e. Obviously, people have underestimated the true price level at this point. However, over time

FIGURE 10.5

Unanticipated versus Anticipated Increase in Aggregate Demand

Suppose aggregate demand is expected to be at AD_0 and expected price at P_0^e and then there is an *unanticipated* increase in aggregate demand to AD_1. The new short-run equilibrium will be at point B. Once expectations are revised, the expected aggregate demand and the short-run aggregate supply shift to AD_1 and AS_1, respectively, and the economy returns to full employment at point C. If the initial increase in aggregate demand was *anticipated* then the equilibrium would shift to C instantly.

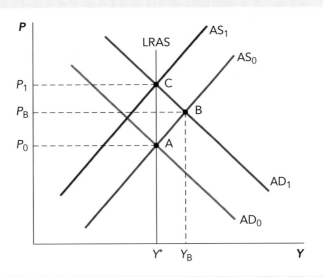

people obtain information about the true price level in the economy and revise their expectations accordingly. The expected aggregate demand will then be at AD_1 and the new expected price will be P_1^e. Given this higher expected price, the short-run aggregate supply curve shifts up to AS_1, and the economy returns to full employment at point C where the actual and expected price are equal to P_l (i.e., $P = P_1^e = P_l$). Point C is the new long-run general equilibrium for the economy.

ANTICIPATED SHOCKS

Suppose instead, the increase in aggregate demand to AD_1 is *anticipated*. This may result, for example, from a pre-announced expansionary monetary policy by the Bank of Canada that is credible and believed by all people. If the increase in aggregate demand is thus anticipated, expectations will be revised to P_1^e immediately, and the aggregate supply curve will shift to AS_1 accordingly. Hence, in this case, both the aggregate demand and the aggregate supply curves shift simultaneously, and the new long-run equilibrium will be established at point C instantly. The reason for this is that when the increase in aggregate demand is anticipated, then people expect that all prices will increase, leaving relative prices unchanged. As output in any sector depends on the price level in that sector relative to the general price level, output will not be affected in any sector.

Thus, in this model it is important to make a distinction between anticipated and unanticipated changes in aggregate demand. While in this model unanticipated changes in aggregate demand have some effect on output, anticipated changes have no effect on output.

AGGREGATE SUPPLY BASED ON LABOUR CONTRACTS

This approach of deriving the aggregate supply function relies more on the Keynesian assumption of wage and price rigidities due to the existence of labour contracts that fix the nominal wage for the duration of the contracts. In what follows, first we discuss one-period **non-overlapping contracts** signed at the same time for everyone in the labour market and show how this approach gives rise to an aggregate supply function similar to that given by equation (10.2), and shown in Figure 10.3. We then analyze the effects of unanticipated and anticipated shocks in this framework. Finally, we outline an extension of the basic model when contracts are signed at different points in time by different groups of workers and firms, and discuss the important differences that such **overlapping contracts** make for the adjustment process to macroeconomic equilibrium.

ONE-PERIOD NON-OVERLAPPING LABOUR CONTRACTS AND AGGREGATE SUPPLY

The basic assumptions of the model that emphasizes labour contracts are simpler than those of the misperception model. There is only one sector in the economy, and workers and firms sign contracts at the beginning of each period based on their expectations about the general price level that will prevail for the duration of the contract, which is assumed to be *one period* for simplicity. These labour contracts fix the nominal wage for the duration of the contract.

Suppose expectations about the general price level are correct or rational. Then the level of output produced will be identical to that of the model with perfectly flexible wages and prices; that is, output will be at its full-employment level. Hence, the aggregate supply curve (AS) will intersect the long-run aggregate supply curve (LRAS) when the expected price P^e is equal to the actual price P, as in Figure 10.3.

On the other hand, if the actual price is higher than the expected price then, with fixed wages, firms will try to reap the benefits of higher prices, and hence higher profits, by raising output. They will raise output by asking their workers to work overtime, and by speeding up the conveyor belts. The higher is the actual price from the expected price the larger will be the level of output relative to its full-employment level. Hence, with one-period labour contracts the aggregate supply curve will also be upward sloping, and can be represented by equation (10.2).

THE EFFECTS OF SHOCKS WITH ONE-PERIOD NON-OVERLAPPING LABOUR CONTRACTS

Now consider the effects of unanticipated and anticipated changes in aggregate demand in the model with one-period non-overlapping labour contracts. First, consider the effects of an unanticipated increase in aggregate demand. Suppose contracts are signed at the beginning of the period with the expectation that aggregate demand will be at AD_0 in Figure 10.5, and the price equal to P_0 (i.e., $P_0^e = P_0$). Then there is an *unanticipated* increase in aggregate demand, and actual aggregate demand turns out to be at AD_1. With nominal wages fixed, the short-run equilibrium will be at point B, with output Y_B.

Nevertheless, at the beginning of the next period expectations will be revised. The expected aggregate demand will then be at AD_1 and the new expected price will be P_1^e. The labour contracts will then be revised accordingly, and the aggregate supply curve will shift up to AS_1, and the economy returns to full employment at point C where the actual and expected prices are equal to P_1 (i.e., $P = P_1^e = P_1$).

On the other hand, if the initial shift in aggregate demand was fully anticipated then the equilibrium would jump from point A to point C immediately, since in that case the initial labour contracts would be signed with the expectation that aggregate demand will be at AD_1, with the corresponding expected price P_1^e equal to P_1.

One could then conclude that the implications of the model with labour contracts are the same as the misperception model. Nevertheless, this is based on the assumption that all workers and firms sign contracts at the same time. If different groups of workers and firms sign contracts at different times, then nominal wages will exhibit a great deal of inertia, and the implications of the model will be different. Stanley Fischer of MIT and John Taylor of Stanford University first developed such a model with "overlapping" or "staggered" contracts.

OVERLAPPING LABOUR CONTRACTS AND AGGREGATE SUPPLY

In reality, labour contracts are rarely signed at the same time; it is more realistic to assume that labour contracts overlap, with half the workers and firms signing contracts at the beginning of each period, and the other half signing contracts in the middle of the period. With such overlapping labour contracts, when a group of workers and firms is signing a contract, it has to take into account the fact that the other group of workers and firms is already locked into a contract with fixed wages. This adds a great deal of inertia to the movement of nominal wages.

With overlapping labour contracts wage increases will be resisted by firms while wage cuts will be resisted by workers. Firms engaged in wage negotiations will resist wage increases because they do not want to lose competitiveness relative to the other group of firms that are locked in contracts that are due for renegotiation at a later date. On the other hand, workers engaged in wage negotiations will resist wage cuts because they are worried about their social position relative to the other group of workers whose wages are fixed until a later date.

Suppose half the workers and firms sign contracts at the beginning of each period, and the other half in the middle of the period. Also suppose all contracts last for one period. Consider the case of an unanticipated increase in aggregate demand in this setting. In Figure 10.6, start from a full-employment equilibrium at point A, where all contracts are signed with the expectation that aggregate demand will be at AD^e, with the corresponding expected price P_0 (i.e., $P_0^e = P_0$) and aggregate supply at AS_0. Suppose there is then an unexpected increase in aggregate demand to AD_1 that takes place in the first half of a period. The equilibrium in the first half of the period, in which no contract can be revised, will then shift to point B.

In the middle of the period half the contracts are ready to be revised. The workers and firms that are involved in the negotiations worry about their competitive position relative to other firms and workers. Thus they raise their nominal wages by a relatively small amount, because they do not wish to raise their production costs substantially and lose their competitive position relative to the other group of workers and firms. This increase in nominal wages shifts the AS_0 schedule up by a small amount, to AS_1, establishing the equilibrium in the second half of the period at point C.

Similarly, at the beginning of the next period, the other half of workers and firms negotiate their contracts. This group of workers and firms also increases their nominal wages by a relatively small amount in order to maintain their competitiveness relative to the first group of workers and firms. This increase in their nominal wages shifts the AS_1 schedule up to AS_2 in the first half of the next period, taking the

FIGURE 10.6
Unanticipated Increase in Aggregate Demand with Overlapping Labour Contracts

Start from a full-employment equilibrium at point A, where all contracts are signed with the expectation that aggregate demand will be at AD^e. An unanticipated increase in aggregate demand to AD_1 shifts the equilibrium to point B. Because contracts are signed at different points in time, workers and firms worry about their position relative to others; and nominal wages adjust very slowly. Hence, the AS curve shifts up gradually over time until the economy reaches a new full-employment equilibrium at point F.

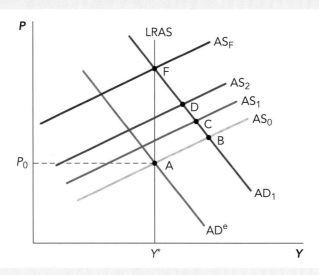

equilibrium to point D. This process goes on, and the aggregate supply curve shifts very gradually over time until the economy reaches full-employment equilibrium at point F, with the aggregate supply curve at AS_F.

Similarly, in response to an unexpected fall in aggregate demand wages will adjust downward very slowly, as workers will resist wage cuts. The complete discussion of the adjustment process in response to an unanticipated fall in aggregate demand is left to an exercise at the end of this chapter.

RECAP   AGGREGATE SUPPLY

The aggregate supply curve gives the total output supplied by firms at any given price level. The "misperception model" and the one-period non-overlapping labour contract model give rise to an aggregate supply curve that depends on the expected price, which is determined by the intersection of expected aggregate demand and the *long-run* aggregate supply curves. With these models, an anticipated change in aggregate demand shifts the aggregate supply curve and does not affect output, while an unanticipated change in aggregate demand affects output for only one period. With overlapping labour contracts, however, there is a lot of inertia in nominal wages, and changes in aggregate demand have prolonged effects on output.

10.3 DETERMINATION OF OUTPUT AND THE INFLATION RATE

We have studied how equilibrium output and price level are determined by the intersection of aggregate demand and aggregate supply curves. Most of the time in macroeconomics we are not so much interested in the determination of the price level as in the determination of the inflation rate. In this section we will study how the aggregate demand and aggregate supply relations that we derived in previous sections could be extended to study the determination of the inflation rate. To this end, we first study the *Taylor Rule* regarding the conduct of the monetary policies of the central bank. Second, we use the Taylor rule in order to express aggregate demand as a curve that gives us the total quantity of output demanded for any given inflation rate. Third, we recast the aggregate supply as a curve that gives us the total output that will be produced for any given inflation rate. Finally, we use the new aggregate demand and aggregate supply curves in order to determine the equilibrium output and inflation rate.

TAYLOR RULE

Central banks around the world no longer fix the money stock and then sit by passively watching the business cycle. They intervene in the economy rather routinely by following active rules that target interest rates and inflation rates. Modern central banks monitor closely movements in the inflation rate and output. When the inflation rate and output rise, the central bank tends to reduce the money supply to reduce aggregate demand and cool off the economy. When the inflation rate and output fall, the central bank tends to increase the money supply to increase aggregate demand and stimulate the economy.

In practice, the conduct of monetary policy is very complicated. It takes a relatively long time for changes in the money supply to affect inflation and output. The central bank has to derive the relationship between money supply and the inflation rate or output for the economy in order to deduce a target for the money supply.

Recently, in conducting their monetary policies the Bank of Canada and other central banks in industrialized countries have opted for controlling the **overnight lending rate** rather than the money supply directly; the overnight lending rate being the rate at which the chartered banks borrow and lend from each other overnight in order to cover their daily transactions. The reason is that chartered banks set their own interest rates following the overnight lending rate, and as a result by controlling the interest rate this way the central bank can speed up the process in which changes in their monetary policies can affect the inflation rate and output.

John Taylor of Stanford University has proposed a simple rule that describes the monetary policy followed by most central banks in industrialized economies. According to the **Taylor rule**, the central bank has a *target* value for the inflation rate, a *target* value Y^* for output, and an estimate r^* of what the *normal* (or neutral) real interest rate should be. If inflation or output are higher than their target values, the central bank follows a contractionary monetary policy and raises the real interest rate above r^*. Whenever inflation or output are lower than their target values, the central bank follows an expansionary monetary policy and lowers the interest rate below r^* according to the rule

$$r = r^* + \phi'' \times (\pi - \pi') + \delta \times (Y - Y^*) \tag{10.3}$$

where the parameters ϕ'' (the Greek letter "phi" with a double prime symbol) and δ (the Greek letter "delta") determine, respectively, how aggressively the central bank reacts to inflation and output.

MONETARY POLICY, AGGREGATE DEMAND, AND INFLATION

The Taylor rule shows how the central bank sets the real interest rate as a function of the deviations of the inflation rate and output from their target levels. We now discuss the relationship between the Taylor rule and the LM curve, and derive the monetary policy reaction function (MPRF), which in effect gives aggregate output demanded for each inflation rate.

With the Taylor rule the central bank is willing to supply as much money as is demanded at the interest rate given by equation (10.3). In this manner, the central bank ensures that the money market is in equilibrium for any combinations of r, π, and Y that satisfy equation (10.3). Therefore, the effective LM curve, or TR for Taylor rule, which describes the **money market equilibrium**, is given by this equation.

In the upper panel of Figure 10.7 this effective TR curve is drawn for a given value of π. It is clear from equation (10.3) that if there is an increase in π then, for each

FIGURE 10.7
The Monetary Policy Reaction Function
The actions of an inflation-fighting central bank lead to the same kind of downward-sloping relationship between prices and output as in the previous section. But in this case it is a higher inflation rate, not a higher price level, that is associated with lower real GDP.

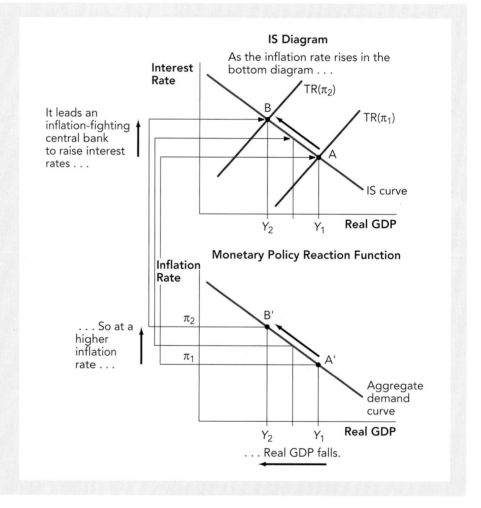

value of Y, there must be a higher r that is consistent with money market equilibrium. Hence, if, for example, the inflation rate rises from π_1 to π_2, the TR curve shifts up from $TR(\pi_1)$ to $TR(\pi_2)$.

In the lower panel of Figure 10.7 we use the equilibrium in the IS-TR diagram in order to derive the monetary policy reaction function (MPRF). Suppose the initial inflation rate is π_1. Then aggregate demand, as given by the intersection of IS and $TR(\pi_1)$ at point A will be at Y_1. When the inflation rate rises to π_2, the TR curve shifts to $TR(\pi_2)$, reducing aggregate demand to Y_2. The MPRF plots different quantities of aggregate demand, as given by the intersection points of the IS and TR curves, corresponding to each level of inflation. Hence, the intersection points A and B in the IS-TR diagram correspond to points A′ and B′ on the MPRF, which is also referred to as the aggregate demand curve.

In order to simplify the analysis, from now on we assume that the central bank cares only about inflation, and not about output. Hence, $\delta = 0$, and the Taylor rule has the simple form

$$r = r^* + \phi'' \times (\pi - \pi') \tag{10.4}$$

In this case, the central bank does not care about the level of output Y when it decides the level of interest rate r. Hence, the money market equilibrium will not depend on the Y; and the TR curve will be horizontal. The TR curve will still shift up when there is an increase in inflation, giving rise to a downward sloping MPRF.

To obtain a mathematical expression for the MPRF corresponding to the simpler form of the Taylor rule given by equation (10.4), substitute for real interest rates from equation (10.4) into the IS-equation

$$Y = \frac{A_0}{1 - MPE} - \frac{I_r + X_\varepsilon \varepsilon_r}{1 - MPE} \times r \tag{10.5}$$

to obtain

$$Y = \left[\frac{A_0}{1 - MPE} - \frac{I_r + X_\varepsilon \varepsilon_r}{1 - MPE} \times r^* \right] - \frac{\phi'' \times (I_r + X_\varepsilon \varepsilon_r)}{1 - MPE} \times (\pi - \pi') \tag{10.6}$$

This equation is too complex to work with, so once again it is useful to simplify. Define Y_0 to be the level of real GDP when the real interest rate is at its long-run normal value r^*:

$$Y_0 = \frac{A_0}{1 - MPE} - \frac{I_r + X_\varepsilon \varepsilon_r}{1 - MPE} \times r^* \tag{10.7}$$

And define a new parameter ϕ', "phi prime," to be

$$\phi' = \frac{\phi'' \times (I_r + X_\varepsilon \varepsilon_r)}{1 - MPE} \tag{10.8}$$

Then we can write our combination of the Taylor rule and the IS curve in the simple-looking form

$$Y = Y_0 - \phi' \times (\pi - \pi') \tag{10.9}$$

which is called the *monetary policy reaction function*, shown in Figure 10.7.

This monetary policy reaction function looks akin to the aggregate demand curve of the previous section. When prices increase — in this case, when inflation is higher than the central bank wants it to be — real GDP declines. There are, however, differences. The aggregate demand curve of the previous section was a relationship between the price *level* and real GDP. This monetary policy reaction function is a relationship between the inflation rate and real GDP. The previous aggregate demand curve assumed that the Bank of Canada sat like a potted plant while the business cycle proceeded. The monetary policy reaction function assumes that the Bank of Canada is engaged in the economy, trying to manage it to keep inflation close to the inflation target, and is a good model of how central banks actually behave.

This monetary policy reaction function offers a glimpse, once again, into how adjustments in prices and wages might carry the economy, over time, from the sticky-price equilibrium with potentially high unemployment and a gap between GDP and potential output back to the flexible-price equilibrium in which real GDP is equal to potential output. If real GDP is less than potential output, inflation might fall over time, and the central bank's reducing interest rates in response to low inflation would carry the economy down and to the right along the monetary policy reaction function, increasing real GDP. If real GDP is greater than potential output, inflation might rise over time, and the central bank's raising interest rates in response to high inflation would carry the economy up and to the left along the aggregate demand curve, reducing real GDP.

SHIFTS OF THE MPRF CURVE

We now consider the factors that will shift the MPRF curve. We will first study the effects of a fall in the inflation target on the MPRF curve and then consider the effects of other factors on the position of the MPRF curve.

First, consider the effect of the central bank reducing the inflation target π'. As can be seen from the Taylor rule

$$r = r* + \phi'' \times (\pi - \pi') + \delta \times (Y - Y*)$$

the reduction in π' will lead the central bank to raise the real interest rate r, for any given inflation rate and output Y. The resulting effect on the MPRF curve is shown in Figure 10.8. The increase in the real interest rate will reduce investment

FIGURE 10.8

Effects of a Reduction in the Inflation Target

The reduction in π' will lead the central bank to raise the real interest rate r, for any given inflation rate and output Y, which will reduce investment expenditures and net exports, shifting the MPRF curve to the left.

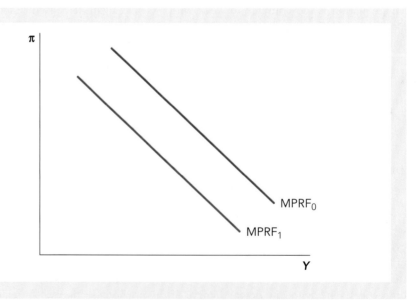

expenditures and the real exchange rate ε (recall, $\varepsilon = \varepsilon_0 + \varepsilon_r \times (r - r^f)$), which, in turn, will reduce net exports. Hence, the reduction in the inflation target reduces aggregate output demanded at any given actual inflation rate π; that is, the MPRF curve shifts to the left.

One can readily infer the effects of other shocks on the MPRF curve. Any shock that shifts the IS curve to the left will result in a lower demand for goods at any given inflation rate, resulting in a leftward shift of the MPRF curve. Such shocks were discussed in detail in Chapter 9, and include a fall in government expenditures, a fall in investment as a result of pessimism on the part of firms regarding the future level of economic activity, and a gain in confidence by currency speculators about the fundamental value of the real exchange rate.

AGGREGATE SUPPLY AND INFLATION

Inflation is an increase in the general, overall price level. An increase in the price of any one particular good — even a large increase in the price of any one particular good — is not inflation. Inflation, then, is an increase in the price of just about everything. Together, the prices of all or nearly all goods and incomes rise by approximately the same proportional amount.

In order to discuss the determinants of the inflation rate we first transform the aggregate supply equation (10.2) into a form that relates output produced to the inflation rate. We then use the resulting relation in conjunction with the monetary reaction function in order to determine the equilibrium inflation rate. Recall from equation (10.2), the aggregate supply equation is given by

$$\frac{Y - Y^*}{Y^*} = \theta \times \frac{P - P^e}{P^e}$$

It will be convenient, for the analysis of the next section, to express the aggregate supply equation in terms of the differential $\pi - \pi^e$, between actual and expected inflation, rather than the price differential $P - P^e$, as is the case in equation (10.2). This can be accomplished easily, since it can be shown, after some algebra, that $(P - P^e)/P^e$ is approximately equal to $\pi - \pi^e$; (See Analytical Exercise 5 at the end of this chapter). Thus, the aggregate supply equation can be written, alternatively, as:

$$\frac{Y - Y^*}{Y^*} = \theta \times (\pi - \pi^e) \tag{10.10}$$

This is a variant of the short-run aggregate supply function that relates the percentage deviation of actual output Y from its potential level Y^* to the deviation of actual inflation rate from its expected level π^e. According to this aggregate supply equation, whenever real GDP is greater than potential GDP, there will be stronger inflationary pressures in the economy than people had previously anticipated. Thus, inflation will accelerate, and actual inflation will be higher than people had previously anticipated. Conversely, whenever real GDP is smaller than potential GDP, there will be weaker inflationary pressures in the economy than people had previously anticipated. Thus, inflation will decelerate, and actual inflation will be lower than people had previously anticipated. Figure 10.9 plots this version of the short-run aggregate supply curve.

Equation (10.10) has a simple explanation in terms of labour contracts. In an economy in which there is ongoing inflation workers and firms will be signing

FIGURE 10.9

Output Relative to Potential and the Inflation Rate

When production is higher than potential output, prices will be higher than businesses, consumers, and workers had anticipated — and inflation will be higher than expected inflation.

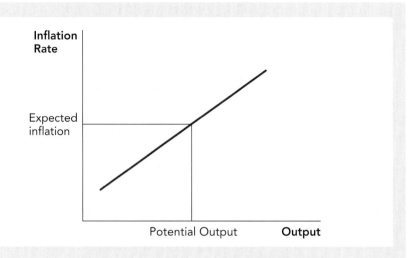

FIGURE 10.10

Effects of an Increase in Expected Inflation on AS

When the expected inflation rate increases from π^e_0 to π^e_1, the terms of the labour contracts change and wages increase at a higher rate. This shows up as a higher actual inflation rate π, at each level of output Y, thus shifting up the AS curve.

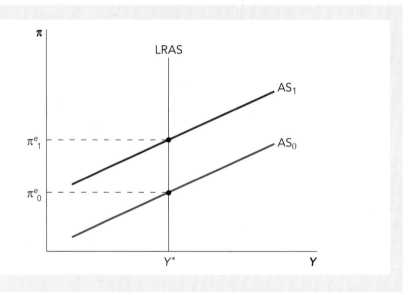

contracts with an **expected inflation** rate π^e in mind and nominal wages will be adjusted in line with π^e. Nevertheless, once a contract has been signed, the terms of the contract remain fixed for the duration of the contract; in this sense, wages are "fixed."

In this setting, if the actual inflation rate π turns out to be larger than π^e, then the revenues of the firms will be increasing at a faster rate than wages; revenues will be increasing at the rate π while wages will be increasing at the rate π^e. Consequently, firms will take advantage of the unexpectedly high profits by pushing output above its potential level. This is why the aggregate supply curve in Figure 10.9 is upward sloping.

Of course, as explained in Figure 10.10, when the expected inflation rate increases the aggregate supply curve shifts up, because when π^e increases the terms of the labour contract will change accordingly and wages will increase at a higher rate. Hence, when expected inflation π^e increases there will be higher actual inflation π, at each level of output Y, as higher rates of wage increases are passed on to the consumers in the form of higher rates of price increases.

Notice the important difference between Figures 10.3 and 10.10. Both figures measure real GDP on the horizontal axis. However, on the vertical axis, Figure 10.3 measures the price level P, whereas Figure 10.10 measures the rate of inflation π. Thus, the two figures correspond to the aggregate supply equations (10.2) and (10.10) respectively. Even though Figure 10.3 is standard in macroeconomic texts, Figure 10.10 is a very useful device because when we bring together aggregate supply and aggregate demand in inflation-output space, in the next section, we can determine the equilibrium inflation rate in the economy, rather than the equilibrium price level. The inflation rate is, certainly, a much more important variable to economists and policy makers than is the aggregate price index. Economists, politicians, and newspapers are concerned mostly with the inflation rate in the economy and much less with the level of prices.

There are other interpretations for the aggregate supply curve, which are discussed in Box 10.1.

MORE ON SHORT-RUN AGGREGATE SUPPLY

There are many possible reasons why high levels of real GDP should be associated with higher inflation and a higher price level. The "misperception model" and the labour contract models studied above give us some plausible explanations. Here we discuss other explanations.

First, when demand for products is stronger than anticipated, firms raise their prices higher than they had previously planned. When aggregate demand is higher than potential output, demand is strong in nearly every single industry. Nearly all firms raise prices and hire more workers. Employment expands beyond its average proportion of the adult population and the unemployment rate falls below the "natural" rate of unemployment — the rate at which the rate of inflation is stable. High demand gives workers extra bargaining power, and they use it to bargain for higher wage levels than they had previously planned. Unions threaten to strike, knowing that firms will have a hard time finding replacement workers. Individuals quit, knowing they can find better jobs elsewhere. Such a high-pressure economy generates wages that rise faster than anticipated. Rapid wage growth is passed along to consumers in higher prices and accelerating inflation. Thus high real GDP generates higher inflation.

Second, when aggregate demand is higher than potential output, individual economic sectors and industries in the economy quickly reach the limits of capacity: Bottlenecks emerge. Confronted with a bottleneck — a vital item, part, or process where production cannot be increased quickly — potential purchasers bid up the price of the bottlenecked item. Since a car is useless without brakes, car manufacturers will pay any price for brake assemblies if they are in short supply. Such high prices signal to the market that the bottleneck industry should expand, and triggers investment that in the end boosts productive capacity. But developing bottlenecks lead to prices that increase faster than expected — thus to accelerating inflation.

To some degree the puzzle is not why high levels of real GDP (and low levels of unemployment) are associated with higher prices and inflation, but why the association is as weak as it is. In the model of Chapter 7, after all, changes in total nominal spending show up exclusively as changes in prices and not at all as changes in real GDP. But that is a subject for the next chapter.

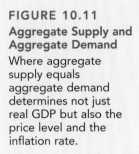

FIGURE 10.11

Aggregate Supply and Aggregate Demand

Where aggregate supply equals aggregate demand determines not just real GDP but also the price level and the inflation rate.

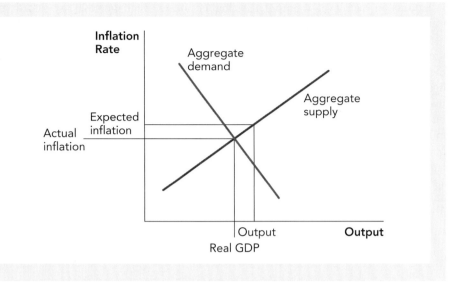

THE DETERMINATION OF OUTPUT AND INFLATION

Whatever form of the aggregate supply function we use, we can combine it with the aggregate demand or monetary policy reaction function to see not just the equilibrium level of real GDP but also what the economy's price level and inflation rate will be, as Figure 10.11 shows. The aggregate supply curve slopes upward because a higher inflation rate calls forth the more intensive use of resources and thus a higher level of production. A higher inflation rate either reduces the real money stock by raising the price level directly and thus increases the real interest rate, or induces the central bank to raise the real interest rate, and so cuts aggregate demand. Where aggregate supply and aggregate demand are equal — where the two curves cross — is the current level of real GDP and the current inflation rate.

ON THE GREAT CANADIAN SLUMP

In the early and mid-1990s, the Canadian economy experienced a slowdown in economic activity with accumulated losses in employment and output. The causes of this slowdown were hotly debated among Canadian economists at the time. Among others, Pierre Fortin of the University of Quebec at Montreal provided an excellent discussion of the potential causes of the slow growth of the Canadian economy during that period, in his presidential address to the Canadian Economics Association in 1996.[1] According to Fortin, the main cause of the slowdown of the Canadian economy in the 1990s was the high real interest rates in Canada relative to the U.S. that were brought about by the Bank of Canada in its efforts to fight inflation by setting very low inflation targets — the so called "zero inflation" policy of the Bank of Canada during that period. The framework developed in this chapter can be easily used to illustrate Fortin's arguments.

---

[1] Pierre Fortin (1996) "The Great Canadian Slump," *Canadian Journal of Economics* 29, 761–87.

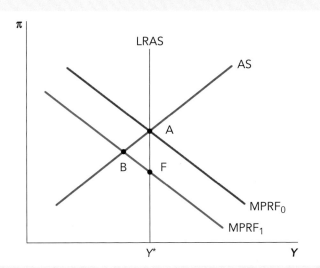

FIGURE 10.12

Effects of a Reduction in the Target Inflation Rate

If the target inflation rate is unexpectedly reduced the MPRF will shift to the left. The short-run equilibrium will be at point B. With overlapping labour contracts the aggregate supply curve will shift down very gradually, until the new long-run equilibrium is reached at point F.

Assume, as in Figure 10.12, that the Canadian economy is initially at full equilibrium at point A. Suppose next that the Central Bank unexpectedly sets the inflation target π' at a lower level. As discussed above, in relation to Figure 10.8, the Central Bank's action will shift the MPRF curve to the left. As a result, the economy's new equilibrium will be at point B, corresponding to lower actual inflation and output, compared to point A. Clearly, the Bank has achieved lower inflation at the expense of higher unemployment and lower output than potential — a slump.

The equilibrium at point B is only short-run equilibrium. With overlapping labour contracts, wages will be revised very gradually over time, and the aggregate supply curve will be shifting down slowly over time until the new long-run equilibrium is established at point F (draw the AS_F curve yourself). Just such a prolonged adjustment period followed the low inflation target adopted by the Bank of Canada in the 1990s, and is referred to as the Great Canadian Slump.

RECAP   DETERMINATION OF OUTPUT AND THE INFLATION RATE

Most of the time in macroeconomics we are not so much interested in the determination of the price level as in the determination of the inflation rate. Hence, the equations for aggregate supply and aggregate demand are usually expressed in terms of relations between output and the inflation rate. The equation for aggregate supply can be easily expressed in this form, while to transform the equation for aggregate demand, the Taylor rule, regarding the conduct of monetary policy, is used. According to the Taylor rule, the central bank has a *target* value for the inflation rate. If the inflation rate is different from its target value, the central bank changes the real interest rate.

CHAPTER SUMMARY

1. The aggregate demand relationship arises because changes in the price level and inflation rate cause shifts in the determinants of aggregate demand — either directly as changes in the price level change the money stock, or indirectly as changes in the inflation rate change the interest rate target of the central bank.

2. The aggregate supply curve captures the relationship between the aggregate output supplied by firms and the price level. The higher the price level and the inflation rate the larger the aggregate output supplied by firms is likely to be.

3. Together the aggregate supply and aggregate demand curves make up the AS-AD framework, which allows us to analyze the impact of changes in economic policy and the economic environment not just on real GDP but also on the price level and the inflation rate.

4. The Great Canadian Slump of the 1990s was caused by the Bank of Canada's policy of reducing its inflation target, which shifted the MPRF to the left. With overlapping labour contracts the aggregate supply curve shifted down very gradually, giving rise to a protracted slowdown of the economy.

KEY TERMS AND EQUATIONS

aggregate demand curve (p. 312)

aggregate supply curve (p. 314)

expected inflation (p. 326)

money market equilibrium (p. 322)

non-overlapping contracts (p. 318)

overlapping contracts (p. 318)

overnight lending rate (p. 321)

rational expectations (p. 315)

Taylor rule (p. 321)

Short-run aggregate supply curve:	$\dfrac{Y - Y^*}{Y^*} = \theta \times \dfrac{P - P^e}{P^e}$	(10.2)
Taylor rule:	$r = r^* + \phi'' \times (\pi - \pi') + \delta \times (Y - Y^*)$	(10.3)
Simplified Taylor rule:	$r = r^* + \phi'' \times (\pi - \pi')$	(10.4)
Monetary policy reaction function:	$Y = Y_0 - \phi' \times (\pi - \pi')$	(10.9)
Short-run aggregate supply curve:	$\dfrac{Y - Y^*}{Y^*} = \theta \times (\pi - \pi^e)$	(10.10)

ANALYTICAL EXERCISES

1. Describe the "overlapping labour contracts" model. Explain the effects of an unanticipated fall in aggregate demand with overlapping labour contracts.

2. Explain what would be the effect on the monetary policy reaction function of a decrease in the normal interest rate r^* in the Taylor rule
$$r = r^* + \phi'' \times (\pi - \pi') + \delta \times (Y - Y^*).$$

3. *a.* Consider the more general Taylor rule according to which the central bank has a target value π' for the inflation rate, a target value Y^* for output, an estimate r^* of what the normal real interest rate should be, and it adjusts interest rates according to
$$r = r^* + \phi'' \times (\pi - \pi') + \delta \times (Y - Y^*).$$

Derive the monetary policy reaction function corresponding to this Taylor rule.

b. Consider an extension of the Taylor rule:
$$r = r^* + \phi'' \times (\pi - \pi') + \delta \times (Y - Y^*) + \gamma \times (\varepsilon - \varepsilon^*)$$
where γ is the Greek letter "gamma," and ε^* is the target level of the real exchange rate.

Derive the monetary reaction function corresponding to this version of the Taylor rule.

c. Discuss which version of the Taylor rule best describes the current objectives of the Bank of Canada.

4. Suppose the economy has a given money stock M, price level P, and real demand for money given by the

liquidity preference schedule $L = 20 - 1000 \times (r + \pi^e) + 0.01 \times Y$. Further assume that the economy's IS curve is given by $Y = 1000 - 2000 \times r$.

a. Derive the economy's LM curve for given M, P, and π^e.

b. Combine the IS and LM curves to derive the equation for the aggregate demand curve, AD.

c. Draw the AD curve when $M = \$3000$ billion and $\pi^e = 0.03$. What is the value of Y when $P = 100$?

d. Use the IS and LM equations to solve for the equilibrium levels of r and Y when M, P, and π^e have the same values as in question *c*, above. Comment on your results.

e. Show what happens to the AD curve when i) M increases by \$30 billion and ii) π^e increases by 1 percent.

5. Show that $(P - P^e)/P^e$ is approximately equal to $\pi - \pi^e$. (Hint: Let $P/P^e - 1 \equiv \eta$ and take a first-order Taylor series approximation of e^{η} around $\eta = 0$.)

POLICY EXERCISES

1. It is sometimes argued that governments should announce their policies in advance in order to minimize surprises to the private sector. Discuss.

2. In the year 2000, faced with a stock market crash, the U.S. Federal Reserve reduced real interest rates. Discuss what would be the effects of a stock market crash on different components of aggregate expenditures and how it will affect the aggregate demand curve. How would the response of the Federal Reserve help stabilize the economy?

3. Explain as completely as you can the effect of a fall in aggregate demand with overlapping wage contracts.

4. Explain whether in the long run target inflation should be equal to the expected and actual inflation rates.

Is there a reason why when a country adopts a low inflation target it also reduces government expenditures?

5. In the early 1990s the Bank of Canada embarked on a tight monetary policy in order to reduce the inflation rate, while the government followed a contractionary fiscal policy in order to reduce the budget deficit. What does the AD-AS model predict about the effects of these policies on interest rates and the exchange rate? What would be the effect of these policies on investment? Does your answer support the view expressed by some economists that these policies contributed to a substantial reduction in growth in Canada in the early 1990s?

11

The Phillips Curve and Expectations

QUESTIONS

What is the Phillips curve?

How has the natural rate of unemployment changed in Canada over the past two generations?

What determines the expected rate of inflation?

How can we tell how expectations of inflation are formed — whether they are static, adaptive, or rational?

How useful is the aggregate demand–aggregate supply framework — the IS-LM model and the Phillips curve — for understanding macroeconomic events in Canada over the past two generations?

How do we connect the sticky-price model of this part, Part IV, with the flexible-price model of Part III?

This chapter has two major goals: to complete the construction of the sticky-price model begun in Chapter 8, and to link the sticky-price macroeconomic model analysis of Part IV with the flexible-price macroeconomic model analysis of Part III. The key to accomplishing both of these is an analytical tool called the Phillips curve. The Phillips curve, a version of the aggregate supply relationship, describes the relationship between inflation and unemployment, according to which a higher rate of unemployment is associated with a lower rate of inflation.

11.1 AGGREGATE SUPPLY AND THE PHILLIPS CURVE

UNEMPLOYMENT

So far in this book one of our six key economic variables, the unemployment rate, has been largely absent. In Part II, the long-run growth section, unemployment was not a significant factor. In Part III, the flexible-price macroeconomic model section, there were no fluctuations in unemployment. Wages and prices were flexible, and so labour supply balanced labour demand.

Now it is time to bring unemployment to centre stage. Back in Chapter 2 we studied **Okun's law,** the simple yet strong relationship between the unemployment rate and real GDP. Letting u stand for the rate of unemployment and u^* for the economy's natural rate of unemployment at which there is neither upward nor downward pressure on inflation, and letting Y stand for real GDP and Y^* for potential output, Okun's law is

$$u - u^* = -0.6 \times \frac{Y - Y^*}{Y^*} \qquad (11.1)$$

Because of Okun's law, we do not have to separately keep track of what is happening to real GDP (relative to potential output) and to the unemployment rate. Using Okun's law, you can easily go back and forth from one to the other. It is usually more convenient to work with the unemployment rate than with the output gap — real GDP relative to potential output — if only because the unemployment rate is easier to measure. Box 11.1 presents examples of how to use Okun's law to go back and forth.

FORMS OF OKUN'S LAW

As we saw in Chapter 2, Okun's law relates the unemployment rate u (relative to the natural rate of unemployment u^*) to real GDP Y (relative to potential output Y^*). When real GDP Y is equal to Y^*, then the unemployment rate u is equal to the natural rate of unemployment u^*. When real GDP Y is different from Y^*, unemployment u will be different from the natural rate of unemployment u^* by an amount

$$u - u^* = -0.6 \times \frac{Y - Y^*}{Y^*}$$

When real GDP is above potential output, unemployment will be relatively low. When real GDP is below potential output, unemployment will be relatively high. The percentage point gap between unemployment and its natural rate will be three-fifths the magnitude of the percentage point gap between real GDP and potential output.

We can reverse Okun's law to put the output gap between real GDP and potential output on the left-hand side:

$$\frac{Y - Y^*}{Y^*} = -1.7 \times (u - u^*)$$

It can sometimes be more useful to write Okun's law in its year-to-year change form. Once again we use the Greek capital letter delta Δ as a symbol for the annual change in a variable. If the natural rate of unemployment u^* is constant, and if we identify the proportional rate of growth of potential output with the trend rate of population growth n plus the trend rate of productivity growth g, then we can derive the year-to-year change form of Okun's law from the equation above. We start with

$$\Delta u - \Delta u^* = -0.6 \times \frac{\Delta Y - \Delta Y^*}{Y^*}$$

Since the natural rate of unemployment u^* is constant, this is equivalent to

$$\Delta u = -0.6 \times \left(\frac{\Delta Y}{Y^*} - \frac{\Delta Y^*}{Y^*} \right)$$

Using the definition of the proportional rate of growth of potential output:

$$\Delta u = 0.6 \times \left(\frac{\Delta Y}{Y^*} - (n + g) \right)$$

This equation tells us that in any year the unemployment rate will fall (or rise) by an amount equal to 0.6 times the gap between the proportional growth rate of real GDP minus n plus g, the proportional growth rate of potential output.

Alternatively, we can put the change in real GDP proportional to potential output on the left-hand side:

$$\frac{\Delta Y}{Y^*} = (n + g) - 1.7 \times \Delta u$$

All these forms of Okun's law can be useful at one point or another in helping us to go back and forth between movements in the unemployment rate and changes in real GDP.

Moreover, the unemployment rate is of special interest because a high unemployment rate means low social welfare (see Box 11.2).

11.2   BOX   POLICY

COSTS OF HIGH UNEMPLOYMENT

In a typical Canadian recession, unemployment rises by 2 percentage points. By Okun's law, that means that the **output gap** — real GDP relative to potential output — falls by some 3.4 percent. Moreover, recessions are not permanent; with rare exceptions, they are over in a year or two and are followed by periods of rapid growth that return real GDP to its pre-recession growth trend. Even the steepest post–World War II recession raised the unemployment rate by only 4 percentage points, and it took only three years after the recession trough for unemployment to fall back to a normal level.

Yet people fear a deep recession much more than they appear to value an extra four years' worth of economic growth. For example, the memory of the 1981–1982 and 1991–1992 recessions has substantially altered Canadians' perceptions of how the economy works, how much they dare risk in the search for higher wages, and how confident they can be that their jobs are secure.

Why do episodes of high recession unemployment have such a large psychological impact? The most likely answer is that recessions are feared because they do not distribute their impact equally. Workers who keep their jobs are only lightly affected, while those who lose their jobs suffer a near-total loss of income. People fear a 2-percent chance of losing half their income much more than they fear a certain loss of 1 percent. Thus it is much worse for 2 percent of the people each to lose half their income than for everyone to lose 1 percent. It is the unequal distribution of the costs of high unemployment that makes recessions so feared — and that makes voters so anxious to elect economic policy makers who will successfully avoid them.

THREE FACES OF AGGREGATE SUPPLY

In the last part of Chapter 10, we looked at the aggregate supply relationship. Looking at it one way, we saw that when real GDP is greater than potential output, the price level is likely to be higher than people had expected. In this case aggregate supply relates the price *level* P relative to the previously expected price level P^e to the *level* of real GDP Y relative to potential output Y^*:

$$\frac{Y - Y^*}{Y^*} = \theta \times \left(\frac{P - P^e}{P^e} \right) \tag{11.2}$$

Looking at it a second way, we saw aggregate supply as a relationship between the inflation *rate* π relative to the previously expected inflation rate π^e, and the *level* of real GDP, Y, relative to potential output Y^*:

$$\frac{Y - Y^*}{Y^*} = \theta \times (\pi - \pi^e) \tag{11.3}$$

Because inflation this year minus what inflation was expected to be is the same as the proportional difference between the price level now and what the price level was expected to be, these are different ways of looking at the same economic process.

We can use Okun's law to look at aggregate supply in yet a third way. Because

$$\frac{Y - Y^*}{Y^*} = -1.7 \times (u - u^*) \tag{11.4}$$

we can substitute the right-hand side of the equation above for $(Y - Y^*)/Y$ in our aggregate supply function

$$-1.7 \times (u - u^*) = \theta \times (\pi - \pi^e) \tag{11.5}$$

If we rearrange to put the inflation rate by itself on the left-hand side:

$$\pi = \pi^e - \frac{1.7}{\theta} \times (u - u^*) \tag{11.6}$$

and then define the parameter β (the Greek letter "beta") as $\beta = 1.7/\theta$, the resulting function is

$$\pi = \pi^e - \beta \times (u - u^*) \tag{11.7}$$

This function is called the Phillips curve, after the New Zealand economist A. W. Phillips, who first wrote in the 1950s of the relationship between unemployment and the rate of change of prices. We will usually want to add an extra term to the Phillips curve:

$$\pi = \pi^e - \beta \times (u - u^*) + \varepsilon^s \tag{11.8}$$

where ε^s represents supply shocks — like the 1973 oil price increase — that can directly affect the rate of inflation.

FIGURE 11.1

The Phillips Curve

When inflation is higher than expected inflation and production is higher than potential output, the unemployment rate will be lower than the natural rate of unemployment. There is an inverse relationship in the short run between inflation and unemployment.

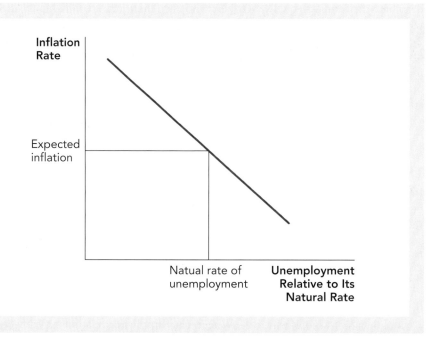

Figure 11.1 sketches the **Phillips curve** on a graph with the unemployment rate on the horizontal axis and the inflation rate on the vertical axis. As you can see, it is an inverse relationship between inflation and unemployment. The Phillips curve is the third way of expressing the aggregate supply function. The underlying economic meaning is the same no matter which form — output-price level (Figure 10.3), output-inflation (Figure 10.7), or unemployment-inflation (Figure 11.1) — you use. From this point on, however, we will almost always use the unemployment-inflation Phillips curve form. It is simply more convenient than the other forms.

THE PHILLIPS CURVE EXAMINED

The slope of the Phillips curve depends on how sticky wages and prices are. The stickier they are, the smaller the parameter β is, and the flatter the Phillips curve is. The parameter β varies widely from country to country and era to era. In Canada today θ is about 4.7 and $\beta = \dfrac{1.7}{4.7} = 0.36$. When the Phillips curve is flat, even large movements in the unemployment rate have little effect on the price level. When wages and prices are less sticky, the Phillips curve is nearly vertical. Then even small movements in the unemployment rate have the potential to cause large changes in the price level.

Whenever unemployment is equal to its natural rate, inflation is equal to **expected inflation**. Thus we can determine the position of the Phillips curve if we know the **natural rate of unemployment** and the expected rate of inflation. A higher natural rate moves the Phillips curve right. Higher expected inflation moves the Phillips curve up. (See Figure 11.2.) If the past 40 years have made anything clear, it is that the Phillips curve shifts around substantially as *both* expected inflation and the natural rate change. Neither is a constant. The current natural rate of unemployment u^* is about 7.5 percent. The current rate of expected inflation π^e is about 2 percent per year. But both will be different in the future. One other important factor affects the

FIGURE 11.2
Shifts in the Phillips Curve
When expected inflation changes, the position of the Phillips curve changes too.

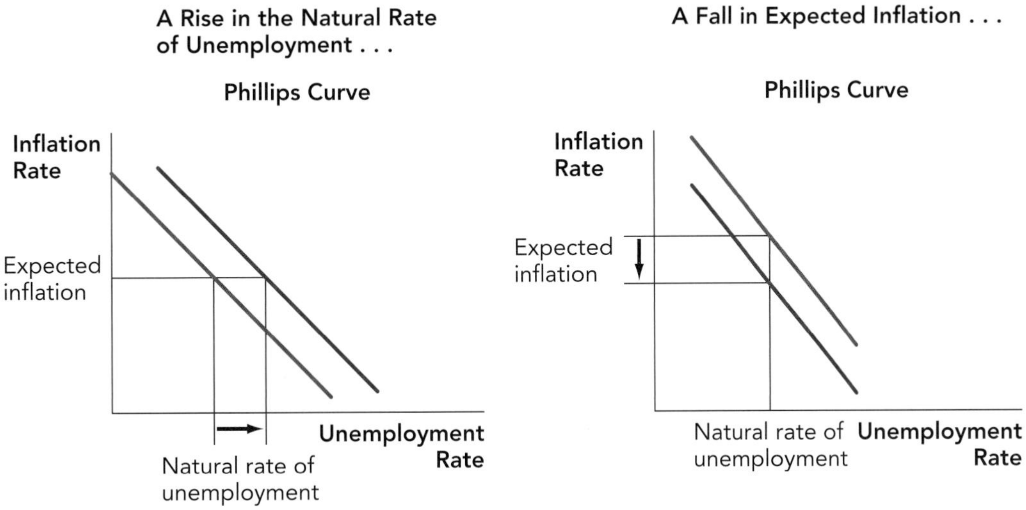

position of the Phillips curve. Adverse supply shocks (like the 1973 tripling of world oil prices) move the Phillips curve up. Favourable supply shocks (like the 1986 worldwide declines in oil prices) move the Phillips curve down.

RECAP   AGGREGATE SUPPLY AND THE PHILLIPS CURVE

The Phillips curve is an inverse relationship between inflation and unemployment. It is the most convenient form of the aggregate supply relationship, so it is the one that we use. The Phillips curve tells us that when unemployment is below its natural rate, inflation is higher than expected inflation; conversely, when unemployment is above its natural rate, inflation is lower than expected inflation. The stickier wages and prices are, the flatter the Phillips curve is. When the Phillips curve is flat, even large movements in the unemployment rate have little effect on the price level. When wages and prices are less sticky, the Phillips curve is nearly vertical. Then even small movements in the unemployment rate have the potential to cause large changes in the price level.

11.2 AGGREGATE DEMAND AND INFLATION

In Chapter 10 we combined the IS curve with the Taylor rule for setting monetary policy and produced an aggregate demand function that showed how real GDP depended on the inflation rate. This **monetary policy reaction function (MPRF)** is

$$Y = Y_0 - \phi' \times (\pi - \pi') \tag{11.9}$$

However, we would prefer an aggregate demand equation with the unemployment rate on the left-hand side so we can use it along with the Phillips curve. So we use Okun's law to replace real GDP with the unemployment rate on the left-hand side:

$$u = u_0 + \phi \times (\pi - \pi') \qquad (11.10)$$

where the parameter ϕ is the product of three different things, as is shown at great length in Box 11.3:

- How much the central bank raises the real interest rate in response to a rise in inflation.
- The slope of the IS curve — how much real GDP changes in response to a change in the real interest rate.
- The Okun's law coefficient — how large a change in unemployment is produced by a change in real GDP.

Together, this unemployment form of the aggregate demand relationship and the Phillips curve equation, which is

$$\pi = \pi^e - \beta(u - u^*) + \varepsilon^s,$$

allow us to determine what the inflation and unemployment rates will be in the economy. (And when we have determined the unemployment rate, Okun's law

---

BOX 11.3

DETAILS

FROM INCOME-EXPENDITURE TO THE PHILLIPS CURVE AND THE MPRF
We have spent little time on the deeper parameters and functions that underpin the parameter, β, that governs the slope of the Phillips curve. The most we can say is that $\beta = 1.7/\theta$, where θ is the proportional amount of extra productive effort called forth by an extra 1-percent rise in the price level. Each of the competing theories of aggregate supply mentioned in Chapter 10 hopes to account for why θ is what it is. But none would claim to be able to do so yet.

By contrast, four chapters worth of detail underpins the parameter, ϕ, that governs the slope of the monetary policy reaction function.

$$u = u_0 + \phi \times (\pi - \pi')$$

The determinants of ϕ are:

$$\phi = \frac{1}{1.7} \times \phi' \times (I_r + X_\varepsilon\varepsilon_r) \times \frac{1}{1 - (C_y \times (1 - t) - IM_y)} \times \frac{1}{Y^*}$$

All four of these terms have been analyzed at considerable length.
The first term

$$\frac{1}{1.7}$$

comes from Okun's law. It is the change in the unemployment rate produced by a 1-percent change in real GDP relative to potential output.
The second term

$$\phi'$$

is a measure of how much central bankers raise interest rates in response to higher inflation.

The third term — $(I_r + X_\varepsilon \varepsilon_r)$ — comes from Chapter 9. It is the interest sensitivity of autonomous spending. It incorporates both the effect of interest rates on investment spending, and the effect of interest rates on the exchange rate and hence on exports spending too. The fourth term

$$\frac{1}{1 - (C_y \times (1-t) - IM_y)}$$

comes from Chapter 8. It is the multiplier — 1 divided by 1 minus the *MPE*. And the fifth term — $1/Y^*$ — is needed to transform the dollar change in aggregate demand into a percentage-point change in demand so that Okun's Law can be applied.

Almost all of the work of the preceding three chapters is thus encapsulated in this single parameter ϕ.

allows us to immediately calculate real GDP as well.) Once again, the economy's equilibrium is where the curves cross: The Phillips curve determines inflation as a function of the unemployment rate, the MPRF determines the unemployment rate as a function of the inflation rate, and the two must be consistent, as Figure 11.3 shows.

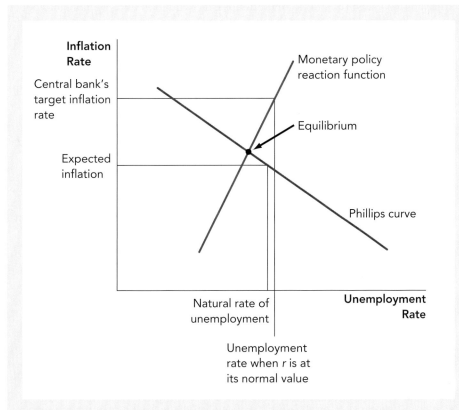

FIGURE 11.3
Equilibrium Levels of Unemployment and Inflation

As we have seen before, the position of the Phillips curve depends on:

- u^*, the natural rate of unemployment.
- π^e, the expected rate of inflation.
- ε^s, any current supply shocks affecting inflation.

The position of the aggregate demand curve, the MPRF, depends on

- u_0, the level of unemployment when the real interest rate r is at what the central bank thinks of as its long-run average rate.
- π', the **central bank's target level of inflation.**

All five of these factors together, along with the parameters θ and β — the slopes of the monetary policy reaction function and of the Phillips curve — determine the economy's equilibrium inflation and unemployment rates. Box 11.4 takes a more detailed look at precisely how.

11.4

BOX

DETAILS

SOLVING FOR EQUILIBRIUM INFLATION AND UNEMPLOYMENT
From our aggregate demand relationship, the MPRF:

$$u = u_0 + \phi \times (\pi - \pi')$$

and our aggregate supply relationship, the Phillips curve:

$$\pi = \pi^e - \beta(u = u^*) + \varepsilon^s$$

it is straightforward to find, algebraically, the economy's unemployment rate and inflation rate. Substitute the second Phillips curve equation into the monetary policy reaction function and solve for the unemployment rate:

$$u = \left(\frac{1}{1 + \phi\beta} u_0 + \frac{\phi\beta}{1 + \phi\beta} u^* \right) + \frac{\phi}{1 + \phi\beta} (\pi^e - \pi') + \frac{\phi}{1 + \phi\beta} \varepsilon^s$$

And substitute the first monetary policy reaction function equation into the Phillips curve and solve for the inflation rate:

$$\pi = \left(\frac{1}{1 + \phi\beta} \pi^e + \frac{\phi\beta}{1 + \phi\beta} \pi' \right) + \frac{\beta}{1 + \phi\beta} (u^* - u_0) + \frac{1}{1 + \phi\beta} \varepsilon^s$$

We see that the unemployment rate is equal to

- A weighted average of the natural rate of unemployment u^* and the unemployment rate u_0 when the central bank has set the real interest rate to its normal average value r^* (the greater the product of the slope parameters θ and β, the higher the relative weight on the natural rate u^*).
- A term that depends on the difference between the expected rate of inflation π^e and the central bank's target rate of inflation π'; when the first is higher than the second, unemployment is higher because the central bank has raised interest rates to fight inflation.
- A term that depends on current supply shocks ε^s.

We see that the inflation rate is equal to

- A weighted average of the expected rate of inflation π^e and the central bank's target rate of inflation π' (the greater the product of the slope parameters ϕ and β, the higher the relative weight on the target rate π').
- A term that depends on the difference between the natural rate of unemployment u^* and the unemployment rate u_0 when the central bank has set the real interest

rate to its normal average value r^*; when the first is higher than the second, inflation is higher because there is an inflationary bias to demand when the real interest rate is at its normal average value r^*.

- A term that depends on current supply shocks ε^s.

We can use this framework to analyze the effects of a shift in policy on the economy's equilibrium. For example, consider a depression abroad that lowers demand for exports. If the central bank takes a hands-off approach to this fall in exports and does not lower its estimate of r^*, the normal value for the real interest rate, then this change in the economic environment causes a rise in u_0, the unemployment rate when the real interest rate is at its normal value r^*, by an amount Δu_0. Since none of the other parameters of the inflation-unemployment framework change, the effect on the equilibrium levels of unemployment and inflation can be calculated immediately as

$$\Delta u = \frac{1}{1 + \phi\beta} \Delta u_0$$

Substitute the first monetary policy reaction function equation into the Phillips curve and solve for the change in the inflation rate:

$$\Delta \pi = \frac{-\beta}{1 + \phi\beta} \Delta u_0$$

The fact that the central bank has not reacted to the fall in export demand by lowering its r^* means that the monetary policy reaction function has shifted to the right, as Figure 11.4 shows, and the economy's equilibrium has moved down and to the right along the Phillips curve.

FIGURE 11.4
Effects of a Fall in Exports
A fall in exports with no countervailing change in the central bank's view of the normal target interest rate r^* shifts the MPRF right, raises the equilibrium unemployment rate, and lowers the inflation rate.

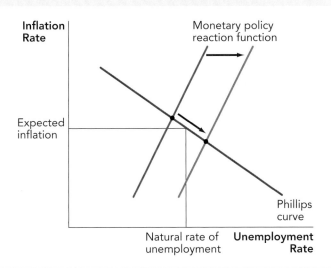

RECAP   **AGGREGATE DEMAND AND INFLATION**

We need a form of the aggregate demand function expressed in terms of the unemployment rate in order for the function to be useful alongside the Phillips curve. So we write an unemployment-rate version of the monetary policy reaction function (MPRF), which was set out in Chapter 10 as follows: $u = u_0 + \phi \times (\pi - \pi')$. The unemployment rate u is equal to u_0, the unemployment rate when the real interest rate is at what the central bank estimates is its normal value, plus a parameter ϕ times the difference between the current inflation rate π and the central bank's target inflation rate π'. This MPRF arises because the central bank raises the real interest rate above normal whenever inflation accelerates, and so higher inflation produces lower demand and higher unemployment.

The parameter θ is the product of three different things: (1) how much the central bank raises the real interest rate in response to a rise in inflation; (2) the slope of the IS curve — how much real GDP changes in response to a change in the real interest rate; and (3) Okun's law — how large a change in unemployment is produced by a change in real GDP.

11.3 THE NATURAL RATE OF UNEMPLOYMENT

In English, the word "natural" normally carries strong positive connotations of normal and desirable, but a high natural rate of unemployment is a bad thing. Unemployment cannot be reduced below its natural rate without accelerating inflation, so a high natural rate means that expansionary fiscal and monetary policy are largely ineffective as tools to reduce unemployment.

The natural rate of unemployment is measured by "filtering" the data on the actual unemployment rate in such a way as to remove the short-term random fluctuations and retain only the long-term trend unemployment. The specific filtering technique that we use in this book is called the Hodrick-Prescott filter (or HP filter for short). The same technique can be used to calculate the long-term trend for other macroeconomic variables, such as potential output (in Chapter 8) or cyclically adjusted budget balance (in Chapter 13). The smooth curve in Figure 11.5 shows Canada's natural rate of unemployment, estimated with the HP filter over the period 1961–2004. Clearly, Canada's natural rate of unemployment has changed over time, but in a much smoother fashion than the actual unemployment rate.

Today, most estimates of the current Canadian "natural" rate of unemployment lie between 7 and 8 percent. But all agree that uncertainty about the level of the natural rate is substantial. And the natural rate has fluctuated substantially over the past two generations, as Figure 11.5 shows.

Notice since early 1992 the natural rate of unemployment has been falling over time. It is not easy to identify the determinants of the natural rate of unemployment, because the natural rate itself is not observed; we simply compute it from the data of the actual unemployment rate, using statistical techniques like the HP filter. Nevertheless, we can point to some plausible factors. First, the fall in the natural rate of unemployment has coincided with gains in productivity during this period, which are attributed primarily to the adoption of information technology into the production process. Second, the new information and communications technologies, combined with higher education levels, have allowed more women to enter the labour force in recent years, and this is another factor for the decline in the natural rate of

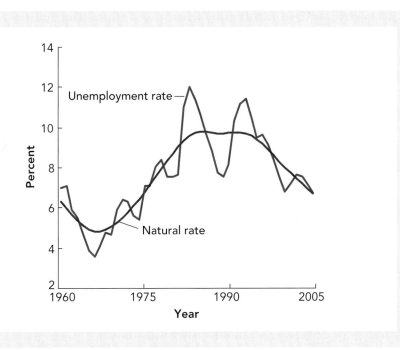

Source: Adapted from the Statistics Canada CANSIM II database, V2064894.

FIGURE 11.5
Fluctuations in Unemployment and the Natural Rate
The natural rate of unemployment is not fixed. It varies substantially from decade to decade.

unemployment in Canada in recent years. Further, reduced unemployment insurance benefits and relatively weaker labour unions in Canada have increased labour market flexibility, by reducing downward rigidity in wages, and may have also contributed to the observed reduction in the natural rate of unemployment in Canada.

Broadly, four sets of factors have powerful influence over the natural rate. We explain each, in turn, below.

DEMOGRAPHY AND THE NATURAL RATE

First, the natural rate changes as the relative age and educational distribution of the labour force changes. Teenagers have higher unemployment rates than adults; thus an economy with a lot of teenagers will have a higher natural rate. More experienced and more skilled workers find job hunting an easier experience and take less time to find a new job when they leave an old one. Thus the natural rate of unemployment will fall when the labour force becomes more experienced and more skilled. Women used to have higher unemployment rates than men — although this is no longer true in Canada. The more educated tend to have lower rates of unemployment than the less well educated.

A large part of the estimated rise in the natural rate from 5 percent or so in the 1960s to 9 percent by the end of the 1970s was due to changing demography. Some component of the decline in the natural rate since then was due to the increasing job-hunting experience of the very large baby-boom cohort. But the exact, quantitative relationship between demography and the natural rate is not well understood.

INSTITUTIONS AND THE NATURAL RATE

Second, institutions have a powerful influence on the natural rate. Some economies have strong labour unions; other economies have weak ones. Some unions sacrifice

http://www.statcan.ca/english/
freepub/11-516-XIE/sectiona/
toc.htm
http://cansim2.statcan.ca/

employment in their industry for higher wages; others settle for lower wages in return for employment guarantees. Some economies lack apprenticeship programs that make the transition from education to employment relatively straightforward; others make the school-to-work transition easy. In each pair, the first increases and the second reduces the natural rate of unemployment. Barriers to worker mobility raise the natural rate, whether the barrier be subsidized housing that workers lose if they move (as in Britain in the 1970s and the 1980s) or high taxes that a firm must pay to hire a worker (as in France from the 1970s to today).

However, the link between economic institutions and the natural rate is neither simple nor straightforward. The institutional features that many observers today point to as a source of high European unemployment now were also present in the European economies in the 1970s, when European unemployment was low. Once again the quantitative relationships are not well understood.

PRODUCTIVITY GROWTH AND THE NATURAL RATE

Third, in recent years it has become more and more likely that a major determinant of the natural rate is the rate of productivity growth. The era of slow productivity growth from the mid-1970s to the mid-1990s saw a relatively high natural rate. By contrast, rapid productivity growth before 1973 and moderate productivity growth after 1995 seem to have generated a lower natural rate.

Why should a productivity growth slowdown generate a higher natural rate? A higher rate of productivity growth allows firms to pay higher real wage increases and remain profitable. If workers' aspirations for real wage growth depend on the rate of unemployment, then a slowdown in productivity growth will increase the natural rate. If real wages grow faster than productivity for an extended period of time, profits will disappear. Long before that point is reached, businesses will begin to fire workers and unemployment will rise. Thus if productivity growth slows, unemployment will rise. Unemployment will keep rising until workers' real wage aspirations fall to a rate consistent with current productivity growth, as shown in Figure 11.6.

THE PAST LEVEL OF UNEMPLOYMENT AND THE NATURAL RATE

Fourth and last, the natural rate will be high if unemployment has been high. Before 1980 western European economies had unemployment rates lower than the 5 to 6 percent that the United States averaged back then. But the mid-1970s brought recessions. European unemployment rose, but did not fall back much in subsequent recoveries. Workers left unemployed for two or three years had lost their skills, lost their willingness to show up on time, and lost their interest in even looking for new jobs. Thus the natural rate rose sharply in Europe with each business cycle. By the late 1990s European unemployment averaged 8 percent, and inflation was stable (see Figure 11.7). Long-term unemployment appears especially poisonous for an economy.

This laundry list of factors affecting the natural rate is incomplete. Do not think that economists understand much about why the natural rate is what it is. Almost every economist was surprised by the large rise in the natural rate in western Europe over the past quarter century. Almost every economist was surprised by the sharp fall in America's natural rate in the 1990s. And economists cannot confidently account for these shifts even in retrospect.

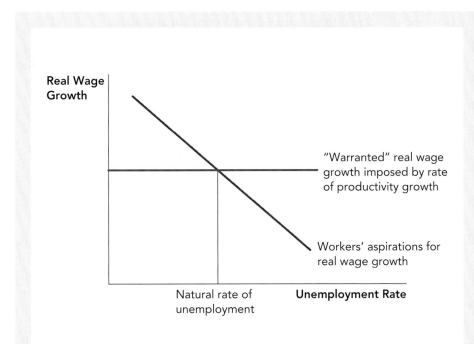

FIGURE 11.6
Real Wage Growth Aspirations and Productivity
Workers aspire to earn higher real wages. How much workers demand in the way of increases in the average real wage is a function of unemployment: The higher unemployment is, the lower workers' aspirations for real wage growth are. But in the long run real wages can grow no faster than productivity. Hence the natural rate of unemployment is whatever rate of unemployment curbs real wage demands so that they are consistent with productivity growth.

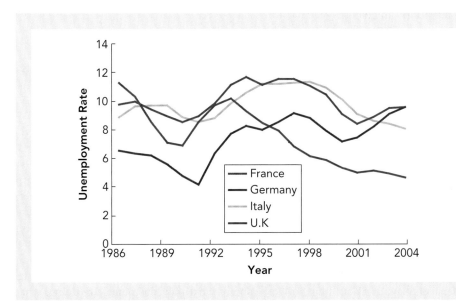

FIGURE 11.7
Patterns of European Unemployment, 1986–2004
The growth of unemployment in the U.S. and western European countries, 1986–2004.

Source: OECD Economic Outlook (No. 78), Table 14.

Concerning the Canadian experience, while the actual unemployment rates in Canada were comparable to the U.S. rates in the 1960s, they were persistently higher than the U.S. rates in the 1970s and 1980s. As a result, the natural rate in Canada remained substantially above the U.S. natural rate. The current natural rate in the U.S. is between 4.5 and 5 percent, whereas the current natural rate in Canada is between 6.5 and 7 percent.

http://www.oecd.org

> **RECAP   THE NATURAL RATE OF UNEMPLOYMENT**
>
> The natural rate of unemployment is not a constant. It has fluctuated substantially over the past two generations, and it will continue to fluctuate. Four sets of factors drive fluctuations in the natural rate of unemployment. First, the natural rate changes as the relative age and educational distribution of the labour force changes. Second, countries with inflexible labour markets are likely to have high natural rates of unemployment. Third, faster productivity growth brings a lower natural rate with it. Fourth, the natural rate will be high if unemployment has been high in the past and large numbers of workers have become discouraged.

11.4 EXPECTED INFLATION

The natural rate of unemployment and expected inflation together determine the location of the Phillips curve because it passes through the point where inflation is equal to expected inflation and unemployment is equal to its natural rate. Higher expected inflation would move the Phillips curve upward. But who does the expecting? And when do people form expectations relevant for this year's Phillips curve?

Economists work with three basic scenarios for how managers, workers, and investors go about forecasting the future and forming their expectations:

- **Static expectations** of inflation prevail when people ignore the fact that inflation can change.
- **Adaptive expectations** prevail when people assume the future will be like the recent past.
- **Rational expectations** prevail when people use all the information they have as best they can.

The Phillips curve behaves very differently under each of these three scenarios.

THE PHILLIPS CURVE UNDER STATIC EXPECTATIONS

If inflation expectations are *static,* expected inflation never changes. People just don't think about inflation. In some years unemployment will be relatively low; in those years inflation will be relatively high. In other years unemployment is higher, and then inflation will be lower. But as long as expectations of inflation remain static (and the natural rate of unemployment unchanged), the trade-off between inflation and unemployment will not change from year to year (see Figure 11.8).

If inflation has been low and stable, businesses will probably hold static inflation expectations. Why? Because the art of managing a business is complex enough as it is. Managers have a lot of things to worry about: what their customers are doing, what their competitors are doing, whether their technology is adequate, and how applicable technology is changing. When inflation has been low or stable, everyone has better things to focus their attention on than the rate of inflation. Box 11.5 discusses the classic example of how the economy behaves under static expectations: The 1960s.

THE PHILLIPS CURVE UNDER ADAPTIVE EXPECTATIONS

Suppose that the inflation rate varies too much for workers and businesses to ignore it completely. What then? As long as inflation last year is a good guide to inflation

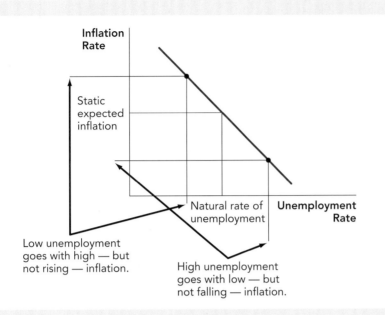

FIGURE 11.8
Static Expectations of Inflation
If inflation expectations are static, the economy moves up and to the left and down and to the right along a Phillips curve that does not change its position.

this year, workers, investors, and managers are likely to hold *adaptive* expectations and forecast inflation by assuming that this year will be like last year. Adaptive forecasts are good forecasts as long as inflation changes only slowly; and adaptive expectations do not absorb a lot of time and energy that can be better used thinking about other issues.

Under such adaptive inflation expectations, the Phillips curve can be written

$$\pi_t = \pi_{t-1} - \beta(u_t - u_t^*) + \varepsilon_t^s \tag{11.11}$$

where π_{t-1}— inflation last year — stands in place of π_t^e because that's what expected inflation is: inflation last year. Under such a set of *adaptive expectations*, the Phillips curve will shift up or down depending on whether last year's inflation was higher or

STATIC EXPECTATIONS OF INFLATION IN THE 1960S

The standard example of static expectations is expectations of inflation in the 1960s. When unemployment was above 5.5 percent, inflation was below 1.5 percent. When unemployment was around 4 percent, inflation was around 2 percent. When unemployment was around 3.6 percent inflation was around 4 percent. This Phillips curve, shown in Figure 11.9, did not shift up or down in response to changes in expected inflation during the decade. Instead, the economy moved along a stable Phillips curve.

But inflation expectations remained static — and the Phillips curve unchanged — only when inflation was low and steady: As inflation rose and became more variable at the end of the 1960s, firms and workers began changing their expectations to *adaptive* ones. And in the early 1970s increases in expected inflation shifted the Phillips curve upward. In Figure 11.9, we can see initial signs of such an upward shift in the Phillips curve from 1967 to 1968, when there was a simultaneous increase in both inflation and unemployment.

BOX 11.5

EXAMPLE

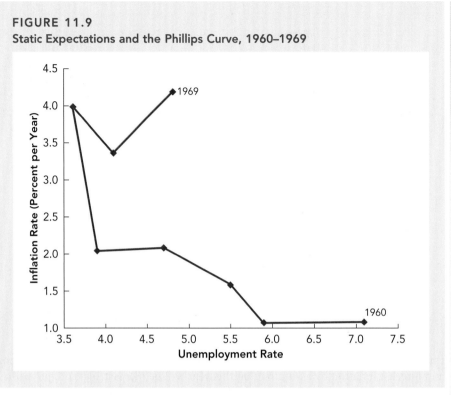

FIGURE 11.9
Static Expectations and the Phillips Curve, 1960–1969

Source: Adapted from the Statistics Canada CANSIM I database, Series P100000 (Consumer Price Index) and from the Statistics Canada publication, "Historical Statistics of Canada," Catalogue 11-516, 1983, Series D233.

lower than the previous year's. Under adaptive expectations, inflation accelerates when unemployment is less than the natural unemployment rate, and decelerates when unemployment is more than the natural rate. Hence this Phillips curve is sometimes called the accelerationist Phillips curve. Box 11.6 presents an example of this "acceleration." And Box 11.7 discusses the dilemmas of economic policy under adaptive expectations.

THE PHILLIPS CURVE UNDER RATIONAL EXPECTATIONS

What happens when government policy and the economic environment are changing rapidly enough that adaptive expectations lead to significant errors, and are no longer good enough for managers or workers? Then the economy will shift to "rational" expectations. Under rational expectations, people form their forecasts of future inflation not by looking backward at what inflation was, but by looking forward. They look at what current and expected future government policies tell us about what inflation will be.

ECONOMIC POLICY UNDER RATIONAL EXPECTATIONS

Consider an economy where the central bank's target inflation rate π' is equal to the current value of expected inflation π^e, and where u_0, the unemployment rate

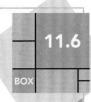

A HIGH-PRESSURE ECONOMY UNDER ADAPTIVE EXPECTATIONS

Suppose the government tries to keep unemployment below the natural rate for a long time in an economy with adaptive expectations. As a result, inflation will be higher than expected inflation year after year, and so year after year expected inflation will rise. Specifically, suppose that the government pushes the economy's unemployment rate down 2 percentage points below the natural rate, that the β parameter in the Phillips curve is $\frac{1}{2}$, and that last year's inflation rate was 4 percent. Because each year's expected inflation rate is last year's actual inflation rate, and because:

$$\pi_{t-1} + \beta \times 2 = \pi_t$$

FIGURE 11.10
Accelerating Inflation

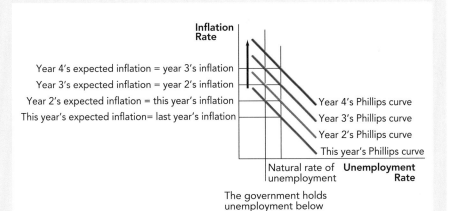

The government holds unemployment below the natural rate.

inflation rates are as follows:

This year's inflation rate will be	$4 + \frac{1}{2} \times 2 = 5$
Next year's inflation rate will be	$5 + \frac{1}{2} \times 2 = 6$
The following year's inflation rate will be	$6 + \frac{1}{2} \times 2 = 7$
The inflation rate the year after that will be	$7 + \frac{1}{2} \times 2 = 8$

as shown in Figure 11.10.

As long as expectations of inflation remain adaptive, inflation will increase by 1 percent per year for every year that passes. But expectations of inflation will not remain adaptive forever if the inflation rate keeps rising.

when the real interest rate is at its normal value, is equal to the natural rate of unemployment u^*. In such an economy, the initial equilibrium has unemployment equal to its natural rate and inflation equal to expected inflation.

Suppose that workers, managers, savers, and investors have rational expectations. Suppose further that the government takes steps to stimulate the economy: It cuts taxes and increases government spending in order to reduce unemployment below

ADAPTIVE EXPECTATIONS AND DISINFLATION OF THE 1980S AND 1990S

At the end of the 1970s the high level of expected inflation gave Canada an unfavourable short-run Phillips curve trade-off. Between 1981 and 1985, the Bank of Canada under its Governor Gerald Bouey reduced inflation in Canada from 12 percent per year to about 4 percent.

Because inflation expectations were adaptive, the fall in actual inflation in the early 1980s triggered a fall in expected inflation as well. The early 1980s also saw a downward shift in the short-run Phillips curve, which gave Canada a much more favourable short-run inflation-unemployment trade-off by the mid-1980s than it had in the late 1970s, as shown in Figure 11.11.

To accomplish this goal of reducing expected inflation, the Bank of Canada raised interest rates sharply, discouraging investment, reducing aggregate demand, and pushing the economy to the right along the Phillips curve. Unemployment rose, and inflation fell. Reducing annual inflation by 8 percentage points required sacrifice: During the disinflation unemployment averaged some 1½ percentage points above the natural rate for the five years between 1981 and 1985. That was the cost of reducing inflation from 12 to 4 percent.

In the early 1990s the Bank of Canada, under Gerald Bouey's successor, John Crow, followed the policy of achieving an inflation rate of 2 percent (plus or minus 1 percent). This target was achieved in 1992, and it has been maintained ever since.

The expected inflation rate has fallen correspondingly, shifting the Phillips curve further down. This policy led to a substantial increase in the unemployment rate between 1991 and 1995, when the actual unemployment rate was on average 0.8 percentage points above its natural rate. Thus, in Figure 11.11 one can trace three distinct Phillips curves: one for the period before 1985, one for the mid- to late-1980s, and one for the period after 1992.

FIGURE 11.11
The Phillips Curve, 1980–2005

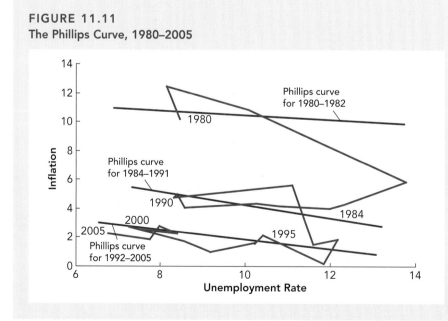

Source: Adapted from the Statistics Canada CANSIM II database, Series V2064894 (unemployment) and V735319 (CPI).

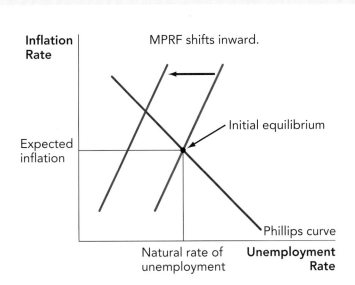

Inflation Rate

MPRF shifts inward.

Initial equilibrium

Expected inflation

Phillips curve

Natural rate of unemployment

Unemployment Rate

FIGURE 11.12
Government Attempt to Stimulate the Economy
A government pursuing an expansionary economic policy shifts the MPRF. Remember that on the Phillips curve diagram an increase in production is associated with a reduction in unemployment, so an expansionary shift is a shift to the left in aggregate demand on the Phillips-curve diagram.

the natural rate, as shown in Figure 11.12, and so reduces the value of u_0. What is likely to happen to the economy?

If the government's policy comes as a *surprise* — if the expectations of inflation that matter for this year's Phillips curve have already been set, in the sense that the contracts have been written, the orders have been made, and the standard operating procedures identified — then the economy moves up and to the left along the Phillips curve in response to the shift in aggregate demand produced by the change in government policy (Figure 11.13).

But if the government's policy is *anticipated* — if the expectations of inflation that matter for this year's Phillips curve are formed after the decision to stimulate the economy is made and becomes public — then workers, managers, savers, and investors will take the stimulative policy into account when they form their expectations of inflation. The inward shift in the MPRF will be accompanied, under rational expectations, by an upward shift in the Phillips curve as well (see Figure 11.14). How large an upward shift? The increase in expected inflation has to be large enough to keep expected inflation after the demand shift equal to actual inflation. Of course the assumption here is that there are no overlapping labour contracts.

Thus an anticipated increase in aggregate demand has, under rational expectations and no overlapping labour contracts, no effect on the unemployment rate or on real GDP. Unemployment does not change: It remains at the natural rate of unemployment because the shift in the Phillips curve has neutralized in advance any impact of changing inflation on unemployment. It will, however, have a large effect on the rate of inflation. Economists sometimes say that under rational expectations "anticipated policy is irrelevant." But this is not the best way to express it. Policy is very relevant indeed for the inflation rate. It is only the effects of policy on real GDP and the unemployment rate — effects that are associated with a divergence between expected inflation and actual inflation — that are neutralized. Moreover, even

FIGURE 11.13

Results If the Shift in Policy Comes as a Surprise

A surprise expansionary policy shifts the economy up and to the left along the Phillips curve, raising inflation and lowering unemployment (and raising production) in the short run.

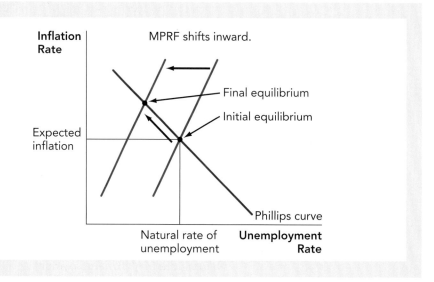

FIGURE 11.14

Results If the Shift in Policy Is Anticipated

If the expansionary policy is anticipated, workers, consumers, and managers will build the policy effects into their expectations: The Phillips curve will shift up as the aggregate demand curve shifts in, and so the expansionary policy will raise inflation without having any impact on unemployment (or production).

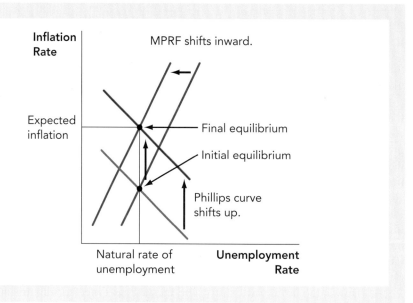

output and the unemployment rate would be affected in the presence of overlapping contracts.

When have we seen examples of rational inflation expectations? The standard case is that of France immediately after the election of the Socialist President Francois Mitterand in 1981. Throughout his campaign Mitterand had promised a rapid expansion of demand and production to reduce unemployment. Thus when he took office French businesses and unions were ready to mark up their prices and wages in anticipation of the expansionary policies they expected. The result? From mid-1981 to mid-1983 France saw a significant acceleration of inflation, but no reduction in unemployment. The Phillips curve had shifted upward fast enough to keep expansionary policies from having any effect on production and employment.

WHAT KIND OF EXPECTATIONS DO WE HAVE?

If inflation is low and stable, expectations are probably static: It is not worth anyone's while to even think about what one's expectations should be. If inflation is moderate and fluctuates, but slowly, expectations are probably adaptive: To assume that the future will be like the recent past — which is what adaptive expectations are — is likely to be a good rule, and is simple to implement.

When shifts in inflation are clearly related to changes in monetary policy, swift to occur, and are large enough to seriously affect profitability, then people are likely to have rational expectations. When the stakes are high — when people think, "had I known inflation was going to jump, I would not have taken that contract" — then every economic decision becomes a speculation on the future of monetary policy. Because it matters for their bottom lines and their livelihoods, people will turn all their skill and insight into generating inflation forecasts.

Thus the kind of expectations likely to be found in the economy at any moment depend on what has been and is going on. A period during which inflation is low and stable will lead people to stop making, and stop paying attention to, inflation forecasts, so expectations of inflation tend to revert to static expectations. A period during which inflation is high, volatile, and linked to visible shifts in economic policy will see expectations of inflation become more rational. An intermediate period of substantial but slow variability is likely to see many managers and workers adopt the rule of adaptive expectations.

PERSISTENT CONTRACTS

The ways that people make contracts and form and execute plans for their economic activity are likely to make an economy behave *as if* expectations in it are less rational than expectations in fact are. People do not wait until December 31 to factor next year's expected inflation into their decisions and contracts. They make decisions about the future, sign contracts, and undertake projects all the time. Some of those steps govern what the company does for a day. Others govern decisions for years or even for a decade or more.

Thus the "expected inflation" that determines the location of the short-run Phillips curve has components that were formed just as the old year ended, but also components that were formed two, three, five, ten, or more years ago. People buying houses form forecasts of what inflation will be over the next 30 years — but once the house is bought, that decision is a piece of economic activity (imputed rent on owner-occupied housing) as long as they own the house, no matter what they subsequently learn about future inflation. Such lags in decision making tend to produce "price inertia." They tend to make the economy behave as if inflation expectations were more adaptive than they in fact are. There will always be a large number of projects and commitments already under way that cannot easily adjust to changing prices. It is important to take this price inertia into account when thinking about the dynamics of inflation, output, and unemployment.

RECAP   **EXPECTED INFLATION**

Higher expected inflation shifts the Phillips curve upward. Lower expected inflation shifts the Phillips curve downward. Thus the dynamics of how expectations evolve are key to understanding the economy. Economists work with three basic scenarios for how managers, workers, and investors go about forecasting the future and forming their expectations: *Static expectations* of inflation prevail when people ignore the fact that inflation can change. *Adaptive expectations* prevail when people assume the future will be like the recent past. *Rational expectations* prevail when people use all the information they have as best they can.

The Phillips curve behaves very differently under each of these three scenarios. Under static expectations the Phillips curve doesn't shift, so changes in policy have powerful effects on unemployment and real GDP. Under rational expectations the Phillips curve shifts immediately and drastically in response to policies so that anticipated changes in policy have powerful effects on inflation, but not on unemployment and real GDP. And adaptive expectations are in the middle.

11.5 FROM THE (STICKY-PRICE) SHORT RUN TO THE (FLEXIBLE-PRICE) LONGER RUN

RATIONAL EXPECTATIONS

Our picture of the determination of real GDP and unemployment under sticky prices is now complete. We have a comprehensive framework to understand how the aggregate price level and inflation rate move and adjust over time in response to changes in aggregate demand, production relative to potential output, and unemployment relative to its natural rate. There is, however, one loose end. How does one get from the short-run sticky-price patterns of behaviour that have been covered in Part IV to the longer-run flexible-price patterns of behaviour that were laid out in Part III?

In the case of an anticipated shift in economic policy under rational expectations, the answer is straightforward: You don't have to get from the short run to the longer run; the longer run is now. An inward (or outward) shift in the monetary policy reaction function on the Phillips curve diagram caused by an expansionary (or contractionary) change in economic policy or the economic environment sets in motion an offsetting shift in the Phillips curve. In the absence of supply shocks, inflation is

$$\pi = \pi^e - \beta \times (u - u*).$$

If expectations are rational and if changes in economic policy are foreseen, then expected inflation will be equal to actual inflation:

$$\pi = \pi^e$$

which means that the unemployment rate is equal to the natural rate, as shown in Figure 11.15. The economy is at full employment. All the analysis of Chapters 5, 6, and 7 holds immediately.

ADAPTIVE EXPECTATIONS

If expectations are and remain adaptive, then the economy approaches the long-run equilibrium laid out in Chapters 5 and 6 gradually, as is shown in Figure 11.16. An

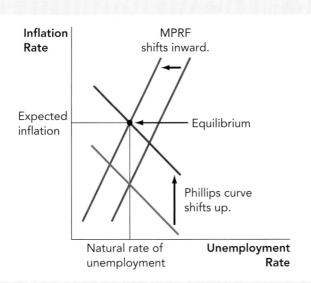

FIGURE 11.15
Rational Expectations: The Long Run Is Now
Under rational expectations there simply is no short run, unless changes in policy come as a complete surprise.

expansionary initial shock that shifts the aggregate demand relation inward on the Phillips curve diagram generates a fall in unemployment, an increase in real GDP, and a rise in inflation. Call this Stage 1. Stage 1 takes place before anyone has had any chance to adjust their expectations of inflation.

To reach Stage 2, workers, managers, investors, and others look at what inflation was in Stage 1 and raise their expectations of inflation. The Phillips curve shifts up by the difference between actual and expected inflation in Stage 1. If the aggregate demand relation does not shift when plotted on the Phillips curve diagram, between Stage 1 and Stage 2 unemployment rises, real GDP falls, and inflation rises.

Moving toward Stage 3, workers, managers, investors, and others look at what inflation was in Stage 1 and raise their expectations of inflation. The Phillips curve shifts up by the difference between actual and expected inflation in Stage 2. If the aggregate demand relation does not shift when plotted on the Phillips curve diagram, between Stage 2 and Stage 3 unemployment rises, real GDP falls, and inflation rises. As time passes the gaps between actual and expected inflation, between real GDP and potential output, and between unemployment and its natural rate shrink toward zero.

Under adaptive expectations, people's forecasts become closer to being accurate as more time passes. Thus the "long run" arrives gradually. Each year the portion of the change in demand that is not implicitly incorporated in people's adaptive forecasts becomes smaller. Thus each year a larger proportion of the shift is "long run," and a smaller proportion is "short run."

STATIC EXPECTATIONS

Under static expectations, the long run never arrives: the analysis of Chapters 5 through 7 never becomes relevant. Under static expectations, the gap between expected inflation and actual inflation can grow arbitrarily large as different shocks affect the economy. And if the gap between expected inflation and actual inflation becomes large, workers, managers, investors, and consumers will not be so foolish as to retain static expectations.

FIGURE 11.16

Adaptive Expectations Convergence to the Longer Run

Under adaptive expectations, shifts in policy have strong initial effects on unemployment and production, but those effects slowly die off.

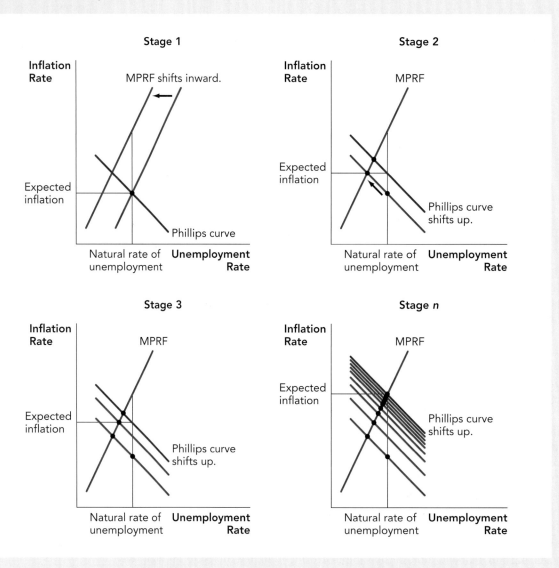

RECAP   STICKY PRICES OR FLEXIBLE PRICES?

The amount of time that must pass before the relevant framework shifts from the sticky-price Part IV framework to the flexible-price Part III framework depends on the type of inflation expectations held in the economy. Under static expectations, Part III is never relevant. Under rational expectations, Part III is always relevant.

CHAPTER SUMMARY

1. The location of the Phillips curve is determined by the expected rate of inflation and the natural rate of unemployment (and possibly by current, active supply shocks). In the absence of current, active supply shocks, the Phillips curve passes through the point at which inflation is at its expected value and unemployment is at its natural rate.

2. The slope of the Phillips curve is determined by the degree of price stickiness in the economy. The stickier prices are, the flatter the Phillips curve is.

3. The natural rate of unemployment in Canada has exhibited moderate swings in the past two generations: from less than 5 percent in the 1960s to around 9.5 percent in the mid-1980s, and now down to 7 percent.

4. Two significant supply shocks have affected the rate of inflation in Canada over the past two generations: the (inflationary) oil price increases of 1973 and 1979.

5. The principal determinant of the expected rate of inflation is the past behaviour of inflation. If inflation has been low and steady, expectations are probably *static,* and the expected inflation rate is very low and unchanging. If inflation has been variable but moderate, expectations are probably *adaptive* and expected inflation is probably simply equal to last year's inflation. If inflation has been high, or has been moderate but varied extremely rapidly, then expectations are probably *rational* and expected inflation is likely to be households' and businesses' best guesses of where economic policy is taking the economy.

6. The best way to gauge how expectations of inflation are formed is to consider the past history of inflation. Would adaptive expectations have provided a significant edge over static ones? If yes, then inflation expectations are probably adaptive. Would rational expectations have provided a significant edge over adaptive ones? If yes, then inflation expectations are probably rational.

7. How fast the flexible-price model becomes relevant depends on the type of inflation expectations in the economy. Under static expectations, the flexible-price model never becomes relevant. Under adaptive expectations, the flexible-price model becomes relevant gradually, in the long run. Under rational expectations the long run is now: the flexible-price model analysis is relevant always and immediately.

KEY TERMS AND EQUATIONS

adaptive expectations (p. 346)

central bank's inflation target (p. 340)

expected inflation (p. 336)

monetary policy reaction function (MPRF) (p. 337)

natural rate of unemployment (p. 336)

Okun's law (p. 333)

output gap (p. 334)

Phillips curve (p. 336)

rational expectations (p. 346)

static expectations (p. 346)

Okun's law:	$u - u^* = -0.6 \times \dfrac{Y - Y^*}{Y^*}$	(11.1)
Phillips curve:	$\pi = \pi^e - \beta \times (u - u^*) + \varepsilon^s$	(11.8)
Monetary policy reaction function:	$u = u_0 + \phi \times (\pi - \pi')$	(11.10)

ANALYTICAL EXERCISES

1. What is the relationship between the three views of aggregate supply? Why do economists tend to focus on the Phillips curve to the exclusion of the other two views?

2. Under what circumstances will a government expansionary fiscal or monetary policy do nothing to raise GDP or lower unemployment?

3. Under the circumstances in which an expansionary government policy fails to raise GDP or lower unemployment, what would the policy manage to do?

4. If expectations of inflation are *adaptive*, is there any way to reduce inflation without suffering unemployment higher than the natural rate? What would you advise a

central bank that sought to reduce inflation without provoking high unemployment to do?

5. What do you think a central bank should do in response to an adverse supply shock? How does your answer depend on the way in which expectations of inflation are being formed in the economy?

6. Explain the effects of an anticipated expansionary government policy in the MPRF–Phillips curve framework with overlapping labour contracts.

7. Use the "warranted" real wage growth and the "aspirations" for real wage growth model in order to explain why the productivity slowdown of the 1970s led to an increase in the natural rate of unemployment.

POLICY EXERCISES

1. What factors do you think have led the natural rate of unemployment to be so high in Europe and so low in the U.S today?

2. What factors do you think have led the natural rate of unemployment to be what it is in Canada today?

3. Do you think that inflation expectations in Canada today are static, adaptive, or rational? Why?

4. Outline the factors that may have contributed to the recent decline in the natural rate of unemployment since the early 1990s.

5. What may explain the "jobless recovery" in the U.S. in recent years?

6. Suppose that the economy has a Phillips curve

$$\pi_t = \pi_t^e - \beta \times (u_t - u_t^*)$$

with the parameter β = 0.5 and the natural rate of unemployment u^* equal to 6 percent. And suppose that the central bank's reaction to inflation, the IS curve, and Okun's law together mean that the unemployment rate is given by

$$u_t = u_0 + \phi \times (\pi_t - \pi_t')$$

with the central bank's target level of inflation π' equal to 2 percent, the parameter ϕ equal to 0.4, and the normal real rate of interest level of aggregate demand corresponding to a value of u_0 of 6 percent. Suppose that initially — this year, in the year zero — expected inflation is equal to actual inflation.

a. What is the initial level of unemployment?

b. Suppose that the government announces that in year one and in every year thereafter its expansionary policies will reduce u_0 to 4 percent, that this announcement is credible, and that the economy has *rational expectations* of inflation. What will unemployment and inflation be in year one? What will they be thereafter?

c. Suppose that the government announces that in year one and in every year thereafter its expansionary policies will reduce u_0 to 4 percent, that this announcement is credible, and that the economy has *adaptive*

expectations of inflation. What will unemployment and inflation be in year one? What will they be thereafter?

d. Suppose that the government announces that in year one and in every year thereafter its expansionary policies will reduce u_0 to 4 percent, that this announcement is credible, and that the economy has *static expectations* of inflation. What will unemployment and inflation be in year one? What will they be thereafter?

7. Suppose that the economy this year, in the year zero, is the same as presented initially in question 6.

a. What is the initial level of unemployment?

b. Suppose that the central bank raises its target inflation rate for next year — year one — to 4 percent, and announces this change. Suppose the economy has *rational expectations* of inflation. What will happen to unemployment and inflation in year one? What will happen thereafter?

c. Suppose that the central bank raises its target inflation rate for next year — year one — to 4 percent, and announces this change. Suppose the economy has *adaptive expectations* of inflation. What will happen to unemployment and inflation in year one? What will happen thereafter?

d. Suppose that the central bank raises its target inflation rate for next year — year one — to 4 percent, and announces this change. Suppose the economy has *static expectations* of inflation. What will happen to unemployment and inflation in year one? What will happen thereafter?

8. Suppose that the economy this year, in the year zero, is as depicted in question 6 initially.

a. What is the initial level of unemployment?

b. Suppose that the natural rate of unemployment u^* falls to 4 percent in year one and remains at that level indefinitely. And suppose that this fall in the natural rate of unemployment does not come as a surprise. Suppose the economy has *rational expectations* of inflation. What will happen to unemployment and inflation in year one? What will happen thereafter?

c. Suppose that the natural rate of unemployment u^* falls to 4 percent in year one and remains at that level indefinitely. And suppose that this fall in the natural rate of unemployment does not come as a surprise. Suppose the economy has *adaptive expectations* of inflation. What will happen to unemployment and inflation in year one? What will happen thereafter?

d. Suppose that the natural rate of unemployment u^* falls to 4 percent in year one and remains at that level indefinitely. And suppose that this fall in the natural rate of unemployment does not come as a surprise. Suppose the economy has *static expectations* of inflation. What will happen to unemployment and inflation in year one? What will happen thereafter?

Macroeconomic Policy

We now have all the tools we need to understand business cycles: Part III showed how to analyze business cycles in a flexible-price macroeconomy. Part IV showed how to analyze business cycles in a sticky-price macroeconomy, and how to understand when the flexible-price model and when the sticky-price model is the best one to use.

Part V uses the tools built up earlier in this book to conduct a guided tour of the major issues in modern macroeconomic policy. Chapter 12 considers stabilization policy: how the government attempts to keep unemployment low, growth steady, inflation low, and recessions shallow. Chapter 13 moves on to consider fiscal policy, and the effect of the government's taxes, spending, and national debt on the level of investment and long-run growth.

Chapter 14 discusses how the macroeconomy has changed over the past century, and how the changes in the macroeconomy have affected macroeconomic policy.

12 Stabilization Policy

QUESTIONS

What principles should guide stabilization policy?

What aspects of stabilization policy do economists argue about today?

Is monetary policy or fiscal policy more effective as a stabilization policy?

How does uncertainty affect the way stabilization policy should be made?

How long are the lags associated with stabilization policy?

Is it better for stabilization policy to be conducted according to fixed *rules,* or to be conducted by authorities with substantial *discretion?*

Part IV of this book set out the sticky-price model in which short-run changes in real GDP, unemployment, interest rates, and inflation are all driven by changes in the economic environment and by shifts in two kinds of government policy: fiscal policy and monetary policy. Changes in *fiscal policy* shift the IS curve out and back. Central-bank-driven changes in interest rates and moves of the LM curve — *monetary policy* — raise and lower real interest rates, and cause the economy's equilibrium to move along the IS curve.

These policies and the economic environment together set the level of aggregate demand. They move the economy along the Phillips curve, raising and lowering inflation and unemployment. Changes in expectations of inflation, changes in the natural rate of unemployment, and supply shocks shift the position of the short-run Phillips curve, and thus play a powerful role in determining the options open to government.

It is in this context that the government tries to manage the macroeconomy. It attempts to *stabilize* the macroeconomy by minimizing the impact of the shocks that cause business cycles. The first part of this chapter looks at the institutions that make macroeconomic policy: the Bank of Canada, which makes monetary policy, and the Ministry of Finance, which makes fiscal policy. After looking at the institutions it will be time to look at how macroeconomic policy is actually made, and at how well it works.

12.1 MONETARY POLICY INSTITUTIONS

THE BANK OF CANADA

Monetary policy in Canada is formulated and implemented by the central Bank of Canada. The Bank of Canada is the counterpart to the Federal Reserve in the United States. It is a publicly owned institution, and was established in 1934, following the Bank of Canada Act.

http://www.bank-banque-canada.ca/
http://www.fin.gc.ca/

The head of the Bank of Canada is its Governor. The main decision-making body is its board of directors, which includes the Governor, the Senior Deputy Governor, 12 outside directors, and the Deputy Minister of Finance. The Minister of Finance, with the approval of the Cabinet, appoints the 12 outside directors for three-year terms. The 12 outside directors, in turn, with the approval of the Cabinet, appoint the Governor and the Deputy Governor for seven-year terms. The present Governor of the Bank of Canada is David Dodge, who was appointed in 2001.

Because monetary policy is an important tool for stabilizing the economy, the Bank of Canada plays a leading role in stabilization policy. The other institution that is responsible for stabilization policy is the Ministry of Finance, which is responsible for formulating and implementing fiscal policy, which includes policies regarding government expenditures, taxation, and issuing of government bonds. Although these two institutions operate independently, in case of serious disagreements, the Minister of Finance, with the approval of the Cabinet, could issue a written directive to the Governor of the Bank of Canada specifying a policy change.

AN OVERVIEW OF THE MONETARY POLICIES IN CANADA

In the post–World War II period up until 1970, with the exception of the period 1950–1962, Canada had mainly a fixed exchange rate system. Monetary policy was, therefore, directed at maintaining a stable value for the Canadian dollar in the foreign exchange market. The exact workings of a fixed exchange rate system will be discussed in Chapters 15 and 16. Essentially, to maintain a fixed exchange rate the Bank of Canada stands ready to exchange Canadian dollars for foreign currencies on the foreign exchange markets at pre-specified rates. Other monetary policy considerations were subservient to this goal.[1]

In 1970, Canada adopted a flexible exchange rate system that allowed the Bank of Canada to follow independent monetary policies without being burdened by consideration of the foreign exchange markets. In his Donald Gow Lecture in 2002, David Dodge gives an overview of the monetary policies followed by the Bank of

---

[1] In Chapter 15 we discuss in detail the workings of a fixed exchange rate system, and the reason why under this system the central bank loses monetary independence. Also, in Chapter 16 we give a detailed discussion of the circumstances that led to the adoption of different foreign exchange arrangements in Canada.

Canada from 1970 to the present.[2] He states three reasons for the sharp increase in the inflation rate in Canada in the first half of the 1970s: the sharp increase in oil prices; the slowdown in productivity growth; and the increase in the long-run unemployment rate. These three factors pushed up the inflation rate by adversely affecting the supply side of the economy, reducing the rate of growth of GDP.

In order to control the inflation rate, which had reached 10 percent by 1975, the Bank of Canada adopted the policy of targeting the rate of growth of the M1. For the period 1975–81 a specific target range for M1 growth was adopted for every three months; and the M1 growth rate was maintained within the target. For the period April–June 1975, the target range for the growth rate of M1 was 10–15 percent, and this was gradually reduced to 4–8 percent for August–October 1980.

Although, as seen from Figure 12.5, from 1975 until 1980 there was a substantial reduction in the rate of growth of M1, the inflation rate stayed high. The reason was that in this period there were several financial innovations that reduced the demand for the narrow measure of money M1, and increased the demand for the broader measure M2, which unlike M1 included savings deposits. These financial innovations include the introduction of electronic banking, which made savings accounts close substitutes for chequing accounts. With savings accounts close substitutes for chequing accounts, M2 becomes the more relevant measure of money in determining inflation. Again, as seen from Figure 12.5, during this period the rate of growth of M2 did not fall by a sufficiently large amount; and, as a result, the inflation rate stayed high, around 10 percent. One could, therefore, argue that the Bank of Canada was targeting an inappropriate measure of the money supply in this period. This problem was compounded by the inflationary expectations of this period that had shifted the Phillips curve.

In 1982 the Bank of Canada abandoned the policy of targeting M1. Its primary objective remained the reduction of the inflation rate; but instead of targeting M1, it adopted the policy of targeting a set of variables that affected the inflation rate, primarily the interest rates, the exchange rate, and M2. Following this strategy, the Bank of Canada succeeded in reducing the inflation rate from 11 percent in 1982 to little over 4 percent in 1985. Nevertheless, as we will see in the next chapter, the 1980s was also a period of high budget deficit and expansionary fiscal policies that put upward pressures on interest rates. As a result, by 1988 the Bank of Canada found it increasingly difficult to meet its targets for interest rate and money supply growth rate.

In 1988 the Bank of Canada abandoned its policy of targeting a set of variables, and adopted the policy of having the inflation rate as the only target. In 1988, John Crow, the newly appointed Governor of the Bank of Canada at the time, made **price stability** the main objective of the Bank of Canada policy. It was recognized that monetary policy plays an important role in protecting the value of the Canadian money and in promoting economic growth and living standards for all Canadians. The value of money is protected by keeping inflation low and stable. This in turn helps people to make better spending and investment decisions that lead to job creation, greater productivity, and long-lasting economic growth.[3]

In 1991 the Bank of Canada and the federal government made inflation-control targeting the main objective of monetary policy in Canada. The inflation target is

---

[2] The 2002 Donald Gow Lecture: "The Interaction between Monetary and Fiscal Policies." School of Policy Studies, Queen's University, Kingston, Ontario.

[3] Recall the costs of inflation that we discussed in Chapter 7.

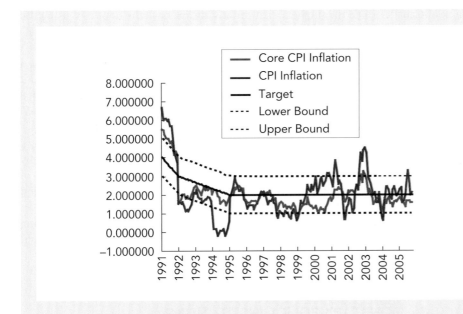

FIGURE 12.1

Inflation as measured by the CPI, Core CPI and Target Range, 1990–2005

In 1991, the Bank of Canada and the federal government made inflation-control targeting the main objective of monetary policy in Canada. The inflation targets are measured in terms of CPI inflation and core inflation. The Bank of Canada has been quite successful in keeping inflation within its target range.

Source: CANSIM II, Series V731319 (CPI) and V2007197 (Core CPI).

Note: Inflation is calculated as the growth in CPI from same month in previous year.

measured by the total CPI inflation, but core inflation is also used as an operational target.[4] By the end of 1993, inflation had been reduced to 2 percent and a target range was set between 1 and 3 percent. The target range has been reviewed periodically and then renewed. In May 2001 the Bank of Canada and the government decided to renew the 1 to 3 percent target range until the end of 2006. In the mean time, monetary policy will be directed at keeping inflation at the 2 percent midpoint of the target range. Figure 12.1 shows Canada's inflation target record from 1991 to the end of 2005. As seen from the graph, the Bank of Canada has been quite successful in keeping inflation within the target range.

The Bank of Canada uses its policy instruments in order to contain inflation within its target range. Its ultimate instrument is the rate of money growth that is used to influence short-term interest rates. The Bank's key policy interest rate is called the **target for the overnight rate**. This is the midpoint of an **operating band** set by the Bank of Canada for financial transactions made in the overnight market. This is the market used by major financial institutions (chartered banks, credit unions, finance companies) to borrow and lend from each other in order to cover their daily transactions. The rate charged for these loans is called the overnight rate.

The Bank of Canada operates in such a way as to keep the overnight rate within the operating band, which is one-half of a percentage point wide with the target rate at its centre. For instance, currently the operating band is 3.75 to 4.25 percent, and the overnight rate is 4 percent. The upper limit of the band is the **bank rate**, which is the interest rate charged to financial institutions when they borrow from the Bank of Canada, and the lower limit is the interest rate paid on deposits made with the

---

[4] Core inflation differs from CPI inflation because its calculation excludes eight commodities with the most volatile prices (fruit, vegetables, gasoline, fuel oil, natural gas, mortgage interest, intercity transportation, and tobacco products) as well as the effect of changes in indirect taxes on the remaining commodities in the CPI basket.

Bank of Canada. Since the financial institutions always have the option of using the Bank of Canada for their financing needs, they have no incentive to trade funds outside the band.

The overnight target rate may change according to a schedule of eight fixed announcement dates each year, determined by the Bank of Canada.[5] When the Bank changes the overnight target rate, it sends a strong signal on the direction of change of short-term interest rates, such as the prime rate, mortgage rates, and interest paid on consumer loans and savings accounts.

When the Bank of Canada lowers the overnight target rate, interest rates fall and individuals and firms spend and invest more and the economy expands thereby increasing inflation and economic growth. On the other hand, when the Bank of Canada raises the overnight target rate, interest rates increase and aggregate demand falls, thereby reducing inflation and economic growth.

This way, Canada's monetary policy is tied to controlling inflation and stabilizing the country's economic growth. In recent years, this policy has been successful and has kept the Canadian economy on a smooth growth path with low inflation.

RECAP   MONETARY POLICY INSTITUTIONS

Monetary policy in Canada is formulated and implemented by the Bank of Canada. In the post–World War II period up until 1970, with the exception of the period 1950–1962, Canada had mainly a fixed exchange rate system and monetary policy was directed at having a stable value for the Canadian dollar in the foreign exchange market. In 1971, Canada adopted a flexible exchange rate system. During the period 1975–81 the Bank of Canada was targeting the M1 measure of the money supply. During the period 1982–88 the Bank was targeting a number of variables that affected the inflation rate, such as the interest rate, the exchange rate, and M2. Since 1988 the Bank has been targeting the inflation rate alone.

12.2 FISCAL POLICY INSTITUTIONS

Fiscal policy is formulated and implemented by the Ministry of Finance, which is responsible for the federal government's expenditures on various goods and services, transfers of funds to provinces and territories, transfers of funds to individuals and businesses, federal income taxes, federal goods and services taxes, and tariffs. The Ministry of Finance is also responsible for issuing government bonds and managing the government's debt.

http://cansim2.statcan.ca/

FACTS AND FIGURES

The Ministry of Finance prepares the government's budget, and the Minister of Finance presents it to Parliament early in the year. The budget is then implemented with the approval of Parliament. In the next chapter we will have a detailed discussion of budget deficits in Canada. At this stage we discuss major federal government expenditures by categories, and how they have changed over time.

---

[5] For 2007, the dates are January 16, March 6, April 24, May 29, July 10, September 5, October 16, and December 4.

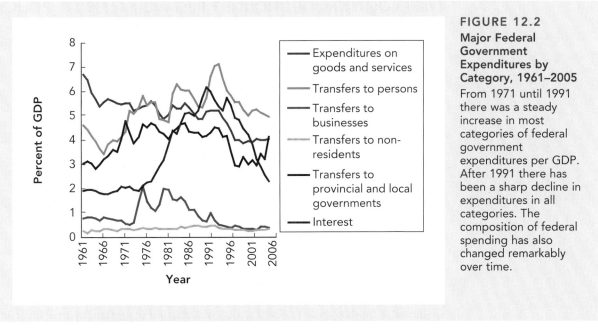

FIGURE 12.2

Major Federal Government Expenditures by Category, 1961–2005

From 1971 until 1991 there was a steady increase in most categories of federal government expenditures per GDP. After 1991 there has been a sharp decline in expenditures in all categories. The composition of federal spending has also changed remarkably over time.

Source: Adapted from Statistics Canada CANSIM II database, Series V499762 (expenditures on goods and services), V499768 (transfers to persons), V499778 (transfers to businesses), V499779 (transfers to non-residents), V449782 (transfers to provincial and local governments), V499798 (interest), and V498086 (nominal GDP).

As seen in Figure 12.2, from 1971 until 1991 there was a steady increase in most categories of federal government expenditures per GDP. On the other hand, after 1991 there has been a sharp decline in expenditures in all categories, as the federal government was committed to reducing the size of the government budget deficits.

The composition of federal spending has also changed remarkably over time. Spending on goods and services has declined steadily from nearly 7 percent of GDP in 1961 to close to 4 percent in 2005. From 1970 to the early 1990s there was a steady increase in the amount of transfers to persons, primarily for two reasons. First, in 1970 there were revisions to the unemployment insurance systems in Canada, which made such payments more generous. Second, there has been a steady increase in the number of elderly in Canada who receive pensions. Since the early 1990s, however, transfers to persons as a percentage of GDP has been falling, primarily because of government cut backs. The federal government in Canada has always made generous transfers to the provinces, in order to maintain comparable public services across the country. As a percentage of the GDP, these transfers were relatively stable, at a little above 4 percent, until the 1990s; but they declined in the 1990s, and reached around 3 percent of GDP in 2001. Since then, however, these transfers have increased over time to 4 percent of GDP in 2005. Due to high interest rates in the 1970s and 1980s, there was a substantial increase in interest payments, rising from 2 percent of GDP in 1970 to about 5 percent by the 1990s. The decline in interest rates in the 1990s reduced the interest payments to around 2.5 percent of GDP in 2005. There was a sharp increase in federal government transfers to businesses in the mid-1970s, when they reached a peak of 2 percent of GDP in 1975. This was due to the sharp increase in the price of oil in 1973, and the government's attempt to support businesses. These transfers have declined over time, and were at less than 0.5 percent of GDP in 2005.

THE EVOLUTION OF THOUGHT REGARDING FISCAL POLICY

In his 2002 Donald Gow Lecture, David Dodge gave a clear explanation of the evolution of fiscal policy in Canada in the 1980s and 1990s. Before the early 1970s, fiscal policy was geared towards providing important social programs and economic stabilization. Fiscal authorities were not concerned very much about the evolution of government debt. However, the economic slowdown of the early 1970s, along with the dramatic increase in interest rates in the late 1970s, had a fundamental impact on views regarding fiscal policy. With high interest rates on government debt and a decline in economic growth, there was a substantial increase in the debt-to-GDP ratio not only in Canada, but also in other industrialized countries.

Fiscal authorities then came to realize that the stock of public debt could not grow indefinitely faster than the rate of growth of the economy. The government, like every individual, faces the constraint that eventually it has to pay back its debt. This important constraint means that the debt-to-GDP ratio cannot grow without limit over time. Unless it is brought under control, either taxes would have to increase or social programs would have to be downsized in the future, which would place a burden on future generations. Moreover, it was recognized that budget deficits, which represent dissaving by the government, reduce total (i.e., private *plus* government) saving in the economy. The fall in total saving then reduces funds that are available for investment, which leads to a reduction in growth. In an open economy, with access to international capital markets, the fall in total savings also leads to an increase in the country's external borrowing, increasing its foreign debt.

For these reasons, in the mid-1980s the federal government recognized the need to control the debt-to-GDP ratio. Nevertheless, it was not until the early 1990s that significant enough policies were adopted in order to bring the debt-to-GDP ratio under control. By 1995, the deficit reduction policies started producing results and the debt-to-GDP ratio was under control. Since then, the federal government's debt-to-GDP ratio has fallen from 70 percent to 50 percent. Canada's federal debt reduction policies of this period have been hailed as one of the most successful among the industrialized countries. At the same time, the provincial governments have also managed to bring their deficits under control. Both federal and provincial governments are now committed to following these policies in the foreseeable future.

Making fiscal policy is complicated, baroque, and time-consuming. The **inside lag** — the time between when a policy proposal is made and when it becomes effective — for fiscal policy is measured in years. By contrast, the inside lag associated with changes in monetary policy is measured in days, weeks, or at most two months. This is a key advantage of monetary policy over fiscal policy.

RECAP **FISCAL POLICY INSTITUTIONS**

Fiscal policy is formulated and implemented by the Ministry of Finance. The economic slowdown of the 1970s and the sharp increase in interest rates in the late 1970s led to a substantial increase in debt-to-GDP ratio. As the stock of public debt cannot grow indefinitely faster than the rate of growth of the economy, in the 1990s government policies were geared towards controlling the debt-to-GDP ratio. Since 1991 there has been a sharp decline in expenditures in all categories of government expenditures. By 1995 the government had succeeded in bringing the debt-to-GDP ratio under control. Since then, the debt-to-GDP ratio has continued to fall, from 70 percent to 50 percent.

12.3 THE DEVELOPMENT OF STABILIZATION POLICIES

Governments did not always view themselves as responsible for stabilizing the economy and taming the business cycle. Indeed, for much of the nineteenth and early twentieth centuries the dominant view among economists was that prices and wages were sufficiently flexible that the economy would converge very rapidly to its full-employment equilibrium, and therefore there was no need for government intervention in order to stabilize business fluctuations. The government was supposed to follow a *laissez-faire* (i.e., "let it be") policy. This was the view of the classical school of economists, dating back to Adam Smith, who viewed the private sector as having an "invisible hand" that led it to the equilibrium without any need for intervention. It was believed that monetary and fiscal policies designed to fight recessions would keep workers and firms producing in unsustainable lines of business and levels of capital intensity, and would make the depression less deep only at the price of making it longer.

This doctrine that in the long run even deep recessions like the Great Depression would turn out to have been "good medicine" for the economy drew anguished cries of dissent even before World War II. John Maynard Keynes tried to ridicule this "crime and punishment" view of business cycles, concluding that he did not see how "universal bankruptcy could do us any good or bring us any nearer to prosperity." Indeed, it was largely due to Keynes's writings, especially his *General Theory of Employment, Interest and Money,* that economists and politicians became convinced that the government could halt depressions and smooth out the business cycle. But Keynes was not alone. For example, Ralph Hawtrey, an adviser to the British Treasury and the Bank of England, called worry about government action the equivalent of "crying, 'Fire! Fire!' in Noah's flood." But you still can see traces of this view in economics in places (like the real business cycle theories discussed at the end of Chapter 6). These arguments led to substantial activist policies by governments not only in Canada but also other industrialized countries in the 1960s.

The 1970s, however, erased that confidence. Economists Milton Friedman and Edward Phelps had warned that attempts to keep the economy at the upper left corner of the Phillips curve would inevitably cause an upward shift in inflation expectations — that even if expectations had truly been static during the 1950s and early 1960s, they would become adaptive if unemployment were pushed too low for too long. Friedman and Phelps were correct: The 1970s saw a sharp upward shift in the Phillips curve as people lost confidence in the commitment of the Bank of Canada to keep inflation low, and raised their expectations of inflation. (See Figure 12.3.) The result was *stagflation:* a combination of relatively high unemployment and relatively high inflation. The lesson learned was that attempts to keep unemployment low and the level of output stable were counterproductive if they eroded public confidence in the central bank's commitment to keep inflation low and prices stable.

Towards the end of the 1970s many economists were convinced that "activist" monetary policy did more harm than good, and that the country might be better off with an "automatic" monetary policy that fixed some control variable like the money stock on a stable long-run growth path. But the sharp instability of monetary velocity since the start of 1975 (see Figure 12.4) has greatly reduced the number of advocates of an automatic central bank that lets the money stock grow by a fixed proportional amount every year.

FIGURE 12.3
The Canadian Phillips Curves, 1955–1980

Between the mid-1950s and the late 1960s, unemployment and inflation in Canada were low and stable, and productivity growth was rapid. Economists in government and their politician bosses thought that the new tools of economic policy had licked the business cycle. They were wrong. Between 1970 and 1975 expected inflation increased, the Phillips curve shifted up, and stagflation set in.

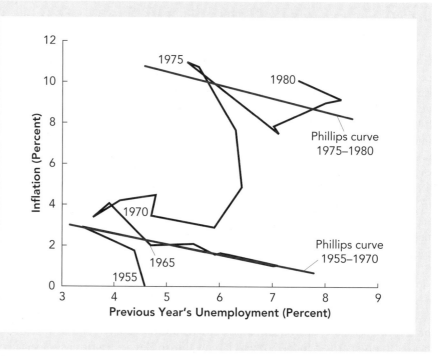

Source: CPI inflation: CANSIM I–P100000; Unemployment rate: CANSIM I–D980745.

FIGURE 12.4
The Velocity of Money, 1961–2005

Before 1975 monetarists argued that the velocity of money was stable and predictable. It had a constant upward trend as new technology was introduced into the banking system, and nearly no other fluctuations. Keep the money supply growing smoothly, they argued, and the smooth trend of velocity will keep the economy stable. They too were wrong. After 1975 the velocity of money became unstable indeed.

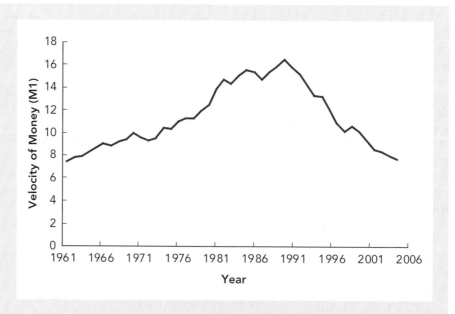

Source: Adapted from Statistics Canada CANSIM II database, Series V498086 (nominal GDP) and V37200 (M1).

RECAP   **THE DEVELOPMENT OF STABILIZATION POLICIES**

Before the Great Depression, the government viewed the business cycle much like people today view hurricanes and tornadoes. They are catastrophes, and the government should help those who suffer, but it makes no sense to ask the government to prevent or manage them. Largely as a result of the writings of the British economist John Maynard Keynes, this attitude vanished during the Great Depression and World War II. After World War II, economists and politicians believed that the government could and should prevent great depressions and smooth out the business cycle. Overconfidence in the government's ability to manage the macroeconomy vanished in the 1970s, a decade of both relatively high unemployment and relatively high inflation. Today we have a more limited confidence in the government's ability to stabilize and manage the business cycle.

12.4 THE POWER AND LIMITS OF STABILIZATION POLICY

Economists today arrange themselves along a line with respect to their views as to how the central bank (the Bank of Canada) and fiscal authorities (the Ministry of Finance) should manage the economy. At one end are economists like Milton Friedman, who holds that activist attempts to manage the economy are likely to do more harm than good. Government should settle on a policy that does not produce disaster no matter what the pattern of shocks or the structure of the economy. This end of the spectrum holds that most of the large business cycles and macroeconomic disturbances experienced in the past century were the result of well-intentioned but destructive economic policy decisions based on faulty models of the economy (see Box 12.1).

At the other end of the spectrum are those who hold that shocks to the economy are frequent and substantial. They believe that appropriate government policy can do a lot to stabilize the economy — to avoid both high unemployment and high inflation.

This economic policy debate has been going on for generations. It will never be resolved, for the differences are inevitably differences of emphasis rather than sharp lines of division. Even the most "activist" economists recognize the limits imposed on stabilization policy by uncertainty about the structure of the economy and the difficulties of forecasting. Even the greatest believer in the natural stability of the economy — Milton Friedman — believes that the economy is naturally stable only if government policy follows the proper policy of ensuring the smooth growth of the money stock.

UNCERTAINTY ABOUT THE ECONOMY

Because economic policy works with long and variable lags, stabilization policy requires that we first know where the economy is and where it is going. If future

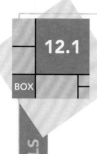

THE STRUCTURE OF THE ECONOMY AND THE LUCAS CRITIQUE

Economist Robert Lucas has argued that most of what economists thought they knew about the structure of the economy was false. Expectations of the future have major effects on decision making in the present: workers' nominal wage demands, managers' investment decisions, households' consumption decisions, and practically every other economic decision hinge, in one way or another, on what is expected to happen in the future. And expectations depend on many things — including the policies followed by the government. Change the policies followed by the government, and you change the structure of the economy as well.

Thus, Lucas argued, the use of economic models to forecast how the economy would respond to changes in government policy is an incoherent and mistaken exercise. Changes in policy would induce changes in the structure of the economy and its patterns of behaviour that would invalidate the forecasting exercise. Economic forecasts based on a period in which inflation expectations were *adaptive* would turn out to be grossly in error if applied to a period in which inflation expectations were *rational*. Forecasts of consumption spending based on estimates of the marginal propensity to consume when changes in national income were permanent would lead policy makers astray if applied to forecast the effects of policies that cause transitory changes in national income.

This **Lucas critique** is an important enough insight that for it Robert Lucas was awarded the Nobel Prize in 1995.

conditions cannot be predicted, policies initiated today are as likely to have destructive as constructive effects when they affect the economy 18 months or two years from now.

In general economists take two approaches in trying to forecast the near-term future of the economy. The first approach is to use large-scale macroeconometric models — more complicated versions of the models of this book. The second approach is to search for **leading indicators:** one or a few economic variables not necessarily noted in this book that experience tells us are strongly correlated with future movements in real GDP or inflation. Statistics Canada publishes a monthly index of leading economic indicators — ten factors averaged together that many economists believe provide a good guide to economic activity nine or so months in the future.

Of the components that go into the index of leading indicators (see Box 12.2), perhaps the most broadly watched is the stock market. The level of the stock market is a good indicator of the future of investment spending because the same factors that make corporate investment committees likely to approve investment projects — optimism about future profits, cheap sources of financing, willingness to accept risks — make investors eager to buy stocks and to buy stocks at higher prices. We can read likely future decisions of corporate investment committees from the current value of the stock market. But the stock market is far from perfect as a leading indicator: As economist Paul Samuelson likes to say, the stock market has predicted nine of the past five recessions.

WHAT ARE LEADING INDICATORS?

The index of leading indicators contains ten different components. The index is constructed by Statistics Canada, which weights all ten of these components to try to create the best possible index of leading indicators, which is called the "Composite Leading Indicator." The recent values of the components of the index are shown in Table 12.1.

TABLE 12.1
Components of the Composite Leading Indicator

	February 2006	March 2006
Composite leading indicator (1992 = 100)	**211.8**	**213**
Housing index (1992 = 100)*	146.6	150.8
Business and personal services employment (000's)	2,682	2,684
TSE 300 stock price index (1975 = 1000)	11,223	11,568
Money supply, M1 ($ millions, 1992)**	142,883	144,443
U.S. composite leading indicator (1992 = 100)***	126.5	127.1
Manufacturing average workweek (hours)	38.1	38
Manufacturing new orders, durables ($ millions, 1992)****	26,700	26,513
Manufacturing shipments/inventories of finished goods****	1.86	1.87
Retail furniture and appliance sales ($ millions, 1992)****	2,339	2,382
Retail other durable goods sales ($ millions, 1992)****	8,079	8,090

Source: Adapted from Statistics Canada CANSIM II database, Table 377-0003.

Notes: *Composite index of housing starts (units) and house sales (multiple listing service).
** Deflated by the Consumer Price Index for all items.
*** The figures in this row reflect data published in the month indicated, but the figures themselves refer to data for the month immediately preceding.
**** The figures in these rows reflect data published in the month indicated, but the figures themselves refer to data for the second preceding month.

THE MONEY SUPPLY AS A LEADING INDICATOR

The leading indicator that has been most closely watched is the *money supply*. Before the instability of the 1980s *monetarists* used to claim that the appropriate measure of the money stock is the only leading indicator worth watching. If the central bank can guide the money stock to the appropriate level through open-market operations, then success at managing the economy will immediately and automatically follow.

As we saw in Chapter 7, there is no sharp, bright line separating assets that are easy to spend from other assets. A dollar bill is clearly "money" in economists' sense

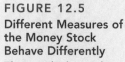

FIGURE 12.5

Different Measures of the Money Stock Behave Differently

The graph shows the different annual growth rates of money stock measures. Since 1974 these different measures have ceased to move together. A year like 1997, in which M1 increases, can also see M2 fall, with a difference between the two of more than 16 percentage points per year.

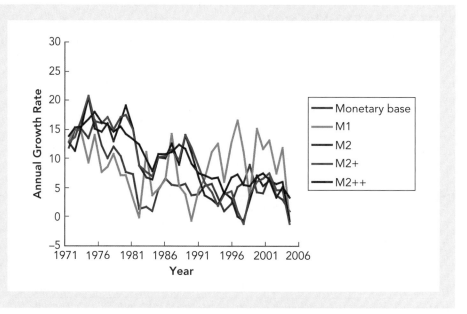

Source: Adapted from Statistics Canada CANSIM II database, Series V37253 (monetary base), V37200 (M1), V37198 (M2), V37131 (M2+), and V37150 (M2++).

of being readily spendable purchasing power. But what about a 90-day certificate of deposit with an interest penalty if you cash it in before it matures? Each place you draw the line gives you a particular total dollar amount of the assets that make up the economy's "money" — a different monetary aggregate. In order from the smallest to the largest, with each a superset of the one before, the most often used measures are called by the shorthand names M1, M2, M2+, and M2++.

As seen from Figure 12.5, these three monetary aggregates do not behave the same. During 1997, for example, M1 — the narrow measure — grew by more than 16 percent while M2++, the broad measure, grew by less than 7 percent, and there was a fall in M2. As gauged by M1, monetary policy in 1997 was expansionary: the Bank of Canada's monetary policy was forcing M1 to grow rapidly, pushing down interest rates and boosting demand. But as gauged by total M2, monetary policy in 1997 was contractionary. The Bank of Canada was reducing M2, and pushing up interest rates. Different measures of the money stock say different things about monetary policy. In fact, there are several other monetary aggregates that the Bank of Canada monitors when conducting its monetary policies (see Box 7.2 in Chapter 7).

LONG LAGS AND VARIABLE EFFECTS

Even if economists have good, reliable forecasts, changes in macroeconomic policy affect the economy with long lags and have variable effects. Estimates of the slope of the IS curve are imprecise: This isn't rocket science, after all. Economists are estimating the reactions of human beings to changes in the incentives to undertake different courses of action. They are not calculating the motions of particles that obey invariant and precisely known physical laws.

Moreover, changes in interest rates take *time* to affect the level of aggregate demand and real GDP. It takes time for corporate investment committees to meet and evaluate how changes in interest rates change the investment projects they wish

http://www.cdhowe.org/

to undertake. It takes time for changes in the decisions of corporate investment committees to affect the amount of work being done that builds up the country's capital stock. It takes time for the changes in employment and income generated by changes in investment to feed through the multiplier process and have their full effect on equilibrium aggregate demand. Thus the level of total product now is determined not by what long-term real risky interest rates are now, but by what they were more than a year and a half ago.

RECAP THE POWER AND LIMITS OF STABILIZATION POLICY

During the 1970s, especially, economists and policy makers painfully learned that the ability of the government to successfully conduct stabilization policy was limited by three factors. First, it became clear that any loss by the public of their belief that the central bank was committed to low inflation produced *stagflation* — a combination of relatively high unemployment and relatively high inflation. Second, a lack of accurate forecasts combined with the long and variable lags with which economic policies take effect means that monetary and fiscal policy must be slow to respond to sudden falls in production and rises in unemployment. Third, because economic policies have uncertain effects, policies to aggressively fight recessions may well wind up being counterproductive. Good policy makers must be cautious policy makers.

12.5 MONETARY POLICY AND THE LIQUIDITY TRAP

As we studied in detail in Chapter 7, the central bank changes interest rates through open market operations. When the central bank buys government bonds, it reduces their supply available for private investors. This reduction in supply raises the price of short-term government bonds. As each government bond pays a fixed amount each period to its holder, this increase in the price of bonds is equivalent to a reduction in the rate of return on each dollar invested in government bonds: a decline in its interest rate.

There is one important restriction on the Bank of Canada's power to set interest rates. When the nominal interest rate is close to zero government bonds and money become such close substitutes that it may not be worthwhile for households and firms to go through the trouble or incur the transaction cost to switch between the two assets in order to maximize the return on their wealth. At very low nominal interest rates, therefore, if there is an increase in real money holdings by households and firms they will not convert part of it into bonds; bond prices will not change, and there will be no change in the nominal interest rate.

In Figure 12.6 we show the money market equilibrium that we studied in detail in Chapter 10. At nominal interest rates close to zero, the demand for real money balances will be very sensitive to falls in the nominal interest rate; and the liquidity preference curve $L(r + \pi^e, Y)$ will be flat. Suppose we start from initial equilibrium at point A, with initial real money supply of M_0/P. If there is a change in the real money supply, the equilibrium nominal interest rate will not change, and any amount of real balances that is supplied will be held at the nominal interest rate i_0. Economists refer to such a situation as a **liquidity trap**.

FIGURE 12.6
Money Market Equilibrium and the Liquidity Trap
At nominal interest rates close to zero, the demand for real money balances is very sensitive to decreases in the nominal interest rate; and the liquidity preference curve is flat. Suppose we start from initial equilibrium at point A, with initial real money supply of M_0/P. If there is a change in the real money supply, to M_1/P or M_2/P, say, the equilibrium nominal interest rate will not change. Economists refer to such a situation as a *liquidity trap.*

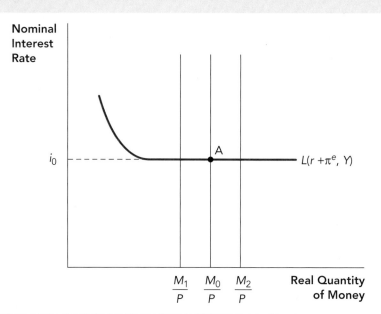

A country may fall into a liquidity trap after a crash in stock or real estate prices. Examples of such crashes include the 1929 Wall Street crash, which sent the U.S. economy into the Great Depression, and the stock and the real estate market crashes in Japan in the early 1990s, which sent that economy into a decade-long recession. After a crash in stock or real estate markets households and firms lose a large portion of their wealth; households cut back on their consumption expenditures and firms cut back on their investment expenditures. The resulting fall in aggregate expenditures sends the economy into a deep recession. Once the country is in this situation, the central bank responds by reducing interest rates. If the recession is deep enough even when interest rates fall the economy stays stagnant; eventually, interest rates hit such low levels that the economy falls into a liquidity trap.

Once the country is in a liquidity trap matters will get worse. Because of the recession, output demanded is substantially below potential and prices will start to fall. With the nominal interest rates i fixed due to the liquidity trap, and with prices expected to fall, the real interest rate r will increase, because the real interest rate is the difference between the nominal interest rate and the expected inflation rate (π^e):

$$r = i - \pi^e$$

If the expected inflation rate is sufficiently far below zero, the real interest rate will be high, and investment low, no matter what the Bank of Canada does. As Box 12.3 discusses, this may be relevant to Japan's economic stagnation in the 1990s.

JAPAN'S LIQUIDITY TRAP

The possibility that monetary policy might lose its power because expected deflation kept *real* interest rates high used to be dismissed as a theoretical curiosity irrelevant to the real world. But for a decade since the mid-1990s the Japanese economy looked very much as though it was caught in such a "liquidity trap." Real GDP was far below potential output. Nominal interest rates on short-term government bonds at times fell to 0.04 percent — that is four-hundredths of 1 percent a year; the annual interest on $100 invested at such an interest rate would be four cents. (See Figure 12.7.) But a combination of expected deflation, high risk premiums, and steep term premiums meant that businesses found that the real interest rate they had to pay to borrow money was quite high.

This situation continued until 2002. From the banks' perspective there were few creditworthy borrowers. Yet from the businesses' perspective there was little afford-able capital. Japan's stagnation dragged on for nearly a decade.

Two obvious policies might have improved matters. The first was fiscal expansion: Cut taxes or increase spending to shift the IS curve to the right and raise the level of aggregate demand even if real interest rates were relatively high. The second was to create expectations of inflation by announcing that monetary policy would be expansionary not just in the short run but for the indefinite future.

FIGURE 12.7

Japan's Liquidity Trap in the 1990s: Nominal Safe Interest Rates
The graph shows the official discount rate of the Bank of Japan. Despite a decade of extremely low interest rates on government bonds in Japan, investment has not boomed. Why not? Because risk premiums and expected deflation have made businesses believe that the real interest rates at which they can borrow remain high.

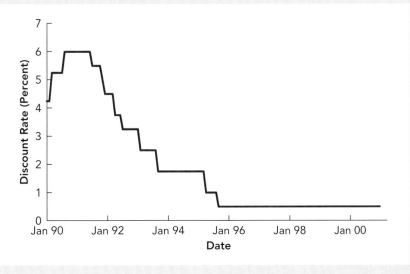

Source: Bank of Japan.

THE IS-LM MODEL AND THE LIQUIDITY TRAP

Now we use the IS-LM model to analyze an economy in a liquidity trap. To this end, we should examine the shape of the LM curve in a liquidity trap. First, notice from Figure 12.6 that once the economy is in a liquidity trap, the liquidity preference schedule is infinitely sensitive to changes in interest rates; that is, the parameter L_i in the equation for the liquidity preference

$$L = L_0 - L_i \times i + L_y \times Y$$

is infinitely large. With such a large value for L_i the ratio L_y/L_i (the slope of the LM curve) will be zero; that is, the LM curve will be horizontal.

In other words, even though an increase in income will shift the liquidity preference curve to the right, changes in income will not affect the nominal interest rate that clears the money market. As a result, a country that is in a liquidity trap will have its money market in equilibrium at any income level as long as the nominal interest rate is at i_0.

Figure 12.8 shows two LM curves for a country in a liquidity trap. It is important to notice that, in this figure, the vertical axis measures the *real* interest rate $r = i - \pi^e$. With the nominal interest rate fixed at i_0, each LM curve corresponds to a different expected inflation rate. If π^e falls, then the real interest rate required to clear the money market must increase; that is, the LM curve will shift up.

Suppose the initial equilibrium is at point A in Figure 12.7, with initial output Y_0 substantially below its potential level Y^*. Then, as prices start to fall, the expected inflation rate becomes negative, and the LM curve shifts up, resulting in a new equilibrium point at B, with lower output than Y_0. This situation places even stronger deflationary pressures in the economy, reducing expected inflation (or increasing deflation) further, and shifting LM up again. Hence, unless the government takes fiscal measures in order to shift the IS curve to the right, output will be falling over time.

Now consider the question of what policies can help a country get out of a liquidity trap. Recall the expression for the money supply multiplier derived in Chapter 9:

FIGURE 12.8

Liquidity Trap and Deflation

Suppose the initial equilibrium is at point A, with initial output Y_0, below its potential level Y^*. Then, as prices start to fall, the expected inflation rate becomes negative, and the LM curve shifts up, resulting in a new equilibrium point at B, with lower output than Y_0. This situation places even stronger deflationary pressures on the economy, reducing expected inflation (or increasing deflation) further, and shifting LM up again.

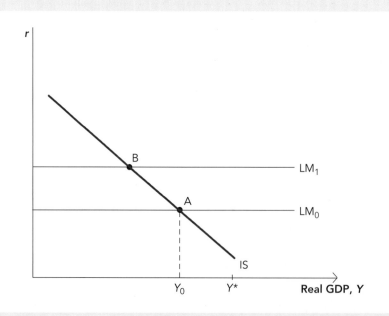

$$Y_M = \frac{1/L_i}{(1 - MPE) + (I_r + X_\varepsilon \times \varepsilon_r) \times \dfrac{L_y}{L_i}}$$

Clearly, in a liquidity trap, when L_i is infinitely large, this multiplier is zero, and monetary policy is ineffective. In contrast, in a liquidity trap, when the interest rate is unaffected by shifts of the IS curve, the government expenditures multiplier Y_G has the same value as in Chapter 8, when interest rate effects were absent; that is, in a liquidity trap $Y_G = \dfrac{1}{1 - MPE}$. Hence, in this case fiscal policy is very effective in changing output.

RECAP   MONETARY POLICY AND THE LIQUIDITY TRAP

When the nominal interest rate is close to zero government bonds and money are very close substitutes. As a result, if there is an increase in real money holdings by households and firms they will not convert part of it into bonds. Bond prices will not change, and there will be no change in the nominal interest rate. Monetary policy will then be ineffective in changing output, and fiscal policy should be used to get the country out of a recession. Japan experienced such a liquidity trap in the 1990s and early 2000s, with nominal interest rates close to zero and falling prices (deflation). The associated ineffectiveness of monetary policy kept that country in the liquidity trap for more than a decade. Only recently has Japan been able to escape from the liquidity trap, showing positive economic growth and rising prices.

12.6 MONETARY VERSUS FISCAL POLICY

RELATIVE POWER

At the end of the World War II era, most economists and policy makers believed that the principal stabilization policy tool would be *fiscal policy*. Monetary policy had proved to be of little use during the Great Depression: Risk premiums and term premiums were too high and too unstable for changes in the short-term nominal safe interest rates controlled by central banks to have reliable effects on production and employment. In contrast, changes in government spending and in taxes were seen as having rapid and reliable effects on aggregate demand. But over the past 50 years opinion has shifted. Today the overwhelming consensus is that monetary policy has proved itself faster acting and more reliable than discretionary fiscal policy.

When the Ministry of Finance tries to stabilize the economy by fiscal policy — by passing laws to change levels of taxes and spending — it cannot realistically hope to see changes in the level of output and employment in less than two years after the bill is first introduced into the Houses of Parliament. It takes time for the bill to be enacted. And it takes more time for the change in government purchases or in net taxes to have its full effect through the multiplier process.

Monetary policy lags are shorter. The Bank of Canada can move rapidly; once its decisions are made they affect long-term real interest rates on the same day. There are substantial lags between when interest rates change and when output reaches its new equilibrium value: Monetary policy still takes more than a year to work. But **monetary policy lags** are shorter than those associated with **discretionary fiscal policy**.

The nature of the international monetary arrangements also plays a very important role in determining the relative strengths of fiscal and monetary policies. After World

War II the world economy had a fixed exchange rate system; and the central bank of every country was obliged to maintain a fixed exchange rate by buying and selling its currency in return for foreign exchange. All other monetary considerations were subservient to this obligation of the central bank. Monetary policy was, therefore, ineffective, and stabilization was done mainly through fiscal policies.

On the other hand, since the early 1970s most countries have adopted a flexible exchange rate system. Monetary authorities, therefore, are independent to follow stabilization policies. Furthermore, under a flexible exchange rate system fiscal policy is relatively ineffective as a stabilization tool. As government expenditures increase, and the domestic interest rate rises, by our fundamental equation for the determination of the exchange rate

$$\varepsilon = \varepsilon_0 - \varepsilon_r \times (r - r^f)$$

there is a real appreciation, which reduces net exports. Hence, under a flexible exchange rate system an increase in government expenditure "crowds out" net exports. These important issues will be dealt with in detail in Chapter 15.

FISCAL POLICY: AUTOMATIC STABILIZERS

There is, however, one kind of fiscal policy that does work rapidly enough to be important. The so-called fiscal **automatic stabilizers** swing into action within three months to moderate business cycle–driven swings in disposable income and so moderate the business cycle.

Whenever the economy enters a recession or a boom, the government's budget surplus or deficit begins to swing in the opposite direction. As the economy enters a boom, tax collections and withholdings automatically rise because incomes rise. Spending on social welfare programs like unemployment insurance falls because higher employment and higher wages mean that fewer people are poor. Thus the government budget moves toward surplus, without the Houses of Parliament passing or signing a single bill. And if the economy enters a recession, tax collections fall, social welfare spending rises, and the government's budget swings into deficit.

As unemployment rises and national income falls, taxes fall by about 30 cents for every dollar fall in national product. Spending rises by about 7 cents for every dollar fall in national product. A $1 fall in national product produces a fall of only 70 cents in consumers' disposable income. Thus automatic stabilizers provide more than $1's worth of boost to aggregate demand for every $3 fall in production.

Such fiscal automatic stabilizers would be large enough to reduce the marginal propensity to spend from about 0.6 to about 0.4. This would imply a reduction in the size of the multiplier from about 2.5 to about 1.67. Business cycles could be considerably larger if these automatic stabilizers did not exist, if the Bank of Canada found itself unable to compensate for their disappearance, and if their disappearance did not lead to counteracting changes in the marginal propensity to spend.

HOW MONETARY POLICY WORKS

For monetary policy to work, the Bank of Canada must first recognize that there is a problem. It takes three to six months for statistical agencies to collect and process the data, for the Bank of Canada to recognize the state of the economy, and for it to conclude that action is needed.

Once the Bank of Canada acts, the response of financial markets is immediate. At the latest, interest rates shift the very day the policy change is announced. Often interest rates change in advance of the policy change, because traders can often

MONETARY POLICY INSTRUMENTS

Today the Bank of Canada focuses on controlling interest rates. In the past it has occasionally let interest rates be more volatile and focused on controlling the rate of growth of the *money supply* — also called the money stock — which is the economy's total supply of liquid assets.

Should the Bank of Canada target real interest rates — try to keep them stable, perhaps allowing them to climb when inflation threatens and to fall during a recession? Or should it focus on keeping the money stock growing smoothly because the money stock is a good leading indicator, and stabilizing the growth path of this indicator is a good way to stabilize the economy as a whole?

It depends.

If the principal instability in the economy is found in a shifting IS curve, then targeting interest rates will do little or nothing to reduce the magnitude of shocks to the economy. Better to have a monetary policy *reaction function* that reacts to leading indicators and outcomes. But if the instability lies instead in the relationship between the money stock and real output (the result of volatile money demand) or in a shifting relationship between the monetary base and the money supply (because the currency-to-deposits and reserves-to-deposits ratios vary), then targeting interest rates is wiser.

In recent years instability has been primarily in the velocity of money and the sign of the money multiplier. The money multiplier has fluctuated unexpectedly and widely in the 1980s and 1990s, chiefly because of unexpected fluctuations in the currency-to-deposits ratio. Since 1980, the Bank of Canada's control over the monetary base has not been enough to allow the Bank of Canada to exercise control over the money supply. And the velocity of money has fluctuated as well. By contrast, the position of the IS curve has been relatively stable.

Thus in the past two decades it has been better for the Bank of Canada to have as its monetary target the level of interest rates than the growth of the money supply.

guess what it is going to do beforehand. However, it takes over a year for changes in interest rates to change national product and unemployment.

This means that the Bank of Canada is essentially powerless to smooth out fluctuations in less than a year. The average recession in post–World War II Canada has lasted less than 18 months. This means that by the time monetary policy changes initiated at the beginning of the recession and aimed at reducing its size have their effect on the economy, the recession is likely to be nearly over (see Box 12.4).

RECAP　MONETARY VERSUS FISCAL POLICY

Under a flexible exchange rate system policy makers favour monetary rather than fiscal policy as a stabilizing tool, because with flexible rates fiscal policy is relatively ineffective. In addition, monetary policy lags are shorter than fiscal policy lags. On the other hand, under a fixed exchange rate system most policy makers favour fiscal policy, because with a fixed exchange rate system all monetary policy considerations are subservient to the obligation of the central bank to buy and sell its currency in return for foreign exchange in order to stabilize the exchange rate.

12.7 RULES VERSUS DISCRETION

In the late 1940s Chicago School economist Henry Simons set the terms for a debate over macroeconomic policy that continues to this day. He asked, Should macroeconomic policy be conducted "automatically," according to **rules** that would be followed no matter what? Or should macroeconomic policy be left to authorities — bodies of appointed officials — provided with wide discretion over how to use their power and given general guidance as to what goals to pursue?

COMPETENCE AND OBJECTIVES

The first reason for automatic rules is that we fear that the people appointed to authorities will be incompetent. If people are appointed because of friendships from the past, or because of their ability to rally campaign contributions for a particular cause, there is little reason to think that they will be skilled judges of the situation or insightful analysts. Better then to constrain them by automatic rules. Even if those appointed to authorities are well intentioned, they may fail to find good solutions to macroeconomic problems. The stream of public discourse about macroeconomics is polluted by a large quantity of misinformation.

A second reason for fixed rules is that authorities might not have the right objectives. To institute a good rule it is only necessary for the political process to make the right decision once — at the moment the rule is settled. But an authority making decisions every day may be more likely to start pursuing objectives that conflict with the long-run public interest. The state of the economy at the moment of the election is a powerful influence on citizens' votes. Thus politicians in office have a personal power incentive to pursue policies that will sacrifice the health of the economy in the future in order to obtain good reported economic numbers during the election year.

The substitution of technocratic authorities — like the Bank of Canada — in the place of prime ministers and finance ministers provides some insulation. The fear that politicians will have objectives different from the long-run public interest has led many to advocate that monetary policy be made by *independent* central banks. If stabilization policy is to be made by authorities, it should be made by authorities placed at least one remove from partisan politics (see Box 12.5).

BOX 12.5 POLICY

CENTRAL BANK INDEPENDENCE

A number of economists have investigated the relationship between macroeconomic performance and the degree to which central banks are insulated from partisan politics. They have examined the legal and institutional framework within which central banks in different countries operate, and constructed indexes of the extent to which their central banks are independent.

Alberto Alesina and Lawrence Summers concluded that the more independent a central bank, the better its inflation performance. More independent central banks presided over lower average inflation and less variable inflation. Moreover, countries with independent central banks did not pay any penalty. Countries with independent central banks did not have higher unemployment, lower real GDP growth, or larger business cycles.

Interpreting this correlation is not straightforward. Perhaps the factors that lead countries to have independent central banks lead them to have low inflation. Perhaps independent central banks do reduce economic growth, but only countries likely to have high economic growth for other reasons are likely to have independent central banks. Nevertheless, at least the post-1950 experience of the industrialized countries strongly suggests that insulating central banks from partisan politics delivers low inflation without any visible macroeconomic cost (see Figure 12.9).

FIGURE 12.9

Inflation and Central Bank Insulation from Politics

Countries whose central banks are more independent — rate higher on an average index of independence — have lower average inflation rates.

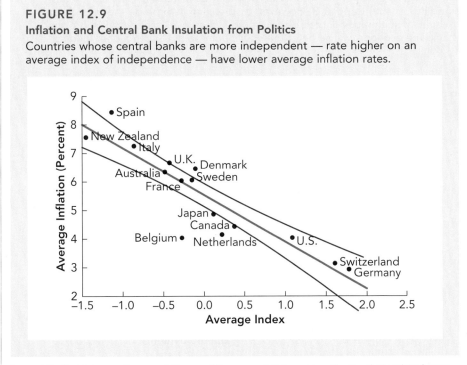

Source: J. Bradford DeLong and Lawrence H. Summers, "Macroeconomic Policy and Long-Run Growth," in *Policies for Long-Run Economic Growth* (Kansas City: Federal Reserve Bank of Kansas City, 1993), pp. 93–128; replicating an analysis carried out by Alberto Alesina, "Macroeconomics and Politics," *NBER Macroeconomics Annual 1988* (Cambridge, MA: MIT Press, 1988).

DYNAMIC INCONSISTENCY AND POLICIES WITH INFLATIONARY BIAS

An important implication of the rational expectations hypothesis is that, because workers and firms take the behaviour of the government into account when forming their expectations, it is important that the government should not break its promises. Government polices that are announced but not ultimately carried out are said to be dynamically inconsistent. Here we provide a simple illustration of why governments may have an incentive not to implement the policies they promise; and why broken promises may lead the economy to an inferior equilibrium.

To this end, we consider the incentives of a central bank to break its promises of a low inflation policy; and we illustrate how this may lead to inflationary policies. The key to understanding the source of dynamic inconsistency in the central banks' low inflation policy is to keep in mind the distinction between the short-run and the long-run Phillips curves. In the short-run, there is always a trade-off between inflation and unemployment, given the public's expectations of inflation. However, no such trade-off exists in the long-run as expected inflation is *always* equal to actual inflation and the Phillips curve is vertical at the natural rate of unemployment, as shown in Figure 12.10.

FIGURE 12.10

Dynamic Inconsistency and Inflationary Bias

The best policy is to achieve the equilibrium point A, with low inflation and unemployment at the natural rate, u^*. But if the expected inflation rate is at $\pi^e = \pi_0$ and the short-run Phillips curve at PC ($\pi^e = \pi_0$), it is tempting for the central bank to reduce the unemployment rate below u^* by increasing the inflation rate, and moving the economy along PC ($\pi^e = \pi_0$) to point B. However, by breaking its promise the central bank loses its *reputation*. The expected inflation rate will then be set at the higher level, placing the short-run Phillips curve at PC ($\pi^e = \pi_1$); and the economy will settle at the equilibrium point D, with higher long-run inflation at π_1.

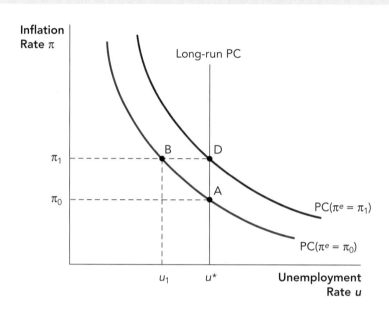

Suppose the central bank promises that it will implement a policy of achieving a low inflation rate, corresponding to the natural rate of unemployment u^* at point A. Suppose, further, that workers and firms believe the central bank, and set their expected inflation rate at $\pi^e = \pi_0$. In Figure 12.10, with $\pi^e = \pi_0$ the short-run Phillips curve will be at PC ($\pi^e = \pi_0$). Next, notice once the short-run Phillips curve is at PC ($\pi^e = \pi_0$) it is tempting for a politically motivated central bank to reduce the unemployment rate below its natural level u^* by increasing the inflation rate and moving the economy along PC ($\pi^e = \pi_0$) to point B. Notice that the central bank will be willing to raise the inflation rate to π_1 in this manner as long as the political benefits of having the unemployment rate at u_1 rather than u^* dominate the political costs of having the inflation rate at π_1 rather than π_0.

Hence, with central banks that do not mind breaking their own promises, low inflation policies are dynamically inconsistent; they are promised policies that will not be implemented. Notice also that with higher inflation rates the political costs of raising the inflation rate further are much higher, and the central bank is less likely to break its promise.

When the central bank loses its reputation by breaking its promises, workers and firms will set their expected inflation rate at the higher level π_1, placing the short-run Phillips curve at PC ($\pi^e = \pi_1$). Once the Phillips curve is at PC ($\pi^e = \pi_1$), the political costs of increasing it further are just equal to the political benefits of having an unemployment rate that is slightly below its natural rate. The economy, therefore settles at the equilibrium point D along the long-run Phillips curve.

The important point to note is that a central bank that breaks its words by reneging on its promises of low inflation cannot credibly promise a low inflation policy, and it cannot attain the equilibrium at point A in Figure 12.10. Such a central bank has to choose a point like D, with the same unemployment rate as A, but a higher inflation rate. As inflation reduces welfare, the economy is worse off at D.

In the late 1970s, economists managed to convince central bankers in industrialized countries that promises should not be broken, and low inflation policies should be implemented in order to make low inflation equilibriums attainable. For this reason, in the early 1980s the central banks in most industrialized countries followed inflation reduction policies, even though at that time such policies seemed to be too painful. It is because of these policies that the central banks today have regained **credibility**, and we now enjoy the benefits of low inflation, and relatively low unemployment.

MODERN MONETARY POLICY

Whether monetary policy is guided by strict and rigid rules or made by authorities using their discretion to come up with the best policy for the particular — unique — situation, one question remains: What sort of rules should be adopted, or how should the authority behave? What sort of *guidelines* for monetary policy should those who set the rules or those who staff the authorities follow?

Economists believe that one set of rules to avoid are those that command the central bank to attain values for real economic variables, like the rate of growth of real GDP or the level of the unemployment rate. The rate of growth of real GDP is limited in the long run by the rate of growth of potential output. The level of the unemployment rate is controlled in the long run by the natural rate of unemployment. A central-bank target of too high a rate of real GDP growth, or too low a level of the unemployment rate, is likely to end in upward-spiralling inflation. A policy that targets *nominal* variables — like the nominal money stock, or nominal GDP, or the inflation rate — is robust, in the sense that it does not run the risk of leading to disaster if our assessment of the macroeconomic structure of the economy turns out to be wrong.

One proposal is for the central bank to choose a target for the inflation rate (call it π'), to estimate what the real interest rate should be on average (call it r^*). It would then raise interest rates when inflation is above and lower interest rates when inflation is below this target. A 1-percentage-point increase in inflation would cause the central bank to raise real interest rates by an amount represented by the parameter ϕ'':

$$r = r^* + \phi'' \times (\pi - \pi')$$

An activist central bank concerned with unemployment as well might also reduce the real interest rate when unemployment is above the natural rate, and raise it whenever unemployment falls below the natural rate, with a 1-percentage-point increase in unemployment causing the central bank to reduce real interest rates by an amount represented by the parameter γ:

$$r = r^* + \phi'' \times (\pi - \pi') - \gamma \times (u - u^*)$$

Stanford University macroeconomist John Taylor put this *Taylor rule* forward as a way of adding some structure and order to the process by which monetary policy is made. The Taylor rule provides a way to think about how strongly the Bank of Canada should move to counter shocks to the economy. Do you believe that the Bank of Canada should act more aggressively to boost the economy when unemployment is high? Then you are arguing for a larger parameter γ in the Taylor rule. Do you believe that the Bank of Canada reacts too strongly to cool the economy when inflation rises? Then you are arguing for a smaller parameter ϕ'' in the Taylor rule.

> **RECAP   RULES VERSUS DISCRETION**
>
> The short-run trade-off between inflation and unemployment, given the public's expectations of inflation, gives the central banks the incentive to promise low inflation (keeping expectations low) but to create surprise inflations instead — in order to reduce unemployment. However, central banks that follow such policies lose credibility, leading to high inflation expectations, and are unable to reduce the unemployment rate below the natural rate.

12.8 EXTREME SITUATIONS: FINANCIAL CRISES

Open-market operations are not the only tool by which the central bank affects the economy. Because the long-term interest rate is an average of expected future short-term interest rates, expectations of future Bank of Canada policy — closely tied to central-bank credibility — are also important influences on aggregate demand today. Even more important, however, are the existence of *deposit insurance* to insulate bank depositors from the effects of financial crises, and the expectation that should a financial crisis become deep enough the Bank of Canada will act as a lender of last resort. In extreme situations such alternative policy levers become important tools to try to stem depressions.

For nearly 400 years market economies have undergone *financial crises* — episodes when the prices of stocks or of other assets crash, everyone tries to move their wealth into safer forms at once, and the consequent panic among investors can lead to a prolonged and serious depression. Managing such financial crises has been one of the responsibilities of monetary policy makers for more than a century and a half.

A financial crisis — like the financial panics in East Asia in 1998 — sees investors as a group suddenly (and often not very rationally) become convinced that their investments have become overly risky. As a result, they try to exchange their investments for high-quality bonds and cash. But as everyone tries to do this at once, they create the risk that they hoped to avoid: Stock and real estate prices crash, and interest rates spike upward as everyone tries to increase their holdings of relatively safe, liquid assets.

The sharp rise in real interest rates that occurs in a financial crisis can severely reduce investment, and send the economy into a deep depression. Moreover, once the crisis gathers force, the ability of monetary policy tools to boost investment may well be limited. Financial crises are accompanied by steep rises in risk premiums. They are often accompanied by sharp rises in term premiums as well, as investors decide that they want to hold their wealth in as liquid a form as possible. And financial crises frequently generate deflation as well.

All of these drive a large wedge between the short-term nominal safe interest rates that the central bank controls and the long-term real interest rate relevant for the determination of investment and aggregate demand. The central bank may have done all it can to reduce interest rates, and it may not be enough: Real interest rates may remain high.

LENDERS OF LAST RESORT

In such a situation a central bank can do a lot of good easily by rapidly expanding the money supply, so that the increase in the demand for liquid assets to hold doesn't lead to a spike in interest rates and a crash in other asset prices. It can also do a lot of good by lending directly to institutions that are fundamentally *solvent* — that will, if the crisis is stemmed and resolved rapidly, be able to function profitably — but that are temporarily *illiquid* in the sense that no one is willing to lend to them because no one is confident that the crisis will be resolved. Such a *lender of last resort* can rapidly reduce risk and term premiums as it reduces safe short-term nominal interest rates and end the financial crisis.

The problem is that a central bank can also do a lot of harm if it bails out institutions that have gone bankrupt, and thus encourages others in the future to take excessive risks hoping that the central bank will bail them out. Thus the central bank has to (a) expand the money supply and lend freely to institutions that are merely illiquid — that is, caught short of cash but fundamentally sound — while (b) forcibly liquidating institutions that are insolvent, those that could never repay what they owe even if the panic were stemmed immediately. This is a neat trick, to save one without saving the other.

A central bank can take institutional steps in advance to reduce the chance that the economy will suffer a financial crisis, and reduce the damage that a financial panic will do. The first and most obvious is to do a good job as a supervising regulator over the banking system. Depositors will panic and pull their money out of a bank when they fear that it is bankrupt — that it no longer has enough capital, and that the capital plus the value of the loans that it has made are together lower than the value of the money it owes to its depositors. If banks are kept well capitalized, and if banks that fail to meet standards for capital adequacy are rapidly taken over and closed down, then the risk of a full-fledged financial panic is small.

The potential problem with this strategy of supervision and surveillance is that it may be politically difficult to carry out. Bankers are, after all, often wealthy and influential people with substantial political connections. Bank regulators are midlevel civil servants, subject to pressure and influence from politicians.

DEPOSIT INSURANCE AND MORAL HAZARD

The most recent major financial crisis in industrialized countries, the Great Depression, was also the most destructive. Although there were no bank failures in Canada, in the U.S. at the beginning of 1933 more than one in three of the banks that had existed in 1929 had closed its doors. When banks failed, people who had their money in them were out of luck; years might pass before any portion of their deposits would be returned. Hence fear of bank failure leads to an immediate increase in households' and businesses' holdings of currency relative to deposits. In the Great Depression this flight from banks reduced the money supply.

With banks failing, more and more people felt that putting their money in a bank was not much better than throwing it away. Since a rise in the currency-to-deposits ratio carries with it a fall in the money multiplier, fear of bank failures shrank the money stock. That only deepened the Depression.

http://www.cdic.ca/

One of the reforms adopted by several developed countries since the 1930s is the institution of deposit insurance provided by the government. If your bank fails, the government will make sure your deposits do not disappear. In Canada such insurance is provided by the Canada Deposit Insurance Corporation (CDIC), which was established by the federal government in 1967. The purpose of such insurance schemes is to diminish monetary instability by eliminating swings in the money supply and interest rates that are driven by failures of banks and other financial institutions, such as trust companies.

Government deposit insurance acts as a **monetary automatic stabilizer**. A financial panic gathers force when investors conclude that they need to pull their money out of banks and mutual funds because such investments are too risky. Deposit insurance eliminates the risk of keeping your money in a bank — even if the bank goes belly-up, your deposit is still secure. Thus there is no reason to seek to move your money to any safer place. Deposit insurance has broken one of the important links in the chain of transmission that used to make financial panics so severe.

The availability of deposit insurance and the potential existence of a lender of last resort do not come for free. These institutions create potential problems of their own — problems that economists discuss under the heading of *moral hazard*. If depositors know that the Canada Deposit Insurance Corporation has guaranteed their deposits, they will not inquire into the kinds of loans that their bank is making. Bank owners and managers may decide to make deliberately risky high-interest loans. If the economy booms and the loans are repaid, then they make a fortune. If the economy goes into recession and the risky firms to which they have loaned go bankrupt, they declare bankruptcy too and leave the CDIC to deal with the depositors. It becomes a classic game of heads-I-win-tails-you-lose.

The principal way to guard against moral hazard is to make certain that decision makers have substantial amounts of their own money at risk. Making risky loans using government-guaranteed deposits as your source of funding is a lot less attractive if your personal wealth is the first thing that is taken to pay off depositors if the loans go bad. Hence deposit insurance and lenders of last resort function well only if there is adequate supervision and surveillance: only if the central bank and the other bank regulatory authorities are keeping close watch on banks, and making sure that every bank has adequate capital, so that it is the shareholders' and the managers' funds, rather than those of the CDIC, that are at risk if the loans made go bad.

RECAP   FINANCIAL CRISES

Financial crises are episodes when the prices of stocks or of other assets crash and everyone tries to move their wealth into safer forms at once. The consequent panic among investors can lead to a prolonged and serious depression. Managing such financial crises has been one of the responsibilities of monetary policy makers. To reduce the risks of financial crises, central banks act as a lender of last resort, and governments provide deposit insurance.

CHAPTER SUMMARY

1. Macroeconomic policy should attempt to stabilize the economy: to avoid extremes of high unemployment and also of high and rising inflation.

2. Long and variable lags make successful stabilization policy extremely difficult.

3. Economists arrange themselves along a spectrum, with some advocating more aggressive management of the economy and others concentrating on establishing a stable framework and economic environment. But compared to differences of opinion among economists in the past, differences of opinion today are minor.

4. In today's environment, monetary policy is the stabilization policy tool of choice, largely because it operates with shorter lags than does discretionary fiscal policy.

5. Nevertheless, the fiscal "automatic stabilizers" built into the tax system play an important role in reducing the size of the multiplier.

6. Uncertainty about the structure of the economy or the effectiveness of policy should lead policy makers to be cautious: Blunt policy tools should be used carefully and cautiously lest they do more harm than good.

7. The advantage of having economic policy made by an authority is that the authority can use judgment to devise the best response to a changing — and usually unforeseen — situation.

8. The advantages of having economic policy made by a *rule* are threefold: First, rules do not assume competence in authorities where it may not exist; second, rules reduce the possibility that policy will be made not in the public interest but in some special interest; third, rules make it easier to avoid so-called dynamic inconsistency.

9. Dynamic inconsistency arises whenever a central bank finds that it wishes to change its previously announced policy in an inflationary direction: It is always in the central bank's short-term interest to have money growth be higher, interest rates lower, and inflation a little higher than had been previously expected.

10. Today, however, central banks are by and large successful in taking a long-term view. They pay great attention to establishing and maintaining the credibility of their policy commitments.

KEY TERMS

automatic stabilizers (p. 380)

bank rate (p. 365)

credibility (p. 385)

discretionary fiscal policy (p. 379)

dynamic inconsistency (p. 383)

inside lag (p. 368)

leading indicators (p. 372)

liquidity trap (p. 375)

Lucas critique (p. 372)

monetary automatic stabilizers (p. 388)

monetary policy lags (p. 379)

operating band (p. 365)

price stability (p. 364)

rules (p. 382)

target for the overnight rate (p. 365)

ANALYTICAL EXERCISES

1. What is the Lucas critique? How would the Lucas critique suggest that you should design a policy to try to reduce annual inflation from 10 percent to 2 percent?

2. What is "dynamic inconsistency"? Why does dynamic inconsistency strengthen the case for having policy rules rather than having authorities with discretionary power over economic policy?

3. Under what circumstances do you think that the Bank of Canada should shift from targeting the interest rate to targeting the money stock growth rate?

4. What would be the economic advantages and disadvantages of eliminating federal deposit insurance?

5. Why do economic policy makers think it important to get the best available forecasts?

6. Suppose the Taylor rule followed by the monetary authorities is

$$r - r^* + 2 \times (\pi - \pi^*) - 0.3 \times (u - u^*).$$

Assume the target level of inflation is 2 percent, the target interest rate is 3 percent, and the target level of unemployment rate is 7 percent. If the actual inflation rate is 1 percent and the actual unemployment rate 9 percent, what will be the interest rate that the central bank would want to maintain? If the actual inflation rate is 5 percent and the actual unemployment rate 5 percent, what will be the actual interest rate?

7. Consider the money market equilibrium, and the derivation of the LM curve that we studied in Chapter 9. Explain what will be the shape of the LM curve in a liquidity trap. How will the LM curve shift if there is an increase in the money supply? Would fiscal policy be effective in changing the equilibrium output?

8. In this chapter we discussed the dynamic inconsistency problem with reference to the Phillips curve. The same issue can be discussed using the aggregate demand–aggregate supply model of Chapter 10. Can you explain how?

9. Recall the money supply and government expenditures multipliers derived in Chapter 9. Explain how the slopes of the IS and LM curves determine the relative strengths of monetary versus fiscal policies.

POLICY EXERCISES

1. Suppose that the economy's Phillips curve is given by

$$\pi = \pi^e - \beta \times (u - u^*)$$

with β equal to 0.4 and u^* equal to 0.06 — 6 percent. Suppose that the economy has for a long time had a constant inflation rate equal to 3 percent per year. Suddenly the government announces a new policy: It will use fiscal policy to boost real GDP by 5 percent relative to potential — enough by Okun's law to push the unemployment rate down by 2 percent — and it will keep that expanded fiscal policy in place indefinitely.

Suppose that agents in the economy have *adaptive expectations* of inflation — so that this year's expected inflation is equal to last year's actual inflation. What will be the course of inflation and unemployment in this economy in the years after the shift in fiscal policy? Track the economy out 20 years, assuming that there are no additional shocks.

2. Suppose that all conditions given in question 1 are the case. In addition, suppose that for each 1 percentage point that the inflation rate rises above 3 percent, the central bank raises nominal interest rates by 2 percentage points — and that each 1-percentage-point increase in real GDP moves the economy along the IS curve sufficiently to shrink real GDP by 1 percent.

As in question 1, suppose that agents in the economy have *adaptive expectations* of inflation — so that this year's expected inflation is equal to last year's actual inflation. What will be the course of inflation and unemployment in this economy in the years after the shift in fiscal policy? Track the economy out 20 years, assuming that there are no additional shocks.

3. Suppose that all conditions in question 2 are the case, except that β equals 0.5 and that for each 1 percentage

point the inflation rate rises above 3 percent, the central bank raises real interest rates by 1 percentage point. Again, suppose that each 1-percentage-point increase in real interest rates moves the economy along the IS curve sufficiently to shrink real GDP by 1 percent.

Finally, suppose that agents in the economy have *rational expectations* of inflation — so that this year's expected inflation is what an economist knowing the structure of the economy and proposed economic policies would calculate actual inflation was likely to be.

What will be the course of inflation and unemployment in this economy in the years after the shift in fiscal policy? Track the economy out 20 years, assuming that there are no additional shocks.

4. Suppose that an expensive government program is proposed: it is to spend money helping unemployed workers find new jobs, learn new skills, and possibly move to cities where unemployment is low. What effect is this program likely to have on the location of the Phillips curve in the long run?

5. Why do economists today tend to believe that monetary policy is superior to discretionary fiscal policy as a stabilization policy tool? In what circumstances that you can imagine would this belief be reversed?

6. In the 1970s the central banks of industrialized countries had developed a reputation for pursuing high inflation policies. Then, in the 1980s the central banks promised that they would bring inflation under control. Use the Phillips curve to explain why these policies led to high unemployment in the 1980s. Why are both unemployment and inflation so low now relative to the 1980s?

13

The Budget Balance, the National Debt, and Investment

QUESTIONS

From the standpoint of analyzing stabilization policy, what is the best measure of the government's budget balance?

From the standpoint of analyzing the effect of changes in the national debt on long-run growth, what is the best measure of the government's budget balance?

What is the typical pattern that the Canadian national debt follows over time?

How has experience in the past generation deviated from this traditional pattern of debt behaviour?

What are the reasons that we should worry about a rising national debt?

What are the reasons that we shouldn't worry too much about a rising national debt?

The *national debt* — the amount of money that the government owes those from whom it has borrowed — changes each year. In a year when government spending is less than tax collections, the difference is the government **surplus**. The national debt shrinks by the amount of the surplus. In a year when government spending is greater than tax collections, the difference is the government **deficit**. The national debt grows by the amount of the deficit. Call the debt D and the deficit d (and recognize that a surplus is a negative value of d). Then the relationship between the **debt** and the deficit is

$$\Delta D = d$$

where Δ (the Greek capital letter "delta") is, as before, a standard symbol for change. The change in the debt from year to year is equal to the deficit.

A government spending more than it collects in taxes (including the inflation tax noted in Chapter 7) must borrow the difference in order to finance its spending. A government borrows by selling its citizens and foreigners bonds: promises that the government will repay the principal it borrows with interest. These accumulated promises to pay make up the national debt.

Economists are interested in the debt and the deficit for two reasons. First, the deficit is a convenient and often handy — though sometimes treacherous — measure of fiscal policy's role in stabilization policy. It is an index of how government spending and tax plans affect the position of the IS curve. Second, the debt and deficit are closely connected with national savings and investment. A rising debt — a deficit — tends to depress capital formation. It lowers the economy's long-run steady-state growth path and reduces the steady-state GDP per worker. Moreover, a high national debt means that taxes in the future will be higher to pay higher interest charges. Such higher taxes are likely to further discourage economic activity and reduce economic welfare.

What to do about the national debt is one of the current flashpoints of Canadian politics. Canada ran its national debt up by a large amount during the high-deficit governments in the 1980s. One of the main questions facing Canadian voters and politicians now is: What (if anything) should be done to undo the rise in the debt? Should the government run large surpluses in order to push the debt down to its late-1970s level (or even lower)? Or should the government cut taxes and not worry as much about reducing the national debt? At the moment this issue hangs in the balance.

13.1 THE BUDGET DEFICIT AND STABILIZATION POLICY

THE BUDGET DEFICIT AND THE IS CURVE

An increase in government purchases increases aggregate demand. It shifts the IS curve out and to the right, increasing the level of real GDP for each possible value of the interest rate. A decrease in government tax collections also increases aggregate demand, also shifts the IS curve out. The government's budget deficit is equal to purchases minus net taxes. Why bother with two measures of fiscal policy — purchases and taxes — when you can just keep track of their difference?

This drive for simplification is the reason for focusing on the government's budget balance as a measure of fiscal policy. But it turns out that the right measure of budget balance is not the government's actual deficit (or surplus), as Box 13.1 explains. Instead, the right measure of fiscal policy is the full-employment or cyclically adjusted deficit (or surplus): what the government's budget balance would be if the economy were at full employment. (See Figure 13.1.)

MEASURING THE BUDGET BALANCE

There are different measures of the government budget balance that are frequently used in Canada. The most frequently reported is the **actual budget balance**, which is equal to the government revenues from its tax collections, minus its purchases of goods and services, minus government transfer payments, such as social security and welfare payments, minus the interest on the government debt. If the actual balance is negative then total government expenditures are larger than its revenues,

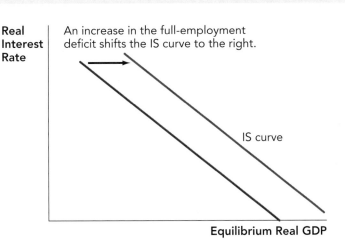

FIGURE 13.1

An Increase in the Full-Employment Deficit Shifts the IS Curve Outward

Either an increase in government purchases or a decrease in net taxes shifts the IS curve to the right. To keep track of the impact of government taxes and spending on the position of the IS curve, it is (approximately) sufficient to look at the difference between the two — the government deficit (or surplus).

and the government is paying for part of its expenditures by borrowing. If the actual balance is positive then total government revenues are larger than its expenditures, and the government is paying back part of the amount it borrowed in the past.

Why is the **full-employment** or **cyclically adjusted budget balance** a better index than either of the more frequently mentioned actual budget balance measures? Consider a situation in which the government does not change either its purchases or its tax rates, and so there is no change in government fiscal policy. But suppose that monetary policy tightens: Real interest rates are raised, and so the economy

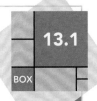

THE DEFICIT AS AN INDEX OF FISCAL POLICY

To see how the budget deficit can be used as an index of the effect of government policy on real GDP, return to the IS curve–based analysis of the determinants of real GDP that was conducted in Chapters 8 and 9. The effect on real GDP of a change in government spending is proportional to the value of the multiplier $1/(1 - MPE)$ (or $1/[1 - C_y(1 - t) + IM_y]$):

$$\Delta Y = \frac{1}{1 - C_y(1 - t) + IM_y} \times \Delta G$$

If the economy starts out at full employment with real GDP equal to potential output Y^*, then a change in tax rates has an effect on real GDP proportional to the product of the multiplier, the marginal propensity to consume C_y, and potential output Y^*:

$$\Delta Y = \frac{-1}{1 - C_y(1 - t) + IM_y} \times C_y Y^* \Delta t$$

Thus if both government purchases and tax rates change, the effect on real GDP will be given by the sum of these two formulas, which is

$$\Delta Y = \frac{1}{1 - C_y(1 - t) + IM_y} \times (\Delta G - C_y Y^* \Delta t)$$

Use ΔT^* to stand for the change in *full-employment tax collections* $Y^* \Delta t$, and add and subtract this change in full-employment tax collections from the right-hand side:

$$\Delta Y = \frac{1}{1 - C_y(1 - t) + IM_y} \times [(\Delta G - \Delta T^*) + (1 - C_y)\Delta T^*]$$

And use Δd^* to stand for the change in the *full-employment deficit* $\Delta G - \Delta T^*$ (or, when spending is low, the full-employment surplus): the difference between government purchases and what tax collections would be if the economy were at full employment:

$$\Delta Y = \frac{1}{1 - C_y(1 - t) + IM_y} \times [(\Delta d^*) + (1 - C_y)\Delta T^*]$$

Changes in government policy shift real GDP by (a) the product of the multiplier with the sum of the change in this full-employment deficit, Δd^*, and (b) an extra term equal to the multiplier by $(1 - C_y)\Delta T^*$.

Where does this extra term come from? Changes in government purchases affect aggregate demand directly and immediately, while changes in tax collections (and transfer payments) affect aggregate demand only to the extent that they affect consumption spending. The degree of this asymmetry depends on how far C_y is from 1.

If we are willing to simplify by ignoring this final term, then the change in the *full-employment* deficit Δd^* is a good approximate index of how changing fiscal policy affects the position of the IS curve, and real GDP. Perhaps the final term can be ignored because C_y is close to 1. Perhaps the final term can be ignored because of other, unmodelled factors. In any event, economists often do use the change in the full-employment deficit as an index of changes in fiscal policy.

moves up and to the left along a stable IS curve (see Figure 13.2). As the economy moves along the IS curve, real GDP falls and tax collections fall too. The government's actual deficit increases, even though there has been no change in government policy to shift the IS curve. The full-employment budget balance, however, remains constant. The fact that the actual budget balance changes as the economy moves along a constant IS curve means that it is not a good indicator of how the government's fiscal policy is affecting the location of the IS curve: The full-employment budget balance is better.

To turn the actual balance into the full-employment balance, we must adjust the budget deficit (or surplus) for the automatic reaction of taxes and spending to the business cycle, as done in Figure 13.3. When unemployment is high, taxes are low and social welfare spending high. The budget balance swings toward deficit. When unemployment is low, taxes are high and the budget balance swings toward surplus. For this reason, welfare programs and taxes, especially progressive taxes with higher tax rates for higher income people, are called *automatic stabilizers*.

In practice, the cyclically adjusted budget balance is obtained by "filtering" the data on the actual budget balance in such a way as to remove the short term cyclical fluctuations around the long term trend, employing the HP (Hodrick-Prescott) filter that we used earlier in the book to estimate potential output or the natural rate

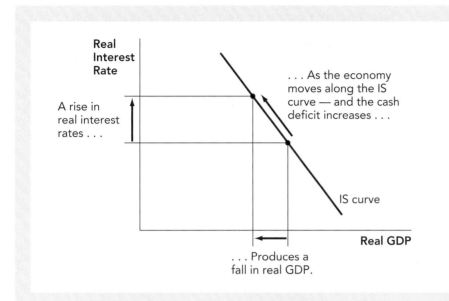

FIGURE 13.2
A Fall in Real GDP

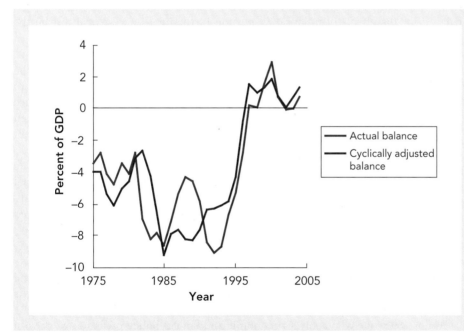

FIGURE 13.3
The Full-Employment, or Cyclically Adjusted, and Actual Budget Balances, 1970–2004
The difference between the actual budget balance and the cyclically adjusted balance can be substantial when the economy is either suffering from a deep recession or undergoing an uplifting boom.

Source: Department of Finance, *Fiscal Reference Tables* (September 2005), Table 46.

of unemployment. The red curve in Figure 13.3 shows the HP filtered or cyclically adjusted budget balance.

However, the cyclically adjusted budget deficit is not a perfect measure of the effect of taxing and spending on the position of the IS curve. And the standard budget deficit you see reported in the newspapers is not even a good measure of the effect of taxing and spending on the position of the IS curve.

13.2 MEASURING THE DEBT AND THE DEFICIT

In addition to cyclical adjustment, we could consider making three other adjustments to the reported budget balance. These adjustments matter, as we discuss below.

INFLATION

One adjustment economists make is to correct the officially reported actual budget balance for the effects of inflation. A portion of the debt interest paid out by the government to its bondholders merely compensates them for inflation's erosion of the value of their principal.

A good measure of the budget balance should be a measure of whether the government is spending more in the way of *resources* than it is taking in: a measure of the change in the *real* debt that the government owes. Inflation tends to reduce the real value of government debt; and this should be taken into account when measuring the budget balance. The reduction in the real value of government debt due to inflation is $\pi \times D$, where D is the nominal value of the debt.

On the other hand, when calculating the actual balance this erosion in the value of government debt is not taken into account. In fact, when calculating the actual balance the *nominal* interest payments, $i \times D$, are used. To correct for this shortfall, the **inflation-adjusted budget balance** or **real budget balance** is therefore calculated from the actual balance as follows:

$$\text{Inflation-adjusted budget balance} = \text{actual balance} + \pi \times D \qquad (13.1)$$

Thus, if, for example, the actual balance is zero but $\pi \times D$ is positive, then the real value of the government debt falls, and the inflation adjusted budget balance is positive.[1]

Almost everyone who analyzes economic and budget policy prefers to work with these inflation-adjusted measures of the budget balance and debt. Figure 13.4 plots the actual budget balance and the inflation-adjusted budget balance for Canada (sum for the federal, provincial, and local governments). The inflation adjusted balance was in deficit during the period 1977–1996, except for the year 1981; and it has been in surplus ever since.

http://fin.gc.ca/purl/frt-e.html

---

[1] Notice, Real budget balance = Tax revenues (T) – Government expenditures (G) – $r \times D$ = T – G – $(i - \pi) \times D$, while Actual balance = T – G – $i \times D$. Comparing these two definitions for the real budget balance and the actual balance we obtain equation (13.1).

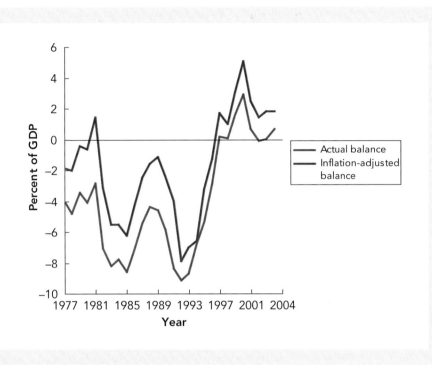

Source: Department of Finance, *Fiscal Reference Tables* (September 2005), Table 45.

FIGURE 13.4

The Actual Balance and the Inflation Adjusted Balance as a Percentage of GDP, 1977–2004

The sum of the inflation adjusted federal, provincial, and local budgets was in deficit during the period 1977–1996, except for the year 1981; and it has been in surplus ever since.

PUBLIC INVESTMENT

Yet another adjustment corrects for an asymmetry between the treatment of private and public assets. Private spending on long-lived capital goods is called "investment." A business that has total sales of $100 million, costs of goods sold of $90 million, and spends $20 million on enlarging its capital stock reports a profit of $10 million — not a deficit of $10 million. Standard and sensible accounting treatment of long-lived valuable assets in the private sector is definitely not to count their entire cost as a charge at the time of initial purpose, but instead to spread the cost out — a process called "amortization" — over the useful life of the asset. The government should do its accounting the same way, like a business, and amortize rather than expense its spending on long-lived assets.

There are periodic calls for a reform of the federal government budget to use *capital budgeting*. But few people use numbers based on capital budgeting. The principal reason that capital budgeting is resisted is political. Which government expenditures are capital expenditures? Defence expenditures? Expenditures on the highway system? Improvements to trails in the national parks? Money spent on education? (After all, it is an investment in the future of the new generation.)

It is hard to see any long-run dividing line between government investment and government consumption expenditures that would be sustainable from a political point of view. Thus critics regard capital budgeting as simply too difficult to implement in a helpful way. Supporters, however, point out that not doing capital budgeting at all is, in a sense, worse than even the least helpful implementation. Nevertheless, relatively few of the uses to which budget balance numbers are put do correct for public investment. The fact that the numbers usually reported do not correct for public investment should be kept in mind: It tends to overestimate the real value of the outstanding national debt.

PRIMARY VERSUS ACTUAL BALANCE

Another measure of the budget balance that has received attention in Canada is called the primary balance. The **primary budget balance** is the actual budget balance *plus* the interest payments on the government debt.

To appreciate the importance of the primary balance, first notice that interest payments on the government debt is a cost paid by the government today for the expenditures it incurred in the *past* and did not pay with taxes. These interest payments can, therefore, be regarded as a burden on the economy today for expenditures that were incurred in the past.

If the primary balance is negative the total government revenues are not large enough to cover its expenditures for the goods and services provided to the current residents of the country. The government is then borrowing to pay for part of these goods and services, and future residents will be paying for them. Similarly, if the primary balance is positive, then the revenues of the government today are larger than the value of the goods and services it provides today. In this case, therefore, the current residents are paying for part of the government goods and services that were provided in the past, or they are paying for some government goods and services that will be provided in the future.

Figure 13.5 compares the behaviour of the actual cyclically adjusted and the primary–cyclically adjusted budget balance for Canada for the period 1970–2004. During this period the government always had some debt, and the primary balance was always larger than the actual balance. The gap between the two balances

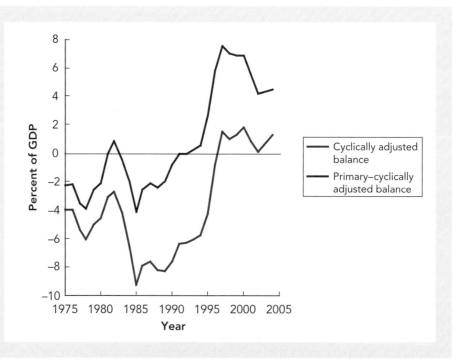

FIGURE 13.5

The Primary–Cyclically Adjusted and the Actual Cyclically Adjusted Budget Balances, 1970–2004

During the period 1970–2004 the government always had some debt and the primary–cyclically adjusted balance was always larger than the actual cyclically adjusted balance. The gap between the two balances widened from the second half of the 1970s, until the mid-1990s, because during this period there was a substantial increase in the size of the government debt.

Source: Department of Finance, *Fiscal Reference Tables* (September 2005), Table 46.

widened from the second half of the 1970s until the mid-1990s, because during this period there was a substantial increase in the size of the government debt.

> **RECAP   MEASURING THE DEBT AND THE DEFICIT**
>
> The inflation-adjusted balance takes into account the fact that inflation tends to reduce the real value of government debt, while the primary balance takes into account the fact that interest payments on the government debt are a cost paid by the government today for the expenditures it incurred in the *past* and did not pay with taxes. Figures for government expenditures do not correct for the fact that some of these expenditures are public investment expenditures — and, as such, they tend to overestimate the real value of the outstanding national debt.

13.3 ANALYZING DEBTS AND DEFICITS

SUSTAINABILITY

The first question to ask about a government that is running a persistent deficit is: "Can it go on?" Is it possible for the government to continue running its current deficit indefinitely, or must policy change — possibly for the better, but also quite possibly for the worse?

THE STEADY-STATE DEBT-TO-GDP RATIO

The variable to look at to assess whether the government's current fiscal policy is sustainable is the time path of the ratio of the government's total debt to GDP, or the debt-to-GDP ratio, D/Y. Fiscal policy is *sustainable* if the debt-to-GDP ratio is heading for a steady state.

As in Chapters 3 and 4, we can analyze the debt-to-GDP ratio D/Y by looking to see if it heads for some steady-state value. At a steady-state value, both the numerator D and the denominator Y will be growing at the same proportional rate. We know that real GDP grows in the long run at a proportional annual rate $n + g$, where n is the annual growth rate of the labour force and g is the annual growth rate of the efficiency of labour.

What is the proportional growth rate of the debt, D? Adding time subscripts to keep things clear, the debt next year will be equal to

$$D_{t+1} = (1 - \pi)D_t + d$$

The real value of the debt shrinks by a proportional amount π as inflation erodes away the real value of the debt principal owed by the government, and grows by an amount equal to the officially reported actual deficit, d. As the economy grows, tax revenues grow roughly in proportion to real GDP and spending grows in proportion to real GDP too. So it makes sense to focus not on the deficit itself but on the deficit as a share of GDP, which we can call little delta (δ):

$$\delta = d/Y$$

Then the proportional growth rate of the debt is

$$\frac{D_{t+1} - D_t}{D_t} = -\pi + \delta \times \frac{Y_t}{D_t}$$

The debt-to-GDP ratio will be stable when these two proportional growth rates — of GDP and of the debt — are equal to each other:

$$n + g = -\pi + \delta \times (Y/D)$$

which happens when

$$\frac{D}{Y} = \frac{\delta}{n + g + \pi}$$

This is the steady-state level toward which the debt-to-GDP ratio will head (see Box 13.2). This is the level consistent with a constant actual balance deficit of δ percent of GDP in an economy with long-run inflation rate π, and with long-run real GDP growth rate $n + g$.

IS THE STEADY-STATE DEBT-TO-GDP RATIO POSSIBLE?

Why then do economists talk about deficit levels as being "unsustainable"? For any deficit as a share of GDP δ, the debt-to-GDP ratio heads for its well-defined steady-state value $\delta/(n + g + \pi)$.

This, however, is only half the story. The ratio of GDP to the debt that the government wants to issue heads for a stable value, yes. But are there enough investors in the world willing to hold that amount of debt? The higher the debt-to-GDP ratio, the riskier an investment financiers judge the debt of a country to be, and the less willing they are to buy and hold that debt.

A higher debt-to-GDP ratio makes investments in the debt issued by a government more risky for two reasons. First, revolutions — or other, more peaceful changes of government — happen. One of the things a new government must decide is whether it is going to honour the debt issued by previous governments. Are these debts the commitments of the nation, which as an honourable entity honours its commitments? Or are these debts the reckless mistakes made by and obligations of

---

EXAMPLE · **BOX 13.2**

THE EQUILIBRIUM DEBT-TO-GDP RATIO

Suppose that the economy is running a constant budget deficit of 4 percent of GDP year after year. Suppose further that the growth rate of the labour force is 2 percent per year, the growth rate of output per worker is 1 percent per year, and the inflation rate is 5 percent per year. What then will be this economy's **steady-state ratio of government debt to GDP?**

To determine the answer, simply plug the parameter values into the formula

$$\frac{D}{Y} = \frac{\delta}{n + g + \pi} = \frac{4\%}{2\% + 1\% + 5\%} = \frac{1}{2}$$

The steady-state debt-to-GDP ratio will be ½. If the current debt-to-GDP ratio is less than ½, the debt-to-GDP ratio will grow. If the current debt-to-GDP ratio is greater than ½, the debt-to-GDP ratio will fall.

Notice a similarity to the analysis of the equilibrium capital–output ratio way back in Chapter 3? The mathematical tools and models are the same, even though the phenomena in the world to which they apply are very different. Such recycling of a formal model in a different context is yet another trick economists use to try to keep their discipline and their models simple.

a gang of thugs, unrepresentative of the nation, to whom investors should have known better than to lend money for the thugs to steal? The holders of a government's debt anxiously await every new government's decision on this issue.

The higher the debt-to-GDP ratio, the greater the temptation for a new government to *repudiate* debt issued by its predecessor, hence the riskier it is to buy and hold a portion of that country's national debt.

Second, a government can control the real size of the debt it owes by controlling the rate of inflation. The (nominal) interest rate to be paid on government debt is fixed by the terms of the bond issued. The real interest rate paid on the debt is equal to the nominal interest rate minus the rate of inflation — and the government controls the rate of inflation.

Thus a government that seeks to redistribute wealth away from its bondholders to its taxpayers can do so by increasing the rate of inflation. The more inflation, the less the government's debt is worth and the lower the real taxes that have to be imposed to pay off the interest and principal on the debt. Whether a government is likely to increase the rate of inflation depends on the costs and benefits — and raising the rate of inflation does have significant political costs. But the higher the debt-to-GDP ratio, the greater the benefits to taxpayers of a sudden burst of inflation. When the debt-to-GDP ratio is equal to 2, a sudden 10 percent rise in the price level reduces the real wealth of the government's creditors and increases the real wealth of taxpayers by an amount equal to 20 percent of a year's GDP. By contrast, when the debt-to-GDP ratio is equal to 0.2, the same rise in the price level redistributes wealth equal to only 2 percent of a year's GDP.

Thus the government's potential creditors must calculate that the greater the debt-to-GDP ratio, the greater the benefits to the government of inflation as a way of writing down the value of its debt. The higher the debt-to-GDP ratio, the more likely it is that the government will resort to inflation. Thus the higher the debt-to-GDP ratio, the riskier it is to invest in a government's debt.

A deficit is *sustainable* only if the associated steady-state debt-to-GDP ratio is low enough that investors judge the debt safe enough to be willing to hold it. Think of each government as having a *debt capacity* — a maximum debt-to-GDP ratio at which investors are willing to hold the debt issued at reasonable interest rates. If this debt capacity is exceeded, then the interest rates that the government must pay on its debt spike upward. The government is faced with a much larger deficit than planned (as a result of higher interest costs). Either the government must raise taxes, or it must resort to high inflation or hyperinflation to write the real value of the debt down.

EFFECTS OF BUDGETARY DEFICITS

Even if a given deficit as a share of GDP is sustainable, it still may have three types of significant effects on the economy. It may affect the political equilibrium that determines the government's tax and spending levels. It may, if the central bank allows it, affect the level of real GDP in the short run. And it will (except in very special cases) affect the level of real GDP in the long run.

Canada's national debt today is below the level at which economists begin to watch the debt with anxious concern. There seems little chance that the deficit and debt will spiral upward out of control. The fears during the 1980s that Canada had put itself on a course for national disaster through a mounting national debt are now passed, as the government's cash balance is now in surplus.

The typical pattern Canada has followed is one of sharp spikes in the debt-to-GDP ratio during wartime, followed by paying off the national debt during peacetime. It is easy to understand why governments usually run up large debts during wartime. Their survival, and perhaps the survival of their nation and their civilization, is at stake. So during major wars, governments use all the tools they have to gain control of resources for their fleets, armies, and airforces. And one of those tools is a substantial dose of government borrowing (through the sale of government bonds).

Figure 13.6 shows the Canadian government debt as a share of total domestic product from 1926 until 2005. There was a great peak in the debt-to-GDP ratio during World War II, where the debt as a percentage of GDP reached almost 150 percent. There are only two upward movements in the debt as a share of GDP not connected to wars: the rise in the national debt during the Great Depression of the 1930s, and the rise in the national debt during the 1980s and the first half of the 1990s.

The reason that during peacetime the size of the government debt as a share of GDP falls is also straightforward. Economic growth raises real GDP and inflation provides an additional boost to nominal GDP. As long as the government's tax and spending programs are not grossly out of whack, in peacetime government debt tends to fall as a share of GDP. Before 1930 the government's tax and spending programs could not get out of whack in peacetime: There was barely any peacetime federal government. Since 1930, however, the peacetime federal government has increased its share of the economy. Thus it was a surprise in the 1980s to see the emergence of substantial peacetime government budget deficits and a rising national debt-to-GDP ratio.

The rise in the debt-to-GDP ratio in the 1980s could be attributed to four main factors. First, the high unemployment rates during this period raised the unemployment benefits paid by the government. Second, in the 1980s the Bank of Canada

http://cansim2.statcan.ca/

FIGURE 13.6
Canadian Debt-to-GDP Ratio, 1926–2005

There was a great peak in the debt-to-GDP ratio during World War II. For this period, there are only two upward movements in the debt as a share of GDP not connected to wars: the rise in the national debt during the Great Depression of the 1930s, and the rise in the national debt during the 1980s and the first half of the 1990s.

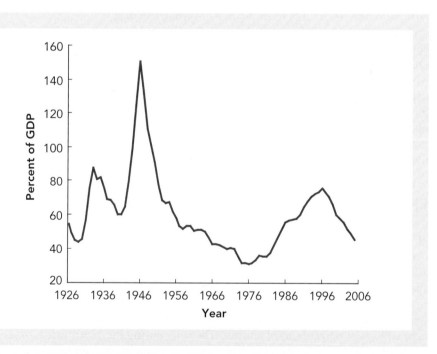

Source: Statistics Canada, Historical Statistics of Canada, Series F13 (nominal GNP, 1926–1960); and Statistics Canada CANSIM II database, Series V49086 (nominal GDP, 1961–2005) and V1511537 (debt).

followed tight monetary policies in order to reduce inflation, which led to substantial hikes in interest rates. High interest rates implied high interest payments on the public debt, which further increased government expenditures. Third, as we saw in the last chapter, in the 1980s there was a substantial increase in the transfer payments by the federal to the provincial and local governments. These generous transfers led to a dramatic increase in the size of the public sector at the provincial level, as well as increasing the size of the federal debt. Fourth, in the last two decades there has been an increase in the size of the elderly population, which has increased the pension payments by the government. These four factors raised the ratio of government expenditures to GDP, as shown in Figure 13.7.

Despite these increases in their expenditures, Canadian governments were reluctant to adopt politically unpopular policies that raised tax rates. As a result, government revenues per GDP were relatively stable in the 1980s and 1990s, as shown in Figure 13.7. With government expenditures per GDP rising in 1980s, and their revenues per GDP relatively stable, there was a sharp increase in government debt per GDP during this period.

In the 1990s the federal and provincial governments were committed to deficit reduction, which resulted in substantial declines in government expenditures, and budget surpluses by the mid-1990s. The efforts of these governments were eased by the growth increases in the mid-1990s, reductions in the unemployment rate, and declines in interest rates. As a result, the debt-to-GDP ratio has been declining since 1996.

How important was the doubling of the debt as a share of GDP that took place in the 1980s and early 1990s? One view, held by a majority of economists, is that such large government deficits had three sets of effects. First, they had uncertain but

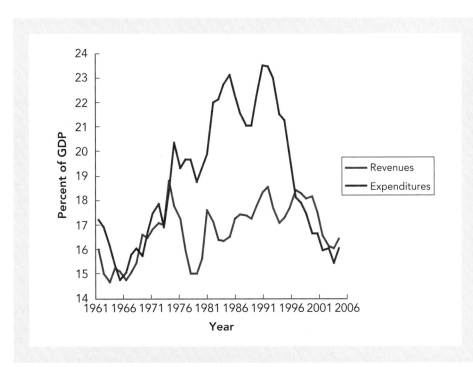

FIGURE 13.7

Federal Revenues and Expenditures as a Share of GDP, 1961–2005

From 1973 until 1997 federal government expenditures significantly outran revenues. But since 1997 revenues have been larger than expenditures.

Source: Adapted from Statistics Canada CANSIM II database, Series V499730 (revenues), V499761 (expenditures), and V498086 (nominal GDP).

probably destructive effects on the formulation of government spending and tax plans. Second, they had the potential to have *expansionary* effects on the economy in the short run. Third, they had contractionary effects on the economy in the long run. Thus the end of the era of deficits was, by the late 1990s, trumpeted as an amazing and important political success, a policy accomplishment that would significantly improve the lives of Canadians. Were they correct? On balance, probably yes.

BUDGET DEFICITS: POLITICAL CONSEQUENCES

One thread of political economic analysis holds that deficits have destructive political consequences: The possibility of financing government spending through borrowing makes the government less effective at advancing the public welfare. Electoral politics suffers from a form of institutional voter myopia: The benefits from higher government spending now are clear and visible to voters, and the costs of the higher taxes later that will be needed to finance the debt built up via deficit spending are distant, fuzzy, and excessively discounted. Moreover, the unborn and underage do not vote: Many of those who will be obligated to pay taxes to make interest payments on tomorrow's national debt do not vote today. The principle of "no taxation without representation" would seem to call for no long-term national debt — or, rather, for a national debt that is not larger than the government's capital stock.

Thus economists like Nobel Prize-winner James Buchanan have argued for a stringent balanced-budget rule. In Buchanan's view, only if political dialogue must simultaneously confront both the benefits of spending and the pain of the taxes needed to finance that spending can we expect a democratic political system to adequately and effectively weigh the costs and benefits of proposed programs.

Since the start of the 1980s, another argument has appeared: an argument for deficits created by tax cuts. The political system, its proponents argue, delivers steadily rising government spending unless it is placed under immediate and dire pressure to reduce the deficit. Therefore the only way to avoid an ever-growing inefficient government share of GDP is to run a constant deficit that politicians feel impelled to try to reduce. And should they ever succeed, the appropriate response is to pass another tax cut to create a new deficit. Only by starving the beast Leviathan that is government can it be kept from indefinite expansion.

The Canadian experience of the 1980s and 1990s tends to support James Buchanan's position, and to count against the alternative position. Few today are satisfied with the decisions about government spending and tax policy made in the 1980s and early 1990s. Moreover, the deficits of the 1980s do not seem to have put downward pressure on federal spending. *Program* spending fell, but total spending rose because of the hike in interest payments created by the series of deficits in the 1980s. Because of the fact that interest payments are part of government spending, the deficits of the 1980s appear to have put not downward but upward pressure on the size of government.

BUDGET DEFICITS: SHORT-RUN CONSEQUENCES

In the short run, the income-expenditure diagram tells us that a deficit produced by a tax cut stimulates consumer spending. A deficit produced by an increase in government spending increases government purchases. Either way, it shifts the IS curve out and to the right: Any given interest rate is associated with a higher equilibrium value of production and employment. If monetary policy is unchanged — if the LM curve does not shift — then output and employment rise in response to the tax cut. A deficit is expansionary in the short run.

Of course, the belief that deficits are expansionary — that they increase production and employment — in the short run hinges on the Bank of Canada's not changing monetary policy in response to the rise in the deficit. If the Bank of Canada does not want inflation to rise, it will respond to the rightward expansionary shift in the IS curve by tightening monetary policy and raising interest rates, neutralizing the expansionary effect of the deficit. Because the decision-making and policy implementation cycle for monetary policy is significantly shorter than the decision-making and policy implementation cycle for discretionary fiscal policy, the central bank can keep legislative actions to change the deficit from affecting the level of production and unemployment. The question is whether it will. The answer is yes. The central bank is trying its best to guide the economy along a narrow path without excess unemployment and without accelerating inflation. It has made its best guess as to what level of aggregate demand leads us along that path. In all likelihood its senior officials are uninterested in seeing the economy pushed away from that path by the fiscal policy decisions of legislators.

BUDGET DEFICITS: OPEN-ECONOMY EFFECTS

Such an increase in the government's budget deficit also leads to an increase in the trade deficit. The outward shift in the IS curve pushes up interest rates. Higher interest rates mean an appreciated dollar — a lower value of the exchange rate and of foreign currency — therefore imports rise and exports fall.

Up to now we have implicitly assumed that the composition of aggregate demand has no effect on the productivity of industry. Businesses have been implicitly assumed to be equally happy and equally productive whether they are producing consumption goods, investment goods for domestic use, goods and services that the government will purchase, or goods for the export market. Yet this is unlikely to be true. Recall from your microeconomics courses that the point of international trade is to trade goods that your economy is especially productive at making for goods that your economy is relatively unproductive at making.

As large deficits that increase interest rates raise the value of the exchange rate, export industries — likely to be highly productive — shrink as exports shrink. This presumably reduces total productivity. Nobody, however, has a very sound estimate of how large these effects might be.

LONG-RUN EFFECTS OF BUDGET DEFICITS

THE POLICY MIX: DEFICITS AND ECONOMIC GROWTH

Higher full-employment deficits lead to low investment. On the IS-LM diagram, a deficit — whether from more government purchases or lower taxes — shifts the IS curve to the right, as shown in Figure 13.8. In any run long enough for the full-employment flexible-price model of Chapter 6 to be relevant, large full-employment deficits lead to lower total savings, higher real interest rates, and lower investment.

In the flexible-price context the analysis of persistent deficits is straightforward. Such deficits reduce national savings. Flow-of-funds equilibrium thus requires higher real interest rates and lower levels of investment spending.

Even in a sticky-price context it may well be that higher deficits reduce investment. The central bank can, and probably will, change monetary policy to neutralize the effect of the higher deficit on real GDP. The central bank chose its baseline monetary policy in order to try to strike the optimum balance between the risk of higher-than-necessary unemployment and the risk of rising inflation. The central

FIGURE 13.8
Higher Full-Employment Deficits Reduce Investment

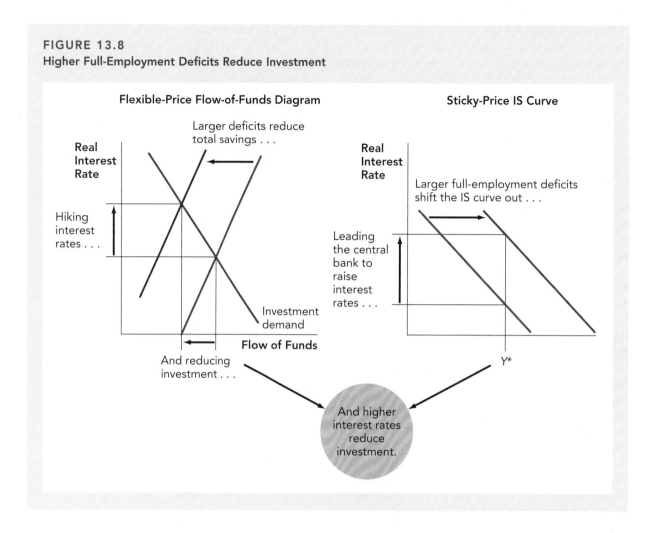

bank does not want this balance disturbed by shifts in the IS curve, so it is highly likely to use monetary policy to offset the effect of the deficit-driven shift in the IS curve on the level of real GDP and employment. The IS curve shifts out, but interest rates rise, leaving real GDP unchanged and investment lowered.

Low investment reduces capital accumulation and productivity growth, putting the country on a trajectory to a lower steady-state growth path. Since the early 1960s, economists have argued that economic growth is fastest and the economy is best off when the **policy mix** pursued by the government and the central bank is one of tight fiscal policy (a government surplus) and loose monetary policy (a relatively low interest rate). Together this policy mix can produce full employment, high investment, and relatively rapid economic growth.

Over time, it has seemed that the Canadian government has the opposite bias. Certainly for a period of a decade and a half from the late 1970s until the early 1990s, the Canadian economy had loose fiscal policy and tight monetary policy. Now Canada has a budget surplus and relatively high investment. Partly these are a result of good luck, but partly they are a result of politicians' taking economists' advice on the policy mix for the first time in more than a generation.

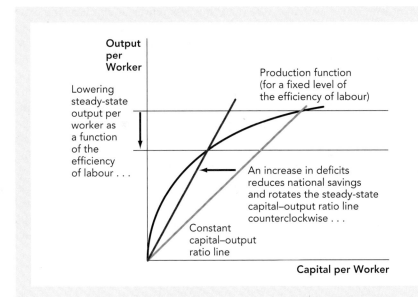

FIGURE 13.9
Long-Run Effects of Persistent Deficits on Economic Growth

If the deficits continue for long, they will begin to have an effect on the economy's capital intensity. The reduction in national savings as a share of GDP will reduce the economy's steady-state capital–output ratio.

A lower steady-state capital–output ratio implies a lower level of output per worker along the steady-state growth path for any given level of the efficiency of labour (see Figure 13.9). Thus a policy of persistent deficits will — as long as the rise in the deficit reduces national savings — reduce the long-run level of output per worker below what it would otherwise have been. (This, at least, is the conventional analysis of the interaction between deficits and long-run growth. It has been challenged by a group of professors centered on Harvard's Robert Barro — as discussed in Chapter 17 on the future of macroeconomics.)

DEBT SERVICE, TAXATION, AND REAL GDP

But there are still more long-term effects. A higher deficit means a higher debt, which means that the government owes more in the way of interest payments to bond-holders. Over time — even if the level of the deficit is kept constant — the increase in interest payments will require tax increases. And these tax increases will discourage entrepreneurship and economic activity. In addition to the reduction in output per worker resulting from the lower capital–output ratio, there will be an additional reduction in output per worker: The increased taxes needed to finance the interest owed on the national debt will have negative supply-side effects on production.

The interaction of macroeconomic policy, tax policy, incentives for production, and the level of real GDP deserves more space. No discussion of fiscal policy could be complete without noting, for example, a possible drawback of the progressive tax rates that create strong fiscal automatic stabilizers. The higher the marginal tax rate, the greater the danger that at the margin taxes will discourage economic activity — leading either to hordes of lawyers wasting social time executing negative-sum tax-avoidance strategies, to a shift away from aggressive entrepreneurship toward more cautious, less growth-promoting activities taxed at lower rates, or to a depreciated exchange rate (and thus less power to purchase imports) as capital flows across national borders to jurisdictions that have lower tax rates at the margin.

Thinking through these issues is complicated. Are government expenditures on infrastructure, basic research, and other public goods themselves productive? Do they raise total output by more than the increased tax rates threaten to reduce it? And what is the government's objective? After all, maximizing measured total output is the same thing as maximizing social welfare only if externalities are absent, and only if the distribution of total wealth corresponds to the weight individuals have in the social welfare function — with the tastes and desires of the rich being given more weight.

These topics are traditionally reserved for public finance courses, and are not covered in macroeconomics courses. But no one should think that an analysis of fiscal policy can start and end with the effects of discretionary fiscal policy and automatic stabilizers on the business cycle, and the effects of persistent deficits on national saving. There is much more to be thought about.

> **RECAP   ANALYZING DEBTS AND DEFICITS**
>
> A high government budget deficit has three types of significant effects on the economy. First, it will tend to swell the absolute size of the government in relation to GDP. Myopic voters will see the benefits of spending increases and not count the costs of future tax increases to finance them. Higher national debt levels increase interest payments, and the government must eventually raise taxes to make these interest payments. A high government budget deficit may — if the central bank allows it — raise real GDP in the short run by shifting the IS curve to the right. A high government budget deficit will in the long run slow economic growth, and lower real GDP below what it would otherwise have been.

13.4 THE RICARDIAN EQUIVALENCE

So far in this chapter we have expounded the economists' standard view of debts and deficits. Fiscal deficits stimulate the economy in the short run; but in the long run debts and deficits crowd out investment and shift the economy to a less favourable steady-state growth path. But there is an alternative view, originating in the writings of the nineteenth century English economist David Ricardo, which was further developed and formalized by the Harvard economist Robert Barro. According to this alternative view, it does not matter whether the government finances its expenditures by incurring debt or by taxing current income, and therefore studying the effects of budget deficits on income and long run growth is not an important issue.

Think of it this way: The government is, in a sense, our agent. It buys goods and services (government purchases) on our behalf, and it collects taxes from us in order to pay for them. Sometimes the government collects as much taxes from us as it buys on our behalf: Then the government budget is balanced. Sometimes the government collects less in taxes from us than it spends on our behalf: Then the government budget is in deficit, and it pays for it by borrowing money now and implicitly committing to raise taxes to repay the debt (interest and principal) at some time in the future.

Suppose that the government spends an extra $1,000 on your behalf and at the same time it raises your taxes by $1,000. Because your after-tax income has gone down by $1,000, you cut back on consumption spending. Now suppose that the government spends an extra $1,000 on your behalf, but doesn't raise taxes — instead it borrows the $1,000 for one year, and announces that it is going to raise taxes next year to repay the debt.

What is the difference between these two situations? In the first case, the government has collected an extra $1,000 in taxes from you this year. In the second case, the government has announced that it will collect an extra $1,000 in taxes from you next year. In either case you are poorer. In the first case you cut back on your consumption. Shouldn't you cut back on your consumption in the second case too — set aside a reserve to pay the extra taxes next year, and invest it, perhaps in the bonds that the government has issued? After all, the effect of the government policy on your personal private wealth is identical in the two cases.

According to the Ricardo-Barro view the answer to the last question is yes; what matters for the determination of consumption spending is not what taxes are levied on you this year, but what all of the changes in government policy tell you about the value of the total stream of taxes this year, next year, and so on in the future. Government policy thus ought to affect consumption only to the extent that it tells you how much the government is going to spend — and thus what will be the total lifetime tax bill levied on your wealth.

Nevertheless, many economists point out that the theoretical elegance of the Ricardo-Barro view is broken by a number of different considerations, including the following:

Myopia Perhaps people are not far-sighted enough to fully work out what an increased deficit in the present implies for their future taxes.

Liquidity Constraints Barro's argument implicitly assumes that it is easy for people to borrow and lend. Nevertheless, there are good many people who cannot borrow and lend because our financial markets are imperfect; they are liquidity constrained. For example, there are informational problems, so that the banks cannot fully distinguish worthy from unworthy borrowers. In such an imperfect market, you would expect several consumers to react to tax cuts by increasing consumption spending even if they knew full well that the government was going to recapture those tax cuts with tax increases later. In essence, the government would be borrowing on behalf of liquidity-constrained consumers.

Beneficiaries and Payers May Differ You may be the beneficiary of increased spending this year and be fortunate enough not to have to pay the future taxes on the implied future debt. If there is, for example, a lot of immigration into the economy then you expect the immigrants and their children to pay some of these extra taxes. In such situations budget deficits reduce the burden of taxes on you now, inducing you to consume more today than you would have done had these expenditures been financed by taxes today.

> **RECAP** **THE RICARDIAN EQUIVALENCE**
>
> According to the Ricardo-Barro view it does not matter whether the government finances its expenditures by incurring debt or by taxing current income; what matters for the determination of consumption spending is not what taxes are levied on you this year but what all of the changes in government policy tell you about the value of the total stream of taxes this year, next year, and so on in the future. This result can be broken if people are liquidity constrained, are myopic, or if the beneficiaries of government expenditures and the tax payers differ.

CHAPTER SUMMARY

1. Canada is usually a moderate-debt country. Only immediately after total wars does the Canadian national debt reach a high value relative to real GDP.

2. The 1980s and 1990s, however, saw steep rises in the national debt — unprecedented rises in peacetime. The era of deficits is now at an end. And the Canadian national debt is still significantly below the level at which economists begin serious worrying about the consequences of the debt for the health of the economy.

3. From the standpoint of analyzing stabilization policy, the best measure of the government's stance is the full-employment, or the cyclically adjusted, deficit. The full-employment deficit is not a bad measure of the net effect of government policy on the location of the IS curve.

4. From the standpoint of analyzing the effect of changes in the national debt on long-run growth, the debt and deficit need to be adjusted for (a) inflation and (b) government investment.

5. Persistent deficits — a rising national debt — threaten to diminish national savings, reduce the level of output per worker along the economy's steady-state growth path, and retard economic growth.

6. Past deficits — a high ratio of current debt to GDP — threaten to reduce national prosperity because the higher taxes required to service the national debt act as a drag on economic activity.

KEY TERMS

actual budget balance
(p. 392)

cyclically adjusted budget balance
(p. 393)

debt (p. 391)

deficit (p. 391)

full-employment budget balance
(p. 393)

inflation-adjusted budget balance
(p. 396)

policy mix (p. 406)

primary budget balance (p. 398)

real budget balance (p. 396)

Ricardian equivalence (p. 408)

steady-state debt-to-GDP ratio
(p. 400)

surplus (p. 391)

ANALYTICAL EXERCISES

1. What is the typical pattern followed by the debt-to-GDP ratio in Canada over time?

2. How does the experience of the 1980s and 1990s differ from the typical Canadian pattern as far as the debt-to-GDP ratio is concerned?

3. Why are the deficits of the 1980s generally seen to have been a bad thing? What are the arguments that the deficits of the 1980s were a good thing?

4. Suppose someone asks you which measure of the government budget balance they should look at. How does

your answer depend on the purpose for which they wish to use the budget balance?

5. Why might there be a long-run link between government budget deficits on the one hand and the inflation rate on the other?

6. Consider the IS-LM model of Chapter 9.
   a. Suppose there is an increase in government expenditures, and the government finances these by issuing bonds. What would be the effect on the equilibrium?

b. How would your answer to part (a) be affected if the government, instead, financed these expenditures by imposing a lump sum tax on all households, whereby each household pays a fixed additional amount T in taxes regardless of its income level?

c. How would your answers to parts (a) and (b) be affected if the Ricardian equivalence were to hold in this economy?

POLICY EXERCISES

1. Why might it make sense for a government to finance roads and other investments in public infrastructure through borrowing rather than through taxing today's taxpayers?

2. What effect in today's world do changes in tax and spending programs have on the level of real GDP in the short run?

3. What are likely to be the long-run effects of a fiscal policy that involves ever-present large budget deficits?

4. In 2001 and 2002 the world economy experienced dramatic declines in stock prices. What do you think would be the consequences of this decline for government budget deficits?

5. Suppose that the economy is running a constant budget *surplus* of 1 percent (that is, a deficit of –1 percent) of GDP year after year. Suppose further that the growth rate of the labour force is 2 percent per year, the growth rate of output per worker is 1 percent per year, and the inflation rate is 2 percent per year. What then will be this economy's steady-state ratio of government debt to GDP?

6. Suppose that in a debate you claim that large deficits lead to high interest rates and lowered investment spending, but your opponent claims that it is not fiscal policy that leads to high interest rates — it is too-tight monetary policy on the part of the central bank. How would you respond?

14

Changes in the Macroeconomy and Changes in Macroeconomic Policy

QUESTIONS

How has the structure of the economy changed over the course of the past century?

How has the business cycle changed over the past century?

How has economic policy changed over the past century?

What are future prospects for successful management of the business cycle?

Why does unemployment in Europe remain so high?

Why was growth in Japan so low for much of the 1990s?

14.1 CHANGES IN THE MACROECONOMY

THE PAST

The structure of the macroeconomy is not set in stone. As time passes the economy changes. The patterns of aggregate economic activity studied in macroeconomics change too. Consumers' opportunities and spending patterns change, industries grow and shrink, the role of international trade steadily expands. The role of the government changes too, rising during the post–World War II period to accommodate the new welfare state of the 1960s and 1970s. It would be surprising indeed if the patterns of macroeconomic fluctuations remained unchanged as all these factors that underpin the macroeconomy change.

Over the past century the structure of modern industrial economies has changed, by some measures at least, more than in the entire millennium (see Figure 14.1). In Canada, between 1911 and 2005 the share of the labour force engaged in agriculture fell from 35 percent to 2 percent. Today, in Canada, there are more gardeners,

FIGURE 14.1

Occupational Distribution of the Labour Force

A thousand years ago almost everyone was a farmer. Even in 1900, nearly one-third of the labour force was made up of farmers. Today the occupational distribution of the labour force is very different. The industries of the industrial revolution — manufacturing, mining, and construction — still employ a quarter of our labour force. But most of today's workers are in the service sector, many of them in information-intensive services.

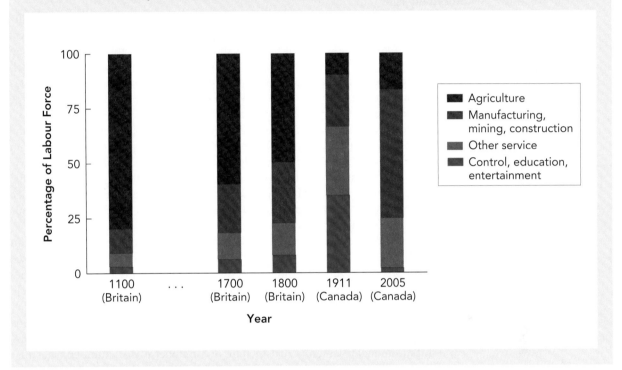

Source: Adapted from the Statistics Canada CANSIM database, http://cansim2.stat.can.ca/cgi-win/CNSMCGI.EXE, Table 282–0008 (2005) and from the Statistics Canada publication, "Historical Statistics of Canada" Catalogue 11–516, 1983 Series D8-D85 (1911).

groundskeepers, and producers and distributors of ornamental plants than there are farmers and farm labourers.

The decline in agriculture is not the only major shift in the economy's occupational and industrial distribution. At the start of the last century 31 percent of the labour force were engaged in mining, manufacturing, and construction. Today only 24 percent of the labour force are so engaged. The fall in relative employment in these industries has been offset by a rise in service-sector employment. Between 1911 and 2005, employment for government control, education, and entertainment rose from 10 percent to 16 percent of the labour force. Similarly, in all the other service industries employment has risen from 24 percent to 58 percent of the labour force, over the same time period.

Moreover, a hundred years ago the government's social insurance state was barely in embryo, the tax system was not at all progressive, and most households found it very difficult to borrow in order to see themselves through a year of low income and of unemployment. Today, by contrast, the Canadian financial system lends immense amounts of money to all kinds of consumers. In standard economic theory, that should allow them to smooth their consumption spending.

Households should be able to greatly reduce the impact of changes in their incomes on changes in consumption, and so reduce the marginal propensity to consume. Such reductions in the marginal propensity to consume *should* carry along with them a substantial reduction in the size of the multiplier. The same holds true for the fiscal automatic stabilizers of progressive taxes and social insurance, which appear to exert a powerful stabilizing force on the economy. They were not present a century ago.

The past century has also seen the rise of **financial automatic stabilizers** like deposit insurance. One major factor making depressions (most notably the Great Depression) larger in the distant past was the fear that your bank might fail, so you needed to pull your money out of the bank and hide it under your mattress. Such sudden increases in the demand for cash during financial panics caused interest rates to spike, investment to fall, and production to decline. Today the existence of a large deposit insurance system has all but eliminated this fear.

Still another change is in the pace and direction of material progress. Back in the early twentieth century the bulk of improvements in labour productivity came from capital deepening: the buildup of the infrastructure and the factories of the country. In the late twentieth century the bulk of improvements in labour productivity came from improvements in the efficiency of labour as a result of improvements in science and technology: inventions and innovations in materials production, materials handling, and organization.

Yet in spite of all of these changes in the structure of the economy, the Canadian economy's business cycle has continued. The patterns of the business cycle we see today would seem familiar to those who watched business cycles late in the nineteenth century. Everything else in the economy changes, yet the business cycle seems to remain largely the same. As Table 14.1 shows, there are some signs that fluctuations in unemployment have become smaller in recent years (and many signs that the Great Depression of the 1930s involved an extraordinarily violent business cycle). But the major lesson is that in spite of a number of structural changes that would seem likely to diminish the size of the business cycle, it remains and has remained largely the same.

http://www.statcan.ca/english/
freepub/11-516-XIE/sectiona/
toc.htm
http://cansim2.statcan.ca

TABLE 14.1
Business Cycle Indicator

Period	Typical Swing in Unemployment	Proportion of Time Spent in Recession
1921–1945	5.4%	26.0%
1921–1930	2.2%	32.5%
1931–1945	5.9%	21.7%
1946–2001	2.6%	17.9%
1946–1975	1.5%	14.2%
1976–2001	1.7%	22.1%

Source: Unemployment: 1921–1945: Historical Statistics of Canada – Series D132 (unemployed persons) and D128 (civilian labour force); 1946–1975: Historical Statistics of Canada – Series D233; 1976–2001: CANSIM I – Series D980745; Recessions: Calculated from Table 14.2 below.

FUTURE CHANGES

We should not imagine that change is over: It will continue. We can already see some of the future changes that will transform the macroeconomy in the future.

The increase in **financial flexibility** that allows consumers to borrow will continue. The increase in financial flexibility will also make it more difficult to read the financial markets — and is thus likely to make monetary policy somewhat more difficult to conduct. International trade will continue to expand. The odds are that international investments will become easier to make, and so the speed at which capital flows across national borders will increase. And labour markets are likely to continue to change as well.

CONSUMPTION

Already **liquidity constraints** — the inability to borrow and the consequent fact that consumption spending is limited by income — play a relatively small role in determining consumption spending in Canada. They certainly play a much smaller role than at the beginning of this century, or even early in the post–World War II period. Economists' theories tell us that if liquidity constraints are absent, then the marginal propensity to consume should be very low. The level of consumption should depend on one's estimate of one's lifetime resources, and be affected by changes in current income only to the extent that changes in current income change one's estimate of lifetime resources.

Now economists' theories may overstate the case. Tying your current level of spending to your current level of income is a reasonable rule of thumb for managing one's affairs. And it just isn't worth the time spent to do better than one does by using reasonable rules of thumb. So the marginal propensity to consume may remain at some noticeable fraction, and increasing ease of borrowing may not lead the multiplier to completely disappear. Nevertheless, the multiplier is likely to grow still smaller over time. It will surely play a smaller role in the economy (and in economic policy, and in economics textbooks) in the future.

GLOBALIZATION

The future is likely to see international trade continue to expand. The growth in trade, depicted in Figure 14.2, will also lower the multiplier: A greater portion of changes in domestic spending will show up as changes in demand for foreign-made goods. So the economy at home will be even less vulnerable to domestic shocks that disturb employment and output. However, increased international integration means that the domestic economy is more vulnerable to foreign shocks: Recession abroad that lowers demand for exports will have repercussions at home.

Accompanying the increase in international trade will be an increase in the magnitude of international financial flows. The odds are that international investments will become easier to make. And the odds are — as means of international communication increase — that investors in one country will become much more confident in making investments in another. So the speed with which capital flows across national borders will increase.

Yet in Chapter 16 we will see that increased flow of capital across national borders is a potential source of financial crisis and macroeconomic volatility. In the East Asian crisis of 1997–1998 a sudden shift in investors' expectations meant that $100 billion a year in international capital flows that had financed investment in

FIGURE 14.2

Globalization: Merchandise Imports as a Share of Total Goods Production, 1961–2005

Since 1960 in Canada, the share of merchandise imports has tripled relative to total production of goods.

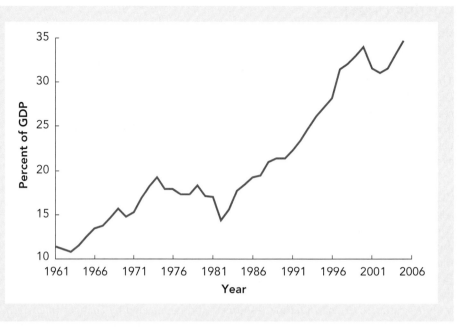

Source: Adapted from Statistics Canada CANSIM II database, Series V1992064 (real imports) and V1992067 (real GDP).

East Asia was no longer there. That $100 billion a year had financed the employment of 20 million people working in investment industries, who dug sewer lines, built roads, erected buildings, and installed machines as both domestic and foreign investors bet that there was lots of money to be made in East Asia's industrial revolution. These 20 million East Asian workers had to find new jobs outside of investment industries.

The fall in the value of East Asian currencies has gone a long way to bringing the supply of and demand for foreign exchange back into balance. Falling exchange rates make East Asian goods more attractive to European and American purchasers. East Asia's economies are growing rapidly again.

But what caused the sudden sharp shift in investment patterns? Unfortunately for economists, and unfortunately for economics as a social science, we cannot find any disturbing cause proportional to the large effect. The shift in international investors' desires to invest in East Asia appears to have been impelled much more by the trend-chasing and herd instincts of investors — a community of people who talk to each other too much, and whose opinions often reflect not judgments about the world but simply guesses about what average opinion expects average opinion to be — than by any transformation in the fundamentals of East Asian economic development.

And here we have reached the limits of economics. Economists are good at analyzing how asset markets work if they are populated by far-sighted investors with accurate models of the world and long horizons. Economists are even good at pointing out that such asset markets can be subject to multiple equilibria — situations in which it is rational to be optimistic and rational investors are optimistic if they think that everyone else is optimistic, and in which it is also rational to be pessimistic and rational investors are pessimistic if they think that everyone else is pessimistic. But that is all they can say.

Note that the process of international investment may still be worth supporting. It does promise powerful benefits: faster industrialization on the developing periphery, and higher rates of return for investors from the industrial core, as well as diversification to reduce risk. These benefits may well outweigh the costs of international financial crises. Nevertheless, it is likely that the next generation of business cycles will be judged to have gone well or ill depending on whether the financial crises generated by cross-border financial flows are handled well or badly.

MONETARY POLICY

The increase in financial flexibility that reduces the multiplier will also make it more difficult to read the financial markets, and probably to conduct monetary policy. Monetary policy works, after all, because the central bank's open-market operations change interest rates. These operations have large effects on interest rates because the assets traded — Treasury bills on the one hand, and reserve deposits of the chartered banks on the other hand — play key roles in finance. Few substitute assets can serve the functions that they serve.

But as financial flexibility increases, any one kind of asset will become less and less of a bottleneck. There will be more ways of structuring transactions, and more kinds of financial instruments will be traded. Thus in the future, changes in the supply of Treasury bills likely will have less effect on interest rates than they do today. Open-market operations are likely to become somewhat less effective, and monetary policy somewhat more difficult to conduct, in the future.

Will this make much of a difference? Nobody knows. But monetary policy today is *plenty* effective at controlling production, employment, and prices — albeit with long and variable lags. Even a considerable reduction in the power of open-market operations would still leave central bankers with more-than-ample tools to carry out whatever kinds of policies they wished. The fear that increases in financial instability will rob central banks of their power to control economies is at least a generation in the future.

Will these ongoing and future changes in the structure of the macroeconomy have as little effect on the relative size of the business cycle as past changes appear to have had? To answer that question we need to look at the history of macroeconomic fluctuations, which we do in the next section.

INVENTORIES

Fourth and last of the changes that we can foresee is that improvements in information technology will improve businesses' ability to control their inventories. Mismatches between production and demand — unanticipated large-scale inventory accumulation or drawdowns — have been a principal source of fluctuations in unemployment and output over the past century. There is reason to think that better information technology will reduce this component of macroeconomic instability.

But how large this reduction will be is, once again, something that nobody knows.

> RECAP   **CHANGES IN THE MACROECONOMY**
>
> The future is likely to bring a continued increase in liquidity. People will find it easier and easier to borrow, hence their spending will be less closely tied to their current income, and the marginal propensity to consume will fall. International trade and financial markets are likely to become increasingly integrated, but at least as far as financial markets are concerned it is not clear that this is a good thing. It's likely that over time the power and effectiveness of monetary policy will decline as increased financial options erode the key role played by commercial bank deposits in finance. And firms will probably become better at managing their inventories, so that inventory fluctuation–driven business cycles will become a thing of the past.

14.2 THE HISTORY OF MACROECONOMIC FLUCTUATIONS

ESTIMATING LONG-RUN CHANGES IN CYCLICAL VOLATILITY

http://www.nber.org
http://www.stat.ca/english

Macroeconomic fluctuations are the subject of the business cycle theory. The modern empirical research of business cycles started with Mitchell and Burns[1] in the 1920s, at the National Bureau of Economic Research (NBER) in the United States. Today there is a huge literature on the theory and empirics of business cycles.[2] Mitchell and Burns define a **business cycle** as fluctuations in the level of aggregate economic activity that consist of expansions occurring simultaneously in many economic activities followed by similar general contractions. See Box 14.1 for some theories regarding the causes of business cycles.

Figure 14.3 shows a hypothetical business cycle. The vertical axis measures the level of economic activity and the horizontal axis measures time, usually in quarters or years. The highest point of the expansion phase is called the **peak**, while the lowest point of a contraction phase or recession is called the **trough**. The time period it takes economic activity to move from a trough to the level of the previous peak is called a **recovery**. A complete business cycle includes an expansion and a recession; that is the time period from one peak to another or from one trough to another. The peaks and troughs in the business cycles are called the turning points.

Assessing the changes in the size of the overall business cycle turns out to be harder than it looks. First, aggregate economic activity is not defined precisely. In the early business cycle studies NBER researchers developed business cycle chronologies and identified turning points by examining the behaviour of about 600 variables. Later in the post–World War II period, with the development of national income accounting, aggregate economic activity has been identified by a few economic variables such as real GDP, employment, industrial production, consumption, investment, the trade balance, inflation, stock prices, and interest rates.

Second, the quality of the data and the measurement of these variables have changed over time. Typically, pre–World War II economic data have been assembled

---

[1] See, for example, *Measuring Business Cycles*, by Burns, A. and M.C. Mitchell (1946), NBER: New York.
[2] An excellent review of business cycle theory and evidence for Canada is provided by P. Cross, "Alternative Measures of Business Cycles in Canada: 1947–1992," *Canadian Economic Observer*, February 1996, Statistics Canada-Catalogue no. 11-010-XPB.

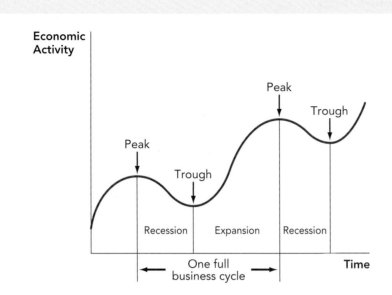

FIGURE 14.3

The Stages of Business Cycles

Business cycles are fluctuations in aggregate economic activity that consist of expansions in many economic activities followed by similar contractions. The highest point of the expansion is called the *peak*, and the lowest point of the contraction is called the *trough*. A complete business cycle includes an expansion and a contraction.

THEORIES OF BUSINESS CYCLES

As on many other issues, economists are divided on the causes of business cycles. Broadly speaking, there are four schools of thought on the causes of business cycles: the Keynesian theory, the Austrian theory, the real business cycles theory, and policy-induced theory.

The Keynesian Theory

The Keynesian theory of business cycles originated in the writings of John Maynard Keynes in his book *The General Theory*. According to this theory, business cycles are driven by fluctuation in the expectations of the entrepreneurs regarding the future level of business activities, which Keynes termed "Animal Spirits." If entrepreneurs are optimistic that in the future there will be a lot of economic activity and large profits will be made, then they will invest more. On the other hand, if they are pessimistic, they will invest less. These fluctuations in investment expenditures will lead to fluctuations in the aggregate demand for goods and services, which will lead to fluctuations in output and economic activity if wages are relatively sticky.

Keynesian theory maintains that wages are sticky because of the overlapping structure of wage contracts, which we studied in Chapter 10. Firms engaged in wage negotiations will resist wage increases because they do not want to lose competitiveness relative to the other group of firms which are locked in contracts that are due for renegotiation at a later date. On the other hand, workers engaged in wage negotiations will resist wage cuts because they are worried about their social position relative to the other group of workers whose wages are fixed until a later date. As a result, fluctuations in investment lead to substantial fluctuations in output, and to business cycles.

Therefore, the Keynesian theory views business cycles as originating on the demand side of the economy; and it implies that governments can stabilize business fluctuations through monetary and fiscal policies.

The Austrian Theory

This theory was developed by the Austrian economists such as Ludwig von Mises and Friedrich Hayek. The Austrian theory views business cycles as being inherent in the workings of the capitalist system.

According to the Austrian theory at any point in time there is some industrial restructuring going on in the economy, with old, obsolete, firms exiting and new, innovative, firms entering the economy; what Joseph Schumpeter called "creative destruction." As it takes time for workers to be retrained, it takes time for them to move from old to new industries. As a result, there is always some unemployment in the economy. The Austrian theory argues that business cycles arise because the intensity of industrial restructuring varies from time to time. In time of intense industrial restructuring the unemployment rate is high and we have a recession, while in time of low industrial restructuring the unemployment rate is low and we have a boom.

According to the Austrian theory recessions are necessary in order to force inefficient firms out of the economy. If the government tries to stabilize business cycles by reducing interest rates in recessions, then it will be interfering with the workings of the system, leading to a buildup of inefficient firms, and reducing overall productivity in the economy. The buildup of inefficient firms will eventually lead to more severe recessions.

The Real Business Cycle Theory

The real business cycle theory originated with the writings of Finn Kydland and Edward Prescott of the University of Minnesota, in the early 1980s. The real business cycle theory models business cycles as arising from shocks to overall productivity in the economy. Booms are periods of high productivity, with applications of new innovations to the production process; examples include the applications of information technologies to the production process. Recessions are times of relatively low productivity because, for example, major investment projects did not turn out to be as promising as they were originally thought.

According to the real business cycle theory the economy is assumed to be always at full employment, with shocks to productivity resulting in fluctuation in the full employment level of output. As such, according to this theory business cycles originate in the supply side of the economy; and it implies that there is no need for government stabilization policies. We discussed such supply shocks and how they will affect the economy in the flexible-price model of Chapter 6.

Policy-Induced Theory

This theory of business cycles is based on the observation that several post–World War II recessions were the result of government policies to curb inflation or to reduce budget deficits. Examples of policy-induced recessions are the recessions of the early 1980s and the early 1990s, both of which were primarily caused by the Bank of Canada's commitments to reduce inflation, and the high interest rates that resulted. These policies, which were viewed as being optimal for the long-run well-being of Canadians, did result in rather severe recessions. The same was true of the deficit reduction policies of the 1990s.

In comparing these theories, notice the Keynesian and the policy-induced theories rely on price rigidities; and, as such, they view fluctuations in unemployment as being primarily due to fluctuations in its cyclical component, $u - u^*$. On the other hand, the Austrian and the real business cycle theories assume that prices and wages are fully flexible; and, as such, they view fluctuations in unemployment as being primarily due to fluctuations in the natural rate u^*. Also, whereas the Keynesian theory has very strong policy prescriptions, the other three theories advocate no government intervention in order to stabilize business cycles.

from different sources and are of poorer quality than post–World War II data that have been compiled by official statistical agencies such as Statistics Canada. For this reason, comparing business cycles over different time periods may not be a very informative exercise.

Table 14.2 shows the historical record of Canada's business cycles in the twentieth century. This includes year and quarter dates for the peaks and the troughs of the business cycles as well as the duration of expansions and contractions measured in quarters. The selection of the peaks and troughs is based on the methodology used at the NBER; that is, looking at the behaviour of several economic variables and

TABLE 14.2

Length of Recessions and Expansions in Quarters since 1900

The average pre-WWII recession was larger than the average post-WWII recession. But the average pre-war expansion is smaller than the average post-war expansion.

Pre-WWII				Post-WWII			
Peak	Length of Contraction	Trough	Length of Expansion	Peak	Length of Contraction	Trough	Length of Expansion
1900:2	3	1901:1	7	1947:3	3	1948:2	12
1902:4	6	1904:2	10	1951:2	2	1951:4	5
1906:4	7	1908:3	6	1953:1	5	1954:2	11
1910:1	6	1911:3	5	1957:1	4	1958:1	9
1912:4	9	1915:1	15	1960:2	3	1961:1	36
1918:4	2	1919:2	4	1970:1	1	1970:2	16
1920:2	5	1921:3	7	1974:2	3	1975:1	20
1923:2	5	1924:3	21	1980:1	2	1980:3	4
1929:2	15	1933:1	14	1981:3	5	1982:4	14
1937:3	5	1938:4	35	1986:2	2	1986:4	10
				1989:2	14	1992:4	–
Average	6.3		12.4		4.0		13.7

Source: 1900–1919: Keith A. J. Hay, "Early Twentieth Century Business Cycles in Canada," *Canadian Journal of Economics and Political Science*, August 1966, pp. 354–65.
1919–1938: Edward J. Chambers, "Canadian Business Cycles since 1919: A Progress Report," *Canadian Journal of Economics and Political Science*, May 1958, pp. 166–89.
1947–1992: Philip Cross, "Alternative Measures of Business Cycles in Canada: 1947–1992," *Canadian Economic Observer*, February 1996, pp. 3.1–3.40.

making a determination about the timing of peaks and troughs. Since 1900, the Canadian economy has gone through 19 complete business cycles, of which nine took place before and ten after World War II.

We can reach a few conclusions about the changing cyclical variability of the Canadian economy. The first and most obvious fact is the extraordinary large size of the business cycle during the interwar period — the 1920–1940 period that came after World War I and before World War II. The Great Depression that began in 1929 was only the largest of three interwar business cycles. Other major contractions in economic activity took place in 1920–1923 and 1937–1938 (see also Figure 14.4).

As shown in the last row of Table 14.2, a second clear conclusion is that the average pre–World War II contraction was 2.3 quarters larger than the average post–World War II contraction. But the average pre-war expansion was 1.3 quarters shorter than the average post-war expansion. Overall the post-war business cycle is a somewhat smaller animal, but it would seem to be of the same species.

Thus many of the changes in the economy since 1900 must have roughly cancelled each other out. The decline of agriculture as a share of employment and production (as a rule not very susceptible to the industrial business cycle) has been offset by the rise in importance of relatively acyclical services (also not very susceptible to the business cycle). An increase in the life span of capital equipment built with more durable materials might seem likely to increase cyclical volatility because more economic activity takes the form of long-term bets on the future. But this has apparently been offset by faster technological obsolescence, which reduces the effective economic life of investments in fixed capital. A smaller multiplier due to reduced liquidity constraints on households has presumably had some effect. But perhaps keeping spending proportional to income remains a useful rule of thumb even as credit becomes widely available, and so perhaps credit availability has not done as much to reduce the multiplier as economists' theories claim.

FIGURE 14.4

The Great Depression Relative to Other Business Cycles: Canadian Unemployment, 1921–2005

The Great Depression pushed the unemployment rate to about 20 percent of the Canadian labour force. The other recessions had a much smaller impact on the unemployment rate in Canada.

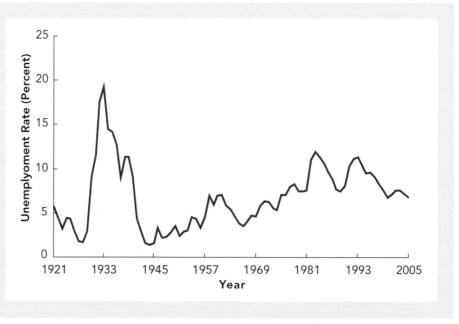

Source: Statistics Canada, Historical Statistics of Canada, Series D129 (labour force, 1921–1945), D132 (unemployed, 1921–1945), and D233 (unemployment rate, 1946–1975); and Statistics Canada CANSIM II database, Series V2064894 (unemployment rate, 1976–2005).

ECONOMIC POLICY

HOW ECONOMIC POLICY HAS WORKED

Yet if we look a little deeper, we see that business cycles today are not the same animals as they were before the Great Depression. The fall in the multiplier, the arrival of automatic stabilizers, and the increasing power of central banks have allowed monetary policy to offset many of the kinds of shocks that generated pre-Depression business cycles. The absence of significant stabilization springs from the fact that the increasing power of central banks has created a new class of shocks to the economy: recessions deliberately induced by monetary authorities to curb rising inflation. The post–World War II economy appears to have had fewer small recessions caused by shocks to the IS and LM curves. **Stabilization policy** has worked, in that it allows for the central bank working in combination with automatic stabilizers to react when the economy threatens to turn down into recession because of any sudden shock.

Before World War II it was impossible for the Canadian government to have a large effect on aggregate demand. Government purchases and net taxes were so small relative to economic activity that no fiscal policy variation short of fighting a major war could materially shift the IS curve and change equilibrium real GDP. The pre–World War II government also lacked, until the founding of the Bank of Canada in 1935, the ability to affect the level of interest rates. Neither fiscal stabilization policy nor monetary stabilization policy as we know them today was possible before World War II.

By the end of World War II the power of stabilization policy and the government's commitment to manage aggregate demand were both firmly established. The war left Canada with a federal government committed to countercyclical fiscal policy. Before World War II it had been a commonplace of political and policy-making discourse that taxes should be raised and spending cut to try to balance the budget in a recession. By the 1950s this doctrine was dead: The automatic stabilizers of the federal budget were in place.

The emergence of a significant progressive income tax made government revenues substantially procyclical, and the emergence of unemployment compensation and welfare led government spending to have a substantial automatic procyclical component as well. By the 1960s the federal government believed that it ought to be undertaking countercyclical discretionary fiscal policy as well (even though it has never been able to succeed in doing so). In monetary policy a similar shift had been accomplished near the beginning of the post–World War II period. By the early 1950s the principal task of the Bank of Canada was to use monetary policy to stabilize the economy.

Since then the Bank of Canada has attempted to use monetary policy, within the limits placed on it by long and variable lags, to stabilize the economy and to moderate recessions. Both overall survey studies and detailed studies of cases like the interest rate cuts that followed the stock market crash of 1987 teach the lesson that the Bank of Canada has had considerable success in cutting short recessions and in accelerating growth in the early stages of the subsequent economic expansion.

http://www.bank-banque-canada.ca/

HOW ECONOMIC POLICY HAS NOT WORKED

But if economic policy since World War II has prevented or moderated many recessions, it has caused recessions as well. The existence of **policy-induced recessions** like those of 1981–1982 and 1990–1992 is what explains why there has not been a more dramatic reduction in the size of the business cycle over time. At least four times in Canada since World War II the Bank of Canada has engineered a recession, or has willingly accepted a substantial risk of a recession, in order to accomplish its policy goal of curbing inflation. It has had to curb an inflation rate that has crept upward into an uncomfortably high range.

If the pre-war boom-and-bust business cycle was driven by, in John Maynard Keynes's phrase, the "animal spirits" of investors' shifts from optimism to pessimism and back again (and by financial panics), the post–World War II boom-and-bust business cycle has been driven by economic policies that have allowed rises in inflation, followed by the development of a consensus within the Bank of Canada that the rise in inflation must be reversed.

Why have economic policy makers in the post–World War II era found themselves repeatedly driven to risk recession in order to fight inflation? In the 1960s and 1970s inflation was allowed to accelerate for reasons that economists still debate. We have stressed historical accidents and the lingering memory of the Great Depression. The Stanford economist John Taylor stresses mistaken economic theories held in the early 1960s — in particular, the Phillips curve model of Samuelson and Solow constructed under the assumption that inflation expectations were and would remain static.

At the first, surface level, Canada had an unstable macroeconomy in the 1970s because until the 1980s no influential policy makers would place a sufficiently high priority on keeping inflation from rising. As long as inflation remained relatively low, it was not seen as a crisis, and so other goals took precedence among every group of economic policy makers. Thus, the federal government and the Bank of Canada were willing to accept the risk of increasing inflation to achieve other goals. Only after inflation had risen — only after it had reached the level of a political crisis — did a consensus develop that priorities needed to be changed, and steps were taken to reduce inflation.

Under this interpretation, Canada after World War II had a boom-bust, stop-go business cycle because the political system could pay attention to only one phenomenon at a time: When inflation wasn't a crisis, it wasn't an issue.

Only with the acceleration of inflation toward the end of the 1970s did political sentiment begin to shift. For rising inflation did become a severe political problem in 1979. And Gerald Bouey, the Governor of the Bank of Canada at that time, following the U.S. lead, made inflation the focus of monetary policy. The Bank of Canada under Bouey quickly signalled its intention to place first priority on controlling inflation. This policy was pursued with more vigour in the early 1990s under the next Bank of Canada Governor, John Crow. Many commentators now believe that the recession of 1990–1992 was in a large measure the result of the "zero inflation" policy of the Bank of Canada.

At a second, deeper level, Canada had a burst of inflation in the 1970s that required a painful recession cure in the 1980s because economic policy makers during the 1960s dealt their successors a bad hand: an unfavourable Phillips curve. Thus the policies of the 1960s left economic policy makers of the 1970s with a painful dilemma: either higher-than-usual inflation, or higher-than-usual unemployment. Bad cards coupled with bad luck made inflation in the 1970s worse than anyone expected it might be. And unsuccessful attempts to find a way out of this dilemma gave the economy the boom-bust cycle of the 1970s.

And at a third, deepest level, the truest cause of the inflation of the 1970s was the memory of the Great Depression. The Great Depression made it impossible for a while to believe that the business cycle was a fluctuation *around* rather than a shortfall *below* potential output and potential employment. The memory of the Great Depression made everyone skeptical of taking the average level of capacity utilization or the unemployment rate as a measure of the economy's sustainable productive potential.

Only after the experiences of the 1970s were economic policy makers persuaded that the flaws and frictions in the Canadian economy made it unwise to try to use stimulative macroeconomic policies without limit. Only after the experiences of the 1970s were policy makers persuaded that the minimum sustainable rate of unemployment attainable by macroeconomic policy was relatively high, and that the costs — at least the political costs — of even moderately high one-digit inflation were high as well.

It is somewhat depressing that the post–World War II gains from stabilization policy appear to have been relatively small. Nearly 50 years ago Milton Friedman warned that stabilization policy, if pursued overly aggressively by policy makers who did not understand its limits, could easily turn into destabilization policy. It looks as though his gloomy warning was very close to being correct. Yet important lessons may have been learned.

RECAP   PRE-WWII VERSUS POST-WWII BUSINESS CYCLES

The pre-WWII boom-and-bust business cycle was driven by investors' shifts from optimism to pessimism and back again. The post-WWII boom-and-bust business cycle has been driven by economic policies that have allowed rises in inflation, followed by a policy-caused recession to reverse the rise in inflation. There is reason to hope that the modern Bank of Canada has learned how to eliminate or at least reduce the size of these inflation-fighting recessions. The magnitude of the business cycle has been much smaller since the mid-1980s.

THE GREAT DEPRESSION

But if the business cycle has remained in spite of — and in part because of — active macroeconomic policy, it is important to remember that active macroeconomic policy has made a disaster on the order of magnitude of the Great Depression inconceivable. To see how bad things could get in an extreme situation when economic policy does not do its job, we need only to look back 74 years at the Great Depression.

THE MAGNITUDE OF THE GREAT DEPRESSION

The speed and magnitude of the economy's collapse during the first stages of the Great Depression was unprecedented: Nothing like it had been seen before, and nothing like it has been seen since. From above full employment in 1929, real GDP fell until it was nearly 30 percent below potential output by 1933 (see Figure 14.5). Investment collapsed: By 1932 real investment spending was negative. And by 1933 unemployment had reached a fifth of the labour force.

In our analytical framework it is straightforward to understand why investment and real GDP fell so far so fast between 1929 and 1933. They did so because of an extraordinary rise in real interest rates. Real interest rates that had been 4 percent in 1929 spiked to nearly 13 percent by 1931, and stayed high throughout 1932. With such high real interest rates, naturally investment spending fell off.

After 1932 investment spending remained low, averaging less than half its 1929 value for the rest of the Great Depression decade even though real interest rates returned to more normal values. Why didn't the return of real interest rates to normal

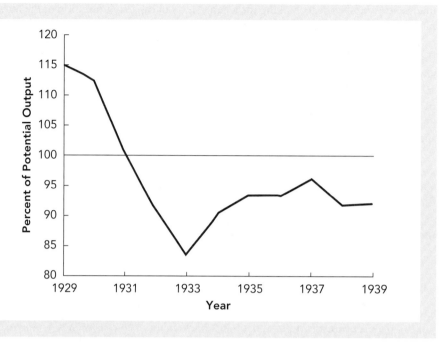

FIGURE 14.5

Real GDP Relative to Potential Output during the Great Depression

The Great Depression saw the steepest fall ever in real GDP relative to potential output.

Source: Adapted from the Statistics Canada CANSIM I database, Series D22432 (Imports of Goods) and D22435 (GDP).

Note: This series is calculated as (Real GDP/Real Trend GDP) × 100 where Real Trend GDP is the Hodrick-Prescott Trend of Real GDP from 1929–1939. Real GDP is measured in constant 1986 dollars.

values cause a revival of investment? Because the magnitude of the Great Depression itself caused businesses to put off expanding their capacity. In 1933, with real GDP less than two-thirds of potential output, practically every business in Canada had excess capacity and hence no immediate incentive to invest at all. The very depth of the Great Depression caused a steep fall in the baseline investment coefficient I_0 in the investment equation

$$I = I_0 - (I_r \times r)$$

Thus even a restoration of real interest rates to normal levels was not sufficient to restore the economy to full employment.

DEFLATION AND HIGH REAL INTEREST RATES

So why did real interest rates rise so high between 1929 and 1932? The immediate, proximate cause of high real interest rates was rapid deflation: rapid sustained falls in prices that, when combined with moderate nominal interest rates, produced very high real interest rates.

What caused the deflation? The first thing was the depth of the Great Depression itself: Falling production, employment, and demand produced steep falls in prices, which caused high real interest rates that reduced demand, production, and employment still further. But it makes little sense to say that the Great Depression caused itself. There must have been an initial shock to start the downward spiral that was the Great Depression.

THE INITIAL SHOCK

Economists have proposed many candidates for the shock that triggered the Great Depression. Perhaps the stock market crash of 1929 reduced wealth and increased uncertainty, and caused a downward shift in the baseline level of consumption. Perhaps the availability of consumer credit in the 1920s caused a consumption spending boom that then came to a natural end. Perhaps there was excessive residential investment in the 1920s because builders failed to realize how the restrictions on immigration put into place in the mid-1920s would affect housing demand in the long run. Perhaps the recognition that the housing stock was too large triggered a downward shift in the baseline level of investment. Perhaps the U.S. Federal Reserve's 1928 increases in interest rates, an attempt to reduce stock market speculation, triggered the initial slump.

Practically any analyst soon reaches the conclusion that the response was disproportionate to the initial shock. Somehow the American economy at the end of the 1920s was very vulnerable in the sense that a small shock could cause a big depression. It is this disproportion between the hard-to-find initial shock and the subsequent depression that makes many economists fear that the economy will be unstable if not managed by appropriate government policies.

CONSEQUENCES OF THE PRICE LEVEL DECLINE

Economists have reached a consensus that a sufficiently aggressive and activist monetary policy could have stemmed the price decline, and so ended the Great Depression much earlier, if undertaken rapidly and aggressively enough. Policies of massive federal deficits funded by money-printing, coupled with aggressive open-market operations to increase the monetary base could have, if carried far enough, produced inflation. And without the high real interest rates produced by deflation in the early 1930s, it is hard to see how there could have been a Great Depression.

Falling price levels reduce real GDP through two separate channels. The first is the real interest rate channel that we saw above: The real interest rate is the nominal interest rate minus the inflation rate, so deflation leads to high real interest rates, to a move up and to the left along the IS curve, and to falling real GDP and employment.

But there is a second channel as well. Unexpected falls in the price level redistribute wealth from debtors to creditors. Those businesses that are heavily in debt find that they cannot pay, and so they go bankrupt. Those financial institutions that have loaned to heavily indebted businesses find that their loans are worthless, and so they go bankrupt as well. Deflation destroys the web of credit that channels funds from savers through banks and other financial institutions to businesses wanting to invest. And without the web of financial intermediaries to channel investment through the financial markets, maintaining or restoring the flow of investment becomes very difficult.

These effects of deflation are long-lasting. Even after real interest rates have returned to normal, the deflation-driven destruction of the web of financial intermediation will continue to depress investment. So it was in the Great Depression.

RECAP THE GREAT DEPRESSION

The extreme depth of the Great Depression led to deflation: Falling price levels reduce real GDP by raising real interest rates, moving the economy up the IS curve, and by redistributing wealth, destroying the web of credit that channels funds from savers to businesses wanting to invest. A sufficiently aggressive and activist monetary policy could have stemmed the price decline in the 1930s and so ended the Great Depression much earlier — if undertaken rapidly and aggressively enough.

14.3 MACROECONOMIC POLICY: LESSONS LEARNED

STABILIZATION

For almost all of your lives — "you" being the typical reader of this textbook — the business cycle has been relatively quiescent. A substantial difference in business-cycle behaviour comes from dividing the post–World War II era into two periods with the breakpoint chosen at the end of the deflation period in the early 1980s. The pre-1984 years show much more business-cycle volatility than do the post-1985 years, as Table 14.3 indicates.

One possibility is that the period since 1984 has been the result of good luck — that business-cycle macroeconomic performance has been good because there have not been many shocks nor any truly large shocks to the economy. But just as the relatively placid 1960s were followed by the disruptive 1970s, perhaps the 1990s is turning out to be followed by an equally turbulent decade.

LEARNING

A second possibility is that lessons have truly been learned from the experience of the 1960s and 1970s. The late 1980s and the 1990s were not only an era of relatively stable economic growth but also an era of low inflation. Recessions have been few and growth relatively steady since the early 1980s in large part because inflation has been firmly under control: A lack of inflation has meant that the Bank of Canada has not had to risk a recession to control inflation.

This leads to the hope that the monetary policy authorities have gained sufficient experience and expertise at using their policy tools to successfully carry out stabilization policy. Perhaps the first three decades of the post–World War II era saw

---

TABLE 14.3

Stabilization of the Canadian Economy: Standard Deviation of Percentage Changes

Since the mid-1980s the Canadian economy has been relatively stable. Typical business-cycle movements in the unemployment rate or in real GDP have been much lower than they were from 1948 to 1984.

Series	1948–1984	1985–1999
Industrial production	4.3%	3.3%
Real GDP	3.3	2.7
Inflation	3.9	1.7
Unemployment rate	2.4	1.3

Source: Ind. Production: 1948–1971: CANSIM I – Series D5760.
              1972–1984: CANSIM I – Series D142851.
              1985–1999: IMF, International Financial Statistics – Series 15666.
      Real GDP : 1948–1960: Historical Statistics of Canada – Series D13 (nominal GNP) and CANSIM I – Series D15689 and P100000 (CPI).
              1962–1999: CANSIM I – Series D15689 (nominal GDP) and P100000 (CPI).
      Inflation : CANSIM I – Series P100000 (CPI).
Unemployment rate : CANSIM I – Series.

little stabilization of the business cycle because of repeated policy mistakes: over-optimism with respect to the possible sustainable rate of economic growth, followed by recessions to demonstrate that the central bank was, after all, serious about controlling inflation.

14.4 MACROECONOMIC POLICY: LESSONS UN- OR HALF-LEARNED

One can also be pessimistic about the future of macroeconomic policy. One can count up all the lessons that economists and policy makers have not learned, or have half-learned, or have learned and then forgotten over the course of the twentieth century. Certainly a look outside North America, either at Japan, or at the financial-crisis-ridden emerging economies, or at Europe with its stubbornly high unemployment, does not lend strength to the claim that traditional business-cycle patterns have come to an end.

LESSONS UNLEARNED: HIGH EUROPEAN UNEMPLOYMENT

Europe at the end of the 1990s was not in a Great Depression. Nevertheless, unemployment rates in western Europe at the end of the 1990s were within hailing distance of the rates achieved during the Great Depression. Unemployment averaged 10 percent in the zone of countries that now share the common currency of the euro (see Figure 14.6).

Up until the end of the 1970s, unemployment in western Europe had been lower — sometimes substantially lower — than unemployment in North America. But

http://www.access.gpo.gov/eop/

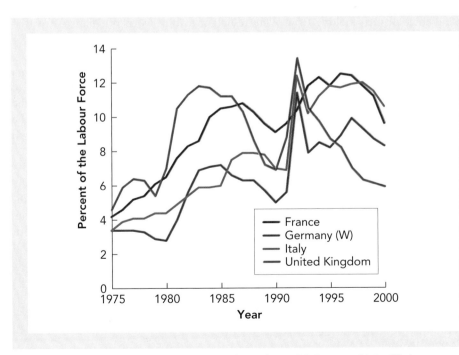

FIGURE 14.6
European Unemployment
The growth of unemployment in the four largest western European countries, 1975–2000.

Source: The 2001 edition of *The Economic Report of the President* (Washington, DC: Government Printing Office).

starting in the 1970s European unemployment began to ratchet upward. Unemployment rose during recessions, yet it did not fall during economic expansions. During the recession of the Volcker disinflation in the U.S. at the start of the 1980s, western European and U.S. unemployment rates were about equal. But during the later 1980s and 1990s the trend of U.S. unemployment was down; the trend of European unemployment was stable or upward.

In the United States it is possible to understand the co-movements of unemployment and inflation over 1960–2000 using the standard Phillips curve. The Phillips curve shifts out in the 1970s as everyone begins to expect higher inflation and demographic factors cause the natural rate of unemployment to rise. The Phillips curve shifts back in the 1980s and 1990s as people regain confidence in the Federal Reserve's commitment to low inflation and as changing demographic factors cause the natural rate of unemployment to fall. The story does not fit badly. The same can also be said about the Canadian economy in the 1980s and 1990s (recall Box 11.7 in Chapter 11). Movements in the expected rate of inflation reflect changes in the economic policy environment. Movements in the natural rate of unemployment are relatively small, and can be linked to plausible factors.

In western Europe, by contrast, the accelerationist Phillips curve *never* fit the historical experience very well. Each policy episode from 1970 on — supply shocks, the Volcker disinflation, the recession of the early 1990s — seemed to shift the Phillips curve further out, and to further raise the natural rate of unemployment. It seemed as if this year's natural rate of unemployment was equal to whatever unemployment had happened to be last year.

The dominant view expressed in Europe in the early 1990s was that high European unemployment was the result of labour market rigidities. Europe possessed laws, restrictions, and regulations that made it too difficult for firms to hire new workers cheaply at a relatively low wage, and too difficult for firms to fire workers (and thus forward-looking firms were reluctant to hire workers). Thus it was too expensive to conduct a labour-intensive business in Europe or to adjust to changes in the economic environment.

According to this dominant view, high unemployment in Europe is an *equilibrium* level that is what economists call "**classical**": It arises not from any deficiency of aggregate demand, but simply from the fact that the state's regulations keep the labour market from clearing. The state's regulations boost the cost of employing the marginal worker far above the extra revenue the typical firm would gain from employing an extra worker.

But the "rigidities" in the European labour market were stronger in the 1960s — when European unemployment was very low — than they are today. It is not that the natural rate of unemployment in Europe has always been high; it is that each additional adverse shock that increases unemployment seems to increase the natural rate as well. Thus many economists who have examined European unemployment dissent from the conventional wisdom of the editorial writers and the politicians. They tend to see western Europe not as locked into high unemployment, but as in a reversible situation. Just as increases in unemployment in the 1970s and 1980s raised the natural rate of unemployment in Europe, so decreases in the rate of unemployment in the 2000s would in all likelihood lower the natural rate of unemployment in Europe.

A GRAND BARGAIN?

Economists' views of western European unemployment thus suggest there is potential for much improvement. Have central bankers and governments shifted to a more expansionary monetary policy? As demand expands, people will find that the natural rate of unemployment is falling. The falling natural rate of unemployment will create still further room for demand expansion, and for further unemployment rate reduction.

Central bankers may fear that the economists' view is wrong and that the conventional wisdom is right — that attempts to expand demand and reduce unemployment a little bit will lead to accelerating inflation as unemployment falls below its (high) current natural rate. Therefore begin the process with some steps to eliminate labour-market rigidities: Reduce employers' contributions to social security, reduce severance costs, transfer unemployment insurance money from the payment of benefits to assistance with job searching, and allow the minimum wage to fall. These steps should leave central bankers confident that there is room to expand demand in the context of a falling natural rate of unemployment.

But governments find that such steps to initiate the process of demand expansion can be portrayed as an attack on the standard of living of the unemployed — as an antiworker, antihuman policy. Only if governments are confident that reform of the social insurance system will be accompanied by stronger demand and higher employment will they be willing to undertake their part of the grand bargain. Otherwise they will fear that — with high interest rates and slow demand growth — social insurance system reform will merely change high classical unemployment to high Keynesian unemployment, and in the process create mass poverty. And only if central banks are confident that their expansionary monetary policies will be accompanied by social insurance system reform would it make sense for them to risk lower interest rates and a change in monetary policy.

Even if the conventional wisdom is right, such a grand bargain promises to make everyone — the currently unemployed, the currently employed who pay taxes to support the social insurance system, politicians dealing with high unemployment, central bankers accused of being out of touch with human experience — better off. And if the economists' view is right — if the principal determinant of a high natural rate of unemployment in Europe is the fact that unemployment has been high in Europe for a long time — then the benefits to such a grand bargain are overwhelmingly large.

Yet European politicians and central bankers have been unable to learn how to deal with their high, stubborn rates of unemployment.

LESSONS HALF-LEARNED: JAPANESE STAGNATION

THE END OF THE BUBBLE ECONOMY

The standard analysis of how the Japanese economy entered its period of stagnation in the 1990s is straightforward. The Japanese stock market and real estate market rose far and fast in the 1980s, to unsustainable "bubble" levels. And eventually the market turned, and both the real estate and stock markets collapsed.

When stock and real estate prices collapsed, it was discovered that lots of enterprises and individuals had borrowed heavily against their real estate and security holdings, putting up their real estate and their stocks as collateral. After the collapse, not only were those who had borrowed heavily bankrupt, but the banks and other institutions that had loaned them money were bankrupt as well: The value of the collateral they had accepted was no longer enough to repay the *lenders'* creditors.

One problem was that no one was exactly sure which institutions were bankrupt — which institutions had liabilities in excess of their assets. Thus no one was anxious to lend money to anyone: You might well never see your money again if the organization you loaned it to was one of those that had extended itself during the bubble economy of the late 1980s. A second problem was regulatory forbearance: the belief that the best way to solve the problem was to pretend that it did not exist, try to let business go on as usual, and hope that a few good years would allow all of the institutions that were "underwater" to make enough in profits to repay their debts even given the low value of the collateral that they had accepted.

These two problems together meant that investment spending was depressed. Financial institutions exist to channel money from savers with purchasing power to businesses that can use that purchasing power to expand their capital. But in the aftermath of the collapse of the bubble, no one really wanted to lend — for you could not know whether the organization wanted your money to invest, or to try to paper over some of its previous losses.

The situation was analogous to the collapse of investment spending in the Great Depression, where the chain of deflation and bankruptcies had similar effects. The collapse of the Japanese financial bubble of the 1980s depressed consumption and investment spending. Banks' and other institutions' large bets on the real estate market meant that the collapse of the bubble put them underwater — with assets and lines of business that were worth less than the debt they already owed that they had borrowed to speculate in real estate. Who will invest in a business — or a bank — if they fear that their money will be used not to boost profitability but instead to pay back earlier creditors?

Thus Japan fell into a decade of economic stagnation. Growth from 1990 until 2002 was almost zero, as Figure 14.7 shows. Unemployment rose to levels previously unheard-of in Japan. The IS curve shifted far to the left. And nothing seemed to correct it: Even extremely low nominal interest rates were not sufficient to boost

FIGURE 14.7

The Japanese Bubble Economy: Before, during, and After

(Real and potential GDP are graphed on the scale on the left side.) Since the Japanese stock market crash at the beginning of the 1990s, Japanese economic growth has been extremely slow. For a decade, what was the fastest growing of the Group of Seven (G-7) major industrial nations' economies became the slowest growing of them all.

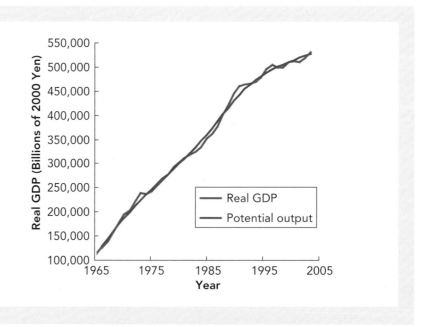

Source: World Bank, World Development Indicators.

investment and aggregate demand. And for an entire decade Japanese economic growth was extremely slow and stagnant.

What should economic policy makers do in such a situation? The answer to what you should do in order to recover from such a state of depressed aggregate demand is "everything." You should have the government run a substantial deficit (although, as E. Cary Brown of MIT pointed out in the 1950s, it requires truly awesome deficit spending — on the order of deficit spending in World War II — to reverse a Great Depression like that in the United States in the 1930s or a Great Stagnation like that in Japan in the 1990s). You should have the central bank push the interest rate it charges close to zero (to make it very easy and cheap to borrow money).

If that isn't enough you should try to deliberately engineer moderate inflation. If demand is depressed because people think investing in corporations is too risky, change their minds by making the alternative to investment spending even more risky. If the alternative is hoarding your money in cash, then eat away a share of its real purchasing power every year with inflation.

Japan changed its fiscal policy to run big deficits (but, as any student of the Great Depression would suspect, they were not big enough). Japan lowered its short-term safe nominal interest rates to within kissing distance of zero. But these did not do enough good. Only in 2003 did the Japanese economy start to recover from its decade-long recession. The lessons of the Great Depression have been only half-learned.

LESSONS HALF-LEARNED: MORAL HAZARD

Even in Canada, it seems that some of the lessons on economic policy taught by the past century of experience have been only half-learned. Consider the problem of dealing with financial crises: those moments when large and highly leveraged financial institutions have failed or are about to, and when there is a genuine fear that a chain of bankruptcies is about to be triggered.

In such a situation the fear that the organization to which one might lend will fail greatly retards lending. The flow of funds through financial markets will slow to a trickle, as savers conclude that keeping their wealth close at hand in safe forms is a much better opportunity than lending it to organizations that are probably bankrupt. Thus such a financial crisis is likely to see the IS curve shift far and fast to the left as the level of investment spending collapses. If this leftward shift in the IS curve is not stemmed, there will be a recession and the financial crisis will rapidly become worse as businesses that were solvent at normal levels of production and sales find that the fall-off in demand has bankrupted them.

What to do in such a situation was first outlined by Bagehot a century and a quarter ago. The government needs to rapidly close down and liquidate those organizations that are fundamentally bankrupt. If they would be bankrupt even if production and demand were at normal levels relative to potential, then they should be closed. The government needs to lend money — albeit at a high, unpleasant, penalty rate — to organizations that would be solvent if production and demand were at normal levels, but that nevertheless suffer a cash crunch now.

The key is twofold: Government support is necessary in order to prevent a deep meltdown of the entire financial system. Government assistance must be offered on terms unpleasant enough and expensive enough that no one would wish in advance to get into a situation in which they need to draw on it. Moreover, the government must accept that its ability to distinguish between these two classes of institutions is imperfect, and that it will inevitably make mistakes.

Yet more and more in the political discussion over economic policy one hears the claim that government provision of liquidity and support in a financial crisis is dangerous — that it causes "**moral hazard**" because organizations place riskier and riskier bets counting on government support to bail them out if things go wrong. The right policy in a financial crisis is a completely hands-off one. A century and a quarter of experience suggests that this is only a half-truth. Moral hazard is a problem, but so is a Great Depression. The balancing point is hard to determine: Bank and financial regulators must impose rules that restrict the growth of moral hazard, assistance in times of financial crisis must be expensive and painful to the organization drawing on the government, and yet the worst outcome — a freezing-up of the financial system and a severe recession — must be guarded against. To focus on only one of these three rather than balancing between them is to recommend bad economic policy.

THE ULTIMATE LESSON

It is strange that neither European nor Japanese governments appear to have learned the lessons that macroeconomists have to teach. It is also strange that fundamentals of crisis policy that seemed settled more than a century ago are still up for grabs in Canada's political debate. The principal lesson is that it seems very hard to learn the lessons of history.

Thus the future of economic policy seems likely to be similar to the past. Gross mistakes will be made, historical analogies will be misapplied, and economists and other observers after the fact (and sometimes during the fact) will find major policy mistakes made by governments and central banks to be inexplicable: We will genuinely be unable to figure out just what the people who made the decisions were thinking.

So do not mistake the steady hand on the monetary policy tiller and the relatively placid business cycle that Canada has experienced since the mid-1980s for the way things will be in the future.

RECAP   **MACROECONOMIC POLICY: LESSONS
UN- OR HALF-LEARNED**

Economists and economic policy makers have learned much over the past century, but many lessons appear unlearned or imperfectly learned. European unemployment remains high in spite of the prospect that a two-handed approach to both stimulate aggregate demand and remove restrictions on aggregate supply would allow for more rapid growth and expanded employment without inflation. The Japanese government was very slow in reacting to a decade-long financial crisis in the 1990s, thus keeping its economy stagnant. And the economic policy debate within Canada fails to note that financial crises pose a choice between evils and not a situation in which one single principle of economic governance — whether "avoid moral hazard" or "avoid chains of bankruptcies" — can be applied to the fullest. Perhaps the most important lesson is that the lessons of history are hard to learn.

CHAPTER SUMMARY

1. The structure of the economy has undergone mammoth changes over the past century, yet these changes appear to have had relatively little impact on the size of the business cycle.

2. Stabilization policy as we know it was impossible a hundred years ago; yet it is now performed routinely and aggressively.

3. Since World War II, stabilization policy has had successes and failures. Its principal failure has been that it has generated recessions to fight inflation, and these policy-induced recessions have kept policy from successfully stabilizing the economy to a greater degree.

4. In the past two decades, stabilization policy in Canada has been very successful. Is this just good luck, or is it a pattern? We shall see.

5. Certainly from the Canadian perspective there is every reason to be optimistic about the future of macroeconomic policy, and of the macroeconomy.

6. From a European perspective there is less reason to be optimistic: European governments and central banks have not learned how to deal with their high levels of unemployment.

7. From a Japanese perspective there is less reason to be optimistic: The Japanese government has not learned how to deal with its financial meltdown.

8. Even from a Canadian perspective, it seems to be hard to learn the lesson that good economic policy during an economic crisis is not a matter of clinging to one principle, but of balancing the conflicting requirements of several valid principles.

KEY TERMS

bubble economy (p. 431)

business cycle (p. 418)

classical unemployment (p. 430)

cyclical volatility (p. 418)

financial automatic stabilizers (p. 414)

financial flexibility (p. 415)

globalization (p. 415)

liquidity constraints (p. 415)

moral hazard (p. 434)

peak (p. 418)

policy-induced recessions (p. 423)

recovery (p. 418)

stabilization policy (p. 423)

trough (p. 418)

ANALYTICAL EXERCISES

1. What changing factors since the start of the twentieth century would make one expect business cycles to become larger?

2. What changing factors since the start of the twentieth century would make one expect business cycles to become smaller?

3. As the macroeconomy continues to change in the twenty-first century, do you expect business cycles to become larger or smaller?

4. Why has production become more stable in Canada since the early 1980s?

5. Why does unemployment remain high in Europe today relative to the U.S?

6. Explain which business cycle theory subscribes to each one of the following statements.

   a. Workers are worried about their position relative to other workers and do not accept wage cuts in recessions.
   b. Recessions force relatively unproductive firms out of the economy.
   c. Business cycles are caused by misguided government policies.
   d. Business cycles are driven by changes in productivity.
   e. Business cycles are driven by fluctuations in the expectations of entrepreneurs regarding the future levels of business activities.
   f. Business cycles are driven by changes in aggregate demand, which are, in turn, caused by fluctuations in government spending.
   g. Governments should intervene to stabilize recessions, otherwise the economy will head into even more severe recessions.

POLICY EXERCISES

1. How, in your view, is the way the Bank of Canada conducts monetary policy likely to change over the next generation?

2. If the government's share of GDP in spending shrinks over the next generation, what in your view is likely to happen to the size of the business cycle?

3. How, in your view, will increased ease of international trade and increased international capital mobility change the workings of the macroeconomy over the next generation?

4. What steps would you take to try to reduce European unemployment, and how might those steps backfire?

5. What steps would you have taken in the 1990s in order to try to end Japan's depression of that decade, and how might those steps have backfired?

PART VI

Open Economy Macroeconomics: Theory and Policy

In the past several chapters we have introduced elements of an open economy in the basic model with flexible and sticky prices. Nevertheless, the models we used in Chapters 5, 6, 8, and 9 did not analyze the details of the foreign exchange market and the determinants of the long-run level of the real exchange rate. Moreover, so far we have focused exclusively on flexible exchange rates and ignored fixed exchange rates.

In this part of the book we provide a more detailed examination of the open economy theory and policy. In Chapter 15 we focus exclusively on the theory of open economy macroeconomics and provide a complete analysis of the balance of payments, exchange rate regimes, capital mobility, international interest parity conditions, and the Mundell-Fleming model. We then use the Mundell-Fleming model to study the effects of fiscal, monetary, and other economic shocks, in the short and the long-run, under flexible and fixed exchange rates.

In Chapter 16 we provide a detailed examination of international policy issues since the early twentieth century. We study the workings of the fixed exchange rate system under the gold standard and the Bretton Woods system, along with the circumstances that led to its replacement by flexible exchange rates in the early 1970s. We then discuss the advantages and disadvantages of fixed and flexible exchange rate systems. We end the chapter with a discussion of some major currency crises in the European, Mexican, and East Asian economies in recent years.

15

Open Economy Macroeconomics: The Balance of Payments, International Parity Conditions, and the Mundell-Fleming Model

QUESTIONS

What are the components of the balance of payments account?

What is the relation between the balance of payments and the demand and supply of currencies on the foreign exchange markets?

What are the interest rate parity conditions?

How does a fixed exchange rate system work?

What are the effects of monetary and fiscal policies under fixed and flexible exchange rate systems?

Why is there so much fluctuation in exchange rates under a flexible exchange rate system?

I n the past several chapters we have introduced elements of an open economy in the basic model with flexible and sticky prices. Our discussion of the national income accounts in Chapter 2 took explicit account of goods and services trade with the rest of the world. Asset trade was not discussed. Asset trade and goods and services trade are closely related, and are usually discussed in the context of the balance of payments accounts, which records all the transactions a country makes with the rest of the world. The models we used in Chapters 5, 6, 8, and 9 did not analyze the details of the foreign exchange market and the determinants of the long-run level of the real exchange rate. In fact, the balance of payments and the foreign exchange market are closely related, and should be studied in conjunction with each other. Also, so far we have focused exclusively on flexible exchange rates and ignored fixed exchange rates, even though the latter have been an important feature of the international monetary system. For instance, currently a lot of developing countries fix their exchange rates to major currencies such as the US dollar, and in the post-war period up until 1973 most industrialized countries operated under a fixed exchange rate system.

In this chapter we focus exclusively on the theory of open economy macroeconomics and provide a complete analysis of the balance of payments, exchange rate regimes, capital mobility, international interest parity conditions, and the well-known Mundell-Fleming model for a **small open economy** that cannot affect world interest rates and prices. We then use the Mundell-Fleming model to study the effects of fiscal, monetary, and other economic shocks on the equilibrium of the economy, in the short and the long run, under flexible and fixed exchange rates. We close the chapter with a discussion of the related issues of devaluation, balance of payments crises, imperfect asset substitutability, and imperfect capital mobility.

15.1 THE BALANCE OF PAYMENTS ACCOUNT

The **balance of payments account** records the international transactions a country makes with the rest of the world. It keeps record of both payments to and receipts from foreigners. Any transaction that results in a payment to foreigners is a *debit,* and is recorded with a negative (−) sign. Any transaction that results in a receipt from foreigners is a *credit,* and is recorded with a positive (+) sign. The balance of payments is divided into two parts: (i) the current account and (ii) the capital account.

Transactions involving goods, services, investment income, and unilateral transfers are recorded in the current account.[1] For example, when a European consumer imports Canadian beer, the transaction is recorded as a credit in the current account of Canada's balance of payments. Why a credit? Because, in this case, Canada is exporting (selling) a good to Europeans; hence a payment is received from abroad.

Transactions involving assets are recorded in the capital account. An *asset* is any one of the forms in which wealth can be held, such as money, bonds, stocks, factories, or land. When a Canadian buys stocks in a U.S. company, the transaction enters the Canadian balance of payments as a debit in the capital account. Why a debit? Because, in this case, Canada is "importing" (purchasing) an asset from abroad; hence a payment to the U.S. is in order.

In general, it is useful to keep in mind the following taxonomy of debits and credits in the current and capital accounts. For the current account we have,

	Credits	*Debits*
Exports of goods and services	+	
Imports of goods and services		−
Investment income received from abroad	+	
Investment income paid to foreigners		−
Transfer payments received from foreigners	+	
Transfer payments paid to foreigners		−

The balance on the current account is all the credits minus all the debits on the current account.

---

[1] Unilateral transfers are international gifts such as foreign aid and immigrant remittances that do not correspond to the purchase of any good, service, or asset exchanged between countries.

For the capital account we have,

	Credits	Debits
Sales of domestic assets to foreigners *(capital inflow)*	+	
Purchases of foreign assets by domestic residents *(capital outflow)*		−

The balance on the capital account is all the credits minus all the debits on the capital account.

Notice that the sale of domestic assets abroad is a **capital inflow** because foreigners buy these assets and capital flows into the domestic economy. Equivalently, we say that the domestic economy is *borrowing* internationally. Similarly, the purchase of foreign assets by domestic residents is a **capital outflow** and corresponds to international *lending* by the domestic economy.

The recording of all international transactions in the balance of payments follows the principle of *double-entry* bookkeeping: every transaction enters the balance of payments twice, once as a credit and once as a debit. For instance, suppose you buy a Sony TV from Japan and pay for it with a $1,000 cheque written against your chequing account with the Bank of Montreal. This transaction generates two offsetting bookkeeping entries in the Canadian balance of payments:

	Credit	Debit
Purchase of Sony TV *(Current Account, Good import)*		−$ 1,000
Sale of bank deposit by the Bank of Montreal *(Capital Account, Asset export)*	+$ 1,000	

Because every international transaction gives rise to two offsetting entries in the balance of payments, the current and capital account balances add up to zero automatically. In practice, however, debits and credits are often collected from different sources and thus discrepancies arise. Such discrepancies are collected and recorded under the name *statistical discrepancy* in the balance of payments.

Further, the purchase and sale of *official foreign exchange reserves* by the central bank enter the capital account separately, and are referred to as the **official reserve transactions**. Foreign exchange reserves consist of gold and reserves of major international currencies, such as the US dollar, the European euro, the Japanese yen, or the British pound, that are held by the central bank. Official transactions involving foreign exchange reserves are often used by central banks to influence the behaviour of the exchange rate. Such activities of the central bank are referred to as **foreign exchange intervention**.

For example, the Bank of Canada can support the Canadian dollar against the euro by selling euros in exchange for dollars on the **foreign exchange market**. This transaction decreases the supply of dollars and increases the supply of euros in the foreign exchange market, thereby helping to maintain the dollar/euro exchange rate against market pressures for depreciation of the dollar. Notice that the sale of euros by the Bank of Canada enters the capital account as a credit, as it represents the export of an asset. Moreover, because this credit in the capital account involves the foreign exchange reserves of the central bank, it is recorded as an "official reserve transaction." On the other hand, the receipt of dollars in exchange for euros by the Bank of Canada is recorded in the capital account as a debit, because it involves the import of an asset. The dollar receipts are not part of the central bank's foreign exchange reserves, and are recorded as a debit in the "short-term capital" component of the capital account.

The balance of payments (BP) is the balance on the current account (CA) plus the balance on the capital account other than official reserve transactions (KA):

$$BP = CA + KA \qquad (15.1)$$

As we shall see in the next section, for the demand for the Canadian dollar to be equal to the supply of the dollar on the international market for currencies, the sum of BP and the balance on the official reserve transactions must always be equal to zero. Hence, if BP is positive then it must be offset by a debit of the same absolute value on the balance on the official reserve transactions. This debit comes about through the central bank's operations on the foreign exchange market: purchase by the Bank of Canada of foreign currencies, such as the euro, in exchange for Canadian dollars.

Hence BP is equal to the change in the foreign exchange reserves of the central bank. If BP is positive, then the central bank must have purchased foreign exchange reserves. This purchase of foreign assets is an import of an asset; and it shows up as a negative entry under "official reserve transactions." On the other hand, if BP is negative then the central bank must have sold foreign exchange reserves. This is an export of an asset; and it shows up as a positive entry under "official reserve transactions."

Table 15.1 shows the Canadian balance of payments for the year 2005. The table shows a 2005 current account balance of $30,243 million ($568,945 million − $538,702 million = $30,243 million), a surplus. This means that Canadian residents used less output than they produced, and they exported the difference. Since these current account transactions were paid for somehow, we know that this positive entry of $30,243 million must be offset by a negative entry of the same amount in the capital account, which is referred to as "Capital and Financial Accounts" by the Government of Canada.

The "Capital and Financial Accounts" of Canada consists of the "Capital Account" and the "Financial Account." The "Capital Account" of Canada's balance of payments records transactions involving the funds belonging to migrants, inheritances, and patents. According to Table 15.1, the balance on Canada's "Capital Account" in the year 2005 was $5,866 million.

The "Financial Accounts" of Canada's balance of payments accounts records transactions involving *investments*, which could be in real or financial assets. Real investments in firms are recorded as "Direct Investments," while financial investments are recorded under "Portfolio Investments." All other investments are recorded under "Other Investment." From Table 15.1, the balance on the "Financial Account" was −$28,027 million in 2005.

The balance on the "Capital and Financial Accounts" is the sum of the balance on the "Capital Account" and the balance on the "Financial Account." For the year 2005, the balance on the "Capital and Financial Accounts" was −$22,161 million (i.e., $5,866 million − $28,027 million). Accordingly, net foreign assets owned by Canadians increased by $22,161 million in 2005. Recall that these are net capital outflows and enter the "Capital and Financial Account" with a negative sign, which signifies that Canada was a net importer of assets in the year 2005. Since the amount −$22,161 falls short of the current account surplus, the statistical discrepancy is −$8,082 million.

TABLE 15.1
Canadian Balance of Payments for 2005 (millions of dollars)

	Credits	Debits
Current Account Receipts	**568,945**	
Goods and Services Receipts	516,396	
Investment Income Receipts	44,661	
Transfer Receipts	7,889	
Current Account Payments		**−538,702**
Goods and Services Payments		−463,105
Investment Income Payments		−67,485
Transfer Payments		−8,113
Total Current Account Balance	**30,243**	
Capital Account Balance	**5,866**	
Financial Account Balance		**−28,027**
Purchases of Foreign Assets by Canadians:		**−112,114**
Canadian Direct Investment Abroad		−37,818
Canadian Portfolio Investment Abroad		−42,165
Other Canadian Investment Abroad		−32,131
Sales of Canadian Assets to Foreigners:	**84,087**	
Foreign Direct Investment in Canada	39,931	
Foreign Portfolio Investment in Canada	15,497	
Other Foreign Investment in Canada	28,658	
Total Capital and Financial Accounts Balance		**−22,161**
Statistical discrepancy		**−8,082**

Source: Adapted from Statistics Canada CANSIM II database, Tables 376-0001 and 376-0002.

http://cansim2.statcan.ca/

Having defined the various components of the balance of payments accounts for Canada, we will from now on revert to the traditional convention of reserving the term "capital account" as the account that records all transactions that involve assets, i.e., the "Capital and Financial Accounts" of Canada's balance of payments.

RECAP   THE BALANCE OF PAYMENTS ACCOUNT

The Balance of Payments Account records the international transactions a country makes with the rest of the world. The balance of payments is divided into two parts: (i) the current account and (ii) the capital account. Transactions involving goods, services, investment income, and unilateral transfers are recorded in the current account. Transactions involving assets are recorded in the capital account.

15.2 THE EXCHANGE RATE AND EXCHANGE RATE REGIMES

We have defined the nominal exchange rate, e, as the price of the foreign currency in terms of the domestic currency. For example, currently we observe the domestic price of one euro to be around \$1.50; that is, $e = 1.5$. This is the convention we have used in this textbook, and we will continue to use it, although in the media sometimes it is the value of dollars in terms of euros ($1/e = 1/1.5 = 0.67$) that is reported. What determines this exchange rate? The determination of the exchange rate depends on the exchange rate regime under which a country operates. In reality there is a whole spectrum of exchange rate regimes, which includes a system of purely floating or flexible exchange rates, a system of fixed exchange rates, and combinations of these two extremes.

Under a flexible or floating exchange system, the exchange rate is allowed to fluctuate in the foreign exchange market in order to set supply equal to demand for each currency. Under a fixed exchange rate system, the exchange rate is set by government agreements and the central banks of the countries concerned are obliged to undertake the necessary official transactions to maintain the fixed value of the exchange rate. Next we study each exchange rate regime in more detail.

FLEXIBLE OR FLOATING EXCHANGE RATES

Under a system of *pure* flexible exchange rates, the exchange rate is determined strictly by the forces of supply and demand for foreign exchange in the international money markets without any official foreign exchange intervention. The *supply* of foreign currency is generated from the foreigners' need to convert their foreign currency into dollars in order to pay for our exports of Canadian goods, services, and assets. The higher is the exchange rate, the more competitive are Canadian exports, and the greater is the quantity of foreign currency supplied by foreign importers. The *demand* for foreign currency is generated from the Canadians' need to convert their dollars into foreign currency in order to pay for their imports of foreign goods, services, and assets. The lower is the exchange rate, the cheaper are foreign exports, and the greater is the quantity of foreign currency demanded by Canadian importers.

Figure 15.1 shows the upward sloping supply curve of euros, denoted by $S_\euro$, and the downward sloping demand curve for euros, denoted by $D_\euro$. Whereas changes in the exchange rate induce movements along these supply and demand curves, changes in any variable other than the exchange rate that affect imports and/or exports of goods, services, and assets will result in shifts of these curves. For example, the imports and exports of assets depend on the difference between the domestic and foreign interest rates; and changes in the interest rate differential will result in shifts of $S_\euro$ and $D_\euro$.

The intersection of the supply and demand curves for euros in Figure 15.1 determines the equilibrium exchange rate in the foreign exchange markets. In this case, the equilibrium dollar/euro rate, e^*, is at \$1.50, which corresponds to the equilibrium quantity of euros traded in exchange for dollars on the horizontal axis of the graph.

At the equilibrium point the market for euros clears. There is neither a surplus nor a shortage of euros, and the balance of payments is in equilibrium. With no official reserve transactions we have $BP = 0$, and the identity equation (15.1) implies $CA + KA = 0$, so that a current account surplus is exactly offset by a capital account deficit, and vice versa.

FIGURE 15.1

The Equilibrium Dollar/ Euro Exchange Rate

The equilibrium dollar/ euro exchange rate, e^*, is given by the intersection of the supply curve and the demand curve for euros at point A. In this case, the equilibrium exchange rate is $e^* = \$1.50$. If the exchange rate were initially at $e_1 = \$1.60$, there would be a surplus of euros and a shortage of dollars in the foreign exchange market. The shortage of dollars and the abundance of euros cause the dollar/euro exchange rate to fall toward its equilibrium level.

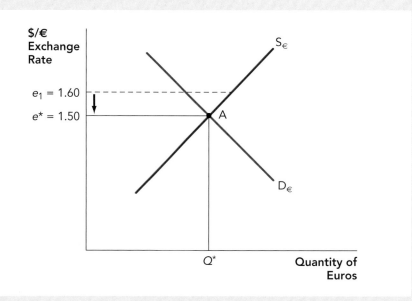

The equilibrium is attained by *adjustment* in the exchange rate. For example, if the exchange rate was initially at $e_1 = \$1.60$ in Figure 15.1, there would be a surplus of euros and a shortage of dollars in the foreign exchange market. Equivalently, Canadian exports to Europe would exceed Canadian imports from Europe and the Canadian balance of payments would be in a surplus position. But the surplus is short-lived. The shortage of dollars and the abundance of euros in the foreign exchange market appreciates the dollar vis-à-vis the euro and the dollar/euro rate falls toward the equilibrium exchange rate. The appreciation of the dollar makes Canadian exports less competitive abroad; Europeans buy less of them and this eliminates the balance of payments surplus. Analogous arguments apply if the exchange rate is initially below the equilibrium value.

Actual exchange rates fluctuate in foreign exchange markets because demand and supply conditions change over time. An economic disturbance that shifts either the demand for or the supply of foreign exchange displaces the equilibrium point and changes the equilibrium value of the exchange rate. For instance, an economic recession in Europe reduces the demand for Canadian exports and shifts the supply of euros curve to the left, thereby causing a depreciation of the dollar.

FIXED EXCHANGE RATES

Under a fixed exchange rate system the value of the exchange rate is set by the central banks. A country's central bank may choose to fix the value of its currency in terms of other currencies, as is currently done by several developing countries. Alternatively, the exchange rates may be fixed through an explicit multilateral agreement among the governments of two or more countries. In the next chapter we discuss the gold standard and the Bretton Woods system, which are examples of multilateral agreements among countries operating under a fixed exchange rate system.

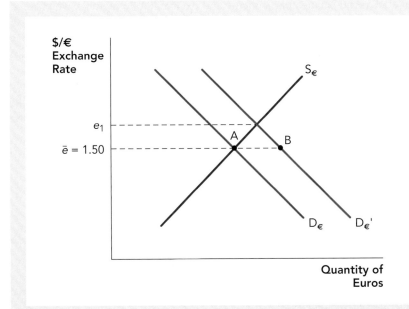

FIGURE 15.2

Fixed Exchange Rates and the Central Bank Intervention

Suppose the Bank of Canada decides unilaterally to fix the dollar/euro rate at the initial equilibrium value $\bar{e} = \$1.50$. Suppose, next, that the demand curve for euros shifts to the right, to $D_{\in}'$. At the fixed dollar/euro rate there is now an excess demand for euros equal to distance AB. To maintain the fixed exchange rate, the Bank of Canada must intervene in the foreign exchange market and sell reserves of euros in the amount AB in exchange for Canadian dollars.

An important part of any fixed exchange system is the *obligation* of all the governments involved to undertake the necessary official reserve transactions to maintain the fixed exchange rates in the presence of economic shocks. For instance, assume for simplicity that the Bank of Canada decides unilaterally to fix the dollar/euro rate at the initial equilibrium value $\bar{e} = \$1.50$. Suppose next that, due to an increased demand for European cars by Canadians, the demand curve for euros shifts to the right, to $D_{\in}'$, as shown in Figure 15.2. The free market equilibrium exchange rate is higher, at e_1, corresponding to a depreciated dollar. Further, at the fixed dollar/euro rate there is now an excess demand for euros equal to distance AB. Clearly, the fixed exchange rate can be maintained only by foreign exchange intervention. To do so the Bank of Canada must intervene in the foreign exchange market and sell reserves of euros in the amount AB in exchange for Canadian dollars.

This situation cannot go on indefinitely. There is a limit to foreign exchange intervention by the Bank of Canada dictated by the stock of euros available in its reserves. If this situation persists, the Bank of Canada will eventually run out of its euro reserves and will be no longer able to sustain the fixed exchange rate. Thus, the fixed exchange rate will then collapse in favour of flexible exchange rates. The next chapter discusses in greater detail the sustainability problems associated with fixed exchange rates in the long run.

Notice the following important property of fixed exchange rates. The commitment to hold the exchange rate fixed forces the Bank of Canada to intervene in the foreign exchange market and exchange euros for dollars, thereby causing changes in the Canadian money supply in this process. Thus, under fixed exchange rates the Bank of Canada loses control of the money supply and cannot pursue its own independent monetary policy.

http://www.bank-banque-canada.ca/

Having studied the balance of payments and exchange rate regimes, we proceed next to analyze the nature of the general economic equilibrium in the context of the well-known **Mundell-Fleming model** of a small open economy. Then we move on to study fiscal and monetary policy issues using this model. Two important assumptions of the Mundell-Fleming model are high capital mobility and perfect asset substitutability across assets of different countries. These assumptions imply certain international interest "parity" conditions that are important building blocks of the model. For this reason we analyze these conditions first in the following section.

RECAP   THE EXCHANGE RATE AND EXCHANGE RATE REGIMES

Under a flexible or floating exchange system, the exchange rate is allowed to fluctuate in the foreign exchange market in order to set supply equal to demand for each currency. Under a fixed exchange rate system, the exchange rate is set by government agreements and the central banks of the countries concerned are obliged to undertake the necessary official transactions to maintain the fixed value of the exchange rate.

15.3 INTERNATIONAL INTEREST PARITY CONDITIONS

One of the central equations in our analysis of the international currency markets has been the following condition, relating the differential between the domestic and foreign interest rates $(r - r^f)$ to the real exchange rate ε:

$$\varepsilon = \varepsilon_0 - \varepsilon_r \times (r - r^f) \tag{15.2}$$

where ε_0 is the investors' expectation about the equilibrium value of the real exchange rate *if domestic and foreign interest rates were equal*, and ε_r measures the effects of a given interest rate differential on the exchange rate. As we saw in Chapter 5, ε_r relates to the investors' balancing of greed and fear in their portfolios of assets.

Equation (15.2) was very useful in simplifying the analysis of the previous chapters. Moreover, it shows how useful it is in practice when financial market conditions are such that real interest rates do not necessarily have to be equal across different countries. In that case, for example, the Bank of Canada is able to conduct its own monetary policy by setting the domestic interest rate at a different level from that of other industrialized countries.

Nevertheless, using equation (15.2) does have its own limitations. An important limitation is that ε_0 is taken as fixed. Notice that ε_0 is a relative price; and relative prices do change over time when economic conditions change. We would like to be able to say what factors affect ε_0. For instance, as shown in Box 15.1 the real value of the Canadian dollar relative to the US dollar is substantially higher today than it was in 2001, while the interest rate differential between Canada and the U.S. today is not that much different from what it was in 2001. In terms of equation (15.2), therefore, one would expect that factors other than the interest rate differential $(r - r^f)$ have led to the increase in the real value of the Canadian dollar. Increasing primary commodity prices, and improving business sector productivity are all important factors that may have led to a fall in ε_0, and hence in the observed increase in the real value of the Canadian dollar.

Another limitation of equation (15.2) is that it does not describe how the real exchange rate adjusts towards its expected long-run level. In order to have a clearer view of the determination of the equilibrium exchange rate, it is important to have a complete model that shows the way in which the exchange rate adjusts towards its long-run level. To this end, we modify equation (15.2), and write it in the form of one of the standard international interest parity conditions.

One assumption that underlies standard **interest rate parity** conditions is that international assets have similar risk characteristics and are thus *perfect substitutes* for each other. This implies that the rate of return on domestic and foreign assets will differ only in the short run, or during the adjustment to the long-run equilibrium. However, with perfect asset substitutability, if the domestic and foreign economies are in long-run equilibrium, then interest rates in the two countries should be equal. Hence, in the long run we will have $r = r^f$, and from equation (15.2), $\varepsilon = \varepsilon_0$. Thus, with perfect asset substitutability the term ε_0 in equation (15.2) can be regarded as the investors' expectation of the *long-run* equilibrium value of the real exchange, which we denote by ε^e.

THE CANADA/U.S. REAL EXCHANGE RATE AND REAL INTEREST RATES

BOX 15.1

DATA

FIGURE 15.3
The Canada/U.S. Real Exchange Rate and Real Interest Rates
(a) The CAD/USD Real Exchange Rate, 1973Q1 to 2005Q4

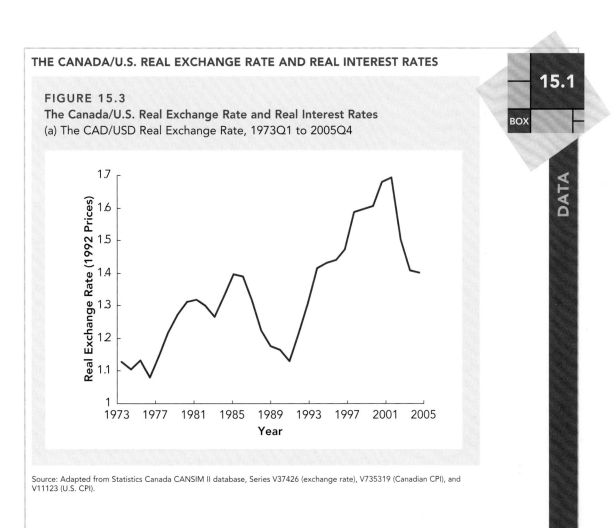

Source: Adapted from Statistics Canada CANSIM II database, Series V37426 (exchange rate), V735319 (Canadian CPI), and V11123 (U.S. CPI).

(b) Real Interest Rates in Canada and the U.S., 1973Q1 to 2005Q4

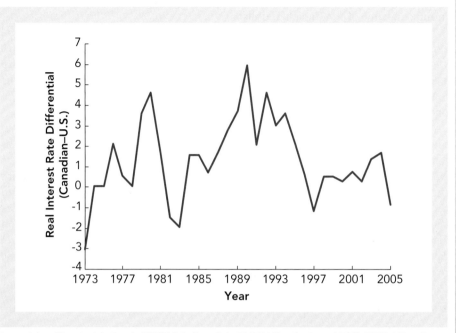

Source: Adapted from Statistics Canada CANSIM II database, Series V122484 (Canadian 3-month T-bill), V735319 (Canadian CPI), and V11123 (U.S. CPI); and St. Louis Federal Reserve, FRED, Series TB3Ms (U.S. 3-month T-bill).

Figure 15.3 shows the quarterly behaviour of the Canada/U.S. real exchange rate (panel (a)) and the quarterly Canadian real interest rate minus the quarterly U.S. real interest rate (panel (b)), for the period 1973Q1 to 2005Q4. If the interest rate differential were the most important factor in determining the real exchange rate, one would expect an increase in the real interest rate differential to lead to a real appreciation of the Canadian dollar, and a fall in the real interest rate differential to lead to a real depreciation.

A close inspection of the two graphs reveals that this is not always the case. For example, between 1973 and 1980 the interest rate differential widened, while there was a real depreciation, instead of appreciation. There was a very sharp decline in the interest rate differential between 1980 and 1982, while there was little change in the real exchange rate. Between 1982 and 1990 there was a general widening in the interest rate differential, while there was a real depreciation between 1982 and 1986, and a real appreciation between 1986 and 1990. Between 1992 and 2001 we saw continuous real depreciation and sharp real appreciations after that, while interest rate differential declined between 1992 and 1995, but it has been relatively stable ever since.

Clearly, there does not seem to be a clear long-run relation between the two variables as predicted by the theory. At best, we can say that there is a short-run relation, in the sense that short-run fluctuations in the interest rate differential are associated with short-run fluctuation of the real exchange rate. The conclusion that we must draw is that variables other than the interest rate differential are important in affecting the long-run behaviour of the real exchange rate. For Canada, such variables include commodity prices, fiscal policy, the relative productivity of the manufacturing sector, and other real shocks hitting the economy.

The next step in expressing equation (15.2) as a standard interest rate parity condition is to replace ε_r by ε. We can then rewrite equation (15.2) as

$$r = r^f + \frac{\varepsilon^e - \varepsilon}{\varepsilon} \tag{15.3}$$

Equation (15.3) is called the uncovered real interest parity condition. It states that, with perfect asset substitutability, the domestic real interest rate, r, should be equal to the foreign real interest rate, r^f, plus the expected rate of change in the real value of the domestic currency $(\varepsilon^e - \varepsilon)/\varepsilon$. If the term $(\varepsilon^e - \varepsilon)/\varepsilon$ is positive, investors expect a *real depreciation* of the domestic currency, and if it is negative they expect a *real appreciation*. Notice that the right-hand side of equation (15.3) is the real return on domestic assets, whereas the left-hand side is the real return on foreign assets expressed in terms of the domestic goods.[2] Thus, equation (15.3) can be interpreted as an equilibrium condition in financial markets. That is, financial markets are in equilibrium when the real rates of return on assets from different countries are equal when expressed in terms of a common basket of goods. For example, if the real return on European bonds is 4 percent and investors expect an annual real depreciation of 2 percent of the Canadian dollar vis-à-vis the euro, then they will invest in Canadian bonds if their real rate of return is 6 percent (i.e., .06 = .04 + .02).

The domestic and foreign interest rates will be equal $(r = r^f)$ only in the long run, where $\varepsilon = \varepsilon^e$, that is, when the real exchange rate is expected to remain constant over time. In this case we say that *relative purchasing power* holds, which implies that the expected change in the *nominal* exchange rate is equal to the expected inflation differential between the domestic and foreign economies; see equation (15.4) below. More generally, however, real interest rates in different countries need not be equal, even in the long run, if the economies are subject to continuous shocks that change the long-run equilibrium, and hence ε, continuously.

Equation (15.3) has a nominal counterpart, called uncovered interest parity. To derive this, we take proportional rates of change on both sides of the real exchange rate equation, $\varepsilon = e \times P^*/P$, to obtain *ex ante*, or in expectation,

$$\frac{\varepsilon^e - \varepsilon}{\varepsilon} = \frac{e^e - e}{e} + \frac{P^{*e} - P^*}{P^*} - \frac{P^e - P}{P} \tag{15.4}$$

Substituting for $(\varepsilon^e - \varepsilon)/\varepsilon$ from equation (15.4) into equation (15.3), we can rewrite the equation as

$$r + \frac{P^e - P}{P} = r^f + \frac{P^{*e} - P^*}{P^*} + \frac{e^e - e}{e} \tag{15.5}$$

Now notice $(P^e - P)/P$ is the domestic expected inflation rate, and $r + (P^e - P)/P$ is the domestic nominal interest rate, denoted by i. Also, $(P^{*e} - P^*)/P^*$ is the foreign

---

[2] Suppose an investor wishes to acquire one unit of foreign goods and invest it for a period of one year. The initial domestic cost of acquiring the foreign good is simply ε. If the annual foreign interest rate is r^f, one year later the investment will have grown to $1 + r^f$, which will be equivalent to $(1 + r^f)\varepsilon^e$ in terms of domestic goods. Hence the exact annual real rate of return on the foreign goods expressed in terms of domestic goods is $\frac{(1+r^f)\varepsilon^e - \varepsilon}{\varepsilon}$. This exact formula can be rewritten, however, as $r^f + \frac{\varepsilon^e - \varepsilon}{\varepsilon} + r^f \times \left(\frac{\varepsilon^e - \varepsilon}{\varepsilon}\right)$. The third term in this expression is a small number that can be ignored, thus arriving at the right-hand side of equation (15.3).

expected inflation rate, and $r^f + (P^{*e} - P^*)/P^*$ is the foreign nominal interest, denoted by i^f. Hence, we can re-write equation (15. 4) as

$$i = i^f + \frac{e^e - e}{e} \tag{15.6}$$

Equation (15.6) is the uncovered interest parity condition. It states that, under perfect asset substitutability, the domestic nominal interest rate is equal to the foreign nominal interest rate plus the expected rate of change of the domestic currency. If the term $(e^e - e)/e$ is positive investors expect a *nominal depreciation* of the domestic currency; and if it is negative they expect a *nominal appreciation*. Equation (15.6) is also an equilibrium condition. It says that asset markets are in equilibrium when the *nominal* rates of return on assets from different countries are equal when expressed in terms of the same currency.[3] Further, the domestic and foreign nominal interest rates will be equal $(i = i^f)$ only in the long run when $e = e^e$.

RECAP   INTEREST PARITY CONDITIONS

The uncovered real interest parity condition states that, with perfect asset substitutability, the domestic real interest rate should be equal to the foreign real interest rate plus the expected rate of change in the real value of the domestic currency. The uncovered interest parity condition states that, under perfect asset substitutability, the domestic nominal interest rate is equal to the foreign nominal interest rate plus the expected rate of change of the domestic currency.

15.4 THE MUNDELL-FLEMING MODEL FOR A SMALL OPEN ECONOMY

The Mundell-Fleming model has been the dominant model for analyzing macroeconomic issues pertaining to small open economies in the last 40 years.[4] The model has three components: the IS curve, the LM curve, and the uncovered interest parity (UIP) condition. As usual, the IS curve describes equilibrium in the goods and services market, the LM curve describes equilibrium in the money market, and the UIP condition describes equilibrium in the foreign exchange market that corresponds to a balance of payments equilibrium. For completeness we write the IS and LM equations in general form together with the real UIP equation:[5]

(IS) $$Y = C(Y - T) + I(r) + G + NX(\varepsilon, Y, Y^f) \tag{15.7}$$

(LM) $$\frac{M}{P} = L(r + \pi^e, Y) \tag{15.8}$$

---

[3] Using the nominal counterpart of the exact formula in footnote 2, it can be easily shown that the (approximate) nominal rate of return of foreign assets expressed in terms of the domestic currency is $i^f + \frac{e^e - e}{e}$.

[4] The model is named after the two economists who developed it: the Canadian economist Robert Mundell of Columbia University who received the Nobel Prize in Economics in 1999 for his important contributions in international macroeconomics, including this model and his theories on optimum currency areas and monetary unions, and the late Marcus Fleming who was a researcher at the International Monetary Fund in the 1960s.

[5] The detailed analysis in Chapters 8 and 9 should help you understand the more general specifications of the IS and LM equations in this section. Notice, however, that the IS curve here does not depend on the parameter ε^r because we substituted it with ε in Section 15.3 to obtain the UIP equation (15.3).

(UIP) $$r = r^f + \frac{\varepsilon^e - \varepsilon}{\varepsilon}$$ (15.9)

The IS equation shows that consumption is a function of disposable income, $Y - T$, where T is aggregate taxes, investment is a function of the real interest rate, r, and net exports is a function of the real exchange rate, ε, domestic income, Y, and foreign income Y^f. An increase in r reduces investment demand and reduces equilibrium income, Y. That is, as usual the IS curve is downward sloping in the familiar (Y, r)-space. An increase in ε, or real depreciation of the domestic currency, makes home exports cheaper relative to imports and shifts the IS curve to the right. Similarly, a decrease in ε shifts IS to the left. An increase in Y^f shifts IS to the right as foreigners buy more of the country's exports.

In the LM equation the demand for real money balances is a function of the nominal interest rate, $r + \pi^e$ and real income Y. An increase in $r + \pi^e$ increases the opportunity cost of holding money and reduces the demand for real money balances. Thus, given M and P, Y must increase to maintain equilibrium in the money market. That is, the LM curve is upward sloping in (Y, r)-space. Further an increase in M shifts LM to the right and an increase in P shifts it to the left.

The UIP condition embodies the assumptions of high capital mobility and perfect asset substitutability, both of which are realistic descriptions of modern capital markets. It is a simple relation but it has powerful implications in the present analysis. UIP is an equilibrium condition both for the foreign exchange market and for the balance of payments. To see the latter more clearly, let us consider the BP equation, and see what happens when it does not hold.

Recall, that $BP = CA + KA$. The current account, CA, depends on the same variables as net exports above (that is, ε, Y, and Y^f), while the capital account depends on the real *interest rate differential* expressed in terms of domestic goods and services. Hence, we can write the BP equation as

$$BP = CA(\varepsilon, Y, Y^f) + KA(r - r^f - (\varepsilon^e - \varepsilon)/\varepsilon)$$ (15.10)

If UIP does not hold and the interest rate differential is positive, there will be a massive capital inflow in the home economy as investors favour domestic over foreign assets and the balance of payments will be in huge surplus. True, the surplus will induce domestic currency appreciation that will tend to reduce the surplus via the current account, but given high capital mobility the overall BP balance will be dominated by the developments in the capital account. Similarly, if the interest differential is negative, there will be a massive capital outflow and the balance of payment will be in huge deficit. The only case where the balance of payments will be in equilibrium is when UIP holds and there are no induced capital flows in or out of the economy. Then the particular equilibrium value of the BP can be chosen by government authorities to achieve a target value. For convenience here we choose this target to be zero (i.e., $BP = 0$). As discussed earlier, this target value is the natural one under flexible exchange rates.

The economy is in equilibrium when it is simultaneously in internal and external balance. **Internal balance** exists when goods and money markets are in equilibrium at the intersection of the IS and LM curves. **External balance** exists when the balance of payments is at its desired target value. In addition, in the long run the economy is in *full equilibrium* when it is in internal and external balance at the full-employment level of output Y^*.

The Mundell-Fleming model makes the following three simplifying assumptions:

- The domestic economy is a *small open economy*. It can borrow and lend unlimited amounts from the international financial markets at the going world interest rate but it cannot affect either r^f or P^*. Both of these variables are taken as given.

- The domestic price level P is fixed, so that $\pi^e = 0$. This assumption makes the model appropriate only for short-run analysis. We relax this assumption later for the long-run analysis. Notice that with P and P^* fixed, nominal and real interest rates are equal and changes in the real exchange rate, $\varepsilon = e \times P^*/P$, are proportional to changes in the nominal exchange rate, e. Thus we do not need to distinguish between the real and the nominal UIP condition in the short run. Under these assumptions equations (15.2) and (15.6) are the same.

- The expected change in the exchange rate is zero (i.e., $\varepsilon^e = \varepsilon$), so that the UIP condition reduces to $r = r^f$ or $i = i^f$. With r^f fixed in view of the first assumption above, this means that the UIP condition is represented by a *horizontal* line at the foreign interest rate, as shown in Figure 15.4. Points above the line correspond to balance of payments surpluses and points below it correspond to balance of payments deficits. This assumption is appropriate in the long run, but it deprives the model of some interesting dynamics in the transition of the economy from the short run to the long run. We relax this assumption below when we analyze some issues relating to the dynamics of the model such as the adjustment process to the long-run equilibrium, and nominal exchange rate overshooting following a permanent increase in the money supply.

Figure 15.4 shows the small open economy's equilibrium based on these three simplifying assumptions. When the economy is in equilibrium the IS, LM, and UIP curves intersect at the same point A. Economic forces at work make sure that this is the case. To see this, assume that the IS and LM curves intersect at point B above the horizontal UIP line, as shown in Figure 15.5. Then the domestic interest rate is higher than the world interest rate and the balance of payments will be in surplus.

FIGURE 15.4

The Equilibrium of the Small Open Economy

The intersection of the IS and LM curves gives us the internal balance, while the UIP curve gives us the external balance. The economy is in equilibrium when it is in both internal and external balance, that is, when the IS, LM, and UIP curves intersect at the same point. The equilibrium is given by point A.

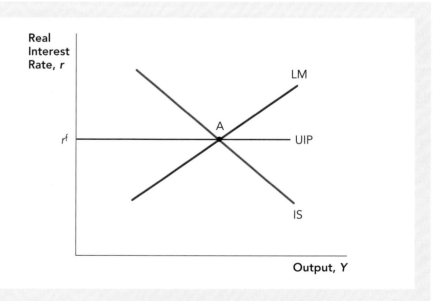

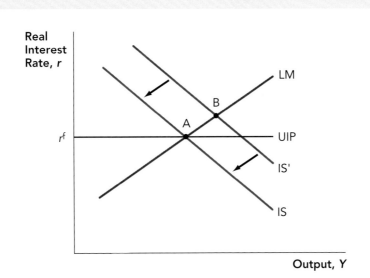

FIGURE 15.5
The Equilibrium of the Small Open Economy
Suppose the IS and LM curves intersect at point B above the UIP line. Then the domestic interest rate is higher than the world interest rate, r^f, and the balance of payments will be in surplus. The surplus will cause an appreciation of the domestic currency and a shift of the IS curve to the left until the three curves intersect at the same point A.

With flexible exchange rates, the surplus will cause an appreciation of the domestic currency and a shift of the IS curve to the left until the three curves intersect at the same point A. Similar but opposite arguments apply if the IS and LM curves intersect below the UIP line.

Having presented the Mundell-Fleming model, we next discuss its predictions under **flexible** and **fixed exchange rates** following fiscal, monetary, and other economic shocks. For simplicity, we refer to Canada as the home country, and to the European Union as the foreign country.

> **RECAP** **THE MUNDELL-FLEMING MODEL FOR A SMALL OPEN ECONOMY**
>
> The Mundell-Fleming model has three components: the IS curve, the LM curve, and the uncovered interest parity condition. *Internal balance* exists when goods and money markets are in equilibrium at the intersection of the IS and LM curves. *External balance* exists when the balance of payments is at its desired target value and the uncovered interest parity condition holds. The economy is in equilibrium when it is simultaneously in internal and external balance. In addition, in the long run the economy is in *full equilibrium* when it is in internal and external balance at the full-employment level of output.

15.5 THE MUNDELL-FLEMING MODEL WITH FLEXIBLE EXCHANGE RATES

With flexible exchange rates, the exchange rate adjusts to attain external balance. In this section we consider the effects of three types of economic shifts: a fiscal contraction, a fall in commodity prices, and a monetary contraction. We also analyze the phenomenon of nominal exchange rate overshooting following a permanent monetary contraction. We distinguish between the short-run and long-run effects. For the short-run analysis we assume that the domestic price level P is fixed, and also the expected change in the exchange rate is zero (i.e., $\varepsilon^e = \varepsilon$). For the long-run analysis, we allow for both changes in the price level P and deviations of the actual from the expected exchange rate during the adjustment process to the full-employment equilibrium.

THE EFFECTS OF A FISCAL CONTRACTION: FLEXIBLE EXCHANGE RATES

THE SHORT-RUN EFFECTS OF A FISCAL CONTRACTION

Consider the effects of a fiscal contraction in the Mundell-Fleming model with flexible exchange rates. Suppose that starting from the long-run equilibrium point A in Figure 15.6, there is a decrease in government expenditures, G. This policy change shifts the IS curve to the left, to IS_1. At the new internal equilibrium point B, given by the intersection of the IS_1 and LM curves, the domestic interest rate is below the foreign rate. Hence, Canadian assets become less attractive than foreign assets. Now investors try to sell their Canadian assets, convert their dollars into euros, and use these euros to purchase European assets. This action reduces the demand for the Canadian dollars and the supply of euros in the foreign exchange market. As a

FIGURE 15.6

The Effects of a Decrease in Government Expenditures

Starting from the long-run equilibrium point A, a decrease in government expenditures shifts the IS curve to the left, to IS_1. At the new internal balance point B, the domestic interest rate is below the foreign interest rate. Hence, investors try to sell their Canadian assets, convert their dollars into euros, and use these euros to purchase European assets. As a result, the Canadian dollar depreciates vis-à-vis the euro, increasing net exports, and shifting the IS curve to the right, back to its original position.

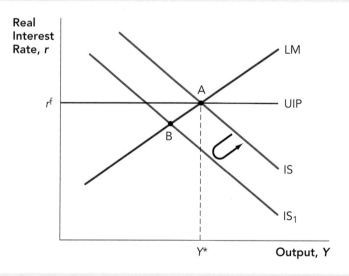

result, the Canadian dollar will depreciate vis-à-vis the euro and the dollar/euro real exchange rate will increase (ε will increase). With ε increasing, Canadian goods become more competitive relative to foreign goods. Thus, Canada's net exports increase and the IS curve shifts to the right, back to its original position where it intersects the LM curve along the UIP curve at Y^*.

Hence, with high capital mobility and perfect asset substitutability fiscal policy cannot affect output under a flexible exchange rate system. Fiscal policy ineffectiveness results from a "crowding in" effect through net exports: the decrease in G reduces Y, but the increase in ε increases net exports and hence output Y. On balance, the two effects cancel out and there is no net change in Y.

THE LONG-RUN EFFECTS OF A FISCAL CONTRACTION

The long-run effect of a fiscal contraction on output is the same as the short-run effect. Since output remains unchanged in the short run, there will be no adjustment to the long-run equilibrium. Hence, the new short-run equilibrium after a fiscal contraction is also the long-run equilibrium.

What is the effect of the fiscal contraction on the nominal and real exchange rates? In the short run, the real exchange rate, ε, increased as a result of the fiscal contraction. Since P and P^f are fixed in the short run, this implies that the nominal exchange rate, e, also increased. Further, since there was no long-run effect on P, the nominal and real exchange rates have increased permanently. Consequently, the fiscal contraction leads to an overall depreciation of the domestic currency. This prediction is useful in explaining the behaviour of the Canadian dollar in the 1990s. The restrictive fiscal policies that have been followed by the Canadian government since the mid-1990s, turning government budget deficits to surpluses, contributed to the real and nominal depreciation of the dollar in the 1990s.

THE EFFECTS OF A DECLINE IN COMMODITY PRICES

Another reason for the fall in the real and nominal value of the Canadian dollar in the 1990s, which has been widely cited by the Bank of Canada, was the decline in the prices of primary commodities, such as oil, minerals, and agricultural products during that decade.[6] The prices of primary commodities are set in international markets and depend on the international supply and demand for these goods. Because Canada has a relatively large primary goods sector, the fall in the world prices for commodities reduces the value of the country's stocks of these commodities, which reduces the country's wealth.

Recall from our discussion of the consumption function in Chapter 5, consumption depends not only on current disposable income, but also on wealth. Hence, if the fall in commodity prices reduces wealth, it also reduces consumption and other expenditures such as expenditures on public infrastructure, all of which shift the IS curve to the left. As with a fiscal contraction, this results in a real depreciation of the Canadian dollar that shifts the IS curve to the right, back to its original position.

In the 2000s we have observed a substantial real appreciation of the Canadian dollar. The increase in primary commodity prices is the main cause of this real appreciation.

---

[6] Yet another reason for the real and nominal depreciation of the Canadian dollar in the 1990s was the widening of the productivity gap between Canada and the U.S. This issue was discussed in Chapters 1 and 4.

FIGURE 15.7

The Short-Run Effects of a Monetary Contraction

Starting from the long-run equilibrium point A, a decrease in the money supply shifts the LM curve to the left, to LM_1. The resulting increase in the domestic interest rate makes Canadian assets more attractive relative to foreign assets, increasing the demand for the dollar in the foreign exchange market. Hence, the dollar appreciates relative to the euro, reducing Canada's net exports and shifting the IS curve to the left, until it intersects LM_1 along the UIP curve at point B, with output at Y_B.

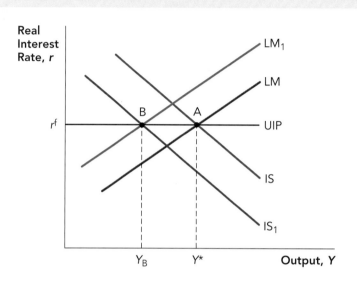

THE EFFECTS OF A MONETARY CONTRACTION: FLEXIBLE RATES

THE SHORT-RUN EFFECTS OF MONETARY CONTRACTION

Suppose that the economy is initially in long-run equilibrium at point A in Figure 15.7 and then there is a decrease in the money supply. Given that P is fixed in the short run, this policy shifts the LM curve to the left, to LM_1. The resulting increase in domestic interest rates makes Canadian assets more attractive relative to foreign assets. Again, investors try to sell their foreign assets, convert their euros into dollars, and use the dollars to buy Canadian assets. This increases the demand for the dollar in the foreign exchange market, and the dollar appreciates relative to the euro (i.e., ε falls). The fall in ε makes Canadian goods less attractive relative to European goods, reducing Canada's net exports and shifting the IS curve to the left, until it intersects LM_1 along the UIP curve. Figure 15.7 shows the economy's short-run equilibrium at point B corresponding to output level Y_B. Clearly, monetary policy is quite effective in reducing output Y in the short run. Output falls for two reasons, once from the initial monetary contraction and once from the subsequent appreciation of the dollar that makes Canadian exports more expensive abroad.

THE LONG-RUN EFFECTS OF MONETARY CONTRACTION

One of the simplifying assumptions that we made for the short-run analysis was that the expected long-run exchange rate ε^e is equal to the current exchange rate ε. This

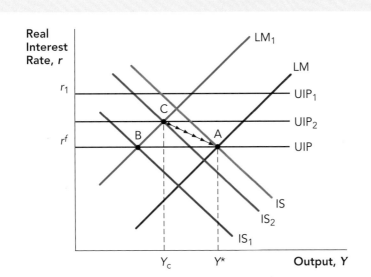

FIGURE 15.8

The Adjustment to Long-Run Equilibrium after a Monetary Contraction

After the monetary contraction, the equilibrium jumps from point B to point C to maintain interest parity. Thereafter, the gradual fall in the price level shifts the intersection of the IS, LM, and UIP curves along the trajectory CA, until the economy returns to the initial long-run equilibrium point A.

assumption may be reasonable for the short run but not for the long-run analysis. As time passes, people will realize that the exchange rate ε is not at its new long-run level and has to adjust towards it. Then, unlike the short run, people would expect the exchange rate to change over time ($\varepsilon^e \neq \varepsilon$) until the long-run equilibrium is reached. This means that along with the other curves the UIP curve will shift as well.

Consider now the economy's adjustment process to the long-run equilibrium following the monetary contraction. In Figure 15.8, the short-run equilibrium at point B is momentary. The reason for this is twofold. First, the monetary contraction raises the domestic interest rate above the foreign interest rate, r^f, and causes an *instantaneous* appreciation of the domestic currency (i.e., ε jumps down on impact). Second, money supply changes do not affect any real variable in the long run. Hence, in the long run the nominal exchange rate e and the price level P fall in proportion to the money supply so as to leave the real exchange rate, ε, unaffected. Since investors understand this fact, they do not change their expectations and thus the expected real exchange rate ε^e remains the same. With fixed ε^e and lower ε, the UIP curve shifts up to UIP_1 where the domestic interest rate is at level r_1. But now the interest rate that is consistent with internal balance at point B is below the interest rate that is consistent with external balance at UIP_1. Hence, the dollar depreciates in real terms, shifting the IS_1 curve to the right to IS_2 and the UIP_1 curve down to UIP_2 until both curves intersect the LM_1 curve at the equilibrium point C.

Notice that the dynamics of the model are such that the economy jumps immediately from point B to point C. However, the new equilibrium at point C is temporary. At point C output Y_C is below its full-employment level Y^* and the factors of production are not fully employed. Therefore, the price level P starts falling, reflecting lower wages and other production costs.

As prices in Canada fall, both the IS_2 and LM_1 curves shift to the right. The IS_2 curve shifts because the fall in P increases Canada's net exports, while the LM_1 curve

FIGURE 15.9

Adjustment of the Real Exchange Rate after a Monetary Contraction

The initial long-run equilibrium real exchange rate is at ε_L. Immediately after the monetary contraction, at time t_0, ε falls to ε_1 in order to maintain uncovered real interest parity. Then, as the price level falls over time, ε rises smoothly until it returns to its initial value before the monetary contraction.

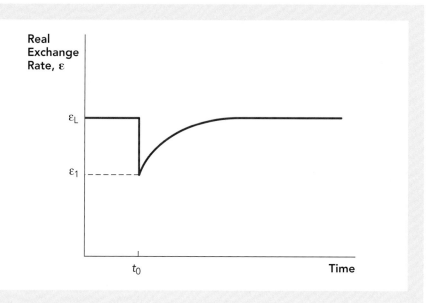

shifts because the fall in P increases real money balances. Further, as P declines the real exchange rate ε rises towards its long-run level ε^e, thereby causing the ratio $(\varepsilon^e - \varepsilon)/\varepsilon$ to become smaller over time, shifting the UIP_2 curve downward. The three curves stop shifting when they intersect at full-employment output. During the adjustment process to full equilibrium, the intersection of the IS, LM, and UIP curves will move along the trajectory CA as shown in Figure 15.8. The long-run equilibrium is at point A, with the IS, LM, and UIP curves intersecting at the full-employment level of output Y^*.

It is useful to examine the behaviour of the real exchange rate following the monetary contraction. First as noted above, at the long-run equilibrium the nominal exchange rate e and the price level P have increased in the same proportion as the money supply so as to keep the long-run real exchange rate fixed at e_L in Figure 15.9. This is an instance of the long-run *neutrality of money*, which states that money supply changes cannot affect real variables in the long run. Nonetheless, the monetary contraction does affect the real exchange rate during the adjustment to the long-run equilibrium. Just after the monetary contraction, at time t_0, ε jumps down to ε_1 in order to maintain uncovered real interest parity. Then, as P falls, ε rises smoothly over time until it returns to its initial value before the monetary contraction, as shown in Figure 15.9.

NOMINAL EXCHANGE RATE OVERSHOOTING

As shown in Box 15.2, a striking feature of the flexible exchange rate system is the large and frequent fluctuations in the nominal exchange rate e. At the same time, unlike the nominal exchange rate, goods' prices and the overall price level adjust slowly, and are less volatile over time. The late economist Rudiger Dornbusch[7]

---

[7] Rudiger Dornbusch died in July 2002. He taught at MIT for the majority of his career and made important contributions in the areas of exchange rate volatility and the monetary approach to the balance of payments.

THE CANADA/U.S. NOMINAL EXCHANGE RATE AND CANADA/U.S. PRICE LEVEL RATIO

15.2

BOX

DATA

FIGURE 15.10
Variability of the Canada/U.S. Nominal Exchange Rate and Canada/U.S. Price Level Ratio, 1973Q1 to 2005Q4

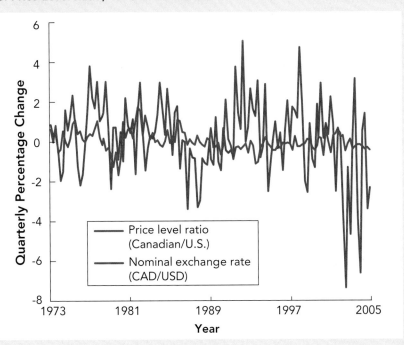

Source: Adapted from Statistics Canada CANSIM II database, Series V735319 (Canadian CPI), V11123 (U.S. CPI), and V37426 (nominal exchange rate).

Note: The quarter-to-quarter variability of the price ratio is much smaller than the variability of the nominal exchange rate, suggesting price stickiness in the short run.

The exchange rate overshooting model assumes that the nominal exchange rate is much more flexible than goods prices in the short run. Thus, when the demand and supply conditions change, the exchange rate adjusts quickly to restore equilibrium in the foreign exchange market, whereas prices adjust slowly to clear the goods markets. Figure 15.10 provides empirical support for these assumptions based on data from Canada and the U.S. It compares quarter-to-quarter percentage changes in the Canada/U.S. nominal exchange rate, CAD/USD, with quarter-to-quarter percentage changes in the Canada/U.S. price level ratio, CPI_{CDN}/CPI_{US}, for the period 1973Q1 to 2005Q4. As can be seen, the exchange rate is much more volatile than the price level ratio between the two countries. This evidence is consistent with the view of short-run "price stickiness" and exchange rate flexibility. Similar evidence exists for most industrialized countries since the early 1970s.

combined these features of the foreign exchange and goods markets and developed a convincing theory to explain the excessive volatility of the exchange rate following a permanent change in the money supply.

The starting point of Dornbusch's theory is the fact that the foreign exchange market is a lot more efficient than the goods market, in the sense that the exchange rate continuously adjusts to clear the foreign exchange market while goods prices are "sticky" and the goods markets clear slowly over time. As a result, when the money supply falls, for example, and goods prices are sticky, the nominal exchange overreacts initially and falls (i.e., the domestic currency appreciates) by more than it does in the long run; that is, the exchange rate *overshoots* its new long-run equilibrium level in order to maintain equilibrium in the foreign exchange market, and then it adjusts smoothly to attain goods market equilibrium.

Since foreign exchange markets are in equilibrium when international rates of returns are equal, we can use the nominal uncovered interest rate parity condition to illustrate the phenomenon of **exchange rate overshooting**:

$$\text{(UIP)} \qquad\qquad i = i^f + \frac{e^e - e}{e} \qquad\qquad (15.11)$$

Notice that the expected future exchange rate e^e is also the long-run level of the exchange rate. Suppose the initial long-run level of the exchange rate is at e_1^L. Let the new long-run level of the exchange rate, after the fall in the money supply at time t_0, be e_2^L, which is less than e_1^L. Notice after the fall in the money supply we will have $e^e = e_2^L$. Further, immediately after the fall in the money supply the domestic interest rate, i, increases. With the foreign interest rate i^f unchanged, UIP can hold only if the exchange rate overshoots its long-run level, that is, the exchange rate falls to a level e_1 such that $e_1 < e_2^L$, as shown in Figure 15.11.

FIGURE 15.11

Adjustment of the Nominal Exchange Rate after a Monetary Contraction

Immediately, after the fall in the money supply, at time t_0, the nominal exchange rate jumps down from its initial long-run equilibrium level, e_1^L, to e_1. Because goods prices are sticky in the short run, e_1 is below its new long-run level e_2^L. Then goods prices slowly adjust over time, which reduces the pressure on the nominal exchange rate. As a result, over time the nominal exchange rate rises until eventually it reaches its long-run level e_2^L.

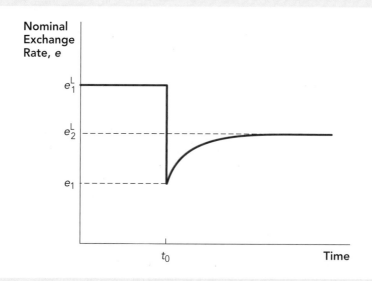

Then, over time, the nominal interest rate will be falling until it is eventually equal to i^f. For this to be consistent with the nominal interest rate parity condition, the nominal exchange rate e must be rising over time until in the long run it reaches e_2^L. Again, the argument is based on the assumption that, unlike the goods market, the foreign exchange market is very efficient; and the exchange rate adjusts in order to maintain the nominal interest rate parity condition at all times.

To sum up, unlike the real exchange rate, the long-run level of the nominal exchange rate e is affected by the monetary contraction. In the long run, e falls in proportion to the fall in the money supply. In the short run, following the monetary contraction the domestic currency appreciates by more than it does in the long run, thus producing the phenomenon of nominal exchange rate overshooting.

RECAP **THE MUNDELL-FLEMING MODEL WITH FLEXIBLE EXCHANGE RATES**

With high capital mobility and perfect asset substitutability fiscal policy cannot affect output under a flexible exchange rate system. A fall in government expenditures leads to a real depreciation of the domestic currency that increases net exports by the same amount as the fall in government expenditures. A monetary contraction, on the other hand, leads to an increase in domestic interest rates, which in the short run leads to a real appreciation of the domestic currency and a fall in net exports and output. Because goods prices are rigid in the short run while the exchange rate is flexible, in the short run the nominal exchange rate overshoots its long-run level. Over time, as goods prices adjust, output and the nominal exchange rate converge to their long-run levels.

15.6 THE MUNDELL-FLEMING MODEL WITH FIXED EXCHANGE RATES

The Mundell-Fleming model is particularly simple for studying policy issues for a small open economy with fixed exchange rates. As discussed above, a fixed exchange rate entails a commitment by the country's central bank to buy and sell its currency at fixed, unchanging prices in terms of other currencies. To carry out this commitment, the country's central bank must maintain *foreign exchange reserves*, that is, foreign assets including foreign denominated bonds, foreign currencies, and precious metals.

In this section, we first assume that the central bank has enough foreign reserves that it can *credibly* commit to maintain the nominal exchange rate at a level $\bar{e}$ indefinitely. In this case, the expected long-run level of the nominal exchange rate will be equal to the current value of the exchange rate, which is $\bar{e}$. Hence, $e = e^e = \bar{e}$. To simplify the analysis we also assume that the expected inflation rate is zero; that is, $\pi^e = 0$. Under these assumptions, the expected change in the real exchange rate is also zero; that is, $\varepsilon = \varepsilon^e = \bar{\varepsilon}$ where $\varepsilon = \bar{e} \times P^f/P$. This means that the real interest rate parity condition reduces to $r = r^f$.

FIGURE 15.12

Effects of a Monetary Contraction with Fixed Exchange Rates

Starting from the full equilibrium point A, a decrease in the money supply shifts the LM curve to the left, to LM_1. At the new internal balance point B, the domestic interest rate is above the foreign rate, which brings about a capital inflow and puts downward pressure on the dollar/euro exchange rate. To keep the exchange rate fixed the central bank sells dollars in exchange for euros. This increases the money supply in Canada and shifts the LM curve back to its original position, re-establishing the full-employment equilibrium at point A.

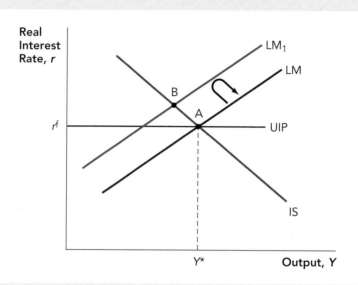

THE EFFECTS OF A MONETARY CONTRACTION: FIXED EXCHANGE RATES

THE SHORT-RUN EFFECTS OF A MONETARY CONTRACTION

Figure 15.12 shows the effects of a decrease in the money supply with a fixed exchange rate system. Suppose we start from full equilibrium at point A. The decrease in the money supply shifts the LM curve to the left, to LM_1. At the new internal balance point B, the domestic interest is above the foreign rate, and there is a huge increase in the demand for Canadian assets, thereby increasing the demand for the dollar in the foreign exchange market. To prevent the appreciation of the dollar and to maintain the exchange rate at its fixed level, the central bank intervenes in the foreign exchange market, and purchases euros in exchange for dollars. This intervention increases both the foreign exchange reserves of the central bank and the quantity of dollars in circulation, shifting the LM curve back to its original position.

Hence, unlike flexible exchange rates, with fixed exchange rates monetary policy cannot affect output even in the short run. The reason is that with fixed exchange rates the central bank gives up control of the money supply. Instead, its monetary policy objective is to control the exchange rate.

THE LONG-RUN EFFECTS OF MONETARY CONTRACTION

Under fixed exchange rates the dynamics of the model are such that, following the monetary contraction, the economy returns to its initial full-employment equilibrium in the short run. Hence, in this case, there will be no adjustments from the short run to the long run. The new short-run equilibrium after the monetary contraction is also the long-run equilibrium.

Further, with the nominal exchange rate fixed and the price level P unchanged, the real exchange rate remains the same at $\bar{\varepsilon}$. Thus, like flexible exchange rates, the monetary contraction does not alter the long-run equilibrium real exchange rate.

THE EFFECTS OF A FISCAL CONTRACTION: FIXED EXCHANGE RATES

THE SHORT-RUN EFFECTS OF A FISCAL CONTRACTION

Suppose that starting from full equilibrium at point A in Figure 15.13, there is a decrease in government expenditures, G. The decrease in G shifts the IS curve to the left, to IS_1. At the new internal balance point B, the domestic interest rate is below the foreign interest rate, which makes Canadian assets less attractive than European assets. As a result, there is a capital outflow from Canada and downward pressure on the dollar/euro exchange rate. To maintain the exchange rate at its fixed level, the central bank intervenes in the foreign exchange market and buys dollars in exchange for euros. The central bank's foreign exchange intervention reduces the money supply in Canada and shifts the LM curve to the left. This process continues until the IS_1 and LM_1 curves intersect along the UIP curve. The new short-run equilibrium will be at point C, with output at level Y_C.

FIGURE 15.13

The Short-Run Effects of a Fiscal Contraction with Fixed Exchange Rates

Starting from full equilibrium at point A, a decrease in G shifts the IS curve to the left, to IS_1. At the new internal balance point B, the domestic interest rate is below the foreign interest rate, which brings about a capital outflow, and puts downward pressure on the dollar/euro exchange rate. To keep the exchange rate fixed, the central bank buys dollars in exchange for euros, which reduces the money supply, and shifts the LM curve to the left, to LM_1. The new short-run equilibrium will be at point C, with output at Y_C.

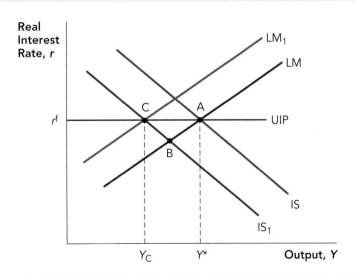

FIGURE 15.14

Adjustment to the Long-Run Equilibrium with Fixed Exchange Rates

Start from the short-run equilibrium point C after a fall in G. As Y_C is below the full-employment output Y^*, prices start to fall, which shifts the IS_1 and LM_1 curves to the right, to IS_2 and LM_2, respectively. If the intersection point D of the IS_2 and LM_2 curves lies below the UIP curve, then the resulting capital outflow will require the central bank to buy dollars in exchange for euros. The money supply will, thus, fall and the LM_2 curve will shift to LM_3. In effect, when the price level falls the money supply adjusts to maintain the internal balance along the UIP curve; and the equilibrium adjusts along the UIP curve until the full long-run equilibrium is established at point A.

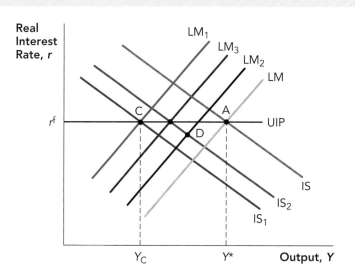

THE LONG-RUN EFFECTS OF FISCAL CONTRACTION

In Figure 15.14 the short-run equilibrium at point C is temporary because output Y_C is below its full-employment level Y^*. Hence, there will be downward pressures on prices in Canada. As P falls, Canadian goods become more competitive relative to foreign goods and Canada's net exports increase, shifting the IS_1 curve to the right to IS_2. The fall in P also increases the supply of real money balances in the economy, shifting the LM_1 curve to the right, to LM_2, where it intersects the IS_2 curve below the UIP line at point D.[8] Now, the Canadian interest rate is lower than the foreign interest rate. As a result, investors favour European over Canadian assets, and put pressure on the Canadian dollar to depreciate. To maintain the exchange rate at its fixed level, the central bank intervenes in the foreign exchange market and purchases dollars in exchange for euros. The resulting reduction of the money supply in Canada shifts the LM_2 curve to the left, to LM_3 until it intersects the IS_2 curve along the UIP curve. In effect, when the price level falls the money supply adjusts to maintain the internal balance along the UIP curve; and the equilibrium adjusts along the UIP curve until the full long-run equilibrium is established at point A.

What is the effect of the fiscal contraction on the *long-run* level of the real exchange rate? Notice that in the new long-run equilibrium the price level P is lower

---

[8] It is possible that the leftward shift in the LM_2 curve is large enough to intersect the IS_1 curve above the UIP line. In this case the adjustment process would be the opposite from the one described in the text. For the sake of brevity, we ignore this case.

while the nominal exchange rate $\bar{e}$ is the same. Hence, there must have been an increase in the long-run level of the real exchange rate, ε. The fiscal contraction has caused a real depreciation of the long-run equilibrium value of the Canadian dollar.

THE EFFECTS OF DEVALUATION

THE SHORT-RUN EFFECTS OF DEVALUATION

With a fixed exchange rate system it is possible that the pressures on the economy could be such that the central bank will be losing foreign exchange reserves. In order to reverse this loss, the central bank may decide to set the nominal exchange rate at a higher level by raising the level of $\bar{e}$. We call this **devaluation**.[9]

Suppose that starting from full equilibrium at point A in Figure 15.15, the central bank devalues the Canadian dollar. Given that P is fixed, the devaluation increases the real exchange rate ε, and makes Canadian goods cheaper relative to foreign goods. Thus, net exports increase, shifting the IS curve to IS_1, and raising the domestic interest rate above the foreign rates. Canadian assets are now more attractive than European assets, thereby causing a capital inflow in Canada, and a downward pressure on the dollar/euro exchange rate. To maintain the exchange rate

---

FIGURE 15.15

The Effects of a Devaluation

The initial full equilibrium is at point A. When the central bank devalues the Canadian dollar, the real exchange rate ε increases, which increases net exports, shifting the IS curve to IS_1. The increase in the domestic interest rate causes a capital inflow and puts upward pressure on the dollar/euro exchange rate. As a result, the central bank sells dollars in exchange for euros, which increases the money supply, and shifts the LM curve to the right, to LM_1. At point B, output Y_B is above its full-employment level Y^*. Hence, prices increase, shifting IS_1 and LM_1 to the left. The equilibrium shifts along the UIP curve towards its initial long-run equilibrium at point A.

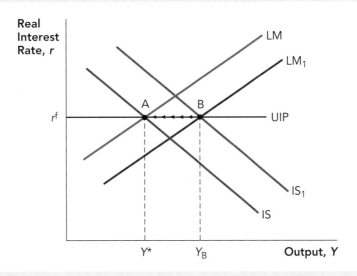

---

[9] Conversely, if the central bank raised the level at which it fixes the value of the domestic currency (i.e., if it reduces $\bar{e}$) we say it *revalued* the domestic currency. Notice also that devaluation/revaluation is caused by the central bank under a fixed exchange rate system, whereas depreciation/appreciation is caused by the free market forces of supply and demand for currencies under a flexible exchange rate system.

at its fixed level the central bank intervenes in the foreign exchange market by selling dollars in exchange for euros. This action increases the money supply in Canada and shifts the LM curve to the right. The process continues until the IS_1 and LM_1 curves intersect along the UIP curve. This is the short-run equilibrium, which is denoted by point B in Figure 15.15.

THE LONG-RUN EFFECTS OF DEVALUATION

At point B in Figure 15.15 output Y_B is higher than the full-employment level of output Y^*. Hence, there will be upward pressures on prices in Canada. As the price level P increases, the equilibrium shifts along the UIP curve towards its long-run equilibrium at point A, with the IS, LM, and UIP curves intersecting again at the full-employment level of output Y^*.

What is the effect of the devaluation on the *long-run* level of the real exchange rate? To answer this question, recall the goods market equilibrium condition that requires output Y to be equal to aggregate expenditures: $Y = C + I + G + NX$. Notice that the long-run equilibrium both before and after the devaluation is at point A in Figure 15.15. Hence, output and interest rates are the same in both equilibria. This means that C, I, and G are the same in both equilibria, which also requires NX to be the same. Now, for NX to be the same it must be the case that the real exchange rate ε is the same in both long-run equilibria. Thus, the long-run level of the real exchange rate is unaffected by the devaluation: $\overline{e}$ and P increase in the same proportion in the long run.

What is the effect of the devaluation on the long-run level of the foreign exchange reserves of the central bank? First, notice that the long-run price level P rises in proportion to $\overline{e}$, while the long-run interest rate and output remain unchanged. Hence, for the money market to be in long-run equilibrium it must be the case that the nominal money supply must have increased in proportion to P. This way, the long-run level of the real money supply will be unaffected by the devaluation. Next, notice that with fixed exchange rates the money supply adjusts following the central bank's foreign exchange intervention, with the money supply increasing when the central bank sells domestic currency in exchange for foreign currency. Hence, as the long-run level of the nominal money supply has increased, it must be the case that the long-run foreign exchange reserves of the central bank have also increased. On balance, the central bank has sold dollars for euros in the foreign exchange market.

THE EFFECTS OF A BALANCE OF PAYMENTS CRISIS

With fixed exchange rates, an often recurring problem is loss of confidence on the part of the private sector, leading to *runs* on the domestic currency and a substantial loss of foreign exchange reserves by the central bank. Recent examples of such crises are the runs on the Mexican peso in 1994–1995 and the crisis in the East Asian economies in 1997–1998. Both of these cases will be discussed in detail in the next chapter. Here, we will use the Mundell-Fleming model in order to discuss the effects of balance of payments crises on output, interest rates, the money supply, and the foreign exchange reserves of the central bank.

The basic scenario for a **balance of payments crisis** is as follows: There is a general belief on the part of the private sector that the central bank will devalue the domestic currency in the near future. The reason may be because there is a recession, and the central bank may be trying to boost production by devaluing the

FIGURE 15.16

The Effects of a Balance of Payments Crisis

Assume the economy is initially at full-employment equilibrium at point A. A sudden general belief by speculators that the central bank will in the near future devalue the domestic currency raises the expected return on foreign assets from r^f to $r^f + (\bar{\varepsilon}_1 - \bar{\varepsilon})/\bar{\varepsilon}$, which shifts the UIP curve up to UIP_1. The domestic interest rate, as given by point A, is then below the return on foreign assets, as given by UIP_1. Thus, there is a capital outflow, an excess demand for euros, and excess supply of dollars in the foreign exchange market. To keep the exchange rate fixed, the central bank buys dollars in exchange for euros, which reduces the money supply, shifting the LM curve to the left, until it intersects the IS curve along UIP_1.

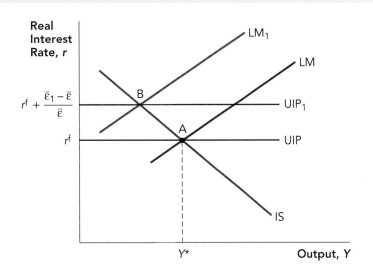

currency; or the foreign exchange reserves of the central bank may be running low, and the bank may be trying to replenish them.

Let $\bar{e}$ be the level at which the central bank is currently fixing the exchange rate. Recall, in our analysis of fixed exchange rates so far we have assumed that the central bank's policy is credible, and as a result the expected future exchange rate is equal to the current exchange rate, $e^e = \bar{e}$. With this requirement, and the simplifying assumption $\pi^e = 0$, we have $\varepsilon^e = \bar{\varepsilon}$, and the UIP condition reduces to $r = r^f$.

To illustrate the balance of payments crisis using the IS-LM-UIP model, suppose the economy is initially at full equilibrium point A in Figure 15.16. Suppose now there is suddenly a general belief by speculators that the central bank will in the near future devalue the domestic currency, and fix the exchange rate at a higher level $\bar{e}_1$. Hence, the expected future real exchange rate becomes $\varepsilon^e = \bar{\varepsilon}_1$; and the expected return on foreign assets increases from r^f to $r^f + (\bar{\varepsilon}_1 - \bar{\varepsilon})/\bar{\varepsilon}$. The uncovered interest parity will then be given by $r = r^f + (\bar{\varepsilon}_1 - \bar{\varepsilon})/\bar{\varepsilon}$, which shifts the UIP curve up to UIP_1.

Domestic interest rates, as given by the internal balance point A, are then below the expected return on foreign assets, as given by UIP_1. Thus, there is a capital outflow, an excess demand for euros, and an excess supply of dollars in the foreign exchange market. To keep the exchange rate fixed, the central bank buys dollars in exchange for euros, which reduces the money supply, shifting the LM curve to the left, until it intersects the IS curve along UIP_1.

The new short-run equilibrium is at point B. Along with the decrease in the money supply, the crisis has increased interest rates, reduced output, and reduced the foreign exchange reserves of the central bank. We will not discuss the dynamic adjustment to the new long-run equilibrium here, but the short-run analysis is rich enough to bring out the salient features of a balance of payments crisis.

RECAP   **THE MUNDELL-FLEMING MODEL WITH FIXED EXCHANGE RATES**

Under a fixed exchange rate system monetary policy is directed at having a stable value for the exchange rate. An increase in the money supply will be completely neutralized by the activities of the central bank in the foreign exchange market. On the other hand, a fall in government expenditures will, in the short run, put downward pressure on interest rates, leading to a balance of payments deficit, and a fall in the money supply and output. A devaluation of the domestic currency will, in the short run, increase the relative price of the domestic good, raising net exports, output, and the money supply. A balance of payments crisis happens when speculators anticipate that in the near future the central bank will devalue the currency. The crisis will lead to an increase in domestic interest rates, a fall in the money supply and output.

15.7 IMPERFECT ASSET SUBSTITUTABILITY AND IMPERFECT CAPITAL MOBILITY

Our analysis so far has assumed that international assets are perfect substitutes and that capital can move freely across international borders without any impediments. When these assumptions do not hold, the interest parity conditions have to be modified to reflect **imperfect asset substitutability** and **imperfect capital mobility**.

Assets are said to be *imperfect substitutes* when they have different risk characteristics and therefore different rates of return even at the long-run equilibrium. For example, bonds issued by a less developed country that has a large national debt are much riskier than bonds issued by a developed country with a sound fiscal position. Therefore, in order for investors to be induced to purchase the bonds of the less developed country, they will require a risk premium over and above the rate of return paid by the bonds of the developed country.

Under imperfect asset substitutability the relation between the real rates of return on domestic and foreign assets can be written as

$$r = r^f + \frac{\varepsilon^e - \varepsilon}{\varepsilon} + \rho \tag{15.12}$$

where ρ is a risk premium associated with holding domestic assets. Notice that the risk premium drives a wedge between the equilibrium rates of returns of domestic and foreign assets. Thus, it is clear from equation (15.12) that even in the long-run equilibrium where $\varepsilon^e = \varepsilon$, r and r^f differ by the value of the risk premium ρ.

Imperfect asset substitutability has implications for the effectiveness of government policies. For example, to the extent that policy makers can affect the value of ρ, they can set the domestic interest rate at a different level from the foreign interest rate, thereby gaining some monetary policy independence relative to foreign countries. This is true even under conditions of perfect capital mobility.

The risk premium in general depends on many factors such as the state of a country's economy, political uncertainty, and a country's national debt. Governments have some control over these factors and hence they can affect the risk premium and, in turn, the domestic interest rate. For instance, if a government decides to reduce the level of its national debt by buying back some of its bonds from the public, they can reduce the risk premium associated with the remaining outstanding bonds, and thus cause a fall in the domestic interest rates.

Imperfect capital mobility, like imperfect asset substitutability, can also cause deviations from the uncovered real or nominal interest parity conditions. *Imperfect capital mobility* exists if there are sufficient barriers to international capital flows to make it difficult and costly to move assets and money across national borders. Thus the government's foreign exchange reserves are sizable relative to flows of capital. Capital mobility today is limited for many developing countries with "thin" financial markets. Capital mobility was limited for all countries only a few decades in the past. It may be limited in the future as well, either as future governments impose explicit controls on some types of transactions or as taxes on international transactions levied by future governments put sand in the wheels of international finance.

If capital mobility is low, the rate at which the government buys or sells its currency for foreign exchange has an impact on foreign exchange supply and demand and thus on the current exchange rate and interest rates. Hence, the real interest parity condition has to be modified to account for imperfect capital mobility. A convenient expression is the following

$$r = r^f + \frac{\varepsilon^e - \varepsilon}{\varepsilon} + \theta \times \Delta R \qquad (15.13)$$

where θ is a positive parameter and ΔR is the change in the foreign exchange reserves of the central bank. When the central bank buys foreign currency (i.e., $\Delta R > 0$) it raises its demand and the domestic currency depreciates or ε rises. Similarly, when it sells foreign currency (i.e., $\Delta R < 0$) it lowers its demand and the domestic currency depreciates or ε falls.

Under imperfect capital mobility, the central bank regains some freedom of action to use monetary policy for domestic uses under fixed exchange rates. Suppose, for instance, that an adverse shock abroad increases the foreign interest rate r^f and creates pressure for domestic currency depreciation. To maintain the exchange rate at some fixed level, $\bar{\varepsilon}$, and prevent the domestic interest rate from rising, the central bank can run down its foreign exchange reserves by selling them on the foreign exchange market.

But the amount of freedom of action for monetary policy is limited by the sensitivity of the exchange rate to the magnitude of foreign exchange intervention as measured by the parameter θ, and by the amount of reserves. The level of foreign exchange reserves must be positive. As discussed earlier, policies that spend reserves cannot be continued forever because once the government's foreign reserves have fallen to zero it can no longer finance interventions in the foreign exchange market.

> ### RECAP   IMPERFECT ASSET SUBSTITUTABILITY AND IMPERFECT CAPITAL MOBILITY
>
> Assets are said to be imperfect substitutes when they have different risk characteristics and therefore different rates of return even at the long-run equilibrium. Imperfect capital mobility exists if there are sufficient barriers to international capital flows to make it difficult and costly to move assets and money across national borders. With imperfect asset substitutability or imperfect capital mobility policy makers can set the domestic interest rate at a different level from the foreign interest rate, thereby gaining some monetary policy independence relative to foreign countries.

15.8 IMPERFECT CAPITAL MOBILITY AND THE IS-LM-BP MODEL

In this section we briefly outline the Mundell-Fleming model with imperfect capital mobility, and illustrate how it works with reference to a fiscal contraction under a flexible exchange rate system. We show that with imperfect capital mobility fiscal policy can affect output in the short run under a flexible exchange rate system, which is in contrast to the case with perfect capital mobility. Before discussing the model it is important to mention that imperfect asset substitutability will work in a way very similar to what is described in this section, even though we refer to the model as a model of imperfect capital mobility.

THE IS-LM-BP MODEL

With imperfect capital mobility the IS and LM curves are as before. On the other hand, the combinations of Y and r that are consistent with a balance of payment equilibrium do not lie on a horizontal line at r^f as they do under perfect capital mobility. Instead, they lie on an upward sloping curve, which we call the BP curve. To see this, recall equation (15.10) for the balance on the official reserve transactions:

$$BP = CA(\varepsilon, Y, Y^f) + KA(r - r^f - (\varepsilon^e - \varepsilon)/\varepsilon)$$

where CA is the current account and KA is the capital account.

For our analysis of the IS-LM-BP model we consider the benchmark case where $BP = 0$, both under flexible and fixed exchange rates. Under a flexible exchange rate system, this is the level of BP that is attained by market forces without any official foreign exchange intervention by the central bank. Also, under a fixed exchange rate system when $BP = 0$ there are no official reserve transactions, no corresponding changes in the money supply, and, therefore, no shifts of the LM curve.[10]

With imperfect capital mobility, the capital account no longer dominates the balance of payments in the sense that a change in the interest rate differential no

---

[10] Alternatively, setting $BP = X$, where X is a non-zero amount under fixed rates would complicate the analysis because of the implied endogenous changes in the domestic money supply and therefore the LM curve. Recall that BP is the current account (CA) plus the balance on the capital account other than official reserve transactions (KA). Hence, as explained in Section 15.1, BP is equal to the change in the foreign exchange reserves of the central bank. If $BP > 0$ the central bank must be gaining foreign exchange reserves; that is, it must be buying foreign assets in exchange for dollars. Hence, if $BP > 0$ then the money supply in Canada is increasing. This cannot go on forever, with the central bank accumulating an infinite amount of foreign exchange reserves. Similarly, if $BP < 0$ the central bank will be losing foreign exchange reserves and the money supply in Canada must be falling. This too cannot go on forever, as the central bank has a limited amount of foreign exchange reserves. Hence, $BP = 0$ is the natural long-term target for BP in a fixed exchange rate system, with its implicit fixed level for the real exchange rate.

longer induces infinite amounts of capital inflows or outflows. Now, an increase in the domestic interest rate, r, induces a *finite* amount of capital inflows and causes a capital account surplus. To restore the balance of payments to zero the domestic income, Y, must increase, thereby reducing net exports and inducing a current account deficit. This demonstrates that the BP curve is upward sloping in (Y, r)-space, as shown in Figure 15.17. The BP curve will be steeper the lower the degree of capital mobility (or the lower is the degree of asset substitutability). The reason is that the lower the degree of capital mobility (or asset substitutability) the smaller will be the amount of capital inflow corresponding to a given increase in the domestic interest rate; and, therefore, the smaller is the required increase in output in order to maintain a balance of payments equilibrium. In the extreme case of no capital mobility (or no asset substitutability) the BP curve will be vertical.

The balance of payments is zero on points along the BP curve. Points below the BP curve correspond to balance of payments deficits, and points above it correspond to balance of payments surpluses. To see this, start from a point like A on the BP curve in Figure 15.17 and then increase r, while keeping Y fixed, to reach point B vertically above A. With a higher interest rate differential at point B than at point A, there is now a balance of payments surplus. Similarly, all points above the BP curve signify a balance of payments surplus, and all points below it signify a balance of payments deficit.

Next, we consider shifts in the BP curve when there is an increase in the real exchange rate ε. For simplicity, we consider the case of a flexible exchange rate

FIGURE 15.17

Imperfect Capital Mobility and the BP Curve

With imperfect capital mobility, an increase in the domestic interest rate induces a *finite* amount of capital inflow. The balance of payments can then be restored if output increases to reduce the net exports of goods and services. Hence, the BP curve is upward sloping. Above the BP curve domestic interest rates are high and there is a balance of payments surplus. Below the BP curve there is a balance of payments deficit. An increase in the real exchange rate increases net exports for each interest rate and shifts the BP curve to the right.

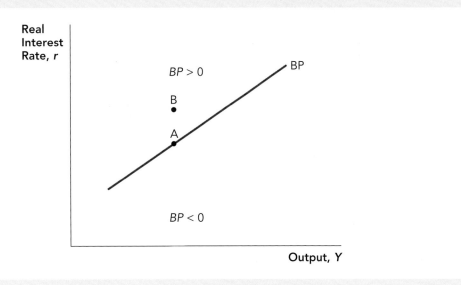

system, in which case $BP = 0$. Further, we confine the analysis to the short run only, where $(\varepsilon^e - \varepsilon)/\varepsilon = 0$, and thus KA depends only on $r - r^f$. The increase in ε increases net exports. In order to maintain BP at zero, for each Y there must be a decrease in r, to induce a capital outflow and balance out the increase in net exports. Hence, the BP curve shifts down if there is an increase in the real exchange rate.

FISCAL CONTRACTION WITH FLEXIBLE EXCHANGE RATES AND IMPERFECT CAPITAL MOBILITY

We can readily work out the short-run effects of a decrease in government expenditures, with flexible exchange rates using this model. For brevity, we assume that the BP curve is flatter than the LM curve. In Figure 15.18 start at the initial equilibrium A, where the IS_0, LM_0, and BP_0 curves intersect, and suppose there is a fall in government expenditures on domestically-produced goods that shifts the IS curve from IS_0 to IS_1.[11] There will then be an instantaneous equilibrium at point B, which lies below the BP curve, signifying a balance of payments deficit. There will thus be a nominal and real depreciation of the Canadian dollar (an increase in ε), which will shift up the IS curve, to IS_2, and shift down the BP curve, to BP_1. A new short-run equilibrium will then be established at intersection point D of the IS_2, LM_0, and BP_1 curves.

Unlike with perfect capital mobility, with imperfect capital mobility fiscal policy has some effect on output in the short run with flexible exchange rates. The reason

FIGURE 15.18
A Fiscal Contraction with Imperfect Capital Mobility
Starting from an initial equilibrium point A, a fall in government expenditures on domestically-produced goods shifts the IS curve from IS_0 to IS_1. The instantaneous equilibrium is at point B, which lies below the BP curve, signifying a balance of payments deficit. There is then a nominal and real depreciation of the Canadian dollar that shifts up the IS curve, to IS_2, and shifts down the BP curve, to BP_1. The new short-run equilibrium is at the intersection point D of the IS_2, LM_0, and BP_1 curves.

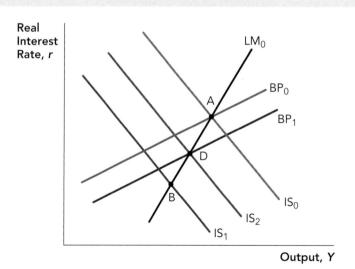

[11] Because the increase in government expenditures does not fall on foreign-produced goods the BP curve does not shift.

is that with imperfect capital mobility the domestic equilibrium interest rate can deviate from the foreign rate, and the adjustment of the model retains some features of the closed economy. As government expenditures decrease, there is an increase in e and an increase in the size of the current account balance CA. Hence, to have $BP = 0$, it must be the case that in the new equilibrium we should have a smaller balance on the capital account KA, which is attainable if r is lower than it was before the policy change. With lower interest rates but fixed prices, the only way the money market will clear in the short run is if output stays below its original level. In terms of Figure 15.18, we move along the LM_0 curve from point A to point D.

RECAP   IMPERFECT CAPITAL MOBILITY AND THE IS-LM-BP MODEL

With imperfect capital mobility the combinations of Y and r that are consistent with a balance of payments equilibrium lie on an upward sloping curve, called the BP curve. Points below that BP curve correspond to balance of payments deficits, and points above it correspond to balance of payments surpluses. The BP curve shifts down if there is an increase in the real exchange rate, and it shifts up when there is a decrease in the real exchange rate. With imperfect capital mobility the domestic equilibrium interest rate can deviate from the foreign rate, and the adjustment of the model retains some features of the closed economy. Hence, for example, fiscal policy has some effect on output in the short run with flexible exchange rates.

CHAPTER SUMMARY

1. The balance of payments account records the international transactions a country makes with the rest of the world. The balance of payments is divided into two parts: (i) the current account and (ii) the capital account.

2. The uncovered real interest parity condition states that, with perfect asset substitutability, the domestic real interest rate should be equal to the foreign real interest rate plus the expected rate of change in the real value of the domestic currency.

3. The Mundell-Fleming model has three components: the IS curve, the LM curve, and the uncovered interest parity condition. *Internal balance* exists when goods and money markets are in equilibrium at the intersection of the IS and LM curves. *External balance* exists when the balance of payments is at its desired target value, and the uncovered interest parity condition holds.

4. With high capital mobility and perfect asset substitutability fiscal policy cannot affect output under a flexible exchange rate system, while monetary policy is very effective.

5. Under a flexible exchange rate system the nominal exchange rate overshoots its long-run level after a monetary policy change. The reason for overshooting is that goods prices are rigid in the short run while the exchange rate is flexible.

6. Under a fixed exchange rate system monetary policy is directed at having a stable value for the exchange rate. As a result, under a fixed exchange rate system monetary policy is not effective in affecting output, while fiscal policy is very effective.

7. A balance of payments crisis happens when speculators anticipate that in the near future the central bank will devalue the currency. The crisis will lead to an increase in domestic interest rates and a fall in the money supply and output.

8. With imperfect asset substitutability or imperfect capital mobility policy makers can set the domestic interest rate at a different level from the foreign interest rate, thereby gaining some monetary policy independence relative to foreign countries.

9. With imperfect asset substitutability or imperfect capital mobility the BP curve is upward sloping, and the adjustment of the model retains some features of the closed economy.

KEY TERMS AND EQUATIONS

balance of payments account (p. 439)

balance of payments crisis (p. 466)

capital inflow (p. 440)

capital outflow (p. 440)

devaluation (p. 465)

exchange rate overshooting (p. 460)

external balance (p. 451)

fixed exchange rates (p. 453)

flexible exchange rates (p. 453)

foreign exchange intervention (p. 440)

foreign exchange market (p. 440)

imperfect asset substitutability (p. 468)

imperfect capital mobility (p. 468)

interest rate parity (p. 447)

internal balance (p. 451)

Mundell-Fleming model (p. 446)

offical reserve transactions (p. 440)

small open economy (p. 439)

Balance of payments:	$BP = CA + KA$	(15.1)
Uncovered real interest rate parity:	$r = r^f + \dfrac{\varepsilon^e - \varepsilon}{\varepsilon}$	(15.3)
Uncovered interest parity:	$i = i^f + \dfrac{e^e - e}{e}$	(15.6)
The IS curve:	$Y = C(Y - T) + I(r) + G + NX(\varepsilon, Y, Y^f)$	(15.7)
The LM curve:	$\dfrac{M}{P} = L(r + \pi^e, Y)$	(15.8)
The BP equation:	$BP = CA(\varepsilon, Y, Y^f) + KA(r - r^f - (\varepsilon^e - \varepsilon)/\varepsilon)$	(15.10)

ANALYTICAL EXERCISES

1. Recall, the real exchange rate was defined as $\varepsilon = e \times P^*/P$. Assuming that the real exchange rate is expected to remain *constant* over time, derive the relationship between the rate of change of the nominal exchange rate and the inflation rates at home and abroad. The relationship you have derived is called "*ex ante* or expected relative purchasing power parity." What does it say about the purchasing power parity in the two countries?

2. Absolute purchasing power holds when $P = e \times P^*$, that is, the value of domestic and foreign goods is the same when expressed in terms of the same currency. If that is the case, what is the implied value of the real exchange rate? Does the real exchange rate change over time?

3. Suppose the uncovered real interest parity and the expected relative purchasing power parity conditions hold. If the nominal interest rate in Canada is 2 percent, and the nominal interest rate in Europe 3 percent, what is the expected rate of increase in the value of the euro? If, in addition, the expected inflation rate in Canada is 2 percent, what is the real interest rate in Europe?

4. Consider a small open economy with a fixed exchange rate system. Suppose there is a general expectation that the central bank will *revalue* the domestic currency

(i.e., that it will reduce the nominal exchange rate) in the future. Explain the short-run effects of this on the economy.

5. Consider an extension of the Mundell-Fleming model with imperfect international mobility of assets. Show that the BP curve is upward sloping in this case. Explain whether there is a balance of payments surplus or deficit above the BP curve. How will the BP curve shift if there is a real depreciation of the domestic currency?

6. It is particularly easy to do short-run policy analysis with imperfect international mobility of assets, using the standard assumptions that underlie the short-run in the Mundell-Fleming model. Explain the short run effects only of an increase in government expenditures with fixed exchange rates. Explain the effects of an increase in the money supply with fixed exchange rates. Does the central bank have monetary independence in this setup?

7. Explain the short-run effects only of an increase in the money supply with imperfect international mobility of assets in the Mundell-Fleming model with flexible exchange rates.

8. Recall the money creation process discussed in Section 7.6 (Chapter 7). Suppose the money multiplier is m and

the central bank sells $1 million on the foreign exchange market in exchange for euros. Explain what will be the effects on the monetary base and the money supply.

9. Suppose investment is very volatile because of changes in the expectations of firms regarding the level of economic activity. What type of exchange rate system will reduce fluctuations in output? Is a fixed or a flexible exchange rate system better at insulating the economy from disturbances originating in the goods market?

10. Suppose money demand is very volatile because of financial innovations. What type of exchange rate system will reduce fluctuations in output? Is a fixed or a flexible exchange rate system better at insulating the economy from disturbances originating in the money market?

POLICY EXERCISES

1. Explain why recessions starting in the U.S. are so easily transmitted to Canada. Is Canada better insulated from these recessions with fixed or with flexible exchange rates?

2. During the recession of 2001–2002 the U.S. Federal Reserve substantially reduced the interest rates in the U.S. What would be the effects of these U.S. interest rate cuts on the Canadian economy? Why did the Bank of Canada lower Canadian interest rates following the U.S. interest rate cuts?

3. Suppose the Bank of Canada were to unilaterally fix the value of the Canadian dollar in terms of the US dollar. Explain what would then be the effect of an increase in the money supply in the U.S. on the money supply in Canada.

4. Use your answers to Policy Exercises 1, 2, and 3, and any other issues that you can think of, in order to discuss whether the Bank of Canada should adopt a policy of fixing the value of the Canadian dollar.

5. What would be the effect of a substantial discovery of oil on the real value of the Canadian dollar? What would be the effect on the size of the manufacturing sector in Canada? What would be the effect on the price of housing in Canada?

16 International Economic Policy

QUESTIONS

How has the world organized its international monetary system?

What is a fixed exchange rate system?

What is a floating exchange rate system?

What are the costs and benefits of fixed exchange rates vis-à-vis floating exchange rates?

Why do most countries today have floating exchange rates?

Why has western Europe recently created a "monetary union" — an irrevocable commitment to fixed exchange rates within western Europe?

What were the causes of the major currency crises of the 1990s?

I n Chapter 15 we studied in detail the workings of fixed and flexible exchange rate systems. In this chapter we provide a historical perspective on the alternative international monetary arrangements in the world economy during the past century. We discuss two alternative multilateral arrangements of fixed exchange rate systems: the gold standard and the Bretton Woods system. Then we explain how each of these systems was replaced; and how we arrived at the current system of largely **floating exchange rates**.

In this chapter we also study the different costs and benefits of fixed versus floating exchange rates. The chapter concludes by analyzing some of the major international shocks to the world economy in the 1990s. Three separate major international financial crises (and a host of more minor crises) struck during that decade: the European crisis of 1992, the Mexican crisis of 1995, and the East Asian crisis of 1997–1998.

16.1 THE HISTORY OF EXCHANGE RATES

THE CLASSICAL GOLD STANDARD

WHAT THE GOLD STANDARD IS

In the generation before World War I nearly all of the world economy was on a particular **fixed exchange rate** system: the **gold standard**. A government would *define* a unit of its currency unit as worth such-and-such an amount of gold. It would stand ready to buy or sell its currency for gold at that price at any time, in any amount. Such a currency was *convertible,* for it could be converted into gold freely (and gold could be converted into it freely). The currency's price in terms of gold was its *parity*.

When two countries were on the gold standard, their nominal exchange rate was fixed at the ratio of their gold parities. Someone wishing to turn British currency — pounds sterling — into Canadian currency — Canadian dollars — could begin by taking British currency to the Bank of England and exchanging it for gold at the pound's parity. They would then ship the gold across the Atlantic to Canada, and exchange it for dollars.

In the early 1910s, one Canadian or US dollar was worth 0.053 ounces (or 1.504 grams) of gold, and one British pound sterling was worth 0.258 ounces (or 7.321 grams) of gold. Thus, the exchange rate of the dollar for the pound (that is, the dollar price of the pound) was £1.00 = $(0.258/0.053) = $4.87. Suppose that supply and demand in the market for foreign exchange in 1910 had balanced not at £1.00 = $4.87 but at some other value — say £1.00 = $5.00. Someone with an idle pound sterling note could then get $5 for it if they sold it on the foreign exchange market. But with their $5 they could then buy enough gold in Canada to recover their original £1, and have 13 cents left over. So if the market exchange rate ever drifted up from £1.00 = $4.87 to £1.00 = $5.00, a huge mass of people selling pounds would enter the market and drive the exchange rate back to £1.00 = $4.87 as they attempted to carry out this **currency arbitrage**, outlined at greater length in Box 16.1.

Thus under the gold standard, nominal exchange rates were fixed at the ratio of countries' gold parities, as Box 16.1 explains. The gold standard was a fixed exchange rate system.

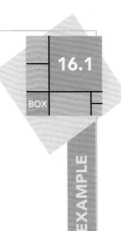

CURRENCY ARBITRAGE UNDER THE GOLD STANDARD

As long as central banks or treasuries stood ready to keep their currencies *convertible* at their gold parities, the ratio of two gold *parities* determined the nominal exchange rate. Why? Because of currency arbitrage. Anyone buying or selling one currency at any price other than the ratio of the two gold parities would find themselves facing an unlimited demand, and would soon find themselves losing a nearly unlimited amount of money.

Suppose that the monetary authorities in Canada stood ready to buy or sell gold from qualified parties at the price of $18.87 an ounce, that the British Treasury stood ready to buy or sell gold from qualified parties at the price of £3.88 an ounce, but that the pound sterling was trading in the foreign exchange market not for the $4.87 that was the ratio of the gold parities, but instead for 10 percent more — $5.36.

Then someone with an ounce of gold could

- Trade it to the British Treasury for £3.88.
- Then trade those pounds sterling for dollars in the foreign-exchange market and wind up with $20.80.

- Trade that $20.80 to the monetary authorities in Canada for 1.1 ounces of gold.
- Repeat the process as rapidly as possible, making a 10 percent profit each time the circle is completed.

Figure 16.1 shows these steps. Note that those who sell dollars for pounds at the rate of $5.36 = £1.00 are losing 10 percent of their value each time the circle is completed. The only things hindering this round-trip "arbitrage" process — as long as currencies remain convertible and parities remain fixed — are the costs of transporting and insuring the gold. Thus there can be very small fluctuations of exchange rates within the "gold points," but gold is cheap to transport and straightforward to insure: These fluctuations are minor indeed.

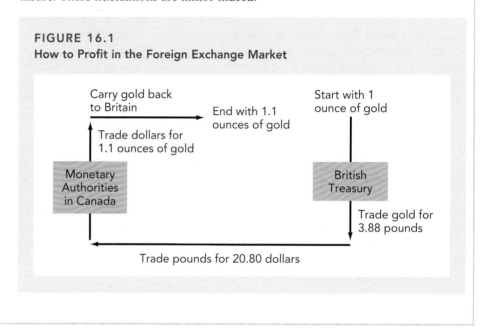

FIGURE 16.1
How to Profit in the Foreign Exchange Market

This system grew up gradually. It originated when Sir Isaac Newton, in his government job as master of the mint in Britain, fixed the gold parity of the British pound sterling. Because the industrial revolution began in Britain, Britain became the largest trading nation in the world in the nineteenth century. Other countries' governments sought easy access to the British market for the products made by their citizens. A fixed gold parity meant the prices their countries' producers charged would appear stable to British customers. It also meant that British investors would not fear that depreciation and devaluation would erode the value of the principal that they had lent. Throughout the late nineteenth century, country after country joined the gold standard, as Figure 16.2 shows. By the eve of World War I the overwhelming fraction of world commerce and investment flowed between countries on the gold standard.

A GOLD STANDARD TENDS TO PRODUCE CONTRACTIONARY POLICIES

Even in its turn-of-the-century heyday around 1900 it was already apparent that the gold standard had certain serious weaknesses as an international monetary system. The most important of these weaknesses was that the gold standard tended to be deflationary. In some circumstances it pushed countries to raise their interest rates

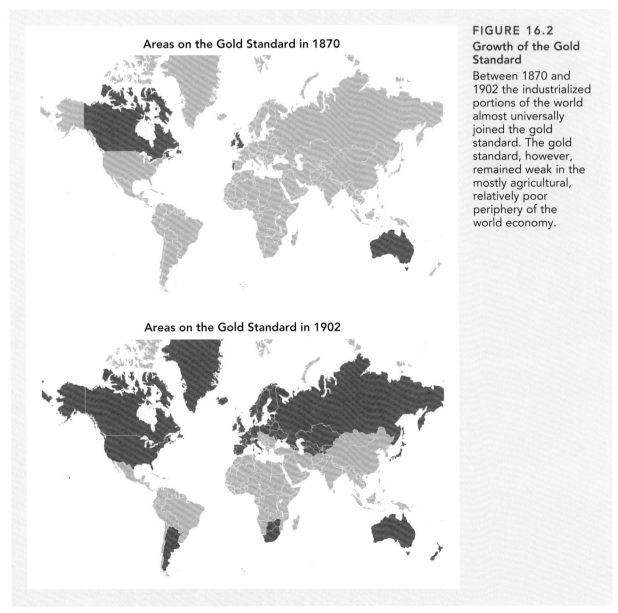

FIGURE 16.2
Growth of the Gold Standard
Between 1870 and 1902 the industrialized portions of the world almost universally joined the gold standard. The gold standard, however, remained weak in the mostly agricultural, relatively poor periphery of the world economy.

Source: Chris Meissner, http://econ161.berkeley.edu/~meissner/.

to reduce production and raise unemployment. And it never provided a counter-vailing push to other countries to lower their interest rates to raise production and to lower unemployment.

To see why, we need to digress for a moment into the role played under a gold standard by a country's gold and other **foreign exchange reserves**. If the exchange rate is floating in country A, foreigners' earnings in currency A must be used to buy A's exports or be invested in country A: Nothing else can be done with them. Under a floating rate system a country's current account (*CA*) plus capital account (*KA*) must add up to zero:

$$CA + KA = 0$$

The exchange rate moves up or down in response to changes in the supply and demand for foreign exchange in order to make this so.

Under a gold standard things are different. There is an extra participant in the market: the country's treasury or central bank. One can do something else with foreign-currency earnings besides using them to buy imports or make investments abroad: Take them to the foreign country's treasury, turn them into gold, ship the gold back home, take the gold to the treasury there, and turn the gold into real spendable cash. Under a gold standard it is net exports plus net investment from abroad minus the flow of gold into your country — FG — that together add up to zero:

$$CA + KA - FG = 0$$

What happens if a country finds that net exports plus net investment from abroad are less than zero? Its treasury will find itself losing gold, as a long line of foreigners come into its office, demand gold in exchange for currency, and then ship the gold out of the country. With each such transaction the country's gold reserves shrink. Eventually the government's gold reserves are gone.

At this point the country has a choice. One option is to abandon the fixed exchange rate system. It "closes the gold window," announces that the country will no longer buy back its currency at the established gold parity, abandons its fixed exchange rate, and lets the exchange rate float. The only other option is to solve its gold-outflow problem by making it more attractive for foreigners to invest. The way to increase net investment from abroad is to raise domestic interest rates. If net investment from abroad rises enough, gold will no longer flow out.

Thus under a gold standard countries running persistent balance-of-payments deficits — losing gold — must eventually raise interest rates to stay on the gold standard. However, surplus countries — those gaining gold — face no symmetrical crisis in which they must lower interest to stay on the gold standard. Their central banks can lower interest rates if they wish. But if they do not so wish, they can keep interest rates constant and watch their gold reserves grow.

This asymmetry means that a fixed exchange rate system like the gold standard puts periodic contractionary pressure on the world economy. Such pressure turned the interwar period into a disaster; the gold standard's contractionary pressure on countries to raise interest rates played a major role in generating the worldwide Great Depression of the 1930s.

THE COLLAPSE OF THE GOLD STANDARD

The international gold standard was suspended when World War I began in 1914. Every country used inflation to help finance its massive war expenditures. Inflation was inconsistent with the gold standard. Under the gold standard attempted inflation simply leads everyone to immediately trade their currency for solid gold.

After World War I was over, politicians and central bankers sought to restore the gold standard. They believed that the pre–World War I system of a fixed exchange rate on the gold standard had been a success. They saw restoring it as an important step to restoring general economic prosperity. The gold standard had, after all, delivered 40 years of more rapid economic and industrial growth than the world had ever seen before.

It took more than half a decade to fully restore the gold standard. But the revived gold standard did not produce prosperity. Instead, in less than half a decade the Great Depression began, and the restored gold standard broke apart. The consensus of economic historians today is that the Great Depression had its principal origin in the

United States, where for reasons not fully understood some combination of small shocks set off a downward spiral of destabilizing deflation. But a combination of mistaken policies and flaws in the functioning of the post–World War I gold standard then quickly amplified the Great Depression and propagated it around the world.

Economists Barry Eichengreen and Ben Bernanke argue that four factors made the post–World War I gold standard a much less secure monetary system than the pre–World War I gold standard:

- Everyone knew that governments could abandon their gold parities in an emergency. After all, they had done so during World War I. Thus everyone was eager to turn their holdings of currency into gold at the first sign of trouble. This meant countries had to maintain much larger gold reserves in order to keep the gold standard functioning.

- Everyone knew that governments had taken on the additional responsibility of trying to keep interest rates low enough to produce full employment.

- After World War I countries held their reserves not in gold but in foreign currencies. This was fine in normal times, but it meant that at the first sign of trouble not only would citizens show up trying to turn their currency into gold, but foreign central banks would do so too, greatly multiplying the magnitude of the gold outflow.

- The post–World War I surplus economies, the United States and France, did not lower their interest rates as gold flowed in.

These factors meant that as soon as a recession set in and gold drains began from countries with weak currencies, their governments found themselves under immediate and massive pressure to raise interest rates and lower output further if they were to stay on the gold standard. If they stayed on the gold standard, they guaranteed themselves high real interest rates and deep depression. If they abandoned the gold standard, they went against all the advice of bankers and gold standard advocates.

There was a clear divergence in the 1930s between those countries that abandoned the gold standard early in the Depression and those that stubbornly clung to gold, as shown in Figure 16.3. Those that clung to their gold parities found themselves forced to raise interest rates and contract their money supplies in order to avoid large gold losses that would rapidly exhaust their reserves. Those that abandoned the gold bloc and floated their exchange rates could avoid deflation, and avoid the worst of the Great Depression. By the middle of the 1930s the Great Depression was in full swing, and the gold standard was over.

THE BRETTON WOODS SYSTEM

After World War II, everyone took careful note of what they thought had gone wrong after World War I. Led by Harry Dexter White for the United States and John Maynard Keynes for Great Britain, governments tried to set up an international monetary system that would have all the advantages and none of the drawbacks of the gold standard. The system they set up came to be called the "Bretton Woods system," after a New Hampshire mountain resort town that was the location in late 1944 of a key international monetary conference.

Three principles guided this post–World War II international monetary system:

- In ordinary times, exchange rates should be fixed: Fixed exchange rates encourage international trade by making the prices of goods made in a foreign country predictable, and so have powerful advantages.

FIGURE 16.3
Economic Performance and Degree of Exchange Rate Depreciation during the Great Depression
The further countries moved away from their gold-standard exchange rates, the faster they recovered from the Great Depression.

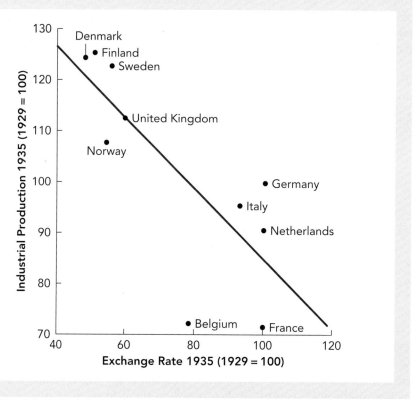

Source: Barry Eichengreen and Jeffrey Sachs, "Exchange Rates and Economic Recovery in the 1930s," *Journal of Economic History* (December 1985), pp. 925–946.

Note: The exchange rate is in units of gold per unit of domestic currency.

- In extraordinary times — whenever a country found itself in recession with a significantly overvalued currency that discouraged its exports, or found itself suffering from inflation because an undervalued currency raised the prices of imports and stimulated export demand — exchange rates should be changed. Such "fundamental disequilibrium" could and should be corrected by revaluing or devaluing the currency.
- An institution was needed — the International Monetary Fund — to watch over the international financial system. The IMF would make bridge loans to countries that were adjusting their economic policies. It would ensure that countries did not abuse their privilege of changing exchange rates. Exchange rate devaluation and revaluation would remain an exceptional measure for times of "fundamental disequilibrium," rather than becoming a standard tool of economic policy.

The Bretton Woods system was the "gold exchange" standard. Under this system the central banks of all the countries involved, except for the U.S. Federal Reserve, fixed the price of their currencies in terms of the US dollar; and they all carried sufficient reserves of US dollars in order to maintain their commitments. The U.S. Fed., on the other hand, fixed the price of the US dollar in terms of gold; and it stood ready to buy or sell gold in exchange for US dollars at the price of US$35 an ounce.

OUR CURRENT FLOATING-RATE SYSTEM

The Bretton Woods system in its turn broke down in the early 1970s. The United States saw inflation accelerate in the 1960s. It found itself with an overvalued exchange rate and a significant trade deficit at the end of the 1960s. As a result, the United States sought to devalue its currency: to reduce the value of the dollar in terms of gold. Because all other countries were fixing the prices of their currencies in terms of the US dollar, a devaluation of the US dollar would have a tremendous impact on the international monetary arrangement.

Policy makers in other countries thought that the United States should instead raise interest rates. Higher U.S. interest rates would make foreigners more willing to invest in the United States. The foreign currency committed to those investments could then be used to finance the excess of imports over exports that was the U.S. trade deficit. In the end the deadlock was broken by the unilateral American action to stop fixing the price of gold in terms of US dollars; and the Bretton Woods system fell apart.

Since the early 1970s the exchange rates at which the currencies of the major industrial powers trade against each other have been "floating" rates. The exchange rate is not fixed by the government, but fluctuates according to the balance of demand and supply on that day in the foreign exchange market. There seem to be few if any prospects for a restoration of a global system of fixed exchange rates over the next generation. Thus this book has assumed as its standard case that exchange rates are free to float and are set by market forces.

http://www.bank-banque-canada.ca/

Nevertheless, the older system is worth studying for three reasons. First, understanding the functioning of a fixed-rate system sheds light on how a floating-rate system works. Second, economic policy makers still debate the costs and benefits of a fixed-rate system relative to our current floating-rate system. Third, perhaps the pendulum will swing back in a generation and we will find ourselves once more in a fixed exchange rate system.

THE CANADIAN DOLLAR IN HISTORICAL PERSPECTIVE

In the first half of the twentieth century Canada had a fixed exchange rate system. In September 1939 the Canadian dollar was fixed at US$0.909. During World War II, continued capital inflows, mainly from the U.S., contributed to a revaluation of the Canadian dollar in 1946. The new rate was set at par value with the US dollar, but it did not last very long. Rising imports from the U.S. and a major realignment of most European currencies vis-à-vis the US dollar forced the Canadian authorities to devalue the currency by 9.1 percent in September 1949, and re-establish the pre-1946 exchange rate against the US dollar.[1]

Once again, though, international conditions changed and required yet another change in Canada's foreign exchange policy. Rising commodity prices, the beginning of the Korean War in June 1950, and strong inflows into Canada of short-term capital and foreign direct investment intensified expectations of a Canadian dollar revaluation. Faced with this situation, the Canadian authorities were concerned about the inflationary effects of maintaining a fixed exchange rate and in September 30, 1950 they decided to float the dollar within a system of foreign exchange controls that were subsequently removed at the end of 1951.

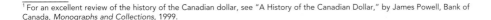

[1] For an excellent review of the history of the Canadian dollar, see "A History of the Canadian Dollar," by James Powell, Bank of Canada, *Monographs and Collections*, 1999.

The floating dollar lasted until 1962 while the rest of the world operated under the Bretton Woods system of fixed exchange rates. During this period, substantial capital inflows caused the dollar to appreciate and reach a peak of US$1.0614 in August 1957. The resulting loss of competitiveness and current account deficits combined with rising unemployment in the late-1950s forced the government to seek expansionary policies to support aggregate demand and reduce unemployment, despite the objections of James Coyne, the then Governor of the Bank of Canada. The policy dispute cost the governor his job in July 1961, and in May 1962 Canada returned to fixed exchange rates. In agreement with the IMF, the government fixed the Canadian dollar at US$0.925 with a fluctuation band of plus or minus one percent. Canada would go back to flexible exchange rates in June 1970 and remain with this exchange rate regime until the present.

The Canadian experience with fixed and floating exchange rates in the 1940s and 1950s inspired considerable academic work about the merits of fixed and flexible exchange rates. It was against this background, in the early 1960s, that the famous Mundell-Fleming model of a small open economy was developed to study the effectiveness of fiscal and monetary policies in an environment of high international capital mobility.

RECAP **HISTORY OF EXCHANGE RATES**

In the generation before World War I nearly all of the world economy was on a fixed exchange rate system called the gold standard, under which nominal exchange rates were equal to the ratio of currencies' gold *parities*. The international gold standard was suspended when World War I began in 1914. After World War I attempts to rebuild the gold standard created a system vulnerable to shocks that played a key role in causing the Great Depression. Therefore, after World War II economists built a fixed exchange rate system — the Bretton Woods system — that they hoped would combine the advantages of fixed and floating rate systems. But this system collapsed in the early 1970s, and was followed by our current floating exchange rate system.

16.2 THE CHOICE OF EXCHANGE RATE SYSTEMS

Economists either applaud or deplore the breakdown of the Bretton Woods system and the resort to floating exchange rates, depending on their underlying philosophy. For some, like Nobel Prize–winner Milton Friedman, the exchange rate is a price. Economic freedom and efficiency require that prices be set by market supply and demand. They should not be set by the decrees of governments. Thus the replacement of the fixed exchange rate, administered-price Bretton Woods system by the floating exchange rate, market-price system of today is a very positive change.

For others, like Nobel Prize–winner Robert Mundell, the exchange rate is the value that the government promises that the currency it issues will have. A stable exchange rate means that the government is keeping the contract it has made with investors in foreign countries. To let the exchange rate float is to break this contract — and everyone knows that markets work only if people do not break their contracts. Thus the replacement of the fixed exchange rate, administered-price Bretton Woods system by the floating exchange rate, market-price system of today is a very negative change.

We think that the right answer is "It depends." High philosophy is all very well, but what should really matter are the details of how the choice of an exchange rate regime affects the economy.

BENEFITS OF FIXED EXCHANGE RATES

Under a floating exchange rate system, exporters and firms whose products compete with imported goods never know what their competitors' costs are going to be. Exchange rate–driven fluctuations in the costs to their foreign competitors are an extra source of risk, and businesses do not like unnecessary risks. The fact that exchange rates fluctuate discourages international trade, and makes the international division of labour less sophisticated than it would otherwise be. Fixed exchange rate systems avoid these costs, and encourage international trade by reducing exchange rate fluctuations as a source of risk. They avoid the churning of industrial structure — the pointless and inefficient shift of resources into and out of tradable goods sectors — as the exchange rate fluctuates around its fundamental value. That is an important advantage. That advantage was behind the decision of nearly all western European countries at the start of 1999 to form a **monetary union**: to fix their exchange rates against each other irrevocably, so that even their national currencies will eventually disappear.

Fixed exchange rate systems avoid some political vulnerabilities as well. Large exchange rate swings are a powerful source of political turmoil. This political turmoil is avoided by fixed exchange rate systems.

With a fixed exchange rate system the central bank has a well defined monetary policy, which involves controlling the money supply in order to maintain the exchange rate at its predetermined level. This monetary constraint imparts a discipline on monetary authorities and is an important advantage of a fixed exchange rate system. It is often argued that the high inflation policies of the 1970s, which followed the adoption of a flexible exchange rate system, point to an important disadvantage of the flexible exchange rate system: monetary independence of the flexible exchange rates may lead to lack of monetary discipline with adverse consequences, as was discussed in Chapters 11 and 12.

Also, with fixed exchange rates the central bank controls the money supply in order to keep the exchange rate fixed; that is, it stands ready to absorb all monetary shocks in order to achieve this objective. As such, if the economy is going through a period in which there are several shocks originating in the money market, fixed exchange rates will reduce fluctuations in output more than flexible exchange rates. Essentially, when the LM curve shifts as a result of a monetary shock, with fixed exchange rates the monetary authorities adjust the money supply in order to offset the shift.

COSTS OF FIXED EXCHANGE RATES

Under fixed exchange rates, monetary policy is tightly constrained by the requirement of maintaining the exchange rate at its fixed parity. Interest rates that are too low for too long exhaust foreign exchange reserves, and are followed either by a sharp tightening of monetary policy or by an abandonment of the fixed exchange rate. A floating exchange rate allows monetary policy to concentrate on maintaining full employment and low inflation at home — on attaining what economists call

internal balance. By contrast, under a fixed exchange rate system the level of interest rates must be devoted to maintaining **external balance** — the fixed exchange rate. And fixed exchange rates have the disadvantage of rapidly transmitting monetary or confidence shocks: Interest rates move in tandem all across the world in response to shocks. The central bank must respond to any shift in international investors' expectations of future profitability or future monetary policy by shifting short-term interest rates.

When shocks originate in the goods market, which shift the IS curve, the adjustment of the exchange rate under a flexible exchange rate system are such that they tend to offset the original IS shift. Hence, if, for example, firms are optimistic and investment expenditures increase, the IS curve shifts out and real interest rates increase, which then appreciates the domestic currency, thereby reducing net exports and shifting the IS curve back to its original position. Hence, we say when shocks originate in the goods market flexible exchange rates will reduce fluctuations in output more than fixed exchange rates.

This is the cost–benefit calculation facing those who have to choose between fixed and floating exchange rates. Is it more important to preserve the ability to use monetary policy to stabilize the domestic economy, rather than dedicating monetary policy to maintaining a constant exchange rate? Or is it more important to preserve the constancy of international prices, and thus expand the volume of trade and the scope of the international division of labour?

RECAP   THE CHOICE OF EXCHANGE RATE SYSTEMS

Fixed exchange rate systems encourage international trade by reducing exchange rate fluctuations as a source of risk, but they also tightly constrain monetary policy. Is it more important to preserve the ability to use monetary policy to stabilize the domestic economy, or to reduce risk by eliminating exchange rate fluctuations? That is the question — the reason that central bankers and finance ministers get paid the big bucks.

16.3 CURRENCY UNIONS AND CURRENCY BOARDS

In this section we discuss other types of fixed exchange rate systems that have emerged in the past: currency unions and currency boards. The most important currency union was formed in 2002 when several European countries decided to give up their distinctive currencies in favour of a single currency, the euro. Examples of currency boards are those established by Hong Kong and some Latin American countries. In a currency board arrangement the monetary base of a country is fully backed by foreign assets alone.

CURRENCY UNION

Robert Mundell's (1961) theory of **optimum currency areas** set out the terms under which fixed exchange rates would work better than floating rates.[2] Mundell argued,

---

[2] See R. Mundell, "A Theory of Optimum Currency Areas," *American Economic Review*, (1961), pp. 657–65. This theory is one of the reasons that he was awarded the Nobel Prize in Economics in 1999.

the major reason not to have fixed exchange rates is that floating exchange rates allow adjustment to shocks that affect two countries differently. This benefit would be worth little if two countries suffer the same shocks, and react to them in the same way. It would also be worth little if factors of production possessed high mobility: because then the effects of shocks would be transient since labour and capital would adjust rapidly, and the benefits from different policy reactions to economic shocks would be small.

The theory of optimum currency areas provides the foundation for a successful monetary union among a group of countries or regions. A currency area is basically a collection of countries or regions that operate under a tight form of fixed exchange rates. In this system, bilateral exchange rates among countries can fluctuate within narrow bands around agreed upon central rates that cannot be changed unilaterally. The European Monetary System, until the financial crisis of 1992, is an example of a currency area. Based on Mundell's work, a currency area is *optimal* if the following criteria are met: (a) the regions are exposed to common economic shocks, (b) the shocks are similar or symmetric, (c) the regions have similar response to common shocks, and (d) if the regions are subject to asymmetric shocks, they need to be capable of quick adjustment, by means of high factor mobility, wage-and-price flexibility and fiscal transfers. (See Box 16.2.)

The most rigid form of an optimum currency area is a *monetary union*, in which there is a common currency, one central bank, and one monetary policy. The European Union is a recent example of a monetary union, with the European Central Bank being responsible for formulating and implementing the whole union's monetary policy.

The creation of the euro in the European Union and the signing of the North American Free Trade Agreement (NAFTA) in January 1994 have helped intensify the debate in Canada about the prospects of creating a monetary union in North America. Currently, there is an ongoing debate among Canadian economists and policy makers about the appropriate monetary and exchange rate regime for Canada. One group of economists, associated mainly with the research group at the Bank of Canada, adopts the view that a flexible exchange rate system is better for Canada than any type of fixed exchange rates including a monetary union within NAFTA. This view emphasizes structural differences between Canada and the U.S., as well as the desire to retain an independent monetary policy. In particular, it is pointed out that Canada has relatively large primary goods sectors that are subject to asymmetric shocks. NAFTA itself does not provide for free labour mobility within North America or fiscal cross-border transfers in order to smooth out these shocks. Consequently, it is important for Canada to retain flexible exchange rates, and hence an independent monetary policy to deal with the domestic impact of economic shocks.

Another group of economists, primarily from Simon Fraser and Queen's Universities, has reached different conclusions. They point out that Canada's experience with flexible exchange rates has been disappointing given the high volatility of real exchange rates and the prolonged misalignment of the Canadian dollar from its equilibrium value. A weak Canadian dollar contributes to the low productivity of the Canadian firms competing in the foreign sector and it biases investment in physical and human capital towards the U.S. Since NAFTA means greater trade links with the U.S., this group of economists favours the elimination of exchange rates and the creation of a North American monetary union — with a common currency that could perhaps be called the "*amero.*"

16.2

BOX

EXAMPLE

ARE WESTERN EUROPE AND THE UNITED STATES OPTIMAL CURRENCY AREAS?

Today the two largest economic regions within which exchange rates are fixed are the United States and western Europe's "euro zone." California, for example, does not have a separate exchange rate vis-à-vis the rest of the United States. Almost all of the countries of western Europe are now committed to their common currency, the euro. Does this make economic sense? Or should there be a separate "California dollar" to allow California to have a different monetary policy than the rest of America?

Few economists today would maintain that western Europe's euro zone meets Robert Mundell's criteria for an optimal currency area. Shocks to the economy of Portugal are very different from shocks to the economy of western Germany. Southern Italy has few similarities in economic structure with Denmark. Vulnerability to different shocks would be relatively unimportant if factors of production were mobile. But the fact that different European countries have different languages means there is little chance that a boom in Denmark and a bust in Portugal will see large-scale migration to compensate.

Why then has western Europe embarked on monetary union? One reason is that some economists and policy makers hope that the benefits from economic integration are very large indeed — large enough to offset even substantial costs from adopting a common currency. But the main reason is that European monetary unification is not so much an economic as a political project: an attempt to knit Europe together as a single entity whether or not monetary union makes narrow economic sense.

Practically all economists today believe, by contrast, that the United States is an optimal currency area, although the U.S. economy's regions are no more subject to common shocks than western Europe's countries are. The mid-1980s saw the high dollar decimate midwestern manufacturing while leaving most of the rest of the country much less affected. The health of the economies of Texas and Oklahoma still depends substantially on the price of oil. Southern California's defence-industry boom and bust of the 1980s and early 1990s and northern California's high-tech boom of the 1990s make it clear that California is so big a state that its component parts experience very different economic shocks. But even though the United States' component parts experience different shocks, factor mobility across the United States is remarkably high. Capital and workers move to where returns and wages are high with remarkable speed — fast enough that it is hard to believe that different parts of the United States could gain substantially from following the different monetary policies that separate currencies and floating exchange rates would allow.

A new currency within NAFTA may be politically infeasible in the near future given the importance and prominence of the US dollar in international monetary transactions. An alternative monetary arrangement that has received more media attention in Canada is **dollarization**. Dollarization is defined as the adoption of another country's currency to perform the main functions of money — medium of exchange, unit of account, and store of value. For Canada, naturally, dollarization would involve adoption of the US dollar.

Dollarization can occur either as *policy dollarization* or *market dollarization*. Policy dollarization involves an official decision by the authorities of a country to adopt another country's currency. This may be motivated by a desire to reduce inflation and improve the credibility of the country's monetary policy. Market dollarization, on the other hand, occurs through a market process, in which private individuals and firms use a foreign currency for their market transactions.

Canada's inflation rates have been close to the U.S. inflation rates historically and even below the U.S. level in recent times. Also, Canada's monetary policies have been similar to those of the U.S., including the credibility of these policies. Consequently, policy dollarization does not seem plausible for Canada in the near future. Further, the evidence for Canada shows that only a small fraction of Canadian businesses and individuals do their market transactions using the US dollar.[3] This evidence points to a slow process of market dollarization in Canada as well.

There are also other issues related to dollarization. One issue is the loss of *seigniorage* to the U.S. Fed. Seigniorage is the inflation tax that a central bank imposes on the economy when it needs to print new money. If Canada adopts the US dollar, all the seigniorage would go to the U.S. government. Another issue is the politics of dollarization. Once Canada is dollarized its monetary policy will be decided mainly by officials at the U.S. Fed, appointed by U.S. politicians, and not voted for by Canadians. Thus, dollarization may be associated with a lack of political accountability in Canada. For these reasons, we can conclude that the Canadian loonie will be around for a while longer.

As far as Canada, the United States, western Europe, and Japan are concerned, the issue of fixed versus floating exchange rates appears to have been decided: None of these countries is willing to sacrifice its freedom of action in monetary policy. Within western Europe the answer also appears clear: Monetary union means that there is now one pan-European monetary policy, and Italy, for example, no longer retains the ability to use monetary policy to lower interest rates in Milan when unemployment is relatively high. Elsewhere in the world, the question is still under debate.

Moreover, fixed exchange rate systems have one more major disadvantage: They seem to make large-scale currency crises more likely. The decade of the 1990s has seen three major large-scale currency crises, all of which have threatened prosperity in the immediately affected countries, and all of which raised fears (initially at least) of their much wider spread to the world economy as a whole.

CURRENCY BOARDS

A currency board is another example of a "hard currency fix" within the spectrum of fixed exchange rates. As will be seen shortly, it is a more stringent exchange rate arrangement than the Bretton Woods system of fixed exchange rates that was created by the major powers after the Second World War. A currency board arrangement has two important features. First, a country is committed to fixing the value of its currency relative to a major currency like the US dollar or the euro. Second, the country's monetary base (or central bank liabilities) must be fully backed by foreign currency assets.

Currency boards were originally created by the colonial powers of Europe and particularly by the British Empire, as a way of conducting the monetary policies of their colonies and collecting all the seigniorage from the printing of new money for them.

---

[3] See John Murray and James Powell (2003), "Dollarization in Canada: Where Does the Buck Stop?" *North American Journal of Economics and Finance*, 14, pp. 145–172.

The oldest currency board seems to be that of Falkland Islands, which began in 1899 with a fixed exchange rate: 1 Falkland pound = 1 UK pound. The Hong Kong currency board also originated the same way and had its currency linked to the British pound, although since the Second World War it has been pegged to the US dollar to date, at the exchange rate: 1$US = 7.80 $HK. Other more recent currency boards include those of Bosnia, Bulgaria, and Estonia that were created in the 1990s and linked their currencies to the German mark first, and later to the euro, and most notably Argentina's US dollar–based currency board that was created in 1991 and fell apart in 2002.[4]

Why would a country, in modern times, choose a currency board as its official exchange rate regime? Like any other monetary arrangement, there are always benefits and costs associated with a currency board. So for a country to adopt such a system voluntarily, it must be the case that the perceived *net* benefits are positive. A main cost of a currency board relates to a country's inability to pursue its own monetary policy, as it is the case under conventional fixed exchange rates. Another disadvantage relates to the second feature of a currency board, which means that the monetary authority of the country cannot buy and sell domestic assets to carry out open market operations if economic conditions dictate it. A currency board also places a severe constraint on a country's ability to carry out its fiscal policies, as then the government cannot finance its expenditures by printing money.

On the other hand, a currency board benefits a country because it removes the power from domestic monetary and government authorities of pursuing irresponsible monetary and fiscal policies that may lead to inflation, budget deficits, and a weak currency. Countries with a long history of high inflation gain directly from the adoption of a currency board because, this way, they buy the credibility of the monetary policies of the country to which they fix their currency. For example, Argentina had an inflation rate of 4,927 percent in 1989! In 1992, one year after the adoption of its currency board, inflation dropped to 17.5 percent and to 7.4, 3.9, and 1.6 percent in the following three years.

Currency boards provide monetary credibility and work smoothly if they coexist locally with flexible labour markets, efficient banking systems, and sound government finances. If these conditions are not met, currency crises that arise from expected devaluations can deal a serious blow to any currency board arrangement. For example, during the East Asian financial crisis in the mid-1990s the Hong Kong exchange rate was attacked by speculators, leading to high real interest rates and a recession. Similarly, inflexible labour markets and poor government finances were the main causes for the collapse of Argentina's currency board.

RECAP   CURRENCY UNIONS AND CURRENCY BOARDS

A currency union is formed when a group of countries give up their distinctive currencies in favour of a single currency. Robert Mundell set out the basic conditions that would make a currency union an optimal arrangement for a group of countries. A currency board is an arrangement whereby the central bank of a country backs up its currency by foreign assets alone. A country may decide to adopt a currency board in order to gain credibility after a period in which it has followed irresponsible monetary policies.

---

[4] For an overview of Argentina's currency board see Herbert G. Grubel, "The Merit of Hard Currency Fixes and Argentina's Experience with a Currency Board," pp. 49–74, in *Exchange Rates, Economic Integration and the International Economy*, edited by Leo Michelis and Mark Lovewell, APF Press, 2004.

16.4 CURRENCY CRISES

THE EUROPEAN CRISIS OF 1992

The first of the three major financial crises that hit the world economy in the 1990s came in the fall of 1992. In 1990 West German Chancellor Helmut Kohl reunified Germany, a country that had been divided since the end of World War II first into zones of occupation — French, British, American, and Russian — and then into two separate countries — East Germany and West Germany.

The two parts of Germany had very similar levels of economic development and economic structures before World War II. But since World War II they had diverged. West Germany had become one of the richest and most developed economies on earth, while East Germany had turned into a standard communist economy with dirty industry, inefficient factories, and inadequate infrastructure. Chancellor Kohl undertook a program of massive public investment to try to bring East Germany up to the West German standard as quickly as possible.

The expansion of German government purchases shifted the German IS curve to the right in the years after 1990. The German central bank, the Bundesbank, responded by raising real interest rates in order to keep real GDP in the range thought to be consistent with the Bundesbank's inflation targets (see Figure 16.4).

The rise in the real interest rate generated a rise in the German exchange rate vis-à-vis the dollar and the yen, and a sharp fall in net exports as capital flowed into Germany. The other countries of western Europe had then fixed their exchange rates relative to the German mark as part of the European Exchange Rate Mechanism (ERM). Britain, France, Italy, and other countries found themselves trapped: The rise in interest rates in Germany required that they too increase interest rates because r^f had risen in the equation

$$r = r^f + \frac{\varepsilon^e - \overline{\varepsilon}}{\overline{\varepsilon}}$$

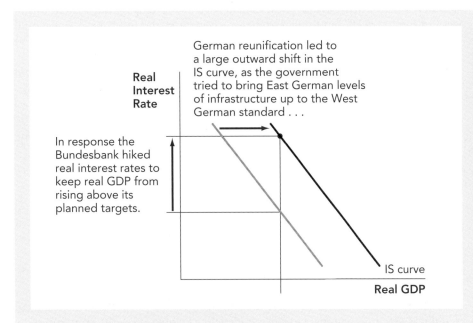

In response the Bundesbank hiked real interest rates to keep real GDP from rising above its planned targets.

German reunification led to a large outward shift in the IS curve, as the government tried to bring East German levels of infrastructure up to the West German standard . . .

Real Interest Rate

IS curve

Real GDP

FIGURE 16.4

German Fiscal Policy and Monetary Response in the Early 1990s

The reunification of Germany in 1990 led to a large outward shift in the IS curve, and a large increase in real interest rates as Germany's central bank, the Bundesbank, fought to keep real GDP from rising above potential output.

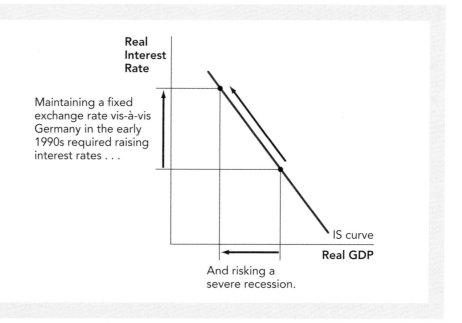

FIGURE 16.5

Effect of German Policy on Other European Countries

At the start of the 1990s governments in other western European countries were raising interest rates and contracting their economies, risking a recession, in order to maintain the parities of ERM exchange rates.

and r had to rise in response if the ERM was to be maintained. (In this equation $\overline{\varepsilon}$ is the real exchange rate set by the ERM.) Without the surge of spending found in Germany and without the ability or desire to rapidly shift policy to run large deficits, such increases in interest rates threatened to send the other European economies into recession (see Figure 16.5).

Politicians in other European countries — Britain, Sweden, Italy, France, and elsewhere — promised that their commitment to their fixed exchange rate parity was absolute. They promised that high interest rates and the risk of a domestic recession were prices worth paying for the benefits of a fixed exchange rate system within western Europe itself. But foreign exchange speculators did not believe they would keep their promise to maintain the fixed exchange rate parity when unemployment began to rise.

Thus foreign exchange speculators' expectations of the long-run fundamental real value of the exchange rate, ε^e, rose as well. This expectation that other European currencies would lose value vis-à-vis the German mark in the long run put their values under pressure in the short run as well.

The domestic real interest rate required to maintain the exchange rate parity, given by

$$r = r^f + \frac{\varepsilon^e - \overline{\varepsilon}}{\overline{\varepsilon}}$$

was rising not just because of higher real interest rates in Germany but also because of foreign exchange speculators' more pessimistic expectations. The governments of much of western Europe found themselves in a trap. Different governments undertook different strategies:

- First, some tried to avoid the consequences of the shift in expectations. They spent reserves like water in the hope that a demonstrated commitment to maintain the parity would reverse the shift in speculator expectations. All this did was give international currency traders like George Soros the opportunity to make profits measured in the billions by betting on the abandonment of the fixed exchange rate. Economists Maurice Obstfeld and Ken Rogoff report that the British government may have lost $7 billion in a few hours during the September 1992 speculative attack on the pound.

• Second, some tried to demonstrate that they would defend the parity no matter how high the interest rate required to keep the exchange rate fixed. The Swedish government raised its overnight interest rate to 500 percent per year for a brief time. But all this did was reinforce speculators' opinion that the political and economic cost of keeping the exchange rate parity was too high for governments that sought to win re-election.

• Third, some abandoned their parity against the German mark, and let their currencies float as they turned monetary policy for a while to setting interest rates consistent with *internal balance.*

In less than two months what had seemed a durable framework of fixed exchange rates in western Europe had collapsed into a floating-rate system.

But governments interested in long-run exchange stability within Europe regrouped. They proposed to try again to fix their exchange rates, with the European Economic and Monetary Union that began in January 1999. This time, however, they decided not to peg their exchange rates while keeping their national currencies (thus retaining at least the possibility of someday changing parities), but to eliminate their separate national currencies entirely: not fixed exchanged rates, but monetary union. The hope was to eliminate once and for all any fear or expectation that exchange rates might ever change again.

THE MEXICAN CRISIS OF 1994–1995

In the winter of 1994–1995 the second of the major currency crises of the 1990s hit the world economy. The Mexican peso crisis came as a shock to economists and to economic policy makers. Previous speculative attacks on and collapses in the value of currencies had occurred for one of two reasons: In situations of limited capital mobility, governments with overvalued exchange rates and large inflation-financed budget deficits had suffered speculative attacks. And in cases like western Europe in 1992, currencies had suffered speculative attacks when speculators judged that the policies needed to maintain fixed exchange rates had become inconsistent with the government's political survival.

Mexico, however, fit neither of these two cases. The government's budget was balanced, so an outbreak of renewed inflation was not generally expected. The government's willingness to raise interest rates was not in question: In the end the government of Mexico raised real interest rates to 40 percent per year during the crisis. The Mexican peso was not clearly overvalued: In the winter of 1993–1994 the Mexican government had conducted large exchange rate interventions and had eased monetary policy to try to keep the value of the peso from rising. Yet the Mexican peso lost half of its value in four months starting in December of 1994. The peso fell from about 3.5 to about 7 to the US dollar before recovering somewhat in the summer of 1995 (see Figure 16.6).

The sudden reversal of investor expectations about the long-run value of the Mexican peso was startling. At the start of 1994 Mexico had just joined the world's club of industrialized countries, the Organisation for Economic Cooperation and Development (OECD). It had just entered into the North American Free Trade Agreement (NAFTA), which granted Mexico guaranteed tariff-free markets for its

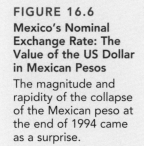

FIGURE 16.6

Mexico's Nominal Exchange Rate: The Value of the US Dollar in Mexican Pesos

The magnitude and rapidity of the collapse of the Mexican peso at the end of 1994 came as a surprise.

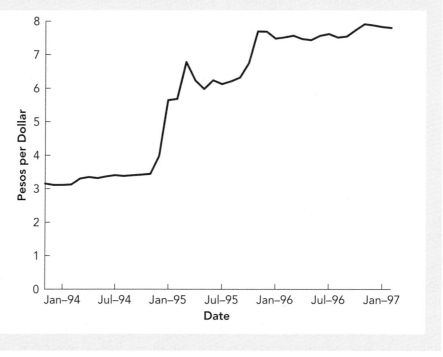

Source: J. Bradford DeLong and Barry J. Eichengreen, "Between Meltdown and Moral Hazard: Clinton Administration International Monetary and Financial Policy," in Jeffrey Frankel and Peter Orszag, eds., *American Economic Policy in the 1990s* (Cambridge, MA: MIT Press, 2002).

products in the largest consumer economy on earth. Expectations were that the Mexican peso would strengthen in real terms in the future, and that the profits from investing in Mexico were high.

Optimism eroded in 1994. At the start of the year a guerrilla uprising in the poor southern Mexican province of Chiapas cast doubt on political stability. Further doubt was cast by a wave of assassinations killing, among others, Luis Donaldo Colosio, the presidential candidate of the ruling Party of the Revolution (Institutionalized) (PRI). During the presidential election year of 1994 itself, the central bank raised the money supply, causing some international investors to worry that macroeconomic policy was more political and less "technocratic" than they had thought. All of these events plus a wave of pessimism reduced foreign exchange speculators' estimates of the long-run value of the Mexican peso, and raised their assessment of the value of the long-run exchange rate, fundamental ε^e.

During 1994 the Mexican government spent $50 billion in foreign exchange reserves supporting the peso, believing at each moment that the adverse shift in expectations had to turn around. It did not. By the end of 1994 the Mexican government was out of foreign exchange reserves. And so it devalued the peso, and let it float against the dollar.

The devaluation of the peso had destructive consequences, however. First, a great many — naïve — investors in New York and elsewhere had believed the Mexican government when it said that it would do whatever was necessary to defend the value of the peso. The increase in the value of the Mexican exchange rate ε led to a further fall in the perceived fundamental value of the peso — a rise in the expected exchange rate ε^e — which added to pressure for further depreciation and a further rise in the exchange rate ε. A more serious problem soon became clear: Much of the Mexican government's debt was indexed to the dollar in the form of securities called *tesebonos*. Each depreciation of the peso raised the peso value of the Mexican government's debt, increasing the temptation for the Mexican government to default on its debt, and the resulting financial distress led to further rises in foreign exchange speculators' opinions of ε^e.

The Mexican government seemed faced with a horrible choice. The first option was to raise interest rates to defend the peso, but adverse movements in foreign exchange speculator expectations meant that the level of interest rates that would be required by the formula

$$r = r^f + \frac{\varepsilon^e - \overline{\varepsilon}}{\overline{\varepsilon}}$$

was a level that would produce a Great Depression in Mexico. This first option would produce catastrophe.

The second option was to keep interest rates low and let the value of foreign currency rise much further. This would mean that Mexican companies — and the Mexican government — would be unable to pay their dollar-denominated and dollar-interest debts. Companies would declare bankruptcy. The government would default on its debt. Mexican exports would fall because foreign creditors would try to seize Mexican goods as soon as they left the country. Mexican imports would fall because foreign creditors would try to seize goods purchased by Mexico before they entered the country.

The result would be to delink Mexico from the world economy. Mexico's foreign trade would fall drastically. Meanwhile, international committees of lenders and creditors would thrash out a settlement of the bankruptcies with Mexican companies and the default with the Mexican government. This second option would produce catastrophe too. The Mexican government of Presidents Salinas and Zedillo had bet Mexico's economic future on increased integration with the world economy and the use of foreign capital to finance domestic industrialization.

The U.S. government and the IMF tried to give the Mexican government more options. The U.S. administration proposed loan guarantees to Mexico. But these guarantees fell through because neither then Speaker of the House Newt Gingrich nor then Majority Leader of the Senate Robert Dole nor other congressional leaders were willing to spend political capital on the issues. The administration then made direct loans to Mexico out of the U.S. Treasury's Exchange Stabilization Fund. These built Mexico's foreign-exchange reserves back to a level where it could support the peso to some degree without pushing domestic interest rates to Great Depression–causing levels.

These loans allowed the Mexican government to refinance its debt, and helped restore confidence that the Mexican government would not be forced into hyperinflation or resort to default. As time passed, Wall Street investors calmed down too. They recognized that Mexico was still the same country with relatively bright economic growth prospects, with promises of financial support if necessary from the U.S. Treasury and the IMF, and with NAFTA-guaranteed tariff-free access to the largest market for exports in the world. Thus the Mexican economic meltdown of 1994–1995 was a short, sharp recession that reduced Mexican real GDP by about 6 percent, but that was then followed by resumed economic growth.

The central lessons were two: First, the views of foreign exchange speculators could change radically with extraordinary speed. Second, developing countries that had not carefully prepared beforehand were extremely vulnerable to the shocks that such changes in international expectations could deliver.

THE EAST ASIAN CRISIS OF 1997–1998

Two and a half years after the beginning of the Mexican crisis, the third international financial crisis of the 1990s hit the world economy. For 20 years before 1997 the economies of the East Asian Pacific rim had been the fastest-growing economies the world had ever seen. But in mid-1997 foreign investors began to worry about the long-run sustainability of the East Asian miracle and the growing overhang of non-performing loans in East Asian economies. They began to change their opinions of the fundamental long-term value ε^e of East Asia's exchange rates.

In Thailand, Malaysia, South Korea, and Indonesia the values of domestic currency fell, and once again falling currency values caused a further swing in foreign exchange speculators' expectations of ε^e. Indonesia was hit the worst: Real GDP fell by one-sixth in 1998; the Indonesian currency, the rupiah, lost three-quarters of its nominal value against the dollar; and short-term real interest rates rose to 30 percent and nominal interest rates to 60 percent. Figure 16.7 shows the shock to two other currencies' exchange rates.

Once foreign exchange speculators began lowering their estimates of the long-run value of investments in East Asia, other, deeper problems in the Asian economies became apparent and were magnified. As East Asian exchange rates fell, it became clear that many of East Asia's banks and companies had borrowed heavily abroad in amounts denominated in dollars or yen. They had used those borrowings to make loans to the politically well connected, or to make investments that turned out not to be profitable in the long run.

The fact that East Asia's financial system was based on close links between governments, banks, and businesses — and that it was very difficult to obtain financial accounts from any East Asian organization — increased fear that more East Asian banks and companies were bankrupt than had been thought. This caused a further increase in foreign exchange speculators' views of the long-run exchange rate fundamental.

The vicious circle continued. Each loss of value in the exchange rate increased the burden of foreign-denominated debt and increased the likelihood of general bankruptcy. Each increase in the perceived burden of foreign-denominated debt caused a further loss of value in the exchange rate. Poor bank regulation had created a situation in which a small initial shock to exchange rate confidence could produce a major crisis. The shorter term the debt held by a country and its citizens, the more easily capital can flee — and the larger is the impact of the crisis.

As the Asian crisis developed, the IMF stepped in with substantial loans to boost foreign exchange reserves, made in return for promises to improve bank regulation and reform the financial system. The hope was that short-term loans would allow East Asian economies to avoid catastrophe until the pendulum of Wall Street expectations began to swing back. The hope proved sound. Since mid-1998, investors in New York and elsewhere have remembered that East Asia's economies had been the fastest-growing in the world in the previous generation, and were in all likelihood good places to invest.

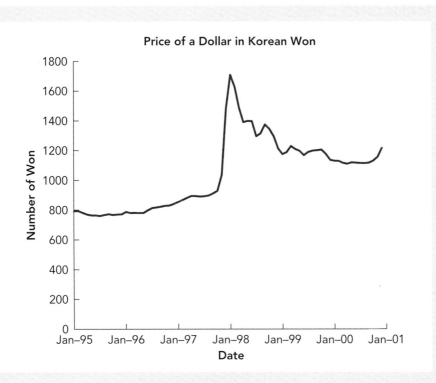

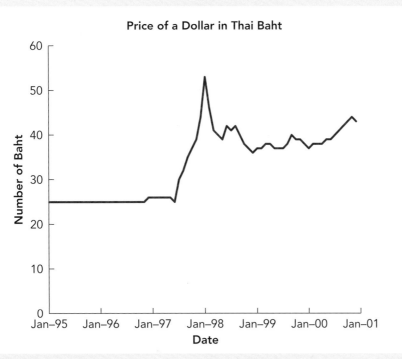

Source: J. Bradford DeLong and Barry J. Eichengreen, "Between Meltdown and Moral Hazard: Clinton Administration International Monetary and Financial Policy," in Jeffrey Frankel and Peter Orszag, eds., *American Economic Policy in the 1990s* (Cambridge, MA: MIT Press, 2002).

FIGURE 16.7

Exchange Rates during the Asian Currency Crisis

Before 1997 everyone saw East Asia's economies as having the best growth prospects in the world. In 1997 foreign investor opinion suddenly became much more pessimistic. But now it is optimistic again: Those who pulled their portfolios out of Korea, Thailand, and Malaysia during 1997 and 1998 have a hard time explaining what they were thinking.

MANAGING CRISES

We can see the interest parity condition:

$$r = r^f + \frac{\varepsilon^e - \varepsilon}{\varepsilon}$$

as offering a country a menu of choices for the value of foreign goods and currency ε and the value of the domestic real interest rate r. The higher the domestic real interest rate r, the more appreciated is the exchange rate, and the lower is the value of ε.

If for any of a number of reasons speculators lose confidence in the future of the economy, their assessment of the fundamental price of foreign goods and currency, ε^e, suddenly and massively shifts. The menu of choices that a country has for its combination interest rate r and the exchange rate ε suddenly deteriorates. If the interest rate r is to remain unchanged, the value ε of the real home currency price of foreign exchange must rise a good deal. If the exchange rate ε is to remain unchanged, then the domestic real interest rate r must rise a good deal. Raising interest rates appears unattractive because it will create a recession. No domestic purpose would be served by such a recession: it is just the result of foreign investors' change of opinion. Thus, letting the exchange rate depreciate would seem to be the natural, inevitable policy choice. A sudden panic by foreign-exchange speculators is a sudden fall in demand for your country's products: international investors are no longer willing to hold your country's bonds at prices and interest rates that they were happy with last month. What does a business firm do when all of a sudden demand for the products it makes falls? The firm cuts its price. Perhaps a country faced with a sudden fall in demand for the products it makes should do the same: it should "cut its price." And the easiest way for a country to cut its price is to let the home-currency value of foreign currency and goods rise.

Yet throughout the 1990s, whenever international investors have suddenly turned pessimistic about investing in a country, observers have reacted with shock and horror when the value of foreign currency rises. This was the story in the collapse of the European Monetary System in 1992, the collapse of the Mexican peso in 1994–95, and the East Asian financial crisis of 1997–98. In all these cases the trigger of the crisis was a sudden change of heart on the part of investors in the world economy's industrial core — in New York, Frankfurt, London, and Tokyo.

Economists will long argue the question as to whether it was the relative optimism of investors before the crisis or the relative pessimism of international investors after the crisis that was the irrational speculative wave. The right answer is probably "yes"; financial markets were excessively enthusiastic before the crisis and were excessively pessimistic afterwards. But why did such changes in international investor sentiment cause a *crisis* rather than an embarrassment? Why not let the exchange rate depreciate — the value of foreign currency rise — and keep domestic monetary and fiscal policy aimed at maintaining internal balance?

The answer appears to be that letting the value of foreign currency rise is dangerous if banks, businesses, and governments have borrowed massively abroad in foreign currencies. Then a depreciation of the exchange rate bankrupts the economy: the foreign-currency value of all the foreign-currency and business assets are halved by the depreciation, while the home-currency value of their liabilities is unchanged. Such an interlinked chain of general bankruptcies destroys the economy's ability to transform household savings into investment and shifts the IS curve far and fast back to the left. Such chains of bankruptcies are the stuff of which Great Depressions are made.

There are some things that should surely have been done to reduce vulnerability to a crisis. Strongly discourage — that is, tax — borrowers from borrowing in foreign currencies. If you are going to accept free international capital flows (in an attempt to use foreign financing for your industrial revolution), then be sure that your exchange rate can float without causing trouble for the domestic economy. If your exchange rate must stay fixed (for inflation fighting or other reasons), then recognize that an important part of keeping it fixed is controls over capital movements.

But once the crisis has hit, good options are rare. Is there a possible path to safety? Can you raise interest rates enough to keep the depreciation from triggering bankruptcy and hyperinflation while still avoiding a high-interest-rate-generated recession? Can you depreciate the exchange rate far enough to restore demand for home-produced goods without depreciating it so far as to bankrupt local businesses and banks?

Maybe.

The dilemmas are real. It is economic policy malpractice to claim that it is obvious that in a financial crisis interest rates should not be raised and the exchange rate allowed to find its own panicked-market level even if banks and firms have large foreign-currency debts. It is also economic policy malpractice to claim that in a financial crisis interest rates should be raised high enough to keep the exchange rate from falling at all. It's not that simple. So if sudden changes of opinion by international investors cause so much trouble, shouldn't we keep such sudden changes of opinion from having destructive effects? Shouldn't we use capital controls and other devices to keep international flows of investment small, manageable, and firmly corralled?

Once again, maybe.

The first generation of post–World War II economists — John Maynard Keynes, Harry Dexter White, and their students — would have said, "Yes." Sudden changes of opinion on the part of international investors can cause enormous damage to countries that allow free movement of capital. Such sudden changes of opinion are a frequent fact of life. Therefore, make it illegal, or at least very difficult, to borrow from and lend to, invest in, or withdraw investments from foreign countries. The second and third generations of post–World War II economists had a different view. They regretted that capital controls kept people with money to lend in the industrial core away from people who could make good use of the money to expand economic growth. The balance of opinion shifted to the view that too much was sacrificed in economic growth at the periphery for whatever reduction in instability capital controls produced. Moreover, a regime of capital controls encouraged corruption. Often it was the cousin of the wife of the vice minister of finance who received permission to borrow abroad. Thus, capital controls paved the way to kleptocracy: rule by the thieves.

So today we have the benefits of free international flows of capital. The ability to borrow from abroad does promise to give successful emerging market economies the power to cut a decade or two off the time it would take for them to industrialize. It promises to give investors in the world economy's industrial core the opportunity to earn higher rates of return. But this free flow of financial capital also is giving us a major international financial crisis every three years or so.

What is to be done will be one of the major economic policy debates of the next decade. Should we try to move toward a system in which capital is even more mobile than it is today, but in which international financial crises may become an even more

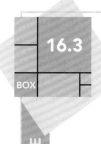

BOX 16.3

THE ARGENTINEAN CRISIS

During the 1990s, some economists argued that the reason that economies such as Mexico, Korea, Thailand, Malaysia, Indonesia, and Brazil were subject to such sharp financial crises was that their exchange rates were not fixed enough. When a crisis developed, the fact that the government *could* change the exchange rate meant that financiers feared that the government *would* change the exchange rate. The result was large-scale capital flight, which triggered the devaluation financiers had feared, and the devaluation of the home currency set off the chain of threatened bankruptcies that turned an adjustment of international prices into a full-blown crisis. If, some economists argued, the government lacked the power to change the exchange rate, no one would fear devaluation, capital flight would be avoided, and the crisis would never occur.

The collapse of the Argentinean economy at the end of 2001 provides a test case for this theory. And the answer appears to be, "No." Even if — as the Argentinean government did — the government delegates control over the exchange rate to an external authority, a "currency board," and assigns the currency board the mission of keeping the exchange rate fixed, a large-scale financial crisis is still possible. And Argentina has had one: Argentinean GDP declined by 7.5 percent in 2002.

What happened? Argentina's federal and state governments did not balance their budgets. As long as the Argentinean economy was growing, the fiscal deficits were of little concern. But internal inflation made Argentina's exports uncompetitive. The fear that the currency board might someday end made Argentina's interest rates higher than those elsewhere. High interest rates tended to discourage investment. The resulting decline in real aggregate demand meant recession. Recession meant larger fiscal deficits.

In the end, a government deficit must lead to one of three things: taxes must be raised, inflation must take hold and expropriate the debt holders, or the government must formally default. The failure of Argentina's government to effectively collect the taxes due it under law meant that as 2000 and 2001 proceeded, confidence that taxes would be raised diminished. Faced with a growing national debt, the currency board no longer served as a source of confidence — that the government lacked the power to change the exchange rate was no longer reassuring. And so the same process of large-scale capital flight that had produced the earlier crises was set in motion in Argentina at the end of 2001 as well. The crisis in Argentina was so severe that the government defaulted on its debt in 2001.

In recent years, the IMF has been willing to make loans to countries in severe economic crises, such as Argentina, conditional on certain economic reforms. Such IMF loans were very helpful for East Asian countries during their economic crisis in the late-1990s and for Argentina in its crisis of the early 2000s.

common occurrence? Or should we try to move toward a system in which capital is less mobile — more controlled — and in which some of the benefits of international investment are traded for less vulnerability to financial crises? We don't have to have a global economy as vulnerable to currency crises as the economy of the 1990s was.

http://www.imf.org/
http://www.worldbank.org/

CHAPTER SUMMARY

1. For most of the past century, the world has operated with fixed exchange rates — not, as today, with floating exchange rates.

2. Under fixed exchange rates, monetary policy has only very limited freedom to respond to domestic conditions. Instead, the main goal of monetary policy is to adjust interest rates to maintain the fixed exchange rate.

3. Why would a country adopt fixed exchange rates? To make it easier to trade by making foreign prices more predictable and less volatile. Fixed exchange rate systems increase the volume of trade and encourage the international division of labour.

4. Nevertheless, in the past generation countries have usually concluded that freedom to set their own monetary policies to satisfy domestic concerns is more important than the international integration benefits of fixed exchange rates.

5. An exception is western Europe, which is in the process of permanently and irrevocably fixing its exchange rates via a monetary union.

6. Wide swings in foreign exchange speculators' views of countries' future prospects have caused three major currency crises in the 1990s.

7. Such currency crises, although triggered by speculative changes in opinion, were greatly worsened by poor bank regulation and other policies that threatened to send economies subject to capital flight into a vicious spiral ending in depression and hyperinflation.

KEY TERMS

currency arbitrage (p. 477)

currency crisis (p. 491)

dollarization (p. 488)

external balance (p. 486)

fixed exchange rates (p. 477)

floating exchange rates (p. 476)

foreign exchange reserves (p. 479)

gold standard (p. 477)

internal balance (p. 486)

monetary union (p. 485)

optimum currency areas (p. 486)

ANALYTICAL EXERCISES

1. Why does a country's fixing the value of its currency in terms of gold also fix its nominal exchange rate?

2. Why do many economists think that a gold standard tends to put contractionary and deflationary pressure on economies that adhere to it?

3. What are the principal benefits of fixed exchange rates?

4. What are the principal costs of fixed exchange rates?

5. Why did the 1990s see so many international financial crises?

POLICY EXERCISES

1. What were the main principles that guided the Bretton Woods system? What were the circumstances that led to the demise of the Bretton Woods system?

2. Define the concept of arbitrage, and describe how it helps equate the price of a good across locations.

3. According to Robert Mundell, what constitutes an "optimal currency area"? What is the rationale behind his reasoning?

4. Suppose that a developing country with low capital mobility finds that foreign exchange speculators' views of the long-run value of its currency ε^e have suddenly shifted upward to 130, but that it wishes to maintain its pegged exchange rate $\bar{\varepsilon}$ of 100 and also keep domestic interest rates from rising above foreign interest rates. In the formula

$$r = r^f + \frac{\varepsilon^e - \bar{\varepsilon}}{\bar{\varepsilon}} + \theta \times \Delta R$$

if $\theta = 1$, and the relevant period of time is one month, how fast will the country lose reserves if it tries to maintain both its pegged exchange rate and the (relatively) low real interest rate? How high would it have to raise the domestic real interest rate above foreign rates to stop its loss of reserves?

5. Suppose you are asked to analyze whether Europe's monetary union was a mistake. What kinds of evidence would you look for to try to make up your mind?

6. Suppose you are asked whether Canada should *dollarize* — that is, fix its exchange rate with the United States once and for all by adopting the US dollar as its own internal currency. What kinds of evidence would you look for to try to determine whether such dollarization is a good idea or not?

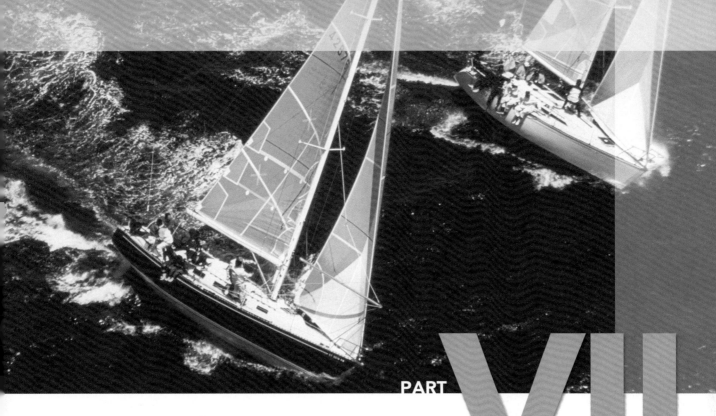

PART VII

Future Prospects and Epilogue

So far in this book, we have studied models and important issues that are relevant to any economy, with special emphasis on the workings of the open economy and the issues that have confronted the Canadian economy.

In this Part of the book we sum up what we have studied so far, and discuss what lies ahead for macroeconomists. In Chapter 17 we discuss how macroeconomics has been changed by the writings of great twentieth century economists, and how it is expected to be changed by the works of current and future economists. The Epilogue sums up the book.

17

The Future of Macroeconomics

QUESTIONS

What might the future of macroeconomics bring? How might the macroeconomics taught two decades from now differ from the macroeconomics that is taught today?

What have been the principal changes in the way macroeconomics is taught over the past 20 years?

What additional changes took place in the 20 years before that — from roughly 1960 to roughly 1980?

What direction will macroeconomics take if the real-business-cycle research program is successful?

What direction will macroeconomics take if the new Keynesian research program proves successful?

How will economists understand the foundations behind the power of monetary policy?

The past 16 chapters of this book have given a historically informed long-run, growth-stressing, new Keynesian view of macroeconomics. But that is not all of macroeconomics — there are other currents of thought and other live research programs. What is the past, and what might be the future of macroeconomics? This chapter takes a look back at the history of macroeconomics, and then looks forward and sketches a few outlines of what the future of macroeconomics might be.

If one thing is certain it is that we will know different (and, we hope, know more about) macroeconomics in a decade than we do today. What will be taught in macroeconomics courses in 20 years will not be the same as what is taught today.

17.1 THE PAST OF MACROECONOMICS

THE AGE OF JOHN MAYNARD KEYNES

Macroeconomics as a discipline is to a remarkable extent the creation of John Maynard Keynes. His 1936 book *The General Theory of Employment, Interest, and Money* shifted economic research and macroeconomic thought into new and different directions that have led us where we are today. The *General Theory's* extraordinary impact was in large part a result of the then-ongoing Great Depression. Other and previous approaches to understanding business cycles had little useful to say about it. Keynes had a lot to say.

Keynes's book emphasized (a) the role of expectations of future profits in determining investment, (b) the volatility of expectations of future profits, (c) the power of the government to affect the economy through fiscal and monetary policy, and (d) the multiplier process, which amplified the effects of both private-sector shocks and public-sector policies on aggregate demand. It swept the intellectual field, and shaped modern macroeconomics.

By a decade or so after World War II much of the analytical apparatus used in this textbook was already in place. The IS-LM model was developed by economists John Hicks and Alvin Hansen. Other economists developed the approaches used in this textbook to understanding consumption (Milton Friedman and Franco Modigliani), investment (Dale Jorgenson, James Tobin, and many others), and the relationship between interest rates and the money supply (James Tobin once again, along with many others). The difference between the behaviour of the macroeconomy in the flexible-price long run and the fixed-price short run was clarified by many economists (here Franco Modigliani was again the major contributor). The Solow growth model of Chapter 3 was developed by — no surprise — Robert Solow.

This is not to say that the bulk of this textbook stands as it would have been written back in 1960. Macroeconomics textbooks in 1960 had next to no discussion of the relationship between production and inflation. They had little discussion of expectations. The short run was seen as lasting for decades, and analysis of the long-run flexible-price model was rarely included in undergraduate courses. Textbooks in 1960 also downplayed monetary policy and emphasized fiscal policy: Investment was seen as responding little to changes in interest rates, and estimates of the multiplier were much higher than we believe today to be correct for now or for then.

THE AGE OF MILTON FRIEDMAN AND ROBERT LUCAS

Between 1960 and 1980 a good deal of the rest of the meat of this textbook was added to macroeconomic views. Powerful critiques of the then-established conventional wisdom of macroeconomics were made first by Milton Friedman and then by Robert Lucas, both of whom made their intellectual home at the University of Chicago.

Milton Friedman's critique of the then-dominant tradition in macroeconomics had four major parts. The first was that the standard models of the time greatly overestimated the government's ability to manage and control the economy. Great uncertainty, long lags, and variable effects of policy actions placed extremely tight limits on the ability of the government to smooth out recessions and avoid periods of high unemployment. The second was that the standard models greatly overestimated the power of fiscal policy and greatly underestimated the power of monetary policy. The third was that the measurement of the money supply told you most of what you needed to know about how economic policy was working.

The fourth was the idea of the natural rate of unemployment, developed by Friedman and Edward Phelps in the second half of the 1960s. To the extent that macroeconomists in the early 1960s talked about aggregate supply and inflation at all, they tended to follow the lead of economists who took the location of the short-run Phillips curve to be fixed. A given level of unemployment would produce a fixed, unchanging rate of inflation with no feedback of past inflation on expected inflation and no shifts in the natural rate of unemployment. Friedman and Phelps argued that high past inflation would raise expected inflation, and that if unemployment were kept below its natural rate then the Phillips curve would shift upward over time, generating higher and higher inflation.

The "stagflation" of the 1970s proved Friedman and Phelps to be completely correct on their fourth point. In less than a decade the economics profession shifted to the "accelerationist" Phillips curve that we use today. Friedman's first and second points also became part of the received wisdom. Only the claim that the money supply was the sole important variable for understanding macroeconomic policy failed to win broad acceptance.

But Milton Friedman's "**monetarist**" critique was only the first half of the successful revisionist challenge to the doctrines of the post–World War II **Keynesians.** The "rational-expectations" macroeconomists — Robert Lucas, Thomas Sargent, Robert Barro, and others — argued that Keynesian economics had failed to think through the importance of expectations.

The rational-expectations economists assumed that people were doing the best they could to figure out the structure of the economy in which they lived. Because standard Keynesian models did not pay enough attention to expectations, the models failed to recognize that systematic changes in economic policy would change the parameters of the consumption and investment functions as well as the location of the Phillips curve. Thus macroeconomic models that took estimated consumption functions, investment functions, and Phillips curves as building blocks would blow up in the face of policy makers.

Once again the critique was incorporated into the mainstream quite rapidly. As MIT economist Olivier Blanchard puts it, the "idea that rational expectations was the right working assumption gained wide acceptance … not … because all macro-economists believe that people, firms, and participants … always form expectations rationally … [but because] rational expectations appears to be a natural benchmark, at least until economists have made progress … understanding … actual expectations." By the mid-1980s the intellectual structure of the version of modern macroeconomics presented in this book was largely complete.

And since? The late 1980s and 1990s were a time of idea generation and exploration. They saw macroeconomists exploring and testing a large number of different ideas and models. It was an age in which the set of possible approaches expanded, but in which the mainstream policy-analytic position of macroeconomists did not shift much. If the past is any guide, such a period of exploration and experimentation will eventually be followed by another period of successful critique, during which the mainstream of macroeconomics will once again change substantially and rapidly as it did in the 1970s and early 1980s.

What might the future of macroeconomics bring?

17.2 THE FUTURE OF MACROECONOMICS: "REAL" BUSINESS CYCLES

ONE POSSIBLE ROAD

One place where the future of macroeconomics might lie is in the theory of "**real**" **business cycle**s, briefly sketched in Chapter 6. The fundamental premise of this line of thinking is that all the other macroeconomists took a wrong turn a long time ago. It is more than half a century since economists turned away from the line of analysis of Joseph Schumpeter and toward that of the monetarists and Keynesians. One possibility is that this was, in the long run, a mistake.

John Maynard Keynes, Irving Fisher, Milton Friedman, Paul Samuelson, and all of the economists working in both Keynesian and monetarist traditions believe that there are two key elements to understanding business cycles. First, you need to understand the determinants of nominal aggregate demand. Second, you need to understand the division of changes in nominal aggregate demand into changes in production (and employment) on the one hand and changes in prices (inflation or deflation) on the other. Thus Keynesians and monetarists think about the velocity of money, the determinants of investment spending, the multiplier, crowding out, the natural rate of unemployment, the rate of expected inflation, the Phillips curve, and other related topics.

To real-business-cycle economists in the Schumpeterian tradition like Edward Prescott, most of this is a waste of time. There are changes in nominal aggregate demand, but their impact falls mostly on prices and only a little in output and employment. To understand the roots of real fluctuations — fluctuations in the real economy — you need to follow a different road.

The theory of real business cycles begins with the fundamental assumption that the same theory that determines what happens in the long run — the theory of economic growth — should also be applied to explain fluctuations in production and employment in the short run. It is not that real-business-cycle theorists assume that prices are never rigid, or that markets always clear, or that every price paid for every good balances supply and demand at that moment. Instead, real-business-cycle theorists assume that the price rigidities and patterns of sluggish adjustment that Keynesians and monetarists see are simply not very relevant. They assume that a reasonable first approximation is to suppose that the money supply and the level of potential output determine the price level, and that the level of potential output at any moment is more or less equal to actual real GDP. They believe strongly in the *classical dichotomy*: Real fundamentals effectively determine the values of real quantities like GDP even in the short run, and nominal variables (like the money stock) determine the values of nominal quantities (like the price level).

THE UNEVENNESS OF ECONOMIC GROWTH

Some years there are adverse cost shocks — the tripling of world oil prices in 1973, for example. In such years it makes no sense to produce at what had been the normal level of economic output. The normal level balances social benefits and social costs: When social costs increase, the last 1 percent of output produced is certainly no longer worth the resources in people's time, used-up capital, depleted natural resources, and so on, that it consumes. So when an adverse cost shock hits the economy, a recession ought to follow and people ought to spend less time working: That's what an efficient economy would look like. Conversely, when a favourable cost shock hits the economy, it is advantageous to produce as much as possible: Because goods and services can then be produced at low cost, workers should work extra shifts and heavy demands should be placed on other resources.

But these are not the only "real" shocks to the economy's production possibilities that happen. Entrepreneurs have to guess at the future of technological development, and the value of new investment. There are moments when rapid technological innovation opens up new industries and new possibilities for investment. At such moments the stock market will be high, the returns to investment large, and so investment spending will be high and an efficient economy will be in a boom even though the new technologies have not yet increased real output. Current productivity is not especially high. But putting lots of new capital in place is uniquely profitable.

At other moments entrepreneurs will realize that they and those who came before them have been overly optimistic. Branches of industry that have been built up turn out to be unpromising. The socially optimal thing to do is not to invest, but instead to retrench: to cut back on investment spending and scrap capital until it becomes clear where there will be opportunities for profitable large-scale investment. Most of the work on real-business-cycle theory has concentrated on the effect of cost — supply — and productivity shocks on output. But shocks to future technologies are just as "real" in that they involve changes in the economy's long-run production possibilities. And they are large: Just look at the technology section of your newspaper, or visit Silicon Valley.

Is this theory of real business cycles a promising theory of economic fluctuations? Economists disagree. Perhaps fewer economists think that real-business-cycle theory is a progressive research program this year than thought so a decade ago, but that could change. Whether you think that real-business-cycle theory is promising depends on answers to three questions:

- Should the fact that a reduction in work hours shows up as some people becoming wholly unemployed change one's interpretation of what causes a decline in total hours worked?

- Should the fact that many wages and prices are not flexible lead one to assign a prominent role to monetary factors as causes of real fluctuations in output and employment?

- How large are technology shocks to the economy, anyway?

PROBLEMS OF REAL-BUSINESS-CYCLE THEORY

UNEMPLOYMENT

Real-business-cycle theory assumes that the total amount of hours worked at any moment is largely determined by how many hours it makes sense for people to work. The supply of hours worked is set at the point where the marginal displeasure of working an extra hour is just about equal to the marginal social product of an extra hour's work, given the marginal value of extra goods for consumption or for investment purposes.

When the marginal social product of labour is high — when labour is more than usually productive, or when there are extremely valuable opportunities to invest that an increase in work hours and thus of total product can take advantage of — workers are willing to work more hours. When labour is relatively unproductive, or when highly valuable investment opportunities are scarce, it makes sense for total work hours to fall. Instead of spending extra time on the job producing output of relatively little marginal value, take a week or two off and go on an extra vacation, or spend some extra time with the kids.

Such a willingness to work more hours when the incentive to work is relatively high and fewer hours when the incentive to work is relatively low is called an intertemporal substitution of labour. As an example, consider a student who needs to (a) take classes and (b) earn money to save toward some goal. It's hard to take classes and earn money at the same time, so the choice is between either working in the summer and taking classes in the winter, or working in the winter and taking classes in the summer. If the student works in the summer and gets paid at the end of the summer, then at the end of the winter the student will have $W_s(1 + r/2)$ dollars — the sum of his or her summer wage and the interest for half a year that he or she would earn by banking that money until it is needed at the end of the winter. If the student works in the winter, then at the end of the winter the student would have W_w dollars.

The real relative wage between the summer and the winter is thus equal to

$$\frac{W_s(1 + r/2)}{W_w}$$

The higher this quantity, the more likely the student is to choose summer rather than winter work. Thus the incentive to work hard now — accept lots of overtime, say — depends on three things: (a) the wage now, (b) the wage expected in the future, and (c) the real interest rate. Increases in the first and the third tend to lead people to postpone recreation and other nonwork uses of time to the future. Increases in the second tend to lead people to cut back on work effort now. If people are highly willing to shift their hours of work from season to season or from year to year, then one would expect fluctuations in current productivity and technological opportunities to lead to substantial fluctuations in employment.

But critics of real-business-cycle theory think that it makes little sense to analyze the total number of hours worked in the economy as if they were determined by the decisions of a representative worker. They point out that people change their weekly work hours by relatively little. People in the labour force want to work. When total work hours fall it isn't because people have chosen to work shorter shifts and avoid overtime, it is because people have lost their jobs. The unemployment rate fluctuates substantially over the business cycle. And high unemployment in a recession is not a market-clearing phenomenon: People don't say they are "taking an extra vacation" or "out of the labour force because wages will be higher next year"; people say they are "unemployed."

Advocates of real-business-cycle theory say that this critique misses the point. People stay unemployed because they would rather spend more time searching for a better job that matches their skills and pays more than the job they could get today. And the job they could get today pays relatively little either because labour productivity is not high, or because there are no extremely valuable uses in investment or consumption for the good produced by an extra amount of work.

TECHNOLOGY AND REAL BUSINESS CYCLES

According to real-business-cycle theories, production fluctuates because of the changing value of output and the changing productivity of the economy. When production technology improves, more is produced. When unique opportunities for investment open, more is produced. Perhaps recessions are times in which increases in costs — the tripling of oil prices in 1973, say — make it socially inefficient to run factories near capacity. Perhaps recessions are times in which everyone now recognizes that too much has been invested, and that it is better to cut back on investment than to continue to build up capital that adds little to the economy's productive capacity.

Critics of real-business-cycle theory concentrate their fire on the claim that the economy experiences large negative shocks to productivity. They claim that increases in costs like the 1973 oil shock are the exception rather than the rule. Critics tend to be silent on whether downturns in investment are to be understood as rational reactions to news about future growth and productivity, and have little to offer as alternative explanations of why investment fluctuates so much.

MONEY AND REAL BUSINESS CYCLES

http://www.bank-banque-canada.ca/

Real-business-cycle theorists tend to argue that monetary policy has little impact on production and employment, and that fluctuations in the money stock and interest rates are mostly reactions to changes already taking place in output and employment. But the Bank of Canada certainly believes that it affects the level of interest rates, that it makes decisions about the level of the money supply, and that its decisions cause changes in the level of production and output. Either everyone in the Bank of Canada's conference room is hopelessly deluded (and what they think are their decisions are instead the result of fluctuations in real activity that they do not consciously know about at the time they make their votes) or monetary policy has a powerful impact on production and employment.

ASSESSMENT

If we thought this line of research was truly the future of macroeconomics, we would have written a different book. Nevertheless these theorists make important points, especially those in what we see as the Schumpeterian wing of the real-business-cycle tradition. Economic growth is *not* smooth. It *does* proceed sector by sector. Shifts in investment — big backward-and-forward moves in the position of the IS curve — do arise out of changing beliefs about the current productivity of the economy and the future value of new investment.

The existence of real-business-cycle theory is a call for all economists to spend more time thinking about the determinants of investment fluctuations: either tying them to changes in productivity and the value of investment, or developing useful social-psychological theories of the shifts in animal spirits that cause such large movements in investment over time. Our guess is that a lot of what is now called real-business-cycle analysis will be incorporated into mainstream macroeconomics over the next two decades as the theory of growth is integrated with the theory of business cycles, and as economists make progress in understanding why investment is so volatile.

> **RECAP   THE FUTURE OF MACROECONOMICS: "REAL" BUSINESS CYCLES**
>
> Real-business-cycle theorists see booms as generated when rapid technological innovation opens up new industries and new possibilities for investment. At such moments the stock market will be high, the returns to investment large, and so investment spending will be high. Real-business-cycle theorists see recessions as generated when entrepreneurs conclude that those who came before them have been overly optimistic. The socially optimal thing to do is not to invest, but instead to retrench: to cut back on investment spending and scrap capital until it becomes clear where there will be opportunities for profitable large-scale investment.

17.3 THE FUTURE: NEW KEYNESIAN ECONOMICS

The second possible future for macroeconomics sees the continued development of the mainstream research program, as its weaknesses and incoherencies are slowly repaired.

Certainly the area of modern macroeconomics that is in least satisfactory shape is the area of aggregate supply. Why do changes in nominal aggregate demand show up as changes in the level of production and employment, and not just as changes in the level of prices? Since at least the 1930s, the mainstream of macroeconomics has attributed the sluggishness of aggregate supply — the fact that the Phillips curve has a slope, and is not vertical — to stickiness in wages and prices. Thus fluctuations in the nominal level of aggregate demand cause fluctuations in output and employment. But where does this stickiness and slow adjustment of wages and prices come from? After all, business cycles appear to be so unpleasant and costly to society as a whole that by now we should have found a way to greatly reduce the harmful macroeconomic consequences of price stickiness.

Thus a possible future direction for macroeconomics is a deep investigation into the sources of sluggish wage and price adjustment, and of aggregate supply. This research program has gained the name *new Keynesian economics*.

MENU COSTS

Prices do not adjust immediately and completely in the short run because it is costly to change them. A restaurant must print up a new menu; a mail-order firm must send out a new catalogue. Economists call these costs of changing prices **menu costs**. They are what lead firms to adjust prices once in a while — not, with a few exceptions, every second. In most cases such menu costs are small: It doesn't cost a firm very much to change its prices. But "small" does not mean "unimportant." As macroeconomists George Akerlof, Janet Yellen, and Greg Mankiw have stressed, it is entirely possible, in theory at least, for small menu costs at the level of an individual firm to have large effects on the economy as a whole.

A price adjustment or a failure to adjust prices on the part of one firm affects other firms. Whenever one particular business lowers its price, it frees up a little bit of nominal purchasing power. The extra nominal purchasing power that would have been spent buying that particular firm's product (but that wasn't spent because the price was lowered) is instead free to be spent on products made by other firms. As long as total nominal spending remains constant, a decline in one firm's price slightly increases demand for other firms' products. New Keynesian economists call this phenomenon an *aggregate demand externality*.

Because of such aggregate demand externalities, as long as total nominal demand is fixed, the economy as a whole benefits more by one firm's reduction in price than that one firm does. But the firm decides whether to cut its price depending on whether the benefit *to the firm* from cutting its price exceeds the menu costs the firm must pay. Thus the economy can get stuck in a situation in which no firm reduces its price — because no firm can see a private benefit in excess of its menu cost — even though the economy as a whole would benefit by vastly more than the sum of menu costs if all businesses were to reduce their prices.

STAGGERED PRICES AND COORDINATION FAILURES

Even if menu costs are not important, the fact that one firm's best choice for its price depends on the prices that other firms are charging may lead to sluggish adjustment in wages and prices even though individual prices are theoretically free to move without hindrance.

Macroeconomist John Taylor was the first to consider an economy in which large groups of workers sign three-year labour contracts. Those who negotiate their wages in years divisible by three will look forward at what demand and supply on the labour market is likely to be, but they will also look sideways, at firms that negotiated their labour contracts one or two years ago. Thus the wage negotiated this year will depend not just on what will happen but on what people one or two years ago — when the last set of contracts were signed — thought was likely to happen. The aggregate wage and price levels will thus exhibit inertia even without barriers to price flexibility when renegotiations occur, just because of the institutional structure of the economy.

Are such "**coordination failures**" caused by the fact that agents in the economy do not all make long-run decisions at the same time or are unable to commit to deciding in similar ways important causes of business cycles? Two decades ago economists thought that the answer was almost surely yes. Many studies were written comparing the U.S. system of wage negotiation with other, more centralized systems found in Germany and Japan that seemed less likely to lead to coordination failures.

Today, because of the relatively good macroeconomic performance of the U.S. economy, theories that point out structural flaws in U.S. macroeconomic institutions receive little attention. The theoretical point, however, remains unsettled.

ASSESSMENT

At the moment these ideas about the microfoundations of price stickiness are at the stage of just-so stories: plausible and possible mechanisms, but only that. There are no convincing quantitative analyses of just how much sluggishness in wage and price adjustment is contributed by each possible cause. There are no tests of one theory against another, and no predictions of the magnitude of price inertia that should emerge from any of the possible theoretical causes. In this sense, the theory of aggregate supply today is in a position roughly analogous to the position of the theory of aggregate demand just before John Maynard Keynes.

We have no doubt that the mechanisms of business cycles should be a large part of the future of economics. We should be able to learn a lot about which models of business cycles are potentially useful by turning theories loose on perhaps the greatest macroeconomic laboratory available: the extant record of macroeconomic historical statistics. A robust and useful theory of business cycles should be able to account for the patterns seen in the long-run data for many countries.

Our reading of the historical evidence is that business-cycle models that do not put monetary economics at the centre of analysis are inconsistent with the evidence on the behaviour of real exchange rates. Events like the comparative pattern of national recoveries from the Great Depression cannot be understood without placing prices that are sticky at the centre of the analysis as well. Thus we think that the new Keynesian research program is likely to play a stronger role in the future of macroeconomics than the real-business-cycle research program. But we have been wrong before.

RECAP   THE FUTURE: NEW KEYNESIAN ECONOMICS

Why do changes in nominal aggregate demand show up as changes in the level of production and employment, and not just as changes in the level of prices? The mainstream of macroeconomics has attributed this to stickiness in wages and prices. But where does this stickiness come from? One possibility is that small costs of changing prices on the part of individual firms have large effects because a price adjustment or a failure to adjust prices on the part of one firm affects other firms through *aggregate demand externalities*. Another possibility is that prices and wages are sticky because agents in the economy do not all make long-run decisions at the same time.

17.4 DEBTS AND DEFICITS, CONSUMPTION AND SAVING

Chapter 13 detailed two competing view of debts and deficits. According to one view fiscal deficits stimulate the economy in the short run as long as the central bank does not take action to neutralize the fiscal stimulus. In the long run, however, debts and deficits crowd out investment and shift the economy to a less favourable steady-state growth path. According to the alternative view, also known as the Ricardo-Barro view, it does not matter whether the government finances its expenditures by current taxes or by issuing bonds (debt); the two modes of financing a given amount of expenditures are equivalent, since debt-financing entails taxes in the future.

This controversy has very important implications regarding the way fiscal policy issues should be discussed. If one subscribes to the first view, then in studying fiscal policy issues one should concentrate on the effects of deficits on income and growth, as was discussed at length in Chapter 13. On the other hand, if one subscribes to the second view then it is more important to study the effects of distortions created by taxes, rather than the effects of debt. This view has led to a relatively new literature, which has found that variations in tax rates over time lead to large distortions in the economy. According to this view, again originating in the works of Robert Barro, the government should maintain fluctuations in tax rates at a minimum, by running deficits in times of relatively high expenditures and surpluses in times of relatively low expenditures. The debate on this issue, and the political economy implications of it, will occupy macroeconomists for many years to come.

In any case, the issue of whether government deficits matter is very closely related to the question of how and why people divide their income between consumption and saving. In the early part of the twentieth century it was relatively easy to justify a relatively high marginal propensity to consume. Most households had little if any savings. Most households found themselves unable to borrow. Hence they were *liquidity constrained:* They wished to spend more today, but could not find anyone to lend them the liquid wealth to enable them to do so. Thus one would expect a boost to income today to generate a large rise in consumption spending. Add to this the fact that buying consumer durables is in a sense as valid a way of saving for the future as putting money in the bank; then a high marginal propensity to consume and a strong multiplier process seem easy to understand.

The past 50 years, however, have seen steady and large increases in the flexibility of the financial system. Few Canadians today are without the ability to borrow to increase current consumption should they so wish. Those Canadians whose liquidity is constrained today receive a very small portion of total income, and a small portion of increases in total income. Thus economists' theories would predict that the marginal propensity to consume would have dropped far by today, and that the multiplier process would be more or less irrelevant to aggregate demand. Nevertheless, consumption still declines significantly when the economy goes into recession.

This consumption puzzle is another substantial hole in today's current macroeconomic knowledge. Many economists are trying to close it. Some, like Johns Hopkins macroeconomist Chris Carroll, argue that typical consumers are both impatient and strongly **risk averse.** Risk aversion makes them unwilling to borrow. Impatience makes them eager to spend increases in income. Thus the fact that improvements in financial flexibility means that consumers could borrow doesn't mean that they will. Other economists focus on the persistence of income changes, and say that current income is a good proxy for permanent income and hence should be a strong determinant of consumption. Still others — led by Chicago economist Richard Thaler — argue that it is time for economists to throw the simple-minded psychological theory of utility maximization overboard, and to take seriously what psychologists have to say about how humans reason.

It is unclear how this hole in macroeconomists' understanding will be resolved. It is clear, however, that whatever answer is reached to the puzzles regarding consumption and saving will also have a powerful impact on the debate over debts and deficits.

17.5 DOES MONETARY POLICY HAVE A LONG-RUN FUTURE?

When the Bank of Canada uses open-market operations to affect interest rates, it does so because its purchases or sales of T-bills raise or lower the supply of bank reserves in the economy, and so make it easier or harder for businesses to borrow money. But total commercial bank reserves in Canada amount to less than half a percent of GDP. A typical open-market operation is a few hundred million dollars.

In the context of an economy in which annual GDP is more than $1 trillion how is it that a swap of one government promise to pay (a T-bill) for another (a dollar bill) can cause big changes in the cost of borrowing money, and ultimately in the level and composition of economic activity?

This question has not been asked often enough in the past hundred years. Economists have tended to assume that monetary policy is powerful and that the reasons for its power are relatively uninteresting. They have by and large ignored the fact that to shift from an extremely tight monetary policy in which long-run nominal GDP growth is zero to a loose one in which long-run nominal GDP growth is 10 percent per year requires that the Bank of Canada increase purchases of T-bills by an average of only some $2 million a day.

Monetary policy is certainly powerful. But in at least one of the potential futures of macroeconomics the reasons for its power become very interesting indeed. For it is at least possible that the future evolution of the financial system might undermine the sources of influence that monetary policy today possesses.

The reasons that monetary policy has power today that economists usually bring forward rest on what Harvard macroeconomist Benjamin Friedman calls — politely — "a series of ... familiar fictions: Households and firms need currency to purchase goods ... nonbank financial institutions [cannot] create credit ... [and] so on."

The standard explanation is that open-market purchases of bills increase the reserve balances held by the bank where the seller of the bills receives payment. Thus the total volume of reserves in the banking system as a whole rises, and the banking system responds to this increase in reserves by increasing total credit in the economy by more than ten times the reserve increase. Because commercial banks must hold reserves, and because only the Bank of Canada can change the total amount of reserves, it has a uniquely strong ability to affect interest rates. In the standard story the central bank's power is further boosted because everyone in financial markets takes its actions today as a powerful signal of what its actions will be in the entire future.

The Bank of Canada's power, however, would be of little use if nobody much cared about keeping deposits at commercial banks, and nobody used reserve-backed commercial bank deposits as transactions balances. Looking to the future, it's likely that more and more transactions will be carried out not through cash or cheque but through credit cards, debit cards, smart cash cards now used in Europe, or other forms of electronic funds transfer at points of sale.

Will the future hold a gradual weakening of central bank power? Macroeconomists know that central banks today are powerful and are likely to remain so for at least a generation. But forecasting beyond that point requires a deeper knowledge and better models of the sources of central bank power than macroeconomists currently possess. This is thus another area in which the macroeconomics taught in the future is likely to be substantially different from the macroeconomics taught in the past.

CHAPTER SUMMARY

1. Modern macroeconomics has its origin in the Keynesian theories of the Great Depression and the immediate post-WWII era.

2. Modern macroeconomics was reforged by the monetarists under Milton Friedman in the 1960s and 1970s, and by the rational-expectations economists led by Robert Lucas in the 1970s and 1980s.

3. Perhaps the focus on aggregate demand will turn out in the long run to have been a false road. Perhaps a better theory of the macroeconomy can be built up out of the theory of real business cycles in the Schumpeterian tradition.

4. Perhaps the future of macroeconomics lies in a more detailed investigation of aggregate supply. Perhaps uncovering the reasons that prices are sticky will lead to the next wave of progress in macroeconomics.

5. The entire conventional analysis of debts and deficits is under challenge by Robert Barro, who argues that individuals are far-sighted and closely linked, and that they take action to neutralize the effects of many government policies.

6. The conventional analysis of consumption — the permanent income hypothesis — is also under challenge by more psychological approaches to understanding consumption.

7. The other possible interesting direction in which macroeconomics might evolve involves the future of monetary policy. How will the coming of the "new economy" and the changing institutional framework of transactions and settlements affect the power of monetary policy?

KEY TERMS

coordination failures (p. 512)

Keynesian (p. 506)

menu costs (p. 512)

monetarist (p. 506)

real business cycle (p. 507)

risk averse (p. 514)

staggered prices (p. 512)

ANALYTICAL EXERCISES

1. What are the principal pieces of real-business-cycle theory?

2. Why is it possible that real-business-cycle theory will play a much larger role in macroeconomics courses in the future than in the present?

3. In what areas do new Keynesian economists concentrate their research?

4. What is Ricardian equivalence? Why might it not be a good approximation to the way individuals actually behave?

5. Why do some economists fear that monetary policy is going to lose its effectiveness?

6. Use the theory of the intertemporal substitution of leisure to explain what will be the effect of an increase in interest rates on the supply of labour. What will be the effect of a permanent increase in income taxes? What will be the effect of a temporary increase in income taxes?

EPILOGUE

Macroeconomics is far from complete. It will not become complete in our or your or anyone's lifetime. One reason for this is that the subject is complicated. A second reason is that macroeconomists are pursuing an ever-changing and ever-moving target: As the economy changes, its macroeconomic behaviour changes as well. Four centuries ago (if there had been a macroeconomics course then) the macroeconomics of harvest failures would have been a big topic. Today it isn't. Many of what we see as important topics today will be dismissed as irrelevant a generation or a century from now. And much of what those societies will need answers to is unimportant to us, or unknown to us.

But here at the end of the book is the place to quickly look back over the entire text. There are a great many things that macroeconomists do know. And this is the place to summarize them, before going on to discuss what macroeconomists don't know, and what we believe macroeconomists will never know.

WHAT ECONOMISTS KNOW . . .

. . . ABOUT THE CURRENT STATE OF THE ECONOMY

Largely relying on government-collected statistics, economists know a substantial amount about the current state of the economy. They have good estimates of the level of potential output. They have good estimates of the current real wage level, of the amount of unemployment, and of the general state of the labour market. They have good estimates of the rate of inflation.

Economists' knowledge of the long-run pace of economic growth is, however, much more partial. The size and extent of the biases inevitably present in the national income and product accounts remain elusive. And economists' knowledge of the current state of the economy comes with a substantial lag: Economists know much more about the state of the economy last year than they do about the state of the economy today.

But all in all, the National Income and Expenditure Accounts — and the other largely government-collected economic statistics — give us a remarkable amount of knowledge about the current state of our economy. Certainly the amount of easily and publicly available information about the state of the Canadian macroeconomy today dwarfs the knowledge that even the best-informed in previous centuries had, or even the knowledge that the leaders presiding over the centrally planned economies of the twentieth century had of the real state of affairs.

. . . ABOUT LONG-RUN ECONOMIC GROWTH

http://www.statcan.ca/english/sdds/1901.htm

Economists also know a surprising amount about the preconditions of long-run growth. We know demography — Malthus, the population explosion, the demographic revolution, and the importance of education. We know that before the industrial revolution living standards were very low because in the race between human fertility, diminishing returns, and technological development the rate of technological progress was slow. We know that once human populations pass through a threshold level of material prosperity and literacy, population growth rates slow down drastically — the experience of western Europe suggests that negative population growth may be in humanity's future after the middle of the next century.

Economists understand the importance of a high rate of investment for achieving successful economic growth — both because capital goods amplify our skills and capabilities, and because much of modern technology that increases total factor productivity works only if it is accompanied by, embodied in, the right kinds of capital goods. A high rate of investment is key to a rapidly growing and relatively prosperous economy.

Economists also know that better *technology* — understood in both a broad and a narrow sense — is the single most important key to sustained progress in material standards of living. And here we believe economists have fallen down on the job: Macroeconomists know much less about the development and diffusion of this truly important source of growth, technology, than we should. But it is completely clear that a high rate of investment to generate a high capital–output ratio, a strong commitment to education to create a skilled and literate workforce (and a low rate of population growth), and better technology are the goals of economic policy as far as the long run is concerned.

Economists also know important things about how to achieve these goals of economic policy: The role of the government in economic development has become increasingly clear over the past generation. It is now clear that it is much easier to achieve successful long-run growth by relying on the market system to coordinate economic activity than by relying on central planning and central commands. Market economies appear to function well only if they are coupled with strong legal and institutional protections for private property. Overly mighty governments — governments that regard other people's things as the government's property — appear to be very bad for economic growth.

It is also clear that government policy needs to provide the market economy with the right incentives and signals if it is to function: Activities with negative externalities like pollution need to be penalized; activities with positive externalities like research and development need to be encouraged. Thus a government that protects property rights, promotes education, and promotes innovation seems important as a precondition for successful economic growth.

But our knowledge of economic growth is incomplete. The links between different kinds of investment and rates of total factor productivity growth and the mechanisms underlying the transfer of technology from rich countries to poor countries remain elusive.

. . . ABOUT BUSINESS CYCLES, UNEMPLOYMENT, AND INFLATION IN THE LONG RUN

Economists know that market economies are robust things. In the long run — and exceptional circumstances like the Great Depression aside — the market economy does tend to return to a position of nearly full employment. Markets for goods and for labour do — absent large blockages — reach something like a supply-and-demand equilibrium. In a recession it is safe to predict that the next five years will bring a boom. In a gigantic boom it is safe to predict that the next five years will bring a slowdown.

Thus economists know that shifts in government spending will crowd out (or crowd in) consumption and investment. They know that shortfalls of national saving or booms in investment will bring inflows of capital and the trade deficits needed to finance them. They know that the central bank's policy is in the long run the absolutely crucial determinant of the price level and the inflation rate.

. . . ABOUT BUSINESS CYCLES, UNEMPLOYMENT, AND INFLATION IN THE SHORT RUN

Economists know that the basic Keynesian sticky-price model still provides a good guide to the basic determinants of the level of aggregate demand. And the aggregate supply–Phillips curve diagram still provides a guide — not necessarily a good guide, but the best one we have — to the relationship between the level of real aggregate demand and the rate of price increase.

Because aggregate demand is the principal determinant of the level of GDP in the short run, anything that affects aggregate demand affects employment and output: fiscal policy, monetary policy, expectations, shocks to components of demand, shocks to the financial markets, changes in the international environment — all of these produce shifts in the equilibrium level of output.

Economists know that aggregate demand interacts with aggregate supply — the Phillips curve — to generate the inflation rate. And economists know that the Phillips curve is extremely volatile. The natural rate of unemployment can undergo substantial shifts much more rapidly than the changing composition of the labour force would suggest is possible. The expected rate of inflation depends critically on expectations of the central bank's competence and commitment to price stability.

. . . ABOUT THE MAKING OF MACROECONOMIC POLICY

Thus governments attempting to stabilize the economy face a hard task of damping out many kinds of shocks. Their task is made harder because shifts in economic policy have uncertain and delayed effects on spending: Policy affects output and prices with long and variable lags. Perhaps the first lesson of stabilization policy is that governments should not overestimate their power and attempt to do too much. The second lesson is that monetary policy is the most useful *discretionary* stabilization policy tool. And the third lesson is that automatic stabilizers — the fiscal automatic stabilizers in the government's budget and the financial automatic stabilizers of deposit insurance — are important factors that help limit the need for discretionary stabilization policy.

Economists have learned over the past two decades that peacetime inflation at a level high enough that it becomes an important part of voters' consciousness — inflation at a rate of even 10 percent per year — is politically unacceptable in modern industrial democracies. Voters appear to hate and loathe politicians who preside over such episodes of inflation. Why even moderate inflation should be viewed so negatively is somewhat of a mystery: Economists' attempts to model costs of inflation have a difficult time coming up with costs that justify the high political value of low inflation. It may be that people simply dislike the greater uncertainty that inflation generates. It may be that people are simply making a mistake — that they should not dislike inflation as much as they do.

But for whatever reason, it is clear that in a modern democracy, successful control of inflation must be a very high priority for public policy.

At the root, the ultimate determinant of inflation is growth in the money supply. Control the rate of growth of the money supply, and you control inflation. A central bank that loses sight of this goal will find itself unable to control inflation.

But that is not all that economists know about controlling inflation. We also know that controlling inflation is easy — can be accomplished at low cost — if and only if investors, managers, and workers have confidence in the central bank's commitment to control inflation. Central bank *credibility* is the most important asset in order to make control of inflation easy and cheap. Central bank *credibility* is the most valuable thing a central bank can have — and is the most costly thing to regain once it is lost.

Economists know that in the short run the level of GDP and of employment depends on the level of aggregate demand for goods and services. Thus a good macroeconomic policy that seeks to avoid unnecessary unemployment and inflation must walk a fine line. Aggregate demand must be high enough to eliminate unnecessary unemployment, but not high enough to generate accelerating inflation or (worst of all) to call into question the central bank's commitment to low inflation.

WHAT ECONOMISTS DON'T KNOW — BUT COULD LEARN

. . . ABOUT THE LONG-RUN RELATIONSHIP BETWEEN KINDS OF INVESTMENT AND PRODUCTIVITY GROWTH

The list of what macroeconomists don't know is even longer than the list of things they do know. First, large chunks of the process of long-run economic growth remain a mystery. Macroeconomists cannot prescribe to poor countries the policy mix that would enable them to duplicate the rapid convergence of Japan or Italy to industrial-core status that we have seen since World War II. Macroeconomists cannot prescribe to rich countries how to maximize their rates of economic growth and appropriately discounted levels of economic welfare. Macroeconomists do not know what is the right degree of "openness" for the world economy. They do not know at what point we would get the most benefits from international trade and investment flows while suffering the lowest costs from international financial market–generated economic instability.

But in these areas, at least, macroeconomists can learn. The history of the world over the past century provides a lot of lessons about the sources of long-run growth and stagnation. And the future will continue to provide more such lessons. As long as economists are willing to take fresh looks at the world and revise their beliefs in response to new information, macroeconomists in a generation will know much more about long-run growth than we do today.

. . . ABOUT THE SHORT-RUN DETERMINANTS OF INVESTMENT

Ultimately the key issue dividing the new Keynesian and the real-business-cycle schools of macroeconomists is the sources of shifts in investment. The most common large-scale macroeconomic shock hitting a modern industrial market economy is an inward (or outward) shift in the IS curve caused by an investment slump (or boom) accompanied by a fall (or a swift rise) in the stock market. Is this shock better thought of as optimal responses of the market to news about future profits and technological opportunities? If so, then the real-business-cycle research program will be the most fruitful over the next generation. Is this shock more accurately seen as one of the less-than-rational shifts in social-psychological opinion that John Maynard Keynes referred to as "animal spirits"? If so, then the new Keynesian research program is likely to pay the highest dividends over the next generation.

This question of the most important determinants of domestic investment booms is closely tied to the key issue in international finance. Why have international financial markets been so vulnerable to financial crises over the past decade? And what is the appropriate response to constrain governments from engaging in disturbing policies? Is it to reduce the magnitude of cross-border trade and financial flows, or to adopt more aggressive policies to intervene to support countries afflicted by financial crises?

The only true answer is that macroeconomists today do not really know. This area will be one of the major political flashpoints of the next generation. It will also be one of the major battlegrounds — and hopefully areas of the progress of knowledge — for macroeconomic theory over the next generation.

. . . ABOUT THE IMPACT OF GOVERNMENT POLICY ON THE ECONOMY

A lot is still not known about how and why government policy affects the economy. Macroeconomists still argue about the relative roles played in generating short-run business cycles of "monetary" shocks and "real" shocks. Macroeconomists for the most part feel there ought to be powerful benefits from eliminating noise in the price system. But these gains from achieving low and stable inflation have not hitherto been demonstrated. And it remains mysterious why voters seem so averse to inflation when its measured economic costs appear relatively low.

Thus many fundamental questions about government policy remain up for grabs. How aggressively should central bankers pursue stabilization policy? The answer to that question depends on the solutions to the mysteries noted in the paragraph above. How much should we worry about large government deficits? The answer turns on whether or not Ricardian equivalence is roughly correct, and that depends in turn on the determinants and motivations of households' consumption and savings decisions.

. . . ABOUT THE MICROFOUNDATIONS OF MACROECONOMICS

Thus we come to the final set of things that economists do not know — but might someday find out. Macroeconomists do not understand aggregate consumption and savings decisions in the economy. They do not understand what determines the large shifts in the natural rate of unemployment seen over the past 30 years. Nor do they understand what can be done to constructively lower the natural rate of unemployment, or even what the natural rate of unemployment should be. Clearly it is worthwhile for the average worker who loses a job to spend some time unemployed searching for a new job. But how much?

And last, what are the underlying reasons that wages and prices are slow to respond to shifts in aggregate demand?

These questions about the "microfoundations of macroeconomics" have been at the top of the agenda for economic research at least since the end of World War II. Looking back, it is somewhat depressing to realize how little progress has been made, and how much the live microfoundational issues of today are those that economists like Franco Modigliani were worrying about immediately after World War II.

WHAT ECONOMISTS WILL NEVER KNOW

CHASING AN EVER-MOVING TARGET

In the natural sciences there is a strong sense of progress toward a goal: knowledge advances, and the number of unknowns left to be understood shrinks. In the social sciences it is not so clear that there is progress. More is known, yes. But we are chasing an ever-moving target: One economist's joke is that you can give the same exam every 20 years, as long as you remember that the right answers will change.

Macroeconomics is a science of what might be called *emergent* phenomena. The marginal propensity to consume, the slope of the IS curve, the velocity of money — these are not basic, unchanging, fundamental quantities that can be measured and described once and for all. They are, instead, summary rule-of-thumb characterizations of phenomena that *emerge* from the billions of economic decisions made by millions of workers, consumers, and firms. Thus we should expect macroeconomic "truth" to change over time as our economy changes.

So if there is a final lesson, it is this: Keep an open mind. Recognize that some of the things taught in this book will turn out to be wrong, or incomplete. And recognize that the questions that people want macroeconomics to answer will change in the future as well, both because the economy will change and because macroeconomics is the handmaiden of policy, which is a sub-branch of politics. And as politics changes, the questions that policy makers will ask of macroeconomists will change as well.

GLOSSARY

A

accelerating inflation A situation in which inflation rises yearly, so that this year's inflation is greater than last year's inflation, which is greater than inflation in the year before. Accelerating inflation is typically found when the unemployment rate is lower than the natural rate of unemployment or when the economy is hit by an adverse supply shock like a sharp oil price increase.

accelerationist Phillips curve An accelerationist Phillips curve is found when inflation expectations are adaptive — that is, the expected rate of inflation that determines the position of the Phillips curve is equal to last year's rate of inflation. Each extra percentage point rise in expectations of inflation shifts the entire Phillips curve upward by 1 percentage point. Thus if unemployment falls and remains below the natural rate, inflation will accelerate.

accommodation A strategy for economic policy in which the central bank does not counteract but reinforces the consequences of a shock. For example, consider an adverse supply shock that boosts inflation. A policy of accommodation would not increase real interest rates to fight inflation, but would instead allow real interest rates to fall and so further boost inflation.

actual budget balance The actual budget balance is equal to government revenues from its tax collections, minus its purchases of goods and services, minus government transfer payments, minus the interest on government debt.

adaptive expectations Expectations of the future formed by assuming the future will be like the past. Usually applied to expectations of inflation: Adaptive inflation expectations forecast future inflation by assuming it will be equal to inflation in the recent past. Adaptive expectations of inflation are one of the three cases economists typically analyze; the other two are *static inflation expectations* and *rational inflation expectations*.

aggregate demand Also called planned expenditure. Total spending — by consumers, investing firms, the government, and the international sector — on final goods and services. When considering the details of national income accounting, there are differences between aggregate demand, national product, GDP, and national income, which are caused by differences in their exact definitions. At the eagle's eye level of analysis used in most of this book, however, the circular flow principle means that aggregate demand, national product, GDP, and national income are all equal.

aggregate demand–aggregate supply diagram (AD-AS diagram) This diagram plots real GDP on the horizontal axis and the price level (or the inflation rate) on the vertical axis. On this diagram the aggregate demand curve shows how planned expenditure varies with the price level (or the inflation rate); the aggregate supply curve shows how firms' total production varies with the price level (or the inflation rate). Equilibrium is where the curves cross, and thus where production is equal to sales, inventories are stable, and there is neither upward nor downward pressure on production or prices.

aggregate demand curve A downward-sloping relationship between aggregate demand and the price level. This inverse relationship is produced because (a) a higher price level means a lower money stock, higher interest rates, lower investment spending, and lower aggregate demand; or (b) a higher price level means that inflation is high and a central bank wishing to control inflation has raised interest rates to reduce aggregate demand.

aggregate demand line Usually called the planned expenditure line. It is found on the income-expenditure (or Keynesian cross) diagram that shows aggregate demand on the vertical and national income on the horizontal axis. An important part of the sticky-price, short-run business-cycle model. The planned expenditure line shows total spending — aggregate demand — as a function of the level of national income. The slope of the planned expenditure line is the MPE — the marginal propensity to expend income on domestic goods. The intercept of the planned expenditure line is the level of autonomous spending.

aggregate supply The quantity of final goods and services that firms produce given their existing stocks of plant, equipment, and other capital and given the prevailing wage and price levels. In the flexible-price business-cycle model of Chapters 5 through 7 (and in the growth model of Chapters 3 and 4), wages and prices adjust so that in equilibrium, aggregate supply is equal to the economy's potential output. In the sticky-price model of Chapters 8 through 11, aggregate supply in the short run is an increasing function of the inflation rate (and thus of the price level). Also see misperception model and labour contracts.

aggregate supply based on labour contracts This approach for deriving the aggregate supply function relies on the Keynesian assumption of wage and price rigidities based on the existence of labour contracts that fix the nominal wage for the duration of the contract. If all labour contracts are signed at the same time, then unexpected shocks lead to deviations of output from its full-employment level only for the duration of the contract. On the other hand, if contacts are signed at different dates (overlapping contracts), then there will be a substantial degree of inertia in wages that will lead to persistent deviations of output from its full-employment level.

aggregate supply curve Gives for each actual and expected price level (or inflation rate) the quantity of output that will be supplied by firms. The aggregate supply curve and the Phillips curve are different ways of expressing the same economic relationship.

animal spirits Waves of optimism and pessimism — perhaps irrational or self-confirming — about the future of the economy that affect investment spending. Shifts in animal spirits push stock market and other asset prices up and down, and lead businesses to increase and decrease how much they spend on investment. *John Maynard Keynes* often used this term as part of his argument that private investment spending was inherently unstable and that strong stabilizing monetary and fiscal policies were needed to control the natural fluctuations of the business cycle.

anticipated monetary policy Found when workers, managers, and investors have rational expectations of inflation. Anticipated monetary policy is those shifts in the money stock or interest rates that have been anticipated in advance. Under rational expectations, anticipated changes in monetary policy have no effect on production or unemployment, but they do have powerful effects on prices.

appreciation An increase in value, usually on the part of a currency. The opposite of depreciation. When an appreciation is sudden and is the result of an explicit change in policy by a government, it is called a revaluation. An appreciation of foreign currency is an increase in the value of the exchange rate. By contrast, an appreciation of the dollar is a fall in the value of the Canadian exchange rate.

arbitrage Earning profits by buying a good or an asset in one place (or at one time) and selling it in another place (or at another time) where (when) its price is higher. In this book, arbitrage is used to derive equilibrium conditions in financial markets: In equilibrium, no arbitrage opportunities are left for financiers to exploit. Thus, for example, any differential in interest rates paid on investments at home and investments abroad must be offset by an expected change in the exchange rate.

automatic stabilizers Mechanisms that automatically stabilize the economy without the need for active intervention (that is, *discretionary policy*) on the part of the government, central bank, or any other party. As an example of fiscal automatic stabilizers, we notice that in a recession, tax revenues automatically decline as incomes fall, and social insurance spending automatically rises as more people qualify for unemployment insurance and other social welfare expenditures. The government budget automatically swings toward a deficit, providing a stimulus to aggregate demand, whenever private demand drops. Similarly, it automatically swings toward a surplus, reducing aggregate demand, whenever private demand rises. The structure of the government's tax and spending programs thus automatically provides a degree of stabilization to aggregate demand. These fiscal automatic stabilizers are the only form of fiscal policy that work rapidly and effectively to reduce the size of the business cycle.

autonomous consumption Written C_0. That component of consumption spending that is independent of the level of national income. You can think of it as the level that consumption spending would be if household income were to fall to zero.

autonomous spending Written A. Those components of planned expenditure or aggregate demand that are independent of the level of national income. A higher level of autonomous spending is an upward shift in the aggregate demand line on the income-expenditure diagram. A higher level of autonomous spending increases equilibrium aggregate demand by an amount equal to the boost in autonomous spending times the multiplier. Autonomous spending, A, is equal to autonomous consumption C_0, plus investment I, government purchases G, and gross exports GX: $A = C_0 + I + G + GX$.

B

"bads" Products or by-products that are undesirable, such as crime or smog. These are not included (as negative amounts) in measures of GDP but perhaps should be.

balance of payments account The accounting system used to measure and comprehend a country's economic relations with the rest of the world. The balance of payments account has three parts: The current account tracks a country's imports and exports of goods and services; the capital account tracks a country's gross investment of capital abroad and foreigners' gross investment of capital at home; and, under a fixed exchange rate system, the official settlements account tracks changes in governments' exchange reserves.

balance of payments crisis A situation, under a fixed exchange rate system, in which international investors lose confidence in the long run value of a currency.

balanced budget When the government's tax receipts equal its spending. Since there are many possible ways of accounting for tax receipts and for spending, the concept of a balanced budget is a fuzzy one.

balanced growth Balanced growth is attained when a country has converged to its long-run steady-state growth path and has a capital–labour ratio equal to its steady-state level.

bank assets The sum of a bank's reserves and the loans it has made (and thus that people owe it). Bank assets are equal to the sum of a bank's liabilities — its deposits and its borrowings — and shareholders' net worth.

bank deposits Sums of money that people and organizations have taken to and placed in the bank for convenience, safe-keeping, and profit. Deposits are usually classified as either chequing-account deposits (which can be transferred to others by writing cheques) or saving-account deposits (which must be withdrawn or transferred into some other form before they can be spent). But there are other forms as well: certificates of deposit or money market account deposits, for example.

bank liabilities How much a bank owes to other people and organizations. The sum of the deposits that people have made in the bank, any direct borrowings that the bank itself has undertaken, and any bonds that the bank itself has issued.

Bank of Canada Canada's central bank. This institution conducts monetary policy and regulates banks. Its open-market operations change the money stock and peg short-term nominal interest rates.

bank rate The interest rate charged to financial institutions when they borrow from the central bank.

bank reserves Cash held in bank vaults or money that banks have on deposit at the Bank of Canada. A bank's reserves are the amount of money it can pay out to depositors easily and immediately, without selling less than perfectly liquid assets, calling in loans, or borrowing.

bank run Before deposit insurance, when the depositors in a bank fear that it is insolvent, and so all at once demand that the bank liquidate their deposits for cash.

base year In the construction of an index, the year from which the weights assigned to the different components of the index are drawn. It is conventional to set the value of an index in its base year equal to 100.

bond A tradable financial instrument that is a promise by a business or a government to repay money that it has

borrowed. A discount bond is a short-term promise to pay a fixed sum on the date that the bond matures. A coupon bond is a promise to periodically pay out coupon interest payments until the bond matures and then to repay the bond's principal value at maturity.

bond market The set of places and communication links along which governments and others bid for, offer, and trade bonds. Economists often say that interest rates are determined by supply and demand in the bond market. These days the bond market is largely a computer network — numbers on bond traders' computer screens and electronic offers to buy and sell.

bond rating Some financial information services rate bonds, thus telling investors how safe and secure an investment a particular bond is. The highest-rated bonds are rated AAA.

boom A situation in which production is above long-run trend and has been growing rapidly, in which employment is high and unemployment is low, and in which nearly everyone is optimistic about the future of the economy.

bubble economy When a country's stock and real estate markets have risen far and fast to unsustainable "bubble" levels that cannot be justified on the basis of fundamental values. Bubbles are driven by investors' belief in the "greater fool" theory: that even though they may be fools for buying stocks and bonds at overvalued prices, somewhere out there is a greater fool who will soon buy the securities from them at even higher prices. At some point, however, the greater fool theory turns out to be false, the markets turn, and values on the stock and real estate markets crash. Today when economists refer to the bubble economy, they are referring to Japan in the late 1980s.

budget balance The net state of the government's finances. When government spending equals tax receipts, economists say that the budget is in balance or that the budget balance is zero. When spending exceeds taxes, the government's budget is in deficit. When taxes exceed spending, the government's budget is in surplus.

budget deficit The difference between government spending and taxes when the first is larger than the second. In sticky-price short-run models, a budget deficit raises aggregate demand: The government's purchases of goods and services inject more spending power into the economy than the government's net taxes are withdrawing from the economy. In flexible-price models, a budget deficit lowers national savings and investment: Money that would otherwise have been borrowed by businesses and used to finance investment in new plant and equipment is borrowed by the government instead.

budget surplus The difference between the government's spending and the government's revenues when the second is larger than the first. In sticky-price short-run models, a budget surplus lowers aggregate demand: The government's purchases of goods and services inject more spending power into the economy than the government's net taxes are withdrawing from the economy. In flexible-price models, a budget surplus raises national savings and investment: The government's retirement of its debt injects purchasing power into financial markets that is then borrowed by businesses and used to finance investment in new plants and equipment.

business cycle The short-run fluctuation in the output, income, and employment of an economy relative to the long-run trend. A political business cycle is one produced by policy actions implemented for political gain. A real business cycle is a boom generated not by stimulative monetary or fiscal policies or by the irrational animal spirits of investors but by rapid technological innovation opening up new industries and new possibilities for investment.

business structures One of the components of investment spending. The construction of buildings, railroad tracks, bridges, or other things that are not machines and not inventory yet improve the productive capacity of businesses.

C

CANSIM The principal macroeconomic database pertaining to the Canadian economy that is compiled by Statistics Canada.

capital Produced goods, such as machines, buildings, transportation infrastructure, or inventories, that amplify the economy's productive potential.

capital account That part of the international balance of payments that covers investment flows from one country to another. When gross investment in foreign countries by domestic citizens is greater than gross investment in the home country by foreigners, economists say that there is a capital outflow. When gross investment in foreign countries by domestic citizens is less than gross investment in the home country by foreigners, we say there is a capital inflow. The capital account and the current account must match: When there is a capital inflow, the current account must show a trade deficit — an excess of imports over exports — of equal magnitude; when there is a capital outflow, the current account must show a trade surplus — an excess of exports over imports — of equal magnitude.

capital accumulation Increases in a country's capital stock when gross investment is greater than depreciation.

capital deepening Increases in an economy's capital–labour ratio.

capital flight When a collapse of confidence in a country's economic policy leads investors to try to pull their investments out of a country and invest them somewhere else. Capital flight is associated with a sharp depreciation in the value of the currency and poses very difficult economic policy choices.

capital flows Net investment by the citizens of one country in another — the "flow" of capital from one country to another. When there is a net outflow of capital from a country, the outflow is equal to its trade surplus — net exports (exports minus imports). When there is a net inflow of capital into a country, the inflow is equal to its trade deficit — net imports (imports minus exports).

capital inflow The net flow of purchasing power that foreigners channel into domestic financial markets; also called *international savings.*

capital intensity A measure of the stock of machines, equipment, and buildings that the average worker has at his or her disposal in order to contribute to an economy's productivity.

capital–labour ratio The economy's capital stock divided by the size of its labour force. In the economic growth chapters, Chapters 3 and 4, the capital–labour ratio is the key variable in the economic growth model. Over time, economies converge to steady-state growth paths along which the capital–labour ratio is at a constant, equilibrium level.

capital mobility The extent to which it is easy for investors to place their money in or pull their money out of other countries.

capital outflow Purchases of foreign assets by the residents of a country. See *capital flows.*

capital share The share of national income that is received as income by the owners of capital: the sum of profits, rent, and net interest divided by total national income. If the economy is competitive — without monopolies — and there are no major external benefits to investment in the economic growth process, then in equilibrium the capital share of an economy will be equal to the diminishing-returns-to-scale parameter of its aggregate production function.

capital stock The economy's, or sometimes a firm's, total accumulated stock of buildings, roads, other infrastructure, machines, and inventories. The greater the capital stock, the more productive the average worker. A substantial chunk of long-run economic growth is due to increases in the capital stock.

cash flow The difference between a business's revenues and its immediate cost of doing business. Cash flow is available for the business to either return to its shareholders in dividends, use to buy back its stock or its bonds on the financial market, or spend on increasing its capital stock through investment.

central bank The arm of a national government that controls the money supply and the credit pattern of an economy and usually oversees and regulates the banking system as well.

central bank's inflation target The inflation rate desired by the central bank.

certificate of deposit A type of bank account that is one step less liquid, and thus one step less moneylike, than a savings account. You give your money to the bank; in return it gives you a "certificate of deposit" that you can redeem after a fixed period of time to get your money back with interest. However, if you try to cash in your certificate of deposit early, you will suffer, as the advertisements all say, "substantial penalties for early withdrawal."

chain-weighted index An index constructed not by choosing one particular year as the base year and calculating the index value for every year using the base-year weights, but by "chaining" together year-to-year changes. That is, each year-to-year change in the index is calculated using that particular year as the base year. These calculated changes in the index are then linked together to create the index level values. Chain-weighted indexes avoid problems that fixed-weight indexes develop as time passes and the base-year weights used to construct the index become less and less relevant.

chequing account deposits Often called *demand deposits,* because the bank pays them out whenever the depositor demands (usually by writing a cheque that the cheque recipient's bank then presents to the depositor's bank). Because it is so easy to use chequing account balances to pay for goods and services, chequing account deposits are included in every possible measure of the money stock.

circular flow The central, dominant metaphor in macroeconomics and the way of looking at the macroeconomy that underlies the national income and product accounts. Every economic transaction is made up of a flow of goods or services and of an offsetting flow of purchasing power in the opposite direction. Every economic agent has an income and an expenditure, and the two must match. Thus purchasing power flows from businesses to households and back in a circular fashion.

classical dichotomy When real variables (like real GDP, real investment spending, or the real exchange rate) can be analyzed and calculated without thinking about nominal variables (like the price level or the nominal money stock). If the classical dichotomy holds, then economists also say that money is *neutral* — changes in the money stock do not affect the real variables, income, production, and employment in the economy. They also say that money is a veil — a covering that does not affect the shape of the face underneath.

classical unemployment When unemployment arises not because aggregate demand is too low but because government regulations or market power keep the labour market from clearing and keep labour demand by firms below labour supply.

closed economy An economy in which international trade is so small a share of national product that exports and imports can be ignored. Contrast with an *open economy*, in which trade and capital flows have important effects on real GDP and other economic variables.

commodity futures A contract that allows you to "lock in" today the price at which you will buy or sell a commodity in the future. The contract can then itself be traded, and, depending on how prices move, a contract that allows you to buy a commodity — euros, say — at a low price can itself be very valuable. Businesses and investors can use such commodity futures contracts to avoid bearing various forms of risk. Other businesses and investors use such commodity futures to gamble.

comparative statics A method of analysis to determine the effect on the economy of some particular shift in the environment or policy. When employing comparative statics, we first look at the initial equilibrium position of the economy without the shift; then look at the equilibrium position of the economy with the shift; and, finally, see the difference in the two equilibrium positions as the response to the shift.

consumer confidence The optimism or pessimism of consumers about the economy. The more confident consumers are, the higher consumption is likely to be for any given level of GDP. Consumer confidence is a powerful determinant of autonomous consumption.

consumer price index (CPI) The most commonly used measure of the cost of living. It measures the cost of a slowly changing basket of consumer goods. The change in the CPI is the most frequently used measure of inflation. Because of difficulties in getting good measurements of components of the cost of living, the CPI probably contains a slight bias. Many economists believe that the CPI overstates true changes in the cost of living by between 0.5 and 1.0 percentage points per year.

consumer prices The average prices paid by households for the goods they buy as consumers. Consumer prices are distinguished from investment-goods

prices, the prices paid by the government, and export prices.

consumption function The relationship between total consumption (C) and disposable income (Y^D): $C = C_0 + (C_y \times Y^D) = C_0 + C_y \times (1 - t)Y$, where C_0 is the autonomous level of consumption, t the tax rate on income (Y) and C_y the marginal propensity to consume out of disposable income.

consumption per worker A measure of the consumption of the workforce — the consumption component of GDP divided by the labour force for the national economy.

consumption spending Spending on goods and services purchased and used by consumers. Consumption spending is the major component of national product, equal to about two-thirds of the total. Consumption spending does not include purchases of existing houses or the construction of new houses. The purchase of an existing house is an asset; housing construction is counted in investment.

contractionary policy The opposite of expansionary policy: shifts in government spending, taxation, or monetary policy that reduce aggregate demand and tend to reduce national product, income, employment, and inflation. A contractionary fiscal policy increases net taxes or reduces government spending. A contractionary monetary policy is usually an open-market operation by which the Bank of Canada sells bonds for cash, thus reducing the money supply and raising short-run interest rates.

convergence The tendency for poor countries or regions to grow faster per capita than rich ones and eventually catch up with them.

coordination failures Failures of firms to change prices to respond quickly to the marketplace or in concert with other firms. Such things as long-term price and labour contracts produce a kind of inertia.

cost-of-living escalators Provisions in contracts that automatically raise wages or prices as official price indexes rise.

countercyclical Something that moves in the opposite direction from the business cycle; something that is low when national product is above potential output and vice versa. The unemployment rate is countercyclical, as is the government's budget balance.

coupon bond A bond that pays its holder not only its principal value at maturity but also a periodic interest payment called a "coupon."

CPI See *consumer price index.*

credibility The degree to which the public believes in the policy action taken by some institution of government (e.g., the Bank of Canada or the Ministry of Finance). As long as people in an economy believe that the central bank

will act to keep inflation low, it is possible that the economy will be able to have both relatively full employment and relative price stability. But if the central bank does not have this credibility, either unemployment will be high or inflation will be high — or both.

currency The sum of paper money and coins. Currency is one of the major components of the money stock. It is the form of money that is easiest to use to buy goods and services.

currency arbitrage A situation, operating under the gold standard, whereby people buying or selling one currency at any price other than the ratio of the two gold parities would find themselves facing an unlimited demand and would soon find themselves losing a nearly unlimited amount of money.

currency board An exchange rate system in which the central bank gives up its power to conduct domestic open-market operations and commits to buying and selling foreign currency at the official exchange rate only. Under a currency board, a country's stock of high-powered money is equal to its foreign exchange reserves. Establishing a currency board system is a way that a central bank can gain credibility: It not only fixes its exchange rate in terms of foreign currency, but it abandons the key lever — open-market operations — that it would use should it wish to begin a policy of inflation.

currency confidence The condition where people, domestic or foreign, have faith in the continuing value of one country's currency relative to one or more other currencies.

currency crisis A situation where a country's currency is in serious trouble relative to the exchange rates of other countries. The most common problems facing that country are the prospect of hyperinflation or the need for significant devaluation.

currency-to-deposits ratio How much individuals and firms wish to hold in currency for every dollar that they hold in the form of bank deposits. When people are nervous about the stability or liquidity of the banking system, the currency-to-deposits ratio will rise, pushing the money multiplier and the money stock down and perhaps causing a recession.

current account In the balance of payments, the account that keeps track of a country's exports and imports. When exports exceed imports, economists say that there is a current account or trade *surplus*. When imports exceed exports, economists say that there is a current account or trade *deficit*. The current account and the capital account must match: Whenever there is a capital inflow, the current account must show a trade deficit — an excess of imports over exports — of equal magnitude; whenever there is a capital outflow, the current account must show a trade surplus — an excess of exports over imports — of equal magnitude.

cyclical unemployment The difference between the current unemployment rate and the current value of the natural rate of unemployment. Cyclical unemployment is associated with deviations of national product from potential output.

cyclical volatility Fluctuations in economic activity due to business cycles.

cyclically adjusted What the value of an economic variable would be if unemployment were at its average rate and the business cycle were in neither a boom nor a depressed state.

cyclically adjusted budget balance The budget balance that would prevail if the economy were at full employment.

cyclically adjusted budget deficit Also called the *high-employment budget deficit*. An estimate of what the budget deficit would be if national product were at potential output and unemployment were equal to the natural rate. This measure removes shifts in the budget deficit that are due to the operation of the economy's automatic stabilizers.

D

debt The national debt of a country is the sum total of all past deficits the government has run. The government owes interest on the national debt — thus taxes must be higher when the debt is higher. And the fact that investors hold the bonds issued by the government that are the national debt means that they have less to use to finance private investment that boosts the country's capital stock.

deficit The amount by which government spending on goods, services, and transfer payments exceeds tax revenues in a given year. A national debt is created when the government borrows to cover the shortfall.

deflation When the price level falls for some substantial period of time. The opposite of inflation: a decrease in the overall price level. Deflation is rarely seen today, but in the Great Depression the deflation of 1929–1933 was a major factor contributing to the depth of the Depression: The falling price level bankrupted firms and banks that were in debt, and so reduced total aggregate demand.

demand deposits Chequing account deposits. Called demand deposits because the bank pays them out whenever the depositor demands (usually by writing a cheque). Chequing account deposits are part of what economists call the *money stock* because it is so easy to use chequing account balances to pay for goods and services.

demographic transition A period in history that sees a rise in birth rates and a sharp fall in death rates as material standards of living increase above "subsistence" levels.

After a while, however, birth rates start to decline rapidly too. The end of the demographic transition sees both birth and death rates at a relatively low level and the population nearly stable.

dependent variable The variable alone on the left-hand side of an equation; this is the variable whose value is determined by the values of the variables on the right-hand side and that changes when the variables on the right-hand side change.

deposit insurance A promise by the government or the central bank that bank failures will not freeze consumers' or firms' bank deposits and thus their ability to spend. Deposit insurance in Canada was instituted by the federal government in 1967 with the establishment of the Canada Deposit Insurance Corporation and has reduced the risk of a classic financial crisis.

depreciation rate The rate at which capital wears out, rusts, or becomes obsolete and is scrapped. Because of depreciation, the economy's capital stock does not grow by the full value of gross investment. It grows by the amount of net investment — the difference between gross investment and depreciation.

depreciation Wearing out of the capital stock due to use or obsolescence.

depression The word used for an economic downturn — a fall in national product and a rise in unemployment — before "recession" was coined as a euphemism. Today the meaning of "depression" is confined to a very severe downturn.

devaluation In a fixed exchange rate system, a reduction in the value of a country's currency so that it takes more units of the home country's currency to purchase one unit of foreign currency. An action taken by a central bank or treasury to decrease the official price of a country's currency relative to the price of other currencies — or in terms of gold. (*Revaluation* is the opposite action.)

diminishing returns Doubling the number of workers on a farm or doubling the value of the capital each employee uses in a factory does not generally double production but rather raises it by some smaller amount. Moreover, as more factors are added, smaller and smaller increases in production are generated. Such diminishing returns prompted nineteenth-century literary critic Thomas Carlyle to call economics "the dismal science."

discounting Figuring out how much money you would have to put aside today and invest at the prevailing interest rate in order to obtain a specified sum at some particular point in the future. We calculate the profitability of investments by discounting future profits from investments and comparing the discounted present value to the cost of the investment.

discouraged workers Potential workers who have left the labour force because

they do not believe they can find worthwhile jobs. Discouraged workers return to the labour force when the labour market tightens. Many think that official unemployment rates understate the problem because of the existence of discouraged workers.

discretionary fiscal policy See *discretionary policy*.

discretionary policy Discretionary policy is policy that results from conscious decisions rather than being automatic — in the sense that automatic stabilizers swing into action without any person or organization having to make an explicit decision (see *financial automatic stabilizers* and *fiscal automatic stabilizers*). Discretionary monetary policy is made by the Bank of Canada's decisions to change interest rates. Discretionary fiscal policy is made by the government's decision to change levels of spending and of taxes.

disinflation A reduction in inflation — that is, a reduction in the rate at which prices are increasing — but not so great a reduction as to cause deflation.

disposable income What is left of income after taxes have been paid. The difference between national income and net taxes. Even when national income is unchanged, changes in the government's tax and transfer programs change disposable income and so are likely to change consumption spending. Disposable income $Y^D = Y - T = (1 - t)Y$ where Y is total income, T is taxes, and t is the tax rate.

divergence The tendency for a per capita measurement (e.g., incomes or standards of living) in various countries to become less equal over a period of time.

dividends Payments by a corporation to its shareholders on a regular, periodic basis. Dividends are the primary way that a firm rewards those who have invested in its common stock by returning a portion of the firm's profits to its investors.

dollarization The adoption of another country's currency to perform the main functions of money: medium of exchange, store of value, and unit of account. For Canada, dollarization would mean the adoption of the US dollar.

domestic exchange rate The domestic currency price of one unit of foreign currency.

domestic investment The same as "investment" in the national income and product accounts. Distinguished from foreign investment, which is investment by one country's citizens in the economy of another country.

durable manufacturing That part of the economy's manufacturing sector that makes durable goods — long-lived goods like refrigerators, large turbine generators, structural steel, and washing machines.

dynamic inconsistency Refers to a situation where the government promises a policy to be implemented in the future but does not implement it when the implementation time arrives.

E

East Asian crisis The remarkably deep and sudden financial crisis that hit East Asian economies in 1997 and 1998. The East Asian crisis came with the least warning of any financial crisis in the 1990s. In other crises — Britain's, Brazil's, or Mexico's — some observers at least had pointed out fundamental problems with the economy that made it vulnerable to a crisis. The East Asian crisis appeared to come out of a blue sky.

East Asian miracle Since the mid-1960s the economies of East Asia have grown more rapidly than any other group of economies, anywhere, anytime.

economic disturbances Shifts in the economic environment or changes in economic policy that disturb the balance of the economy.

economic expansion A sustained increase in GPD bracketed on either side by a period of recession.

economic growth The process by which productivity, living standards, and output increase. It is measured by the growth of real GDP.

Economic Report of the President A "book" prepared once a year (in January) by the U.S. president's Council of Economic Advisers. It gives their view of the U.S. economy's accomplishments, problems, and opportunities.

efficiency of labour The skills and education of the labour force, the ability of the labour force to handle modern technologies, and the efficiency with which the economy's businesses and markets function. The efficiency of labour is very closely linked to an economy's total factor productivity.

elasticity The proportional response of one variable to a proportional change in another variable. If a 1 percent change in one variable generates a 1 percent change in the other, the elasticity is one. If a 1 percent change in one generates a 2 percent change in the other, the elasticity is two.

equilibrium Short-run equilibrium is a state of balance between supply and demand in a particular market or in the economy as a whole. Long-run equilibrium requires that markets balance and also that expectations of inflation and other quantities be correct.

equilibrium capital–labour ratio In the economic growth chapters, Chapters 3 and 4, the equilibrium capital–output ratio is the key to understanding where the economy is headed: what its long-run dynamic trajectory will be. Over time, the economy will converge to its steady-state growth path along which

the capital–labour ratio is constant at its equilibrium level.

equilibrium condition The condition that ensures that the quantity demanded is equal to the quantity supplied.

excess bank reserves Bank reserves held over and above those mandated by law because banks are not confident that they would be paid back if they made additional loans, or because banks believe that some loans they have already made are about to go into default, or because they believe depositors are about to withdraw deposits.

exchange rate The nominal exchange rate is the rate at which one country's money can be turned into another's. The real exchange rate is the rate at which goods produced in one country can be bought or sold for another's. The definition of the exchange rate is either the value of home currency, or the price of foreign currency, depending on the textbook.

exchange rate overshooting See *overshooting model*.

exogenous An exogenous variable is one that is taken as given and is determined outside the model under consideration. The model cannot say anything about how the exogenous variable is determined.

expansion A period in which production grows and unemployment falls; also called a *boom*.

expansionary policy Increases in government spending, decreases in net taxes, or increases in the money stock that lower interest rates. Expansionary policies raise aggregate demand, national product, employment, and inflation.

expectations Everyone in the economy makes plans about what to do that depend on what they think the future will be like. Economists focus on this dependence of behaviour on beliefs about the future: investors', consumers', employers', and workers' expectations are a principal determinant of economic behaviour. As a shorthand, economists usually collapse the range of different and conflicting expectations held by people into a single average number — for example, expectations of inflation.

expectations theory of the term structure The theory that the long-term interest rate is an average of today's short-term interest rate and of the short-term interest rates that are expected to prevail in the future.

expected inflation Expectations of overall price increases between the short run and the long run.

expenditure side That part of the national income and product accounts made up of total expenditure — on consumption spending, investment, net exports, and government purchases.

exports Total goods and services produced at home and sold to

purchasers in foreign countries. Exports are an addition to aggregate demand for home-produced products.

external balance Exists when the balance of payments is at its desired target value. External balance is along the UIP curve or the BP curve. This concept is used in relation to the Mundell-Fleming model of an open economy in Chapter 15.

F

Federal Reserve The central bank of the United States. It consists of a Board of Governors and 12 regional Federal Reserve Banks.

final goods and services Products that are not themselves used by businesses to make other products. Products that are either (a) bought by consumers, (b) bought by firms or individuals as investments that increase their capital stock, (c) bought by foreigners (in excess of intermediate goods bought by domestic producers), or (d) bought by the government.

financial automatic stabilizers Instruments such as deposit insurance that are built into the economy in order to provide financial stability.

financial flexibility A situation in which a large number of different financial instruments are traded on thick and liquid markets. This means that any one kind of asset has less and less potential to become a bottleneck.

financial markets The stock market, the bond market, the short-term borrowing market, plus firms' borrowings from banks. The markets in which the flow of money from savers seeking a return to investors seeking money to finance purchases takes place.

financial panics Sudden falls in stock market and bond market prices and rises in interest rates, driven at least in part by the fear that other people are about to panic and sell.

fine-tuning The goal of having the Bank of Canada and the Ministry of Finance together adjust fiscal and monetary policy so as to keep the economy always near full employment — as you tune a radio to get the strongest signal.

fiscal automatic stabilizers In a recession, tax revenues automatically decline as incomes fall, and social spending automatically rises as more people qualify for unemployment insurance and other social welfare expenditures. The government budget automatically swings toward a deficit, providing a stimulus to aggregate demand, whenever private demand drops. Similarly, it automatically swings toward a surplus, reducing aggregate demand, whenever private demand rises. The structure of the government's tax and spending programs thus automatically provides a degree of stabilization to aggregate demand. These fiscal automatic stabilizers are the only form of fiscal policy in Canada that works rapidly and effectively to reduce the size of the business cycle.

fiscal policy Changes in government purchases or in net taxes that affect the level of aggregate demand. Increases in purchases or in transfer payments are expansionary policy; increases in taxes are contractionary policy.

fixed exchange rates An exchange rate system where the value of the exchange rate is set by the central banks.

fixed exchange rate system A system of international monetary arrangements by which central banks buy and sell in foreign exchange markets so as to keep their relative exchange rates fixed. Between 1945 and 1971 the industrial world was on a fixed exchange rate system called the Bretton Woods system.

fixed investment Investment to build houses and apartments, infrastructure, offices, stores, and other buildings, plus investment in machinery and equipment. The other important component of investment is *inventory investment.*

fixed-weight indexes Indexes formed by taking a weighted average of different quantities, where the weights are fixed and unchanging over the span of years for which the index is constructed.

flexible exchange rates An exchange rate system where the exchange rate is determined strictly by the forces of supply and demand for foreign exchange in the international money markets without any official foreign exchange intervention.

flexible prices When wages and prices in an economy are not sticky but move smoothly and rapidly to keep supply equal to demand in the labor market and in the goods market. Under flexible prices, real GDP is equal to potential output and unemployment is equal to its natural rate. Under flexible prices, changes in monetary and fiscal policy do not affect the level of real GDP but they do affect its composition, and they affect the price level as well.

floating exchange rate system A system of international monetary arrangements by which central banks let exchange rates be decided by supply and demand, so that they "float" against one another as supplies and demands vary. Floating systems can be "clean" — if central banks truly leave the markets alone — or "dirty" — if central banks try at times to nudge exchange rates in one direction or another.

flow of funds The process by which savings — whether private, government, or international — are transformed into purchasing power useful for businesses undertaking investment spending.

The flow of funds through financial markets is the centre of macroeconomic analysis in the flexible-price full employment model of Chapters 5 and 6.

flow variable An economic quantity measured as a flow per unit of time. GDP, investment spending, and inflation are examples of flow variables. The unemployment rate, the capital stock, and the price level are not flow variables — they are *stock variables.*

foreign currency The money of any country save the one you happen to live in. When domestic exporters earn foreign currency by exporting, they have to figure out what to do with it — it's no good in this country, after all. So they need to trade it either to someone who needs foreign currency to buy imports or someone who wants foreign currency to make an investment abroad.

foreign exchange intervention International foreign exchange transactions made by governments in order to stabilize exchange rates.

foreign exchange market The decentralized trading around the world of assets denominated in one currency for assets denominated in another: deutschmarks or dollars, pounds or yen. Exchange rates are set in the foreign exchange market.

foreign exchange rate The foreign currency price of one unit of domestic currency.

foreign exchange reserves Foreign currency–denominated assets held by a country's central bank or treasury to use in foreign exchange interventions. Under a fixed exchange rate system, a government must maintain sufficient foreign exchange reserves so that it can satisfy the people who wish to trade home currency for foreign currency.

formulation lag The lapse of time between the moment that makers of economic policy recognize that a shock has affected the economy and the moment at which their policy response begins to be implemented. The time it takes to formulate policy.

fractional reserve banking A banking system — like the one we have — in which banks hold in their vaults only a portion of deposits they accept as reserves and lend the rest to customers who pay interest.

frictional unemployment The unemployment generated by firms taking time to fill vacancies and workers taking time to find the right job. Frictional unemployment is the labour market counterpart of goods inventories in the goods market: It boosts output and workers' incomes by giving them the opportunity to find jobs that match their skills.

Friedman, Milton One of the four most influential macroeconomists of the twentieth century (the other three being

John Maynard Keynes, Irving Fisher, and Robert Lucas). A leading exponent of monetarism and one of the first to recognize the dominant role potentially played by the U.S. Federal Reserve in stabilization policy.

full-employment budget balance See *cyclically adjusted budget balance.*

full equilibrium An equilibrium in which the goods and money markets are in equilibrium at the intersection of the IS and LM curves (internal balance), the balance of payments is at its desired level (external balance), and output is at its potential level. Full equilibrium describes the long-run equilibrium of an open economy.

future value The inverse of present value — the value that a sum of money or a flow of cash would have at some date in the future, if it were invested and compounded at the prevailing rate of interest.

G

GDP See *gross domestic product.*

GDP deflator The ratio of nominal GDP to real GDP. The second most used estimate of the overall price level (the *consumer price index* is the most-used estimate).

globalization The ongoing process by which barriers to the free flow of commodities, capital, and information across countries are reduced.

GNP See *gross national product.*

gold standard The particular fixed exchange rate system dominant for more than a half century before the Great Depression. A system by which central banks preserve fixed exchange rates by always being willing to buy or sell their currencies at fixed rates in terms of the precious metal gold.

golden rule In growth theory, when an economy's savings rate is equal to its capital share. In such a case the steady-state growth path has a higher level of consumption associated with it than any other steady-state growth path with the same path over time of the efficiency of labour.

goods market The market where people (and firms and the government) buy and sell final goods and services.

goods market equilibrium In the flexible-price model, the point at which prices have adjusted to make total aggregate demand for goods equal to potential output. In the sticky-price model, the point at which firms have responded to their increasing or decreasing inventories by adjusting production to aggregate demand so that inventories are stable.

government expenditure multiplier This number tells us by how much the equilibrium output will increase if government expenditures increase by one unit.

government purchases Government spending on goods or services (including the wages of government employees). Much government spending is not purchases but is instead transfer payments — that is, payments like social security that do not buy any good or service for the government.

Great Depression From 1929–1941, the deepest depression the industrialized countries have ever experienced. At its nadir in 1933, close to one-fifth of the labour force in Canada was unemployed.

gross domestic product (GDP) The most commonly used measure of product, output, and income, gross domestic product is the total amount of final goods and services produced in a given period, usually a year. By the circular flow principle, this is equal to the total income earned through domestically located production; it is also equal to total expenditure on domestically produced goods and services.

gross exports The goods and services produced in the home country that are sold abroad.

gross investment Spending on investment goods that includes spending to simply replace worn-out or obsolete pieces of capital or to keep existing capital in working condition. Subtract depreciation from gross investment to obtain net investment, the net increase in the economy's capital stock.

gross national product (GNP) Equal to GDP minus the income earned by foreign-owned factors of production located in Canada, plus income of Canadian factors of production located abroad.

growth accounting A general framework first developed by Robert Solow for measuring the contributions of factors of production to the growth of output. Growth accounting is discussed in Chapter 3.

growth rate Almost always refers to the annual growth rate of GDP or of GDP per worker. This shows how much real economic product is increasing from year to year.

H

high-employment budget deficit See *cyclically adjusted budget deficit*.

high-powered money See the more usual term for this, *monetary base*.

high-pressure economy An economy in which the "pressure" of economic activity is high: Unemployment is low, production is often higher than potential output, workers are being pulled into the labour force, and inflation is often rising.

hyperinflation Extremely high inflation, so high that the price mechanism breaks down. Under hyperinflation people are never sure what the true value of their money is and spend a great deal of time and energy trying to spend their cash incomes as fast as possible before they lose value. One rule of thumb is that inflation of more than 20 percent per month can be called hyperinflation.

I

imperfect asset substitutability Refers to a situation when assets have different risk characteristics and therefore different rates of return even at the long-run equilibrium.

imperfect capital mobility Exists if there are sufficient barriers to international capital flows to make it difficult and costly to move assets and money across national borders. With imperfect capital mobility even assets that are perfect substitutes will have different rates of return in different countries.

implementation lag The time that passes between when a monetary or fiscal policy action is completed by the Bank of Canada or the Ministry of Finance and when the action affects real GDP, unemployment, and inflation.

imports Goods and services produced in and purchased from other countries. Imports are a reduction in aggregate demand: Consumption and investment spending that are diverted to imports are not part of aggregate demand for domestically produced goods and services.

imputed rent The rent that those who live in owner-occupied housing pay as tenants to themselves as landlords. Imputed rents are included in the calculations of GDP.

income-expenditure diagram The tool for figuring out what the equilibrium level of aggregate demand and national product is. If national product is too low, it is to the left of equilibrium on the income-expenditure diagram, and inventories are rapidly being exhausted. If national product is too high, it is to the right of equilibrium, and inventories are being involuntarily built up.

income side That part of the national income and product accounts made up of total income — income earned by workers, income received by investors, income paid to landlords, and residual economic profits left for entrepreneurs and risk-bearers.

independent variable A variable on the right-hand side of an equation. A variable whose value helps determine the value of the variable on the left-hand side, and that, when it changes, makes the variable on the left-hand side change.

index number A number that isn't a set sum, value, or quantity in well-defined units (like dollars, people, or percent) but that is a quantity relative to a base year. The index number is given a value of 100 in the base year. Index numbers are usually weighted averages of a large number of individual components; the weights can either be fixed or chained.

industrial economies Those economies that have finished the process of industrialization — the United States, Britain, Germany, Japan, France, Canada, Italy, and the smaller economies at roughly the same stage of economic development.

industrial revolution The transformation of the British economy between 1750 and 1850 when largely handmade production was replaced by machine-made production, a change made possible by technological advance. Following the initial British Industrial Revolution, other countries have in turn undergone their own industrial revolutions.

inflation An increase in the overall level of prices in an economy, usually measured as the annual percent change in its consumer price index.

inflation-adjusted budget balance Equal to the actual budget balance minus the loss in the value of total debt due to inflation.

inflation rate The percentage rate of increase in the overall price level.

inflation tax The rate at which the value of real money balances are eroded by inflation. See also *seigniorage*.

inside lag The lapse of time between the moment that a shock begins to affect the economy and the moment that economic policy is altered in response to the shock. The inside lag has two parts — the recognition lag, during which makers of economic policy do not yet recognize the shock, and the formulation lag, during which makers of economic policy are designing the policy response.

insider–outsider theory A theory of how cyclical unemployment that persists for too long becomes transformed into structural unemployment. Workers who remain unemployed gradually lose their skills and their attachment to the labour force. And unions bargain to raise the wages of current members rather than to find jobs for ex-members.

intellectual property Ideas, inventions, processes, or creative works that were invented or created by someone and are considered their property. The owner of intellectual property is entitled to control how it is used and to be paid for its use by other people — at least for a period of time.

interest The periodic sums that you pay to "rent" the money that you have borrowed.

interest rate The price, measured in percent per year, paid for borrowing money. Conversely, the return earned by saving, and the relative price at which purchasing power can be transferred from the present to the future.

interest rate parity See *uncovered interest rate parity condition or uncovered real interest rate parity condition*.

interest rate targeting Controlling interest rates. Recently, in conducting their monetary policies, the Bank of Canada and other central banks in industrialized countries have opted for controlling the rate at which they make loans to the chartered banks, known as the *overnight lending rate*, rather than controlling the money directly. Because chartered banks set their own interest rates following the overnight lending rate, by controlling the interest rate this way, the central bank can speed up the process in which changes in their monetary policies can affect the inflation rate and output.

intermediate goods Goods that are not final goods and services. Goods that are bought by businesses as inputs into some further process of production. Intermediate goods are excluded from product-side counts of GDP: To include them would lead to double counting the same economic product twice, once as an intermediate good and then again as part of the final good that the intermediate good was used to produce.

internal balance This exists when goods and money markets are in equilibrium at the intersection of the IS and LM curves.

international division of labour Resource-rich countries produce and export natural resources and resource-based products, industrialized economies export capital-intensive high-technology manufactures, and other countries export labour-intensive manufactures. All gain by concentrating their production in those sectors in which their economy is most efficient.

international savings See *capital inflow*.

inventory investment A change in the stock of goods that make up firms' inventories: materials and supplies, work in progress, goods in storage, and finished goods that have not yet been sold. Fluctuations in inventory investment are primarily involuntary, the result of quarter-by-quarter differences between national product and aggregate demand.

investment The buildings and goods (both machines and inventories) purchased to add to the economy's stock of capital, plus (sometimes) government creation of infrastructure, plus residential construction.

investment accelerator The dependence of the level of business investment on the level of production. This arises from firms' preference to use internally-generated rather than externally-raised funds to finance investment, as well as from other causes. A strong accelerator increases the value of the Keynesian multiplier.

investment function The function that relates investment spending to the real interest rate: $I = I_0 - (I_r \times r)$, where I_0 is the baseline level of investment, r is the real interest rate, and I_r the responsiveness of investment to a change in real interest rates.

investment requirements The share of GDP that must be devoted to investment spending in order to keep an economy's capital–output ratio from falling.

investment spending That portion of total spending (approximately 20 percent) devoted to increasing business capacity and the economy's capital stock.

investor optimism The principal determinant of baseline investment I_0. When investors are optimistic, I_0 is high. Fluctuations in investor optimism — what *John Maynard Keynes* called investors' "animal spirits" — are a principal cause of the business cycle.

investors' expectations The expectations of investors regarding the future level of economic activity.

IS curve The downward-sloping relationship between the (real, long-term) interest rate and the equilibrium level of national product and aggregate demand. The IS curve summarizes the information about equilibrium national product in an entire family of income-expenditure diagrams, one for each possible value of the interest rate.

IS-LM diagram A diagram with the interest rate on the vertical axis and the level of real GDP on the horizontal axis, used to determine what values of the interest rate and of real GDP together produce equilibrium in the money market and equilibrium in the goods market for a given price level.

K

Keynes, John Maynard One of the four most influential macroeconomists of the twentieth century (the other three being *Milton Friedman*, Irving Fisher, and Robert Lucas). To Keynes we owe the income-expenditure aggregate-demand framework that still dominates intermediate macroeconomics courses and textbooks.

Keynesian cross diagram The income-expenditure diagram by another name. The tool for finding equilibrium aggregate demand and national product. Principally used in the derivation of the multiplier: the amplified response of changes in equilibrium aggregate demand and national product to fluctuations in autonomous spending.

Keynesian multiplier The change in national income and aggregate demand that follows from a one-dollar change in any component of autonomous spending, such as government purchases. To find the value of the *multiplier*, subtract the economy's marginal propensity to expend from 1, and then take that number's inverse.

Keynesian One who adheres to the ideas developed by *John Maynard Keynes*. See *Keynesianism*.

Keynesianism The school of thought, developed from the ideas of *John Maynard Keynes*, that emphasizes (a) the role of expectations of future profits in determining investment; (b) the volatility of expectations of future profits; (c) the power of the government to affect the

economy through fiscal and monetary policy; and (d) the multiplier process, which amplifies the effects of both private-sector shocks and public-sector policies on aggregate demand.

L

labour contracts Institutional agreements between workers and firms that fix the nominal wage for the duration of the contract. Labour contracts give rise to an upward sloping short-run aggregate supply curve.

labour demand The amount of labour that firms wish to employ at a given real wage rate.

labour demand curve This gives the amount of labour that firms would like to employ at different levels of the real wage, holding all the other factors fixed. To maximize profits firms hire workers until the marginal product of labour, *MPL*, is equal to the real wage. Hence, the *MPL* schedule is the labour demand schedule, L^d.

labour force The sum of those who are employed and those who are actively looking for work. (The *unemployment rate* is defined as the number of unemployed divided by the labour force.)

Labour Force Survey (LFS) The survey conducted by Statistics Canada in order to estimate the unemployment rate.

labour market equilibrium When the only kind of unemployment is *"frictional" unemployment*, and there is neither cyclical nor structural unemployment. When, save for those in the process of changing jobs, the economy is at full employment.

labour productivity National product divided by the number of workers (or alternatively, by the total number of hours worked). Such a measure of output per worker is probably the best available measure of long-term economic growth.

labour supply The amount of labour that households are willing to supply to firms at a given real wage rate.

labour unions Organizations of workers that attempt to bargain with employers for higher wages and better working conditions and can threaten to strike if a satisfactory agreement is not met. Multiyear union contracts have been seen as important causes of price inertia.

lags The time between when a policy proposal is made and when it becomes effective in changing the economy in some way. Lags can arise during recognition of a condition, formulation of a policy, or implementation of that policy. The first two are *inside lags*, because they occur inside the government. The last is sometimes called the outside lag.

leading indicators A number of variables correlated with future movements in real GDP or inflation. Many economists believe these indicators can be relied on as a good guide to economic activity nine or so months ahead. Some key indicators are stock prices, new manufacturing orders, the money supply, and the index of consumer expectations.

lender of last resort In a financial crisis, the government may play this role, stepping in and lending money to organizations that are thought to be fundamentally sound but that are critically short of cash.

life-cycle consumption Consumption is depressed below income in peak earning years because people are saving for retirement. Before and after peak earning years, consumption is raised above income, either as a child's upbringing is paid for by parents or as retirees spend their savings.

liquid assets Forms of wealth that can be readily and cheaply converted into spendable form. Forms of wealth that can be easily used to finance purchases.

liquidity Applied to assets whenever they can be easily, quickly, and without cost turned into money.

liquidity constraints A liquidity constraint is an inability to borrow. When consumers suffer from liquidity constraints, their consumption spending is limited by their current income, and the marginal propensity to consume is likely to be high.

liquidity crisis When banks or other institutions cannot make the payments they owe because they lack cash, but there is little doubt that they would be solvent and profitable if the current financial crisis were successfully resolved.

liquidity trap A situation in which households and firms are willing to hold as much real money balances as are supplied at a given interest rate. When a country is in a liquidity trap, monetary policy is ineffective in changing output.

LM curve Gives the combinations of real interest rates and real GDP that result in equilibrium in the money market, for a given expected inflation rate and price level.

loanable funds The total flow of resources available — *private savings*, government savings, and international savings — to finance investment spending and capital accumulation.

long-run growth The path of economic growth once the business-cycle fluctuations have been removed. The long-run pace of growth of potential output.

long-term interest rate The interest rate required if you are going to borrow money not for a short term of months but for a long term of decades.

long-term real interest rate The interest rate required if you are going to borrow money not for a short term of months but for a long term of decades, adjusted for inflation by subtracting the inflation rate from the nominal interest rate.

Lucas, Robert One of the four most influential macroeconomists of the

twentieth century (the other three are John Maynard Keynes, Irving Fisher, and Milton Friedman). The leader of the rational-expectations school of macroeconomics for nearly two decades.

Lucas critique The assertion that much analysis of the effects of economic policy is badly flawed because it does not take proper account of how changing policies induce changes in people's expectations.

M

M1, M2, M2+, M2++ Different measures of the *money stock* — of the total stock of assets in the economy that are liquid enough to be readily used to finance purchases.

macroeconomics The subject of the course you are taking. Macroeconomics is concerned, among other things, with business cycles, the determinants of real income, inflation, exchange rates, interest rates, unemployment, long-run growth, and the effects of monetary and fiscal policies.

Malthusian age A time during which Malthus's beliefs that population growth would be limited by natural-resource scarcity seem to apply.

marginal product of capital The increase in potential output from a unit increase in the economy's capital stock. Often calculated as equal to $\alpha Y/K$ (α, the share of national income received by owners of capital, divided by the capital–output ratio K/Y).

marginal product of labour (MPL) The increase in potential output from a 1-unit increase in the supply of labour to the economy. Often calculated as $(1 - \alpha)Y/L$ (the share of national income received by workers, $1 - \alpha$, times average labour productivity Y/L).

marginal propensity to consume (MPC) The increase in consumption spending resulting from a one-dollar increase in disposable income. The parameter C_y in the consumption function $C = C_0 + C_y(1 - t)Y$, where C_0 is baseline consumption, t is the tax rate, and Y is total national income.

marginal propensity to expend (MPE) The increase in total spending — on consumption goods through the *marginal propensity to consume* and on net exports — from a one-dollar increase in national income. In the model of Chapters 8 through 11, $MPE = C_y(1 - t) - IM_y$, where C_y is the marginal propensity to consume, t is the tax rate, and IM_y is the share of income spent on imports. Note, however, that in more complicated models MPE may be different: Changes in national income may have other effects as higher firm profits lead to higher investment spending and as higher household incomes lead to lower social insurance spending.

maturity The date or the number of years in the future at which a bond's interest

payments cease and its principal sum is returned to the lender.

median The middle one of something. The value such that half or more are as large or larger, and half or more are as small or smaller.

medium of exchange A commodity or an asset that almost everyone will accept as payment for a transaction. The most important function of *money*.

menu costs The costs to a firm of changing the price(s) of a good(s) or service(s). These costs lead firms to adjust their prices infrequently.

microeconomics That field of economics that deals with the behaviour of the individual elements in an economy with respect to the price of a single commodity and the behaviour of individual households and businesses.

Ministry of Finance The department of the federal government that is responsible for the federal government's expenditures on various goods and services, transfers of funds to provinces and territories, transfers of funds to individuals and businesses, federal income taxes, federal goods and services taxes and tariffs. The Ministry of Finance is also responsible for issuing government bonds and managing the government's debt.

misperception model A model that gives rise to an upward-sloping short-run aggregate supply curve even with complete wage and price flexibility. The model was first proposed by Milton Friedman in 1968 and then formalized by Robert Lucas in the 1970s. It assumes that production of goods takes place in a large number of sectors that are separated from each other in terms of the information that is available in each sector about the levels of economic activities in other sectors. This "friction" gives rise to an upward-sloping aggregate supply curve.

mixed economy An economy in which markets control the allocation of resources and of labour to industries and firms, but in which the government plays a not overwhelming but significant role: providing social insurance and social welfare benefits on a large scale, trying to stabilize the macroeconomy, and enforcing contracts. Post-WWII mixed economies have been extraordinarily successful at generating economic growth.

model A construct that aims to establish relationships — usually quantitative — between and among economic variables. Economists describe the process of reducing the complexity and variation of the real-world economy into a handful of equations "building a model."

monetarism The theory, very popular in the 1970s and the early 1980s, that fluctuations in interest rates had little impact on money demand, so that stabilizing national product and employment could be carried out in a smooth and straightforward fashion by stabilizing the rate of growth of the *money stock*.

monetarist One who believes in the principles of *monetarism*.

monetary automatic stabilizers Named by analogy with the *fiscal automatic stabilizers* produced by the structure of the government's budget. Features of the financial system that tend to cushion and prevent declines in the *money stock* that would otherwise occur during a financial crisis. For example, deposit insurance is a monetary automatic stabilizer: It prevents bank deposits and the money stock from dropping when people begin to fear that a depression may bankrupt the bank they use.

monetary base Often called *high-powered money*. The sum total of currency and of bank reserves on deposit at the Bank of Canada. The *money stock* is equal to the monetary base times the *money multiplier*.

monetary neutrality This exists if changes in the money supply do not affect real variables such as consumption, investment, and real output.

monetary policy How the supply of money or the interest rate varies with economic conditions like inflation, unemployment, and the exchange rate.

monetary policy lags The time it takes for real interest rate changes to affect the equilibrium output.

monetary policy reaction function (MPRF) The aggregate demand curve as a function of the inflation rate.

monetary transmission mechanism How changes in the money supply or in interest rates affect spending on consumption, investment, and other components of aggregate demand and thus lead to changes in national income and product.

monetary union A monetary union is formed when a group of countries decide to adopt a single currency and have one central bank and one monetary policy.

money A word that economists use in a technical sense. To an economist, "money" means only "wealth in the form of readily spendable purchasing power." Cash, plus balances in chequing accounts, plus whatever other assets are held primarily as a way to keep purchasing power on hand to spend rather than as long-term investments.

money balances How much *money* — wealth in the form of readily spendable purchasing power — consumers and firms actually hold at a given moment.

money demand How much *money* — wealth in the form of readily spendable purchasing power — consumers and firms wish to hold at the given levels of national income and of interest rates.

money demand curve A curve — drawn for a given and fixed level of national income — that shows how consumers' and firms' demand for money varies with the interest rate: The higher the interest rate, the lower money demand is. On the money demand–money supply diagram, the point where the money demand curve is equal to the supply of money determines the market-clearing interest rate.

money illusion When managers, workers, and others fail to recognize that some of the change in their nominal income and revenue is a result of inflation and is not a change in their real income and revenue.

money market equilibrium The point where the money market is in balance such that the real money supplied is equal to the real money demanded.

money multiplier The change in the money stock that follows a one-dollar change in the monetary base; the ratio between the money stock and the monetary base. Increases in the reserves-to-deposits ratio or in the currency-to-deposits ratio reduce the money multiplier.

money stock The stock of liquid assets that are widely accepted as means of payment for goods and services.

money supply How much in the amount of liquid assets the Bank of Canada has allowed the banking system to create.

money supply curve The money supply considered as a function of the interest rate. In general the higher the interest rate, the lower are the excess reserves that the banking sector holds and the higher is the money stock.

money supply–money demand diagram The building block of the LM curve, the diagram with the nominal interest rate on the vertical and the quantity of money supplied and demanded on the horizontal axis.

money supply multiplier Tells us by how much, in the IS-LM model, the equilibrium output will increase if the money supply increases by one unit, allowing for adjustment in the equilibrium real interest rate.

moral hazard The danger of imprudent, improper, or dishonest behaviour in economic situations where actions are not easily or routinely monitored. A possible drawback of deposit insurance and of lender of last resort activities.

MPC See *marginal propensity to consume*.

MPE See *marginal propensity to expend*.

MPL See *marginal product of labour*.

multifactor productivity The part of total productivity accounted for jointly by all factors of production. Also known as *total factor productivity*.

multiplier The change in equilibrium real GDP and aggregate demand that follows from a one-dollar change in any component of autonomous spending, such as government purchases. To find the value of the multiplier, subtract the economy's *marginal propensity to expend*

from 1, and then take that number's inverse.

Mundell-Fleming model Named after its creators, this is an extension of the basic IS-LM model that is used to analyze the effectiveness of government policies in small open economies with perfect capital mobility.

myopia Short-sightedness. A failure to look far enough ahead into the future. For example, "voter myopia" is the theory that voters react to the immediate economic situation rather than to what has happened in the further past or what is likely to happen in the future.

N

NAIRU Acronym for the nonaccelerating inflation rate of unemployment, which is the same as the *natural rate of unemployment*. The rate of unemployment when inflation is equal to expected inflation. The rate around which unemployment tends to fluctuate, and at which (because actual and expected inflation are equal) there is neither upward nor downward pressure on inflation.

national income The total incomes from all work and asset ownership in an economy. Leaving aside differences in accounting definitions, national income is equal to *national product* (for the only way incomes can be earned is by producing products) and is equal to total expenditure or *aggregate demand* (for all incomes flowing to individuals must be expended one way or another).

National Income and Expenditure Accounts (NIEA) The system that government statisticians use to measure, estimate, and check the flow of economic activity.

national income identity The requirement — built into the national income and product accounts — that total income add up to total expenditure, and that both be equal to the total value added produced by businesses: $C + I + G + NX = Y$, where C is consumption spending, I is investment spending, G is government purchases, NX is net exports, and Y is total national income.

national product The total value of all final goods and services produced in an economy. Leaving aside differences in accounting definitions, national product is equal to *national income* (for the only way products can be produced is by paying people to make them) and is equal to total expenditure or *aggregate demand* (for every product is ultimately purchased).

national product per worker A synonym for labour productivity. It is probably the best measure of an economy's development. Other measures — national product per adult or per capita — fail to take account of the changing mix of market and household production, or imply that adults who spend their money on raising children are impoverished compared to adults who buy DVDs.

national savings The sum of *private savings* and government savings — or since the government is usually not saving but running a deficit, private savings minus the government deficit. *Domestic investment* is equal to national savings plus *net investment* in this country by foreigners.

national savings identity A consequence of the national income identity: that private savings $(Y - C - T)$ plus the government's budget surplus $(T - G)$ plus the net inflow of capital $- NX$ is equal to investment: $(Y - C - T) + (T - G) - NX = I$, where Y is total national income, C is consumption spending, T is net taxes, G is government purchases, NX is net exports, and I is investment spending.

natural rate of unemployment A synonym for *NAIRU*: the rate of unemployment where actual and expected inflation are equal, and there is no downward or upward pressure on inflation. Milton Friedman coined the phrase "natural rate"; those who did not like the hint in the word "natural" that such unemployment was a good thing preferred the colourless acronym NAIRU.

natural-resource scarcity A scarcity of land or other natural resources necessary for human prosperity. Thomas R. Malthus believed that inventions and their consequent higher standards of living would lead to faster rates of population increase, which would in turn lead inevitably to natural-resource scarcity and consequent lowered productivity and standards of living. He maintained that this cycle would keep the overall population growth over time at zero.

net domestic product Another measure of total production, obtained by subtracting capital depreciation from GDP.

net exports The difference between exports and imports. Net exports have to be added to the sum of consumption, investment, and government purchases in order to arrive at aggregate demand, because exports are an addition to and imports a subtraction from aggregate demand for domestically produced goods and services.

net investment The difference between gross investment and depreciation. Net investment is the increase in the economy's capital stock — the stock of buildings, infrastructure, machines, and inventories that amplify worker productivity.

net national product (NNP) Yet another measure of the economy's total output. Net national product subtracts depreciation from *gross domestic product*, and also subtracts payments that foreigners receive for the use of foreign-owned productive resources located in this country. Net national product is, from a conceptual point of view, the best estimate of national product.

net taxes The difference between taxes collected by the government and transfer payments received by households and businesses. Net taxes are the impact of the government's fiscal policy on the disposable income of the private sector. A fall in net taxes raises disposable income and thus consumption spending. Net taxes are the variable T in the models of this book.

neutral See *monetary neutrality*.

NNP See *net national product*.

nominal A quantity that is not adjusted for inflation or for changes in the price level.

nominal exchange rate The exchange rate not adjusted for the changes in countries' relative price levels over time.

nominal GDP Real GDP times the price level as measured by the GDP deflator. Nominal GDP is the total current-dollar value of final goods and services produced.

nominal interest rate The interest rate measured in terms of money: how many dollars you have to pay in the future in exchange for one dollar borrowed today; the nominal interest rate is equal to the real interest rate plus the expected inflation rate.

nominal wage The average level of money wages paid in an economy; the money cost to an employer of an average worker.

nondurable manufacturing Manufacturing that produces relatively short-lived products. Demand for nondurable manufactures is fairly steady — since they wear out, there is always a stable source of replacement demand.

non-overlapping contracts Labour contracts signed simultaneously with the same time duration. With non-overlapping contracts there is no wage inertia and the economy achieves full employment when all contracts are signed.

O

OECD See *Organisation for Economic Co-operation and Development*.

official reserve transactions International transactions among the central banks of different countries.

official settlements account International transactions that are neither current account transactions (payments for imports or exports) nor capital account transactions (payments for investments in other countries) but the purchase or sale of foreign currency assets by governments or central banks.

Okun's law A fall in the unemployment rate of 1 percentage point is associated with a 1.65 percent rise in national product relative to potential output. This association is called Okun's law: Periods of high (or low) unemployment relative to the natural rate are the same as periods of low (or high) national product relative to potential output.

100 percent reserve banking A banking system — never seen in the real world, but sometimes used in economics textbooks as a baseline case — in which banks accept deposits but cannot make loans. When they accept deposits they must either (a) hold them in cash in their vaults or (b) redeposit the money in their own accounts at the central bank.

open economy An economy without substantial tariffs on imports or restrictions on international investments. Alternatively, an economy where imports, exports, and international capital flows are relatively large shares of national product and are important determinants of fluctuations in employment and output.

open-market operation The principal way that central banks affect interest rates: the purchase (or sale) of short-term government bonds to increase (or decrease) the money supply and push interest rates down (or up). Open-market operations are not the only tool that central banks have to affect money supplies and interest rates, but they are by far the most often used.

operating band A band set by the Bank of Canada for the *overnight rate* that is one-half of a percentage point wide, with the target for the overnight rate at its centre.

optimum currency areas A theory developed by Robert Mundell that sets out the conditions under which fixed exchange rates would work better than a flexible exchange rate system.

Organisation for Economic Co-operation and Development (OECD) Originally a club of all countries that received Marshall Plan aid from the United States and Canada. Now a club of the industrialized countries that is used to collect data and try to coordinate economic policy.

output gap The deviation of actual output from potential output.

output per worker The economy's output divided by the number of workers in the economy.

overlapping contracts Labour contracts with overlapping time durations. Overlapping contracts cause inertia in nominal wages, because when groups of workers and firms sign contracts, they are worried about their position relative to other groups of workers and firms. Such inertia in wages leads to persistent deviations of output from full employment.

overnight lending rate or **overnight rate** The *interest rate* charged for loans made in the *overnight market*.

overnight market The market used by major financial institutions (chartered banks, credit unions, finance companies) to borrow and lend from each other in order to cover their daily transactions.

overshooting model Dornbusch's model that accounts for large fluctuations in the exchange rate following a monetary shock under a flexible exchange rate system. The model emphasizes the flexibility of exchange rates at all times versus the stickiness of goods prices in the short run in order to account for the fluctuations in the exchange rate. After a monetary shock the exchange rate "overshoots" its long-run level because it has to do some of the adjustments that should have been done by goods prices to bring the economy to equilibrium.

P

participation rate The fraction of adults (people aged 16 to 65) who are in the *labour force* — that is, they are either employed or are actively searching for work. The participation rate is *procyclical*, because discouraged workers drop out of the labour force when unemployment is relatively high. The participation rate has grown steadily over time, as gender roles have changed and the boundary between market and household work has shifted.

patent laws and copyrights Laws protecting *intellectual property*. Patents give a firm or individual that has discovered something new the right to exclude anyone else from using that discovery for a period of years.

peak The highest point of a business expansion.

permanent income The level of income that households regard as likely to persist in the future. Their income minus any transitory windfalls that they do not expect to receive again in the future.

Phillips curve The downward-sloping relationship between unemployment and inflation. The old-fashioned type implied unemployment could be permanently reduced at the price of a small (permanent) rise in inflation. The location of the more satisfactory "accelerationist" Phillips curve depends on expectations of inflation: the higher expected inflation, the higher the unemployment rate needed to keep inflation at any particular level.

planned-expenditure function The relationship $E = C + I + G + NX$ used to build *aggregate demand* for domestically produced products from the determinants of each of its components: consumption spending (C), investment spending (I), government purchases (G), and net exports (NX).

planned expenditure line Found on the income-expenditure (or Keynesian cross) diagram that shows *aggregate demand* on the vertical and *national income* on the horizontal axis. An important part of the sticky-price short-run business-cycle model, the planned expenditure line shows total spending — aggregate demand — as a function of the level of national income. The slope of the planned expenditure line is the MPE — the *marginal propensity to expend* income on domestic goods. The intercept of the planned expenditure line is the level of autonomous spending.

policy mix The combination of monetary and fiscal policies being followed by a country's government and central bank.

policy-induced recessions Recessions that are brought about by the policies of the government, such as policies designed to reduce the inflation rate or to reduce budget deficits. Examples of policy induced recessions are the recessions of the early 1980s and early 1990s in Canada.

potential growth rate The growth rate of potential output. The growth rate at which the economy's unemployment rate is neither rising nor falling.

potential output The level at which national product would be if expectations were correct, and if unemployment were equal to its natural rate. Potential output grows smoothly over time as technology advances, as net investment augments the capital stock, and as the labour force grows.

present value How much money you would have to put aside and invest today (at prevailing interest rates) in order to match a specified sum or pattern of cash flows in the future. Thus the value in today's dollars (calculated using prevailing interest rates) of a sum or sums of money to be received in the future.

price inertia Inflation can be slow to accelerate and also slow to decline because many decisions on changes in prices and wages are made with a long lead time.

price level The average level of nominal prices in the economy. Changes in the price level are *inflation* (or *deflation*). The concept of the price level is meant to abstract from shifts in relative prices like a rise in the relative price of oil or a fall in the relative price of computers and to capture changes in the value of the unit of account in which goods are priced, workers are paid, and contracts are written.

price stability The goal of central banks. An inflation rate so low that no one worries about it.

primary budget balance The actual government budget balance plus the interest payments on the government debt.

private savings Equal by definition to households' disposable incomes minus their consumption spending. Note that earnings not paid out but retained by corporations and then reinvested are counted in disposable income. Hence private savings includes both saving done directly by households and saving done on their behalf by firms whose stock they own.

procyclical Varying with the business cycle. A procyclical variable tends to be high when national product is high relative to potential output. Investment, especially investment in inventories, is procyclical; employment is procyclical; and inflation is procyclical. Unemployment is *countercyclical*.

producers' durable equipment One of the major components of business investment. The machines that embody the technologies of the industrial revolution bought by businesses: computers, fax machines, large turbine generators, metal presses, and other capital goods that are not structures and not part of inventories.

production function The relation between the total amount of national product produced, and the quantities of labour and capital (and the level of technology) used to produce it. The production function tells us how the productive resources of the economy — the labour force, the capital stock, and the level of technology that determines the efficiency of labour — can be used to produce and determine the level of output in the economy. In the Cobb-Douglas form of the production function: $Y^* = (K)^\alpha (L \times E)^{1-\alpha}$, potential output ($Y^*$) is determined by the size of the labour force (L), the economy's capital stock (K), the efficiency of labour (E), and a parameter α that tells us how fast returns to investment diminish.

productivity Usually a synonym for *labour productivity*: total national product divided by the number of workers, or by the number of hours worked. Sometimes used for total factor productivity: the amount of national product divided by the number of weighted units of labour and capital used in production. Also see *multifactor productivity*.

productivity growth The rate at which the economy's full-employment productivity expands from year to year as technology advances, as human capital increases, and as investment increases the economy's physical capital stock.

productivity slowdown Around 1973, the rate of productivity growth in Canada and other economies suddenly slowed. The causes of this slowdown still remain somewhat a mystery. The most likely explanation is bad luck: a number of small negative factors all affecting the economy at once, each with its own separate causes. The productivity slowdown era appears to have come to an end in the mid-1990s.

profits Income earned by entrepreneurs and equity investors. What is left over from the receipts of an enterprise after it has paid for (a) intermediate goods and materials, (b) wages, salaries, and fringe benefits, (c) rent, and (d) interest.

public savings The government's budget surplus; the flow of funds from the government into the financial markets.

purchasing power parity Valuing production in different countries as if the relative exchange rate gave you equal purchasing power in each country; sometimes also used for the theory that exchange rates ought to fluctuate around the values that correspond to purchasing power parity.

Q

quantity theory of money demand The core belief of *monetarism*: the belief — strongly pushed by Milton Friedman in the 1960s and 1970s — that money demand is insensitive to changes in interest rates and that the *velocity of money* is nearly constant. If true, then successful stabilization policy would require little more than stabilizing the rate of growth of the money stock.

R

rational expectations Expectations about the future formed by using all information about the structure of the economy and the likely course of government policy. When people in an economy have rational expectations, it is extremely difficult for shifts in economic policy to cause anything other than shifts in the rate of inflation or the price level. Contrasted with *static expectations* and *adaptive expectations*.

real Adjusted for inflation; either divided by the price level or with the inflation rate subtracted from it.

real appreciation A rise in the value of the nominal exchange rate under a floating-rate system that is greater than the ongoing difference in inflation rates between the home country and other countries. An increase in the relative price of domestic-made goods in terms of foreign-made goods.

real balances The purchasing power of the *money* — wealth in the form of readily spendable purchasing power — that consumers and firms actually hold at a given moment. Equal to nominal money balances divided by the price level, and thus adjusted for inflation.

real budget balance See *inflation-adjusted budget balance*.

real business cycle A boom generated when rapid technological innovation opens up new industries and new possibilities for investment. At such moments the stock market will be high, the returns to investment large, and so investment spending will be high as well. An adverse *supply shock* — like the sudden and extreme rises in oil prices in the 1970s — can generate a real-business-cycle recession as well.

real depreciation A fall in the value of the nominal exchange rate under a floating-rate system that is greater than the ongoing difference in inflation rates between the home country and other countries. A reduction in the relative price of domestic-made goods in terms of foreign-made goods.

real devaluation A reduction in the value of the exchange rate under a fixed-rate system that is greater than the ongoing

difference in inflation rates between the home country and other countries.

real exchange rate The exchange rate adjusted for changes in relative price levels. The price of foreign-made goods measured relative to the price of domestic-made goods.

real GDP Inflation-adjusted gross domestic product; the most commonly used measure of national product, output, and income. The total income earned through domestically located production. Equal as well to total expenditure on domestically produced goods and services. Real GDP can be calculated by dividing nominal (or money) GDP by the price level.

real GDP per worker Real GDP divided by the number of workers in the economy. This is the most frequently used summary index of the economy and is a measure of how well the economy produces the goods and services people need.

real interest rate The *nominal interest rate* minus the *inflation rate*. The real interest rate measures how expensive it is in terms of goods to borrow purchasing power. It answers the question: "How much more power to purchase goods and services in the future must I offer in order to borrow a fixed amount of power to purchase goods and services today?"

real money balances The total stock of nominal money balances in the economy divided by the price level. Money demand is usually thought of as a demand for real money balances: If the price level doubles while interest rates and (real) national income remain the same, then nominal money demand should double as well in order to keep real money demand constant.

real wage The wage paid to the average worker divided by the price level.

real wage growth The change in the wage paid to the average worker divided by the price level. Found by taking the rate of increase of nominal wages and subtracting the inflation rate.

recession A fall in the level of GDP for at least six months, or two quarters of the year.

recognition lag It takes time for Statistics Canada to compile and analyze data about the economy. The recognition lag is the lag between when a process begins and when those making economic policy recognize that it is going on. Recognition lags are on the order of three to six months.

recovery The time period in a business cycle between a trough and the level of the previous peak.

representative agent A simplification often made in macroeconomics that assumes all participants in the economy are the same (i.e., that the differences between businesses and workers do not matter much for the issues under study). Macroeconomists will analyze a situation by examining the decision making of a

single representative agent and then generalize to the economy as a whole from what would be his or her decisions.

reserve requirements The amount of money that the *central bank* requires other banks to maintain either as cash in their vaults or at the central bank for each dollar of deposits that they hold. Reserve requirements are one of the principal determinants of the *money multiplier*. Their adjustment is a rarely used tool of central banks.

reserves-to-deposits ratio The ratio of *bank reserves* to *bank deposits*; partly the result of mandated government regulations and partly the result of the banks' own desire to avoid getting caught short and of fear that those they lend to will not pay the money back. One of the two determinants (along with the *currency-to-deposits ratio*) of the *money multiplier*.

residential investment New construction of residences, both single-family homes and apartment buildings. An important component of total investment and the principal nonbusiness component of investment. Fluctuations in residential investment are an important source of the business cycle.

revaluation When a central bank raises the value of its currency under a fixed exchange rate system.

Ricardian equivalence The hypothesis that households will cut consumption whenever they see a government deficit, anticipating higher future taxes that will be raised to pay off that deficit. It is named for the nineteenth-century economist David Ricardo but should be named after its principal advocate, the late-twentieth-century economist Robert Barro.

risk averse When individuals and institutions are unwilling to invest in ventures with a reasonable expected return but also with a substantial probability of disaster.

risk premium The higher interest rate that lenders charge some of their borrowers because they fear that the borrower may not repay their money. Risk premiums are measured relative to the interest rates that the Canadian government can borrow using Treasury bills.

risky interest rate The interest rate on assets where there is a significant probability of default.

rules Monetarists believe that central banks should operate by setting fixed rules for how fast they will allow the money supply to grow. Only by setting policy according to fixed rules, they argue, can the central bank minimize uncertainty and let the private sector do its job.

rules versus authorities The debate, started by the early Chicago School economist Henry Simons, over whether macroeconomic policy should be conducted "automatically," according to rules that would be followed no matter what, or determined by authorities with the discretion to respond to specific circumstances as they saw fit.

S

sacrifice ratio The number of percentage points of *unemployment* in excess of *the natural rate* times the number of years such excess unemployment must be endured to reduce annual inflation permanently by 1 percentage point.

safe interest rate The interest rate on assets where there is no significant probability of default.

Samuelson, Paul Nobel Prize–winning MIT economist. The person whose late-1940s economics textbook set the mold for the economics textbooks that you use.

savings rate The share of total GDP that an economy saves. Usually calculated as the difference between the *private savings* rate and the government's *budget deficit.*

seasonal adjustment Over a year, employment and production undergo seasonal fluctuations about as large as in a typical business cycle. They build up in the fall in preparation for the Christmas rush. They fall in the summer as vacations are taken. Seasonal adjustment removes these seasonal variations from economic data to give a better idea of the longer-term evolution of the economy.

seigniorage The tax implicitly levied on an economy's private sector by the government's exercise of its power to print more money. Sometimes known as *inflation tax.*

services Commodities that are not (or are only incidentally) physical objects but are instead useful processes or pieces of information. Services are contrasted with goods — commodities that are principally useful physical objects.

shareholders Those who own the common stock issued by a company and so are entitled to vote for its directors and other officers at the company's annual meetings and to receive dividends (if any).

short-term interest rate The interest rate paid to borrow money for the short term — three to six months.

short-term nominal interest rate The interest rate paid to borrow money for the short term — three to six months. A nominal interest rate is not adjusted for inflation. The short-term nominal interest rate is important because it is the interest rate that has the greatest impact on money demand.

small open economy A trading economy that is small, in the sense that its transactions cannot affect either the foreign real interest rate or international prices and inflation.

Solow residuals The part of the growth rate of output that cannot be accounted for by the growth rates of capital or labour. Solow residuals are calculated as the growth rate

of output minus the weighted sum of the growth rates of capital and labour, where the weights used are the fractions of total income earned by capital and labour.

stabilization policy Policy aimed at avoiding recessions and undue inflation by keeping total aggregate demand growing smoothly, and unemployment near its *NAIRU.* Stabilization policy is *countercyclical* policy.

stagflation The coexistence of recession and rising inflation or of recession and relatively high inflation. Politicians on whose watch economies suffer from stagflation usually lose their jobs at the next election.

staggered labour contracts Labour contracts that are not signed simultaneously. Staggered contracts lead to prolonged recessions and recoveries.

staggered prices Prices of different goods and services that are not set at the same time.

staples Commodities that are produced with a high content of natural resources and are exported to the rest of the world.

staples theory A theory that emphasizes the role of land, natural resources, and primary products in Canada's economic growth.

static expectations Barely deserve the name of "expectations" at all — visions of the future that do not change at all in response to changes in the current economic situation. Contrasted with *adaptive expectations* and *rational expectations.*

statistical discrepancy A fudge factor added to reconcile two measurements of the same quantity that should be equal by definition but that are not equal as measured. The System of National Accounts are full of statistical discrepancies. The statistical discrepancy in the international trade sector is often the largest.

Statistics Canada An agency of the federal government that is responsible for collecting and disseminating important economic data pertaining to the country.

steady-state capital–labour ratio The value of the *capital–labour ratio* to which an economy with constant investment and population growth rates converges over time.

steady-state debt-to-GDP ratio The long run stable value of government debt-to-GDP ratio.

steady-state growth path The path toward which national product per worker tends to converge as the capital–output ratio converges to its steady-state value. In analyzing long-run growth it is often easiest to first calculate an economy's steady-state growth path and then to use the fact that the economy tends to converge to that path.

sticky prices When wages and prices do not move smoothly and immediately to keep supply equal to demand in the labour and goods markets. With sticky prices, inventory adjustment is the principal determinant of short-run equilibrium.

stock market The market on which the shares of common stock that carry ownership of companies are bought and sold. A company's bondholders have a right to be paid their interest and principal out of a company's operating profits. A company's stockholders have the right to elect the company's board of directors and to decide what to do with the rest of its profits. A relatively high stock market indicates optimism about future profits and is likely to be accompanied by a high level of investment.

stock variable An economic quantity or variable that is measured not as a flow over some period of time but as a stock that exists at a single moment in time. For example, the *capital stock* and the *money supply* are stock variables. GDP, consumption, and the government deficit are *flow variables.* The capital stock and the money supply can be measured in dollars. But when you speak of GDP, consumption, or the government deficit, you must always be measuring — implicitly or explicitly — in dollars per year.

structural deficit A synonym for cyclically adjusted or high-employment government budget deficit. The government runs a structural deficit when its budget deficit exists not because real GDP is less than potential output but because taxes are too low or spending too high to balance the budget even when real GDP equals potential output and unemployment is at its *natural rate.*

structural unemployment Unemployment that is not "cyclical" and not "frictional." *Cyclical unemployment* goes away when output expands and real GDP reaches the level of potential output. *Frictional unemployment* serves as the economy's inventory of workers and is part of the normal process of workers changing jobs and finding good matches. Structural unemployment is the result of (a) a real wage level stuck too high for supply to balance demand in the labour market, (b) poor labour-market tax and regulatory policies that drive a large wedge between the earnings that workers receive and the costs firms must pay to employ them, (c) other policies that make it difficult for workers to move to where the jobs are and for jobs to move to where the workers are, or (d) a gross mismatch between the educational and skill levels of the labour force and the levels that employers require. Structural unemployment has been high in western Europe for two decades, was high in Canada and the United States during the Great Depression, and is frequently high in the developing world.

structures Buildings, docks, bridges, and every other component of *investment* that is neither a piece of machinery and equipment nor a component of inventories. One way of looking at investment is to divide it into spending on machinery and equipment, changes in inventories, and spending on structures — residential, business, and government structures.

supply shocks Changes — usually large, sudden changes — in the productivity of the economy. Supply shocks can take the form of a large, sudden change in the price of a key raw material, as happened in the oil shocks of the 1970s. The sudden rise in the price of oil gave businesses a powerful incentive to use less oil and energy and more labour and capital in production; thus the economy's output per worker and its potential output dropped. The sudden rise in the price of oil also set in motion compensating price rises in other sectors and led to higher inflation. The supply shocks of the 1970s were a major contributing factor to the stagflation of that decade. Rapid changes in technology can be seen as supply shocks as well.

surplus A shortened form of "government surplus." The amount by which the government's taxes exceed its spending.

T

target for the overnight rate The midpoint of an operating band set by the Bank of Canada for financial transactions made in the *overnight market*. For instance, if the operating band is 2.50 to 3.00 percent, then the target for the overnight rate is 2.75 percent.

taxes Payments by the residents of the country to the government. *Transfer payments* are subtracted from gross taxes to calculate net taxes, or taxes less transfer payments. Net taxes are the measure of how much purchasing power is removed from the private sector by the government's fiscal policies.

taxes less transfers A synonym for "net taxes." The difference between total gross taxes collected by the government and *transfer payments* issued by the government. Taxes less transfers is a measure of how much purchasing power the government's fiscal policies remove from private households. Taxes less transfers is the variable T in the models of this book and is equal to $t \times Y$, the tax rate t times national income Y.

Taylor rule A simple rule proposed by John Taylor of Stanford University that describes the monetary policy followed by most central banks in industrialized economies: According to the Taylor rule, the central bank adjusts the nominal or real interest rate in order to achieve its target values for the inflation rate and output.

technological progress Invention and innovation in the broadest sense — including innovations in organization and control — that boost economic productivity over time.

technology transfer The rapid advance in *total factor productivity* possible in developing countries as they adopt the more productive technologies already well known in the world economy's industrial core. Since most of the difference between productivity levels across countries is due to differences in total factor productivity and the efficiency of labour, successful technology transfer is at the heart of successful economic development.

term premium The premium in the *interest rate* that the market charges on long-term loans vis-à-vis short-term loans.

term structure The relationship between the lifetime — the maturity — of bonds and the interest rates buyers receive from holding bonds until their maturity. "Term structure" is a synonym for "yield curve." The term structure of interest rates usually has an upward slope: The interest rate on long-term bonds is higher than the interest rate on short-term bonds. When the interest rate on short-term bonds is higher, economists say that the term structure is inverted, and an inverted term structure is one sign of a possible future recession.

time inconsistency See *dynamic inconsistency*.

total factor productivity Also known as *multifactor productivity*, the total factor productivity is not labour productivity — not real GDP Y divided by the labour force L. Total factor productivity is not capital productivity — not real GDP Y divided by the capital stock K. Instead, total factor productivity is real GDP Y divided by a geometric weighted average of the factors of production, where each factor's weight is the share of national income that is paid to it. Total factor productivity is very closely related to the efficiency of labour E: In the Solow growth model of Chapter 3, total factor productivity is equal to $E^{1-\alpha}$. Total factor productivity is the best measure of the technological level and the overall efficiency of an economy.

total savings *Private savings* (by businesses and households) plus *public savings* (the government's surplus; public savings are negative when the government runs a deficit) plus the *capital inflow* (the net amount of money that foreigners are committing to buying up property and assets in the home country, equal to minus net exports). Total savings are equal to total investment. Total savings are distinguished from *national savings*, which are equal to private savings plus the government surplus (leaving out the capital inflow); and total savings are distinguished from private savings, which are just the savings directly undertaken by households plus the business savings undertaken by firms on behalf of the households that are their owners.

trade balance A synonym for *net exports*, equal to gross *exports* minus *imports*.

trade deficit When gross *exports* are less than *imports*, and thus when *net exports* are negative. A country runs a trade deficit when international demand for goods and services it produces is less than home demand for goods and services produced abroad. A trade deficit is a subtraction from aggregate demand for domestically made products. A trade deficit is also necessarily associated with an equal *capital inflow*: net investment by foreigners in the home country.

trade surplus When *gross exports* are greater than *imports*, and thus when *net exports* are positive. A country runs a trade surplus when international demand for goods and services it produces is greater than home demand for goods and services produced abroad. A trade surplus is a boost to aggregate demand for domestically made products. A trade surplus is also necessarily associated with an equal *capital outflow*: net investment by home-country citizens in foreign countries.

transfer payments Spending by the government that is not a purchase of goods or services but instead simply a transfer of income from taxpayers to program recipients. Payments to contractors who have built highways or to bureaucrats who have sold their labour time to the government are not transfer payments. Payments to social security recipients or unemployment insurance recipients are transfer payments. Transfer payments are included in the *National Income and Expenditure Accounts* not as government purchases but under the "taxes" category. Transfer payments are subtracted from gross taxes to arrive at net taxes.

transitory income The difference between a household's current income and its permanent income. A household's transitory income is any portion of its current income that is seen as a windfall and is not expected to continue in the future. Households tend to spend most of changes in their permanent income and to save most of changes in their transitory income. The *marginal propensity to consume* out of transitory income is much lower than the marginal propensity to consume out of permanent income.

Treasury bill A short-term bond issued by the government with a maturity — a period between the date at which the bond is issued and the date at which its principal comes due — of a year or less. A Treasury bill is a discount bond. It has no explicit payment of interest associated with it and pays a positive interest rate to investors solely because it is initially sold at a discount to — for less than — its principal value.

Treasury bond A long-term bond issued by the government with a maturity — a period between the date at which the bond is issued and the date at which its principal comes due — often of years or more. A Treasury bond is a coupon bond: Not only does the government pay the holder the bond's principal at its maturity but it pays the holder periodic "coupon" interest payments throughout the bond's lifetime.

trough The lowest point of a business contraction.

twin deficits During the 1980s the Canadian government *budget deficits* and *trade deficits* mirrored each other: When one rose, the other rose; when one fell, the other fell; they were "twins." The argument was made that the first was driving the second: that high Canadian trade deficits were the result of large government budget deficits, and that the cure for the trade deficit was for the government to get its fiscal house in order and balance its budget — not to impose tariffs and import restrictions on goods coming into the country.

U

uncovered interest rate parity condition States that, under perfect asset substitutability (cf. *imperfect asset substitutability*) and perfect capital mobility (cf. *imperfect capital mobility*), the domestic nominal interest rate is equal to the foreign nominal interest rate plus the expected rate of change of the domestic currency.

uncovered real interest parity condition States that, with perfect asset substitutability (cf. *imperfect asset substitutability*) and perfect capital mobility (cf. *imperfect capital mobility*), the domestic real interest rate should be equal to the foreign real interest rate plus the expected rate of change in the real value of the domestic currency.

unemployment rate The share of the *labour force* who are looking for but have not found an acceptable job. The labour force is calculated by adding (a) the number of people who told the *Labour Force Survey* (*LFS*) interviewers that they were at work and (b) the number of people who told the LFS interviewers they were looking for work but had no job. The number of unemployed is calculated as the number of people who told the LFS interviewers they were looking for work but had no job. The unemployment rate is the number of unemployed divided by the labour force. The conventionally measured unemployment rate is usually seen as an underestimate of the amount of unemployment in the economy. The unemployment rate fails to take account of discouraged workers — those who want to work but are not looking for a job now because they don't think they can find one. It also makes no allowance for those who are working part-time for economic reasons — people who want a full-time job but have found only a part-time one.

unionization rate The share of an economy's workforce that belongs to a labour union.

unit of account One of the three functions that economists traditionally ascribe to *money*: Money is a *medium of exchange*, a store of value, and a unit of account. To say that a form of money — the Canadian dollar, say — is a unit of account is to say that a great many contracts are written promising to exchange such-and-such a good or service for such-and-such a number of dollars. The fact that a form of money is a unit of account means that changes in that form of money's value — *inflation* or *deflation* — can have powerful effects on the distribution of income and the level of production. Falling prices — deflation — increase the real wealth of creditors: The amount of money they are owed buys more real goods and services when the price level is lower. Rising prices —inflation — increase the real wealth of debtors: The quantity of real goods they must sell to raise the money to pay off their debt is lower when the price level is higher. As *John Maynard Keynes* wrote in 1923, "the fact of falling prices injures entrepreneurs; consequently, the fear of falling prices causes [them to] … curtail … their operations" and leads to reduced production and high unemployment.

V

value added The difference between the material costs a business incurs in production by buying raw materials and intermediate goods and the revenue it earns when it sells its products. Value added is equal to the sum of (a) employee compensation (wages, salaries, and benefits), (b) capital costs (depreciation and interest), and (c) profits.

variable lags Part of a phrase from economist *Milton Friedman*: "monetary policy works with long and variable lags." It reflects the idea that shifts in government policy will have powerful effects on *aggregate demand*, but that how long it takes such policy shifts to have their effects is not fixed but varies from time to time, country to country, and case to case. Because changes in economic policy work with long and variable lags, caution in changing economic policies helps avoid doing more harm than good.

velocity of money The rate at which the economy's *money stock* "turns over" in an economy, equal to nominal expenditure or income divided by the money stock. If an economy has $0.1 trillion of monetary assets and annual nominal national income of $1 trillion, economists say that money has an income velocity of ($1 trillion)/ ($0.1 trillion) = 10. The velocity of money is a measure of how often the average monetary asset is used as a means of payment, and thus changes hands, over the course of a year. The higher the interest rate, the greater the velocity of money. A higher interest rate gives businesses and

households an incentive to economize on their use of money — that proportion of their wealth they hold in liquid and readily spendable but low interest-earning form.

W

wage indexation When unions or workers negotiate with managers for wage levels that rise automatically when the price level rises. If, say, a steelworkers' contract provides them with an extra 1 percent increase in wages for each 1 percent rise in the CPI, economists say that their wages are indexed to the CPI. The more prevalent wage indexation is in an economy, the steeper its Phillips curve and the larger the change in inflation produced by any shift in the unemployment rate. When wage indexation is prevalent, changes in prices will immediately and automatically trigger corresponding changes in wages.

Y

yield curve The relationship between the *interest rate* you earn for lending or are charged for borrowing money and the length of time of the loan contract. "Yield curve" is a synonym for "term structure." A yield curve diagram is drawn with the interest rate for a given risk category of bonds on the vertical axis, and the bonds' maturity — the time until the borrower repays the principal — on the horizontal axis. The yield curve usually slopes upward: You pay a higher interest rate to borrow and earn a higher interest rate to lend for a longer term because longer-term investments bear higher risk. Whenever the yield curve slopes downward — whenever short-term interest rates are higher than long-term rates — economists say that the yield curve is inverted. An inverted yield curve is a sign of a possible future recession.

yield-to-maturity The interest rate you will earn over the life span of a bond if you buy it today and hold it until it reaches its maturity and the issuer pays you back the bond's principal. Note that if the bond's current price is different from its face (or principal) value, the yield-to-maturity will be different than the coupon interest rate. Consider a five-year bond with a principal value of $100 that pays annual coupon interest of 5 percent, or $5 a year. If you paid $100 for this bond, its yield-to-maturity would be the coupon interest rate of 5 percent per year. But if you buy the bond for $85, its yield-to-maturity is 8.84 percent. Remember: The lower the price of a bond, the higher the interest rate it pays.

INDEX

Year	Real GDP (millions of 1997 dollars)	Real GDP per Worker (1997 dollars)	CPI Inflation (percent per year)	Unemployment (percent)	Long-Term Real Interest Rate (percent per year; Government of Canada bonds minus current inflation rate)	Real Exchange Rate (1961 = 100)	Real Stock Market Value (TSE 300) (1975 = 1000)	Consumption (millions of 1997 dollars)
1961	245230	40500	1.2	7.1	3.8	100.0	1191	152680
1962	262382	42150	0.9	5.9	4.2	105.8	1142	160424
1963	276306	43342	1.8	5.5	3.3	106.2	1209	166989
1964	294196	44514	1.9	4.7	3.3	105.6	1403	175747
1965	312930	45603	2.3	3.9	2.9	104.7	1514	185798
1966	333724	46662	3.8	3.6	1.9	103.9	1385	194924
1967	343454	46545	3.6	4.1	2.3	103.2	1417	202009
1968	360214	47793	4.0	4.8	2.8	103.4	1433	210711
1969	378344	48630	4.7	4.7	2.9	104.1	1525	220538
1970	389809	49474	3.3	5.9	4.6	103.4	1296	224628
1971	405860	50236	2.7	6.4	4.2	101.5	1340	236722
1972	427962	51382	4.9	6.3	2.3	98.1	1503	252957
1973	457766	52262	7.6	5.6	0.0	97.7	1494	269987
1974	474663	51950	11.0	5.4	−2.1	95.7	1125	283477
1975	483316	51925	10.7	7.1	−1.6	98.1	1000	294303
1976	508445	52162	7.5	7.1	1.6	93.5	963	309395
1977	526028	53042	8.0	8.1	0.7	99.4	869	317993
1978	546825	53504	9.0	8.4	0.3	105.4	916	327480
1979	567631	53206	9.1	7.6	1.1	110.3	1142	334974
1980	579907	52795	10.2	7.6	2.3	113.5	1397	340694
1981	600253	53096	12.4	7.6	2.8	114.2	1262	344779
1982	583089	53281	10.8	11.0	3.5	112.6	865	336080
1983	598941	54340	5.9	12.0	5.9	109.6	1180	344897
1984	633756	56076	4.3	11.4	8.4	115.2	1119	359502
1985	664059	57112	4.0	10.7	7.1	121.0	1247	377329
1986	680144	56742	4.2	9.7	5.3	120.4	1328	391399
1987	709058	57493	4.3	8.8	5.6	114.2	1509	407702
1988	744333	58565	4.0	7.8	6.2	106.0	1342	425265
1989	763837	58774	5.0	7.6	4.9	101.8	1471	439855
1990	765311	58481	4.8	8.2	6.1	100.9	1264	444920
1991	749294	58277	5.6	10.3	4.1	97.8	1214	437916
1992	755848	59371	1.5	11.2	7.3	104.8	1173	444643
1993	773528	60466	1.9	11.4	6.0	113.0	1321	452569
1994	810695	62081	0.2	10.4	8.5	122.6	1447	466296
1995	833456	62688	2.2	9.5	6.1	123.9	1466	475880
1996	846952	63105	1.6	9.6	5.9	124.8	1715	488155
1997	882733	64405	1.6	9.1	4.8	127.6	2069	510695
1998	918910	65420	1.0	8.3	4.5	137.5	2143	524807
1999	969750	67312	1.7	7.6	4.0	138.3	2201	544753
2000	1020488	69119	2.7	6.8	3.2	139.1	2916	566664
2001	1038702	69496	2.5	7.2	3.3	145.5	2313	579513
2002	1070789	69939	2.2	7.7	3.4	146.5	2037	600521
2003	1092388	69702	2.8	7.6	2.5	130.1	2018	618424
2004	1124428	70510	1.8	7.2	3.2	121.9	2392	638825
2005	1157446	71581	2.2	6.8	2.2	114.7	2751	663583